Experiences, Advantages, and Economic Dimensions of Pilgrimage Routes

Vítor João Pereira Domingues Martinho
ESAV, CERNAS-IPV Research Centre, Polytechnic Institute of Viseu, Portugal

João Augusto Guerra da Rocha Nunes
School of Education, Polytechnic Institute of Viseu, Portugal

Maria Lúcia de Jesus Pato
Agricultural S (IPV), 3chool (ESAV), and CERNAS-IPV Research Centre, Polytechnic Institute of Viseu, Portugal

Liliana Andrade de Matos Castilho
School of Education, Polytechnic Institute of Viseu, Portugal

IGI Global
PUBLISHER of TIMELY KNOWLEDGE

A volume in the Advances in Hospitality, Tourism, and the Services Industry (AHTSI) Book Series

Published in the United States of America by
IGI Global
Business Science Reference (an imprint of IGI Global)
701 E. Chocolate Avenue
Hershey PA, USA 17033
Tel: 717-533-8845
Fax: 717-533-8661
E-mail: cust@igi-global.com
Web site: http://www.igi-global.com

Library of Congress Cataloging-in-Publication Data

Names: Martinho, Vítor João Pereira Domingues, editor. | Nunes, João, 1972- editor. | Jesus Pato, Maria, 1974- editor. | Castilho, Liliana Andrade de Matos e, editor.
Title: Experiences, advantages, and economic dimensions of pilgrimage routes / edited by: Vítor João Pereira Domingues Martinho, João Nunes, Maria Jesus Pato, Liliana Castilho.
Description: Hershey PA : Business Science Reference, [2024] | Includes bibliographical references. | Summary: "This book brings more knowledge about the different dimensions of pilgrimage routes and opens a discussion forum on these topics"-- Provided by publisher.
Identifiers: LCCN 2023034560 (print) | LCCN 2023034561 (ebook) | ISBN 9781668499238 (hardcover) | ISBN 9781668499245 (ebook)
Subjects: LCSH: Pilgrims and pilgrimages. | Pilgrims and pilgrimages--Economic aspects. | Religion--Economic aspects.
Classification: LCC BL619.P5 E97 2024 (print) | LCC BL619.P5 (ebook) | DDC 203/.51--dc23/eng/20231026
LC record available at https://lccn.loc.gov/2023034560
LC ebook record available at https://lccn.loc.gov/2023034561

This book is published in the IGI Global book series Advances in Hospitality, Tourism, and the Services Industry (AHTSI) (ISSN: 2475-6547; eISSN: 2475-6555)

British Cataloguing in Publication Data
A Cataloguing in Publication record for this book is available from the British Library.

For electronic access to this publication, please contact: eresources@igi-global.com.

Advances in Hospitality, Tourism, and the Services Industry (AHTSI) Book Series

Maximiliano Korstanje
University of Palermo, Argentina

ISSN:2475-6547
EISSN:2475-6555

Mission

Globally, the hospitality, travel, tourism, and services industries generate a significant percentage of revenue and represent a large portion of the business world. Even in tough economic times, these industries thrive as individuals continue to spend on leisure and recreation activities as well as services.

The Advances in Hospitality, Tourism, and the Services Industry (AHTSI) book series offers diverse publications relating to the management, promotion, and profitability of the leisure, recreation, and services industries. Highlighting current research pertaining to various topics within the realm of hospitality, travel, tourism, and services management, the titles found within the AHTSI book series are pertinent to the research and professional needs of managers, business practitioners, researchers, and upper-level students studying in the field.

Coverage

- Cruise Marketing and Sales
- Customer Service Issues
- Destination Marketing and Management
- International Tourism
- Sustainable Tourism
- Service Design
- Tourism and the Environment
- Hotel Management
- Service Training
- Casino Management

IGI Global is currently accepting manuscripts for publication within this series. To submit a proposal for a volume in this series, please contact our Acquisition Editors at Acquisitions@igi-global.com or visit: http://www.igi-global.com/publish/.

The Advances in Hospitality, Tourism, and the Services Industry (AHTSI) Book Series (ISSN 2475-6547) is published by IGI Global, 701 E. Chocolate Avenue, Hershey, PA 17033-1240, USA, www.igi-global.com. This series is composed of titles available for purchase individually; each title is edited to be contextually exclusive from any other title within the series. For pricing and ordering information please visit http://www.igi-global.com/book-series/advances-hospitality-tourism-services-industry/121014. Postmaster: Send all address changes to above address.

Titles in this Series

For a list of additional titles in this series, please visit: www.igi-global.com/book-series

Sustainable Development Goal Advancement Through Digital Innovation in the Service Sector
Vipin Nadda (University of Sunderland, UK) Pankaj Kumar Tyagi (Chandigarh University, India) Rubina Moniz Vieira (St. Mary's University, London, UK) and Priyanka Tyagi (Chandigarh University, India)
Business Science Reference • copyright 2023 • 272pp • H/C (ISBN: 9798369306505) • US $275.00 (our price)

Management and Practices of Pilgrimage Tourism and Hospitality
S.K. Gupta (Centre for Mountain Tourism and Hospitality Management, HNB Garhwal University, India) Lilibeth C. Aragon (College of International Tourism and Hospitality Management, Lyceum of the Philippines University, Philippines) Pankaj Kumar (Department of Tourism and Hospitality Management, Mizoram University, India) Madhurima S. (Department of Environmental Science, Mizoram University, India) and Rajesh Ramasamy (Department of Tourism and Hospitality Management, Mizoram University, India)
Business Science Reference • copyright 2023 • 264pp • H/C (ISBN: 9798369314142) • US $250.00 (our price)

Critical Social Challenges in the Tourism Industry Labor, Commodification, and Drugs
Barış Çıvak (Anadolu University, Turkey) and Engin Bayraktaroğlu (Anadolu University, Turkey)
Business Science Reference • copyright 2023 • 298pp • H/C (ISBN: 9781668492550) • US $250.00 (our price)

Prospects and Challenges of Global Pilgrimage Tourism and Hospitality
S.K. Gupta (Centre for Mountain Tourism and Hospitality Management, HNB Garhwal University, India) Lilibeth C. Aragon (College of International Tourism and Hospitality Management, Lyceum of the Philippines University, Philippines) Pankaj Kumar (Department of Tourism and Hospitality Management, Mizoram University, India) Madhurima S. (Department of Environmental Science, Mizoram University, India) and Rajesh Ramasamy (Department of Tourism and Hospitality Management, Mizoram University, India)
Business Science Reference • copyright 2023 • 291pp • H/C (ISBN: 9781668448175) • US $250.00 (our price)

Handbook of Research on Innovation, Differentiation, and New Technologies in Tourism, Hotels, and Food Service
Gonçalo Poeta Fernandes (CITUR, Polytechnic Institute of Guarda, Portugal & CICS, Universidade NOVA de Lisboa, Portugal) and António Silva Melo (CiTUR, Polytechnic Institute of Porto, Portugal & CIDTFF, University of Aveiro, Portugal)
Business Science Reference • copyright 2023 • 389pp • H/C (ISBN: 9781668469859) • US $295.00 (our price)

Exploring Niche Tourism Business Models, Marketing, and Consumer Experience
Maria Antónia Rodrigues (CEOS.PP, ISCAP, Polytechnic of Porto, Portugal) and Maria Amélia Carvalho (ISCAP, Polytechnic of Porto, Portugal)
Business Science Reference • copyright 2023 • 397pp • H/C (ISBN: 9781668472422) • US $250.00 (our price)

IGI Global
PUBLISHER of TIMELY KNOWLEDGE

701 East Chocolate Avenue, Hershey, PA 17033, USA
Tel: 717-533-8845 x100 • Fax: 717-533-8661
E-Mail: cust@igi-global.com • www.igi-global.com

Table of Contents

Detailed Table of Contents

The chapter offers a reflection on regional development and pilgrimage itineraries. After proceeding with the review of the geographical literature, the analysis will move to the study of the phenomenon on a regional scale with a focus on Apulia and on the current and potential effects of Apulian pilgrimages. In particular, the case study will focus on the "Via Francigena of Capitanata." The Via Francigena is a historical path that from Canterbury led first to Rome, then to Jerusalem. Traveled in the Middle Ages by pilgrims and crusaders, it crossed the whole of Apulia, starting from the Dauni Mountains. By adopting a geo-economic approach, the chapter intends to analyze the religious and spiritual motivations, political and institutional conditioning, and above all the economic-territorial repercussions of a secular phenomenon but still of great relevance and equally important multiplicative potential.

Religious tourism in Pakistan is a diverse and culturally rich sector poised for growth, yet facing numerous challenges, including infrastructure deficiencies, maintenance issues, security concerns, undiscovered potential, economic factors, cultural disparities, and data gaps. OpenStreetMap (OSM), a community-driven mapping platform, offers transformative solutions. OSM can empower users to map religious sites, provide information, improve accessibility, and advocate for cultural preservation. It can help in route planning, community engagement, tourism promotion, and economic empowerment. OSM can address Pakistan's challenges by mapping infrastructure, supporting maintenance, ensuring safety, promoting lesser-known sites, enhancing economic inclusivity, and fostering cultural harmony. Real-time data from OSM has the potential to empower sustainable tourism development.

The chapter talks about the author's experience as a pilgrim. From 1973 until 2018, he was a pilgrim to Our Lady of Fátima, mapped and walked a centuries-old route to Our Lady of Lapa and was a frequent pilgrim to Santiago de Compostela. In the meantime, in the spirit of the pilgrimage to Santiago, he also became a volunteer, supporting pilgrims in hostels since 2016. In 2019, a serious illness led him to fear that his pilgrimages had come to an end. The fight against fears, uncertainties about the future, but also the solidarity of many friends and, perhaps unexpectedly, of those who have walked the same roads with him.

This study will tackle with the figure of Paulinus of Nola, a Roman senator, and an important figure too during Late Antiquity, for his religious conversion during the primitive Christianity. Through a biographical study the authors delve into this character and his gradual inclusion in the early Church, becoming bishop of Nola. Paulinus was closely linked to the martyr and the saint Felix (3rd century). That is why Paulinus will be the patron of a primitive pilgrimage to the tomb of Felix, introducing patronage for the demands of the pilgrims traveling to Nola, as the repair of the road, the creation of shelters, purchase of offerings, etc.

This chapter investigates the phenomenon of medieval pilgrimages to mountain shrines and their contemporary revival as postmodern physical practices in rural settings. This growth encompasses both religious and secular pilgrimages, unveiling evolving social, economic, and cultural contexts. The research focuses specifically on the unique case of western Castellón and eastern Teruel in Spain, where pilgrimages to mountain shrines have been preserved. Fieldwork was conducted in the pilgrimages between 2017 and 2019, and the data were analyzed to find the motivations and meanings behind these pilgrimages. The findings shed light on the potential benefits that the recovery of pilgrimages can offer to rural communities, such as population stabilization and the promotion of cultural heritage.

The purpose of this study is to provide a deeper understanding and uncover the main topics of discourse regarding emerging trends and follow up on the evolution of the Camino de Santiago to highlight the connections between them by looking at and comparing the papers representing this field's core. Indexed to Scopus, the authors analysed 62 papers, applying content analysis techniques to identify the main research lines. Authors found three main research perspectives: evolution in political trends and tourism strategies, the digitalisation process and its impact on the pilgrimage experience, as well as the globalisation surge in the past years. This research impacts the several stakeholders intertwined with the Camino de Santiago, be it public institutions or private operators that need to explore and understand these collective dynamics.

The activities of the creative economy are characterized by being a new perspective of regional development, occupying local opportunities and using creativity as a driving force. Tourism is one of these segments, providing experiences for offerers (hospitable) and claimants (pilgrims or pilgrims). The objective of this chapter is to analyze the Caminho do Sol route in São Paulo (BRAZIL) and to problematize the relationship of creative tourism as a potential for development among the different aspects of the creative economy through the narratives of a group of pilgrims. Basically, it used a theoretical revision on the subject and interviews with hospitable ones. It was concluded that creative tourism, through the Pilgrimage to the Sun's Path, has potential and offers advantages to the local community, under the socio-economic approach. However, it will still require greater commitment from the authorities to make it a greater possibility of development, involving relations between productive agents, civil society and walkers.

The pilgrimage routes of Southeast Asia are discussed in this chapter, with emphasis on Thailand. It examines the paths that already exist and suggests new ones that incorporate cultural, gastronomic, and ecological elements. The chapter also analyzes the regional impact, particularly the relationship between pilgrimage, cultural heritage, and tourism, and the growth of local economies. It sheds light on the connections between pilgrimage sites and their routes using the Temple of the Emerald Buddha in Bangkok and Phra That Doi Suthep in Chiang Mai as case examples. The goal is to educate those who care about sustainable regional development in Southeast Asia on the best practices for managing and upgrading these sacred paths.

Preface

The book *Experiences, Advantages and Economic Dimensions of Pilgrimage Routes* encompasses a set of contributions associated with the phenomenon of pilgrimage. It arises from the relevance of a phenomenon as an ancient practice, which despite the processes of transformation of societies, at political, social and cultural levels, that is still practiced in different societies and cultures in the contemporary world.

Pilgrimages have been studied in several dimensions. On a historical level, the studies focus mainly on the origins of pilgrimages, in understanding the meanings and contexts in which people in the past did this kind of practice. In sociological terms, the phenomenon has been mainly seen through the meaning of what this venture represents for man in the present, on a religious/spiritual level. In other words, sociologists have made an attempt to observe the meaning and importance of religion and the way in which it is lived in pilgrimage contexts. Other sociological studies have also tried to discover the relevance of the venture in the life of each pilgrim how it affected themselves and their relationship with others. They were focused as well on the importance of the various forms of evasion, discovery and the pilgrims' experiences. Pilgrimage also impacts other realities, namely economic ones due to what it represents and the importance it has in terms of geographic mobility. It contributes to tourism in regions that are often far away from large population centers, thus enhancing the development of communities. They also contribute to the discovery of material and immaterial cultural heritage. It is important to highlight that it is through pilgrimage that natural heritage is often discovered and valued, in its diversity and particularity. In this sense, pilgrimage is seen and has been studied as a tourist, religious/spiritual but also a cultural phenomenon. More recently, attention has been drawn to the issues of sustainable tourism and pilgrimages, particularly in Europe, have been observed through this prism considering the often difficult to operationalize equation that involves development and respect for natural and cultural heritage.

As it is a practice that crosses multiple cultures, it is important to bring together diverse contributions that allow to know, explain and understand the relevance of the pilgrimage. This book has this particularity that distinguishes it from works that focus on certain geographic or sociocultural universes. In effect, it is a work that seeks to discover aspects linked to pilgrimage in distinct societies and cultures on a global scale. The pilgrimages covered in the work are located in diverse geographical locations, on various continents such as America, Europe and Asia. They arise from very different cultural universes, framed in some cases by major religions, such as Buddhism, Christianity, and Hinduism, but equally, in other cases, marked by the new age spirituality that has been highlighted in the Western world since the 1960s.

The studies gathered here are based on the three central axes of the book: experiences, advantages, and economic dimensions of pilgrimages:

Chapter 1 begins with an exploration of regional development intertwined with pilgrimage itineraries, particularly focusing on Apulia, Italy. The historical and economic dimensions of the Via Francigena pilgrimage route are analyzed, emphasizing its relevance and potential impacts on the region.

Chapter 2 delves into the rich and diverse sector of religious tourism in Pakistan, discussing the challenges it faces and the potential transformative solutions provided by OpenStreetMap (OSM). It explores how OSM can empower users to map religious sites, improve accessibility, and promote cultural preservation, contributing to the growth of this sector.

In chapter 3, the author shares their personal pilgrimage experiences, reflecting on their journeys to significant religious sites. From fears of illness to unexpected solidarity, this chapter is a heartfelt account of a pilgrim's spiritual and physical journey.

Chapter 4 offers a biographical study of Paulinus of Nola, a Roman senator turned bishop, and his association with pilgrimage to the tomb of Felix. It highlights Paulinus' role as a patron of pilgrims and how he influenced the early Christian pilgrimage experience.

Exploring the phenomenon of medieval pilgrimages to mountain shrines and their contemporary revival, chapter 5 focuses on the unique case of western Castellón and eastern Teruel in Spain. It analyzes the motivations and meanings behind these pilgrimages, emphasizing their potential benefits to rural communities.

Chapter 6 explores the significance of Anatolia in Christianity, specifically focusing on the seven churches mentioned in the Bible. It delves into faith tourism and pilgrimage within the context of Christianity, offering examples of tours and discussing evaluation criteria.

Focusing on the massive gathering event of Kumbh Mela, chapter 7 examines various dimensions of pilgrimage itineraries, including crowd control, pilgrimage experiences, economic implications, and safety. It emphasizes the importance of proper planning and management to enhance the pilgrim experience.

Chapter 8 delves into the technical ability to survey across land and ice, examining existing large bisects (Norse "vis") and their significance in mapping alignments with churches. It provides insights into the possible origins of church orientations and their geometric determinations.

Chapter 9 offers a deep understanding of emerging trends and the evolution of the Camino de Santiago pilgrimage, based on an analysis of research papers. It identifies three main research perspectives and their impact on stakeholders associated with the Camino de Santiago.

Focusing on the Caminho do Sol route in São Paulo, Brazil, chapter 10 explores creative tourism as a potential for regional development through narratives of pilgrims. It emphasizes the advantages creative tourism offers to the local community from a socio-economic perspective.

Chapter 11 delves into pilgrimage routes in Southeast Asia, particularly in Thailand, highlighting their cultural, gastronomic, and ecological elements. It analyzes the regional impact and explores the relationship between pilgrimage, cultural heritage, and tourism.

Chapter 12 collects data and opinions from pilgrims on the Portuguese Inner Way to Santiago de Compostela, focusing on physical preparation, alternative paths, logistic services, and effective preservation of the itineraries. It offers recommendations for improving the pilgrim experience.

Chapter 13 provides insights into pilgrimage routes by analyzing historical records, specifically focusing on the Ways of Santiago de Compostela. It offers a benchmark to understand the dimensions of pilgrimage routes associated with various pilgrimages.

Chapter 14 examines how the COVID-19 pandemic affected religious customs in Indochina, focusing on three distinct religious rituals. It analyzes the adjustments made by religious organizations and rituals, their challenges, and the role of religion in times of crisis.

Chapter 15 explores the economic dimensions, opportunities, and challenges of developing heritage and spiritual railway tourism train routes in India. It highlights the role of these routes in celebrating India's diverse heritage, promoting tourism, and generating revenue and employment opportunities.

In effect, the pilgrim's vision of his own experiences, allows the reader to understand the pilgrimage process from the image and feelings of the traveler himself. These experiences may be about present or past realities. The role that religions and some figures associated with them play in the emergence and appreciation of pilgrimage routes and the experiences of pilgrims are behold in this book. Pilgrimages were marked by the experiences of individuals that stem from specific ways of feeling the pilgrimage, and some of these individuals ended up enhancing the phenomenon of peregrinatio, due to their own experiences in these contexts. Experiences are framed by religious or spiritual phenomena. However, pilgrimage is much more than a religious or spiritual phenomenon. It is a determining reality, in some cases, transformative for the individual who experiences it and the community through which the route passes. In this book, the issue of pilgrimage is also remarked upon what it can promote in terms of the human development. Infrastructure issues, aspects related to georeferencing technology, as well as issues related to the health and safety of pilgrims, the latter in order to make pilgrimage routes safe places, are also aspects covered. The economic and the relevance of the pilgrimage in its tourist dimension could not fail to be addressed. The impact of pilgrimage as a tourist phenomenon in the economic progress of communities, the involvement of stakeholders, the benefits that translate into the development of spaces, especially rural areas that pilgrimage enhance, permeate several studies of the book. The role that pilgrimage can have in promoting intercultural contacts is also brought to light. This aspect is of capital importance in a contemporary world marked by wars and conflicts. By bringing together people from diverse cultural backgrounds, the pilgrimage contributes to uniting people. In short, this book enriches the knowledge of pilgrimage, an undeniable reality of the present, which despite being a multi-secular practice, still has strength and projection in various physical geographies and cultural latitudes of the contemporary world.

Vítor João Pereira Domingues Martinho
ESAV, CERNAS-IPV Research Centre, Polytechnic Institute of Viseu, Portugal

João Augusto Guerra da Rocha Nunes
School of Education, Polytechnic Institute of Viseu, Portugal

Maria Lúcia de Jesus Pato
Agricultural S (IPV), 3chool (ESAV), and CERNAS-IPV Research Centre, Polytechnic Institute of Viseu, Portugal

Liliana Andrade de Matos Castilho
School of Education, Polytechnic Institute of Viseu, Portugal

Chapter 1
Ancient Roads, New Potential: The Christian Pilgrimages Pivot of Territorial Development

Antonietta Ivona
https://orcid.org/0000-0003-3508-4489
University of Bari Aldo Moro, Italy

ABSTRACT

The chapter offers a reflection on regional development and pilgrimage itineraries. After proceeding with the review of the geographical literature, the analysis will move to the study of the phenomenon on a regional scale with a focus on Apulia and on the current and potential effects of Apulian pilgrimages. In particular, the case study will focus on the "Via Francigena of Capitanata." The Via Francigena is a historical path that from Canterbury led first to Rome, then to Jerusalem. Traveled in the Middle Ages by pilgrims and crusaders, it crossed the whole of Apulia, starting from the Dauni Mountains. By adopting a geo-economic approach, the chapter intends to analyze the religious and spiritual motivations, political and institutional conditioning, and above all the economic-territorial repercussions of a secular phenomenon but still of great relevance and equally important multiplicative potential.

INTRODUCTION

Pilgrimage is one of the most deep-rooted and relevant phenomena in the history of Christianity. Over the centuries, generations of faithful have felt the desire to set out, covering short distances or crossing entire continents, spending a few hours or long years, to seek an encounter with God in "special" places and times. This aspiration has accompanied the development of Christianity, following its progress, tensions, and splits from late antiquity to the contemporary age, up to the present day. This centuries-old but still highly relevant phenomenon has an equally important multiplicative economic potential given its economic-territorial implications.

DOI: 10.4018/978-1-6684-9923-8.ch001

Pilgrimage is a widespread practice on a global level which, in different geographical and chronological contexts, has involved and still involves lay people and ecclesiastics, individuals and communities, masses and elites, regions and places.

As has happened since the dawn of this religious practice, even today pilgrimages can be a boost to the development of the territories crossed. As will be seen in the following paragraphs, the passage of pilgrims generated, along the designed itineraries, ever support activities generated by their needs. From the need for refreshment after long hours of walking (*hospitalia*) to the request for means of transport to reach the holy places.

Historically, Puglia has been among the territories crossed by multiple pilgrimage routes which have contributed to defining the territorial organization over time.

Those ancient flows of pilgrims which reduced over time for various historical, political, and social reasons seem to have returned today and are increasing year after year. Among the most important pilgrimage routes that cross Apulia is the southern Via Francigena.

The not yet definitive data on the statistics on pilgrim flows in 2022 in Apulia record an increase of +24% compared to the previous year. Only by considering the estimated flow projections for the Via Francigena would it be possible to reach a +45% in incoming. Then evaluating the economic impact of the walkers' stay in the Apulia area for 2022, the data stands at a conservative estimate of over two million euros.

To fully understand the value of the current pilgrimage routes, the chapter, after having outlined the geoeconomic approach to the phenomenon of pilgrimage, presents a brief historical excursus to understand its origins and diffusion. The final case study (The Via Francigena of the Capitanata and the Dauni Mountains) is a proposal for a combination of religious tourism, rural areas and economic development which could also be achieved thanks to the various funding currently available and linked to this very purpose.

THE GEOECONOMICAL APPROACH AND THE PILGRIMAGE PHENOMENON

The origins of pilgrimages are difficult to determine, but visiting sacred sites has been a widespread practice since ancient times. Pilgrimages have long been a common feature of many world religions; they were undertaken to fulfill a vow, as expiation for sins, as a gesture of thanksgiving for positive events or as a means of intercession between man and the divine. Before the spread of travel in the modern sense, pilgrimage was the motivation for human movements for "fun", according to the Latin etymology of the term *devertere* ('turning elsewhere').

Today pilgrimage is a complex and changing phenomenon, with different implications at a religious, political, social, and territorial level.

According to the geoeconomic approach, religion is not only a factor in shaping the landscape and defining lifestyles. Religious geography studies therefore aim to explain the relationship between religion and society, to retrace the history of the birth and diffusion of new cults and the marginalization of old cults from a geographical-territorial perspective. This includes the study of the events that have affected the pilgrim routes over the centuries and the analysis of the links between religion and use of the environment, recently revisited from a conservationist perspective. Geographical-religious studies also investigate the relationship between local cultures and environmental peculiarities, in relation to the environments in which cults arose and/or spread, especially with reference to the urban/rural dichotomy. (Levine, 1986; Kong, 1990; Jenkins & Chapple, 2011).

The relationships between religion and tourism today constitute a privileged object of study on a cultural and social level, but also on an economic and political level.

Already in 1948, Deffontaines considered religion essentially as a factor in the transformation of the geographical landscape, abandoning the traditional perspective which described the geographical distribution of different religious forms in the world and the influence of geographical factors on their diffusion. He takes into consideration the manifestations of religion in their repercussions on the landscape starting from the characteristics of the religious sanctuaries, noting how, predominantly, they dotted the highest sites to be easily recognisable. Religion is therefore proposed as a constitutive element of landscape architecture, which shapes pilgrimage itineraries, in a visible way, through the diffusion of places of worship or of the living, of places of the deceased, of places of circulation, with devotional routes.

However, from whatever point of view it is considered, for Deffontaines (1948) religion is an *élément consommateur* of space and resources variable from cult to cult. He ended up replacing the old environmental determinisms with what we could call a religious determinism, attributing to religious beliefs and cult practices a decisive and sometimes almost absolute influence in the construction of geographical landscapes and in the organization of ways of life. (Lefebvre, 1974; Tuan, 1977; Galliano, 2002).

In continuity with the value of Deffontaines' studies for his theoretical reflections on the links between religion and geography and for the methodological proposals in the analysis of the localization processes of human settlements linked to religious facts, Pedreschi's studies on religious centres should also be remembered (Pedreschi, 1966). He highlighted the territorial effects of religious circulation generated by particularly well-known religious centres. These effects can be immediately tangible such as, for example, the partial transformations of the surrounding natural environment (excavations, leveling, diversion of water courses, etc.), the valorisation of some elements (a cave or a group of caves, a spring, erratic boulders, a rocky outcrop, a rock face, a rose garden, etc.), the inclusion of particular cultural elements in the landscape (such as roads, car parks, stairways, cable cars, aqueducts, etc.) and above all the agricultural valorization of some surrounding areas, generally corresponding to those acquired as property, following bequests, donations, etc., to the various religious communities. Or intangible effects such as the increase in local activities linked to the presence of pilgrims and/or religious tourists (accommodation facilities, artisanal, commercial, cultural, folklore activities and much more).

Studies aimed at privileging religion as a "directing factor" for the understanding of cultural globality appear equally important; other significant studies highlight the way in which religious sentiment and the sense of belonging to a religious community are reflected in the organization of the territory. (Caldo, 1990; Santus, 1990; Rocca, 2003, Vallega 2006).

Some scholars including Caldo (1990) highlight the 'sense of place' which compared to the French *espace vécu* appears as an enhanced environmental relationship, because we move from the sense of space linked to social relationships to the sense of sacred space. When an element (a mountain, a tree, a bell tower) of a space becomes the symbol representing a community if the latter attributes to it the functions of a place of worship, its symbolic value is strengthened and it becomes the goal of collective aggregation, and a witness of the religiosity of the inhabitants (Galliano, 2002); it is, therefore, a cultural asset, not artistic or unique, "but an expression of the popular culture shared and internalized by the social group" (Caldo, 1990, p. 4).

Sacred space is something more: it is not only a landscape full of meaning and memories, but it has an evocative power that transcends it. Defining and circumscribing sacred space is one of the topics on which anthropologists, sociologists and historians of religions have most often discussed without ever reaching a univocal agreement on its definition.

Furthermore, the links between geography and religion appear clearly visible in the landscape, which is interwoven with the traces left by cults both in the organization of the territory and in the expressions and models of social behavior. The impact of religious culture on the territory, however, is not limited to legacies that refer to the strictly spiritual aspect but goes beyond them through expressions that have a strong impact on both the morphology of the landscape and the economy of the territorial area concerned. In fact, religions also qualify space with the manifestations of material culture, such as food, clothing, social behavior, with times, cadences, and customs specific to the different faiths. (Brandenburg & Carroll, 1995; Imarisio, 2011).

Understandings of religious tourism have evolved beyond pilgrimage and now encompass the meaningfulness of a destination. Recent explorations have extended beyond visitor motivations to consider their identities, such as individual religious affiliations and religiosity.

One interpretation of religious tourism is as an organic system that encompasses not only holy places, but also the services and relevant facilities associated with official religious organizations and a spectrum of visitors ranging from the devout to the secular. (Lefeuvre, 1980).

In some recent studies, then, the concept of secularized and commodified pilgrimage has emerged in parallel with a paradigm shift towards the contemporary commodification and commercialization of religious tourism and pilgrimage (Collins-Kreiner, 2016a; Hung et al., 2017; Nilsson & Tesfahuney, 2016). Other studies have highlighted secularism in religious tourism by focusing on the post-secular aspect of pilgrimage (Collins-Kreiner, 2016b; Murray & Graham, 1997). Secular pilgrimages are increasingly recognized as a postmodern form, as researchers have sought to understand the needs of new secular pilgrims who are minimally motivated by religious faith (Brown, 2016; Digance, 2003; Hyde & Harman, 2011). Thus, tourism scholars have given widespread recognition to contemporary pilgrimage as a domain of religious tourism and tourism more generally. (Bona et al., 2020).

According to Damari & Mansfeld (2016) "Pilgrimage is an ancient practice which encompasses both tradition and change; and both factors have been motivating millions of people to embark on a journey to holy sites worldwide. Scholars who nowadays try to understand this complex phenomenon are called upon to deal with religious, spiritual, social, economic, political, and geographical issues that stem from the ramifications of globalization and global change." (p. 200).

In the contemporary scholarly landscape, the conflation of pilgrims and tourists or the assimilation of pilgrimage into the broader concept of tourism emerges as a noteworthy paradigm shift. Scholars now converge on recognizing pilgrimage as a seamless integration within diverse modalities of tourism. A critical determinant of tourists' trust in destination brands, including those infused with religious themes, rests upon subjective sentiments. Crucial elements of destination branding encompass the expeditious availability of comprehensive information about scenic locales, the profundity of spiritual experiences proffered, and the distinctiveness of commercial undertakings entwined with these sacred destinations (Guriţă, D.; Scortescu, 2023).

THE UNIVERSAL PHENOMENON OF PILGRIMAGE

Pilgrimage is one of the most deep-rooted and relevant phenomena in the history of Christianity. Over the centuries, generations of faithful have felt the desire to set out, covering short distances or crossing entire continents, spending a few hours or long years, to seek an encounter with God in "special" places and times. This aspiration has accompanied the development of Christianity, following its progress, tensions, and ruptures from late antiquity to the contemporary age, up to the present day. Pilgrimage is in fact a widespread practice on a global level which, in different geographical and chronological contexts, has involved, and still does, lay people and ecclesiastics, individuals and communities, masses and elites, regions and places.

The practice of pilgrimage is still widespread as pilgrims are linked to sacred places due to the roles such places play in their religious belief systems and identities. This approach can still be found in many types of pilgrimages, not just Christian ones. For example, the sacred city of Mecca continues to play a significant role in the identity of every Muslim cleric who is obliged to visit the city at least once in his life. Likewise, in Jewish tradition, Jerusalem is frequently cited as the holiest city, and both the Yom Kippur prayer and the Easter Seder end with the phrase "next year in Jerusalem." In short, sacred places, perhaps always, are filled with meanings and signifiers; they become objects of sacred value only if shared by the same human group.

The pilgrimage establishes a special relationship between the earthly dimension and the sacred dimension. The physical commitment necessary to reach the goal is a metaphor of man's spiritual journey, fraught with sacrifices and renunciations, aimed at renewing the spirit, attaining glory, paradise and eternal salvation depending on the beliefs considered.

There are documents relating to historical and extremely ancient pilgrimages to Mesopotamia, Egypt or Greece. If in Hinduism pilgrimages are almost always linked to waterways, in Buddhism they are linked to the relics of Buddha or to events that characterized his life. Shintoism, also, has numerous places of pilgrimage since the kami or nature spirits dwell in them. Thousands of pilgrims converge towards Jerusalem, Rome, Santiago de Compostela and Mecca, the largest centres of the three major monotheistic religions.

As regards Christian pilgrimage, the places linked to the life of Jesus Christ, the disciples and the first martyrs became soon centres of devotion and destinations for pilgrims since Christianity borrows pilgrimages from the Jewish tradition. Freedom of worship and the imposition of Christianity as the official religion of the Roman Empire in the 4th century favoured the expansion and proliferation of these places. The tombs of the apostles and martyrs or their relics led to the creation of important pilgrimage centres in the Middle Ages. In the 16th century, the sale of indulgences, the excessive veneration of relics and other excesses were the object of reproach both within the Catholic Church, through the figure of Erasmus of Rotterdam, and outside it, through Luther.

In the first centuries of the Christian era there are testimonies of pilgrims who set out to visit the places where the events recounted in the Gospels had occurred. For example, before the Constantinian peace, towards the middle of the 2nd century, Melito, Bishop of Sardi, went to the locations mentioned in the biblical texts and drew up a list of the books of the Old Testament; Origene, expelled from Alexandria, settled in Caesarea and travelled through Palestine to discover the traces of Jesus and his disciples, as well as the prophets; the Cappodoc Bishop Alexander went to Jerusalem to pray and visit the places. But their interest went beyond seeing; they wanted to relive the history of salvation in those places.

After the Edict of Constantine, pilgrimages to biblical places became more frequent. Among others, those of the Pilgrim of Bordeaux, of Egeria, of the Pseudo Eucherio and of the Pseudo Antoninus of Piacenza are known. Subsequently, pilgrimages to the martyria, i.e., to the tombs of the martyrs, spread together with the cult of their relics. Starting from the sec. VI-VII, during and after the inclusion of new peoples within the borders of the Roman Empire, forms of penitential pilgrimage developed.

In the centuries X and XI, the pilgrimage became a form of asceticism: medieval man sought the *fuga mundi* and martyrdom was seen as a journey that crowns earthly existence. The Camino de Santiago de Compostela, for example, experienced in solitude and penance, became emblematic of this form of asceticism and sacrifice. The Crusades also took on spiritual significance. In the crusader there was the belief that through risks and adversities one could conquer divine mercy, purifying the soul from sins and crimes of different nature, precisely because the search for reconciliation with God and the conquest of the holy places where Jesus had lived his earthly life. (Cozzo, 2021).

With the solicitations of the Protestant Reformation, pilgrimage passed from a penitential function to a devotional one; instead of visiting abbeys and monasteries, pilgrims now went to sanctuaries. Marian ones flourished, which originated from apparitions or the discovery of statues, images, or aedicules. Thus, the Marian pilgrimage almost became the model of the journey in faith. In fact, the names of Loreto, Caravaggio, Guadalupe, Aparecida, La Salette, Lourdes, Fatima, Czestochowa traced the spiritual topography of humanity, alongside the endless list of local Marian temples.

Sanctuaries dedicated to the saints also arose, which were based on their tombs or on the places where they had lived, such as San Francesco in Assisi, Sant'Antonio in Padua, Santa Rita in Cascia, etc.

This brief historical *excursus* allows us to identify the typology of Christian pilgrimages, first listing the pilgrimage of devotion, which in ancient times established contact with the sacred places of the Holy Land and the first Christian communities. A famous example of devotional pilgrimage was that made by Saint Helena, mother of Constantine I, in the 4th century AD. She is attributed with the discovery of the tomb of Christ dug into the rock and shortly afterwards the cross of the Lord and those of the

Figure 1. Monte Sant'Angelo, Museo Devozionale: Byzantine-Lombard icon of Saint Michael the Archangel
Source: Ivona, 2023.

two thieves, which occurred in 326. This event produced great emotion throughout Christianity; for this reason, the first and natural destinations of the pilgrim were the two "sacred stones": that of Calvary, on which the cross was raised, and that of the Sepulchre, which remained empty after the resurrection.

The palmiers, as the pilgrims who went to Jerusalem were called and whose name derives from the practice of collecting and bringing back home the palms of Jericho, found themselves in difficulty in fulfilling their pilgrimage with the Islamic conquest of Jerusalem in 637; nevertheless, by the 4th century other goals had already been established; for Italy mainly Rome, with its *memoriae apostolorum* and martyrs, and the rock sanctuary of San Michele Arcangelo on the Gargano (Figure 1). For other destinations, the basis of the pilgrimage was the cult of the relics of saints and martyrs, which throughout the Middle Ages had significant dimensions. It was rare for a city not to celebrate the remains of a saint, a confessor, or the Virgin Mary.

With the custom of penitential pilgrims going to Rome, they overlapped with devotional pilgrims, who visited the tombs and relics of the apostles Peter and Paul there. During the Middle Ages the two forms of pilgrimage converged to the point of becoming confused and uniform: each pilgrim sought the expiation of something.

Subsequently, the Church recognized pilgrimage as a fundamental experience of religious life and regulated it, providing it with a specific vow and related spiritual indulgences. After the year 1000, pilgrimages were one of the drivers of the newfound mobility of people and accompanied the rebirth of trade. The pilgrimage routes were equipped with *hospitalia* (hospices) where they could refresh themselves and be treated if they were sick.

The 12th century was also the scene of a strong spiritual dynamism following the distinction between the vow of crusade (which provided for plenary indulgence) and the vow of pilgrimage. The crusade became a real institution within the Catholic Church, which involved an armed pilgrimage with the aim of liberating Jerusalem and could be called exclusively by the pontiff. (Flori, 2003; Cardini, Musarra, 2019).

Until the late Middle Ages, religious travel was an event that was among the most widespread religious habits of the time, the motivations for which were different and intertwined both the spiritual and human spheres. The motivations that pushed men to undertake the pilgrimage were influenced by historical events, by the evolution of society as well as by the indications of the church for which, over the centuries there was the prevalence of some motivations over others or the combination of some of them (relics, fear of the end of the world, the remission of sins, participation in jubilees, penitential and judicial pilgrimages). (Sumption, 1993; Duccio, 2005).

For the three monotheistic religions of the Mediterranean, Judaism, Christianity and Islam, the desire to experience mercy turns first to Jerusalem, where three rocks act as pillars for the spiritual construction of the experience of internal pacification and celebration that is the basis of their belief. There is the stone of the temple of Zion: "God is in the midst of it: it cannot be shaken... The people trembled; the kingdoms trembled; he thundered: the earth crumbled" (Psalm 46,6-7). There is the overturned stone of Christ's tomb, a sign of victory over death: "An angel of the Lord came down from heaven and rolled back the stone and sat on it" (Gospel of Matthew, New Testament, 28.2). Finally, there is the stone of the "Dome of the Rock", covered and incorporated by the current mosque of Omar, the site of the sacrifice of Isaac (Gen 22) and the ascension into heaven of the prophet of Islam, Muhammad. The Holy Land has been the vital center of pilgrimage, especially Christian pilgrimage, for centuries, starting from Jerome up to the pilgrims of the Middle Ages and those of today. In the place of the crucifixion and resurrection of Jesus, in particular, the pilgrims found an opportunity for solidarity between men and churches, relationships of dialogue between popular piety and official liturgy, between different and sometimes tense rites, which however reflected the same fidelity to the evangelical message. But for Christianity Rome is undoubtedly the other great destination of convergence, the place of the martyrdom of Peter and Paul and the seat of ecclesial communion *ad Petri sedem*. And it is the Jubilee that marks the rhythms of time and calls cosmopolitan pilgrims to experience the gift of mercy. At the same time, however, the network of pilgrimage routes thickens and branches out towards secondary destinations, represented by the tombs of the apostles and martyrs, veritable treasure chests of relics, including Saint Martin of Tours, Santiago de Compostela, Canterbury, and many local sanctuaries, alongside those dedicated to the veneration of the Madonna. Jerusalem, Rome, the sanctuaries of the martyrs and saints and those of Mary are, therefore, the four cardinal points of the Christian pilgrimage.

THE SOUTHERN VIA FRANCIGENA

Over the centuries, since the early Middle Ages, the Via Francigena has represented the itinerary followed by pilgrims from Central-Northern Europe to reach Rome, seat of the Papacy and heart of Christianity. What is known today as the Via Francigena is the 1,800 km (80 stages) itinerary traveled in 79 days by Archbishop Sigeric in the year 990 to return to Canterbury from Rome after the investiture of the Archbishop's Pallium by Pope John XV. Sigeric, at the invitation of the Pope, wrote down all the stages, one for each day, which took him back to Great Britain through Europe. His diary is therefore the most authentic testimony of the route of the Via Francigena from Rome to the English Channel. The name "Francigena" did not only indicate a devotional route for the exclusive use of pilgrims, but a route traveled by merchants, armies, politicians, and men of culture, thus creating a primary channel of communication and exchange, and allowing all those interrelationships that brought to the substantial unity of European culture between the 10th and 13th centuries. With men and goods, the Via Francigena brought ideas, technical and ideological innovations, encouraging comparison and integration of the various cultural currents. (Trono, 2012; Berti, 2012).

Although a conventional route has never existed since late antiquity real pilgrimage routes have been defined along the network of ancient Roman roads. They certainly weren't smooth journeys; the roads were mostly simple tracks covered in mud or ice and it was necessary to face, especially in winter, almost insurmountable natural obstacles such as the Alps. Usually the journeys involved composite routes: a stretch of road, the ferrying of a watercourse, a path through a forest, a stretch of river navigation. In addition to the possible routes on the remains of Roman roads, pilgrims identified other parallel routes along which there were villages, xenodochia (assistance and rest facilities later called hospitium), inns, churches, and abbeys.

In other cases, pilgrims used roads already identified by traditional routes converging on Rome from much of the peninsula. An example of this is the Via Francigena whose route crossed the Alps in the Aosta Valley (Gran S. Bernardo pass), descended from Piedmont and Lombardy into the Po Valley, crossed the Apennines towards Berceto, flowed along Tuscany and Lazio to reach Rome.

The political settlement of the South, between the 6th and 7th centuries, with the domination of the Byzantines first and then the Lombards, made transit safer and favoured various forms of pilgrimage, both lay and religious, through the most important roads in the South of Italy. To these destinations were added several other venerated places because apparitions and wonders of powerful intercessors of God had been confirmed there; among them the most visited were Canterbury in England; Mont-Saint-Michel and Chartres in France; Cologne and Aachen in Germany; Loreto, Assisi, the Cave of the Archangel

San Michele in Monte Sant'Angelo, the Basilica of San Nicola in Bari and many others in Italy; such sanctuaries have thus traced spiritual maps in the Western world.

The strategic position of southern Italy as a shore in the Mediterranean towards the East was of central importance in the pilgrim movement. It was located at the crossroads of the main Mediterranean trade routes. Oldfield (2014) states that "Southern Italy also occupied an integral position in the 'Christianized topography' of medieval Christendom. Cult centres often emerged at key nodes of passage and communication; islands and peninsulas were thus endowed with particular sacred qualities." (p. 182). Without a doubt, the cult centres of southern Italy also represented the final points of the journeys of many pilgrims who arrived from foreign countries attracted by the sanctuaries present throughout the area and who have spread their mystical charm throughout Christianity. However, for an even greater number of pilgrims, southern Italy was experienced as part of that crucial phase of transition that created the penitential dimensions of a journey that had its destination elsewhere. In short, Southern Italy in medieval times was a sort of crossroads for the atonement of sins or, as Oldfield defines it, 'a bridge to salvation'.

Among the southern Italian regions, Apulia combined more functions than that of eastern *finis terrae*; especially in the Crusader era it played a role of notable importance: its ports allowed the embarkation of pilgrims and knights for the Holy Land, it was the outpost of the monastic-chivalric orders whose traces in many cases are still visible in the area north of Bari. Its location in the final stretch of the Via Francigena was fundamental; that pilgrimage itinerary that linked Canterbury to Rome and then to the ports of Apulia, allowed the arrival in the Holy Land. Apulia was long crossed by the Via Francigena del Sud connecting Rome and the Adriatic ports of Apulia; it retraced the Via Appia and the Via Traiana, the consular roads built by the Romans. (Stopani, 1992; Ceraudo, 2015; Musti, 1988).

Between 108 and 110 AD. Emperor Traiano wanted to create an easier and faster itinerary that linked the capital of the empire to the important port of Brindisi. A branch was created in Benevento, starting from Traiano triumphal arch, and used already existing and modernized routes (such as the ancient route of the Via Minucia) which allowed some mountainous sections to be avoided. Passing through Troia (Aecae), Canosa (Canusium), Ruvo di Puglia (Rubi), Bitonto (Butontum), Bari (Barium), Egnazia (Gnatia) and Santa Sabina (Speluncae) and a series of post stations called *stationes*, he managed to reduce the journey by at least a day compared to the original route, for a total of 206 Roman miles (just over 300 km). Overall, the alternative route was 45 km (28 miles) shorter. The roads which until then had been of beaten ground were completely renovated. The Via Traiana thus quickly became the most important road axis crossing northern and central Apulia, encouraging the development of the cities that were located along its route.

In addition to the Via Appia, the Via Minucia and the Via Litoranea, thanks to the discovery of some milestones, other viae publicae are known in northern and central Apulia: a via Aemilia, probably along the borders between Apulia and Campania but there is no historical evidence and certain archaeological; the Via Gellia was a coastal road axis that would have joined Egnatia to Butuntum passing through Barium as an alternative to the internal variant to be identified with the stretch of the Minucia described by Strabo. Another road was the so-called 'short route' Barium-Tarentum (Bari-Taranto) which was a shortcut for those who wanted to reach Taranto directly from Bari, avoiding the longer passage through Brindisi.

The Roman roads described above primarily represented commercial and military routes, but, over the centuries, they had become already established routes that could also be used as pilgrimage networks. (Ivona, 2023).

But Apulia was also a welcoming land. In addition to strategic ports for the embarkation and disembarkation of pilgrims, it offered hospitality and above all devotional sanctuaries among the most venerated in Christianity. Just think of the sanctuary of San Michele in Monte Sant'Angelo and that of San Nicola in Bari, a crucial stop for European pilgrimages; it was also the place of presence of the military orders of the Hospitallers, the Templars and the Teutonic Order who built various structures intended to welcome pilgrims both departing and returning from the Holy Land and to supply their homes in the East with products from the region. Stopani highlighted how in Apulia "the connection between the land routes and the maritime itineraries to the Holy Land took place: the geographical position of the region, projected towards the East with the Salento peninsula, somehow predestined it to become a sort of "carrefour" of the circulation linked to the Jerusalem pilgrimage" (in Bianco, 2016, p. 86).

"The region, already participating in the *peregrinationes maiores* towards the destinations of the holy places of Rome and Santiago de Compostella, defines its sacred geography through a network of land itineraries punctuated by intermediate stages, coinciding with important regional sanctuaries: San Michele Arcangelo a Monte Sant'Angelo, Santa Maria dei Martiri in Molfetta, San Nicola in Bari, Santa Maria di Leuca in the extreme edge of the region. The pilgrimage itineraries and the transhumance routes that crossed central Italy, but also the Adriatic routes that connected the regions overlooking the Adriatic, were the backdrop to the movement of these pilgrims." (Laterza, 2013, p. 251). In support of the long-lasting fortune that the Loreto cult had in Apulia from the 15th to the 18th century, numerous architectural testimonies remain (several churches were built in the Apulian territory to venerate the cult of the Madonna of Loreto) but also documentary and archaeological evidence. As emerges from some historical documents, not only religious but also economic and cultural relations existed between Apulia and the Loreto sanctuary. (Grimaldi, 1993).

In that context thus outlined, the Via Francigena (also defined as Francisca or Romea, depending on whether one wanted to define its departure from France or arrival in Rome) appears of strategic importance according to the itinerary of Archbishop Sigeric. It was part of a group of routes, also called Ways of Rome, which from Western Europe, in particular from France, led to Southern Europe up to Rome and then continued towards Apulia, where there were the embarkation ports for the Holy Land, destination of pilgrims and crusaders.

In particular, the stretch of the Via Francigena in Southern Italy generated by the intricate Roman road system, represented a bridge between Europe and the Mediterranean, and its function as a cultural hinge is still extremely relevant. The Via Francigena in the South, from Rome to Santa Maria di Leuca, was approximately 930 kilometers long (compared to the total 3200 kilometers of the Via Francigena) and included 45 stages.

Furthermore, we must not overlook the fact that the homonym Francigena is also used to indicate those routes that headed towards the Gargano sanctuary of the Archangel Michael. (Figures 2). The sanctuary, in fact, remained an important destination also on the way to the Holy Land. During the early Middle Ages, the pilgrimage to Monte Sant'Angelo on the Gargano became a European phenomenon and starting from the ninth century various itineraries with the name of Via Francisca or Via Longobardorum reached the Gargano sanctuary and the Apulian Adriatic ports. Precisely that of the Archangel Michael testifies how the importance of the Sanctuary itself is not measured only on the basis of what it originated from, but also on the basis of what it has produced. Even today the local economy of the Gargano villages crossed by the roads to the sanctuary is also supported by the flows of pilgrims.

Naturally, the roads didn't always remain the same since due to wear, atmospheric agents and vandalism, route reconstructions and changes occurred, while in the Middle Ages circulation was also

Figure 2. The official map of Via Francigena European stages
Source: Via Francigena Road to Rome, 2023

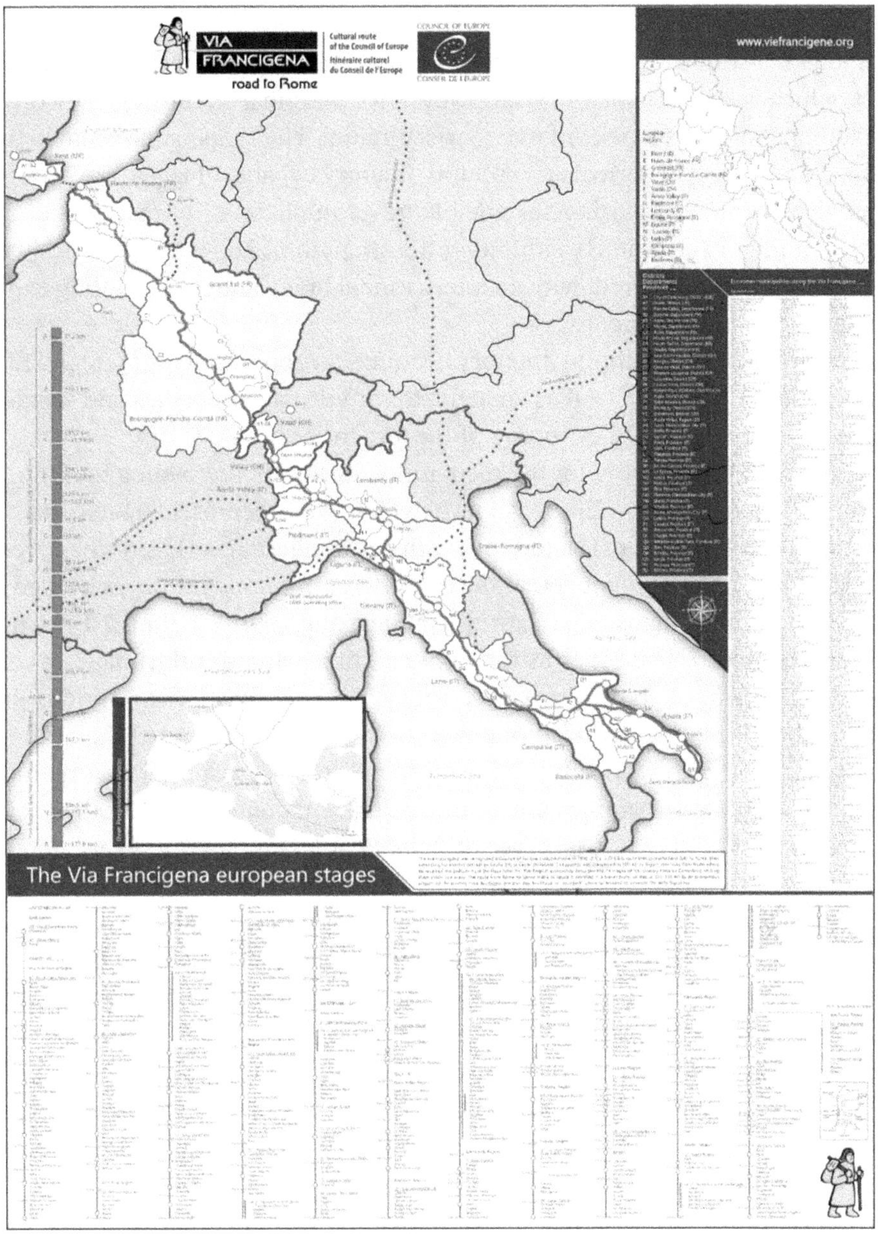

distributed through other routes which constituted the minor roads. The contemporary Via Francigena, from Canterbury to Leuca, obtained the certification of "Cultural Itinerary of the Council of Europe" in 1994. As a cultural itinerary of the Council of Europe it maintains the oldest route for walking, landscape and heritage valorization needs cultural, but the medieval and historical routes do not always coincide with the current routes due to the transformation of the landscape since from the Middle Ages to today it has changed considerably, undergoing intense anthropization especially since the second half of the 15th century. (Paul, 2014).

THE VIA FRANCIGENA IN SOUTHERN ITALY AND THE PROSPECTS FOR TERRITORIAL DEVELOPMENT

The Via Francigena constitutes a concrete possibility of building and promoting a quality tourist or cultural product, which is a reason for valorisation even for marginal territories; they often are excluded from traditional competitive strategies or large tourist circuits. The Francigena route in the South has all the potential to become a great historical and cultural itinerary capable of triggering valorisation actions, respecting the environment and favoring sustainable travel in places of attraction and in often defined territorial realities of minor tourism. By exploiting the strength of network dynamics, new elements of the tourist offer can also be configured, with an international brand and a storytelling capacity perceived by the visitor in a unitary and coherent way.

In this sense, the religious and cultural itinerary becomes an opportunity for integrated valorization of the multiple economies involved, as well as an activator of virtuous processes and sustainable mobility, capable of giving new impetus to the economy of the territories crossed.

Furthermore, it would be desirable for the recognition of the southern stretch of the Via Francigena in Italy as a cultural itinerary also at a European level which would represent a break between the Nordic world where the Via Francigena began (Canterbury) with the Mediterranean basin where it ends (Jerusalem) in the broader perspective of bringing together the three *peregrinationes maiores* headed towards Rome, Jerusalem, and Santiago de Compostela. (Caucci von Saucken, 1999; Chélini & Branthomme, 2004).

Taking up what Cozzi (2021) defines as the political dimension of pilgrimage, it can represent the architect of the development of some territories. Today, as in the past, this religious practice still has a universal value, albeit limited to the Catholic world. As such it constituted the articulation of a language shared and practiced both vertically, i.e., in all social strata of a specific geopolitical context, and horizontally, i.e., between classes and groups of those different contexts. Like other devotional events, pilgrimage represents an idiom that is transversally understood and used in every context, even in the most advanced societies.

To better understand the potential of the Via Francigena (and consequently also of partial sections such as the Apulian one), it is necessary to reflect on the statistical data collected by the European Association of the Via Francigena Routes (EAVF); in 2022, pilgrims returned in large numbers to the Via Francigena, giving strong signs of recovery in international attendance of the route. Despite the Covid-19 restrictions, outdoor slow tourism has shown good growth numbers. The 3,200 km of the Via Francigena, through over 700 municipalities and a route that winds for over 80% in rural areas, were travelled by tourists from all over the world with overall figures that are close to the 2019 trend before Covid pandemic. Around 50,000 pilgrims walked the Via Francigena in 2022 (compared to the 40,000 estimated in 2021) with an average stay on the path of seven days. This is what emerges from the overview of the key indicators; in the following analysis, the data of 3,985 interviewees who filled out the survey at the time of receiving the credentials were considered. The number of AEVF credential distribution points across Europe increased from 95 in 2021 to 115 in 2022. Around 17,500 credentials were distributed to pilgrims. The website's statistics highlight the growing interest in the itinerary: in 2022, the site attracted around 700,000 users and recorded almost 4 million page views, with an average presence of visitors on the site of 3'54". As regards the App, this tool proves to be highly appreciated by pilgrims who have downloaded it 15,113 times (main months: April 1,886, August 1,825, May 1,802). Top 5 user origins: Italy (7,779), United States (1,185), United Kingdom (881), France (872), Switzerland (670). The App is created by AEVF and is made available free of charge to all pilgrims who request it. (Via Francigena Road to Rome, 2023).

If we then cross-reference these global data with those published by the Italian Ministry of Tourism, it becomes clear how much notoriety and curiosity towards the Via Francigena is increasing. In July 2023, data from the Ministry of Tourism reports that "Francigena" is among the most clicked words on search engines, with a +22% and 60,500 clicks compared to June 2022.

Apulia, from the Dauni Mountains to Santa Maria di Leuca, is crossed by the Francigena of the South and the paths, increasingly widespread in Italy, are the cornerstones of sustainable and attentive tourism, capable of filling the streets and centres of the villages of Apulia from the North to the South. The "Road to Rome" event to celebrate twenty years of the Via Francigena with the pilgrims who left Canterbury and arrived in *Finibus Terreae* (Santa Maria di Leuca) passing through Rome, made many people aware of the villages Apulians and contributed to promoting the Francigena of the South.

It therefore seems clear that since roads are integral parts of that anthropic landscape in which men and things interact, the variants become fundamental in a route like this. The same variations are then affected by the historical, political, and economic context of the moment.

A PROPOSAL FOR THE SECTION OF THE VIA FRANCIGENA OF THE CAPITANATA (AND THE DAUNI MOUNTAINS)

The promotion of areas with development difficulties, generally identified with rural, internal, and marginal ones, is the object of various policies activated at national and regional level within specific European programs aimed at improving territorial cohesion and increasing social development and economical. Despite the different measures proposed by the various governments that have followed one another over the years, the situation of the internal areas still presents, in some cases, the characteristics of marginality, albeit with the differences of each territory. The economic-financial crisis of recent years has also accentuated the problems of the weakest areas, such as the Apennine areas or those of southern Italy more generally. Given these premises, it is more necessary than ever to rethink a development model that is mainly oriented towards the recovery of these disadvantaged and weak areas, with the recognition of the diversity of territorial values, which cannot be homogenized (or imposed) by the more developed ones. The development path must be reworked thinking of a dynamic balance between economic growth and valorization of the territory's own resources, such as environmental and cultural assets, food and wine products, knowledge, and artisanal knowledge, according to the consolidated principles of sustainability and social cohesion. Many scholars have confirmed how tourist activities can be a driving force for the development of the local economy although they can sometimes induce a process of deskilling caused by the methods and intensity of tourist use, with effects that are not exactly favourable. Furthermore, the global pandemic emergency has induced a further rethinking of the role of smaller Italian centres as drivers of development considering that the crisis manifested itself differently in the territories, accelerating some pre-existing dynamics and potentially determining further gaps, as well as opportunities to address and reverse restart processes. The strategic desire to survey the state of the art at a national and international level, to compare multidisciplinary and interdisciplinary experiences and methodologies, to investigate the connection between the size of the projects underway for the relaunch, at different scales, and the spaces of economic-economic evaluation financial, is animating the scientific debate on the role of smaller centers by shifting the lens of observation from problem to resource. Further actions and which strategies to implement for the enhancement of the building, landscape, and cultural heritage of territories in internal marginal areas are more than ever at the centre of the reflections and policies of institutional decision-makers. (Ivona & Privitera, 2022).

The small municipalities or *borghi* (with the new terminology) of the internal areas (not only in Italy) are numerous and experience economic and socio-cultural isolation such as to encourage the movement of residents towards larger centers equipped with extensive services, infrastructures and opportunities work; Added to all this is the inadequacy of the housing stock compared to the needs of contemporary society. Because of this long-standing conflict between center and periphery, there is constant depopulation, an overall degradation of places and the loss of a heritage of material values (monuments, architectural structures, naturalistic features and much more) and intangible values (local cultural heritage, cultural traditions, artisanal skills). Despite the aforementioned ongoing process, these territories still bear witness, in many cases, to an unchanged 'spirit of place' at least in its instrumental meaning as the attitude to consider the place primarily as a resource that provides goods, opportunities prevails and authenticity. Add, then, the presence of unique characteristics in terms of identity and memory: a historical-architectural and artistic heritage of widespread interest, a minimally contaminated environmental and landscape context. (Belhassen et al, 2008).

The depopulation of smaller towns is a dynamic of today's society which sees cities as the answer to globalization. Yet, internal areas play a fundamental role not only for the protection of the historical and cultural heritage and the existing landscape, but also for the possibility of promoting lifestyles alternative to metropolitan ones and of encouraging the development of innovative economic and social models capable to combine tradition and contemporaneity. The gaps left by demographic movements can be the opportunity for the rebirth of smaller centers through strategies such as widespread hospitality, production, local culture, identity preservation and cooperation.

The smaller centres with their identity heritage and equally indispensable value as territorial garrisons are at the centre of public interest. Recently the European Union transferred 24.9 billion euros to Italy to support the first 106 projects envisaged in the National Recovery and Resilience Plan (PNRR). Mission 1 Tourism and Culture 4.0 received 436 million euros for the financing of 11 projects, identified as driving ones, including that of the National Plan for *Borghi*, on which more than one centre has placed its hopes of rebirth. Useful resources to enhance the heritage rich in history, art, cultural and natural attractions, traditions present in internal areas with landscape-cultural value and economic growth potential.

Huge economic resources are foreseen for the restoration and redevelopment of historic rural buildings and characteristic elements of the landscape, favouring eco-compatible solutions. Included are rural architecture census activities and the collection and exchange of knowledge on rural heritage and landscape. The word *borghi* is mentioned numerous times and in the PNRR it is reported that many small historic centres offer enormous potential for alternative sustainable tourism, thanks to the cultural heritage, history, arts and traditions that characterize them. Interventions in this area will be implemented through the National Plan for *Borghi*, a program to support the economic and social development of disadvantaged areas based on the cultural regeneration of small historic centres and on the relaunch of tourism. (Ivona & Privitera, 2022).

Religious tourism represents a sector of no secondary importance in the context of cultural tourism and can represent a real engine of development especially for rural areas, the subject of various policies activated at national and regional level within specific European programs tending to improve territorial cohesion and increase social and economic development. If it is true that the main attractors are the most iconic sanctuaries, it is equally true that the minor religious sites represent, if adequately valorised, a potential resource capable of conveying new and more substantial flows of visitors. The itineraries of

Figure 3. The south via Francigena
Source: Terre di Mezzo Editore, 2022, with modifications

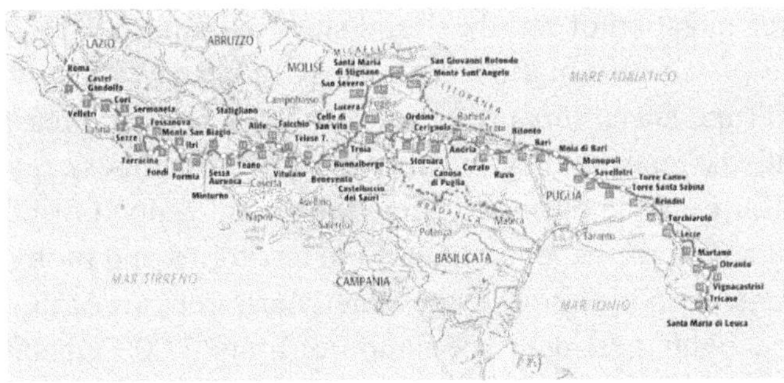

faith, then, could represent a possible response to these development needs given that, as established by the Council of Europe, they constitute a useful tool for increasing the competitiveness and development of the areas crossed, also with the strengthening of the identity. Religious tourism, in fact, in addition to the "renowned" sites, increasingly involves the myriad of small churches, convents and little-known but very widespread places of worship in the more internal areas, which often represent the interconnection network with the cultural poles of greatest attraction, to the point of constituting a real "reticular system". This form of tourism, if adequately stimulated, could be able to involve local institutions and communities, since it would allow an approach to religious heritage free from self-referentiality, as it is inserted in an identity context dominated by tradition, but capable of creating new attractiveness, determining an enrichment in terms of added value". (Podda et al, 2020).

The case of Capitanata, the northern part of Apulia (circled in yellow in Figure 3), appears interesting as a laboratory for an overall tourist development proposal in which the religious itinerary or itineraries can contribute.

Although the Capitanata subregion has had a strategic importance in history (its centers perched on hills represented the defensive outposts of the Byzantine Empire against the Lombard invasions; the valleys, with the large sheep tracks, were those "routes of transhumance" used by nomadic shepherds who descended from the mountains to the plains with their flock in winter), over the years it has undergone a progressive isolation due not only to its morphology but also to its peripherality with respect to the main axes of circulation of goods and ideas from Apulia and the South.

Today the economic measures for a profitable combination between tourism and the religious paths of Apulia are different and could generate the opportunity for the relaunch of those areas previously defined as "lagging in development". At a national level, the Italian Ministry of Tourism has allocated 35 million euros in the "Small Municipalities Fund with a tourist vocation" to be used in the three-year period 2023-2025 to finance projects for the valorization of municipalities with a population of less than 5,000 inhabitants, classified by the National Institute of statistics as municipalities with a tourist vocation, in order to encourage innovative interventions of accessibility, mobility, urban regeneration and environmental sustainability. The municipalities of the Capitanata are 61 in total; among these 27 are among those eligible for the aforementioned ministerial funding and are all also included in the National Strategy for Internal Areas, i.e. a strategy of the Italian Government to support those parts of the national territory that suffer the effects of the decline or aging of the population and where the weakness of development prospects determines increasingly difficult living conditions for the citizens who reside there.

Furthermore, the National Recovery and Resilience Plan (the Italian instrument for the implementation of the European Union's Next Generation). The implementation measure of the "Tourism and Culture" Plan is dedicated to the regeneration of small cultural sites, cultural, religious, and rural heritage. The investments will allow the valorization of the great heritage of history, art, culture and traditions present in small Italian towns and rural areas: supporting the recovery of cultural heritage, activating entrepreneurial/commercial initiatives (for example new accommodation methods), revitalizing the social fabric -economic of the places (for example by encouraging the revitalization of traditional professions, such as craftsmanship), counteracting the depopulation of the territories and promoting the conservation of the landscape and traditions. Also in this case, the beneficiaries of part of the funding are small single or aggregate municipalities with a resident population of up to 5,000 inhabitants in which there is a clearly identifiable and recognizable historic village (or, in the case of municipalities that are dimensionally very small, are themselves like a historic village). The aggregations of municipalities can concern neighboring municipalities or municipalities in the same region that share the same themes. Currently 13 municipalities in the Capitanata area are eligible for this financing.

Finally, the Italian Law of 30 December 2021, n. 234 established, at the Ministry of Tourism, a Fund for Religious Paths, with an initial allocation of 3 million euros for 2022, for the relaunch and tourist promotion of the so-called religious "paths" routes and the recovery and valorisation of the properties that characterize them. Article 1 defines religious paths as "hiking itineraries with a religious or spiritual theme, which can be explored exclusively or mainly on foot or with other forms of slow and sustainable tourism, at an interregional and regional level". To date, the Fund has an endowment of 4.5 million euros for the promotion of Italian religious paths. (Figures 4). The Ministry has also created the Catalog of Italian religious paths, in which since March 2023, the Via Francigena with its many sections has been included.

Figure 4. The financing system for tourism development
Source: Ivona, 2023

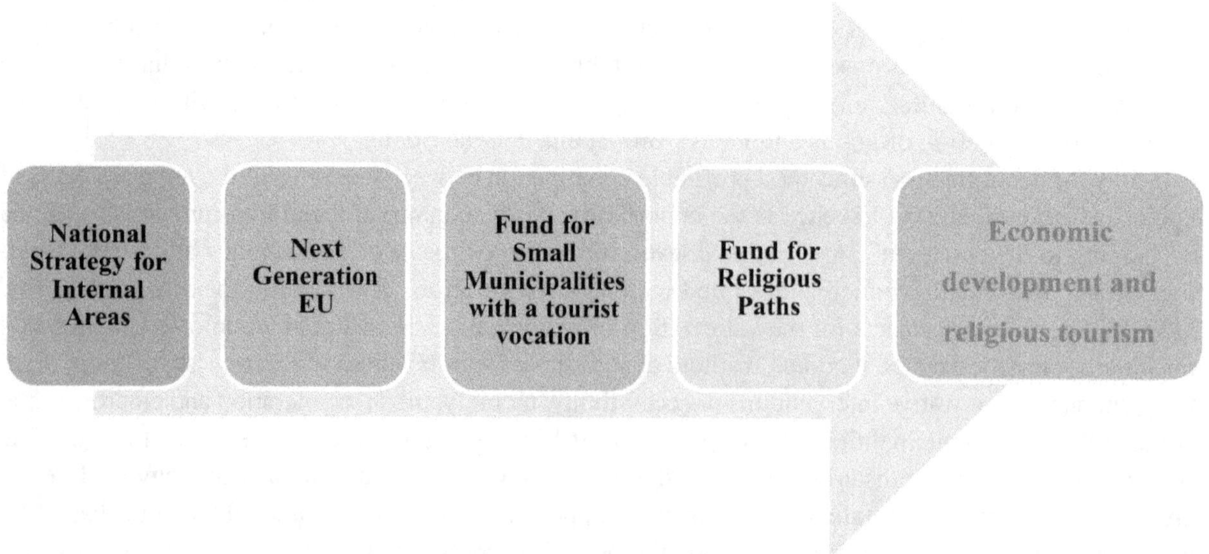

From what has been said so far, religious tourism and that of the Walks and pilgrimages can be an opportunity for territorial development but only if certain conditions exist; in the meantime, it is necessary to design integrated tourist routes that are able to enhance small and large attractions.

In this new planning it will be necessary to take increasingly into account the 'sense of place', which was mentioned previously, which acts as a glue between the idea of space only linked to social relationships and the sense of sacred space. In this sense, the host community can itself become a symbol of religiosity and a communication tool among religious tourists. Moreover, as widely studied in the literature, Cammini tourism also represents an alternative and sustainable development practice, not only from an economic point of view but also from a social point of view thanks to the involvement and promotion of the host communities (Cardia, 2018; Kato & Progano, 2017; Jimura, 2016; Božić & Tomić, 2016).

According to Božić and Tomić (2016) themed routes can play a pivotal role in encouraging local communities to participate in cultural activities raising awareness of the local heritage importance.

Like other slow tourism projects, cultural itineraries can also increase the resilience of local communities (Splendiani et al., 2023; Sheldon & Daniele, 2017; Cheer & Lew, 2017). It, more than other forms of tourism, favors local economies through the synergy between visitors, businesses, artisans, and local services. By supporting local businesses, slow tourism helps diversify an area's economic base, reducing its dependence on a single sector. This diversification improves economic resilience, making the area less vulnerable to economic shocks or recessions.

Third condition is to consider religious itineraries as divisible into different segments and each of those segments as a precious opportunity to attract investments and consequently regenerate the economy of the territories involved. Finally, the overall financing system (Figure 4) will be able to generate a concrete multiplier effect on the economy of the territory and/or territories only if they are used to carry out long-term projects, imagined and planned by all the public decision makers involved. It will be precisely the systemic perspective applied to design, finance and implement a new vision of religious tourism as an integral part of the economy of a territory, which will produce tangible and profitable effects. (Cohen, 1992; Coleman & Eade, 2004; Collins-Kreiner, 2010). As Forlani et al. (2023, p. 64) state "Implications for trail managers are related to the design of routes, which should consider both aspects of tourist attractiveness and those related to community involvement. Lastly, there are implications for the tourism businesses involved in the project, who must understand the importance of participation and sharing in such projects, as the competitiveness of their offerings is closely linked to the competitiveness of the cultural route. Future research should focus on evaluating the long-term impacts of cultural routes on tourism development, assessing visitor satisfaction, and exploring the potential replication of these projects in different marginal areas."

To achieve the objectives of the European Paths, especially those concerning the relationship between spirituality, culture, and rurality of the territory, in a logic of overall development of the Capitanata system, in particular, the capacity for territorial governance is needed. Territorial governance, understood as the capacity for "cooperative" division of institutional, economic, political and cultural tasks, which rethinks a local development model and verifies the feasibility and conditions for the take-off of a local rural tourism system capable of both directing processes broader ones, which arise elsewhere such as the Paths of Europe, for their own benefit (the focus is therefore on the dynamic interactions between local areas and the wider political, institutional, commercial and natural environments; and on the ways in which these interactions are mediated or regulated); and to build coordination with the planning and strategy of all the political-territorial bodies that dictate the development directions of the area; and to create a network of local rural tourism system projected into the Mediterranean and the Middle East. In short, placing the idea of a Southern Via Francigena (in which the Via Francigena della Capitanata is a significant segment) rather than in the local system alone, in a national, European, and Mediterranean dimension. (Longo, 2008).

The integration between plan and strategic planning therefore implies that "Cities and territories act as collective actors, capable of defining a strategy and pursuing it, guaranteeing coherent behavior on the part of the different components of local society. It is the theme of governance that becomes central: the strategic approach, enhancing and promoting social networks, leveraging the sharing of values and elements of identity, can contribute to configuring a new community governance." (Gibelli, 2007, p. 213).

CONCLUSION

Pilgrimage is a universal religious experience, known not only to Christianity, but also to all religions of antiquity, both monotheistic and polytheistic. Over the centuries the pilgrim, mostly male, driven by various motivations whether individual, intimate, or social, undertook his journey with great tenacity, usually in the months of April and May, in small groups, the so-called 'companies' which they formed right along the streets; sometimes with some animal that carried the necessary baggage or the children and the sick, covering many kilometres a day on foot. The trips were organized by the same people, often called 'priors' to whom the community recognized a specific religious function. (Berardi, 2019). As Turner states "In every pilgrimage system, even those in decline, a thin thread of popular devotion persists that recalls the original ardour and sense of communitas" (in Berardi, 2019, p. 5).

The numerous studies on Christian pilgrimage from its origins to the present day show how pilgrimage has changed considerably compared to its origins: if before it was carried out in a more spiritual sense on foot taking the most disparate risks, already after the year 1000 the situation had improved. With the reopening of the roads and the development of internal trade, better services were available also due to the presence of a dense network of hospices along the main routes; pilgrims also began traveling in more organized groups. After the Second World War, pilgrimage progressively transformed into religious tourism also in light of the progress made by means of transport and with the birth of organizations specialized in assisting pilgrims; the journey is therefore quicker, and the risks and difficulties are fewer. A wealth of stories, of religiosity, of respect for the traditions of these people who, perhaps unconsciously, in their wanderings renew an ancient history which, thanks to them, reaches the modernity of today and which cannot and must not be lost.

A land of transit due to its ancient vocation and tradition, a meeting point between East and West, Apulia has seen the passage of countless travellers, traders, and pilgrims throughout its thousand-year history. Since the time of the Crusades, Apulia had a role of notable importance: its ports allowed the embarkation of pilgrims and knights for the Holy Land, it was the outpost of the monastic-chivalric orders whose traces in many cases are still visible in the whole region. In short, that ancient web made up of networks to and from the significant places of worship designed the geography of pilgrimages in Apulia. How many and which of those ancient networks of roads still crossed the Apulian territory today is difficult to establish exactly; what remains unchanged, however, are the geographical dynamics of this land. A place of welcome, of movement of people, of cultural and commercial exchanges over the centuries, even today it has not renounced its geographical vocation as a border land.

Tourism has acquired an increasingly important role in stimulating economic expansion, mainly thanks to its substantial contribution as a primary generator of foreign currency and a fundamental driver of the diversification of economic activities. This trend finds a pronounced example in selected countries such as Italy, Israel, India and France, where pilgrimage-like travel, based on "spiritual" and "spectacular" motivations, persists as a dominant and long-lasting phenomenon. Consequently, religious, faith-based and spiritual tourism, including the sacred practice of pilgrimages, takes on a salient and ongoing position within a broader context of the tourism industry. Pilgrimages, as a particular type of travel, exert their influence far beyond the confines of merely spiritual experience. Embracing multiple political, economic, social and cultural ramifications, they manifest the potential to impact the development of many territories. The inherent spatial mobility intrinsic to the phenomenon of pilgrimage gives it profound meaning and arouses academic interest, thus deserving in-depth investigation.

In conclusion, it should be underlined how the rediscovery of historical paths, one of the social phenomena of this millennium, has favoured, at the same time, the rediscovery of ancient and glorious routes and sites, abandoned and forgotten until a few decades ago. Through the paths, places destined for depopulation are re-evaluated, a small economy made up of reception and refreshment places is recreated, minor and widespread art is rediscovered; in short, a beneficial chain effect. Despite the awareness that many walkers do not make pilgrimages for religious reasons, this motor action accompanied by effort and reflection also develops a spiritual dimension. We can therefore interpret the paths from multiple aspects; what is certain is their potential from whatever dimension you observe them.

REFERENCES

Belhassen, Y., Caton, K., & Stewart, W. P. (2008). The search for authenticity in the pilgrim experience. *Annals of Tourism Research*, *35*(3), 668–689. doi:10.1016/j.annals.2008.03.007

Berardi, C. C. (2019). *Sul cammino di San Nicola e di San Michele*. Progedit.

Berti, E. (2012). *Itinerari Culturali del Consiglio d'Europa tra ricerca di identità e progetto di paesaggio*. Firenze University Press. doi:10.36253/978-88-6655-142-3

Bianco, R. (2016). La Apulia nel camino de Santiago. Culto e iconografia di San Giacomo di Compostella in Apulia. *Ad Limina*, *7*, 83–112.

Bona, K., Seongseop, K., & Brian, K. (2020). Religious tourism studies: Evolution, progress, and future prospects. *Tourism Recreation Research*, *45*(2), 185–203. doi:10.1080/02508281.2019.1664084

Božić, S., & Tomić, N. (2016). Developing the cultural route evaluation model (CREM) and its application on the Trail of Roman Emperors. Serbia. *Tourism Management Perspectives*, *17*, 26–35. doi:10.1016/j.tmp.2015.11.002

Brandenburg, A., & Carroll, M. (1995). Your Place or Mine? The Effect of Place Creation on Environmental Values and Landscape Meanings. *Society & Natural Resources*, *8*(5), 381–398. doi:10.1080/08941929509380931

Brown, L. (2016). Tourism and pilgrimage: Paying homage to literary heroes. *International Journal of Tourism Research*, *18*(2), 167–175. doi:10.1002/jtr.2043

Caldo, C. (1990). Regione e cultura: la presenza religiosa in Piemonte. In C. Lanza Dematteis (Ed.), *Interpretare una regione. Geografa del Piemonte che cambia* (pp. 51–69). Ed. Libreria Cortina.

Cardia, G. (2018). Routes and itineraries as a means of contribution for sustainable tourism development. In V. Katsoni & K. Valander (Eds.), *Innovative approaches to tourism and leisure* (pp. 17–33). Springer Nature Switzerland., doi:10.1007/978-3-319-67603-6_2

Cardini, F., & Musarra, A. (2019). *Il grande racconto delle crociate*. Il Mulino.

Caucci von Saucken, P. (Ed.). (1999). Il mondo dei pellegrinaggi. Roma, Santiago, Gerusalemme. Jaca Book.

Cheer, J. M., & Lew, A. A. (2017). Understanding tourism resilience: Adapting to social, political, and economic change. In J. M. Cheer, & A. A. Lew (Eds.). Tourism, resilience and sustainability: Adapting to social, political and economic change, (pp. 3-17). Routledge.

Chélini, J., & Branthomme, H. (2004). *Le vie di Dio. Storia dei pellegrinaggi cristiani dalle origini al Medioevo*. Jaca Book.

Cohen, E. (1992). Pilgrimage and Tourism: Convergence and Divergence. In E. A. Morinis & V. W. Turner (Eds.), *Sacred Journeys: the anthropology of pilgrimage* (pp. 47–61). Greenwood Press.

Coleman, S., & Eade, J. (2004). *Reframing Pilgrimage. Cultures in Motion*. Routledge. doi:10.4324/9780203643693

Collins-Kreiner, N. (2010). The Geography of Pilgrimage and Tourism: Transformations and Implications for Applied Geography. *Applied Geography (Sevenoaks, England)*, *20*(1), 153–164. doi:10.1016/j.apgeog.2009.02.001

Collins-Kreiner, N. (2016a). Dark tourism as/is pilgrimage. *Current Issues in Tourism*, *19*(12), 1185–1189. doi:10.1080/13683500.2015.1078299

Collins-Kreiner, N. (2016b). The lifecycle of concepts: The case of 'pilgrimage tourism'. *Tourism Geographies*, *18*(3), 322–334. doi:10.1080/14616688.2016.1155077

Cozzo, P. (2021). *In cammino*. Carocci.

Damari, C., & Mansfeld, Y. (2016). Reflections on pilgrims' identity, role and interplay with the pilgrimage environment. *Current Issues in Tourism*, *19*(3), 199–222. doi:10.1080/13683500.2014.957660

Deffontaines, P. (1948). *Géographie et religions*. Gallimard.

Digance, J. (2003). Pilgrimage at contested sites. *Annals of Tourism Research*, *30*(1), 143–159. doi:10.1016/S0160-7383(02)00028-2

Duccio, D. (2005). *La filosofia del camminare*. Cortina Editore.

Flori, J. (2003). *La Guerra santa. La formazione dell'idea di crociata nell'Occidente cristiano*. Il Mulino.

Forlani, F., Picciotti, A., & Splendiani, S. (2023). Improving tourism resilience through Cultural Routes. An exploratory analysis of the Italian case "Via Francigena". *Turistica*, *32*(1), 45–70.

Galliano, G. (2002). Per l'analisi del rapporto geografia-religione. La letteratura geografica. *Geotema*, *18*, 3–31.

Garrod, B. (2008). Exploring place perception, a photo-based analysis. *Annals of Tourism Research, 35*(2), 381–401. doi:10.1016/j.annals.2007.09.004

Gibelli, M. C. (2007). Piano strategico e pianificazione strategica: Un'integrazione necessaria. *Archivio di Studi Urbani e Regionali, 89*, 211–222.

Grimaldi, F. (1993). *La Historia della chiesa di Santa Maria de Loreto*. Carilo.

Guriţă, D., & Scortescu, F. I. (2023). Religious Tourism and Sustainable Development of the Economy in the Context of Globalization in the Northeast Area of Romania. *Sustainability (Basel), 15*(16), 12128. doi:10.3390u151612128

Hung, K., Yang, X., Wassler, P., Wang, D., Lin, P., & Liu, Z. (2017). Contesting the commercialization and sanctity of religious tourism in the Shaolin Monastery, China. *International Journal of Tourism Research, 19*(2), 145–159. doi:10.1002/jtr.2093

Hyde, K. F., & Harman, S. (2011). Motives for a secular pilgrimage to the Gallipoli battlefields. *Tourism Management, 32*(6), 1343–1351. doi:10.1016/j.tourman.2011.01.008

Imarisio, C. S. (2011). Il paesaggio e i segni della religione. Problemi di metodo e casi di studio. *Ambiente Società Territorio, 56*, 17–21.

Ivona, A. (2023). Network of saints, network of roads. Apulia crossroads of pilgrimages. In L. Lopez (Ed.), *Geography of world pilgrimages. Social, cultural and territorial perspectives* (pp. 53–75). Springer Nature Switzerland. doi:10.1007/978-3-031-32209-9_4

Ivona, A., & Privitera, D. (2022). L'attrattività dei piccoli borghi. La resilienza come strumento per una nuova centralità. *IL CAPITALE CULTURALE. Studies on the Value of Cultural Heritage, 25*, 157–178. doi:10.13138/2039-2362/2836

Jenkins, W., & Chapple, C. (2011). Religion and Environment. *Annual Review of Environment and Resources, 36*(1), 441–463. doi:10.1146/annurev-environ-042610-103728

Jimura, T. (2016). World heritage site management: A case study of sacred sites and pilgrimage routes in the Kii mountain range, Japan. *Journal of Heritage Tourism, 11*(4), 382–394. doi:10.1080/1743873X.2016.1146287

Kato, K., & Progano, R. N. (2017). Spiritual (walking) tourism as a foundation for sustainable destination development: Kumano-kodo pilgrimage, Wakayama, Japan. *Tourism Management Perspectives, 24*, 243–251. doi:10.1016/j.tmp.2017.07.017

Kong, L. (1990). Geography and Religion. Trends and Prospects. *Progress in Human Geography, 3*(3), 355–371. doi:10.1177/030913259001400302

Laterza, L. E. (2013). Culto mariano e percorsi di pellegrinaggio: La Madonna di Loreto in Apulia. *Ad Limina, 4*, 249–274.

Lefebvre, H. (1974). *La Production de l'espace*. Anthropos.

Lefeuvre, A. (1980). Religious tourism and pilgrimage: On the move. *Vatican City: Pontifical Commission on Migration and Tourism, 10*(30), 80–81.

Levine, G. J. (1986). The Geography of Religion. *Transactions of the Institute of British Geographers, 11*(4), 428–440. doi:10.2307/621934

Longo, L. (2008). Cammini d'Europa e "Via Francigena della Capitanata". In V. Vecchione, P. Pazienza, M. Russo, R. Infante, L. Longo, M. Del Giudice, & R. Guglielmi (Eds.), *LA VIA FRANCIGENA DELLA CAPITANATA* (pp. 38–49). Dipartimento di Scienze Economiche, Matematiche e Statistiche.

Musti, D. (1988). *Strabone e la Magna Grecia: città e popoli dell'Italia antica*. Ed. Programma.

Nilsson, M., & Tesfahuney, M. (2016). Performing the "post-secular" in Santiago de Compostela. *Annals of Tourism Research, 57*, 18–30. doi:10.1016/j.annals.2015.11.001

Paul, O. (2014). *Sanctity and Pilgrimage in Medieval Southern Italy, 1000-1200*. Cambridge University Press.

Pedreschi, L. (1966). Aspetti geografici di alcuni centri religiosi italiani. *Bollettino della Società Geografica Italiana, IX*(7), 333–443.

Podda C., Secchi P., & Lampreu S. (2020). Turismo religioso e sviluppo delle aree rurali. Considerazioni sul caso della Sardegna. *Bollettino della Società Geografica Italiana, 14, 3*(2), 39-54. DOI: . doi:10.36253/bsgi-1227

Rocca, G. (2003). Luoghi, itinerari e assetti spaziali nella vita di una comunità religiosa. Il caso dell'Ordine Somasco. *Geotema, 21*, 76–97.

Santus, D. (1990). La geografia della religione. Una rassegna. *Rivista Geografica Italiana, XCVII*(2), 251–259.

Sheldon, P., & Daniele, R. (Eds.), *Social Entrepreneurship and Tourism. Tourism on the Verge*. Springer., doi:10.1007/978-3-319-46518-0

Splendiani, S., Forlani, F., Picciotti, A., & Presenza, A. (2023). Social Innovation Project and Tourism Lifestyle Entrepreneurship to Revitalize the Marginal Areas. The Case of the via Francigena Cultural Route. *Tourism Planning & Development, 20*(5), 938–954. doi:10.1080/21568316.2022.2161616

Stopani, R. (1992). *La Via Francigena del sud. L'Appia Traiana nel medioevo*. Le Lettere.

Sumption, J. (1993). *Monaci santuari pellegrini. La religione nel Medioevo*. Ed. Riuniti.

Terre di Mezzo Editore. (2022). *La Via Francigena nel Sud*. https://www.terre.it, Trono, A. (2012). *Via Francigena. Cammini di Fede e Turismo Culturale*. Congedo Editore.

Tuan, Y. (1977). *Space and Place: The Perspective of Experience*. University of Minneapolis Press.

Vallega, A. (2006). *La geografia del tempo. Saggio di geografia culturale*. Utet.

Via Francigena Road to Rome. (2023). *The Free App of Via Francigena*. Vie Francigene. https://www.viefrancigene.org/ en/guides-app

Chapter 2
Exploring the Role of OpenStreetMap in Mapping Religious Tourism in Pakistan for Sustainable Development

Munir Ahmad
https://orcid.org/0000-0003-4836-6151
Survey of Pakistan, Pakistan

ABSTRACT

Religious tourism in Pakistan is a diverse and culturally rich sector poised for growth, yet facing numerous challenges, including infrastructure deficiencies, maintenance issues, security concerns, undiscovered potential, economic factors, cultural disparities, and data gaps. OpenStreetMap (OSM), a community-driven mapping platform, offers transformative solutions. OSM can empower users to map religious sites, provide information, improve accessibility, and advocate for cultural preservation. It can help in route planning, community engagement, tourism promotion, and economic empowerment. OSM can address Pakistan's challenges by mapping infrastructure, supporting maintenance, ensuring safety, promoting lesser-known sites, enhancing economic inclusivity, and fostering cultural harmony. Real-time data from OSM has the potential to empower sustainable tourism development.

INTRODUCTION

Religious tourism finds its main impetus in religious motivations and stands as one of the most ancient expressions of travel (Rinschede, 1992). This can be described as "Faith Tourism," a term used to describe journeys undertaken by individuals to manifest their religious convictions and explore centers of faith, away from their regular living, working, and everyday needs (Demircioğlu, 2020). Travelers embark on religious tourism with the aim of strengthening their faith, pursuing spiritual encounters, establishing a link with their religious legacy, and taking part in religious ceremonies and customs (Tsironis, 2022).

DOI: 10.4018/978-1-6684-9923-8.ch002

Pakistan, with its rich cultural and religious heritage, stands as a tapestry of diverse spiritual traditions, drawing pilgrims and tourists from around the globe to its sacred sites and historic pilgrimage routes. Pakistan possesses a wealth of diverse religious heritage, rendering it a prominent hub for religious tourism. This encompasses Islamic landmarks such as mosques and shrines, alongside sites of significance to Sikhism, Hinduism, and Buddhism (Bari & Khan, 2020). However, the full potential of religious tourism in Pakistan remains largely untapped due to challenges related to mapping and infrastructure (Irfan & Ali, 2020). Inadequate geospatial data and underdeveloped facilities have hindered the growth of this sector.

OpenStreetMap is an open-source platform that empowers users to contribute to and access geospatial information. OSM has the power to improve interactive visualization of tourist sites (An et al., 2023). It can help to automatically identify tourist attractions (Vaziri et al., 2020). By mapping religious sites and enhancing geospatial data, OSM can play a pivotal role in promoting sustainable tourism practices, empowering local communities, and nurturing cultural and heritage preservation. OSM data can provide a fairly accurate representation of official tourism statistics for most variables, making it a valuable tool for analyzing tourism competitiveness in various countries (Bustamante et al., 2021).

The primary objective of this chapter is to delve into the utilization of OpenStreetMap as a tool to address the challenges impeding the development of religious tourism in Pakistan. This chapter embarks on a journey to explore the transformative potential of OSM in mapping religious tourism sites across Pakistan and fostering sustainable tourism development. To achieve this objective, the chapter is organized into several key sections.

RELIGIOUS AND PILGRIMAGE TOURISM

Religious tourism comprises diverse manifestations driven by spiritual incentives. These encompass brief journeys to sacred pilgrimage hubs, devout conventions, as well as extended sojourns to both domestic and global pilgrimage destinations (Rinschede, 1992). Religious tourism has equal importance for urban and rural areas. For example, Mafudi et al., (2021) have identified four potential opportunities for educational visits related to religious experiences in rural areas, which encompass the following: simulated pilgrimage routes, designated swimming facilities for Muslims, prayer facilities, and venues for archery activities. This form of tourism involves individuals or groups traveling for purposes such as pilgrimage, missionary work, or leisure. It can be categorized into two primary types: one involves tourists actively participating in pilgrimages, while the other comprises tourists seeking to gain insights into religious practices and visit locations associated with their faith (Ramos & Mafé-García, 2018).

Pilgrimage constitutes a distinctive category within religious tourism, characterized by a voyage to a sacred site or a shrine of profound religious importance. For instance, within Islam, the Hajj represents a momentous pilgrimage directed towards Mecca (Luz, 2020). pilgrimage is not confined to Islam, Judaism, and Christianity but extends to other major religious traditions like Buddhism, Hinduism, and Sikhism (Almuhrzi, 2020). Pilgrimage tourism entails the journey of individuals or groups to particular religious or sacred locales. These expeditions are frequently driven by religious reverence, the pursuit of spiritual encounters, or the fulfillment of religious duties. The sites of pilgrimage encompass religious temples, shrines, sacred cities, or locales linked to revered religious personalities. Pilgrims often partake in rituals, prayers, and religious observances during their sojourn to these revered destinations. Pilgrimage tourism carries profound historical and cultural importance and represents an age-old mode of exploration (Di Giovine Michael A.and Elsner, 2016).

RELIGIOUS TOURISM IN PAKISTAN

Pakistan boasts a rich tapestry of cultural, spiritual, and natural wonders waiting to be explored. The domain of religious tourism remains vibrant, yet largely untapped, within the borders of Pakistan (Irfan & Ali, 2020). Pakistan stands as a testament to its multicultural heritage, offering a kaleidoscope of religious experiences. It is a land where the echoes of Islam, Sikhism, Buddhism, and Hinduism resonate through revered sanctuaries. Pakistan has the potential to become a significant player in the global religious tourism industry if it invests in infrastructure, security, and a tourism-friendly environment (Post, 2022).

Religious Diversity

The partition of India in 1947 marked a momentous event in South Asian history, resulting in the migration of people based on their religious affiliations. This partition had a profound impact on the demographic landscape of the region, with millions of people moving to either India or Pakistan. As per the 2017 Pakistan Census (PBS, 2018), the nation predominantly consists of Muslim citizens, forming the majority of the population. However, it's important to note that Pakistan is characterized by its religious diversity, with significant Hindu, Christian, and other religious communities contributing to the country's vibrant cultural fabric (Bari & Khan, 2020).

In Pakistan, Sikhism has a strong and deeply rooted presence. Sikhism's spiritual heartbeats find resonance in Pakistan at sites like Gurdwara Nankana Sahib and Gurdwara Darbar Sahib, drawing thousands of pilgrims annually to reconnect with their faith (Shaukat, 2023). Nankana Sahib stands as one of the holiest cities in Sikhism, hosting a cluster of revered Sikh Gurdwaras and historical sites associated with Guru Nanak and Maharaja Ranjit Singh. Despite its immense significance, Pakistan's Sikh religious tourism has yet to reach its full potential (Iips, 2022b). The opening of the Kartarpur border has initiated increased tourism activities and interfaith harmony.

Buddhism also has a significant heritage in Pakistan, with sites like Dharmarajika Stupa, Taxila, and Swat attracting tourists interested in the religion's history (Shaukat, 2023). The splendor of Buddhist sites like Gandhara and Taxila remains an untapped resource, with immense potential to attract visitors seeking spiritual and historical enlightenment (Iips, 2022b). Hindu devotees embark on significant pilgrimages to temples like Shri Hinglaj Mata and Shri Ramdev Pir, reflecting the profound spiritual significance embedded in these hallowed grounds (Iips, 2022b).

Pakistan's architectural treasures extend to mosques of unparalleled beauty, exemplified by the grandeur of Badshahi Masjid and Faisal Mosque, attracting admiration from tourists and worshippers alike. The Sufi heritage is celebrated in Pakistan through revered shrines such as Sehwan Sharif and Data Ganj Bakhsh, beckoning both Muslim and Hindu visitors to seek solace and spiritual connection (Iips, 2022b; Post, 2022). Pakistan is home to a small Zoroastrian population, and preserving their religious sites can improve interfaith harmony (Iips, 2022b).

Economic Impact

Religious tourism plays a pivotal role in Pakistan's economy, encompassing not only devout pilgrims but also secular tourists intrigued by the rich cultural and historical value of religious sites. This multifaceted form of tourism contributes significantly to the country's economic prosperity and cultural exchange. As per the Pakistan Tourism Development Corporation (PTDC), the nation boasts an impressive array of

480 tourist destinations, with a noteworthy 120 being of religious significance. These spiritual gems draw a considerable number of visitors, including around 900,000 international tourists each year, making a substantial contribution to Pakistan's economic landscape. The tourism sector comprises approximately 1.2 percent of Pakistan's Gross Domestic Product (GDP). It's crucial to note that a significant portion of this economic activity stems from domestic tourism, underlining the importance of catering to the needs and aspirations of local travelers (Shaukat, 2023). In the global arena, Pakistan currently occupies the 83rd position out of 117 countries in the Travel and Tourism Development Index (TTDI) Report for the year 2021 (World Economic Forum, 2022). This underscores the potential for growth and development in the tourism sector.

Challenges

Inadequate Infrastructure

The challenge of inadequate infrastructure poses a significant obstacle to religious tourism in Pakistan. Insufficient resources and underdeveloped facilities can deter tourists from visiting these sacred sites, ultimately affecting their overall experience (Ahmad et al., 2022; Iips, 2022a; Tasneem et al., 2022). To fully harness the potential of religious tourism, it is essential to address these infrastructure deficiencies and enhance the visitor experience.

Maintenance of Tourist Spots

Challenges associated with the maintenance of tourist spots pose a serious threat to the preservation of religious sites. Protecting and preserving these sites is of paramount importance in order to safeguard their cultural and historical significance for future generations (Ahmad et al., 2022; Tasneem et al., 2022). Measures should be taken for the maintenance of tourist spots and ensure the long-term integrity of these invaluable religious landmarks.

Security Concerns

Pakistan has encountered security challenges in the past, which may raise safety concerns for religious tourists. To encourage more visitors, it is imperative to prioritize and ensure the safety and security of travelers (Ahmad et al., 2022; Iips, 2022a; Tasneem et al., 2022). Implementing robust security measures and creating an environment that fosters a sense of safety will be instrumental in attracting a greater number of religious tourists to the country.

Undiscovered Religious Tourism

Religious tourism often doesn't receive the attention it truly deserves from the government and tourism authorities (Ahmed et al., 2022; Arshad et al., 2018). To address this challenge, it is vital to actively promote and invest in religious tourism. By recognizing the cultural, historical, and economic significance of religious sites and allocating resources and efforts toward their development and promotion, governments and tourism authorities can unlock the vast potential of this important sector, benefiting both the tourism industry and the preservation of cultural heritage.

Economic Factors

Economic factors, including the affordability of travel and accommodations, play a crucial role in determining the accessibility of religious sites. To broaden the appeal of religious tourism and attract a more diverse range of tourists, efforts should be made to make it more affordable and accessible (Arshad et al., 2018; Iips, 2022a). This can be achieved through various means, such as offering budget-friendly travel options, reasonably priced accommodations, and special packages for pilgrims and tourists. By addressing these economic factors, religious tourism can become more inclusive and inviting to a wider audience.

Cultural Differences

Cultural differences can indeed sometimes lead to negative reactions towards visitors of different religions (Iips, 2022a). These reactions may stem from misunderstandings, stereotypes, or deep-seated biases. To foster positive interactions and promote cultural and religious harmony, it's crucial to engage in intercultural dialogue and education. Encouraging mutual respect, empathy, and understanding can help mitigate the impact of these differences and create a more welcoming environment for travelers of diverse religious backgrounds.

Lack of Reliable Data

In the realm of the tourism sector, a notable challenge emerges from the absence of dependable data and research. Remarkably, none of the provincial governmental bodies overseeing the tourism sector possesses robust records capturing the flow of foreign and domestic tourists to specific destinations. This deficiency in trustworthy data presents a significant impediment to the formulation of well-informed policies and strategic planning within the tourism domain (Tasneem et al., 2022).

OPENSTREETMAP

OpenStreetMap (OSM) represents a collaborative endeavor with the overarching goal of crafting a comprehensive and openly accessible global map. Its inception dates back to 2004, and over the years, it has evolved into one of the most expansive and impactful crowdsourced mapping initiatives (Weber & Haklay, 2008). OSM thrives on the contributions of a diverse global community of volunteers. These dedicated individuals employ GPS devices and aerial imagery to gather and refine geographic data, encompassing a wide spectrum of features, from road networks and architectural structures to natural landscapes and recreational spaces. The beauty of OSM lies in its commitment to openness, permitting anyone to both utilize and enrich its extensive dataset. This inclusivity renders OSM an invaluable asset spanning numerous domains and applications.

Academic research has delved into various dimensions of OSM, with a particular focus on assessing its data quality and precision. Scholars have crafted quality metrics and frameworks tailored to evaluate the dependability of OSM data, especially concerning specific geographical regions and types of features (Mooney et al., 2010). Furthermore, OSM data has found utility in the realms of machine learning and remote sensing, underscoring its potential in domains like geoscience and related fields (Vargas-Munoz et al., 2021). In addition to these research endeavors, OSM has been the focal point of studies exploring its historical trajectory and inherent quality. Researchers have meticulously traced the evolution of OSM data and scrutinized its contemporaneity, effectively highlighting its sustained enhancements and enduring relevance (Minghini & Frassinelli, 2019). OSM can play a pivotal role in promoting sustainable development across various sectors, encompassing the economy, environment, and society (M. Ahmad & Ali, 2023). Even OSM green space data has great value for fostering business development (M. Ahmad, 2023).

State of OpenStreetMap in Pakistan

The OSM platform aggregates data in three distinct formats: nodes, relations, and ways. To glean comprehensive statistics from OSM in the context of Pakistan, a web tool accessible at https://ohsome.org/apps/dashboard/ has been employed for data extraction, spanning the time frame from 2007 to 2022 for all three OSM data types such as nodes, relations, and ways. As showcased in Figure 1, this graphical representation vividly illustrates the growth trajectory of OSM across various data types, encompassing nodes, ways, relations, and the cumulative total.

The data depicted in Figure 1 underscores a notable surge in OSM datasets within Pakistan over the past 15 years. Specifically, the expansion of OSM nodes has exhibited an uneven pattern, characterized by steady growth in ways and relation types from 2007 to 2015, followed by a marked acceleration in progress from 2016 onward, surpassing the growth rates of previous years.

When assessing the percentage growth rates, it becomes evident that nodes have experienced a remarkable 1437% increase, ways have witnessed an astonishing growth rate of 65779%, and relations

Figure 1. Growth of OSM in Pakistan between the years 2007-2022

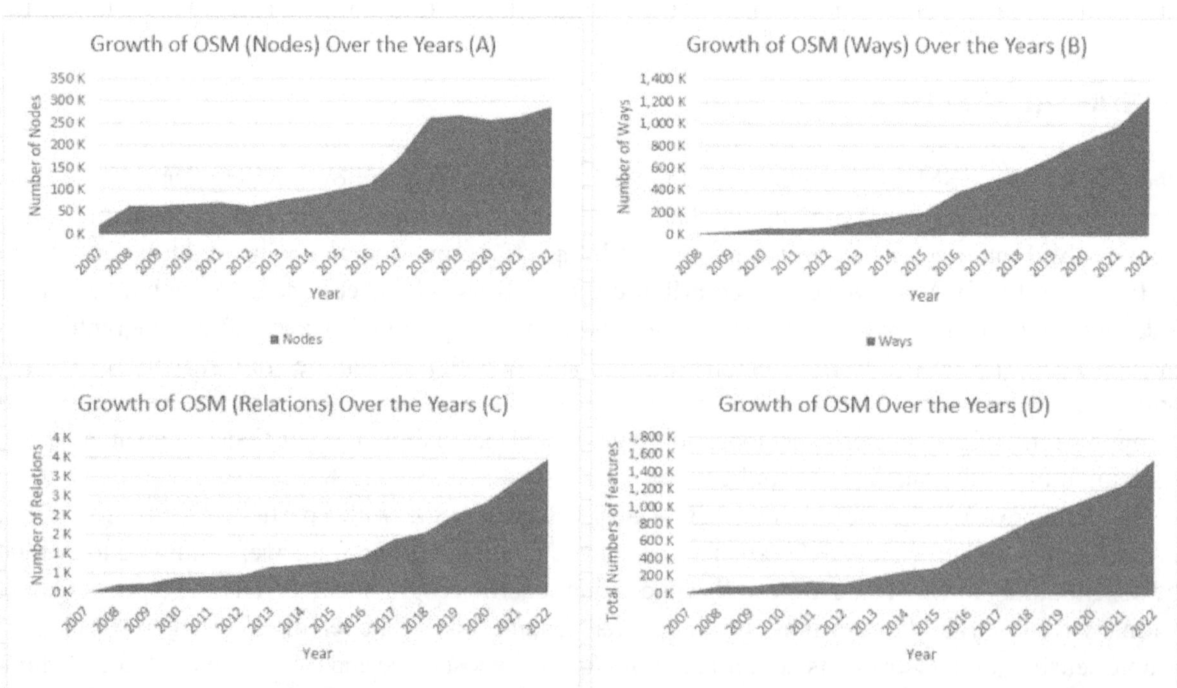

have demonstrated a substantial growth rate of 1498%. In aggregate, these figures collectively signify an impressive overall growth rate of 7416% spanning the years from 2007 to 2022.

ROLE OF OSM IN MAPPING RELIGIOUS TOURISM

OpenStreetMap data generally provides a reasonably accurate representation of official tourism statistics for various variables, rendering it a valuable resource for conducting analyses related to tourism competitiveness among countries (Bustamante et al., 2021). OSM can provide valuable geographic data for mapping religious structures and can be used as an educational resource in human geography courses to help students understand data production and mapping technologies (Dorrell, 2019).

Advantages of Using OpenStreetMap for Mapping Religious Tourism Sites

The benefits of employing OpenStreetMap for the mapping of religious tourism sites are illustrated in Figure 2 and explained in detail below.

Crowdsourced Data

OSM operates on the foundation of a worldwide community of dedicated contributors who engage in a continuous process of updating and verifying map data (See et al., 2015). This crowdsourced approach can serve as the driving force behind the incorporation of comprehensive and current information about religious sites, ensuring that OSM remains a valuable resource for religious tourism and related endeavors.

Customization

Individual users have the flexibility to customize maps according to their particular requirements, allowing them to incorporate layers and data pertinent to religious tourism. This may encompass the pinpointing of temple, mosque, or church locations, delineation of pilgrimage routes, and identification of nearby lodging facilities, all of which enhance the utility of OSM for religious tourism purposes.

Accessibility

The data and maps available through OSM are easily accessible to anyone with an internet connection (Kanthi & Purwanto, 2016). This open accessibility can greatly simplify the process of distributing information to prospective tourists and facilitators of travel planning, contributing to the widespread dissemination of valuable data related to religious tourism sites.

Collaboration

OSM can actively promote collaboration among diverse stakeholders, including governmental entities, religious organizations, and local communities (Budhathoki & Haythornthwaite, 2013; Yordanov et al., 2022). This collaborative ethos serves to nurture a holistic comprehension of the cultural and historical

Figure 2. Advantages of using OSM for mapping religious tourism sites

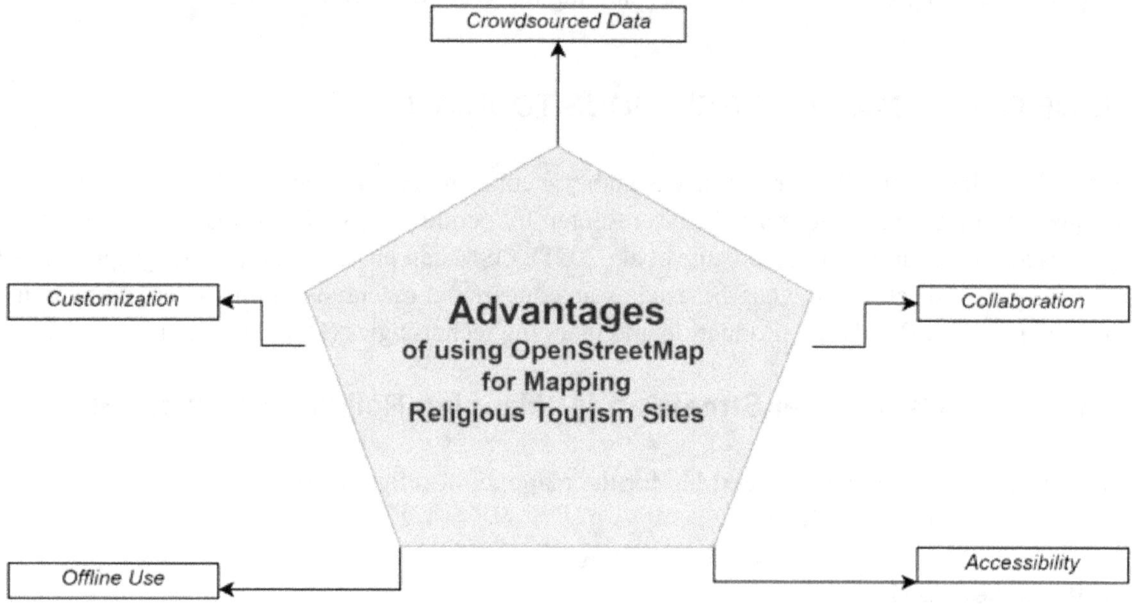

import associated with religious sites. It can facilitate the sharing of knowledge, expertise, and insights, ultimately contributing to a richer appreciation of these sites' significance.

Offline Use

One of the notable advantages of OSM is its capability to be downloaded and utilized offline. This feature proves particularly advantageous in regions characterized by restricted internet connectivity, a common scenario in remote religious pilgrimage sites. Pilgrims and travelers can access and navigate OSM data even when internet access is limited, ensuring that they can make informed and guided journeys to these sacred destinations.

Challenges of Using OpenStreetMap

Figure 3 showcases the obstacles associated with the utilization of OpenStreetMap for mapping religious tourism destinations, which are elucidated in the subsequent discussion.

Data Quality

The precision and comprehensiveness of OSM data can exhibit variability due to its reliance on user contributions. The quality of the data may be subject to fluctuations corresponding to the extent of user participation in a given region or project (Mobasheri et al., 2018). This highlights the importance of considering data quality and potentially supplementing OSM data with authoritative sources for critical applications.

Data Completeness

Relatively obscure or isolated religious sites might encounter constraints in terms of data coverage, and in some cases, the available data may be outdated. These limitations can have repercussions on the overall comprehensiveness of maps within such areas, emphasizing the need for continuous data updating efforts, particularly in lesser-known locations, to enhance the accuracy and inclusivity of OSM maps.

Language and Cultural Considerations

OSM cultural information can be quantitatively rich and demonstrate good positional and semantic accuracy in some parts of the world (Balducci, 2021). However, OSM may not consistently reflect the intricacies of local languages, nuances, or cultural specifics associated with religious sites with pinpoint accuracy. This potential limitation underscores the importance of complementing OSM data with context-specific insights and local knowledge to ensure a more comprehensive and culturally sensitive representation of these sites and their significance.

Reliability

In scenarios where critical applications, like emergency planning, are at stake, official government data sources are frequently deemed more dependable and trustworthy than OSM data. This acknowledgment underscores the need for caution and cross-referencing when it comes to vital tasks and applications that demand the highest levels of data accuracy and reliability. While OSM is a valuable resource, there are situations where government-sanctioned data sources remain the preferred choice for ensuring public safety and well-being.

User Participation

The effectiveness of OSM hinges on the active involvement of users, a factor that can exhibit considerable disparities based on geographical regions and specific projects (Arsanjani et al., 2015; Jokar Arsanjani & Bakillah, 2015). The level of user engagement can fluctuate, highlighting the importance of understanding and addressing regional and project-specific variations in order to maintain the vibrancy and reliability of the OSM platform.

OSM FOR RELIGIOUS TOURISM IN PAKISTAN

OpenStreetMap can be utilized to enhance access to and understanding of religious sites, guaranteeing a more enriching experience for pilgrims and tourists. In general, OSM can support religious tourism in Pakistan in many ways as depicted in Figure 4 and elaborated below.

Figure 3. Challenges of using OSM for mapping religious tourism sites

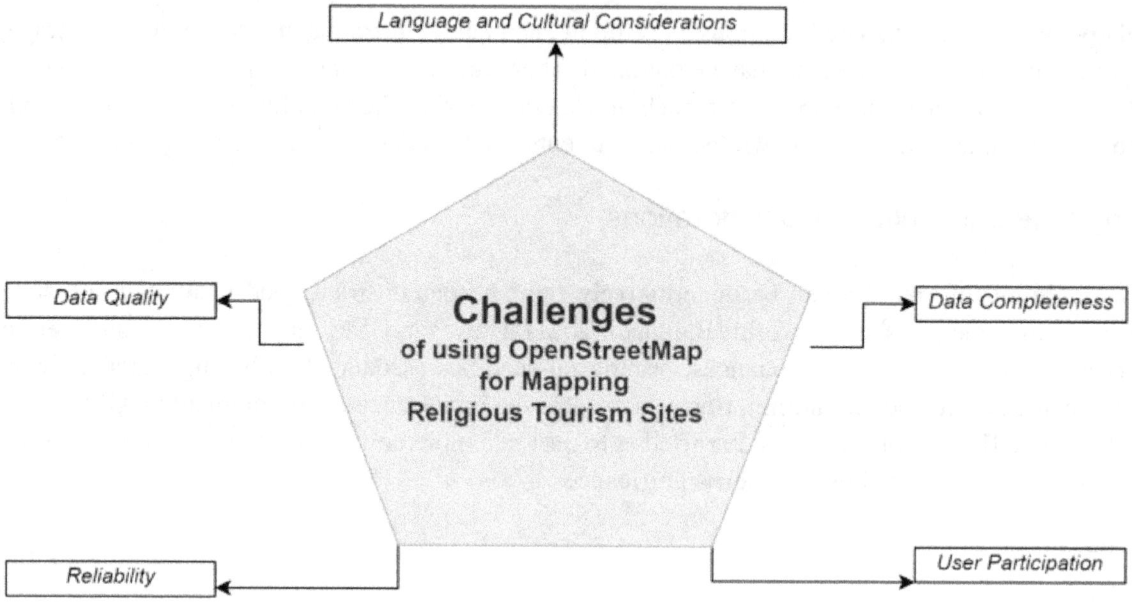

Mapping Religious Sites

OSM provides a platform for users to map and contribute data about various locations, including religious sites. Mapping religious sites on OSM can help in creating accurate and up-to-date geographical information about these places.

Detailed Information

Users can add detailed information about religious sites on OSM, such as historical significance, architectural details, and visiting hours. This information is invaluable for tourists and pilgrims who seek a deeper understanding of the places they are visiting. The availability of such information can enhance the overall experience and educational value of the visit.

Accessibility

Mapping religious sites on OSM can also help in improving accessibility. Users can add information about transportation options, nearby accommodations, and facilities for people with disabilities. This ensures that tourists and pilgrims can plan their visits more effectively and comfortably.

Cultural and Heritage Preservation

OSM can contribute to cultural and heritage preservation by documenting historical and religious sites. This data can be used for conservation efforts and to raise awareness about the importance of preserving these sites for future generations.

Route Planning

OSM offers route planning features that can be particularly useful for religious tourists. Pilgrims can use OSM to plan their journeys, identify nearby attractions, and estimate travel times accurately. This feature is especially valuable for those undertaking religious journeys to remote areas.

Community Engagement

OSM encourages community engagement through its open and collaborative nature. Local communities and religious organizations can actively participate in mapping and updating information about religious sites. This involvement fosters a sense of ownership and responsibility, ensuring that the data remains current and reliable.

Mobile Applications

Several mobile applications have been developed that use OSM data to provide navigation and information about religious sites in Pakistan. These apps make it convenient for tourists to access real-time information while on the move.

Tourism Promotion

The use of OSM for religious tourism in Pakistan can also be a valuable tool for tourism promotion. Government agencies and tourism boards can collaborate with OSM contributors to create interactive maps and promotional materials that showcase the religious and cultural heritage of Pakistan.

In Pakistan, religious tourism is facing several challenges that are endorsed in the previous section. This section will also explore the ways OpenStreetMap can help to address these challenges.

Mapping Infrastructure

OSM can be used to address Pakistan's infrastructure challenges in religious tourism by mapping existing infrastructure and facilities around religious sites, including roads, transportation options, accommodations, and medical facilities. This information can help tourists plan their visits more effectively.

OSM data can help to visualize regions with insufficient infrastructure around religious sites. It can allow users to contribute data about the condition of infrastructure, such as road quality, accessibility, and the availability of amenities. This information can empower tourists to make informed choices about their journeys, while crowdsourced updates on OSM can provide real-time information on areas needing development, helping the country enhance its infrastructure.

Maintaining Tourist Spots

Pakistan is facing the challenge of maintaining its religious tourist spots as noted in the previous section. OSM can serve as a vital tool by accumulating data on the maintenance needs of these sites, helping authorities prioritize resources effectively. Local communities and volunteers can engage with OSM to contribute updates on the condition of tourist spots, safeguarding the cultural and historical significance of these landmarks in Pakistan.

Mapping Safe Zones

Security concerns have been encountered in Pakistan's religious tourism. OSM can be a valuable resource by including data on safe zones and areas with heightened security measures. This can enable tourists to plan secure visits, and information about emergency services can be readily available through OSM, reassuring travelers about their safety while exploring religious sites in Pakistan. OSM can also provide data on the locations of nearby hospitals, police stations, and emergency services, offering tourists a sense of security and access to essential resources in case of emergencies.

Mapping Lesser-Known Sites

Pakistan is home to numerous lesser-known religious sites awaiting discovery. OSM can play a pivotal role in promoting these hidden gems by mapping and highlighting their existence. Through community-driven efforts in Pakistan, OSM can encourage local communities to showcase the cultural and historical significance of their sites, attracting attention from tourists, researchers, and government authorities.

Supporting Economic Factors

Economic factors, such as affordability, impact the accessibility of religious sites in Pakistan. OSM can contribute to making religious tourism more affordable. OSM can include data on budget-friendly accommodations, helping tourists find cost-effective places to stay near religious sites. OSM can also provide information on affordable transportation options, making it easier for tourists to access these sites without breaking their budgets.

Cultural Harmony

Cultural differences can sometimes lead to misunderstandings in Pakistan's diverse religious landscape. OSM can foster cultural sensitivity by incorporating information on local customs and etiquette related to religious sites specifically within Pakistan. This educational aspect can reduce the likelihood of cultural misunderstandings and promote cultural harmony, making religious tourism in Pakistan more welcoming.

Data Provision for Research

The absence of dependable data is a notable challenge in Pakistan's tourism sector. OSM can provide supplemental data about visitor flows and trends within Pakistan, enhancing existing data sources. This crowdsourced information can aid in better-informed policymaking and planning efforts in Pakistan's tourism sector, ensuring sustainable growth.

Figure 4. OSM support for religious tourism in Pakistan

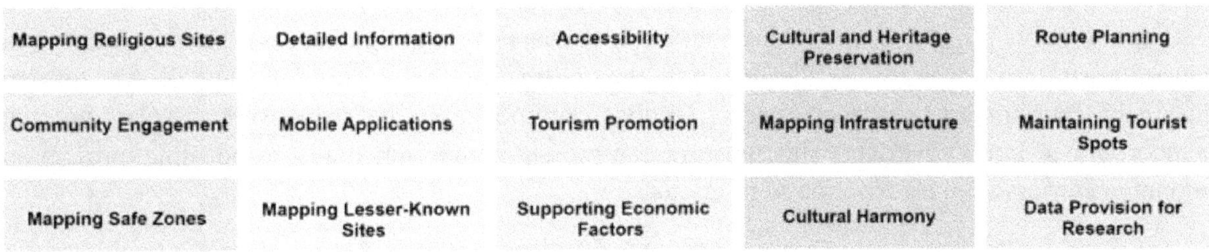

IMPLICATIONS OF USING OSM FOR MAPPING RELIGIOUS TOURISM IN PAKISTAN

The utilization of OpenStreetMap for mapping religious tourism in Pakistan and beyond holds significant implications that extend beyond the realm of tourism itself. OSM has the potential to significantly contribute to sustainable tourism development in Pakistan. It has the potential to catalyze more inclusive and sustainable tourism development by empowering communities and promoting local participation. By providing comprehensive and up-to-date information about religious tourism sites, OSM can empower tourists to make informed choices and explore a wider range of destinations. This, in turn, reduces the strain on heavily visited sites and encourages the development of infrastructure and services in lesser-known areas. Furthermore, the accessibility of OSM data to various stakeholders facilitates collaborative efforts aimed at preserving cultural heritage, protecting the environment, and ensuring the economic well-being of local communities. The ramifications of utilizing OSM for mapping religious tourism in Pakistan are expounded upon in the following sections and visually represented in Figure 5.

Empowering Local Communities

OSM allows local communities to actively participate in mapping and showcasing the religious sites in their areas. This involvement not only recognizes the cultural and historical significance of these sites but also instills a sense of ownership among local residents. By promoting lesser-known religious sites through OSM, local communities can have the opportunity to benefit economically. Increased tourism can generate income for local businesses, fostering economic growth and reducing dependency on centralized resources.

Enhancing Cultural Preservation

OSM's mapping efforts can encourage the preservation of cultural heritage. Local communities become more aware of the value of their religious sites, leading to increased efforts to protect and maintain them. OSM's global accessibility can facilitate cross-cultural exchange. Tourists from diverse backgrounds are exposed to the rich tapestry of cultural and religious diversity, fostering intercultural understanding and appreciation.

Promoting Sustainable Tourism

OSM can promote a more equitable distribution of tourists. By highlighting lesser-known sites, it can reduce the strain on overcrowded destinations, thus mitigating the negative impacts of over-tourism. Sustainable tourism practices, such as eco-friendly accommodations and responsible travel options, can be incorporated into OSM data. This, in turn, can promote environmentally responsible tourism and encourage conservation efforts around religious sites.

Encouraging Responsible Tourism

OSM can include information on cultural norms and customs specific to each religious site. This will educate tourists about the need for respectful behavior, encouraging responsible and considerate tourism. Through OSM, communities can share guidelines for responsible tourism, influencing tourists to engage respectfully with the local environment and culture.

Democratizing Tourism Information

OSM democratizes access to tourism information. It can empower travelers to plan their trips independently, reducing their reliance on commercial tour operators. The open-source nature of OSM can ensure that tourism information remains freely accessible to all, reducing barriers to entry for small-scale tourism entrepreneurs and local communities.

Figure 5. Implications of OSM for mapping religious tourism in Pakistan

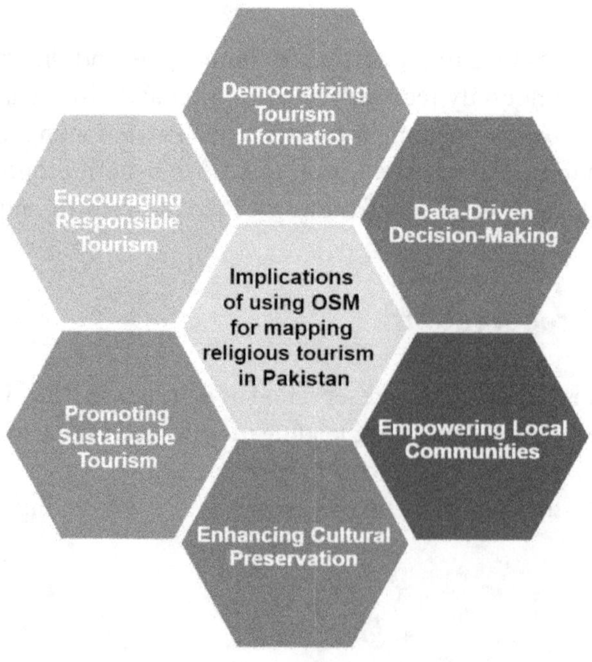

Data-Driven Decision-Making

OSM can provide tourism authorities and policymakers with valuable data to make evidence-based decisions. This can support the development of policies that cater to the diverse needs of tourists and communities. The data collected through OSM can inform the allocation of resources for infrastructure development, maintenance, and security, ensuring that investments are strategically directed.

CONCLUSION

Religious tourism in Pakistan emerges as a rich and multifaceted sector poised for significant growth and development. The nation's diverse spiritual landscape, encompassing Islam, Sikhism, Buddhism, Hinduism, and more, weaves a tapestry of sacred destinations and historical treasures, beckoning exploration. Nonetheless, this sector grapples with a host of challenges, spanning inadequate infrastructure, maintenance deficits, security apprehensions, hidden potential, economic dynamics, cultural disparities, and the absence of dependable data.

In this context, OpenStreetMap emerges as a dynamic and community-driven mapping platform, poised to play a transformative role in surmounting these challenges and unlocking the latent potential of religious tourism in Pakistan. OSM's capabilities extend beyond conventional mapping; it can empower users to chart religious sites, provide comprehensive information, enhance accessibility, and advocate for the conservation of culture and heritage. Additionally, OSM can facilitate route planning, foster community engagement, fuel tourism promotion, and channel economic benefits to local communities.

OSM also rises to address the specific challenges confronting Pakistan's religious tourism sector, such as mapping existing infrastructure, facilitating upkeep, ensuring safety, spotlighting lesser-known sites, supporting economic inclusivity, and nurturing cultural harmony. OSM can empower decision-makers and foster sustainable tourism development by supplying trustworthy, real-time data.

Looking ahead, several promising avenues beckon for the continued evolution and expansion of OSM's role in mapping religious tourism in Pakistan and globally can be surfaced such as encouraging active involvement from local communities through educational initiatives and capacity-building programs to enhance their role in mapping and preserving religious sites; and collaborating with governmental and tourism agencies to seamlessly integrate OSM data into official tourism platforms and apps, delivering a user-friendly experience for travelers.

Future research can also be centered around broadening the scope of OSM to highlight eco-friendly initiatives and environmentally significant areas near religious sites, fostering responsible and sustainable tourism practices; and developing real-time monitoring and alert systems within OSM to address security concerns and offer timely responses to emergencies, bolstering safety. Researchers can also focus on launching campaigns to educate both tourists and locals about the advantages of leveraging OSM for religious tourism and responsible travel; forging partnerships with academic institutions for research endeavors that utilize OSM data to dissect tourism trends, evaluate economic impacts, and delve into cultural dynamics; and garnering support from governmental bodies to recognize the significance of OSM in fostering tourism, safeguarding heritage, and elevating local economies.

REFERENCES

Ahmad, M. (2023). Unleashing Business Potential: Harnessing OpenStreetMap for Intelligent Growth and Sustainability. In *Data-Driven Intelligent Business Sustainability*. IGI Global.

Ahmad, M., & Ali, A. (2023). Mapping the Future of Sustainable Development Through Cloud-Based Solutions: A Case Study of OpenStreetMap. In Promoting Sustainable Management Through Technological Innovation (pp. 153–176). IGI Global.

Ahmad, N. M., Sohail, R., & Ahmad, M. M. (2022). Impact of Religious Tourism on the Development of Smokeless Industry in Pakistan. *Global Social Sciences Review*, *VII*(II), 77–89. doi:10.31703/gssr.2022(VII-II).08

Ahmed, M., Ahmed, S., & Abbas, R. (2022). Tourism in Pakistan, Challenges and Opportunities. *Journal of Social Sciences Review*, *2*(3), 130–137. doi:10.54183/jssr.v2i3.102

Almuhrzi, H. (2020). Islamic tourism: Management of travel destinations. *Journal of Heritage Tourism*, *15*(4), 480–482. doi:10.1080/1743873X.2019.1658351

An, J., Wan Zainon, W. M. N., & Zainon, W. (2023). An interactive visualization of location-based reviews using word cloud and OpenStreetMap for tourism applications. *Spatial Information Research*, *31*(2), 235–243. doi:10.100741324-022-00492-z

Arsanjani, J. J., Mooney, P., Helbich, M., & Zipf, A. (2015). An Exploration of Future Patterns of the Contributions to OpenStreetMap and Development of a Contribution Index. *Transactions in GIS*, *19*(6), 896–914. doi:10.1111/tgis.12139

Arshad, M. I., Iqbal, M. A., & Shahbaz, M. (2018). Pakistan tourism industry and challenges: A review. *Asia Pacific Journal of Tourism Research*, *23*(2), 121–132. doi:10.1080/10941665.2017.1410192

Balducci, F. (2021). Is OpenStreetMap a good source of information for cultural statistics? The case of Italian museums. *Environment and Planning. B, Urban Analytics and City Science*, *48*(3), 503–520. doi:10.1177/2399808319876949

Bari, M. W., & Khan, Q. (2020). Pakistan as a destination of religious tourism. In Global Development of Religious Tourism. IGI Global. doi:10.4018/978-1-7998-5792-1.ch001

Budhathoki, N. R., & Haythornthwaite, C. (2013). Motivation for Open Collaboration: Crowd and Community Models and the Case of OpenStreetMap. In American Behavioral Scientist, 57(5). doi:10.1177/0002764212469364

Bustamante, A., Sebastia, L., & Onaindia, E. (2021). On the representativeness of openstreetmap for the evaluation of country tourism competitiveness. *ISPRS International Journal of Geo-Information*, *10*(5), 301. doi:10.3390/ijgi10050301

Demircioğlu, A. (2020). Introducing the cities of Ghazali in the context of religious tourism. In Global Development of Religious Tourism. IGI Global. doi:10.4018/978-1-7998-5792-1.ch003

Di Giovine Michael, A., & Elsner, J. (2016). Pilgrimage tourism. In H. Jafari Jafar and Xiao (Ed.), Encyclopedia of Tourism (pp. 722–724). Springer International Publishing. doi:10.1007/978-3-319-01384-8_146

Dorrell, D. (2019). Using openstreetmap as a source of religious mapping data in an oer human geography textbook. In Open Educational Resources (OER) Pedagogy and Practices. doi:10.4018/978-1-7998-1200-5.ch006

Iips. (2022a). *Potential of religious tourism in Pakistan*. https://iips.com.pk/potential-of-religious-tourism-in-pakistan/

Iips. (2022b). *Religious tourism and its potential in Pakistan*. Iqbal Institute of Policy Studies – IIPS. https://iips.com.pk/religious-tourism-and-its-potential-in-pakistan/

Irfan, E., & Ali, Y. (2020). Religious tourism in Pakistan: Scope, obstacles & strategies. *Journal of Convention & Event Tourism*, *22*(2), 134–154. doi:10.1080/15470148.2020.1852990

Jokar Arsanjani, J., & Bakillah, M. (2015). Understanding the potential relationship between the socio-economic variables and contributions to OpenStreetMap. *International Journal of Digital Earth*, *8*(11), 861–876. doi:10.1080/17538947.2014.951081

Kanthi, N. S., & Purwanto, T. H. (2016). Application of OpenStreetMap (OSM) to Support the Mapping Village in Indonesia. *IOP Conference Series: Earth and Environmental Science*. IOP Science. 10.1088/1755-1315/47/1/012003

Luz, N. (2020). Pilgrimage and religious tourism in Islam. *Annals of Tourism Research*, *82*, 102915. doi:10.1016/j.annals.2020.102915

Mafudi, M., Sugiarto, S., & Praptapa, A. (2021). Emerging Opportunities for Halal Tourism in Rural Areas: Insights from Indonesia. *Fokus Bisnis : Media Pengkajian Manajemen Dan Akuntansi*, *20*(1), 16–26. doi:10.32639/fokusbisnis.v10i1.726

Minghini, M., & Frassinelli, F. (2019). OpenStreetMap history for intrinsic quality assessment: Is OSM up-to-date? *Open Geospatial Data. Software and Standards*, *4*(1), 9. doi:10.118640965-019-0067-x

Mobasheri, A., Zipf, A., & Francis, L. (2018). OpenStreetMap data quality enrichment through awareness raising and collective action tools—Experiences from a European project. *Geo-Spatial Information Science*, *21*(3), 234–246. doi:10.1080/10095020.2018.1493817

Mooney, P., Corcoran, P., & Winstanley, A. C. (2010). Towards quality metrics for OpenStreetMap. *Proceedings of the 18th SIGSPATIAL International Conference on Advances in Geographic Information Systems GIS 10*, (pp. 514–517). ACM. 10.1145/1869790.1869875

PBS. (2018). *6th Population & Housing Census 2017*. PBS. https://www.pbs.gov.pk/sites/default/files//population_census/National.pdf

Post, F. (2022). Religious tourism in Pakistan. *The Frontier Post*. https://thefrontierpost.com/religious-tourism-in-pakistan-2/

Ramos, C. M. Q., & Mafé-García, A. (2018). Analysis of the contribution of ICT to cultural and religious tourism: In communicating religious heritage to visitors and tourists. In Handbook of Research on Socio-Economic Impacts of Religious Tourism and Pilgrimage. doi:10.4018/978-1-5225-5730-2.ch010

Rinschede, G. (1992). Forms of religious tourism. *Annals of Tourism Research, 19*(1), 51–67. doi:10.1016/0160-7383(92)90106-Y

See, L., Fritz, S., Perger, C., Schill, C., McCallum, I., Schepaschenko, D., Duerauer, M., Sturn, T., Karner, M., Kraxner, F., & Obersteiner, M. (2015). Harnessing the power of volunteers, the internet and Google Earth to collect and validate global spatial information using Geo-Wiki. *Technological Forecasting and Social Change, 98*, 324–335. doi:10.1016/j.techfore.2015.03.002

Shaukat, R. (2023, May). The economy of religious tourism. *The News*. https://www.thenews.com.pk/tns/detail/1074402-the-economy-of-religious-tourism#:~:text=As%20per%20the%20Pakistan%20Tourism,tourists%20visit%20Pakistan%20every%20year

Tasneem, S., Khawar, M., & Hayat, R. (2022). Cultural Tourism in Pakistan: Prospects and Challenges. *Pakistan Vision, 23*(2).

Tsironis, C. N. (2022). Pilgrimage and Religious Tourism in Society, in the Wake of the COVID-19 Pandemic: A Paradigmatic Focus on 'St. Paul's Route' in the Central Macedonia Region, Greece. *Religions, 13*(10), 887. doi:10.3390/rel13100887

Vargas-Munoz, J. E., Srivastava, S., Tuia, D., & Falcao, A. X. (2021). OpenStreetMap: Challenges and Opportunities in Machine Learning and Remote Sensing. *IEEE Geoscience and Remote Sensing Magazine, 9*(1), 184–199. doi:10.1109/MGRS.2020.2994107

Vaziri, F., Nanni, M., Matwin, S., & Pedreschi, D. (2020). *Discovering Tourist Attractions of Cities Using Flickr and OpenStreetMap Data*. doi:10.1007/978-981-15-2024-2_21

Weber, P., & Haklay, M. (2008). OpenStreetMap: User-generated street maps. *IEEE Pervasive Computing, 7*(4).

World Economic Forum. (2022). *Travel & Tourism Development Index 2021*. WEF.

Yordanov, V., Quang Truong, X., Thanh Thuy Pham, T., Dong Khuc, T., & Antonia Brovelli, M. (2022). Open and collaborative tools for disaster management and risk reduction. *Vietnam Journal of Hydrometeorology, 3*(12), 33–38. doi:10.36335/VNJHM.2022(12).33-38

Chapter 3
Pilgrimages and the Sacred Way: My Experience

Luís Maia Rodrigues
Independent Researcher, Portugal

ABSTRACT

The chapter talks about the author's experience as a pilgrim. From 1973 until 2018, he was a pilgrim to Our Lady of Fátima, mapped and walked a centuries-old route to Our Lady of Lapa and was a frequent pilgrim to Santiago de Compostela. In the meantime, in the spirit of the pilgrimage to Santiago, he also became a volunteer, supporting pilgrims in hostels since 2016. In 2019, a serious illness led him to fear that his pilgrimages had come to an end. The fight against fears, uncertainties about the future, but also the solidarity of many friends and, perhaps unexpectedly, of those who have walked the same roads with him.

INTRODUCTION

This article describes aspects and points of view of my "life" as a pilgrim. A continuous search for pilgrimage routes and the pleasure of trying to reach the material and spiritual limits they offer. The multiple feelings along the routes travelled and the experiences as a volunteer in the hostels along the road to Santiago de Compostela. In my experience, I have accompanied others who have made promises, I have been the bearer of promises on behalf of people without hope, believing that they could only find a cure or obtain peace from death through the supernatural. I have supported pilgrims in their various conditions, even when they were desperate, but also many of those who, having no roof over their heads, lived off charity and solidarity up and down the roads to Santiago.

The first eight chapters describe many of these experiences, covering the most memorable moments as a person, pilgrim, and volunteer.

But life always has setbacks. In 2019, after having walked half of the French route, cancer forced me to leave the most travelled pilgrimage route in the Christian world halfway through. The ninth chapter deals with illness, the fight against fears, uncertainties about the future, but also the solidarity of many

DOI: 10.4018/978-1-6684-9923-8.ch003

and, perhaps unexpectedly, of those who have walked the same roads with me. Despite this, some doubts persisted: Would I be able to finish the French way?

The continuous search for information about the Camino de Santiago (Way of Saint James), its origins and development are the basis of the methodology adopted. The "inventio" of the relics of St. James the Greater and the legends surrounding the Apostle, reproduced in the "Codex Calixtinus", ended up transforming history, after being promoted and protected by royal and church elites. The development of pilgrimage routes to Santiago de Compostela is one of the consequences of this protection, plus the commitment of Popes, both in the Middle Ages and today. Also present are the study and knowledge of the evolution of the concept of pilgrim and the existence or not of contradictions between the motivations of the various people who walk the Camino de Santiago.

The methodology for this text was based on experiences that were gathered randomly, guided, and adapted as each moment demanded, through interviews and observation of the behaviour and attitudes of other pilgrims and, when searching for and rediscovering ancestral paths, of elders who had walked them or knew them through tradition.

The main objective, with this article, is to reach the reader in the subject of pilgrimage routes, and to encourage him to become a pilgrim, as well.

1. The Beginning

March 1973. At the Rocha dock, by the Tagus River in Lisbon, a crowd awaited the disembarkation of soldiers who, at the end of a mission in Guinea, were returning home. In that moment, nobody was thinking about the 'Mission accomplished', but only about the fraternal embrace of the son, the brother, the fiancé who, after a nightmare of 2 or more years, was returning home, alive.

In the midst of the crowd, we couldn't find a familiar face. What chaos. The camouflage uniforms were worn, the coloured insignias faded, the boys tanned and their hair lighter. Suddenly, we saw my brother on an army truck leaving the place where we were waiting, heading to RAL1[1], for the necessary demobilization process. A few hours later, at the regiment's gate, the reunion happened: hugs, kisses, and tears of joy. The dream of returning from the war 'safe and sound' was realized.

Now, our family mostly lived in Coimbra, even though my father was in Oliveira do Hospital. Upon arriving in Coimbra, my now returned brother displayed gifts while recounting stories and revealing to the family that he had made a promise: on the day he arrived in Oliveira do Hospital, he would embark on a pilgrimage to Fátima. In our family, there were no habits of making promises to saints, the Virgin, or making pilgrimage vows. Despite that, we all understood that this was an exception, only justified by the unique circumstances of someone who needed an anchor to survive in the midst of wartime conflict. After exchanging opinions on the matter, I volunteered to accompany him on the pilgrimage, with the decision being that only after a few days of physical recovery in Coimbra would we go to Oliveira to fulfil the promise. And so it was, even with my newly returned brother attempting to prevent me accompanying him, pointing out my underage status (I was 18 at the time) and the fear that I might be a burden rather than a companion for him.

This was my first pilgrimage. I will never forget the leg and foot pains, the fatigue at the end of each day, the mistakes typical of beginners, especially the inappropriate footwear, etc. We had only planned the first day, up to Miranda do Corvo. From there, we asked for directions along the way, but in the end, despite all the improvisation, everything was perfect. What marked me indelibly and memorably was the human warmth received throughout the journey. From the snack in a tavern where the elderly almost toasted us as heroes, to the veal chop in Freixienda where, despite the late hour, we were received with extraordinary friendliness and hospitality, to sleeping at the Caxarias train station due to a lack of alternatives. I felt, throughout the experience, that it was the realization of a dream I had harboured for many years. Always ready to continue, even when we stopped to regain our strength, I felt fulfilled by the kilometres travelled and excited about those left to traverse, in a countdown to which only very strong emotions were added.

The fascination and wonder of this pilgrimage have stayed with me ever since. After all, humans have always been eternal pilgrims, always searching for something more, whether mentally or materially. Looking at the evolutionary journey of the human species, and especially how Homo sapiens colonized different continents tens of thousands of years ago and comparing it to the current movements of souls arriving in Europe in search of something, anything, outside their home countries where they would naturally feel secure. How can we fail to understand the significance of current or, in fact, eternal pilgrimages? Contrary to prejudiced conceptions, we know that even in the Middle Ages, there was significant movement of people for various reasons. Wandering beggars, merchants, prelates, lords, pilgrims...

Today, pilgrimage encompasses many different forms and concepts. Looking, for example, along the paths of Santiago, the way they are organized, with yellow arrows, hostels, hotels, bars, restaurants, convenience stores, souvenir shops, tourist offices, etc., it seems more like we're on a tourist circuit than a route for encountering the supernatural, whether religious or not. Many contemporary authors agree that the relationship between tourism and religion is very old, even considering that the origin of contemporary tourism may be related to pilgrimages (Collins-Kreiner et al., 2006); (Margry, 2008); (Sharpley, 2009); (Norman & Cusack, 2015). At the same time, religious or spiritual pilgrimages have developed significantly and constitute an important segment of international tourism (Timothy & Olsen, 2006); (Margry, 2008), (Norman & Cusack, 2015). According to the World Tourism Organization (United Nations|ONU News, 2014), over 300 million tourists visit shrines every year. For MacCannel (1976), tourism can be considered a modern version of a connection with the sacred.

2. The Rediscovery of the Paths of Santiago

A few years and experiences later, news spread that a Spanish priest had revived and marked the ancient path from France to Santiago de Compostela. In 1982, during his apostolic journey to Spain, Pope John Paul II visited Santiago, where he addressed words to all of Europe from the Cathedral's pulpit, affirming that there was a convergence of paths from all across the continent. In his words, the Bishop of Rome stated, '*People and Christians of every social condition arrived here from France, Italy, Central Europe, the Nordic Countries, and Slavic Nations,* (...)', confirming that, after all, from the Middle Ages to our present day, all European paths lead to Santiago de Compostela, contradicting the popular saying that 'all roads lead to Rome.' By saying, '*I, Bishop of Rome and Shepherd of the universal Church, from Santiago, I let out to you, old Europe, a cry full of love: Rediscover yourself. Be yourself. Uncover your origins. Revive your roots*', John Paul reminded the civilized world that 'new crusades' lay ahead of us: the rediscovery of our civilizational origins.

In a different context, Popes have made appeals to old Europe from Santiago. In the Middle Ages, the call was for the reconquest of the Peninsula and the Holy Places in the East, and now, the call is for the values that unite European culture. Seemingly different in terms of means, we must agree that the ultimate goal remains the same.

In 1989, John Paul II returned to Santiago de Compostela for the IV World Youth Day, drawing together around a million people, mostly young. Beyond these events, I couldn't ignore the news of the Jacobean Year in 2004. Over 170,000 pilgrims made their way to Santiago. Throughout the centuries, Santiago has been both a point of departure and arrival, and in this movement, as a pilgrim, I couldn't remain unaffected.

3. The First Pilgrimage to Santiago

The opportunity to pilgrimage to Santiago only arose for me in 2009. A friend, my wife's working colleague, had gone to Santiago in 2004 and was organizing another pilgrimage. I asked what it was like, if there were places to sleep, how to cover so many kilometres. At the end of the conversation, I asked if I could accompany him and, immediately, we began exchanging ideas about how we would do it: the pilgrim's credential, the backpack and equipment, the appropriate footwear, and of course, the number of days we would need. My friend's group was departing from Tomar towards Coimbra through the Portuguese Central Way; then, following an untrodden route through what may have been the Portuguese Interior Way, passing through Viseu, Castro Daire, Lamego, Vila Real, Vila Pouca de Aguiar, Vidago, Chaves, Vila Verde da Raia, and Verin, from where they would continue on the Sanabrian Way (a variant of the Silver Way). Looking at the calendar and the remaining vacation days I had, I would join the group starting from Vila Pouca de Aguiar.

The pilgrimage proved to be an immensely enriching experience. The Interior Way wasn't marked with arrows; we had to plan our overnight stays. From one town to another, we had to ask for directions and, preferably, inquire about "shortcuts." This was the "magical" way to get people to suggest alternatives to the paved roads. The best guides for our orientation were the local farmers, shepherds, and cyclists. In Chaves, there was a contact of a pilgrim who would guide us to Verin. It was a Monday, and there we sat with a map and calendar in front of us. Unlike my companions, I had to finish by Sunday as I had to return to work the following week. Given this context, our friend was peremptory: "you have to go to Laza tomorrow." However, the suggested route had a major issue in the middle. A new road was being constructed in Spain, cutting through the path, making it difficult to follow without getting lost. Therefore, upon entering Spain, we were advised to follow the national road to Verin, which posed no safety issues as Spanish roads had wide shoulders where we could walk safely. Despite all the challenges, we reached Verin almost at dusk. The pilgrim's hostel was located in the garage of Casa do Escudo, which also housed the tourist office.

We were entering a different world. The information provided to pilgrims was excellent, with well-designed magazines, brochures, useful contacts and information, as well as pilgrims' rights and responsibilities. I still keep some of those materials. That night, after taking a shower, I realized I had a blister on one of my right toes. Another pilgrim promptly offered me a blister plaster, a solution that was new to me, and that proved to be miraculous for continuing the journey. During dinner, we reviewed our plans again. My friends reaffirmed that it was possible to reach Santiago by Sunday.

The Sanabrian Way variant passing through Verin continued on to Xinzo de Limia, but the nearest pilgrim's hostel was about 38 kilometres away. However, we knew there was a marked path with yellow arrows leading to Laza, which had a hostel just 22 kilometres away. We decided to head for Laza.

The next morning, the challenges resumed. No one could inform us where the alternative route connecting Verin to Laza began. We decided to follow the road until we found the first yellow arrow. We arrived in Laza by nightfall. During dinner, we revisited the pilgrimage plan, but for me, it was clear that we were behind schedule. Nevertheless, the following day, we had to ascend the mountain to Albergueria. The path was steep and difficult, but the arrival would be welcoming. Back at the hostel, I studied the guide that had been given to us at the Verin tourist office. It was evident that at the pace we had been maintaining, reaching Santiago by Sunday would be very challenging. Therefore, I had a decision to make. Considering the challenges, we had faced since the beginning, if I wanted to reach Santiago by Sunday, I would have to try to change the group dynamic. I knew this would be difficult, both for me and for each of my companions.

Upon reaching Albergueria, a village with around 40 inhabitants, we entered the only shop there, El Rincón del Peregrino. It was very cold, and at the centre of the shop stood a welcoming wood-burning stove. As we entered, the music changed. The waltzes of Strauss were replaced by Cesária Évora's "Sódade". Two Austrian pilgrims who had stayed in Laza with us asked why the music had changed, to which José Luis, the owner, pointed at us and said, "they are Portuguese." The walls were adorned with scallop shells bearing names and dates. We were given one to mark our passage. My friends asked if I knew about another scallop shell, they had signed years ago, and to our surprise, it was there, waiting for us. In the warmth of the stove and José Luis's company, I brought up our plan again. My friends decided to stay in Vilar de Barrio on the mountain's descent. I showed them that I had to continue to Xunqueira de Ambía. If everything went well, I would reach Santiago by Sunday; otherwise, I would wait and continue with them later. They agreed, and we continued.

From Vilar de Barrio onwards, I continued alone. The adventure continued to Santiago de Compostela, after some exhausting stages due to both the kilometres covered and the heat of some of the days. These challenges were compounded by blisters on my feet and a scarcity of hot meals. However, along the journey, I was never truly alone; there was always another pilgrim waiting for me at the next café or shop, and before I set off again, another would arrive. With the repeated encounters characteristic of the pilgrimage, I formed unexpected friendships with fellow travellers who helped me in every way. But like them, many other factors also aided me in moving forward. The widespread warm welcome from the Galician locals, the human warmth of the hostel owners, and, psychologically, the sensation of getting closer and closer to my goal, both physically and mentally: Santiago was waiting for me for an embrace!

After 240 kilometres, one and a half kilograms lighter, feet full of blisters, I arrive at Obradoiro square tired but filled with emotion. I took off my shoes, and for a moment, I stopped feeling the pain and fatigue. A relieved wave of emotion made me cry. A tremendous joy and pleasure overwhelmed me. I had managed to arrive.

I attempted to go to the Portico of Glory to fulfil the tradition – leaning my head against it and placing my right hand on the central pillar, on a hand-shaped mark "sculpted" by countless pilgrims over hundreds of years. However, I couldn't achieve it as access to the Portico was restricted for restoration. After that, I performed the ritual of embracing the image of Santiago, said a little prayer in front of the tomb believed to be that of the apostle and obtained the Compostela. Then came the pilgrim's mass. I had attended this mass during previous visits, but on that day, everything was different. I couldn't control my emotions. The atmosphere, the swinging censer (the Botafumeiro[2]), the celestial voice of the choir soloist nun, the service of the mass, and the spoken word – everything merged and intertwined in such a special, magical way that once again, my joy culminated in a silent, but uncontrollable, weeping.

My family was waiting for me. We embraced, kissed, and after lunch at Manolo's in Cervantes Square, we headed back home.

4. My first Jacobean Year

2010 was another Jacobean year. Very early on, I began to organize my Jacobean journey. The Interior Way to Santiago was not yet defined, so I began by searching the literature for the possibilities that were open to me from the city of Viseu. My attention was drawn to the fact that, from Castro Daire, there were two possible routes: one through Vila Real and another towards Amarante, following Guimarães and Braga. There was still another possibility, close to these options, from Peso da Régua towards Amarante. I looked for nature and outdoor associations, groups of hikers and cyclists, in order to find some guidance. Among many friends I made, however, one remained in my memory because he would become a source I kept going back to: the head of the Marco de Canaveses scouts, Engº Mouro Pinto, a proponent of the path that followed the Roman road from Castro Daire to Braga, passing through Cinfães, Porto Manso, Marco de Canaveses, Guimarães. In the absence of more detailed information, I started looking into different possibilities, ending up, after many miles under my belt, going from Viseu to Castro Daire through Almargem, Calde, Adenodeiro, Cela, Termas de Carvalhal, Ribolhos and Ponte Pedrinha. After Castro Daire, it would pass through Picão, following the Serra de Montemuro (Panchorra, Panchorrinha and Granja) to Cárquere and Resende and then towards Amarante, Guimarães, Braga and Ponte de Lima, from where we would take the Portuguese Central route. By this time, I had been joined by another companion and pilgrim.

We worked out what was possible and set off. Along the way, when meeting people, we were seen either as something strange or bizarre. When they saw us with backpacks and sticks, they asked us if we were looking for pinecones, and when we asked about "shortcuts" to avoid roads, they looked suspiciously: "Why don't you take the road? You will never make a mistake that way, or are you on the run?"

Another common difficulty was the distances to be covered. Usually, when you ask a driver how many kilometres are left, you never get a correct answer: "You'll be there in a jiffy, it's only 5 minutes", and after 1 hour you haven't arrived where you wanted. I remember that, desperate to have lunch, someone told us that there was a restaurant on the road, "just down there". After a lot of wandering, we found a lady on the road with a red scarf, very short clothes and red hair who, in a friendly and attentive way, told us precisely where the restaurant was.

For open minds, even these difficulties are understood as part of the pilgrimage, as atonement for our cross, our fate. It is all part of our experience as pilgrims. We usually forget about them, after laughing a bit, until the next meeting. However, many of these experiences end in unexpected and emotional ways. We were passing through a small village and in a villa a lady was watering her garden. We asked if the water was good and if we could drink it. After the initial conversation, having drunk the water and filled the canteens, she asked us where we were going, because Fatima was in another direction. "We're going to Santiago de Compostela!"; "So far away, and you're going on a personal vow?" When we said no, the lady began to cry: "Then pray and ask for me, Maria da Conceição, to Santiago. I have cancer and I don't know how many more months I have to live...". We ended up crying with her and remembered her all the way to Santiago.

Until arriving in Ponte de Lima, the experience of the pilgrimage is a lot to do with personal emotions. On the one hand, our conversations, our feelings, our difficulties; and on the other hand, the transient relationships with the residents of the villages that we pass. Where we are from, where we are going, why, what personal vow has been made, what is the material interest or the spiritual reason. But the progress of the walk was somewhat erratic. The president of the 'Associação Espaços Jacobeus' (the Jacobean Association) gave us some guidance and there were some sections marked with arrows, from

Guimarães, however they were still difficult to follow because there were lots of mistakes, signs in different directions, directions that ended up in dead-ends. Arriving in Braga we knew that the markings started near the cathedral. We did a reconnaissance in the evening and the next morning we followed the markings to Ponte de Lima.

Leave Ponte de Lima, cross the ancient bridge and arrive at the hostel. Everything started perfectly again. The following days were very simple, just follow the yellow arrows. The need for interaction with people on the way became much less. Even so, we did not stop chatting at the "vendas"[3] where my companion found the vernacular of the language of the people of Minho strange, and much more strange the fact that men and women practised it without concern or feelings of doing something wrong.

However, as we progressed through Galicia, the typical signs of a tourist route returned: the decoration of the bars with Jacobean motifs, the stores of all kinds of "recuerdos"[4], the informal stores with products that pilgrims need, the coin machines for drinks and snacks, flanked by benches or chairs for a short break, etc. Whether we like it or not, to enter the Santiago paths, as they are currently set up, one needs to follow a route that is in no way different from any typical nature tourism route. The road is like a great framework that moulds us, involving us, capturing us in its economic structure all the way to Santiago. Here and there we see numerous groups of people, some of them dressed in cloaks, pilgrim hats, gourds and walking sticks, who, further on, have a bus waiting for them with a small meal, then go to a hotel.

Figure 1. Arriving to Santiago de Compostela (May 2, 2010)

At the opposite end of the spectrum, we saw something very special in Redondela. The municipal hostel was full. Early in the morning, there was more noise than usual, considering that all the pilgrims must leave without disturbing the others. Woken up, I decided to get up and realized that it was a very large group of elderly people going about their morning routines. Since it was an unusual group, I decided to stop and simply observe... Morning ablutions done (which took a while), they started organizing their belongings for the next stage and how great was my surprise when I saw that instead of backpacks, most of them were carrying a shopping bag with wheels, as used in supermarket shopping. One of the pilgrims was even more peculiar because he had attached the straps of a backpack to a trolley. It seemed to me like one of those excursions organized by local associations, except that instead of taking the bus, they were walking.

Own Elaboration

When we arrived in Santiago, my emotions of the previous year were repeated. There were no blisters on my feet, but when I arrived, the tiredness disappeared for a moment. Except that this Jacobean, after the terrorist attacks suffered in recent years in Europe and Spain, security measures had been reinforced and, because of this, the entrance to the pilgrim's Mass resembled the security control of an airport. There was such a queue that, by the time it would be our turn to enter, the Mass would be over. We decided to just go and embrace the figure of Santiago. The queue was shorter, for some reason the security was less, we just couldn't go in with our backpack. We took turns to hold each other's backpacks and went to embrace the figure while Mass was going on, but we couldn't stop. When it came to the Catholic precept of the forgiveness of our sins, this remained unfulfilled. After all, if Santiago was unable to welcome pilgrims in his Cathedral, for logistical reasons, surely, after about 400 kilometres covered in numerous days, deprived of our family, usually without time for meals, with sore legs, our sins would be forgiven.

A pilgrim friend of mine advised me that when we get to Compostela, we should get a new credential. That way we are always prepared for the next pilgrimage.

5. Our Lady of Lapa

After the pilgrimage of the Jacobean year 2010, I started another project. Since time immemorial, a group of women set out from Santar and Moreira (Nelas) towards the Shrine of Our Lady of Lapa, about 60 kilometres away. After the law on the separation of Church and State, during the 1st Republic, this pilgrimage began to lose importance and, after the phenomenon of Fatima, it was almost completely abandoned by pilgrims on foot. I learned about it and realized that there were still some elderly people who knew where the pilgrimage path was, either because they had walked it or because they had heard about it on many evenings, in the days when there was no television to occupy the long winter nights. Today the world comes to us at home, but in other times, people shared with each other experiences, stories, songs with remote origins and their remarkable life experiences.

The Sanctuary of Our Lady of Lapa has been in my memory from when I was very young. My family visited it often in the 1960s and I remember very well the darkness of the cave where an oil lamp illuminated the image of the Virgin. I have to confess that I was afraid, but I held my mother's hand and that gave me complete confidence to go to the cave and then pass through the gap in the rock until I returned to the light. When I learned that such an ancient tradition had existed in Santar and that it could be lost due to lack of records, I began to contact the person who, being a devotee of the Virgin of Lapa, seemed to have the best memory to guide me. At the same time, I would walk the paths, looking for identifying elements, returning to my source, to confirm. Throughout these walks, I got involved with the presidents of the parish councils, to help me in the search for what could have been these pilgrimage paths, over the centuries. After hundreds of miles under my belt, conversations with local councillors and with many people along the way that I was rediscovering, trying to follow the "alminhas"[5] and those places where legends tell us that the Virgin Mary passed in her escape to Egypt, I managed to map out and mark with blue arrows a pilgrimage path that would be the one that those women did, in the past, and for many years to Our Lady of Lapa.

The local parishes involved were fundamental to organize the logistics. Places to sleep, to eat, etc, were needed. After the route was surveyed and marked with blue arrows, a memorandum of understanding was signed involving the Santa Casa da Misericórdia de Santar[6], the parish councils along the way, with the knowledge and signature of the Rector of the Shrine. Involving all these possible stakeholders and interested parties was essential so that, in the future, this pilgrimage path would not be forgotten.

Figure 2. On the way to Our Lady of Lapa (August 15, 2011)

Own elaboration

The 1st overnight stay was at the Germil nursing home, where the pilgrims usually mingled with the elderly at dinner. On arrival in Penalva do Castelo, halfway along the route, we are usually welcomed in Sangemil at the community oven rebuilt by the parish council (with a small ethnographic museum). A group of ladies, masters in the art of making the famous, crispy and fragrant bread of Sangemil, awaits us to re-energize us after the ascent of the river Dão by the way of the courts, with the product of their art, their kindness and warm welcome. The 2nd night takes place at the Guard's house in the Sanctuary of Senhor dos Caminhos[7] in Rãs, in the parish of Romãs, where a local restaurant serves us a delicious breakfast. At the end of the pilgrimage, we fulfil the precept, pray to the Virgin, pass through the gap in the side of the cave and go around the church three times. On arrival, the Mass is always emotional. We rest while listening to the Word. Then you have to register your credentials and get your pilgrimage certificates. Often, because the local restaurants are full, the "little sisters of Lapa", as the nuns who look after the Shrine and the College are known, cook lunch for the pilgrims.

All in all, it is a fantastic pilgrimage. Apart from Fátima, I do not know of any pilgrimages in Portugal that last more than one day, so to re-establish this route would be to restart a tradition that, with the beginning and unfolding of the 20th century, became lost within Portugal.

The inaugural pilgrimage ended on July 17, 2011, after 3 days of pilgrimage and has remained active since then until today, being travelled on foot or by bicycle.

6. The Definition of a Pilgrimage Group

At the end of 2012, a retired friend visited me asking when I would be returning to Santiago and if he could accompany me. With him came another friend of his who asked if he could do some stages and not others, depending on his availability on each day. I said yes, of course, if after Ourense he took the route, we had chosen, without interruption. The group would be joined by another friend of mine, a pilgrim in other experiences.

We followed the Interior Way, which had now been marked, albeit with shortcomings in the bookings and some last-minute diversions due to works on the way. However, from Almargem to Castro Daire we followed the route I had planned and walked in 2010 (Almargem, Calde, Adenodeiro, Cela, Termas de Carvalhal, Ribolhos, Ponte Pedrinha). Just like when you go to any destination by car, there are always several options, and you don't always have to take the highway or the fastest route. As an experienced pilgrim who travelled the Interior Way before it was officially marked, I can't understand the historical or religious reason for abandoning a Roman road (even if only bits of it remain) and tracing this route to Santiago through the village of Cabrum, and then passing some stepping stones bridges that, for example, in the alternative via da prata, outside Xunqueira de Ambía, were excluded from the original route, most likely for pilgrim safety reasons.

Interactions with residents along the way were fortuitous and mainly resulted in them suggesting alternatives, either along the paved road because, according to them, they were easier to travel or because they shortened distances. In general, the hostels were closed, but there were telephone numbers on the doors so that we could use them. When we wanted to stamp the pilgrim's credentials, we usually encountered difficulties: either the stamps were not in the establishment or, more often, it was suggested that we would need a "special stamp" specifically for the Camino de Santiago (The Way of St James), and we would have to go to a tourist office or a local authority office, which were often closed.

Figure 3. At Rincón del Peregrino (May 1, 2013)
Own elaboration

Figure 4. "mira lo tienes en gallego que es lo mismo" (May 2, 2013)
Own elaboration

When we arrived in Verín, even with the time that had passed since 2009, the start of the alternative route to Laza was still not adequately marked. However, as a result of previous intensive research on social media, we knew that it would leave from Verín Castle. However, once we reached the castle, it took us a long time to find the yellow arrow. We continued on the same day to Laza, despite all the setbacks and the many kilometres on our legs. One of the new pilgrims, at breaking point, began to blaspheme: "what evil have I done to God and Santiago", "who sent me on an adventure like this", "I was so well at home" and, after some vernacular in between, "I'll never go on another one". We arrived in Laza after dark. At dinner, after a shower, things got a little quieter. In the centre of the table was a tureen with lentil soup and smoked meats. My colleagues didn't like the look of it, but even though we Portuguese eat more with our eyes than our bellies, once they'd tasted it, they fell in love with the soup, which helped a lot to break the ice created by the difficulties of the stage.

The next day, when we arrived at Albergueria, my friends were enchanted by the magic of the "Rincón del Peregrino" and by José Luis' friendliness and welcoming smile. A place as special as this, we would only find again in Reguengo, just before Cea and after Ourense. On our left, a very rustic stone house, we find "Casa César - La Parada del Peregrino", César is the host, he offers us coffee, wine from his production, bread with garlic butter and, more than anything, conversation, lots of conversation. César was a bus driver and pilgrim. He is now retired and, with his status, missed the world in which he used to travel. To combat the risk of stress that loneliness brought him, César decided to meet the world of people who passed by his door on their way to Santiago. After drinking some wine and a very weak cup of coffee, we read the house's guest book and, fighting off César's resistance, we decided to leave, after a companion had left a poem on the subject of wine, which greatly cheered up our host. On the way out, looking at the sign with the name of the "establishment", we jokingly asked: "César, so many languages there and you don't have anything in Portuguese?" To which he replied "mira lo tienes en gallego que es lo mismo"[8]. By this time, and from Ourense, we were all reunited.

At dinner in Cea, one of the companions had a severe pain in one of his eyes. From the pain he was showing, it looked like something serious. Even so, we decided to continue our journey to Castro de Dózon, where we knew there would be a pharmacy. In the morning he realized that he hadn't brought his European health card, but there was nothing we could do now. At the pharmacy, our friend was advised to go to the medical centre. He went to the health centre where he was very well received, even without the card. The patients were generally elderly and there were several waiting their turn. However, even without documents, everyone let the pilgrim go ahead. He was examined, medicated and we continued our pilgrimage. Among the pilgrims in Laxe, a very young group of three girls and a boy stood out. Unlike us, they had blisters on their feet and didn't know how to treat them. I approached them and helped them by providing bandages for the blisters, which gave some relief. After we had eaten a small meal, they approached us and asked if we would give them the preserves we had left over. After our offer, we realized that they had nothing else to eat, apart from pasta and tomato sauce. When we got to Santiago, after the railway overpass, we stopped at a bar to get something to eat and then, just one of the pilgrims from the youth group arrived. We took the opportunity to talk to her a bit more while we ate. She told us that she was from New Zealand and was studying marketing design in the Netherlands. Her parents were sheep farmers and she didn't feel suited to continuing their legacy. Then she said she was going to visit some friends in Alentejo, Portugal. We offered her a ride, as we had space available in our transport. She politely declined the invitation because she said she would be in Santiago for a while, where the young man in their group lived. We offered him the rest of the things we had left and set off. Arriving in Santiago wasn't as emotional for me, but I felt the emotion of my companions. The Cathedral was under construction, and it wasn't possible to perform the ritual by the Portico de la Gloria. We entered the Cathedral and attended the pilgrim's Mass, with the censer and that angelic voice of the nun soloist in the Cathedral choir. Some of us took part in the Mass by receiving Holy Communion.

After returning home, I went to work the next day, getting into the routine of everyday family life. At the end of the day, I was supposed to meet my wife at the mall to do some shopping. As I entered the mall, I saw a man standing next to a young woman from New Zealand who was looking for something on her cell phone. In disbelief, I asked her how she had ended up there, to which she replied that he had hitched a ride with a truck and that was where the truck driver's journey had ended. She told me he was looking for a cheap hostel where she could sleep. So, I told her not to look any further and to come with me because I wanted to introduce her to my wife. We all met, I introduced the pilgrim to my wife and asked her if we could invite her to sleep at our house. When she said yes, I promised to tell her about the circumstances in which we had met, and we went home. At our house, we prepared her room, had dinner and talked a lot about her experience as a pilgrim, as a student and about her family. She confirmed that livestock farming was not her vocation. As we talked, she drew lots of pictures and, at the end, she asked if she could have some more food, ending up "hoovering up" what was left. In the morning, we made him a good snack for the journey and, at her request, left her at a service station at the entrance to the city. Despite our concern, a few days later she confirmed by email that she had arrived at her destination in Alentejo.

7. A New Challenge Along an Old Path

A few months later, I received a phone call from Eng Mouro Pinto. He told me that he was disappointed with his group of "Vitanatura - life in nature" hikers who, at the last minute, decided that they couldn't accompany him on the pilgrimage to Santiago de Compostela.

In 2006 and 2007, with that group and with the support of archaeologists involved in the Tongóbriga Roman city project "Associação de amigos de tongobriga": *Caminhos romanos e de peregrinação* (N.D.), he had mapped out a route that may have been travelled during the Middle Ages by pilgrims on their way to Santiago de Compostela, and which was in fact partly done in 1723 by João Monteiro Valente da Silva, Lord of the Casa de Telhe in Soalhães (Branco, J. A. C., 2010). The route, according to Pinto (2019), being mostly rural, has many kilometres of Roman layout or Roman and medieval technology.

Unfortunately, and to my great regret, I couldn't join him, but I promised I would try at the next opportunity. I had known about the project by Mr. José Mouro Pinto and his friends for several years (when I was looking for a route to Santiago in the 2010 Jacobean) and this call only confirmed that it had been completed, leaving me anxious and eager to walk it. It stuck in my mind, in that part of the brain where we put away wishes to be fulfilled later, without knowing when. But there are some wishes that leave footprints and "wake up", unintentionally, when everything comes together, and the stars align.

In 2014, my friend who had been "blaspheming" during the previous pilgrimage showed up at my work. Incredibly, he wanted to know when I would be returning to Santiago. He missed that experience and wanted to go back again. I was incredulous. Was it really possible? I agreed on one condition: his wife had to go too. We decided to talk about it again later. We had to organize the group and decide which route to take this time. We met again a few months later. I put forward the idea of taking the route marked out by Eng Mouro Pinto. We all agreed that doing the Camino de Santiago, along the best-known routes, would be an unintentional plunge into the world of tourism, albeit a religious one. The current organization of the Camino de Santiago is increasingly a way of making rural areas commercially dynamic, which, without the pilgrims, we wouldn't even know existed and, in fact, in addition to the desire to achieve a religious, cultural or other form of personal fulfilment, ends up being one of its great virtues. The businesses in the "pueblos" (towns) live from and for the pilgrims; apart from that, as the Spanish say, "no pasa nada"[9].

By coincidence, or because we shared common ideas, we all wanted something different, something that would allow us to experience, as much as possible, the difficulties of medieval pilgrims: no yellow arrows or shells, no shops waiting for us and oriented towards us, etc. I suggested we go via Cinfães and Marco de Canaveses, to which everyone agreed.

While we were getting ready, I decided to do, in stages, what the project author had done. Sometimes with him and other scouts from Marco de Canaveses. I was enchanted by the route, the Roman road that wound through the villages to Portas de Montemuro and then down the valley of the river Bestança to Cinfães and then to the mouth of the Bestança. It was a shame that some of them weren't cleared and the brambles, broom and gorse were taking over. Some mayors I spoke to lament the lack of financial means to keep them clear, despite the commitment they had made to Eng Mouro Pinto. So, having prepared everything, we set off from Viseu in June 2015.

It was exciting. On the 2nd day, shortly after Castro Daire, it started raining in torrents all the way to Cinfães. The deluge repeated itself on the 3rd day, all the way to Marco de Canaveses.

Figure 5. The Douro river and "Porto Manso" on the other side (June 14, 2015)
Own elaboration

To add to this difficulty, which turned into an immense nightmare, some sections of the route had to be abandoned in favour of the asphalt road, and those whose obstruction was only tall grass instead of impenetrable undergrowth, when travelled, acted as a water immersion bath, since to complement the water that was falling from the sky, the grasses above our belts were completely soaked. When we arrived in Marco de Canaveses, we had a feast waiting for us. Our friend welcomed us into his home, along with other friends involved in the journey and given the difficulties of the day, everything was perfect.

As soon as the rain stopped, we began to feel the effects of global warming. After Tui, we inevitably returned to what we didn't want, but couldn't escape: the tourist trails, whether they were pilgrims or simply long-distance walkers. Although we had planned where to sleep, in many of the places we had planned, the public hostels were overcrowded. From Valença, the hostels told us that, after passing Pontesampaio, there would be a diversion that went several kilometres through the industrial estate to Pontevedra. Once there, I noticed that the yellow arrows indicating the alternative were covered in black paint. It was clear that the businesses that had set up along the route through the industrial estate didn't like the alternative and wouldn't accept being excluded from the "official" route, demanding, at the very least, that both options be marked and signposted, for the pilgrim's choice.

In Briallos there was nothing available, neither public nor private, and we had to continue on to Caldas de Reis, a makeshift hostel in an old store. The heat was already unbearable, and our pilgrim's backpack had to be shared between me and her husband, as she was starting to feel exhausted after so many kilometres and so much heat. After talking it over with everyone, I decided to go faster, leaving the group, with a plan of arriving early in Caldas de Reis, accompanied by the Pilgrim's IDs and Credentials, to start registering and try to save time for my companions. Despite the fact that it was past 6pm, the thermometers on the billboards indicated over 40º Celsius, but we managed to arrive and find a place to sleep. By this time, several of us were already feeling the pain of blisters, the result of the heat and the many kilometres we had travelled, without rest, to the hostel. We took care of the blisters after the showers, had dinner and slept "like angels".

The next morning confirmed the "miracle" with which Santiago encourages pilgrims: after the most exhausting day of the pilgrimage and after a shower, a good sleep, we woke up ready for another day, as if nothing was weighing us down, neither the tiredness, nor the weight of the backpacks, nor the blisters. Everything started again, almost as if it were the first day of the pilgrimage. Two days later, we arrived in Santiago. Emotions all over again, as if it were the first time. Now there was a small difference, another service (paid for, of course!) for pilgrims: backpack storage. We went to the pilgrim's mass and then had lunch at Manolo. Relieved of the weight of our backpacks, we even talked to the saleswomen selling walking sticks, Galician witches, arrows, shells, etc. on street stalls. The heat was the big topic of conversation: "How is it possible that it's much hotter in Santiago than in Seville?" Yes, it was true, this was the pilgrimage of extremes, torrential rain on departure, sun and scorching heat on arrival. Perhaps that's why we'll never forget this pilgrimage, because of the experience of overcoming.

Perhaps also because we shared such extreme experiences, the friendship between our group was cemented much more. Since then, this has been my and our group for the pilgrimage to Santiago. This pilgrimage was the cement, the glue that has bound us together. Since then, our friendship has been made of stone and mortar, like the medieval constructions that have reached the present day.

After lunch we went to pray at the tomb and embrace the figure of the Apostle. In the queue was, no less, the youngest son of the Count of Santar, the town where I live, in the municipality of Nelas, accompanied by a lady. We recognized each other, greeted each other and he introduced me to the lady. My companions, a little behind me, didn't notice our initial greetings. When they arrived, I began the introductions. Everything was going very well when one of my friends, who was excellent at telling jokes and crazy stories to cheer us up, realizing that they were Portuguese, decided to jump ahead and introduce me: "Meet the Count of Santar". Without missing a beat, we laughed and I introduced not the Count of Santar, but his son. The introductions ended with a general and collective laugh, having concluded that, in Santiago, you can't even tell a lie when you're joking.

Some time passed. A few more of us were now retired, which apparently made life easier for us when we looked at the calendar. That's in theory, because in the end it's not really like that. Being retired relieves a lot of our stress, but as our children's lives are developing at a dizzying speed and pressure, we end up taking on some of that pressure, acting as an outlet to relieve them. So, even though we have every day available for whatever we feel like doing, in practice it's not quite like that.

8. Volunteering on the Way of Saint James

Towards the end of 2015, I learned via social media that a course for hospitality workers was to be held in Albergaria-a-Velha, promoted by "Hosvol - Hospitaleros Voluntarios", an organization of the Spanish Federation of Associations of Friends of the Camino de Santiago (Federación española de asociaciones de amigos del camino de santiago, N.D.). The first condition for becoming a volunteer was that you were a pilgrim and, according to the organization, the aim was to "assist pilgrims in the hostels and collaborate in spreading the cultural and spiritual content of the Way of Saint James"[10]. I signed up straight away and, a few days later, I received an email containing information about the work of the hospitallers and a questionnaire asking me for my personal details, my motivations for being a hospitaller, my previous experience as a volunteer and as a pilgrim on the Camino de Santiago. Immediately afterwards, I received confirmation of my registration and a very interesting text entitled "PORQUE TE DA LA GANA", which the coordinator of the volunteers called "La bandera de nosotros", asking me if I would subscribe to it.

In February the course began, I believe the only one held in Portugal. We started with a short questionnaire about the rules (often myths about them) of hostels, then we gave a presentation in which everyone introduced themselves and talked about something special they had seen or experienced on the way, as well as their motivations for being a volunteer.

The training went on to look at the relationships between people and the production of endorphins, the feel-good hormones, which, among other things, increase physical and mental disposition, helping to improve people's lives. In the opinion of the trainers, being a volunteer means supporting, but also sharing something of ourselves. We don't volunteer only for the pilgrims, but also for ourselves, because this, just like when we go on pilgrimage, gives us pleasure, producing those stimulating endorphins. To this continuous pleasure we must add welcome, availability, spirituality and cleanliness, receiving a donation in return. At the end of each action, the coordinator had a special word which culminated in explaining the differences of Christian welcome. We should never pass judgement on the condition of any pilgrim, much less show prejudice as to who we would consider to be "true" or "false" or, as they say in slang, pilgrims or "turigrinos". He told us about the indigents who walked the path. He told true stories that explained the "reasons" of each pilgrim and, at the end, he asked who could know the motivations that exist within each person, or who we were to make value judgments if, in fact, we don't know them. Finally, he asked us not to worry about the donation amount. For some reason, in Spanish the donation is also called "la voluntad"[11]. We then talked about the possibility of volunteering on the Spanish paths, explaining that each volunteer would have to pay their own travel and food costs. The exception would be the hostels where we would provide dinner for the pilgrims or those whose sponsors would provide

Figure 6. The course to be volunteer (February 20, 2017)
Own elaboration

lunch for the hospitallers. The training ended on February 21 with an unexpected surprise: there was a cake to celebrate my birthday.

I was embarking on a new dimension of the Santiago de Compostela, which would come to fruition in June in Bercianos del Real Camino, in the heart of the Iberian plateau. When I arrived, I saw an inland town with problems identical to our villages: the exodus of its inhabitants, mainly young people, in search of a better life in the big cities. Almost only inhabited by elderly people, around 200, Bercianos is a municipality belonging to the Sahagún county, which is 9 kilometres away. Sahagún is in the middle of the road that Charlemagne of France would have travelled, according to a legend transcribed (as true) in the "Codex Calixtinus" after Santiago appeared to him in his dreams, asking him to free his tomb from Muslim occupation. In another of the books of the same codex, the route linking France to Santiago de Compostela is described. Alfonso VI of León, probably aware of the legend, was the emperor who promoted this route, encouraging it and offering protection to pilgrims who travelled it. He had the support of the Benedictine order of Cluny, whose abbot in Sahagún, Bernardo de Seridac, made it the largest and most influential religious order in Spain.

Although I had intended to walk this symbolic and historic route in the future, even though I hadn't had the opportunity, here I was exploring the French route.

The hostel had 44 beds, but on many days we could accommodate 60 pilgrims of 18 to 20 different nationalities. At 7 p.m. there was a short prayer for those who wanted to take part, sometimes while enjoying the magnificent sunset over the Iberian plateau.

In addition to accommodation, the hostel offered communal dinner and breakfast. We sang, accompanied by a beat made by drumming our hands on the tables, the "Rap de La Bendición". At the end there was a small gathering where the pilgrims of each nationality got together and sang something from their country. For me it was a really valuable experience. Here, I saw and lived experiences that I had never known before and that I would never repeat in my life. From a pilgrim who offered to cook dinner, despite confessing to us at the end that he had never done so, to those who, arriving late, cried at the reception or in the chapel, happy to have somewhere to sleep and eat. They silently complained, after many kilometres, that they couldn't "compete" with the young people whose pace, more often than not, denied them access to a quiet place to rest and to be able to set off again. Here I returned once again to the atmosphere of the houses of my childhood. I saw again that bedbugs had not become extinct, as I had thought. They travelled with the pilgrims, expanding faster than the reconquest of the Peninsula by the Christian kingdoms. I verified the existence of the indigent who circulated on the road, heading towards Santiago or Roncesvalles. Sometimes they only asked to eat and bathe because they had a tent or just a tarpaulin under which they stayed overnight, along with the animals that accompanied them. They all carried pilgrim's credentials, and they were so stamped that there wasn't even room for new stamps, but that wasn't the most important thing: "puedes sellarlo donde lo quieres, no pasa nada"[12]. One of these groups came with a Dalmatian dog and a dirty old baby carriage. The dog had given birth the day before and everyone was part of the entourage, with no one left behind. In the baby carriage was a litter of six puppies. These were not, in the true sense of the word, pilgrims to Santiago. For me, they were actually "eternal pilgrims", looking to find themselves or, having found themselves, taking on this life as their best option for survival in this troubled world. I learned about a new service for pilgrims that has since been created on the French route: backpack transport by companies that specialize in it and, I must admit, provide a good service.

In March 2017 I went to the "Hospital de San Juan Bautista de Grañon", a hostel that has chosen to keep the more common name of the medieval hostels. Grañon is a municipality in the region of Santo Domingo de la Calzada, in the autonomous community of La Rioja, with around 250 inhabitants. The entrance to the hostel was through the tower of the parish church of San Juan Batista. It had no opening or closing hours. Its doors were available to pilgrims 24 hours a day. In the morning, there were often "eternal pilgrims" who, having slept elsewhere under a porch or in a tent, asked to have a bath. The donation box was always open with the sign "Leave what you can, take what you need". Pilgrims who preferred could register themselves in the appropriate book. Perhaps because it was still a "low" season for pilgrims, it seemed that there were many more destitute people on the road, the "eternal pilgrims". Here I saw mothers alone with their 6 or 7-year-old children, among many other things unexpected to me. One day a Portuguese man, Tóni, arrived. He went to the till to see if there was any money and, seeing me, said he needed 5 euros to get something to eat. I gave him the 5 euros and, hearing my Spanish, he asked if I was Portuguese or Galician. He confessed to me that he was also Portuguese, that he had been a cook on an oil rig and had ended up drifting away and then being abandoned by his family. He had once lived very well, but then lost his way up and down the French road to pay for his sins and relieve his guilt. The only thing that kept him happy was knowing that his daughters were doctors and living well. Then a young American woman entered the hostel. Tóni asked her if she was tired and if she wanted a Shiatsu massage. In the end, he asked for her help because, he said, there were no donation shelters in Santo Domingo de la Calzada.

9. The Sacred Way

After meetings and mismatches, 2018 arrived without us returning to Santiago. We got our group together, but we couldn't agree on a date to do the French route: "after the summer we'll see if we can do it again". I put together a program, but at the end of the summer we reconvened without success. The French route was stuck, we couldn't find the time to do it. Failing to reach a consensus, and having seen on social media that there was only a bus to Saint Jean Pied de Port until November 2, I decided to make a decision. I would leave by that day. If no one else could, I would go alone. I informed my usual pilgrimage friends and publicized my decision on social media, hoping that someone else would be willing to accompany me, but no one was available. In response, I only received messages of dissuasion: "because it was a very bad time, because the days were shorter, because the weather would be much less pleasant, etc.". There was no shortage of arguments to dissuade me, but my decision was made. I argued to those closest to me that the years were passing and, in the future, our abilities would diminish, so we should take advantage of the windows of opportunity that were opening up while we could. I prepared this pilgrimage to be done in two stages. This year I'd do it as far as Sahagún, which marks the halfway point, and in 2019 I'd do it from there to Santiago, probably accompanied by my usual companions.

I'll tell you about this first part of the Camino de Santiago another time. Despite the challenge it posed, it gave me a lot of pleasure, as I walked in a hurry, but without losing my bearings, in the continuous interweaving of legends and history. Walking through villages and towns, you can feel the medieval atmosphere, the real driving force behind their development. The French Way is, in fact, a passage through history and, perhaps for this reason, I found myself as a contemplator and not as a pilgrim looking for something within, for or by myself, in the sense of inner search and fulfilment. Rain and cold were the most common aspects of each day. What was also common were the signs, the people and the pilgrims I came across. The number of pilgrims on the French route is surprising, given their immense qualities, their plurality of nationalities, personalities and motivations. Here we meet many people with all kinds of mental or physical disabilities, either from birth or acquired in the course of their lives. When I arrived in Sahagún, I took the customary photos with Emperor Alfonso VI and Abbot Bernardo de Seridac. Mission accomplished, I returned home in the hope and conviction that in 2019 I would be able to complete this trip with my friends.

2019 turned out to be the year when my life was put on hold and, consequently, also my future pilgrimage plans. In its place, I began a great "Sacred Way".

This year was the most challenging of my life. After New Year's Eve, I began to feel an ache in my stomach that grew stronger with each passing day. When it became unbearable, I had to go to the hospital and, during the tests, the doctor told me it was cancer.

I informed my closest friends and received the biggest surprises from everyone. It is said that "Friends and paths, if they are not taken together, become thorns", and I received much more than I could have imagined from the friends who joined me on my pilgrimage through life. I felt accompanied by each and every one of them on my "Sacred Way".

I felt the human warmth of all my friends who included me in the intentions of their daily prayers. I felt, in a very special way, the prayers that the "Little Sisters of Our Lady of Lapa" offered for me in the grotto of Our Lady of Lapa. I felt very deeply the sadness in the eyes of all my family members, even after they had wiped away their tears, in the hope of not giving me any discouragement. During my friends' visits, I had some completely unexpected surprises. My most regular pilgrim friends called to arrange a visit. After some conversation, they asked me if I had a house in Lisbon, the city where I was going to have my treatment. I said that, whenever necessary, I would have to go to a hotel. At that moment, one of them took the key to an apartment in Benfica, saying at the same time, "Use it as long as you need it, it's unoccupied and available". The couple of regular pilgrims have been the ones to accompany me to Lisbon for most of my treatments, exams and routines. They've all been with me at the start of my Sacred Way, fighting like me to avoid the 11th station and reach the 14th as late as possible.

I completed all the treatment clinically planned for 2019. The plans made for the continuation and completion of the French road were put on hold, waiting for better days to talk. Then came the covid-19 pandemic which, on top of what had been going on all year, almost led us to believe that the end of our pilgrimages to Santiago de Compostela might have come.

Fortunately, everything has been overcome in the meantime. I'm beginning to believe that I may have beaten my cancer, and I managed to complete the French route with my friends and one of my daughters and we arrived in Santiago de Compostela on Good Friday 2022, one of the two Holy Years of this Jacobean, after new encounters and unexpected reunions that, as always, we have on the road to Santiago.

When I arrived, once again thrilled, I felt that the morning wind was bringing me the Irish prayer and blessing:

"May the road rise to meet you,
May the wind be always at your back.
May the sun shine warm upon your face,
And rains fall soft upon your fields
And until we meet again
May God hold you in the hollow of His hand."[13]

CONCLUSION

For me, "going on pilgrimage" has been much more than walking along a more or less long route for several days to a place that is considered sacred or which legends and stories call out to us.

The article was an opportunity to compile and publicise a significant part of my experiences as a person committed to pilgrimage and as a volunteer. Through this article, I intend to show my evolving knowledge of the various stereotypes that accompany each pilgrim. I have concluded that most people's motivations change in a continuous dynamic as the feelings and experiences along the way evolve. Thus, pilgrimage can be much more than travelling along a path, marked with signs that identify it and that lead us to achieve personal goals. This mixture of emotions that we feel when we walk outside our comfort zone, associated with the search for something, concrete or abstract, previously defined, is the essence of the pilgrim.

My motivation and personal goal were to pass on my experience, demonstrating that a pilgrim is never alone throughout life, especially when it becomes a "Way of the Cross" rather than a pilgrimage.

But the main objective was to provide the reader with my knowledge of the subject of pilgrimage routes, especially the Camino de Santiago, to reach the reader and get them involved in the dynamics of going on pilgrimage and, most importantly, to encourage them to become a pilgrim.

Whether these objectives will be achieved, I cannot judge right now, but I leave you with my humble contribution.

REFERENCES

Amigos de Tongobriga. (n.d). *Associação de amigos de tongobriga: Caminhos romanos e de peregrinação.* Amigos de Tongbriga. https://amigosdetongobriga.pt/caminhos-romanos-e-de-peregrinacao/

Branco, J. A. C. (2010). *Itinerário inédito do séc. XVIII dum caminho de santiago, com passagem por Ponte de Lima: Pontedelimacultural.pt.* https://pontedelimacultural.pt/Blog.asp?t=paginas&pid=2247&mpid=2246

Collins-Kreiner, N., & Gatrell, J. D. (2006). Tourism, heritage and pilgrimage: The case of haifa's baha'i gardens. *Journal of Heritage Tourism, 1*(1), 32–50. doi:10.1080/17438730608668464

Federación española de asociaciones de amigos del camino de Santiago. (n.d.). *Hospitaleros voluntários.* Federación española de asociaciones de amigos del camino de Santiago. https://www.caminosantiago.org/cpperegrino/hospitaleros/hospitaleros.asp

MacCannell, D. (1976). *The tourist: A new theory of the leisure class.* Schocken.

Margry, P. J. (Ed.). (2008). *Shrines and pilgrimage in the modern world. New itineraries into the sacred.* Amsterdam University. doi:10.5117/9789089640116

Norman, A., & Cusack, C. M. (Eds.). (2015). *Religion, pilgrimage and tourism.* Routledge.

Pinto, J. M. (2019). Um homem do caminho. (1st ed). Lavra: Letras e coisas.

Sharpley, R. (2009). Tourism, Religion and sirituality. In T. Jamal & M. Robinson (Eds.), *The Sage Handbook of Tourism.* Sage. doi:10.4135/9780857021076.n14

Timothy, D. J., & Olsen, D. (Eds.). (2006). *Tourism, religions and spiritual journeys.* Routledge. doi:10.4324/9780203001073

United Nations. (2014). *ONU News: Agência da ONU realiza primeiro congresso global sobre turismo religioso.* UN. https://news.un.org/pt/story/2014/09/1485471 (Accessed on August 3, 2023)

ENDNOTES

1 Light Artillery Regiment Nr 1
2 Censer in Galician
3 A café and grocery store separated by a door
4 Souvenirs
5 Wayside shrines of the paths
6 Local Charity
7 The Lord of Pathes
8 "look, you have it in Galician, which is the same"
9 No prolem, nothing happened
10 Camino de Santiago El camino de las estrellas. [Accessed on august, 2023 on: https://www.caminosantiago.org/cpperegrino/hospitaleros/hospitaleros.asp]
11 The will
12 You can stamp it wherever you want, no worries.
13 Traditional Irish blessing

Chapter 4
Paulinus of Nola and the Pilgrimage to Saint Felix Tomb in Late Antiquity

Patricia Ana Arguelles Alvarez
University Santiago de Compostela, Spain

Diego Piay Augusto
Oviedo University, Spain

ABSTRACT

This study will tackle with the figure of Paulinus of Nola, a Roman senator, and an important figure too during Late Antiquity, for his religious conversion during the primitive Christianity. Through a biographical study the authors delve into this character and his gradual inclusion in the early Church, becoming bishop of Nola. Paulinus was closely linked to the martyr and the saint Felix (3rd century). That is why Paulinus will be the patron of a primitive pilgrimage to the tomb of Felix, introducing patronage for the demands of the pilgrims traveling to Nola, as the repair of the road, the creation of shelters, purchase of offerings, etc.

INTRODUCTION

Paulinus of Nola is undoubtedly one of the most interesting figures to understand the cult of saints and the development of asceticism among aristocratic elites along the Late Antiquity.

The biography of Meropius Pontius Paulinus is rich in experiences: ranging from his position as a consul of Campania in 381, his escaping from Gaul during the persecution of Priscillian and his followers, the murder of his brother in circumstances never clarified, his marriage to the Hispanic Therasia, the death of his son, his conversion to asceticism, his appointment as bishop by the plebs of Barcelona, his return to Campania and, finally, his consecration as bishop of Nola.

In the eventful life of this outstanding member of Burdigalense society, his trips and mystical experiences played a fundamental role, as can be seen from the study of some works of his authorship such as the *Carmina*[1], also colloquially known as Poems, but also from his copious correspondence with more

DOI: 10.4018/978-1-6684-9923-8.ch004

than twenty different recipients (Mratschek, 2002: p. 325). Among them, are some of the most important characters of the West Christian of that time, such as Sulpice Severus, Augustine of Hippo, Jerome, or the bishop Delphinus of Bordeaux. These are, in any case, characters belonging to the upper classes of late Roman society (Mratschek, 2002: 354-355), among which Sulpicius Severus should be highlighted (Griffe, 1966: p.378). A great friend of Paulinus and to whom the Bishop of Nola will address 13 letters. The correspondence between the two, is essential when it comes to reconstructing the building work of Paulinus in Cimitile and Sulpicius Severus in Primiliacum, in addition to the interest it has in knowing the importance of the cult of relics during Late Antiquity[2].

But the figure of Paulinus is also very important because of his direct relationship with St. Felix, bishop of Nola martyred at the third century, and main protagonist of the work presented. The importance acquired by this saint during the Late Antiquity justifies an exhaustive historical study which allows us to know the origin, diffusion and consolidation of the cult that was paid to him, based on the study of literary sources. The pilgrimage linked to the tomb of the saint allows us to relate directly the argument proposed for this volume with the present work, which aims to trace the Paulinus's life until his establishment at Nola, the study of the the beginning of pilgrimage trips to Cimitile and contextualize the phenomenon and character during the Late Antiquity. However, pilgrimage was not an uncontested movement at the fourth century, and its early challenges to the institution of pilgrimage to Nola, which are the topic of this investigation.

After the discovering of Felix's relics outside the city of Nola, Paulinus used his well-to-do economic position, which included properties in Gaul, Hispania, and Italy, to develop a new type of aristocratic patronage. The relics of St. Felix would be the center of a new cult, which Paulinus consolidated.

The present work will begin with a synthesis of the main known data on the biography of Paulino, made from the available sources and the main contributions of the researchers who have focused their studies on his figure[3]. Knowing his life experience will be the best starting point to analyze his role as a promoter of Christian worship in Cimitile, a place that will become one of the most important pilgrimage centers of antiquity thanks to the attraction exerted by the relics of San Felix.

PAULINUS OF NOLA

Early Life and Education

Little is known about Paulinus' life, due to the absence of a *vita* that tells his facts (Álvarez, Hurtado y Rivas, 1999: p.276)[4]. Most of what is known about him comes from his own work, both in prose and poetry, from which some elements can be extracted to elaborate his biography (especially poem 21st), together with other sources such as Gennadius, which reports about him on his literary production (GENNAD. *vir. ill.* 49). Yes, his place of birth, in Bordeaux, and an approximate date of the event, the year 354 (Babut, 1910: p.99) can be established. He grew up in a senatorial family (VRAN. Ep. 12:9)[5], perhaps a Christian one, judging by Paulinus' statement regarding to a chapel devoted to the memory of his parents (Ep. 12, 12) (Frend, 1969: p.2) and a very well-off situation, with properties in Aquitaine, Gaul Narbonense, Lazio, Campania and, probably, Hispania (Álvarez, Hurtado y Rivas, 1999: p.276). He certainly received a good education, which included knowledge of Latin and Greek (Ep. 46, 2), in addition to having been instructed in rhetoric and oratory. He had a great knowledge of the Bible, since in his works he constantly intersperses biblical quotations (Goldsmith, 1940: p.6). All this would lead him to become the best Latin poet of the ancient church (Babut, 1908: p.18). Aquitaine was a pivotal place in the cultural life of the empire back in the fourth century, and its schools of rhetoric were well known and had a demand among the upper classes (Mratschek, 2002: p.32-33).

Political Career

The protection of the Burdigalese *retor* Ausonius, (a preceptor of the emperor Gratian, who became *quaestor sacri palatii* and *praefectus praetoriense* of Italy, the Illyricum and France, before being appointed ordinary consul in the year 379) would be fundamental in the beginning of Paulinus' career. Thanks to the testimony of Paulinus himself (Carm. 21), it is possible to review his *cursus honorum*: after having left Aquitaine during his youth, he exercised a curule magistracy that would open the doors of the senate to him (perhaps the prefecture) (Desmulliez, 2006: p.268), being appointed *consul suffectus* before the year 379. He later became governor of the wealthy province of Campania, residing in Capua. His first visits to the basilica of San Felix moved him deeply, and it was precisely in this period that he began some of the first constructions in Cimitile, such as the *hospitium* for pilgrims (Carm. 21, 383-394).

Around the year 381 (Goldsmith, 1940: 4), Paulinus, at the request of his mother, returns to his native land (Carm. 21, 398). From Gaul, he traveled to Spain to marry a Hispanic aristocrat originally from *Complutum* (Stroheker, 1963: p.118), named Therasia and settled again in Aquitaine on a property near the sea (Carm. 21, 406-407), where he will live as a wealthy landowner with interests on both sides of the Pyrenees (Matthews, 1975: p. 77-78). Between 381 and 385 he wrote poems, on which he invoked Apollo and the Muses (Babut, 1910: p.101) and exchanged a large correspondence with Ausonius and Sulpicius Severus, among others[6].

Religion Conflicts and the Conversion to Asceticism

4th century is a period in which Hispania and Gaul are shaken by problems of a political and religious nature which, undoubtedly, affected Paulinus' career. The murder of Gratian that followed the uprising of Magnus Maximus in Britain in 383, and the latter's arrival in Trier caused a great commotion in Gaul, and Ausonius and his disciple saw their political influence seriously diminished (Álvarez, Hurtado y Rivas, 1999: p.277). In addition, the Priscillianist controversy disturbed the ecclesiastical peace of Gaul and Hispania. In 382, Delfinus refused the entry into Bordeaux to Priscillian, Instantius and Salvian, on their way to Rome, and these lodged in the estates of the widow Eucrocia, preaching in Aquitaine lands: "*...a Burdigala per Delfinum repulsi, tamen in agro Euchrotiae aliquantisper morati, infecere nonnullos suis erroribus. inde iter coeptum ingressi, turpi sane pudibundoque comitatu, uioribus atque alienis etiam femiuis, iu quis erat Euchrotia ac filia eius Procula*" (Svlp. Sev. Chron. 2, 48, 2-3).

In 384, the Priscillianists returned to Bordeaux, this time to attend a council convened to judge their ecclesiastical conduct. The bishops deposed Instantius from the episcopate and condemned him to exile *in Sylinancim insulam*; Priscillian decided to appeal to Caesar: "*... deduci ad synodum Burdigalensem iubet. ita deducti Instantius et Priscillianus: quorum Instantius prior iussus causam dicere, postquam se parum expurgabat, indignus esse episcopatu pronuntiatus est. Priscilliamis uero, ne ab episcopis andiretur, ad principem prouocauit*" (Svlp. Sev. Chron. 2, 49, 8-9).

He was taken to Trier in 385, where he, finally, by order of the usurper Magnus Maximus. He would be beheaded along with some of his followers, among whom was Eucrocia, the widow of the professor of rhetoric Delphidius, a friend of Ausonius: (Svlp. Sev. *Chron.* 2, 50-51). Also, in Bordeaux the chronicler Prospero recalls how a woman, Pomponia Úrbica, follower of Priscillian, was stoned to death by the fervent population: *Burdigalae quaedam Priscilliani discipula nomine Urbica ob impietatis pertinaciam per seditionem vulgi lapidibus extincta est* (Prosper., Chon., 1187).

Paulinus's opinion is unknown in relation to the briefly narrated events, about which he keeps a suspicious silence, but which he undoubtedly knew better than many other authors, who will opine on the Priscillianist controversy, although in his works he will state absolutely nothing about it. However, it is difficult not to link their own existence with these events, although it is difficult as well to discern their relationship to what is reported, in the absence of testimonies. What can be affirmed is that all the conflict experienced by the Hispanic churches after the execution of Priscillian (years 385-400), had to reach Paulinus´ ears, and it is difficult for him to have declared himself neutral in that context (Babut, 1910: p.109).

In fact, Paulinus has been associated with the Priscillianists on more than one occasion[7]. Undoubtedly, there are similarities between Priscillian and Paulinus himself, since both renounced to worldly goods and embraced asceticism, although the former has gone down in history as a teacher of error and perversion and the latter as a model of Christian perfection (Babut, 1910: p.197). Precisely, the testimony of Paulinus himself allows us to deduce that, during his stay in Aquitaine a conversion of a spiritual character is awakened on him, which leads him to consider his life, as a great own a whole nonsense. Possibly, his personal circumstances would also influence on his dedication to asceticism, and also the role of his wife[8]; it has already been pointed out that the women of the Mediterranean world played a fundamental role in the development and consolidation of Christianity during the fourth century (Frend, 1969: p. 5).

Around the year 389, coinciding with one of the most traumatic events of Paulinus' life, the death of his brother[9], the future bishop of Nola, he will be baptized by Delfino of Bordeaux (Fabre, 1948: p.31), perhaps silencing any rumors whatever about his beliefs, and will move to Hispania, where he will live in some of the main cities of the peninsular Northeast (*Caesaraugusta, Barcino* and *Tarraco*)[10]. Between the year 390 and 393, Celsus, his only son, died only 8 days old. Paulinus and his wife decided to bury him next to the graves of the martyrs Justo and Pastor in Complutum, a place of pilgrimage motivated by the tomb of both saints (Martínez, 1973: p.30).

We leave him in the city of Compluto entrusted to the neighboring martyrs, united to them in the bond of burial, so that from the neighboring blood of the saints he may draw with which to sprinkle our souls when they are in that fire (Carm. 31, 606-611).

Perhaps the terrible losses suffered by Paulinus and Therasia definitively influenced the radical turn of their lives, started years ago. In the year 393 Paulinus renounces to his political career, his worldly life, and puts his goods and those of his wife on sale as well, some decisions that arouse the rejection of Ausonius (Avs. *Ep.* 25); because the actions of his disciple not only seemed to show contempt for the traditional ideals of his own culture, but also because they threatened to shorten the accumulated properties[11]. At that time, he also received letters expressing the condolences of some friends for the violent death of his brother[12], about which Paulinus does not offer too many details:

You, Felix, always abundant with me, so that I might not be unhappy, you were my father and guardian with perpetual love. As I grieved for the blood of my dead brother and that the fraternal cause earned me that danger by reason of kinship, and that a buyer already threw his hands on my estate, you, father, snatch my neck to the sword, my patrimony to the treasury and save me and my property for Christ the Lord (Carm. 21, 415-420).

Contact with St. Felix and Arrival in Nola

As Paulinus clearly states on his poem, the risks that at that time overshadowed his life would be solved, according to his own testimony, thanks to the miraculous intervention of St. Felix.

At Christmas of the year 393 or 394[13], Paulinus is appointed priest in Barcelona by Bishop Lampio, who bows to the pressure of the plebs; however, Paulinus will resign this office and settle definitively in Campania because, as he confessed on a letter to his friend Sulpicius Severus, his mind was already "fixed elsewhere" (Ep. 1, 10). In fact, Paulinus himself begs St. Felix for his protection for the journey he must make, in a work composed on January 14, 393 or 394 (Desmulliez, 2006: p.272):

...seu placeat telluris iter, comes aggere tnto esto tuis; sen magna tua fiducia longo suadeat ire mari, da currere mollibus undis, ut famnlis famulos a puppi suggere uentos, ut Campania simul Christo duce litora uecti ad tua mox alacri rapiamur culmina cursu inque tuo placidus novis sit limine portus (Carm.12, 22-29).

Already in Italy, Paulinus will suffer a campaign against him, by the Roman clergy, and will be ignored by Pope Siricius (Ep. 5, 13-14)[14]. And he will also suffer the criticism of the pagans: the testimony of Ambrose of Milan is meaningful (Ep. 58, 3 PL 16, 1178 = Ep. 27, 3, CSEL 82, p. 181):

I have learned that Paulinus has left his homeland, his home, to consecrate himself entirely to the service of God. It is said that he has chosen for his retirement the village of Nola to end his days away from the tumult of the world. (...) When senators hear this news, what will they say? (Desmulliez 2006: 272).

In the summer of 394 Paulinus and his wife Therasia settled permanently in Nola, where Paulinus was well received by the clergy, monks, and administrative staff. There he will become the religious poet and theologian admired by the whole church[15]. There he created a monastic community near the tomb of St. Felix and organized a community life of asceticism and liturgical celebrations. Paulinus will become in Nola an evergeta for the most disadvantaged classes: Uranium, in his *De obitu Paulini* describes his actions towards the poor, sharing his wealth and getting rid of his goods, which are temporary ones, unlike the spiritual goods granted by God, which are eternal, opening the granaries to the poor and providing them with what is deemed necessary for their survival. Paulinus´ way of life would earn him the respect of all, as Paulinus recalls when narrating his death:

His life was an example of salvation and a source of fresh comfort to all. And it's not just my opinion. All provinces are witnesses. All the lands encompassed by the Roman world are witnesses. Even the barbarian nations to which Bishop Paulinus' fame came are witnesses (VRAN. Ep. 12, 9).

The influence of Paulinus of Nola

The protagonist of this work is one of the most outstanding personalities of Late Antiquity, whose importance lies on having brought to the ecclesiastical world the sap of its high classical culture. In doing so it was not original, as it became customary in the final centuries of the Western Roman Empire, for aristocrats educated according to pagan traditions, to convert to Christianity and indulge in asceticism (Frend, 1969: p.2)[16]. If the case of Hispania and southern Gaul is analyzed, it is observed that the spread of Christianity had a similar development, with the conversion of the upper classes and the progressive evangelization of the countryside. The case of Priscillian is again a paradigmatic one since his doctrine spreads through southern Gaul and Hispania. Like Paulinus, he was a wealthy landowner who renounced his property to devote himself to an ascetic life, although he would be accused of *maleficium* and beheaded in Trier in 385. In Gaul, Sulpicius Severus, Paulinus' great friend who would never visit him at Nola (Mratschek, 2001: p.519-520), would also indulge in asceticism, although in a less radical way. Augustine and Alypius renounced the world in 386 in favor to a life devoted to philosophy and the service of Christ. And in Jerome's famous dream (Ep. 22, 30), the Stridonan also chose for the abandonment of the world and the ascetic life (Frend, 1969: p.4).

The case of Paulinus is, however, a paradigmatic one, since he became one of the main promoters of the cult of saints during Late Antiquity, going down in history for the amazing complex he built in Cimitile, to honor the tomb of St. Felix, where he would earn his reputation as the preeminent ascetic of Western Christian society (Matthews, 1975: p.73-74). It did so, however, at a time when the cult of saints was spreading like a haze across the Western Mediterranean (Brown, 2021: p.123). The discovery of the relics of St. Felix made him a man to whom God had granted a grace (Desmulliez, 2006: p.267), just as he had succeeded Ambrose of Milan after discovering the remains of the martyrs Gervase and Protasius. Thanks to the testimony of Paulinus himself and Martin of Tours, it is possible to know some stories related to Felix, since there is none about his martyrdom (Van Dam, 1990: p.40-43). Paulinus' good work in Cimitile made him one of the most venerated men among the leading Christians of his time, as evidenced by the admiration felt for him by figures such as Ambrose of Milan, (who in 393 gives of him; as an example, in *Ep.* 58th addressed to Sabinus, possibly a bishop of Piacenza)[17], Augustine of Hippo (who calls him *nobilis dei famulus* in *Contra Secundinum,* 1, *CSEL* 25, 2, p. 923), Jerome (who names him as an example for having offered to God not only his riches but also to his people as well) or Gregory of Tours, who will dedicate several chapters in his works and one of the longest chapters of his *Gloria de martyriis* (Van Dam, 1989: p.108). In fact, Paulinus kept correspondence with the first three ones, but also with other relevant characters of Western Christianity, such as Pelagius (Avg., Ep. 186, 1, *CSEL* 57, p. 45-46), Alypius of Tagaste, Aurelius of Carthage, Rufinus or Sulpicius Severus. On the other hand, in Cimitile, Paulinus will be visited by such illustrious personages as Melania the Elder, a Roman aristocrat "famous among the holy women of God", founder of a monastic community in Jerusalem[18]. On an epistle addressed to Sulpicius Severus around the year 400, Paulinus describes this visit, on which Melania and her companions were welcomed into the rooms intended for pilgrims. Paulinus would then receive a tunic of wool - which he would later give to Sulpicius Severus - and a fragment of the true Cross, sent by John of Jerusalem (Ep. 29, 5).

Paulinus´ trajectory is essential to understand the conversion to Christianity of the Roman senatorial aristocracy and their entry into the ecclesiastical career (Álvarez, Hurtado y Rivas, 1999: 298). But also to know the way in which these rich owners managed to assert themselves in a Christianized society from a new form of sponsorship, which did not aim at a social ascent that would allow them to advance in their careers because, by giving their wealth to the poor, they also became poor as well (Desmulliez, 2006: p. 273).[19] Paulinus devoted his life to the creation, development and consolidation of a center of worship and pilgrimage; in doing so, perhaps he continued to act as an aristocrat (Álvarez, Hurtado y Rivas, 1999: p. 299), expressing his senatorial status through public munificence (Sivan, 1996: p.179). But interpreting his conversion and that of other rich proprietors of his time from a purely economic or social perspective seems too reductive, and it is necessary to assess in its proper measure the role played by one's own beliefs and the spread of asceticism. Even more risky seem the theories of Frend, for whom the sale of properties and the conversion to asceticism of large landowners such as Paulinus, motivated great social problems which would explain the emergence of the bagaudas or the circumcellions. In this development, Paulinus of Nola, the Gallic aristocrat-turned-ascetic, "was truly representative of the deeper psychological causes that led to the fall of the Roman Empire in the West" (Frend, 1969: p.11).

THE PILGRIMAGE TO SAINT FELIX SEPULCHRE

The Character of Saint Felix

The cross paths of lives of the characters of both Paulinus and Felix emerged in the year 380 or, perhaps, at the beginning of 381, when Paulinus was already governor in Campania (Carm.13, 7-9; Jones, Martindale y Morris, 1971: p.682). Upon arrival in Nola, Paulinus was to be shocked, after seeing the miraculous episodes that occurred in this city, during the festivities of Saint Felix. Such experience will be key to shaping the future guardianship over the tomb of St. Felix. During these festivities, Paulinus would even dedicate his first beard to Felix, as an offering: *"...tunc etiam primae (puerus) libamina barbae ante tuum solium quasi te carpente totondi*" (Carm. 21.376-378)[20].

Undoubtedly, the *Letters* and *Poems* of Paulinus written throughout his life, reveal themselves as a reference of the spiritual transformation of Paulinus in his new Christian life. His preserved texts were inspired by authors such as Virgil, Horace, Ausonius or Prudentius (Battiston, 2006: p.59-73; Lagrange, 1948: p.15-16, 43; Paulinus of Nola, 1996). The Poems 15th-16th are dedicated to Felix of Nola, bishop of the city that, according to the *Martyrologium Romanum,* (1593: p.14) celebrated his festivity on January 14th. Thus, in Poem 15th, Paulinus recounts the popular festivity of the birth of the saint. Felix transmits an intense spiritual fervour which will be very revealing to understand the spiritual impulse of Nola and which is that Paulinus, who compares Felix to God Himself, being for him the Father, Fatherland, House and Wealth, thus he wrote: *"tu pater et patria et domus et substantia nobis..."* (Carm.15, 15), and goes on in praise, suggesting the omnipotence of Felix as an Almighty being (Carm.15, 49). He praises the noble origins of Felix's Eastern, specifically in Syria, land of the patriarchs and prophets of Christ (Carm.15, 55). About Nola, Paulinus refers that it was Felix who chose it as his home and he surrounded the city with gold and well-being (Carm.15,75-77), although from later poems, it seems that Nola was in a condition of old age and considerable dirt (Carm.28, 212-218).

Likewise, we know Felix´s life through Paulinus' own poems and also later in the work of Bede the Venerable, a British monk who lived on horseback, among the centuries VII-VIII. Bede dedicated in his work "English Ecclesiastical History", a chapter to this saint: "Life of the holy confessor Saint Felix". Here Felix´s virtues and mystical experiences are praised during his pursues before the pagan Romans (Bede, 1896: p.103-114). Later, among other authors, the figure of Felix will be also studied by A. Butler (1750: p.94), who names Felix as Paulinus' confessor. Here he reveals, recovering Bede's text, the moment in which the presbyter Felix, helped by the bishop of Nola, Maximus (both of them pursued and heirs of his bishop's chair), suffered Roman persecution. He also points out that Felix was not martyrized, because he did not die violently, but he was tortured and imprisoned and, therefore, throughout his Poems (known as *Carmina*), Paulinus of Nola refers to Felix equally, both as a confessor or as a martyr (Carm.12, 9; Carm.14, 4; Carm.15, 164).

The impulse generated by Paulinus to praise Saint Felix in the city of Nola, undoubtedly benefited the Church, since it was in these centers where they hoarded more wealth and offerings. It was thus justified that the goods of the Church were necessary to worship the saint in question. Likewise, the bishop, in this case Paulinus, remained as a sponsor and in turn was glorified for such work, creating a new Christian community in his territory that united rich, poor, men and women[21] (Brown, 2018: p.102).

Pilgrimage to Saint Felix´s Tomb: Pilgrims and Roads

With the reading of Poem 14th, Paulinus is able to convey the magnitude of the spiritual ardor that Felix's tomb attracted. One day, during the celebration of the saint´s birthday at the year 397, people arrived during the day and night, lengthening the prayers with torches, in a city crowded with a multitude from many other cities, all with a single desire, to praise the saint with "tears of joy". It seems that the city of Nola welcomed everyone without limits, because Paulinus said that: "*…nec modus est populis coeuntibus agmine denso nec requies*"[22] (Carm.14, 49-54).

About the pilgrims, Paulinus clarifies that they came from Lucania, many young people from Apuglia and they also arrived from the Calabria region, as well as people from villages that bathed the seas to the west and east of Lazio. In addition, people from Campania itself, naming the city of Capua, Naples and Venafro, next to villages near the rivers Sarno (Campania), Ufente (Lazio), Galeso (Calabria), Tanagro (Lucania) or coming from the mountains of the Masico (Falerno) and Gauro (Cumas) (Carm.14, 55-65). That is, almost the whole of Italy approached Nola as the capital of Christian pilgrimage, at the end of the fourth century. Due to Paulinus, Nola attracted as many people as Rome, because the faithful pilgrims came to Rome to glorify the tombs of the apostles Peter and Paul, and in equal importance, Nola went to visit Felix (Carm.14, 82nd-86th)[23].

Concerning the people coming from Rome, Paulinus says that they traveled 120 miles after crossing the Capena gate of the walls of Rome. It is reflected in his poems the great and continuous traffic of pilgrims: *"confertis longe latet Appia turbia"* (Carm.14, 65-70) and:

…cara dies tandem quoniam hic praesentibus orta est, Semper et externum nobis celebrata per orbem, quae te sacrauit terris et contulit astris, ecce uias uario plebs discolor agmine pingit, urbes innumeras una miramur in urbe[24] (Carm.13, 23-25).

Likewise, another communication route that connected with Nola was the Via Latina, from which people arrived by a road *"aspera montosae"* from Paeneste (Lazio), Árdea, Cales and two cities of Teano (Civitate and Teano Sedicino) (Carm.14, 71-79).

All these roads named by Paulinus were a part of the infrastructure necessary for pilgrims to reach Nola, so in Poem 21st, he alludes to the need to promote the repair and paving of the road leading to Nola (the singular citation, "the causeway" and does not specify which one it is referring to, for which he financed its repair). And it is that on the famous Appian Way, later we repeat by reminding the reader that the stone which: *"post hace et ad nos pergere inceptat uiam, qua sternit aggerem silex… terit terentem tramitem; qui ueste trita nauigator uenerat"* (Carm.24, 394-398). Coinciding with this problem posed by Paulinus, it is known that by the year 399, the roads were in such a terrible condition that a compulsory call is made for the collaboration of any man of the Empire (C.Th. III)[25].

The pilgrimage was divided into two stages, on the one hand, to undertake a journey through the old and dangerous imperial roads, and we have already seen that at least travelers from all over the Italian peninsula came to Nola. After the hardness and dangers[26] of this trip the pilgrim arrived at Nola, and this is where the second stage began. The groups that arrived exhausted in the city still had to travel the rural road of almost 3 kilometers that led from the urban area to Cimitile, where Felix's tomb was located. This route favored those villagers, who separated from the city or marginalized, attended to the pilgrims. In addition, Cimitile served as a meeting place for mountain villages, who came to Cimitile to trade and meet instead of in Nola itself. So Cimitile, which was originally a barren area, grew exponentially throughout the 4th. century (at the expense of Nola, the traditional urban center of the region) (Carm.13, 25-59; 18, 105-108; 21, 655-711). And it is that the procession to St. Felix departed from the town of Nola to the outskirts to the tomb of St. Felix in Cimitile.

It is clear that the pilgrimage to Cimitile was continuous and every day of the year the city was crowded with pilgrims, although the day of the death of St. Felix was celebrated with greater effusiveness. On this day, January 14th, processions were organized and the villagers themselves collaborated in the event. On the day that a saint was celebrated, the rituality went beyond any other day, since the most solemn rites were organized by the clergy themselves[27].

On the big day, the whole people were one, united by the same faith, without social or geographical differences (Christian, 1972: p.70). In this regard, we must say that not always the sexes behaved in the same way in the pilgrimage and in the middle of the crowd, the woman would not intermingle with total freedom[28]. We mean that women were subject to public control, fearing possible bad behavior or even scenes of falling in love in the middle of pilgrimage (Turner, 1974: p.208).

Nola Renewal: New Infrastructures for Pilgrimage

It seems that around the year 400, Paulinus conceives a project to modernize the city. He notices that the crowds are increasing and Felix's own basilica, by that time was gloomy and its large pillars prevented many people from accessing the interior at once. The anguish that Paulinus suffered at the sight of this scene, as well as the experience acquired after the restoration of the Gallic church of Alingone, led him to renew and glorify the city of Nola in all aspects within his reach (Lagrange, 1881: p.133-134).

Likewise, Paulinus ordered the building of a roof attached to the tomb, to give shelter to the poor and to anyone who came there from lands far away. But the visits grew so much, that later the roof became scarce, and two buildings were built; first a *hospitium* for the poor and then another one for the community, near the cells, where guests from the community itself could rest (Carm.21, 283-389; Goldsmith, 1940: p.175). For the sick ones he built an attached porch to heal those in need, as well as offering friendship and strength in his prayers to the poorest "brothers" who managed to reach Nola (Carm.21, 390-397).

As we already said, Paulinus would have settled since the year 396 in Nola, founding a cenobitic community that grew progressively. He ruled the male section, meanwhile the female one was managed by his wife Therasia. It was then that they began to live together as "brothers" and not as spouses (Carm.21, 447-450; Hydatius, *Chron.* XXX.) This community was also involved with the care and attention of the people who came to Nola; both men and women (Carm.21, 66-68)[29]. The Monastery also favored ascetic settlements in the surroundings of the city and from which the hospices. This way, in Nola, Paulinus weaves a network of infrastructures linked to the demands of religious travelers and ascetic communities (Carm.21, 90-97). And another thing that the traveler who arrived for the first time in Nola could appreciate were the bells on the churches[30].

Likewise, in Poem 21st Paulinus also names the problem of water. Nola was a renovated city thanks to the movement of Paulinus of Nola, but it had a shortage of water. It seems that at that time there was a drought, the beauty of the fountains that adorned the city were dry. Thus, the repair of an old aqueduct begins, for which all the devout world collaborated, on several occasions. Paulinus alludes to volunteering to undertake such reforms: "*...praebuit ubertim gratis operis"* (Carm.21, 720-721, 728). It was a difficult task because of the mountain cliffs. Task was undertaken by plebs and aristocracy of Nola together, as well as by pilgrims. This way, the water reached from the sources of the city (Carm.21, 744-751). Then the midsummer heat disappeared, and the aqueduct was filled to give water to the pilgrims (Carm.21, 685-686; 830-832).

Along with these reforms, up to five basilicas were built surrounding Felix's tomb (Carm.18, 177-179; Carm.21, 459-466). The houses of the cities, which were previously black and dark, were painted to live up to "updated" Nola. They ornated their doors with white veils and flowers, and the altars of the churches with lamps that were lighted up with perfumed candles (Carm.14. 98-103; 18, 30; 28, 212-217). On Poem 28th of the year 404, Paulinus goes into greater detail regarding these constructions, so it seems that the church that housed the remains of Felix, had an arcaded vestibule where you could lay down to rest, with an *impluvium* type plant (Carm.28, 7-8). On the five basilicas, Paulinus tells us, that they were not exempt and were intertwined by adjoining walls, sharing beams to support their roofs. Churches, in addition, were beautifully decorated with paintings, coffered ceilings, pillars and marbles. Sumptuousness, no doubt, that clashed with the modesty of the monastery and its cells (Carm.28, 10-16). Separate cells for men and women who were identified with the martyrs' paintings of the holy men Job and Tobias, and also with Judith and Esther in the female area (Carm.28, 20-28).

The main square of Nola, in which the pilgrims gathered, was always adorned not only by the sky and its stars, but by white columns and a fountain that allowed the faithful to wash themselves before entering the temple, besides of other smaller fountains, ordered and decorated with marble, offering several fountains to quench their thirsts (Carm.28, 29-38). From this main square three of the five basilicas had direct access to the sepulcher area (Carm.28, 38-39). The porticoes that adorned this main square allowed walking and sheltering from the cold and rain in winter and the sun in summer (Carm.28, 44-52). About the church that housed the tomb of Felix, Paulinus wrote that his chapel was beautiful with a starry and undulating dome with three niches in symmetry, renovated all of it, along with the rest of the city on the same dates (Carm.28, 180-189).

Paulinus reports that the reconstruction of Nola and its embellishment to welcome the faithful crowd who visited the saint, was such that everything became beautiful. Thus, little by little Nola was built as a center of Christian hospitality. Moving from a rural sanctuary to one of the most famous major centers of Christianity in Italy (Mratschek, 2001: p.511-533). However, one day some men planted some horrible huts at the entrance to the church of the tomb. That ugly obstacle, as Paulinus said, could not be demolished because the men who occupied them refused to move from there. So, one day, miraculously, a flame began to erupt so large that people feared it would spread throughout the city. Paulinus believes that it was Felix, because the next day, without injuries, the inhabitants of those huts helped to clear debris and, getting repentant, they decided to leave the place, so the city was again sublime (Carm.28, 60-167).

At the same time Paulinus, in addition to thinking about the infrastructures of the city, he also took in charge about how to praise Felix, so among his poems, it seems that the number 18th, he could have composed it with the purpose of being recited and offered to Felix on the feast of his birth, by all the pilgrims who gathered in Nola to celebrate that day, or maybe, he was doing public readings. With the words: "sing with me my poem" (Carm.18, 8).[31]

Paulinus also offers the reader endless miracles where Felix is the protagonist. One of these miraculous stories had as its main character a pilgrim who departed from Capua. Authors propose that he took the Popilia road, which went south to *Rhegium.* The traveler was on a mule and the beast threw the rider between brambles and stones. Paulinus says that he rose without any harm, so Felix could not allow anything bad to happen to a pilgrim who came from so far away to see his tomb (Lagrange, 1881: p.88). Throughout his verses he devotes several verses to Felix's healing miracles: "*Felici potiore uia persistere fecit, continuans medicos operosi martyris actus, uirtutes ut eas idem celebraret humatus quas in carne manens Christi uirtute gerebat, atque ita susceptae nec mortuus aforet urbi corpore… cum tantum positi sanator adesset spiritus…*"[32] (Carm.19, 289-300).

Felix stands as a saint and healer, and Paulinus justifies that this is one of the reasons by which the saint is visited: *"et magni solium breue confessoris adorat iugiter e uariis conferta frequentia terris"* and it is that an eternal love for San Felix is evident, because his tomb emanates a divine and healing power (Carm.19, 304-310).

Mystical Experiences of Pilgrims

The miracles of Felix were not only associated with medicine and healing but also, there were many stories that we know thanks to Paulinus. Miracles, some of them, that occurred precisely during the trips undertaken to Nola, in the already worn Roman roads.

The set of Poems 13th-33rd seems to have been written between the years 396-409. It is in Poem 20th, with the twelfth birthday of Felix at the year 406, where Paulinus tells the facts of a foreigner who came from Abela (Avellino), 20 km away from Nola, who went on pilgrimage there to fulfill a promise. He had to sacrifice a large pig, and it seems that this pilgrim did not act in good faith and gave up the offering by distributing only the viscera among the poor and taking back the flesh of the animal already dead.[33] Divine faith caused him to fall from his horse and his feet to be anchored to the earth (Carm.20, 70-93). At the same time another fact happens during the trip and is that the pack animal took the owner of the ground and the meat of the slaughtered pig he was carrying, as knowing that that meat should not reach Abela; he turned back to the hospice, which was still attached to the church of Nola. He seemed not being able to walk, as if he were provided with invisible shackles, this faithful begged the "doctor" Felix for help. With the favor of the crowd, which astonished looked at the scene, he came to the holy sepulchral church, weeping and kissing the saint for whom he accepted such punishment and was happy to fulfill it. Recognizing his mistake, he was then healed (Carm.20, 94-300).

Another example of miracles and pilgrims is narrated in the same poem 20th. Some peasants fattened a baby pig to offer the saint and when it was ready, they traveled from Apulia, passing through Benevento to Nola. In this case, it was a much longer journey because, according to the story, these peasants had to make their journey and fulfill the promise with the cap by the well-known Appian way that connected with the coastal city of *Bridisium* in the current region of Apulia.

So fat was the animal, that they could hardly walk, and the peasants could not continue traveling, so they left it lying and bought as many small pigs as the one they had abandoned, thus arriving at the sacred place. They stayed, in that case, not in the hospice that Paulinus had built, near the tomb, but rather far away, so it seems that there were many crowds in the area and all the houses around the church were full. To that secluded hut came the fat abandoned pig, sent by God, so that his master could fulfill his promise, so it was Felix himself who guided it on such a long journey to the animal (Carm.20, 312-389).

One more similar miracle was experienced by a traveler who according to Paulinus came from as far away as the previous one. In this case he was to arrive at Nola with a calf that he would give to the crowd with Felix's favor. When the steer grew up, he then set out on his journey, but when he put the yoke for the cart that he would lead to Nola, it fled and hided. The miracle arises when he sees that two oxen carry the cart and she, the calf, recognizes herself as the debt of the vote, and voluntarily and untethered accompanies her owners on the journey (Carm.20, 390-437). Paulinus interprets that it is heading pleasantly to her own death because she has been offered to Felix.

All these cases are undoubtedly signs and demonstrations of faith to manifest to men and women the healing of Felix and justify the hordes of pilgrims who went to his tomb, since there were "many who were blessed with his wonder". All these miracles were also narrated by St. Augustine (letter 50, Piscitelli,

1989) and St. Gregory of Tours (Hist. Franc.1. II, letter 13). We refer the cases of pilgrims traveling to Nola, and it is that not only faithful travelers or penitents arrived in Nola but also, till this new cultural center, more than 30 monks, several bishops and well-known figures such as younger Melania, Flora or Januarius, among others, arrived by Paulinus´ invitation (Mratschek, 2001: p.552-553).

CONCLUSION

Eighteen centuries later, the cult fostered and favored by Paulinus of Nola is still very active in the Campania region and, particularly, in Cimitile. On January $14^{th.}$ of each year, the event of the Patron Saint Felix is celebrated in this small town, to which is attributed the "miraccolo della manna", dew that flows in a chalice from the wall of the crypt where the remains of San Felix rested. Without doubt the pilgrims, to whom the vast geography of Christianity offered multiple centers of cultural exchanges, decided to visit Cimitile in the hope of finding greater closeness to divinity, to the sacred, and to physical salvation.

Paulinus' life perfectly reflects the development of a new type of patronage, developed by the Christianized upper classes of late Roman society. After the beginning of a career typical of a member of the senatorial ordo, Paulinus would opt for an ascetic life, probably through a conversion based on a spiritual reflection in which his own personal experiences had to play a fundamental role. Permanently installed in Nola, he would develop an unprecedented constructive program planning of roads, basilicas, hostels for pilgrims and a monastic center around the power emanated by the relics of his patron, San Felix.

Undoubtedly, the Poems of Paulinus of Nola, allow us to understand the evolution of the relationship of this character with Nola city, after his Christian conversion, in relation to the devotion to Felix and the pilgrimage to this holy place. There is no doubt that the transformation carried out at the beginning of the 5th century to improve, allows to locate Nola as a reference for welcoming pilgrims better. Nola will be from then on, a crossing point of the main routes of the empire from East to West and from South to North.

We could say then without a doubt, that Paulinus sponsored the pilgrimage to Cimitile, improving the fame of the city both religiously and architecturally. This attitude of Paulinus is still striking when, as we anticipated, he wrote with great scholarly figures of this emerging Christianity, whom he respects and admires. In these letters some of his "colleagues" were against pilgrimage to holy places. While this is another topic of study, these major Church Fathers utilized different approaches to dissuade their audience against pilgrimage (Bitton-Ashkelony, 2007: p.30-64). Jerome tries to dissuade a pilgrim, Paulinus of Nola from traveling to Jerusalem by arguing that location is irrelevant to religious life and spiritual growth. The pilgrims are simply to see face to face persons whom they only know from books or tales (Jerome, letter 53, letter 58; Courcelle, 1947: p.250-280). The same line of thought as other Paulinus colleagues such as Gregory of Nyssa (letter 2; Bitton-Ashkelony, 2005: p.31-64; Williams, 1998: p.94-132) or Athanasius (Brakke, 2001: p.453-481).

NOTE

Work developed under the project: Los escenarios de las micropolíticas: acción colectiva, sociedades locales, poderes englobantes (siglos VI-XII). PID2020-112506GB-C42 – Financiado por: Ministerio de Ciencia e Innovación, Agencia Estatal de Investigación.

Patricia Argüelles: Research Groups: ATAEMHIS- University of Salamanca & GEPN- ATT. GI-1534 – University of Santiago de Compostela

Diego Piay: Research Group FALSARIOS- University of Oviedo

- Both co-first authors.

REFERENCES

Álvarez, F.-E., Hurtado, R., & Rivas, O. (1999). La economía de Dios: La construcción de un santuario cristiano según los *carmina natalicia* de Paulino de Nola. *Arys*, *2*, 275–300.

Argüelles, P. (2021). Peligros, inseguridades y problemas del viajero visigodo. *Espacio, Tiempo y Forma. Serie III, Historia Medieval*, (34), 15–36. doi:10.5944/etfiii.34.2021.28413

Babut E.-Ch. (1908). Paulin de Nole, Sulpice Sévère, Saint Martin. *Recherches de chronologie. Annales du Midi: revue archéologique, historique et philologique de la France méridionale*, *20* (77), 18-44. doi:10.3406/anami.1908.6830

Babut E.-Ch. (1910). Paulin de Nole et Priscillien. *Revue d'histoire et de littérature religieuses, 1*, 97-130, 252-275.

Batisstón, D. (2006). *Mens nova me fateor:* Paulino de Nola, poeta cristiano. *Circe*, *10*(1), 59–73.

Bitton-Ashkelony, B. (2005). *Encountering the Sacred: The Debate on Christian Pilgrimage in Late Antiquity.* California Scholarship online. https://doi.org/ doi:10.1525/california/9780520241916.003.0002

Booth, A. D. (1982). Sur la data de naissance de Saint Paulin de Nole. *Echos du monde claassique: Classica views, XI* (1-1), 56-64.

Brakke, D. (2001). Jewish flesh and Christian spirit in Athanasius of Alexandria. *Journal of Early Christian Studies*, *9*(4), 453–481. doi:10.1353/earl.2001.0055

Brown, P. (2018). *El culto a los santos*. Ed. Sígueme.

Butler, A. (1750). *Live of the Saints.* (revised by P. Burns). Burns & Oates Search Press Limited (reed.1995).

Christian, W. A., Jr. (1972). *Person and God in a Spanish Valley*. Seminar Press.

Courcelle, P. (1947). Paulin de Nole et saint Jérome. *REL*, *XXV*, 250–280.

Desmulliez, J. (2006). Paulin de Nole: Du gouverneur de Campanie à l'évêque de Nole, ruptures e continuités. *Cahiers du Centre Gustav Glotz*, *17*(1), 267–275. doi:10.3406/ccgg.2006.915

Ebanista, C. (2007). Paolino di Nola e l'introduzione della campana in Occidente. *Dal fuoco all'aria. Tecniche, significati e prassi nell'uso delle campane dal Medioevo all'età Moderna*, a cura di Fabio Redi e Giovanna Petrella, 325-353.

Fabre, P. (1948). *Essai sur la chronologie de l'oeuvre de Saint Paulin de Nole*. Publications de la faculté des lettres de l'université de Strasbourg.

Frend, W. H. C. (1969). Paulinus of Nola and the Last Century of the Western Empire. *Journal of Roman Studies*, *59*(1/2), 1–11. doi:10.2307/299842

Geary, P. (1978). *Furta Sacra. Thefts of relics in the Middle Ages.* Princeton University. doi:10.1515/9781400820207

Goldsmith, R. C. (1940). *Paulinus´ Churches at Nola. Texts, translations, and commentary.* N.V. Noord-Hollandsche Uitgevers Maatschappij.

Griffe, E. (1966). *La Gaule chrétienne à l'époque romaine. T.II: Des origines chrétiennes a la fin du IVe siècle.* Nouvelle éd. Rev. Et Augm.

Jones, A. H., Martindale, J. R., & Morris, J. (1971). The prosopography of the Later Roman Empire, Vol. I. (260-395 a. C.). Cambridge University Press.

Lagrange, F. (1881). Histoire de Saint Paulin de Nole. Librairie Pussiel frères.

Lienhard, J. T. (1977). *Paulinus of Nola and Early Western Monasticism. With a Study of the Chronology of His Works and an Annotated Bibliography, 1879-1976.* Peter Hanstein Verlag.

Martínez, J. (1973). Paulino de Nola e Hispania. [BIEH]. *Boletín del Instituto de Estudios Helénicos, V*(2), 27–33.

Matthews, J. M. (1975). Western Aristocracies and Imperial Court (364-425). Clarendon Press; Oxford University Press.

Mratschek, S. H. (2001). Multis enim notissima est sanctitas loci: Paulinus and the gradual rise of Nola as a center of Christian hospitality. *Journal of Early Christian Studies, 9*(4), 511–533. doi:10.1353/earl.2001.0059

Mratschek, S. H. (2002). Der Briefwechsel des Paulinus von Nola: Kommunikation und soziale Kontakte zwischen christlichen Intellektuellen, Hypomnemata 134. Vandenhoeck & Ruprecht.

Piscitelli T. (1989). *Paolino di Nola. Epistole ad Agostino.* Stranae Nolane, 2.

Ruíz, A. (2011). Viajes y prácticas culturales en las provincias romanas de Hispania y la Galia. Iglesias, J. M., Ruíz, A. (eds.), Viajes y cambios de residencia en el mundo romano. Universidad de Cantabria, 203-204.

Sivan, H. (1996). The Death of Paulinus' brother. *Rheinisches Museum für Philologie. Neue Folge, 139*(2), 170–179.

Stroheker, K. F. (1963). Spanische Senatoren der spätrömischen und westgotischen Zeit. *Madrider Mitteilungen, 4*, 107–132.

Trout, D. E. (1991). The dates of the ordination of Paulinus of Bordeaux and of his departure for Nola. *Revue d'Études Augustiniennes et Patristiques, 37*(2), 237–260. doi:10.1484/J.REA.5.104642

Turner, V. (1974). Pilgrimages as social process. Turner, V. (ed.). Dramas, Fields and Metaphors. Cornell University Press, 166-230.

Van Dam, R. (1985). *Leadership and community in Late Antique Gaul.* California Press University. doi:10.1525/9780520341968

Williams, W. (1998). *Pilgrimage and Narrative in the French Renaissance: 'The Undiscovered Country.* Oxford University Press. doi:10.1093/acprof:oso/9780198159407.001.0001

ADDITIONAL READING

Bede the Vererable. (1843). *Ecclesiastical History of the English Nation* (translated and revised by J. A. Giles).

Cato y Varro (1979). *De Re Rustica.* (trad. by W.D. Hooper y H. B. Ash). Loeb classical library.

Cyprian of Carthage. (1998). Cartas. (García, M.L., Introduction, translation, and notes). Ed. Gredos, nº 255.

Gennadius. (1896). *Liber de viris illustribus.* Texte und Untersuchungen, Ernest Cushing Richardson.

Gregory of Tours. (1976). *History of the Francs* (B. Radice & L. Thorpe, Eds.). Penguin Classics.

Gregory of Tours. (1988). *Glory of the martyrs* (R. Van Dam, Ed.). Liverpool University Press.

Gregory of Tours. (1989). *Glory of the confessors* (R. Van Dam, Ed.). Liverpool University Press.

Hydatius. (1993). *Chronicle* (ed. R. W. Burgess). Clarendon Press - Oxford University Press.

John Crysostom. (2013). La Virginidad. (I. Garzón ed.). Ciudad Nueva.

Martyrologium romanum. (1593). (notes by C. Baronio Sorano). Apud miniman Societatem.

Mommsen, T., & Meyer, P. M. (Eds.). (1905). *Codex Theodosianus* (Vols. 1–2). Ed. Weidmann.

Nicene and Post-Nicene Fathers: Series II, Volume V: The Letters of St. Gregory of Nyssa. (2007). (eds. P. Schaff, Wace, H.). Ed. William B. Eerdmans Publishing Co. 2nd ed.

Nicene and Post-Nicene Fathers: Series II, Volume VI: The Letters of St. Jerome. (1980). (eds. P. Schaff, Wace, H.). Ed. William B. Eerdmans Publishing Co.

Paulinus of Nole. (1990). I Carmi (introduction, translation notes by A. Ruggiero). Cittá nuova. Collana di testi patristici, Vol. 85.

Paulinus of Nole. (1996). Letters of St. Paulinus of Nola (translated and annotated by P.G. Walsh). V. 1. Letters 1-22. Newman Press.

Paulinus of Nole. (2005). *Poemas* (introduction, translation, and notes by J. J. Cienfuegos García). Biblioteca Clásica de Gredos, 335.

Prosopographie de la Gaule chrétienne 314-614. (2013). Volume 1, A-H /Volume II, G-Z, sous la direction de Luce Pietri et Marc Heijmans; avec les contributions de Philippe Bernard, Carles Buenacasa-Perez, Janine Desmulliez... [et al.].

Prosperus Aquitanus. (1892). Epitoma Chronicon, (ed. Th Mommsen), Chronica minora saec. IV, V, VI, VII, vol. 1, 9, Ed. Weidmann.

Prudentius. (1950). *Obras completas.* (ed. bilingüe, I. Rodríguez). Biblioteca de Autores Cristianos, B.A.C., 58. La Editorial Católica.

Suetonius. (1889). *Life of the twelve Caesars. An English translation, argumented with biographies of contemporary statesmen, orators, poets, and other associates* (J. E. Reed & A. Thomson, Eds.). Ed. Gebbie & Co.

Sulpicius Severus. (1866). *Libri qui supersunt, CSEL 1* (K. Halm, Ed.).

Uranius. (1847). *Ep. De Obitu Paulini ad Pacatum*, Migne, PL 53.

ENDNOTES

1 Named both *Carmina* or Poems, the reference about the consulted editions is Paulinus of Nole, 1990; 2005.

2 Related to the cult of relics had developed in the late 3rd. and early 4th. centuries, first in the East and then more slowly and moderately in the West it was introduced more slowly and moderately in the West. by the 6th. century ecclesiastical sees considered it essential to acquire the bodily remains and material objects of saints to deposit them under the altars. Likewise, episcopal centers were the main points of demand for the possession of relics, as they provided the bishop with a fundamental support in the consolidation of his status, see Geary, 1978.

3 The biography of Paulinus of Nola is very extensive, and his figure has been analyzed from multiple perspectives. This work will focus especially on the main reference works such as Lagrange, 1881; Fabre, 1948; Frend, 1969; Lienhard, 1977; Booth, 1982; Desmulliez, 2006; Battistón, 2006.

4 An account of his death is available, described by his pupil *Uranius* on an epistle to Pacato (Migne, PL 53, 859-866). His remains were transferred to the church of Saint Barthelemy in Isola in Rome (Goldsmith 1940: p.6).

5 *Taceamus generis nobilitatem, paternis maternisque natalibus in senatorum purpuras admirabiliter rutilantem: praeterea et opulentias divitiarum, quas propter Deum pauperibus erogavit.*

6 Thirteen letters written by Paulinus of Nola to Sulpicius Severus are preserved (Babut, 1908: p.19).

7 Babut was the first to associate Priscillian to Paulinus, for until then, "les deux noms de Paulin de Nole et de Priscillien n'ont jamais été associés, et leur rapprochement produit l'effet d´une boutade et d'une paradoxe" (Babut, 1910: 97). In his opinion the final result of Paulinus' biography proves nothing in relation to his beginnings, and after the sentence of his friend Sulpicius Severus: *ec dubium erat, quin sanctorum etiam maximam turbam tempestas ista depopulata esset, parvo discrimine inter hominum genera* (SVLP. SEV. Dial. III, 11, 3) the Priscillianist past of Paulinus could be hidden. And his conjugal continence, the sale of his goods and his suspicious retirement to Hispania should not be forgotten (Babut, 1910: p. 115). The relationship between Paulinus and Priscillian has been treated again after the work of Babut (Lienhard, 1977), (Mratschek, 2002: p.56-57; 85-87).

8 Van Dam (1989: p.108) underlines the importance that a passage from Matthew's gospel (19:21, 24) would have had in Paulinus of Nola's conversion to asceticism: Jesus said to him: "If you want to be perfect, go, sell what you have and give it to the poor, and you will have treasure in heaven; Then come, and follow me." As soon as this passage reached Paulinus' ears, he would have immediately sold everything he had and made donations to the poor. Freed from all his desires, he would have followed his master, choosing to enrich himself with the riches of paradise.

9 Babut (1910: p.103), places the death of Paulinus' brother during the period of Maximus' usurpation (383-388). Other authors opt for a later dating, between 392-393 (Sivan, 1996: p. 172), and deny a relationship between his death and the Priscillianist controversy.

10 Babut (1910: p.275-276), argues that Paulinus of Nola during the years after his conversion (390-393), lived in the Hispanic Northeast. According to Hydatius (*Chron.*), this region was entirely Priscillianist, since the beheading of Priscillian, so that the scarce information that Paulinus offers about his residence could respond to the suspicions that his eventual presence in the Hispanic Northeast could arouse. In Priscillianist circles he would have acquired, through an assiduous study, the astonishing knowledge of the Scriptures which he possessed at the end of his retirement.

11 Ausoniu's letters to his disciple are full of criticism against Hispania, a province characterized for the Burdigalense by the presence of depopulated forests, destroyed cities, and in which bandits abound (Martínez, 1973: p.31).

12 The cause of his brother's death is unclear. For some authors, his murder, and the risk of confiscation of Paulinus' property, could have been due to religious reasons and, particularly, to a possible link between Paulinus and the Priscillianist movement; for others, Paulinus was not attracted to Priscillianism, and the reasons instead, were of a political nature, perhaps because of his political action against the usurper Eugene (Desmuillez, 2006: p.271, 275).

13 In general, the Fabre´s chronology, (Fabre, 1948), which establishes the ordination of Paulinus as a priest in Barcelona on December 25, 394, and is the 395, the date accepted for his arrival to Nola, among other authors, by Mratschek (2002: p.59) and Matthews (1975: p. 250-251). It is opposed by Desmulliez (Desmuillez, 1985), for whom the ordination would have taken place on December 25, 393 and his establishment in Campania in 394. Other authors place his journey to Nola in the year 396, via Aquitaine, where he would have met Sulpicius Severus (Goldsmith, 1940: p.4).

14 Babut, (1910: p.110), believes that Paulinus of Nola and Therasia were accused in the *Urbs* of Priscillianism, because of their defense of asceticism, which Pope Siricius opposed.

15 Of the literary production of Paulinus of Nola 33 *Carmina* are preserved, 13 of which were composed between 395 and 407 on the occasion of the Saint Felix´s *dies natalis*, the day on which his martyrdom was born for eternity (that is, the day of his death); every January 14th Paulinus recited the *Carmina* before his congregation (see note 23). In addition, 50 letters have been preserved (Ebanista, 2007: p.32).

16 As Griffe (1966: p. 378) pointed out long ago, the period after the year 360 is crucial in the conversion to Christianity of the owners and population residing in Gaul. The bishops of the previous generation, such as Febadius of Agen or Hilary of Poitiers, were known for their political fame, for their fierce opposition to the demands of an Arian emperor. In contrast, bishops of the later generation tend to be presented, not primarily as politicians and doctrinal polemicists, but as men prominent in local activity, as evangelizers and organizers (Matthews, 1975: p.154).

17 *Paulinum splendore generis in partibus Aquitaniae nulli secundum, venditis facultatibus tam suis, quam etiam conjugalibus, in hos sese induisse cultus ad fidem comperi; Ut ea in pauperes conferat, quae redegit in pecuniam: et ipse pauper ex divite factus, tamquam deoneratus gravi sarcina, domui, patriae, cognationi quoque valedicat, quo impensius Deo serviat. Elegisse autem secretum affirmatur Nolanae urbis, ubi tumultum fugitans aevum exigat. Matrona quoque virtuti et studio ejus proxime accedit, neque a proposito viri discrepat. Denique transcriptis in aliorum jura suis praediis, virum sequitur, et exiguo illic conjugis contenta cespite solabitur se religionis et charitatis divitiis. Soboles eis nulla, et ideo meritorum posteritas desiderata.*

18 A prosopography analysis of the more than 40 people who visited Paulinus in Nola, which also includes numerous groups of travelers, is offered by Mratschek (Mratschek, 2001).

19 However, we must be cautious when assessing the poverty of Paulinus, Melania and other wealthy landowners, who gave their lives to asceticism. It would never have been easy to liquidate large estates at a stroke. In fact, Paulinus seems to continue to possess great wealth that will allow him to undertake his construction projects in Cimitile.

20 This fact might seem a paradoxical one, because this was a Pagan rite, the *babitondium,* about which, for example, we have documented the case of Nero, who would have offered his beard to Jupiter Capitolinus. This used to happen around the age of 20 (Suet. Nero, 12), although P. Fabre (1948: p.14-16) indicates that Paulinus would have been 25, since this event occurred in the year 381 (Booth, 1982: p.56-64).

21 Prudentius alludes to the pilgrimage to the holy city of Rome: "The august city pours out and brings out its citizens, and among the patricians, together guided by the same desire, the crowd of the plebs, without distinction of arms, mingle, while faith removes the dividing traits of the nobles" (Perist. 11, 191-192, 199-202).

22 ...Crowds roam in motley columns around the city.

23 It should be said, in this sense, that Paulinus himself made a pilgrimage every year to Rome to visit the apostles (Mratschek, 2001: p. 512).

24 A motley people come dying the roads in a multicolored swarm, while we admire that there are so many cities in one.

25 C.Th= *Codex Theodosianus*. Edition consulted of this compilation of Roman laws: *Codex Theodosianus* (1905).

26 The problems of violence linked to travel have been noted since the ancient world. Thus, in the 3rd century, Bishop Cyprian of Carthage pointed out the latent inconvenience of finding inns at the foot of a road besieged by robbers, as well as the high probability of being ambushed, especially in mountainous areas (Cyprian of Carthage, 1998: p. 334-335 and Ruíz, 2011: p.203-224); problem that will persist for centuries to come (Argüelles, 2021: p.15-36).

27 In this regard, Paulinus of Nola composed a Poem to be recited on that date. See note 31.

28 John Chrysostom alludes to the fact that the upper-class women of Antioch went to the processions by mule (Virg. 66, 1), and the same happened in Rome (Jerome, Ep. 66, 13).

29 Van Dam (1985: p.76) believes that Paulinus considered equally both men and women because women were of virgin condition and viragos (Van Dam, 195: p.76).

30 Paulinus is credited with introducing the bell in the West (Goldsmith, 1940: p.5), although there is no historical confirmation for this tradition (Ebanista, 2007: p.343).

31 Ruggiero (1990: p.313) considers that this was the intention of this poem, written in the year 400, where it proves the veneration professed to Felix and the miracles of this saint.

32 ...lengthening the healing actions of the laborious martyr (Felix), so that himself from his tomb might continue in the practice of the same virtues that he exercised through the mediation of Christ when he lived, ... The healing spirit of the buried saint was present there.

33 He started the way back home with the viands without knowing that the *sourvertaurilia* forbids taking anything home because the banquet is for the gods, and as was the case with Christian offerings (Cat. *De Re Rus*. CXLI).

Chapter 5
Contemporary Significance of Medieval Pilgrimages:
A Post-Modern Physical Practice to Create Value in the Rural Environment

Pablo Vidal-González
https://orcid.org/0000-0002-4695-4489
Catholic University of Valencia, Spain

Josep Capsí
https://orcid.org/0000-0001-6028-3004
Catholic University of Valencia, Spain

ABSTRACT

This chapter investigates the phenomenon of medieval pilgrimages to mountain shrines and their contemporary revival as postmodern physical practices in rural settings. This growth encompasses both religious and secular pilgrimages, unveiling evolving social, economic, and cultural contexts. The research focuses specifically on the unique case of western Castellón and eastern Teruel in Spain, where pilgrimages to mountain shrines have been preserved. Fieldwork was conducted in the pilgrimages between 2017 and 2019, and the data were analyzed to find the motivations and meanings behind these pilgrimages. The findings shed light on the potential benefits that the recovery of pilgrimages can offer to rural communities, such as population stabilization and the promotion of cultural heritage.

INTRODUCTION

It is paradoxical that in the age of immediacy, of uncertainty, in which the only sure thing is constant change, in which the metaphor of the pilgrim no longer serves to illustrate people's life strategy (Bauman, 1996) is at the same time the age of the resurgence of one of the most deeply rooted and traditional practices of European culture: pilgrimages. Today, it is estimated that there are more than 6000 Western

DOI: 10.4018/978-1-6684-9923-8.ch005

European pilgrimage centers (Nolan & Nolan, 2018). In this growth one finds pilgrimages linked to the religious aspect of earlier times, however others are experienced without the slightest attachment to organized religion (Reader, 2007). It is true that, nowadays, both pilgrimages and their pilgrims, as well as the social, economic and value context in which they are framed, have little to do with those of previous times. The world of pilgrimages, halfway between the traditional and the present, has changed as much as its pilgrims (Pazos, 2014).

The first Christian pilgrimages sought to reach the places where Jesus and the apostles had lived. In the 4th century, Constantine, the first Christian Roman emperor, built constructions to facilitate the arrival of pilgrims to places that had become popular destinations such as Jerusalem and Bethlehem (Sorabella, 2011). Subsequently, in the Middle Ages, pilgrims could make long and short journeys, both to major destinations such as Rome and Jerusalem, as well as to countless local shrines (Webb, 2017). Such was the importance of these practices that they are recognized as the germ of today's Europe, since the longer routes allowed for cultural and economic exchange between peoples of different kingdoms, and in turn enjoyed the protection of Christian monarchs and nobles.

However, as industrialization took off in the 18th century, many people left the rural environment to work in the cities where the industries that needed labor were located. This process was also accompanied by economic, social, and technological changes. There is no doubt that religion, the church, and everything related to it went from occupying one of the most privileged and central places in people's lives to being displaced by the push of new institutions and ways of thinking closer to scientific thought and economic profitability. These two factors caused pilgrimages, especially those located in more local contexts, generally rural, to lose what made them alive: the pilgrims and the reasons to go on pilgrimage.

In Spain, which is the focus of this paper, industrialization was late compared to the rest of Europe. Therefore, the effects on pilgrimages were noticeable only later. In the area of influence of the pilgrimages we are studying here, it was not until the second half of the 19th century that the exodus to the cities due to industrialization began to appear (Pajero, 2006). At the beginning of the 20th century, the process of depopulation of rural areas was accentuated by the effect of the transformation and concentration of agricultural production and the opening of the economy. With these transformations, the rogations suffered an important identity crisis and, in some cases, these practices were abandoned.

However, the 19th century saw a major revival of religious pilgrimages in Europe (Pazos, 2020). Inspired largely by the success of the Camino de Santiago de Compostela, pilgrimage is being rediscovered and represented again even in areas where it was long discredited and abandoned (Bowman et al., 2020). However, it is questionable whether this growth is simply a continuation of traditional pilgrimages. Previously, pilgrimage centers were sacred buildings visited by people with religious interest, whereas today one must consider that profiles are multiple, and pilgrimage centers themselves have changed to offer additional cultural and touristic services (Sołjan & Liro, 2022). To better understand what moves people to reproduce the practice of pilgrimage, it is necessary to adopt a theoretical perspective to guide us in this research. We feel close to the new mobility paradigm (Sheller, 2014) because we consider that it has the capacity to bring together the analysis of the material and bodily practices of movement, the infrastructures, the systems that facilitate movement and restrict it, and the associated meanings. Taking into consideration this complex amalgam of elements and relationships of the phenomenon we study can provide us with a comprehensive and multidimensional view of pilgrimage. This perspective, in turn, can contribute to better intervention proposals if we wish to generate value in the territory through the pilgrimage boom.

Although numerous studies have recently been conducted to better understand what drives pilgrims to undertake the journey (Amaro, et al., 2018; Brumec, 2023; Farías et al., 2019; Lois-González & Santos, 2015; Malis et al., 2023), research attempting to relate such information to the phenomenon of growth in pilgrimage participation is scarce. On the other hand, studies are usually conducted on more well-known pilgrimage routes, such as the Camino de Santiago. However, no attention has been paid to this object of study in ancestral but less known pilgrimage sites. This work aims to contribute to fill these gaps in this field of knowledge. Our objectives are: first, to discover what are the contemporary meanings associated with the medieval pilgrimages that have re-emerged in recent years in the inland area of eastern Spain. And second, to uncover the relationships that may exist between these meanings and the resurgence of these practices. In addition, we intend, as a result of this research, to contribute reflections and ideas on the opportunity that the recovery of pilgrimages represents for the rural contexts in which they take place, both in the sense of fixing population and for the promotion of cultural heritage.

Method

The fieldwork was developed between 2017 and 2019, just before the pandemic. The mountain area of the West of the province of Castellón and the East of the province of Teruel, in Spain, was chosen because this territory hosts one of the richest sets of penitential pilgrimages to mountain sanctuaries. The preservation of this tradition is due, on the one hand, to the fact that these are territories far from the cities, where the depopulation process took place relatively late (in the 60s of the last century), which has allowed the preservation of cultural traditions that have disappeared in other territories. However, these pilgrimages were not exempt from a period of crisis, precisely at the end of the 1960s, which caused some to disappear, and others were about to do so at that time (Vidal-González & Cantillo, 2019).

Participant observation was carried out in 6 of the rogations, walking along with the pilgrims the entire route. The results of the interviews were recorded in the field notebook. Subsequently, a classification was made into categories of analysis, in order to proceed to their interpretation (Downe-Wamboldt, 1992; Harword & Garry, 2003). All the people mentioned in the text were pilgrims in the different rogations. These manifestations of religious origin take place in spring, in the months of April, May and June. As an exception, the Vallibona rogation takes place only once every 7 years, so the opportunity to carry out fieldwork is exceptional. The pilgrimages from Mosqueruela to La Estrella (Teruel), from Catí to Sant Pere de Castellfort (Castellón), from Portell de Morella to Sant Pere de Castellfort (Castellón), from Puertomingalvo (Teruel) to Sant Joan de Penyagolosa (Castellón), from Culla (Castellón) to Sant Joan de Penyagolosa, as well as the one from Vallibona (Castellón) to Peñarroya de Tastavins (Teruel) were documented.

It should be noted that two of these pilgrimages have the consideration of Intangible Cultural Heritage, the highest element of protection granted by the Administration to Intangible Heritage. This is a recognition of their singular character, their history, and the excellent preservation of their rituals.

The pilgrimages have a duration of one or two days, staying overnight at the sanctuary or nearby, as in the cases of the pilgrimages of Catí, Vallibona, Les Useres or Culla. In the latter case, the round trip through the mountains is close to 60 km. The close contact established with the pilgrims allowed long conversations about the motivations and meaning of their participation in this religious, cultural, and patrimonial manifestation, which was collected in a field notebook for later study and analysis.

In the case of the rogations from Culla to Sant Joan de Penyagolosa (Castellón) and from Mosqueruela to La Estrella (Teruel), we also conducted in-depth interviews with elderly people who had historically participated in the pilgrimages, outside the time frame of the rogation. These interviews were recorded, with prior informed consent, for subsequent transcription and analysis.

Finally, the historical archives of Culla and Mosqueruela were accessed to compare the historical documentation with the information collected in the fieldwork. Both the interviews with elderly people and the historical documentation confronted have allowed us to study in more detail the changes and historical evolution of these heritage practices from their origins to the present day.

The Pilgrimages Studied and Their Context

The study area has maintained pilgrimages to mountain sanctuaries that have their origins in the epidemic of the Black Death, which reached these lands between 1348 and 49. After the terrible mortality caused by this plague, penitential rogations to sanctuaries of special importance and devotion would begin, highlighting among them that of Sant Joan de Penyagolosa, located in the high mountains of the interior of the province of Castellón. These pilgrimages, organized by means of public votes of the town councils, committed the whole town to celebrate these manifestations of piety once a year. It was therefore the whole town, represented by the people who would participate in person, who prayed to the saint for water (prosperity), health and peace (the absence of war).

These pilgrimages had a strong crisis in the process of depopulation that began in the 1940s, after the postwar period and the process of industrialization of the big cities, which demanded a growing labor force. The crisis was accentuated until the end of the 60s of the last century, when these religious manifestations were seen as signs of an outdated and outmoded past (Vidal-González and Sánchez, 2019). This lack of interest caused many local pilgrimages to disappear or to be transformed until they became almost unrecognizable. Only a few remained and the 8 that we study here did so precisely as a sign of survival in the face of the strong demographic crisis and the consequent loss of identity associated with life in factories and big cities.

We will begin by describing the pilgrimages that go to the sanctuary of Sant Joan de Penyagolosa, located at the foot of the peak of the same name. This temple used to host a good number of pilgrimages, a sign of its importance and prestige, but now it continues to host five pilgrimages every spring.

The best known and therefore the one that gathers more people in its route, is the one that starts from the town of Les Useres and that takes place every year on the last Friday and Saturday of April. Every year twelve pilgrims, children of the village, accompanied by the guide and other people of assistance, make their way to the sanctuary, in a journey through the mountains of 25 kilometers. The pilgrims march in silence, following a precise ritual that has remained practically unchanged since the 14th century. Sacred chants are performed with precision along the route, to ask the saints for their protection. When they reach Sant Joan, after several stops, they spend the night there to return the next day. During this 2023 it is estimated that about four thousand people accompanied the pilgrims at some point in their journey.

The other town that makes its way to Sant Joan is Puertomingalvo, in the nearby province of Teruel. The 11-kilometer route takes place at the beginning of May. As a characteristic, the round trip is done on the same day, with a mass and subsequent meal in the sanctuary. The ritual and chants have been maintained, similar to those of the other pilgrimages in the area, although nowadays most people make the return trip by car.

Also, the population of Xodos makes its pilgrimage to the shrine of Sant Joan. Since the residents of Les Useres passed through the village on their way to the sanctuary, the itinerary is the same, but with a route of only 7 kilometers, maintains the same rituals and songs as the rest of rogations in the area and, like that of Puertomingalvo, makes its round trip on the same day.

Finally, it is the town of Culla that closes the cycle of pilgrimages to Sant Joan, moving along a historic road for 28 kilometers to reach the sanctuary on a mobile date in the calendar, but it is usually in early June. The residents of Culla have taken special care of the ritual, trying to maintain the original from the late 14th century, including stops, Gregorian chants, meals, and the order of the various participants of this religious manifestation and at the same time of intangible heritage.

In the vicinity of the sanctuary of Sant Joan is the village of La Estrella, belonging to the municipality of Mosqueruela. From there, on the last Sunday of May, the inhabitants and visitors make the journey to the village, where the sanctuary of the Virgen de la Estrella is located. This pilgrimage also has a medieval origin, it maintains, with the logical modifications due to the passage of time, the rituals, and songs of medieval origin. The participants, after traveling the 18 kilometers of the road, spend the night in the village, to return at noon the next day. It is a pilgrimage that maintains the plea for peace, water, and health, mixed with a vindication of the historical sense of belonging of La Estrella to the town of Mosqueruela. This tradition is followed by thousands of neighbors, friends, and curious people of the area, in one of the clearest examples of combination between devotion, tradition, return to the origins and interest in contact with nature.

Two more pilgrimages go, from Portell de Morella and Catí, to the imposing sanctuary of Sant Pere de Castellfort, a Gothic hermitage from the beginning of the 14th century located on top of a hill, well visible from many kilometers around. The Catí walk follows a circular route, from the village to the sanctuary and back, in a historical itinerary of great interest. It is followed by a multitude of companions and maintains its rituals and chants. The pilgrims sleep in the vicinity of the hermitage the first night, after a ritual and communal dinner of great cultural interest, to start the long way back the next day.

The Portell de Morella is one of the most interesting and unknown. It maintains the ritual in an exceptional way. Only twelve people participate in the pilgrimage, representing the whole town. As a main characteristic, which accentuates its penitential character, the participants walk in silence and the few people who accompany them, the fewer the better, have to do so at a distance so as not to interfere with this intimate and personal ritual. This rogation preserves the chants of medieval origin and the different steps of the ritual, although it runs a serious risk due to depopulation and the lack of generational replacement. The displacement is 14 kilometers, which makes the round trip the same day.

Finally, we will talk about the pilgrimage that the neighbors of Vallibona make to the sanctuary of the Virgin in Peñarroya de Tastavins, in the province of Teruel. It is a 27-kilometer walk through the mountains. The origins of this practice date back to the 14th century, when after the Plague, seven young men from the village had to leave to look for girls to marry in other towns. They finally found their future wives in Peñarroya de Tastavins and since then this pilgrimage has been made once every seven years. It is clearly a foundational ritual and has been maintained to this day despite the strong demographic crisis of Vallibona, which in 2022 had 66 inhabitants. As it has been verified (Vidal-González, 2018) there are more than a thousand people who participate in this pilgrimage, even from very distant places, in search of its sacred character, but also of its patrimonial character, to learn about historical practices in the middle of nature.

RESULTS

1. Past and Present

In the first place, the older people interviewed speak clearly of a before and a now in relation to the pilgrimages. This is what Pilar, a young mother resident of Culla, says when she indicates that "before, people used to go for devotion, but now they go for walking". Along the same lines, Enrique, a retired person, neighbor of Culla, reminds us that "there was a moral commitment that at least one person per house should participate in the pilgrimage". For Juan, neighbor of Mosqueruela and local farmer "before it was something else, very hard promises were made, although now they are also made". Eusebio, very involved in the rogation and resident of Culla, points out, not without some criticism, that "I make the pilgrimage for devotion and tradition, although some come because they like it, for a walk". Finally, José, a former shepherd from Mosqueruela, points out that "people used to go for sacrifice and devotion".

It is evident that the procession, like all human activity, evolves with time and that the ways of doing and customs of the past have evolved. It is in this line that the reflection that the website of the city council of Catí speaks of the temporal evolution of this manifestation of Intangible Heritage: "Every year that passes is more common the presence of pilgrims from outside Catí on horseback or hikers and city people who take advantage of the weekend for a change of scenery. The aim of these people is not religious devotion but to disconnect from their daily lives. It is a new type of tourism[1]".

2. Postmodern Connection With Tradition

Pilgrimages have been maintained precisely because they have evolved, changed, and adapted to the needs of postmodern society. They maintain their essence, the transcendence, and the recognition of our limitations in the face of the immensity of nature, but have changed their schedules, given the need to adapt to modern rhythms. They also combine religiosity with other more patrimonial attractions or contact with nature.

The crisis of these pilgrimages is also commented on by the people interviewed. Thus, Ángel, regular participant from Culla, says that "at the end of the 1960s very few people went, and it almost disappeared". Javier, from Puertomingalvo, also comments that "the pilgrimage stopped at the end of the 60's because there were no people, although it was recovered at the end of the 80's". David also recalls that "the pilgrimage of Les Useres in the 70's was about to disappear".

We are witnessing a revival of these practices, precisely because the dehumanization and lack of roots of the big cities make us look back and try to recover all that we left behind, our origins.

However, we clearly observe a change in the motivations that lead contemporary actors to participate in the different pilgrimages. Thus, the residents of Portell de Morella say that they participate for "the emotion, to continue with the tradition, for continuity with what my grandfather did, for coexistence". For another resident of the same village, participating in the last years, "it is a path of reflection and coexistence, to show that we love the people and the ancestors.

3. Back to the Roots

Two middle age hikers from Albocasser point out that they participate in the Culla rogation because they practice hiking, for culture, tradition, and religiosity, although they declare themselves non-practicing hikers. Another said that he attends for the cultural and heritage component. He declares himself a non-practicing person, but let's glimpse the transcendent component of his practice..... He is very moved by the atmosphere, coexistence, respect, and solidarity.

For Juan José, a resident of Mosqueruela, participating in the pilgrimage means to cultivate the "religious feeling and also to maintain the traditions of the people". He insists that "people from outside come for the traditions and to walk". For Roberto, a young student, "the ritual, the songs and the atmosphere among the neighbors, being all together, is very special". For Pilar, also from Mosqueruela, "if you don't come, you lose your identity". Finally, Vanessa, a young participant in the rogation, also says that she goes "for tradition, for the culture, for the festivities, because it identifies me with my roots".

Luis, a veteran participant, resident of Culla, points out that there are several motivations. "To see it, to walk, for devotion". In that sense, he concludes that "it has been successful because of faith and devotion, but also because people like to walk through the countryside and walk in the mountains".

For Juan Manuel, neighbor of Mosqueruela, "the devotion remains unchanged". "Since birth people carry the devotion to participate in the pilgrimage". "Some of the participants go because they like it, others go for devotion, but others also come for the festivity". Another young participant confirms that "the young people do it to spend the day and to walk" and that "now they do it for exercise, for a walk", although later he confesses that they also go for devotion.

Carmen, a resident of Catí and member of the organizing committee, tells us that "people participate out of a sense of identity and belonging, to feel rooted in their origins".

Juan, from Culla, speaks of the personal commitment of all the inhabitants of the town, "we have to comply", in line with what Eusebio says, "I go every year", with pride and a smile on his face (Culla). In similar terms expresses Eduardo, from Catí, who points out that participating is "recalling an ancestral tradition, a feeling, going back to the Middle Ages", that is, being part of the origins and history. The participants point out that in view of the high participation "the village is alive", in clear reference to the threat of depopulation that threatens these inland villages.

Undoubtedly, the growing interest in these manifestations of popular religiosity can be explained, as has been observed, by a combination of factors. Undoubtedly, the initial one is the ritual practice with all its symbolic, historical, ritual, and patrimonial load. But together with this, the return to the origins, whether they are one's own, as a descendant of someone from the village, or a generic return to the rural and agricultural origins from which we all come from. Likewise, the growing interest in the practice of sports in the natural environment, contact with nature and physical exercise are factors that make this equation of success more valuable and attractive.

DISCUSSION

The results we have presented demonstrate that there are a few predominant elements that explain the resurgence of pilgrimage participation in the current era, namely: returning to origins, transcendence, and unique cultural experience. These results are aligned with those of other works that highlight similar elements present in other contemporary pilgrimages (Feldman, 2017). The constant presence of these motifs in different research can best be understood as the result of the historical, social and value transformation of a postmodern Western society.

In the first place, the desire to return to the origins arises as an element of interest since contemporary society is dominated by dynamism and constant transformation in aspects of life that were once much more stable. The rural exodus to the cities initiated the path of uprooting, and nowadays the changes of work and residence, the loss of family relationships and participation in collective traditions, mean that our origins are not so present, and that the construction of personal identity requires this search. Secondly, the transcendence of pilgrimages is also proof of social transformations. Institutions, such as the Church, which in other times marked that the importance of pilgrimages was related to the religious, have lost the relevance they once had. However, a common denominator is that for pilgrims, from their personal experience, these activities are sacred or transcendent, even if they are not experienced as religious (Di Giovine & Choe, 2019). Another sign of the transformations in terms of the transcendent is the type of prayers that are professed, nowadays much more linked to the individual (improvement at work, results in exams, health problems of relatives...) while in the past they were linked to the benefit of the community (good harvests, times of peace, avoiding plagues, etc.). Thirdly, the cultural experience of rites, songs, or dances, which are recreated in pilgrimages, makes us think of pilgrims as tourists who collect experiences. Nothing is more characteristic of postmodern leisure than experiential tourism, to the point that, according to Collins-Kreiner (2018) the boundaries between tourism and pilgrimage have blurred.

Our analysis shows that these three elements can be present in isolation or in combination in the participants. That is to say, participation in any of the pilgrimages studied may come fundamentally from an interest in getting in touch with family or cultural origins, from the search for a transcendent meaning, or from the interest in experiencing the traditional or cultural manifestation of a pilgrimage, but in most cases, we are dealing with a combination of these aspects. It is also possible that one of these motivations is the gateway to other interests. The pilgrimages we are studying offer the possibility for people to find these elements in them, and in turn, through their participation, people are reconfiguring pilgrimages as collective manifestations that possess these qualities, which allow for these individual experiences. However, we would like to highlight a fourth element that emerges from the reflection based on the results. An element that is transversal and is present in each of the three elements presented above and that is the physical and spatial experience of the pilgrimage that affects, in the sense of transforming, people.

The conceptualization of pilgrimage as an eminently physical and spatial, but also dynamic and moving socio cultural experience that we propose here, is something that has also been put forward from geography (Scriven, 2014). Specifically, the mobility paradigm in the social sciences (Sheller, 2014) contributes to a more dynamic and comprehensive understanding of pilgrimage by considering the social world as consisting of a set of mobile practices rather than rooted places and people. A view in which the outer physical and inner spiritual/emotional journey is intertwined in a process that defines and shapes the people and places involved (Scriven, 2014). A view that sees cultural meaning as being born, primarily, from the voluntary movement of pilgrims (Coleman & Eade, 2004). The meanings we have highlighted cannot be understood as isolated elements but exist thanks to the bodily practice and physical experience that the pilgrimage entails, and thanks to the physical space in which it takes place. In other words, to better understand the resurgence of the pilgrimages studied, it is necessary to connect the meanings and circumstances that have changed in a postmodern society, with the physical and symbolic spaces of the places of pilgrimage, as well as with the corporal, individual and collective experience that is lived.

The physical and corporal dimension is essential in any pilgrimage and pilgrimage, in combination with the symbolic. Those pilgrims who seek to return to their origins refer to a place, a population, and a material environment, but also to a way of life, to traditions that are remembered on pilgrimages. The pilgrims who expressed the intention of living a unique cultural experience highlighted heritage elements such as sanctuaries, rituals, or ancient roads, as well as the natural environment. However, it is perhaps the personal significance of the pilgrimage that makes us understand that the physical aspect is essential. This is achieved thanks to a symbolic but also spatial journey that each person must make. It is generally by walking that a person carries out the pilgrimage, because, as Margry (2008) states, pilgrimage is, mostly, transitive. That is, pilgrimage is an essentially embodied experience through which both the pilgrim and the journey emerge (Scriven, 2020). Along with them emerge, consolidate, and acquire relevance the spaces and symbolic force of pilgrimages as heritage. We agree with O'Mara (2021) that pilgrimage is best understood in a social context and as a social behavior that brings about positive personal changes, as a result of a complex web of interactions between the physical, social, transcendental, mental or emotional. As Slavin (2003) states, walking is at once a bodily, social, and spiritual practice, which is the nexus between the body and the self.

The body in movement, a prerequisite for pilgrimages, is also an important element in the preferences of a postmodern society. The behavioral patterns related to physical and sporting activity of the population at the beginning of the 21st century show that activities performed outdoors and in nature have become one of the most preferred by the population. Precisely, pilgrimages fit perfectly into the processes of postmodernization, since, as García Ferrando (2006) states, the leisure practices of postmodern societies seek, among others, cultural diversity, self-expression, individualization, recognition of aesthetics and a new look at the past. Such is their fit, that in recent years some pilgrimages have inspired the layouts of international trail running events, in what can be said to be a combination of spirituality and sport (Botella-Carrubi, et al., 2019), and even many pilgrims find a sporting motivation in their journey (Amaro et al., 2018).

We cannot end this discussion without addressing the question we posed at the beginning of this paper, as to whether the medieval pilgrimages that are now re-emerging can provide an opportunity to fix the population in rural areas and to maintain and promote this rich cultural heritage. Our point of view, as we have seen, gives continuity to a consolidated trend within the field of study of pilgrimage that brings it closer to tourism (Collins-Kreiner, 2010). From that position, we understand that in a Western world like todays, where tourism is one of the most democratized activities and where communications have greatly improved, ancient pilgrimages have benefited from this to resurface (Olsen et al., 2018). Rural populations near pilgrimages can also benefit from this tourism industry of postmodern travelers. Public managers have treated pilgrimages as service sector products, and have intervened to adapt them to the new times in search of a return, mainly economic (Pazos, 2014). Some researchers have confirmed the positive impacts on pilgrimage areas that are transformed into permanent thematic routes, from the economic point of view, but also from the point of view of preservation of culture and values (Szerb, et al., 2016). The actions to develop pilgrimage destinations that can bring tourism value to the territories have to consider different aspects such as the variety of pilgrim profiles and their evolution (Damari & Mansfeld, 2016), the management of local heritage, the associationism around heritage or the promotion of a heritage culture among the local population and visitors (Herrero Pérez, 2011), that is, a community heritage strategy of which there is already an example in the studied area (Martínez Muñoz et al., 2019).

CONCLUSION

In this research work we had several objectives. Firstly, we wanted to know the elements that guide pilgrims on their journey to provide relevant information that would allow us to better understand their motives. We also wanted to better understand why pilgrimages are currently experiencing a period of growth. Because of the above, we proposed the second objective, to reflect on the opportunity that this phenomenon represents for the territories in which it takes place, to create economic and cultural value.

The results of our research have placed our proposal in line with the investigations that envision the current pilgrimage as part of the activities that allow us to reproduce -through individual or collective practices of leisure, self-making, tourism and heritage- the predominant values of a postmodern western society. We have highlighted three elements as a result of the analysis of the information obtained in the research process. The first, characterized as 'the return to the origins', involves the return to the origins lost with the exodus to the urban, dehumanized, and stressful environment. The participants try to recover what is considered authentic, original, primordial, which is concretized by resorting to a return to the past and traditions. The second element is the search for transcendent meaning, to find oneself, to be transformed through the journey undertaken with the pilgrimage, which is also an inner journey towards oneself. This second element can be linked to the religious aspects of the activity. And the third is to participate in a unique and extraordinary example of a centuries-old practice, which has been preserved over time, attracted by the cultural aspects, the rites, and the cultural and natural heritage. However, because of the reflection of the results, we consider that there is a fourth element that is essential: the physical and material part. Its importance lies in the fact that, by including the physical and material element, we can better understand the pilgrimages by connecting it with the symbolic elements presented. This connection is dynamic, transforming both the person and the spaces in which these practices take place.

By drawing on the paradigm of mobility within the social sciences, we can better address the second of our objectives: to consider whether the pilgrimages studied are an opportunity to fix population and generate heritage value. In this sense, by understanding pilgrimages as practices in emergence that transform spaces, we highlight the possibility of contexts adapting to the transformation of pilgrimages and pilgrims until they become part of what is currently the tourism industry. A destination that wishes to fix population and enhance its cultural, architectural, and natural heritage, must understand these constant transformations, and open itself to the new variety of pilgrims, motivations, and interests, but maintaining and enhancing its unique and authentic cultural value.

REFERENCES

Amaro, S., Antunes, A., & Henriques, C. (2018). A closer look at Santiago de Compostela's pilgrims through the lens of motivations. *Tourism Management, 64*, 271–280. doi:10.1016/j.tourman.2017.09.007

Bauman, Z. (1996). From pilgrim to tourist or a short history of identity. *Questions of cultural identity, 1*, 18-36.

Botella-Carrubi, D., Curras Mostoles, R., & Escrivá-Beltrán, M. (2019). Penyagolosa trails: From ancestral roads to sustainable ultra-trail race, between spirituality, nature, and sports. A case of study. *Sustainability (Basel), 11*(23), 6605. doi:10.3390u11236605

Bowman, M., Johannsen, D., & Ohrvik, A. (2020). Reframing Pilgrimage in Northern Europe: Introduction to the Special Issue. *Numen, 67*(5-6), 439–452. doi:10.1163/15685276-12341597

Brumec, S., Lavrič, M., & Naterer, A. (2023). Examining Motivations to Walk the Camino de Santiago: A Typology of Pilgrims. *Pastoral Psychology, 72*(4), 479–500. doi:10.100711089-023-01071-1

Coleman, S., & Eade, J. (Eds.). (2004). *Reframing pilgrimage: Cultures in motion*. Psychology Press. doi:10.4324/9780203643693

Collins-Kreiner, N. (2010). Researching pilgrimage: Continuity and transformations. *Annals of Tourism Research*, *37*(2), 440–456. doi:10.1016/j.annals.2009.10.016

Collins-Kreiner, N. (2018). Pilgrimage-tourism: Common themes in different religions. *International Journal of Religious Tourism and Pilgrimage*, *6*(1), 8–17. doi:10.21427/D73428

Damari, C., & Mansfeld, Y. (2016). Reflections on pilgrims' identity, role and interplay with the pilgrimage environment. *Current Issues in Tourism*, *19*(3), 199–222. doi:10.1080/13683500.2014.957660

Di Giovine, M. A., & Choe, J. (2019). Geographies of religion and spirituality: Pilgrimage beyond the 'officially' sacred. *Tourism Geographies*, *21*(3), 361–383. doi:10.1080/14616688.2019.1625072

Downe-Wamboldt, R. N. (1992). Content analysis: Method, applications, and issues. *Health Care for Women International*, *13*(3), 313–321. doi:10.1080/07399339209516006 PMID:1399871

Farias, M., Coleman, T. J. III, Bartlett, J. E., Oviedo, L., Soares, P., Santos, T., & Bas, M. D. C. (2019). Atheists on the Santiago Way: Examining motivations to go on pilgrimage. *Sociology of Religion*, *80*(1), 28–44. doi:10.1093ocrelry019

Feldman, J. (2017). Key figure of mobility: The pilgrim. *Social Anthropology*. *Social Anthropology*, *25*(1), 69–82. doi:10.1111/1469-8676.12378

García Ferrando, M. (2006). *Postmodernidad y deporte: Entre la individualización y la masificación: encuesta sobre hábitos deportivos de los españoles, 2005*. Centro de Investigaciones Sociológicas.

Harwood, T. G., & Garry, T. (2003). An overview of content analysis. *The Marketing Review*, *3*(4), 479–498. doi:10.1362/146934703771910080

Herrero Pérez, N. (2011). La posmodernización de la tradición. Nuevos retos para la gestión del patrimonio. *Revista de Antropología Social*, *20*(0), 293–307. doi:10.5209/rev_RASO.2011.v20.36270

Lois-González, R. C., & Santos, X. M. (2015). Tourists and pilgrims on their way to Santiago. Motives, Caminos and final destinations. *Journal of Tourism and Cultural Change*, *13*(2), 149–164. doi:10.1080/14766825.2014.918985

Malis, J., Masilka, D., & Janeckova, K. (2023). The solo pilgrim phenomenon on the Journey to Santiago de Compostela in Spain. *Journal of Heritage Tourism*, *18*(5), 575–593. doi:10.1080/1743873X.2023.2201451

Margry, P. J. (Ed.). (2008). *Shrines and Pilgrimage in the Modern World: New Itineraries into the Sacred*. Amsterdam University Press. doi:10.5117/9789089640116

Martínez Muñoz, E., Escribano, J., & Pérez Cosín, J. V. (2019). El desarrollo local como satisfactor de salvaguarda del patrimonio rural en un contexto de inflación patrimonial: El caso de los peregrinos Les Useres (Castellón). *Revista PH: Instituto Andaluz del Patrimonio Histórico*, *27*(98), 380–381. doi:10.33349/2019.98.4499

Nolan, M. L., & Nolan, S. (2018). *Christian pilgrimage in modern Western Europe*. UNC Press Books.

O'Mara, S. (2021). Biopsychosocial Functions of Human Walking and Adherence to Behaviourally Demanding Belief Systems: A Narrative Review. *Frontiers in Psychology*, *12*, 654122. doi:10.3389/fpsyg.2021.654122 PMID:34421710

Olsen, D. H., Trono, A., & Fidgeon, P. R. (2018). Pilgrimage trails and routes: the journey from the past to the present. In D. H. Olsen & A. Trono (Eds.), *Religious pilgrimage routes and trails: Sustainable development and management* (pp. 1–13). CABI. doi:10.1079/9781786390271.0001

Parejo, J. A. (2006). De la región a la ciudad. Un nuevo enfoque de la historia industrial española contemporánea. *Revista de Historia Industrial*, *30*, 53–102.

Pazos, A. M. (2014). Introduction. In A. M. Pazos (Ed.), *Redefining pilgrimage: New perspectives on historical and contemporary pilgrimages* (pp. 1–6). Ashgate Publishing, Ltd.

Pazos, A. M. (Ed.). (2020). *Nineteenth-Century European Pilgrimages: A New Golden Age* (1st ed.). Routledge. doi:10.4324/9780429198892

Reader, I. (2007). Pilgrimage growth in the modern world: Meanings and implications. *Religion*, *37*(3), 210–229. doi:10.1016/j.religion.2007.06.009

Scriven, R. (2014). Geographies of pilgrimage: Meaningful movements and embodied mobilities. *Geography Compass*, *8*(4), 249–261. doi:10.1111/gec3.12124

Scriven, R. (2020). Pilgrim and path: The emergence of self and world on a walking pilgrimage in Ireland. *Cultural Geographies*, *27*(2), 261–276. doi:10.1177/1474474019876622

Sheller, M. (2014). The new mobilities paradigm for a live sociology. *Current Sociology*, *62*(6), 789–811. doi:10.1177/0011392114533211

Slavin, S. (2003). Walking as Spiritual Practice: The Pilgrimage to Santiago de Compostela. *Body & Society*, *9*(3), 1–18. doi:10.1177/1357034X030093001

Sołjan, I., & Liro, J. (2022). The changing roman catholic pilgrimage centres in Europe in the context of contemporary socio-cultural changes. *Social & Cultural Geography*, *23*(3), 376–399. doi:10.1080/14649365.2020.1739322

Sorabella, J. (2011). Pilgrimage in Medieval Europe. In *Heilbrunn Timeline of Art History*. New York: The Metropolitan Museum of Art, 2000–. http://www.metmuseum.org/toah/hd/pilg/hd_pilg.htm

Szerb, A. B., Bakucz, M., & Martínez-Cortijo, F. J. (2016). The impact of the santiago pilgrimage way on rural Spain. The case of the French Way (Northern Spain). *Journal of Tourism Challenges and Trends*, *9*(1), 47.

Vidal-González, P. (2018). Patrimonio Inmaterial y rutas senderistas como búsqueda de las raíces culturales. El caso de la provincia de Castellón. In B. Santamarina, A. Coca, & O. Beltrán (Eds.), *Antropología Ambiental. Conocimientos y prácticas locales a las puertas del Antropoceno* (pp. 217–230). Icaria.

Vidal-González, P., & Cantillo, D. (2019). *Un tesoro del patrimonio cultural: la rogativa de Culla a Sant Joan de Penyagolosa*. Diputación de Castellón y Ayuntamiento de Culla.

Vidal-González, P., & Sánchez, V. (2019). Hiking paths and Intangible Heritage: A quest for cultural roots. Cases in the province of Castellón, Spain. *Sport in Society*, *22*(12), 2065–2076. doi:10.1080/17430437.2018.1551368

Webb, D. (2017). *Medieval European Pilgrimage c. 700-c. 1500*. Bloomsbury Publishing..

ENDNOTES

1 www.catimenu.com/santpere.htm, consulted 08/29/2023

Chapter 6
Evaluation of the First Seven Churches as Holy Pilgrimage Centers Within the Scope of Faith Tourism

Leyla Tokgöz
https://orcid.org/0000-0002-0044-6235
Atatürk University, Turkey

Ali İskender
Tourism Faculty, Atatürk University, Turkey

ABSTRACT

Document analysis was used as qualitative research methods while preparing this book chapter. For this purpose, verses related to the seven churches in the Bible have been included in the study. The fact that the seven churches mentioned in the Bible are located in Turkey has made this place a very important position in terms of faith tourism. In the book chapter, faith tourism is first mentioned. Later, the concept of pilgrimage was mentioned in Christianity and the importance of Anatolia from the point of view of Christianity was explained. Examples of tours about the seven churches are also included in the study. Later, it was discussed what should be taken into account when evaluating the seven churches within the scope of faith tourism.

1. FAITH TOURISM

Religious beliefs that people have and the phenomenon of tourism are interrelated concepts. Religion and belief have been one of the important reasons for human beings to migrate or travel from one place to another since ancient times (Rot et al., 2014). Faith tourism includes visits to religious sites that are considered to be related to one's own faith or the faith of others. This type of tourism is defined as visits or activities made to visit holy places, participate in religious ceremonies and fulfill religious duties.

DOI: 10.4018/978-1-6684-9923-8.ch006

Faith tourism focuses on visiting religious places, monuments or destinations whose primary purpose is to establish a relationship with a particular faith (Heidari et al., 2018). In his definition, Woodward emphasized that faith tourism is a consumer-oriented type of tourism. According to Woodward, faith tourism activities are an important source of income for many institutions and organizations that provide funds for repairs and maintenance (Woodward, 2004).

In a more comprehensive way, faith tourism is expressed as trips that people participate in for the purposes of satisfying their religious needs and seeing sacred centers other than the places where they live and meet their needs (Demircan, 2014). Faith tourism destinations usually consist of holy places, pilgrimage centers and religious heritage sites (Shinde, 2010). Religious sites such as cathedrals, temples and mosques attract worldwide visitors not only for their spiritual values, but also for entertainment, educational and cultural purposes (Heidari et al., 2018).

Faith tourism, sometimes called spiritual tourism, has gained an increasing role all over the world. Part of this issue is due to the explosion of the tourism phenomenon in general, supported by technology, income growth, knowledge transfer and promotional activities. In addition, faith tourism develops in direct relation to reasons such as people's hunger for knowledge and their desire to understand religions other than their religion (Tala & Padurean, 2008).

While organizing faith tourism activities, attention is paid to some of the unique features of each religion. Because the places or architectural structures considered sacred in every religion are not the same. For this reason, faith tourism activities are organized in three different ways (Usta, 2005):

- Meetings held on the anniversaries of religious events considered important in different religions,
- Pilgrimage trips to holy places organized individually or as a group,
- Tours organized for the purpose of visiting sacred sites and architectural monuments located on a specific route.

Today, millions of people travel around the world in search of holiness and spirituality and visit places that are considered sacred (Tala & Padurean, 2008). Faith tourism attracts a large number of people as a sociocultural phenomenon for reasons such as meeting with different religions and cultures, providing the opportunity to compare religions and establishing good relations between representatives of different religions (Kurmanaliyeva et al., 2014). In today's world, people participate in faith tourism not only to fulfill their religious duties, but also to have information about the religions of different societies and to be intertwined with different cultures (Guzel, 2010). In fact, the reasons behind people's participation in religious tourism activities differ. These reasons are as follows (Kacar & Türker, 2020):

- Performing the duty of pilgrimage,
- Being close to God,
- Praying,
- Asking for help for some problems and illnesses,
- Bringing peace to the soul.

The concepts of faith and holiday tourism are now often used together. This is particularly noticeable in the United States. To give an example; in regions such as Niagara Falls, St. Louis, Miami and Orlando, activities related to both faith tourism and some other types of tourism are carried out together (Gökdeniz, 1996). A large number of visitors who go to some regions in Europe both fulfill their religious duties and see historical and cultural sites. Among the places evaluated for this purpose; there are examples such as Le Mont St. Michel Monastery in France, Covadonga in Spain, Cologne cathedral in Germany (Avcı, 2011).

Looking at the world in general, it is seen that there are some important destinations that are sacred to almost all belief systems, especially major religions such as Christianity, Islam, Judaism, Buddhism and Hinduism. Mecca and Medina, Jerusalem, Vatican City, Fatima, Varanasi, Lhasa and Bethlehem can be shown as examples of these faith tourism centers that attract attention around the world. These sacred areas welcome millions of visitors every year.

2. PILGRIMAGE TOURISM AND PILGRIMAGE WORSHIP IN CHRISTIANITY

Travels for spiritual and religious purposes are not a new phenomenon and are known as one of the oldest tourism typologies. This type of travel is especially associated with the perception of social duty, which is more important than leisure and entertainment (Abad-Galzacorta et al., 2016). Travels to holy places are not new, of course. There are reports of pilgrimages made in Jerusalem in the third century A.D. (Woodward, 2004). For this reason, it is thought that the first activities related to faith tourism were pilgrimage visits. Religious travels are mentioned in the Old Testament, in the holy book that Hindus believe, and in some ancient works (Jackowski, 2000). In the early ages, temple visits were quite common. It is known that Ephesus and Didim in particular were important visiting regions at that time (Kaçar & Türker, 2020).

When the word Hajj is examined etymologically, it is seen that it is mentioned as "Hag" in Hebrew and this concept is derived from the word "hug-hug", which means to turn around something (Derin, 2004). The pilgrimage is usually defined as a spiritual journey to a place originating from religious reasons (Abad-Galzacorta et al., 2016). As a word; Hajj, which means visiting places and temples that are considered sacred in terms of religion, in order to get rid of sins, has been a practice that manifests itself in every period of history. The sanctuary of Apollo in Delphi in Ancient Greece, the first temple of Zeus in Dodona, the Temple of Amon in Ancient Egypt were important pilgrimage centers of the ancient period. Some clues have been obtained that there were pilgrimage activities in Ancient Egypt. Clues such as "footprints belonging to pilgrims" on the roofs of great temples at that time suggest that there were also pilgrimages in ancient Egypt. During the ancient Egyptian period; there were many places considered as religious centers, especially Busiris, Bubastis, Abydos, Karnak and Memphis. Herodotus mentioned that hundreds of thousands of people flock to these regions every year at certain times to celebrate important holidays. There were pilgrimage activities similar to Ancient Egypt in Ancient Greece. At that time, various trips were organized to places such as Delos, Ephesus, Delphes, Eleusis, where important temples were located. There are also four major pilgrimage centers in Buddhism, especially recommended by the Buddha. These centers are Lumbini Park, Bodh-Gaya, Benares Park and the Complete Extinction Grove in Kushinagara. There is a practice of circumambulation in Buddhism, just like in Islam. During the pilgrimage, they circumambulate the sacred areas in groups (Erbaş, 2002).

Pilgrimage is seen as an important worship in the major heavenly religions. In Islam, pilgrimage is mentioned as one of the conditions of Islam. Pilgrimage is a must-do once in a lifetime for those who can afford it. According to Islam, believers must visit the Kaaba in Mecca and attend the necessary prayers in order to fulfill their pilgrimage. Mecca is one of the important cities for Muslims because it is the heart of Islam and contains the Kaaba (Derin, 2004). According to Islamic sources, pilgrimage goes back to

Adam, the first human being (Köse, 2019). In Judaism, another monotheistic religion, pilgrimage goes back to Abraham and his descendants. In Genesis, one of the sacred texts of the Jews; it is mentioned that Abraham, after leaving Harran, went under the sacred oak tree in the land of Canaan, then somewhere between Bethel and Ati, and later in Hebron, where the god made an altar, presented sacrifices and worshiped the god. Although it is not clearly written in Genesis, in Judaism "the place where God appears" is considered a place of pilgrimage, and "the time when God appears" is considered a time of pilgrimage. Again, in some chapters of the Old Testament, the holy book of the Jews, it is mentioned that Jewish men must be in the presence of Yahweh in Jerusalem three times a year. As it can be understood from this, pilgrimage in Judaism is obligatory for all Jews except for young children, women, those with physical and mental disorders (Erbaş, 2002).

Pilgrimage is a worship that also exists in Christianity. According to Christians, pilgrimage is a journey to holy places that contain memories of the life of Jesus, to holy centers where leaders are located in Rome, or to some holy places dedicated to some religious elders (Derin, 2004). In the Bibles, which are the holy books of Christians, there is no clear information about the subject of pilgrimage. However, there are some verses in some parts of these Gospels that imply hajj worship (Köse, 2019). If an example is given to these verses:

"Sir, the woman said, "I can see that you are a prophet. Our ancestors worshiped on this mountain, but you Jews claim that the place where we must worship is in Jerusalem."

"Woman, Jesus replied, "believe me, a time is coming when you will worship the Father neither on this mountain nor in Jerusalem. You Samaritans worship what you do not know; we worship what we do know, for salvation is from the Jews." (John, 4:19-22).

Although there is no direct mention of pilgrimage in these verses, it is thought that pilgrimage is indirectly mentioned and Jerusalem is a place reserved for worship.

The first pilgrimage for Christians began during the Constantine period when Saint Helene visited the places where Jesus was born, crucified, buried and large churches were built. For this reason, Saint Helene is considered to be the first pilgrim in the history of Christianity. Since the first years of Christianity, the graves of martyrs have also been accepted as sacred places to be visited. Before Constantine I, the tombs of St. Peter and St. Paul were among the places visited (Erbaş, 2002).

In the early days, like everyone else, martyrs were buried in cemeteries outside the city. However, over time, the corpses and holy relics of the martyrs were moved to the city churches and many Christians began to visit these churches (Severn, 2019). During the centuries from the 4th century to the Middle Ages, pilgrimages in Christianity were made in the triangle of Jerusalem, Rome and Compostela. Christians consider Jerusalem as the place of salvation from sin, the center of the world and the place of Christ's return; Rome as the city where the tombs of Saints Peter and Paul and the sacred monuments of many other martyrs are located; and Compostela as the cult center of James, one of the apostles of Jesus. For this reason, these three centers formed the basis of Christian pilgrimage practice for a long time (Erbaş, 2002). In the Middle Ages, there were some developments that increased the popularity and prevalence of pilgrimage. With this period, towns and cities began to be established and trade developed (Severn, 2019).

With the conquest of Palestine by the Muslims, new pilgrimage centers began to emerge in Europe. The first pilgrimage centers in Europe were the tombs where the relics and relics of the saints were found. Pilgrimages to these places were considered legitimate by the clergy until the 13th century (Civil, 2003).

During the age of Enlightenment, some religious practices began to lose popularity. For this reason, pilgrimage worship has lost its importance, albeit slightly. As a result of various activities, especially during the French Revolution in 1789, many temples that have been accepted as places of pilgrimage have remained in the memories of the people. However, many holy places that were forgotten or destroyed in the period after 1815 have been recaptured and pilgrimage activities have started to increase (Erbaş, 2002). Today, Christians perform pilgrimages in Jerusalem and Bethlehem on the dates of these events in memory of Jesus' birth (Christmas), crucifixion (Mourning Friday) and resurrection (Easter), which are three important stages in Jesus' life. Along with these regions, Rome, where the tombs of the first period saints and great clergy are located, is one of the most visited places for pilgrimage (Köse, 2019).

There are holy sites that have been declared as pilgrimage centers of Christians in many countries around the world. For example; Among them are the tombs of Saint Martin of Tours in Gaule, Saint Nicolas in Bari, Italy, Saint Cyprien in Africa and Saint Epiphany in Cyprus. In addition to the tombs, the places where some holy relics are found have also been accepted as pilgrimage centers. As an example to this; The shirt of Christ in Treves, the holy shroud in Turin can be shown. In addition to these, some holy places dedicated to Mary in Europe were determined as pilgrimage centers. For example; the places where it is believed that Mary appeared and spoke to the people she chose were chosen as pilgrimage centers. Among the most important of these places; there are Rue du Bac in Paris, Lourdes, Pontmain and La Salette in France, Fatima in Portugal and Beauraing and Banneux in Belgium (Civil, 2003).

For a Christian, pilgrimage has meanings such as attaining salvation, communicating with divine beings, and obtaining favors from supernatural forces. In addition to this, there are also people who gain goodness without fulfilling the pilgrimage. They also express their gratitude for this favor they have achieved by performing the pilgrimage. For this reason, it is understood that there are two types of pilgrimage in Christianity. One of them is the pilgrimage of those who are looking for grace, and the other is the pilgrimage of those who want to offer gratitude (Derin, 2004). There are some devotions performed by those who go to pilgrimage centers in Christianity. These devotions are as follows (Civil, 2003):

- **Bodily prayer:** In bodily prayer, people perform their prayers by covering their faces or crossing their hands.
- **Silent repentance:** This worship is done by kneeling with bare feet.
- **Using water:** In this type of worship, people pray by touching water or making use of water in different ways.
- Finally, a Christian who goes on a pilgrimage, tries to gain God's approval by increasing his foot movements and exercises.

3. THE IMPORTANCE OF ANATOLIA FOR CHRISTIANITY

Christianity, which appeared on the stage of history as a small Jewish sect under the shadow of the Roman Empire in the 1st century and which was the official religion of Rome in the 4th century, is a great religious tradition with the most members in the world today. Christianity is a religion that developed around Jesus Christ, who began his preaching activities at the age of 28 and ended his life by being crucified at the age of 30 (Aydın, 2022). After the death of Jesus, 12 apostles who believed in him played an important role in the spread of Christianity. The apostles, who were left without a leader, were both afraid of the pressures of the Roman Empire and feared the reactions of the Jews to their new religion. Although the apostles of Jesus Christ and other people who believed in him went through such a difficult period, they continued their efforts to spread the religion both inside and outside of Palestine (Kassa, 2020).

In the spread of Christianity, the second important center after Jerusalem is Anatolia. Anatolian lands hosted the apostles of Jesus and important clergy in the early periods of Christianity (Olcay & Albuz, 2016). This importance of Anatolia in the early Christian period is related to both its geographical location and urban culture. In addition, the apostles Paul, John and Luke visited many cities in Anatolia, as they were on both the land and sea route between Jerusalem and Rome. At that time, the presence of many cities in Anatolia and the organization of Christianity mostly in cities accelerated the Christianization process of the region (Keser, 2019). In particular, Paul, who is described as the founder of today's Christianity, has been one of the most active people in the spread of this religion. Paul was born in Tarsus, which is within the borders of Türkiye, in 10 years AD (Aydın, 2022). Paul is not actually one of Jesus' apostles. While Jesus was alive, Paul did not have the opportunity to meet him. However, one day on his way to Damascus, he claimed to have seen Jesus in a vision and made himself accepted by those around him as an apostle. In the following period, St. Paul traveled to many places and invited people to Christianity in the places he went. He organized trips to various parts of Anatolia and the Balkans in order to spread Christianity to Jews and other communities outside of Jerusalem (Keser, 2019).

Paul is accepted as a missionary, theologian, and intellectual, according to the roles he played in the history of Christianity. He carried out intense missionary work in large regions such as Eastern Europe and the Mediterranean Regions, some interior regions in Anatolia and Jerusalem. In these missionary works, he generally focused on subjects such as Christ, the Bible, baptism and salvation (Kassa, 2020).

The region where Christianity spread the most within the Anatolian lands was Antioch. There are some factors that have been influential in the important place of Antioch in the history of Christianity. Firstly, there was a quiet environment in Antioch, far from Jerusalem. Secondly, there was a tolerant environment in Antioch due to the coexistence of people belonging to different religions. Third, transportation with Rome was easily provided through Antioch. Fourth, the economic prosperity provided in Antioch constituted a peaceful environment. Finally, Antioch was a transit point for Cappadocia, Asia and some countries located in the Mediterranean. Antioch has been a center hosting many important events in Christian history. Those who adopted this newly formed religion were given the name "Christian" for the first time in Antioch. Antakya, where the apostles and first Christian leaders often met and made plans, has been the center of Christians' early holy memories for many years. In addition to these, the first cave church accepted by the Christian world, St. Pierre Church is also located in Antakya (Budak, 2012).

One of the important centers that was effective in the entry and spread of Christianity in Anatolia is the Cilicia Region and especially Tarsus in this region. Because Paul, who spread Christianity to wide geographies with his missionary activities, was born in Tarsus. Paul mentioned in his own texts that he went to Cilicia and carried out religious spreading activities in this region. Another important region in Anatolia during the spread of Christianity is the Lykaonia region. This region, which today covers the provinces of Karaman and Konya in Türkiye, was known as Lykaonia in ancient times. One of the cities in this region, Derbe, became a bishopric center mentioned in the Bible and considered sacred for Christians. St. Paul also traveled to the city three times to spread Christianity. Lystra, another city of the Lycaonia region, was a region where early Christians fled from Roman oppression and hid. After the period when Christianity was free, Lystra became an important religious center (Keser, 2019).

Another Anatolian city considered important by the early Christians is Ephesus. Ephesus was a region that hosted different religions in pre-Christian times. With the spread of Christianity, it was accepted as one of the most important centers of this religion. Christians believe that the Virgin Mary spent the last days of her life in Ephesus and died there. At the same time, it is accepted that the legend of "Seven Sleepers" in the Christian faith was also lived in Ephesus (Budak, 2012).

Today, 9 centers and 11 venues located in these centers have been identified by the Ministry of Culture and Tourism in Türkiye, which are considered sacred by Christians in various regions of Anatolia. These centers and locations are as follows (Olcay & Albuz, 2016):

- Hatay- St. Pierre Church,
- Tarsus- St. Paul's Church,
- İzmir- Virgin Mary House,
- Demre- St. Nicholas Church,
- Iznik- Hagia Sophia Mosque,
- Yalvaç- Pisidia Ancient City,
- Derinkuyu- Orthodox Church,
- Cappadocia Region,
- Manisa-Sard Church,
- Manisa- Alaşehir (St. Jean) Church,
- Manisa-Akhisar Church,
- Denizli- Laodicea Ancient City,
- The First Seven Churches.

4. METHODS AND FINDINGS

This book chapter has been prepared in the form of document analysis from qualitative methods. In this context, the letters mentioned in the Bible about seven churches was included in the research. Later, examples of tours related to the seven churches were mentioned. In the results and recommendations, it was discussed what should be considered when evaluating the seven churches in terms of faith tourism.

Today, when the term" church" is used, architectural structures with mosaics, icons and some artistic features, in which the symbol of the cross is intensively used, come to mind. However, the word "ekklesia" in Greek means "congregation" rather than a religious structure. For this reason, the word church in the Bible should be understood as congregation in Christianity (Madrigal, 2014). Therefore, each of the seven churches mentioned in the Bible and located in Anatolia should be considered as a congregation.

The revelations of St. John were effective in the significant spread of Christianity in Anatolian lands. In fact, the first seven churches in Anatolia are mentioned in St. John's book of Revelation (Işık, 2022). Saint John, it is unclear where and when he was born, is known as a Palestinian religious man. According to some rumors, St. John is the cousin of Jesus (Kunt, 2014).

Saint John is one of the apostles chosen by Jesus himself. According to the narrations, St. John was one of the three closest apostles to Jesus. It is believed that after Jesus was crucified, St. John settled in Ephesus and carried out religious activities there. However, he was exiled to Patmos Island due to these activities. It is narrated that after his exile to the island, he wrote some letters along with the revelation. Revelation, the last book of the New Testament, consists of letters written to seven churches (Keser, 2019).

In Christianity, the number seven is repeated many times in the New Testament. Christians believe that this number is sacred. In the New Testament, it is mentioned that Jesus fed a large crowd with 7 loaves of bread and exorcised 7 demons from Mary Magdalene. In the early Christian community, 7 Diacons were determined by the apostles. In addition to these, different concepts such as 7 communities, 7 angels, 7 seals, 7 spirits, 7 enlighteners, 7 suns, 7 sufferings, 7 headed animals are also mentioned in the holy books of Christians. A person must complete 7 separate sacraments to enter Christianity (Ferah, 2012). The number seven is especially mentioned in the book of Revelation. For example; it is mentioned that letters were sent to 7 churches, 7 seals were opened and 7 plagues were sent. Of course, it is possible to multiply these examples. As can be seen from all these examples, the book of Revelation is based on the number seven. It is believed that this figure was not chosen at random. Christians believe that this figure is the number of God's plan. For this reason, the number seven is very important to them. This figure expresses that everything is proceeding as God planned and God's victory. The letters sent to seven churches in the New Testament are also completed in seven parts (Kunt, 2014). In the next section, the issues related to these seven churches mentioned in the Bible are included.

4.1. Ephesus Church

Today, Ephesus is located in the province of Izmir in the Aegean Region of Turkey (Baranaydın and Baranaydın, 2019). It is known that the historical development process of the city goes back to the Early Bronze Age. The city and its surroundings remained under the rule of different civilizations such as the Lelegs, Akhas, Cimmerians, Lydians and Persians. Ephesus is also known as the hometown of the important names of antiquity, Heraclitus, Rufus, Callinos, Zenodotos and Soranos (Avcı, 2020). According to some myths, Ephesus was founded by Androklos, the son of Kodros, King of Athens. Androklos established the city of Ephesus by placing immigrants from Greece in this region (Keser, 2019). Ephesus, which came under Roman domination in the 2nd century B.C., gradually gained strength and was used as the capital of the Asian provinces of the Roman Empire (Avcı, 2020). The rapidly developing city, with a population of 250 thousand, became the most important and largest city after Rome and Alexandria in the ancient period. Ephesus became the economic, social, cultural and religious center of Anatolia. The presence of the Temple of Artemis, one of the seven wonders of the ancient world, in this city further increased its religious importance. Ephesus, which has great importance in various subjects, was also home to many people mentioned in the Bible. It is narrated that the apostles of Jesus, John, the mother of Jesus, Mary and Luke are in Ephesus and their graves are here (Madrigal, 2014). At the same time, Ephesus is one of the seven churches in Anatolia mentioned in the Bible.

Ephesus is the most important of the seven churches that Christians consider sacred. This situation is also understood from the fact that St. Paul gave the first place to Ephesus in the letters he wrote (Baranaydın and Baranaydın, 2019). Ephesus Church is a place located on Mount Bülbül that is 9 km from Selçuk district of İzmir and called "Panaya Kapulu" by Christians. It is estimated to have been built in the 4th century. The altar part of the church resembles a hearth. This part represents the golden heart of Jesus (Kunt, 2014).

Before Jesus was crucified, he entrusted his mother, Mary, to one of his apostles, St. John. After the death of Jesus, St. John brought her to Ephesus from Jerusalem to protect Mary (Türkoğlu, 1999). However, because he did not want Meryem to enter among the pagans in Ephesus, he built her a hut in a tree-covered place on the slopes of Mount Bülbül. According to some rumors, St. John secretly visited Mary every day and brought her food and drink (Kunt, 2014). Of course, the only purpose they came to Ephesus was not to protect Mary. It was also because John thought it would be easier to spread Christianity in Ephesus. Those living in Ephesus at that time worshiped the Goddess Artemis. Considering the large population of Ephesus, if the people here accepted Christianity, it would be easier to destroy paganism in other regions. Having such an idea, Saint John began to organize meetings for teaching religion secretly after he came to Ephesus (Türkoğlu, 1999).

After St. John and Mary settled on the place known as Mount Bülbül today, the first Christian communities began to emerge in Ephesus. A council meeting was held here after Christianity had spread to the full extent in this region. At this meeting, Christians decided to accept Mary as the "mother of God". The Double Church (Church of Mary) was built by Hadrianus, one of the emperors of that period, dedicated to Mary. The fact that a council meeting was held here, in which the basic principles of Christianity were determined, and that it was the first church to be named after Mary, express the importance of this work. Due to the fact that important council meetings are held here, this church is also called the Council Church (Işık, 2022).

4.1.1. Letter to Ephesus

According to various rumors, St. John wrote the book of Revelation, which is considered holy by Christians, on Mount Patmos. John included the letters he wrote to the Seven Churches in his book of Revelation. He wrote the first of these letters to Ephesus (Kunt, 2014). The letter that John wrote to Ephesus is as follows:

"To the angel of the church in Ephesus write: These are the words of him who holds the seven stars in his right hand and walks among the seven golden lampstands. I know your deeds, your hard work and your perseverance. I know that you cannot tolerate wicked people, that you have tested those who claim to be apostles but are not, and have found them false. You have persevered and have endured hardships for my name, and have not grown weary. Yet I hold this against you: You have forsaken the love you had at first. Consider how far you have fallen! Repent and do the things you did at first. If you do not repent, I will come to you and remove your lampstand from its place. But you have this in your favor: You hate the practices of the Nicolaitans, which I also hate. Whoever has ears, let them hear what the Spirit says to the churches. To the one who is victorious, I will give the right to eat from the tree of life, which is in the paradise of God." (Revelation, 2:1-7).

Saint John sent his first letter, believed to have been written by the Holy Spirit, to the people of Ephesus. At that time, a community of pagans lived in Ephesus. In this letter, John tried to introduce the religion of Jesus to the people of Ephesus and invited them to Christianity. In this letter, St. John focused on the community known as the Nicolaitan and gave them warnings. Looking at who the Nicolaitan are; It is seen that there was an agnostic sect living in the Bergama region in the 1st century. The Nikolais were known as a heretical sect. For this reason, Saint John sent warnings to this community in the letter he wrote. Another issue focused on in the letter is false messengers. After the death of Jesus Christ, people who claim that there are many messengers and give false information to people have emerged. John also addressed this issue in the letter. He warned people that they should not believe people who introduce themselves in this way (Kunt, 2014).

When the letter written to Ephesus is examined thoroughly, it is understood that it is similar to the letter written to Sardis. Because at that time, both Ephesus and Sardis were the centers of the regions they were in. For this reason, it is considered quite natural that the letters sent to these two important cities, which are similar in many ways, are also similar (Ramsay, 1904).

4.2. Izmir (Smyrna) Church

The name Smyrna is not Greek. This name is actually of Anatolian origin, as in many place names in the Aegean Region (Keser, 2019). Smyrna Ancient City is located in Bayraklı district of İzmir today. Numerous archaeological researches have been carried out in the city and as a result of these researches, It has been determined that the settlement in this region dates back to 3000 years BC (Erdoğan, 2020).

In ancient times, Izmir was approximately 60 km from the city of Ephesus. At that time, this city was a rich port city (Kunt, 2014). İzmir, which is said to have been first founded by the Amazons in some rumors experienced many disasters such as fire, epidemics, earthquake and war at various times. But then this region was gloriously revived by Alexander the Great in the 4.century B.C. Izmir, one of the 12 city-states of the ancient Ionian Civilization, had risen to the leadership position. This city with a population of 100 thousand had been one of the richest cities of Anatolia in the ancient period (Işık, 2022). This city is also the birthplace of Homer, one of the famous poets of the ancient period. At that time, Izmir was a city known for its natural beauties and that's why it was nicknamed "Beautiful Izmir" (Madrigal, 2014).

Izmir, which hosted important names of Christianity such as the Virgin Mary, St. John and St. Paul throughout the 1st century, became an important center just like Ephesus or Antakya. Christianity in the city began to spread in the 2nd century (Keser, 2019). It is known that there was an important episcopacy center in Smyrna after the Roman Empire split into two and Christianity became the official religion of Rome. Saint Paul lived in this city for a short time. During the period when St. Paul lived here, the Smyrna community was established (Baranaydın & Baranaydın, 2019). However, the congregation of Smyrna has been a community that has suffered a lot. The first reaction to the congregation came from the religious Jews living in the city. Afterwards, some pressures were applied by the Roman government. While some Christians were imprisoned, others were martyred for their faith. The main reason for this was that one of the cult centers where the Roman emperor was worshipped was in Izmir. The Christian community living in the city has been under pressure for a certain period of time because they did not agree to worship the emperor (Madrigal, 2014).

The second of the Seven Churches mentioned in St. John's book of Revelation is the Izmir Church. This church is said to have meanings such as "follower" or "faithful". However, there is no clear information about whether this church is an architectural structure or a congregation. The Izmir Church was established in the name of Polycarp, one of the first disciples of St. John, and is also known as the St. Polycarp Church. Saint Polycarp became the symbol of the Christian community in Izmir and became a very loved and respected person both by his community and by public. Saint Polycarp carried out various activities for pagan people to accept Christianity. Because of these activities, both pagans and Jews hated him. However, despite all this, Aziz Polycarp was seen by everyone as the "teacher of Asia Minor" (Keser, 2019).

4.2.1. Letter to Izmir

The second of the letters that Saint John wrote to the Seven Churches was sent to the community in Izmir. The letter written to Izmir is as follows:

"To the angel of the church in Smyrna write: These are the words of him who is the First and the Last, who died and came to life again. I know your afflictions and your poverty yet you are rich! I know about

the slander of those who say they are Jews and are not, but are a synagogue of Satan. Do not be afraid of what you are about to suffer. I tell you, the devil will put some of you in prison to test you, and you will suffer persecution for ten days. Be faithful, even to the point of death, and I will give you life as your victor's crown. Whoever has ears, let them hear what the Spirit says to the churches. The one who is victorious will not be hurt at all by the second death." (Revelation, 2:8-11).

There are many contrasts between the letter written to the people of Izmir and the letter to the Ephesians. Although these two letters are similar in form, they are quite different from each other in content. St. John wrote his letter with great sympathy for the community in Izmir. Therefore, this letter consists mostly of praise (Ramsay, 1904).

In this letter he wrote, St. John made a reference to the cult of Cybele with the word "*died and came to life again*". Different issues were addressed in the letter. Among these topics; there are ten days, the devil's synagogue and St. Polycarp. Saint John wanted to describe 10 Roman emperors who would persecute the Christian community with the phrase ten days. During the period when Christianity appeared, some Jewish communities reacted to Christians by uniting with pagans. One of the places where this situation was experienced the most was Izmir. Saint John wanted to describe these events with the term devil's synagogue, which he used in the letter. Another subject mentioned in the letter is Saint Polycarp. As mentioned above, Saint Polycarp was one of the first disciples of John. He was also the first bishop of Izmir. Saint Polycarp, who carried out successful activities in spreading the religion, was killed by Jews and pagans at the age of 86. Some narrations describe that Polycarp was thrown to wild animals, while others describe that he was thrown into the fire (Kunt, 2014).

4.3. Pergamon Church

The first name of Bergama is Bergamos. According to the mythos told about the foundation of the city; Pergamos, the grandson of Achilles, one of the heroes of Troy, came to Anatolia and founded a city on the edge of the Seleinos stream and gave this city his own name. In this way, the city of Bergama was established. Among the cities in the region, Bergama attracted the most attention of travelers (Yılmaz, 2004). Bergama, one of the most beautiful and important cities of the Western Anatolian lands, is located in the Bergama district of İzmir today. The name of Pergamon was first encountered in Xenophon's work called Anabasis. Bergama, which remained under the domination of different societies in the historical process, came under the rule of Alexander the Great in 334 BC. Although it was captured by the Seleucids for a certain period of time, it became independent in 261 BC from the sovereignty of the Seleucids (Keser, 2019).

Bergama, which became the capital of Asia in 29 A.D., had never been as economically developed as Izmir and Ephesus (Işık, 2022). Especially during the Roman period, important reconstruction works were carried out in the city. Within the scope of these zoning works, there were roads, bridges, colonnaded streets and temples (Baranaydın & Baranaydın, 2019). A temple was built for the Egyptian gods Serapis, Harpokrates and Isis in Pergamum during the time of Hadrian, one of the Roman emperors. This temple was built using red brick along with a large garden in front. For this reason, the people called the temple the Red Courtyard. During the early Christian period, the Red Courtyard underwent a restoration process and a church was added to the sanctuary. Kizil Avlu or Bergama Church, as it is also known, is the only church whose location is clearly known from the Seven Churches mentioned in the Bible. Christians think that this church means "repentance" or "marriage-union". The meaning of repentance comes from the Zeus Altar, which was known as the devil's throne in Pergamon in previous periods. The meaning of marriage-union comes from the fact that religious and state affairs are carried out together in the church (Işık, 2022).

Bergama, where one of the first seven churches in Anatolia was founded, has an important place in the Christian world. St. John, in his religious activities in Ephesus, denigrated the polytheistic belief that was widespread in Pergamum. St. Paul, who came to the city between 53-56 years, started to spread Christianity here. With the spread of Christianity, it is known that three people who accepted this religion were killed in the city theater in Bergama (Keser, 2019).

4.3.1. Letter to Bergama

The third letter written by John is addressed to the congregation in Pergamum. This letter is as follows:

"To the angel of the church in Pergamum write: These are the words of him who has the sharp, double-edged sword. I know where you live where Satan has his throne. Yet you remain true to my name. You did not renounce your faith in me, not even in the days of Antipas, my faithful witness, who was put to death in your city where Satan lives. Nevertheless, I have a few things against you: There are some among you who hold to the teaching of Balaam, who taught Balak to entice the Israelites to sin so that they ate food sacrificed to idols and committed sexual immorality. Likewise, you also have those who hold to the teaching of the Nicolaitans. Repent therefore! Otherwise, I will soon come to you and will fight against them with the sword of my mouth. Whoever has ears, let them hear what the Spirit says to the churches. To the one who is victorious, I will give some of the hidden manna. I will also give that person a white stone with a new name written on it, known only to the one who receives it." (Revelation, 2:12-17).

In this letter, John referred to Jesus, who had the power of life and death, with the phrase *"the sharp, double-edged sword"* He stated that Jesus spoke to his congregation in Pergamum. A distinctive feature of this letter is the frequent reference to the prestige of Bergama, the center of Roman authority. In this letter, John spoke as if he had an authority similar or even immeasurably superior to that of the Roman government (Ramsay, 1904). The letter contains words such as manna, sword and white stone. These words have different meanings. Manna refers to the food that God sent to the Hebrews in the desert after they left Egypt. The sword symbolizes the official authority in Rome. The white stone, on the other hand, refers to the stone given to the winner of the games in Rome, on which his name is written. The letter also mentions a person named Antipas. Antipas was actually the bishop of Pergamon during the reign of Emperor Domitian. Antipas was a person who was martyred because of his faith, just like Polycarp. Saint John sent Antipas to Pergamon to spread Christianity. When the people attended the meetings held by Antipas, listened to him and started to turn to Christianity, pagans and other dissidents hated Antipas and killed him in Bergama. Upon this incident, John sent a letter to the people of Pergamon and warned those who wanted to keep the polytheistic religion alive. He also explained that those who accept Christianity and believe in Jesus would be rewarded. In his letter, St. John described Pergamon as "the place where the devil reigns" or "the devil's throne". Because he saw the giant reliefs on the Altar of Zeus in the city as an idol, and the statue of Athena in the Temple of Athena as a symbol of pagan belief (Kunt, 2014).

4.4. Thyateira (Akhisar) Church

Today, Thyateira Ancient City is located in Akhisar district of Manisa province. As a result of the archaeological studies carried out in the city and its surroundings, it has been determined that the settlement history of these lands dates back to the end of the Neolithic Age (Akdeniz and Erön, 2020). In ancient times, Thyateira was located at the mouth of a long valley connecting the Hermus and Caicos valleys. Communication and trade between these two great and important valleys was provided over Thyateira at that time (Ramsay, 1904).

It is told in ancient literary works that Thyateira was founded in the Hellenistic period. Ancient writers had different views on who the city belonged to. While Strabo said that the city belonged to the Macedonians, Stephanos Byzantios claimed that the city was founded by Seleukos I and therefore belonged to the Seleucids (Sarılar Özdemir, 2021). According to some rumors, this city, which is one of the important settlements of Anatolia, was founded by the Amazons in the 14th century BC. The Amazons named the city "Thyateira", the name of their queen. This name was later used by the Seleucids. Thyateira continued to exist as a Lydian city even after the region was conquered by the Lydians (Keser, 2019).

Thyateira became the most important city after Sardes, the capital of Lydia, thanks to its military and commercial power in the 1st century. The geographical location of the city has allowed the development of trade. Especially the purple dye produced in the region was in great demand and sold to neighboring countries. Another traded product was cotton. The people of the city engaged in cotton trade and produced fabric. Thyateira remained under the domination of the Pergamon Kingdom for a certain period of time and then came under the rule of Rome (Işık, 2022).

Thyateira, which did not lose its importance during the Roman period, lived rich and prosperous times. When the city was under Roman rule, it became an industrial city. During this period, people from different professions (potters, tailors, weavers, bakers, blacksmiths, etc.) were organized by establishing associations. Although Thyateira developed under Roman rule, it gained its real popularity during the Byzantine Empire, when Christianity began to spread in the city (Keser, 2019).

There is no clear information about Thyateira Church. However, it is known that the longest of the letters written to the Seven Churches belonged to this church. When Saint Paul went to Greece to spread Christianity, he met a woman named Lydia, known to be from Thyateira. This woman, who was in Greece for trade, attended the meetings organized by St. Paul, listened to him and accepted Christianity. Lydia, baptized by St. Paul, opened her home to them and hosted them. This situation accelerated the establishment of the Christian community in Thyateira. Thus, the fourth of the first seven churches in the city was established and religious activities began. At the time when Christianity began to spread, a woman named Jezebel emerged. It is known that this pagan woman wanted to convert people from Christianity by giving false information. The Thyateira community behaved very patiently, humble and determined towards Jezebel and they were successful in this way (Işık, 2022).

4.4.1. Letter to Thyateira

Saint John wrote the fourth of seven letters to Thyateira. This letter is as follows:

"To the angel of the church in Thyatira write: These are the words of the Son of God, whose eyes are like blazing fire and whose feet are like burnished bronze. I know your deeds, your love and faith, your service and perseverance, and that you are now doing more than you did at first. Nevertheless, I have

this against you: You tolerate that woman Jezebel, who calls herself a prophet. By her teaching she misleads my servants into sexual immorality and the eating of food sacrificed to idols. I have given her time to repent of her immorality, but she is unwilling. So I will cast her on a bed of suffering, and I will make those who commit adultery with her suffer intensely, unless they repent of her ways. I will strike her children dead. Then all the churches will know that I am he who searches hearts and minds, and I will repay each of you according to your deeds. Now I say to the rest of you in Thyatira, to you who do not hold to her teaching and have not learned Satan's so-called deep secrets, 'I will not impose any other burden on you, except to hold on to what you have until I come.' To the one who is victorious and does my will to the end, I will give authority over the nations that one 'will rule them with an iron scepter and will dash them to pieces like pottery' just as I have received authority from my Father. I will also give that one the morning star. Whoever has ears, let them hear what the Spirit says to the churches." (Revelation, 2:18-29).

The longest and most instructive of the seven letters was to Thyateira. The letter was also the most obscure of any other letter. The reason for this uncertainty is that the history of Thyateira, especially the conditions and characteristics of the city in the first century AD (Ramsay, 1904).

In the introductory part of the letter sent to Thyateira, Jesus was described as the supreme son of God, with eyes like fire and feet like shiny bronze. Among the Thyateira congregation were those who at that time tolerated a woman (Jezebel) who promoted idolatry and sexual immorality. The warning of Jesus Christ was aimed at this event that was tolerated and overlooked. In the letter written by John, warnings were sent to the people about these events. John also referred to bronze work in this letter. The reason for this is that bronze work was widespread in Thyateira at that time (Kunt, 2014).

4.5. Sardis (Salihli) Church

Sardis is one of the largest cities in the ancient world. In the opinion of Greek travelers and writers, Sardis was the greatest city of recent times (Ramsay, 1904). The city of Sardis, located in the Salihli district of Manisa today, was located between the Tmolos Mountains and the Hermos Plain to the east of the Paktalos Stream. The city of Sardis and the region where the city was located became one of the most important centers of the ancient period, thanks to its being suitable for agriculture, forests, marble quarries and the gold extracted from the Paktalos Stream. According to Herodotus, the ancestors of the Sardisians were the Heraclids dynasty, which came from Heracles and dates back to the late bronze age (Yegül, 2020).

The city of Sardis was the administrative and religious center of the Lydians. So it was the capital of the Lydians. This ancient city was where the Lydians first produced gold coins. Sardis became the satrap of the Achaemenids in 547 BC. It is known that the city, which was captured by Alexander the Great in 334 B.C, was used as a garrison. Sardes came under the rule of the Kingdom of Pergamon in 180 BC, and then was left to the Roman Empire in AD 133. The city, which preserved its commercial importance during the Roman Empire period, continued to evolve in the 2nd-5th century. During this period, especially major development activities were carried out. A large synagogue was built in the city. This shows that there was a Jewish density in the region. In the process of acceptance and spread of Christianity, the first Christians used the synagogues in the city for a certain period of time. Saint Paul also started his missionary activities from synagogues and gave sermons there (Baranaydın & Baranaydın, 2019).

A Christian community was established in Sardis shortly after the death of Jesus. During the Roman Empire, Christians built a church in the city. However, this church was destroyed due to reasons such as earthquake and war. As a result of the archaeological excavations carried out in the city, the remains of a church built using bricks and small stones with the meanings of "remaining" and "walk with me" were found next to the Temple of Artemis. However, there is no clear information about whether this church ruin belongs to the real Sardis Church (Işık, 2022).

4.5.1. Letter to Sardis

The fifth of the letters written by St. John was sent to Sardis. The letter is as follows:

"To the angel of the church in Sardis write: These are the words of him who holds the seven spirits of God and the seven stars. I know your deeds; you have a reputation of being alive, but you are dead. Wake up! Strengthen what remains and is about to die, for I have found your deeds unfinished in the sight of my God. Remember, therefore, what you have received and heard; hold it fast, and repent. But if you do not wake up, I will come like a thief, and you will not know at what time I will come to you. Yet you have a few people in Sardis who have not soiled their clothes. They will walk with me, dressed in white, for they are worthy. The one who is victorious will, like them, be dressed in white. I will never blot out the name of that person from the book of life, but will acknowledge that name before my Father and his angels. Whoever has ears, let them hear what the Spirit says to the churches." (Revelation, 3:1-6).

There are similarities between the letter sent to Sardis and the one sent to Ephesus. Therefore, the two letters should be evaluated together. There was corruption in both cities where the letters were sent. But this situation was felt more in Sardis. For this reason, although the two letters are similar in general terms, they differ in terms of some of the subjects mentioned (Ramsay, 1904).

In the letter written to Sardis, the Christian community in the city is warned that it is time to wake up. It is said that the sleep of this community also means death. In fact, there is a reproach made to the church in this letter. In other words, it is emphasized that the church in Sardis must come to its senses and revive the dying, that is, they must remember the teachings of Jesus. St. John also touched upon the issue of coming like a thief. In a battle in and around Sardes, the Persians besieged Sardes and, thanks to a careless Lydian soldier, found a secret way into the city and occupied the city. This incident was criticized by John in a letter (Kunt, 2014).

4.6. Philadelphia (Alaşehir) Church

Today, Philadelphia is located in the Alaşehir district of Manisa province. It is a center located 45 km southeast of Sardes, one of the important cities of the ancient period (Erdoğan, 2013). In ancient times, the city of Philadelphia was founded on three hills, dominating the important trade routes leading to the Hermos plain, at the foot of Mount Tmolos in the Late Hellenistic period (Barman, 2022). The city was named after Attalus II whose nickname was Philadelphus. Philadelphus means truth and loyalty (Ramsay, 1904). It is thought that city was founded by King of Pergamon Attalos II between 150-138 BC. Attalos II settled some Macedonian immigrants in this new city he founded and increased the population of the city in this way. Although this city was founded by the Pergamon Kingdom, it did not stay under their rule for long. In 133 B.C, after King Attalos III passed away, the city was given to Rome upon his will (Erdoğan, 2013). During the historical process of Philadelphia, it gained a worldwide reputation due to a large-scale disaster. The area where the city was founded was a region of extinct volcanoes and earthquakes occurred from time to time. In 17 A.D, the biggest earthquake ever experienced in this region occurred. After this great earthquake, 12 cities in the great Lydian Valley, including Sardis and Philadelphia, were destroyed (Ramsay, 1904).

Philadelphia improved its prosperity in the 2nd and 3rd centuries. During the Caracalla period, the city was given the title of Neokoros, or temple protector, in the state religion. In addition, the city became a belief center where patients wish healing by offering offerings (Erdoğan, 2013).

The city of Philadelphia, which was founded on the edge of a wide volcanic plain, had fertile lands. At the same time, due to the strategic, geographical and economic conditions it had, the city was in a very important position in economic, political, social, cultural and religious terms both in the Late Hellenistic Age and during the Roman Empire (Barman, 2022). Christianity began to be accepted in Philadelphia 40 years after the birth of Jesus. This city was one of the first cities in Western Anatolia to adopt Christianity (Keser, 2019). Christianity developed more firmly in Philadelphia over time. Philadelphia is one of the few congregations where St. John did not speak ill of his letters. The congregation in this city worked hard to spread Christianity. Thus, they proved themselves to God. They accepted God as the only savior of mankind. Actually, Philadelphia had a rather small and ordinary church. Despite this, thanks to their belief in God and Jesus, they managed to become the most beloved of God among the Seven Churches (Işık, 2022). Built on behalf of this congregation, St. Jean Church has not survived to the present day, except for the dome legs (Baranaydın & Baranaydın, 2019).

4.6.1. Letter to Philadelphia

The sixth letter written by St. John was sent to the community in Philadelphia. The letter is as follows:

"To the angel of the church in Philadelphia write: These are the words of him who is holy and true, who holds the key of David. What he opens no one can shut, and what he shuts no one can open. I know your deeds. See, I have placed before you an open door that no one can shut. I know that you have little strength, yet you have kept my word and have not denied my name. I will make those who are of the synagogue of Satan, who claim to be Jews though they are not, but are liars I will make them come and fall down at your feet and acknowledge that I have loved you. Since you have kept my command to endure patiently, I will also keep you from the hour of trial that is going to come on the whole world to test the inhabitants of the earth. I am coming soon. Hold on to what you have, so that no one will take your crown. The one who is victorious I will make a pillar in the temple of my God. Never again will they leave it. I will write on them the name of my God and the name of the city of my God, the new Jerusalem, which is coming down out of heaven from my God; and I will also write on them my new name. Whoever has ears, let them hear what the Spirit says to the churches." (Revelation, 3:7-13).

This letter was written in accordance with the character and history of the community in Philadelphia (Ramsay, 1904). In this letter, St. John commends the Christians in Philadelphia for keeping their faith in Jesus. Just like in the Izmir Church, the letter written to the Philadelphia Church did not use bad words for the community there (Kunt, 2014). Therefore, the letters written to Izmir and Philadelphia constitute a different section on their own. The letters sent to these two churches were written more sincerely than the others. Both churches had to contend with various difficulties. The Izmir Church was poor and under pressure. Philadelphia, on the other hand, was a community without much power. For this reason, the letters written to these two churches are similar in content (Ramsay, 1904).

4.7. Laodicea Church

Today, Laodicea Antique City is located 6 km northeast of Denizli province; within the borders of Eskihisar, Korucuk, Goncalı and Bozburun neighborhoods (Keser, 2019). The King Antiochus II founded the ancient city of Laodicea in the middle of the 3rd century BC in the name of his wife, Queen Laodice. Laodicea was located at the crossroads of roads connecting Central, Southern and Western Anatolia. For this reason, the city was at an important point that brought the trade activities carried out in Anatolia to the sea (Şimşek, 2013).

An uninterrupted life was lived in Laodicea from the Early Chalcolithic Period to the 7th century AD. Strabon, one of the ancient writers, emphasized that this city was the largest city of the Phrygian region. Laodicea was destroyed and rebuilt due to major earthquakes in the 1st century B.C. (Baranaydın & Baranaydın, 2019). Laodicea reached its highest level of prosperity during the Roman, early Christian and late Byzantine periods. During these periods, the city used the therapeutic properties of the hot water coming from the vicinity of Hireapolis and started to be known as a treatment center (Kunt, 2014). In addition, Laodicea was a manufacturing center. A precious type of wool, soft and shiny black, was produced in the city. Various clothes were produced using this wool. Laodiceans used these clothes they produced themselves and sold them to other regions (Ramsay, 1904).

Laodicea was a very important center in terms of religion in ancient times. Being a region far from the political centers, hosting different religious beliefs and hosting the Jewish community in the Roman period were important factors in the acceptance of Christianity in the city. The Church of Laodicea, the last of the Seven Churches, was founded by a Christian named Epaphras, who is presumed to be a student of St. Paul (Işık, 2022). In addition to the letter written by St. John, it is known that St. Paul also sent a letter to Laodicea. St. Paul wanted the letter he sent to Laodicea to be read and told in other cities (Keser, 2019). As an architectural structure, the Church of Laodicea was built during the reign of Constantine the Great. The church is also important because it is not similar to any other church plan in terms of architectural features (Şimşek, 2013).

4.7.1. Letter to Laodicea

The last of the letters that St. John wrote to the Seven Churches was sent to the Church of Laodicea. The letter is as follows:

"To the angel of the church in Laodicea write: These are the words of the Amen, the faithful and true witness, the ruler of God's creation. I know your deeds, that you are neither cold nor hot. I wish you were either one or the other! So, because you are lukewarm neither hot nor cold I am about to spit you out of my mouth. You say, 'I am rich; I have acquired wealth and do not need a thing.' But you do not realize that you are wretched, pitiful, poor, blind and naked. I counsel you to buy from me gold refined in the fire, so you can become rich; and white clothes to wear, so you can cover your shameful nakedness; and salve to put on your eyes, so you can see. Those whom I love I rebuke and discipline. So be earnest and repent. Here I am! I stand at the door and knock. If anyone hears my voice and opens the door, I will come in and eat with that person, and they with me. To the one who is victorious, I will give the right to

sit with me on my throne, just as I was victorious and sat down with my Father on his throne. Whoever has ears, let them hear what the Spirit says to the churches." (Revelation, 3:14-22).

According to the letter, Jesus warned Laodicean congregation with these words*; "I know your deeds, that you are neither cold nor hot. I wish you were either one or the other! So, because you are lukewarm neither hot nor cold I am about to spit you out of my mouth"* (Revelation, 3:15-16). The concepts of warmth and coldness mentioned here came from the hot springs of Pamukkale, which could also be seen from Laodicea. It is estimated that Jesus referred to these hot springs. St. John also emphasizes "warm city water" in the letter. In fact, he used the metaphor of warm water for people living in the city. John used this analogy for insensitive people who are unknown to which religion they belong to (Kunt, 2014). The Church of Laodicea is the only church that is completely condemned. St. John also included bad words in some of the letters he sent to other churches. However, the letter sent to Laodicea contains complete condemnation. St. John gave advice to the Laodicean community. However, he also mentioned that they would not listen to these advices (Ramsay, 1904).

When all the letters sent to the Seven Churches in Anatolia are evaluated in general, it is understood that John actually had some purposes. The general purpose of the letters is to gather pro-Christian people around the teachings of Jesus for the second coming of Jesus. Apart from that, these seven letters; It has purposes such as showing bad behavior to people, showing divine judgment to people who do not repent, and declaring that believers will be rewarded by God (Kunt & Güngör, 2017).

4.8. The Use of the Seven Churches Mentioned in The Bible as Faith Tourism

As can be seen from the map, the 7 churches are located quite close to each other. Because of each churches location, a faith tourism route related to the churches can be easily created. Tours organized for this purpose are available in Turkey.

Figure 1. Map of the seven churches mentioned in the Bible.

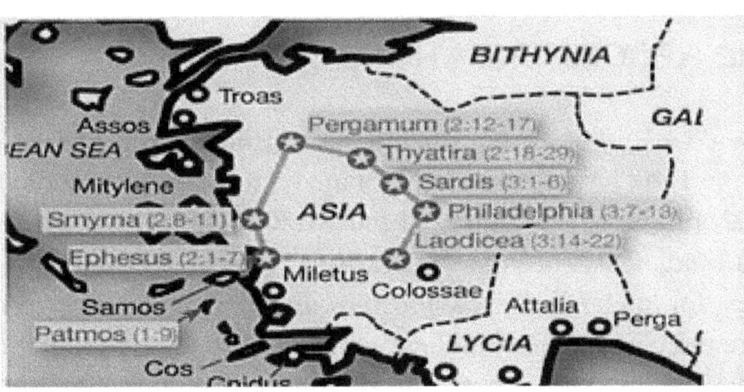

4.8.1. Examples of Tours Organized About the Seven Churches as Biblical Tours

The 7 churches tour organized by the" Epic Encounter" travel agency (in Turkey) is planned as 4 days. The content of the tour is as follows:

1.Day: Ephesus and Izmir: You will be picked up from Izmir Airport today. From there you will tour the unforgettable ruins of Ephesus (Revelation 1:11:2:1-7 Acts 18:19-28:19), including the Terrace Houses, the Ephesus Museum and the Basilica of St. John. After this day full of historical discovery, we will go to Kuşadasi for a delicious dinner and a relaxing evening at our hotel.

2. Day: Izmir and Bergama: Our first stop after breakfast will be Izmir ancient church. We will continue to Pergamon (Revelation 2: 12-17) to visit the Acropolis, the Asclepion and the Red Basilica.
3. Day: Teatira, Sart and Philadelphia: After breakfast, we will visit Akhisar, today's name of the ancient Teatira (Revelation 2: 18-29), a commercial and agricultural center on the highway between Troy and Sart Dec. After lunch, we will go to the ancient capital of the Lydians, Sart (Revelation 3: 1-6). Then we will continue to Alaşehir, where the ancient church of Philadelphia is located (Revelation 3:7-13).
4. Day: Laodicea and Pamukkale: On our last day, we will visit Hierapolis and Pamukkale, one of the most magnificent places in Turkey. We will then visit Eskihisar, where the ancient city of Laodicea is located (Revelation 3:14-22) After lunch, we will continue to Izmir, where you can catch your plane to your next adventure!

Example of 7 Churches of Revelation Tours organized by "Ephesus Shuttle" travel agency (in Turkey):

Day 1: Izmir Arrival (Dinner)
Day 2: Pergamum – Thyatira – Izmir (Breakfast - Dinner)
Day 3: Izmir – Sardis – Philadelphia – Laodicea – Hierapolis (Breakfast - Dinner)
Day 4: Ephesus – Kuşadasi (Breakfast - Dinner)
Day 5: Izmir – Home (Breakfast)

Pick up from the hotel and transfer to Izmir airport for flight back home. The end of services.

CONCLUSION AND RECOMMENDATIONS

The seven churches located in Turkey are considered sacred from the point of view of Christians because they are mentioned in the Bible. Many tours are organized for the seven churches, and the number of overnight stays varies according to the content of these tours. Taking into account the distances of the seven churches to each other, it has been seen that these tours are organized in the form of at least 3 days and 2 nights. Tours for longer periods are also available. In these tours, visits to different tourist areas in the cities where there are seven churches are also included. Although the seven churches are a faith tourism center, they can be considered as both faith tourism and cultural tourism, since they are areas where people from different religions also visit. The fact that seven churches are located in Turkey makes this a very important faith tourism region for Christians. From this point of view, Turkey should not neglect to attach importance to the promotion and protection of the seven churches at the same time by using this power effectively. Tours for the seven churches are held at all times of the year. Even if there is no research that reports problems with the carrying capacity for the seven churches in the studies conducted, the increasing popularity of the area also increases the tourist arrivals there. This, on the other hand, can lead to problems and dissatisfaction for tourists in cases where there are lack of facilities and transportation. In the same way, exceeding the carrying capacity can cause many undesirable events in the region such as environmental pollution, noise pollution, image pollution, damaging historical structures, defacing natural beauties. From this point of view, it is necessary to pay attention to these principles in the promotion of the seven churches as a faith tourism route.

REFERENCES

Abad-Galzacorta, M., Guereno-Omil, B., Makua, A., Iriberri, J. L., & Santoma, R. (2016). Pilgrimage as tourism experience: The case of the Ignatian Way. *International Journal of Religious Tourism and Pilgrimage*, *4*(4), 48–66.

Akdeniz, E., & Erön, A. (2020). Evaluations of the temple ruins in Thyateira. *Anatolian Studies*, *23*, 159–192.

Avcı, E. (2011). *Evaluation of the faith tourism potential of Izmir in terms of travel agencies.* (Thesis No. 312364) [Master's thesis, Adnan Menderes University]. YÖK National Thesis Center.

Avcı, E. (2020). Selçuk/Ephesus, the city where beliefs meet. Eda Avcı, Tolga Akcan & Devrim Ertürk (Eds.), An interdisciplinary view of a UNESCO city in Selçuk (pp. 21-36). Çizgi Bookstore.

Aydın, M. (2022). *History of religions with its main lines, history, belief and worship.* Ensar Publications.

Balcı, F. (2011). *An investigation on the relationship between psychological and subjective well-being and religious beliefs* [Master's thesis, Uludag University]. YÖK National Thesis Center.

Baranaydın, F., & Baranaydın, D. (2019). Apocalyptic churches. *Academy Journal of Social Sciences*, *6*(17), 213–228.

Barman, N. (2022). Economic activities and commercial spaces in Philadelphia, a unique provincial city of Byzantium (XI-XIV centuries). *Journal of Medieval Studies*, *5*(2), 488–497.

Budak, D. (2012). *Evaluation of the lives of saints and saints who lived in Anatolia in terms of the history of religions.* (Thesis No. 350764) [Master's thesis, Necmettin Erbakan University]. YÖK National Thesis Center.

Çakmak, T. F. (2014). *The place and importance of faith tourism in touristic destination marketing: The example of Göbekli Tepe.* [Master's thesis, Istanbul University]. YÖK National Thesis Center.

Civil, Z. (2003). *Hajj in terms of the sociology of religion.* [Master's thesis, Marmara University]. YÖK National Thesis Center. Culture and Tourism Ministry. Laodicea Church. https://kvmgm.ktb.gov.tr/TR-157979/denizli-ili-laodikeia-kilisesi-koruma-ve-onarim-calismalarina-avrupa-birligi-kulturel-miraseuropa-nostra-awards-mansiyon-odulu-verildi.html Retrieved October 9, 2023.

Culture and Tourism Ministry. (2023). *Pergamon Church.* MUZE. https://muze.gov.tr/muze-detay?SectionId=BAZ01&DistId=MRK

Culture and Tourism Ministry. (2023). *Philadelphia Church.* MANISA. https://manisa.ktb.gov.tr/TR-152050/incilde-adi-gecen-7-kiliseden-ucu.html

Culture and Tourism Ministry. (2023). *Sardis Church.* MANISA. https://manisa.ktb.gov.tr/TR-73017/artemis-mabedi.html

Culture and Tourism Ministry. (2023). *Thyateira Church.* https://www.kulturportali.gov.tr/turkiye/manisa/gezilecekyer/thyateira-akhisar-tepe-mezarligi Retrieved October 9, 2023.

Demircan, Ş. (2014). *The importance of faith tourism in local development: The case of Midyat.* [Master's Thesis, Sıtkı Koçman University]. YÖK National Thesis Center.

Derin, H. (2004). *Worship in divine religions (the example of pilgrimage in Islam and its comparison with other religions).* [Master's thesis, Uludağ University]. YÖK National Thesis Center.

Erbaş, A. (2002). Hajj in non-Islamic religions. *Sakarya University Faculty of Theology Journal, 5*, 97–121.

Erdoğan, A. (2020). The ancient city of Smyrna (Bayrakli) in the Classical Period. Olcay Pullukçuoğlu Yapucu, Aylin Ü. Erdem & Aytekin Erdoğan (Eds.), A city in pursuit of the past: İzmir (pp. 17-29). Ege University Press.

Erdoğan, O. (2013). *Philadelphia / Alaşehir in the Middle Ages.* [Master's thesis, Akdeniz University]. YÖK National Thesis Center.

Ferah, H. (2012). *Number symbolism in religions and folk beliefs.* [Master's thesis, Süleyman Demirel University]. YÖK National Thesis Center.

Gökdeniz, A. (1996). Religious travels in international tourism movements and Türkiye. *Anatolia, 7*(1), 101–103.

Gündüz, Y. (2016). *Faith tourism in terms of cultural heritage: The case of Turkey* [Master's thesis, Istanbul University]. YÖK National Thesis Center.

Güzel, F. Ö. (2010). A new dynamic within the scope of touristic product diversification: Faith tourism. *Süleyman Demirel University Visionary Journal, 2*(2), 87–100.

Harrison, V. (2006). The pragmatics of defining religion in a multi-cultural world. *International Journal for Philosophy of Religion, 59*(3), 133–152. doi:10.100711153-006-6961-z

Heidari, A., Yazdani, H. R., Saghafi, F., & Jalilvand, M. R. (2018). The perspective of religious and spiritual tourism research: A systematic mapping study. *Journal of Islamic Marketing, 9*(4), 747–798. doi:10.1108/JIMA-02-2017-0015

Işık, B. (2022). *A study to determine the faith tourism potential of seven churches in the Aegean region within the scope of touristic product diversification.* [Master's thesis, Katip Celebi University]. YÖK National Thesis Center.

Jackowski, A. (2000). Religious tourism-problems with terminology. *Peregrinus Cracoviensis, 10*, 63–74.

Jensen, J. S. (2014). *What is religion?* Routledge Taylor and Francis Group.

Kaçar, F., & Türker, N. (2020). A research on travel motivations and religious place perceptions of faith tourism visitors in the context of Hagia Sophia. *Journal of Tourism and Management, 1*(1), 40–63.

Kartal, E. (2019). *Religious belief and meaning*. [Master's thesis, Yıldırım Beyazıt University]. YÖK National Thesis Center.

Kartopu, A. (2009). *Different views on the definition of religion in the history of religions* [Master's thesis, Çukurova University]. YÖK National Thesis Center.

Kassa, T. T. (2020). *Emperor Constantine I and his place in the history of Christianity*. [Master's thesis, Uludag University]. YÖK National Thesis Center.

Keser, Y. (2019). *The seven churches mentioned in St. John's book of Revelation and their archaeological condition from past to present*. [Master's thesis, Necmettin Erbakan University]. YÖK National Thesis Center.

Köse, S. (2019). *The social importance of pilgrimage*. (Thesis No. 602373) [Master's thesis, Ondokuz Mayıs University]. YÖK National Thesis Center.

Küçük, M. A. (2015). *Religious places in Turkey in terms of faith tourism (Example of Judaism and Christianity)*. Berikan Publishing House.

Kunt, S. (2014). *The seven churches within the framework of St. John's book of Revelation and the place of these churches in the history of Christianity*. [Master's thesis, Ankara University]. YÖK National Thesis Center.

Kunt, S., & Güngör, A. İ. (2017). Seven churches within the framework of St. John's book of Revelation and the place of these churches in religious tourism in Türkiye. *Journal of Gazi University Faculty of Tourism*, *1*, 71–92.

Kurmanaliyeva, A., Rysbekova, S., Duissenbayeva, A., & Izmailov, I. (2014). Religious tourism as a sociocultural phenomenon of the present "The unique sense today is a universal value tomorrow. This is the way religions are created and values are made.". *Procedia: Social and Behavioral Sciences*, *143*, 958–963. doi:10.1016/j.sbspro.2014.07.534

Madrigal, M. (2014). *First Century Anatolian Churches*. The Bible and Archeology.

Madrigal, M. (2017). *First Century Anatolian Churches*. Academia. https://www.academia.edu/42885860/B%C4%B0R%C4%B0NC%C4%B0_Y%C3%9CZYIL_ANADOLU_K%C4%B0L%C4%B0SELER%C4%B0. Retrieved August 4, 2023.

Olcay, A., & Albuz, N. (2016). Faith tourism and its contribution to the promotion of Turkey. Mehmet Özdemir (Ed.), Media and Türkiye in international promotion (pp. 199-229). Dora Publishing House.

Ramsay, W. M. (1904). *The letters to the seven churches of Asia*. Hodder and Stoughton.

Revelation. To the Church in Ephesus. https://www.biblegateway.com/passage/?search=Revelation%202&version=NIV Retrieved July 15, 2023.

Revelation. To the Church in Laodicea. https://www.biblegateway.com/passage/?search=Revelation%203&version=NIV Retrieved August 9, 2023.

Revelation. To the Church in Pergamum. https://www.biblegateway.com/passage/?search=Revelation%202&version=NIV Retrieved August 7, 2023.

Revelation. To the Church in Philadelphia https://www.biblegateway.com/passage/?search=Revelation%203&version=NIV Retrieved August 8, 2023.

Revelation. To the Church in Sardis. https://www.biblegateway.com/passage/?search=Revelation%203&version=NIV Retrieved August 8, 2023.

Revelation. To the Church in Smyrna. https://www.biblegateway.com/passage/?search=Revelation%202&version=NIV Retrieved July 15, 2023.

Revelation. To the Church in Thyatira. https://www.biblegateway.com/passage/?search=Revelation%202&version=NIV Retrieved August 7, 2023.

Rot, E., Mikinac, K., & Bogdan, S. (2014). General characteristics of religious tourism in Croatia. *UTMS Journal of Economics (Skopje)*, *5*(1), 79–87.

Sarılar Özdemir, M. (2021). Thyateira and its coins in the Hellenistic Period. Engin Akdeniz, Barış Gür & Nihal Akıllı (Eds.), 11 years for Thyateira (articles on the results of the 2011-2021 excavations) (pp. 185-205). Dokuz Eylul University Press.

Severn, P. (2019). A history of Christian pilgrimage. *International Journal for the Study of the Christian Church*, *19*(4), 323–339. doi:10.1080/1474225X.2019.1692274

Shinde, K. A. (2010). Entrepreneurship and indigenous enterpreneurs in religious tourism in India. *International Journal of Tourism Research*, *12*, 523–535. doi:10.1002/jtr.771

Şimşek, C. (2013). Studies in the ancient city of Laodikeia. *Colloquium Anatolicum*, *12*, 15–36.

Tala, M. L., & Padurean, A. M. (2008). Dimensions of religious tourism. *Amfiteatru Economic*, *10*, 242–253.

Turkish Language Society. (2023). *Definition of religion*. Sozluk. https://sozluk.gov.tr/

Türkoğlu, S. (1999). *The story of Ephesus*. Archeology and Art Publications.

Tutku Tours. (2023). *Tour program sample*. Turku Tours. https://www.tutkutours.com/images/left/Seven-Churces-2021.pdf

Usta, K. M. (2005). *Evaluation of Iznik in terms of faith tourism potential*. [Master's thesis, Balikesir University]. YÖK National Thesis Center.

Woodward, S. C. (2004). Faith and tourism: Planning tourism in relation to places of worship. *Tourism and Hospitality Planning & Development*, *1*(2), 173–186. doi:10.1080/1479053042000251089

Yegül, F. K. (2020). Sardes: History, architecture and urbanism. *Anatolian Studies*, *23*, 135–158.

Yılmaz, A. A. (2010). *History of religions*. Alter Publishing.

Yılmaz, I. (2004). *Pergamon history and coins during the Roman Empire*. [Master's thesis, Istanbul University]. YÖK National Thesis Center.

ADDITIONAL READING

Schlaepfer, R. (2015). *The seven hope from Jesus in the book of Revelation*. Twin Lakes Church Publishing.

Wilson, M. (2010). *Biblical Turkey a guide to the Jewish and Christian sites of Asia Minor*. Ege Publishing.

KEY TERMS AND DEFINITIONS

Religion: Religion is one of the most basic elements that human beings need from the beginning of human history to the present day, from simple societies to complex ones, from the uneducated to the well-educated, from the weak to the powerful, from the young to the old.

Faith: The concept of faith seen in human beings in every period of history, from the first human to today's people, is defined as the state of being attached to something, trusting, believing in God.

Faith Tourism: Faith tourism is explained as the travels that people participate in for purposes such as fulfilling their religious duties, learning different religions or visiting holy places outside the places where they live.

Pilgrimage: The pilgrimage, which is done in different ways in almost every period of history, means visiting places and temples that are considered sacred in order to be purified from sins.

Christianity: Christianity is a great religious tradition that emerged as a small Jewish sect under the shadow of the Roman Empire in the 1st century, became the official religion of Rome in the 4th century, developed around Christ Jesus and has the largest number of members in the world today.

Diacon: Diacon is a title given to the clergy who come after the bishops and priests in the hierarchy of the clergy in Christianity.

Bishop: In Christianity, the clergy who take responsibility for a part of the Church that has been entrusted to him as the representative of Christ Jesus, in union with all other bishops, are called bishops.

Ekklesia: The word "ekklesia" in Greek is a term used to express the communities also found in Christianity.

Chapter 7
Pilgrimage Itineraries Dimensions With Focus on Kumbh Mela 2019, Prayagraj, India

Ashok Kumar Kanaujiya
Indian Institute of Information Technology, Allahabad, India

Vineet Tiwari
https://orcid.org/0000-0002-5928-8577
Indian Institute of Information Technology, Allahabad, India

ABSTRACT

Mass gatherings are events which can be spontaneous, planned sporting events or religious pilgrimages that attract people from all over the world. Kumbh Mela is the biggest divine and devout assembly on the earth. This chapter provides a holistic approach to pilgrimage itineraries dimensions which include crowd control on pilgrimage routes, pilgrimage experience, advantages, economic dimensions and safety and security of pilgrims etc. It highlights how the better transport facility, hospitality management, infrastructural development, world class amenities, proper planning and management etc. changes the pilgrims experience. The objective is to create mass gathering events free from occurrences. Although this chapter has attempted to cover various aspects of pilgrimage itineraries, still there are many other approaches that can be explored further. Hosting almost millions of pilgrims in the riverbed during Kumbh Mela is important not only for India but also for bringing together scientific forces at the international level for policy making.

INTRODUCTION

The characteristics of religious pilgrims are evolving into a more complex and diversified group, which might have an impact on the creation of new travel opportunities and economic advantages as well as

DOI: 10.4018/978-1-6684-9923-8.ch007

pose difficulties for the administration of pilgrimage sites (Liro, 2023). The Kumbh Mela is the largest gathering of people ever in the world at a given time (Baranwal et al., 2015). During the Mela season, pedestrian movements are huge in the form of crowds. Efficient management of people's movement, crowd regulation on peak days, guaranteeing the well-being of pilgrims and efficient crowd regulation planning should be the primary areas of attention. The occurrence of extensive human gatherings, such as large-scale entertainment events, religious assemblies, sports competitions, political protests, product endorsements, etc., has become increasingly frequent. The preservation of human security, safety, and regulation has become crucial and demanding (Gayathri et al., 2017).During the Kumbh Mela, individuals on a religious journey immerses themselves in the sacred river. The crowd of pilgrims taking bath in river during Kumbh Mela is shown in Figure 1.

Devotees hold the belief that by partaking in this act, they are absolved of their wrongdoings and liberated from the continuous cycle of life and death. A multitude of people attend without invitation. Participants include ascetics, holy individuals, hermits, Kalpavasi (who reside throughout the duration of the Mela and lead a modest existence as shown in Figure 2), and visitors. The festival takes place in Prayagraj (Allahabad), Haridwar, Ujjain, and Nasik on a rotational basis every four years, drawing in millions of individuals regardless of their social status, religious beliefs, or gender.

This gathering encompasses aspects of astronomy, astrology, spirituality, ceremonial traditions, and social and cultural customs, making it an incredibly enriching experience. Due to its occurrence in four different cities in India, the event showcases a diverse range of social and cultural activities, further enhancing its cultural significance. A large assembly occurs when a greater than specified quantity of individuals at a designated venue for a particular purpose come together for a predetermined duration (WHO Press, 2008). During a gathering, influenced by psychological and other significant factors, the quantity of individuals on foot starts to act in an unpredictable manner, making it difficult to control according to the standards of traffic engineering characteristics, and is referred to as a pedestrian crowd. The characteristics of the pilgrims also play a crucial role. Conventional challenges in ensuring the safety and security of pilgrims involve crowd management (regulation, directing, and redirection), planning

Figure 1. The pilgrims taking bath in river during Kumbh Mela
(Source: Prayagraj Mela Authority Report)

Figure 2. The tents of kalpavasis during Kumbh Mela
(Source: Prayagraj Mela Authority Report)

and managing peak days, proactive disaster management planning, and effective response to all emergencies and disasters. A combination of high crowd density, limited access points, inadequate crowd regulation, and insufficient knowledge of the areas and activities can lead to disastrous situations such as a stampede (Soomaroo & Murray, 2012).Some of the biggest human gatherings include the Kumbh Mela, Hajj, and the Shia pilgrimage to Karbala (Gayaṭhri et al., 2017). Makar Sankranti, Paush Purnima, Mauni Amavasya, Basant Panchami, Maghi Purnima and Maha Shivratri are the six peak days during the Kumbh Mela. It also challenges security and surveillance strategies for people coming to the event, prioritizing the needs of pilgrims or participants. This requires a design thinking approach in which the

Figure 3. Inflow of pilgrims during Kumbh Mela

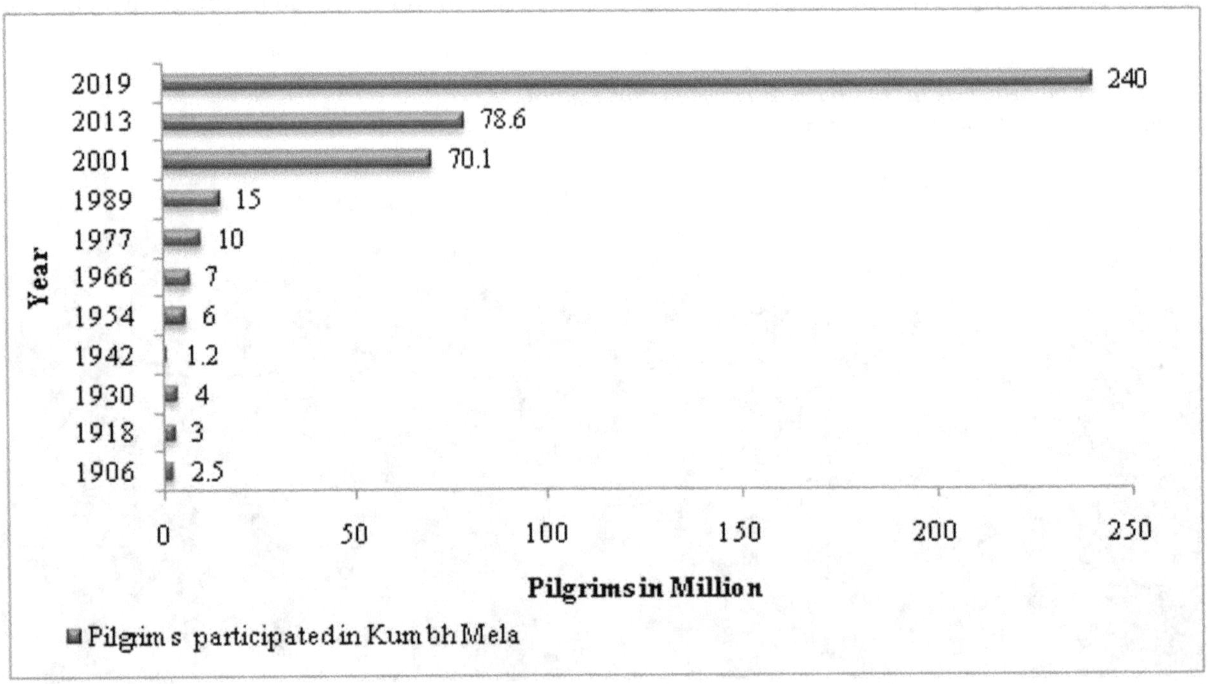

needs of the consumer come first. It relies on observing, with empathy, how people interact with their environments and employs an iterative, hands-on approach to creating innovative solutions. Over the past two decades, there has been a noticeably rising trend of pilgrim immigration, as shown in Figure 3 (Kanaujiya & Tiwari, 2022a).

LITERATURE REVIEW

The topic of crowd management, pilgrimage routes, and associated handling has been extensively studied in the global community (Almutairi et al., 2021). For efficient crowd control, all parties (stakeholders) involved in the realm of crowd management must address the requirements of large gatherings with consideration and empathy (Carter et al., 2020).There are two types of events based on the emergency management field: regular events and special events. Regular events have four unique features (Mair & Whitford, 2013; Richards et al., 2022). Firstly, regular events are planned and conducted regularly in different local communities. Secondly, regular events do not demand significant resources. Thirdly, even though regular events involve a multitude of individuals, they are recurring events. Lastly, regular events do not necessitate special permits. Examples of regular events include private gatherings, political rallies, seminars, the Magh Mela (organized every year in Prayagraj), and more. Emergency planning for typical events does not have a one-sided connection but rather a mutual connection with contingency planning for extraordinary events (Koenti, 2022). However, special occasions possess four unique aspects that define them (FEMA, 2013). They are uncommon occurrences organized within a specific locality. Special events exert a considerable burden on local resources. Moreover, they typically encompass a substantial crowd. Furthermore, special events necessitate local authorities to engage in extra measures for mitigating emergencies, preparing for emergencies, and planning for emergencies like the Maha Kumbh, Kumbh and Ardh Kumbh Melas organized at four locations (Prayagraj, Hardwar, Ujjain, and Nasik) in India in rotation. The objective of emergency management may not be effectively accomplished unless the requirements of all individuals are taken into account when overseeing its extent (Sheehy et al., 2022). In the last decade, several scholars extensively studied crowd simulation, specifically as computational capabilities (including artificial intelligence) significantly improved. One team of researchers explored crowd conduct, motion, and psychology, while the other team concentrated on different catastrophes such as fires, floods, and earthquakes. George Sidiropoulos et al. also researched the subject of crowd simulation (Sidiropoulos et al., 2020).

DATA AND METHODOLOGY

We conducted a thorough search across multiple databases for journals containing terms such as Kumbh Mela, large gathering, crowd control, pilgrimage, pilgrimage routes, pilgrimage safety, spiritual assembly, stampede, crowd management, etc. We utilized platforms such as Google Scholar, PubMed, ResearchGate, etc., and specifically prioritized peer-reviewed literature. We also examined previous reports on the Kumbh Mela published by the Prayagraj Mela Authority as well as reports released by different departments that were relevant to our research. Additionally, news articles pertaining to Kumbh Mela, Magh Mela, and other mass gatherings were utilized as sources of information and data. The approach employed in this research study is qualitative content analysis in systematic evaluations. In

Figure 4. Towards enhanced pilgrim experience
(Source: Prayagraj Mela Authority Report)

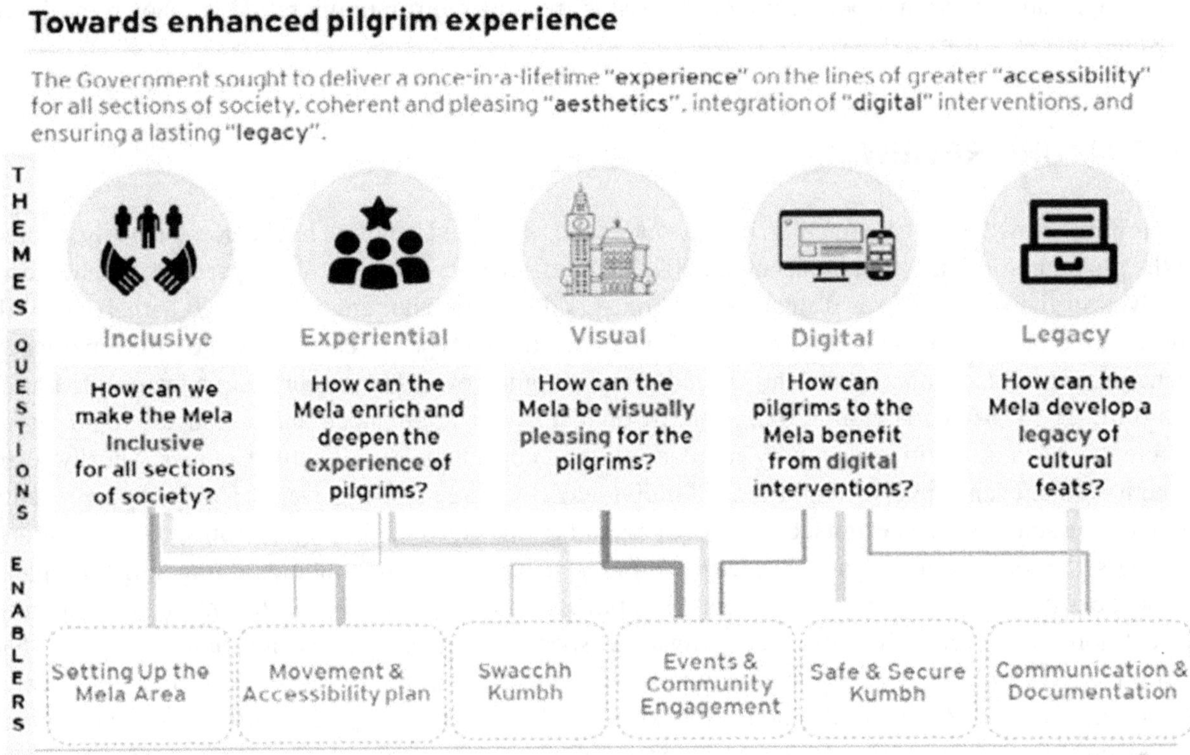

general, systematic evaluations tackle answerable and precise inquiries, while endeavoring to identify the primary problem and subsequently create an alternate strategy (Campbell et al., 2015). The main aim of organizing the mass gathering events should be to deliver a once-in-a-life time experience to the pilgrims. This should include "accessibility" for all sections of society, coherent and pleasing "aesthetics", integration of "digital" interventions, and ensuring a lasting "legacy". In the case of Kumbh Mela, this can be understood by the following Figure 4.

CAUSES FOR STAMPEDES AND DISASTERS DURING MASS GATHERING EVENTS

During mass gathering events, the various types of crowd play a crucial role in the planning of crowd management. In the Kumbh Mela, primarily pilgrims, saints, preachers, and tourists participate, arriving by means of rail, bus, air travel, private vehicles, or on foot. They are driven by their own personal motivations. Drawing from past experiences, the causes of stampedes and disasters can be categorized as structural collapses, fire accidents, crowd behavior, security issues, a lack of clear evacuation plans, and inadequate coordination among stakeholders. Structural collapses can occur due to the failure of temporary structures, bridges, or barricades on the roads. Encroachment on exit routes reduces the capacity for people to exit. Additionally, sloped gradients and slippery or muddy roads can hinder smooth pedestrian movements. In mass gathering events, incidents of fire can arise from the unavailability of fire tenders or extinguishers, illegal and unsafe electrical connections, power outages in the gathering area, short circuits, and violations of building and fire codes (Illiyas et al., 2013). These situations can lead to stampede-like scenarios. Other factors contributing to stampedes or disasters include a larger-than-expected crowd, inadequate circulation areas, more people entering than leaving, limited or no holding areas along the route, closed exits, a lack of crowd classification for seating arrangements, uncontrolled and unregulated parking of vehicles, cross movements from different directions, and limited communication through public address systems regarding arrangements or programs for the public, celebrities, or high-ranking dignitaries. The behavior of the crowd during mass gathering events also affects the flow of pedestrian movements. In the case of the Kumbh Mela, the majority of the public comes from rural areas. They arrive with their families and belongings, including food items. Sometimes they come in small groups and are reluctant to separate from the group out of fear of getting lost. This mindset influences their behavior during pedestrian movements, as they have been trained to follow the leader and walk behind them. They are unwilling to leave the group, so when there is a traffic diversion at cross points; all the group members move together, increasing the normal speed and potentially leading to stampede-like situations (Gayathri et al., 2017). Human stampedes can be triggered by a simple accident, an intentional act, or even a rumor, which can create disturbances in the crowd and alter their psychology (Illiyas et al., 2013). The crowd may attempt to forcefully enter a venue even when there are no available seats in enclosed areas. The insufficient planning, inadequate deployment of security personnel, insufficient training and briefing on crowd control, behavior, emergency plans, and new technology all hinder the ability of security personnel to effectively respond to disasters. Choosing strategic locations for Closed Circuit Television (CCTV) and public address system installations improves surveillance management capabilities. Lack of coordination and communication gaps between organizers, government officials, and other stakeholders negatively impact the immediate response to incidents.

MAJOR INCIDENCES DURING MASS GATHERING EVENTS WORLDWIDE IN THE PAST

There are number of crowd disasters occurred during the mass gathering events worldwide for example, In January 1971, Football Match at Glasgow, UK (66 deaths and 140 injured), in February 1981, Nightclub fire at Dublin, Ireland (48 deaths and 128 injured), in May 1985, Football match at Bradford, UK (53 deaths and 240 injured), in August 1988, Air show at Ramstein, Germany (67 deaths and 346 injured), in April 1989, Football match at Sheffield, UK (96 deaths and 766 injured), in July 1990, The Hajj at Mecca, Saudi Arabia(1426 deaths), in July 2001, Firework event at Akashi, Japan (160 deaths), in January 2006, The Hajj at Mecca, Saudi Arabia (346 deaths) and in November 2010, Water festival at Phnom Penh, Cambodia (347 deaths) (Soomaroo and Murray, 2012).In 2013, around 242 people were killed and 168 injured as a result of a nightclub fire in the city of Santa Maria, in the south of Brazil. According to local authorities, the fire began on stage after members of the band flared a pyrotechnic device that ignited flammable acoustic foam in the ceiling. Other reasons for the high death toll included the lack of emergency exits and the excessive number of people present. In 2015, at least 769 Muslim pilgrims were killed in Mina, Saudi Arabia, in an overcrowding incident during the Hajj pilgrimage. In 2016, at least 24 people were killed near the *Rajghat* Bridge in Varanasi, India, when many times the expected number of people was heading towards a religious retreat, causing a rush and later a stampede due to rumors that the bridge had collapsed. In 2016, around 52 to 300 people were killed during the annual Thanksgiving festival of the Oromo people in Ethiopia after police confronted protesters during Ethiopian protests, resulting in a human stampede. In 2018, at least 58 people were injured at the Bihar Sharif train station in India after an apparent earthquake caused panic among the passengers. In 2019, at least 31 pilgrims were killed and at least 100 others injured in a stampede near a major shrine in the city of Karbala, Iraq, while marking *Ashura*.

MAJOR INCIDENCES DURING THE KUMBH MELA

In Allahabad (now Prayagraj), Uttar Pradesh, India, a stampede took place during the Kumbh Mela in 1954. The tragedy occurred on Mauni Amavasya's (New Moon's) primary bathing day. That year, which was also the first Kumbh Mela after Independence, saw participation from 4-5 million people. In India, around 500 people died, according to the book Law and Order. A stampede occurred at the Allahabad railway station during the 2013 Kumbh Mela, killing 36 people as a result of a train's last-minute platform change that caused pandemonium and the rush to occur over the rail over bridge (ROB).

PILGRIMAGE ITINERARIES DIMENSIONS

Strengthening the Infrastructure for Pilgrims Safety and Security

Planning and Capacity Assessment of the Organizing Agency

There are two perspectives on this: long-term and short-term. The installation of parking, holding spaces, temporary public accommodations, facilities for food, restrooms, and water along the route, as well as the evaluation of the demand for security personnel, are all examples of short-term capacity planning. Long-term capacity planning involves the development of permanent infrastructure, which should be dependent on the event's popularity, regularity, weather, terrain, and local population. Examples of this infrastructure development include building bridges, enlarging roads, building sewage treatment facilities for managing solid waste, developing traffic junctions, electrifying roads, creating multiple routes, and constructing shuttle buses. The locations of the events also have a significant impact and demand careful preparation. As per the Police report, during Kumbh Mela, the details of security personnel deployed are given in Table 1. This was based on previous experiences and the expected participation of pilgrims in Kumbh Mela 2019. Since the police forces were deployed from various parts of the country, it was necessary to provide training for all officers and personnel before deployment.

Security and Surveillance System for Safety of Pilgrims

Security and surveillance structures are required to be reinforced via technological interventions consisting of aerial surveillance (drones), improvements in floor surveillance, good sized anti-sabotage checks, explosive detection structures, etc. Real-time intelligence evaluation and dissemination structures want to be deployed to acquire and offer intelligence to floor employees from diverse forces engaged in ensuring the safety and protection of pilgrims. Initiatives to resource the navigation of pilgrims in an easy and

Table 1. Security personnel deployed during Kumbh Mela 2019

Sl. No.	Officer/ Type of security personal	Number
1	Senior Superintendent of Police	01
2	Superintendent of Police	01
3	Additional Superintendent of Police	13
4	Deputy Superintendent of Police	50
5	Male Civil Police	6976
6	Female Civil Police	478
7	Traffic police	292
8	Mounted police	178
9	Constable from Transport Department	147
10	Local Intelligence Unit	243
11	Water Police	155
12	Home guards	6500
13	Provincial Armed constabulary (PAC)	22 Company
14	State Disaster Relief Force (SDRF)	01 Company
15	Central Armed Police Force (CAPF)	37 Company
16	National Disaster Relief Force (NDRF)	03 Company
17	Bomb Detection and disposal squad (BDDS)	02 Teams
18	Anti-Terrorist Attack Squad (ATS)	02 Teams
19	Special Task Force (STF)	02 Teams
20	National Security Guard (NSG)	01 Teams
21	Spotters	15

* Company refers 120-150 Constables.

powerful way may be taken, like the numbering of major routes, shade coding of parking lots, colored strips on pedestrian routes, variable message display (VMD) boards, and maps. Video analytics may be used for crowd control, detection of unidirectional, bi-directional, or cross-directional movements, and crowd density calculation at important locations. This can assist in head counting to evaluate the crowd density at the important route and facilitate selection for visitor diversion or activating holding regions (Pandey et al., 2020). If the area of the mass gathering event is being prepared in open regions, it's necessary to divide the location into zones and sectors. It facilitates diverting the crowd from a populated region to a less populated region. It additionally facilitates an emergency evacuation of the crowd from a troubled location. A proper circulation area should be given near the area where the main event is being organized. It helps with closer supervision of the flow of the crowd. During Kumbh Mela 2019, there has been integration of the devoted helpline number '1920' and UP Dial 100 (now Dial 112) offerings via the Integrated Command and Control Centre (ICCC) (Figure 5) for actual time and powerful reporting of any emergencies and failures that enabled the emergency responders to reach the location of the incident within brief a span of time. Effective coordination was ensured among the Kumbh Mela Police, Prayagraj District Police, and Railway Police, similarly to different specialized forces including the Anti-terrorism Squad (ATS), Special Task Force (STF), Special Intelligence, National Security Guard

Figure 5. The integrated command and control centre during Kumbh Mela, 2019
(Source: Prayagraj Mela Authority Report)

(NSG), Intelligence Bureau (IB), National Technical Research Organization (NTRO), NDRF, and Central Industrial Security Force (CISF) for protection, making plans and a complete plan for deployment of forces, deployment of era interventions, and responding to incidents (Kanaujiya & Tiwari, 2022b).

Crowd Control, Traffic Management, and Comprehensive Mobility Plan (CMP)

The guiding principle for crowd management should be balancing the demand and supply gap by limiting the crowd's entry, crowd behavior inside the venue, and crowd exit. In order to understand demand, we must first understand the crowd arrival patterns (rail, bus, airways, pedestrian, private vehicle, etc.), past historical numbers, growing popularity of the event through media campaigns, spiritual significance, type of visitors, mass arrival time span creating peak for huge gatherings (seasons, particular times of the day, weekends, festivals, holidays, etc.), advance ticket purchase, and public transportation time tab. The venue's capacity, seating capacity, and duration of the event may all be used to evaluate supply. The capacity of the venue, the seating capacity, the length of the river bank for bathing and circulation, the number of worships or prayers that can be performed every hour, the capacity of the parking and holding areas, the carrying capacity of the roads leading to the venue, the availability of public accommodations in the case of events that are planned to last for a long time, and the availability of the bare minimum facilities, such as water and toilets, can all be used to determine the supply (Ammon & Fried, 1999). Activating the supply input control mechanism is necessary if demand is high. The number of participants can be limited by enforcing a registration requirement, encouraging off-peak hours with discounts, creating distinct lines for advanced reservations, limiting celebrity or very important person (VIP) mobility on peak days, and discouraging the use of private vehicles by making public transportation abundantly available. For crowd control, areas for the movement of pedestrians, public and private transportation, etc. should be designated. Elderly and physically disabled individuals can be exempted from movement by a dedicated vehicle in the designated area. The designated area should be properly planned, and vehicle movement should be limited. Parking and waiting areas should be provided in each sector. During the Kumbh Mela 2019, pilgrims utilized various modes of transportation, such as public transportation, private transportation, pedestrian movement, and movement on water, within and outside the Mela area. Separate initiatives were planned for peak and non-peak days. The capacity of roads was increased by widening them and constructing alternate routes. The goal was to ensure that pilgrim movements were unidirectional. Parking lots were created along the roadside leading to the Mela area, designed to minimize walking distance. Basic amenities were provided, including CCTV cameras at the parking areas. Traffic diversion plans were coordinated with neighboring districts and States. Holding areas and diversion schemes were proposed for pedestrians approaching the Sangam (main area). The concept of unidirectional movement was implemented in the festival area to manage the crowd. The mobility plan for the Kumbh Mela 2019 was inclusive and aimed to provide pilgrims with an enhanced user experience based on the following key features:

- Integration of different modes of transportation for last mile connectivity (Train, shuttle buses, electric rickshaws etc.)
- Sufficient physical infrastructure (Construction of overpasses, rail overpasses, rail underpasses, floating bridges, designated parking areas, temporary bridges etc.)
- One-way movements of vehicles (Avoiding vehicles crossing paths)
- Dispersal of traffic throughout the Mela area (Not all traffic directed towards Sangam area but redirected to different parts of the festival by diverting traffic)
- Planning that prioritizes pedestrians (No vehicle zones during peak days)
- Emphasis on emergency preparedness planning (Designated parking areas and alternate routes)

This mobility strategy was formulated with the input of Government authorities (Prayagraj Mela Authority, Prayagraj District Administration, and City council), enforcing agencies (Prayagraj police department, Kumbh Mela police department, and Transport department), Line departments (Public works department, National highways authority of India, State bridge corporation, City council) and supporting agencies (Health department, Power corporation, Water department, and Transport department). This resulted in the expansion of nine National Highways, the construction of nine ROBs, the construction of 22 Pontoon bridges, the development of 95 parking areas, and the development of a 300-person airport terminal. Prayagraj has nine railway stations, which play a major role during Kumbh Mela. The biggest challenge for railway stations was the peak-day influx of pilgrims. Indian Railways prepared a plan that included increasing the capacity of railway stations, running around 800 special trains, developing holding areas with basic amenities outside every functional railway station, unidirectional movement over bridges at stations, fixing signage boards, etc. During Kumbh Mela around 5500 buses were planned by the Uttar Pradesh State Road Transport. A three Color traffic scheme was planned for the crowd in the Mela area. It was to be implemented outside the Mela areas by making traffic diversion. A mechanism can be developed to control the huge flow of crowds as shown in Figure 6.

Figure 6. Crowd control mechanism
(Source: National Disaster Management Authority)

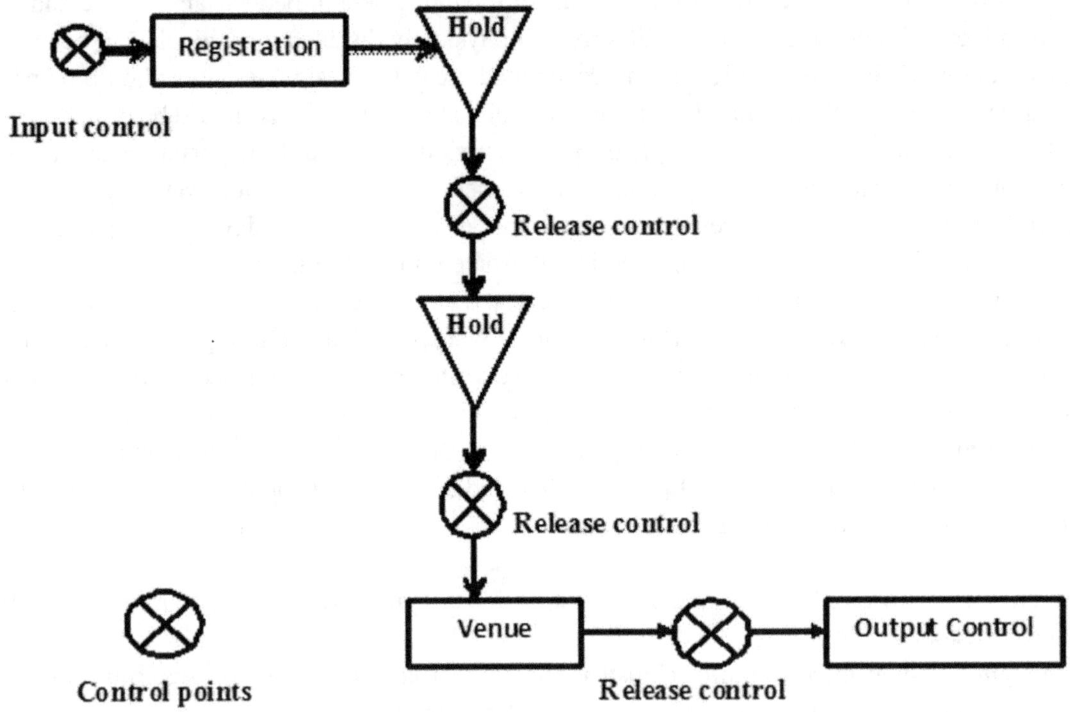

Participation of Stakeholders

Participants, authorities, voluntary groups, Non governmental Organizations (NGOs), welfare committees, etc. should promote active involvement in events for the purpose of unity, prompt decision-making or response, and improved coordination. They have a significant role in non-policing activities such as organizing queues, assisting the elderly and physically challenged individuals, maintaining continuous communication, and urging the crowd to remain patient and calm in case of any issues. Multiple stakeholders must collaborate to attain effective supplementation (Persson & Granberg, 2021). The roles and responsibilities of other individuals or groups with a vested interest should be clearly defined and incorporated into the plan, but they should operate under a unified control system. Crowd management is a collaborative effort, and the successful management of a large-scale event depends on the cooperation and communication among all stakeholders (Martella et al., 2017). Delivering accurate information promptly to the media (electronic, print, and social) aids in curbing the spread of false news among the public. A designated individual should be appointed to supply verified information to the media following any incident, and they should be readily available to media personnel. They should possess all pertinent details concerning the event. The media plays a crucial role in disseminating accurate information about any incident, educating the public, providing feedback on activities, and offering suggestions for improving disaster management and relief efforts.

Risk Evaluation, Readiness, and Planning

Hazard evaluation, readiness, and strategizing possible hazards and origins of calamities must be recognized. The organizer of events should take into account the origins of the previous mishaps, if any, the population of the region, the accessibility of resources, constraints, stress points, possibilities of inundation, widespread disease conditions, etc. After identifying the hazards, the risk should be evaluated. It should include the likelihood of occurrence of any incident, its consequences and seriousness, estimated duration of occurrence, etc. The risk factors, their signs, and management during mass gathering events are given in detail, as shown in Table 2 (Kanaujiya & Tiwari, 2022b).

ICT's (Information and Communication Technology) Role in Mass Communication and Information Dissemination

The analysis of previous events and calamities indicates that the absence of communication or inadequate essential communication with the public increased the severity of damages. The continuous addressing of the public in line through a public address system enhances their patience. People become less panicked, and in cases of stampede, they change their direction while moving. Proper communication regarding any incidents or disasters reduces the curiosity of the public and prevents them from engaging in undesirable behavior. It is a very useful tool for managing and organizing crowds at public transportation locations such as railway stations, bus stations, airports, and pre-booking taxi stands. Providing continuous information about traffic diversions, parking area locations and their availability, distance to the venue, and the starting time of events helps visitors obtain accurate information. Proper dissemination of information is also essential among various stakeholders such as event organizers, government officials, security personnel, voluntary organizations, the media, and local residents. The efficient functioning of command and control is the most important aspect of crowd management. Information and communication technologies help improve the crowd experience and crowd control (Yamin, 2019). The most common technologies include geographical information systems (GIS), short messaging services (SMS), radio frequency identification (RFID) tags, drones, registration database surveys, closed circuit television (CCTV), image processing, crowd simulation, and the use of fog and cloud computing (Abisen et al., 2018). A registration database should be implemented to capture demographic details (gender, age, location, etc.) of the visitors, but it has limitations when there is a large influx of people in a short period of time. ICCC served as the central hub during Kumbh Mela 2019. Its objective was to unite the Mela region with the city region. It proved immensely beneficial to the police department in maintaining law and order and managing the crowds with the help of 1103 CCTV cameras that were installed at 310 strategic positions. These positions encompassed the Mela area, parking area, railway stations, solid waste management area, and city area. The video feed received from the cameras deployed in the Mela area was utilized for head count mapping, analysis of crowd patterns, identification of suspicious individuals, assisting pilgrims by providing updated information on variable message displays, identifying incoming and outgoing traffic in the city and Mela area to prevent stampedes, managing traffic, and analyzing traffic congestion patterns, among other things.

Table 2. Risk factors, their signs and management

Sl. No.	Category	Indicators
1.	Fire Protection	• Number of fire stations, extinguishers, and tenders and distance among them • Average response time • Average time for getting a fire alarm or information from the control center to fire protection team • Fire safety drills
2.	Emergency Health Services	• Number of Ambulances and Air ambulances • Number of advanced life support ambulances • Trauma care facilities • Number of Medical personnel (Doctors, Paramedics etc.) • Average response time • Number of First aid kits availability • Availability of life saving drugs, vaccines, oxygen cylinders etc. • Identification of dedicated Green corridor
3.	Sanitation Facilities	• Dustbins availability and distance between two dustbins • Toilets and urinals in proportion to visitors (separate for men and women) • Timing of picking up garbage and sweeping of roads • Approach to the venue and exit paths are safe, clean and encroachment free
4.	Risk Assessment of Potential Hazard Conditions	• Frequency of crowd and crowd density • Frequency of hazard occurrence, severity, difficulty of detection or control
5.	Emergency Evacuation	• Availability of public address system • Integrated Command and Control Center (ICCC) monitoring • Response time in implementation of emergency exit plan • Response time of implementation of traffic diversion scheme
6.	General Information	• Signage • Information regarding map of area having layout, location of stay, food, information kiosks, entry and exit points, holding areas, police stations, lost and found office, shopping areas, places of interest at venue, medical facilities, local transport, toilets, urinals, parking, peak days, non-peak days, etc. are available online and publicized and given to all security personnel • Variable Message Display and its effective use to communicate masses • Clear guidelines for holding and releasing the visitors from holding areas. • Contact details of event organizers and helpline numbers
7.	Integrated Command and Control Center (ICCC)	• ICCC getting feed from all CCTV installed in Mela areas and outside Mela areas • Able to identify crowd density and its actual location • Able to identify crowd velocity and its actual location • Able to identify the cross pedestrian movements • Properly guided in case of emergency to whom to be contacted • Able to identify crowd density at holding areas to restrict uncontrolled flow movements • Able to identify vehicle density at parking areas to trigger for the activation of the another parking location • Drone monitoring for observing the overall crowd in the case the crowd spread is too big
8.	Roles and Responsibilities and Training	• Roles and responsibilities are clearly identified for officer, security personnel and various stakeholders • Behavioral training are given to each security personnel and NGOs and other stakeholders are also trained for disaster processes • Timely mock drills and safety audits have done
9	Unidirectional Movement Policy	• Ensured unidirectional movement on roads, bridges, flyovers. • No cross movement or intersection of visitors at any locations
10	Coordination	• Coordination between multiple departments has been done • Decisions taken are well documented and communicated • In case of emergency, officers are designated for coordination • Review meetings at regular intervals
11.	Past Incidences/ Disasters	• Previous disasters and their causes are identified • Possible disasters are identified
12.	Documentation	• Communication plan (having Key contacts) • Site plan and master plan are documented • Process of managing hazards • Documentation of events for future • Brief history of any recurring Incidences

Experiences

Cultural Immersion, Spiritual and Personal Growth

Pilgrimage routes provide individuals with opportunities for self-reflection, meditation, and spiritual growth. Walking or traveling along these routes allows pilgrims to disconnect from their daily lives and connect with their faith or beliefs on a deeper level. Religious tourism embodies the past, the genuineness, the personality, and the enduring nature of devoted societies, in a distinctive manner. The gathered tangible and intangible aspects of religious customs depict an intricate portrayal that not only unveils religious legacy but also a vibrant cultural past, multicultural intersections, and the narratives and legends of dedicated travelers and indigenous societies (Tsironis, 2022).Geographically, pilgrimage sites can be divided into three categories: (i) water sites, which are typically associated with sacred immersion on auspicious occasions; (ii) shrines dedicated to specific deities, which are visited by pilgrims of specific sects or with specific needs; and (iii) Kshetra, sacred territory, which traveling along brings special merit (Singh & Rana, 2023). Kumbh Mela is a sacred festival of the Hindu religion that has been observed for centuries (Mehrotra & Vera, 2015). The Kumbh Mela provides an understanding of Hinduism and serves as a representation of spirituality in both thought and practice. Throughout the years, it has attracted millions of individuals from across the globe, irrespective of their beliefs, social status, religion, or gender (Verma & Sarangi, 2019). Philosophers, saints, gurus, preachers, scholars, mahants, aspirants, sadhus, and saints from various sects and regions of India and abroad come together to engage in spiritual discussions, debates, and the sharing of knowledge and beliefs. Pilgrimages hold significance in all faiths. For Muslims, the pilgrimage to Mecca and Medina holds immense spiritual benefits, while for Christians and Jews, a journey to Jerusalem is a lifelong aspiration. In Hinduism, the concept of Kumbh Mela originated from the Vedic worship of rivers, which are associated with water in the hymn "Nadistuti". It is believed that the riverbanks during the Kumbh Mela absorb the sins and sorrows of countless pilgrims. The holy rivers Ganga (Prayagraj and Haridwar), Godavari (Nasik), and Kshipra (Ujjain)acquire their divine nature during the auspicious planetary positions of the Kumbh period. Temporary tents are set up to accommodate approximately two million pilgrims. The peak of the festival spans over six days, while the entire Kumbh Mela in 2019 lasted for 49 days. One of the busiest events during the Kumbh Mela was the Mauni Amavasya, which was attended by around 50 million pilgrims. Estimated pilgrims' participation during Kumbh Mela 2019 on peak days is shown in Figure 7.

The Kumbh Mela is celebrated at different locations (i.e., Prayagraj, Haridwar, Ujjain, and Nasik) depending upon the positions of planet. The Kumbh Mela in each location takes place every twelfth year. The essence of the Kumbh Mela is for pilgrims to bathe at certain sacred spots on certain auspicious days. A holy bath in the river Ganges is of great importance. It is believed that it washes away all the sins and ends the cycle of rebirth and death. Some of the bathing days are designated as royal or peak days. These include Makar Sankranti, Paush Purnima, Mauni Amavasya, Basant Panchami, Maghi Purnima, and Mahashivratri Snan (bathing). Akhadas translates literally into circle or core and refers to monastic schools where students of a sect were trained. There are 13 Akhadas divided into three categories: Shaiva, Vaishnava, and Advaita. Each Akhada has their own deity and weapon, and they do shahi snan (royal bath). Their procession is called peshwai, in which they move with their groups on horses, and lavish carriages into the Mela area (Figure 8).

Figure 7. Estimated pilgrims participated on peak days during Kumbh Mela 2019

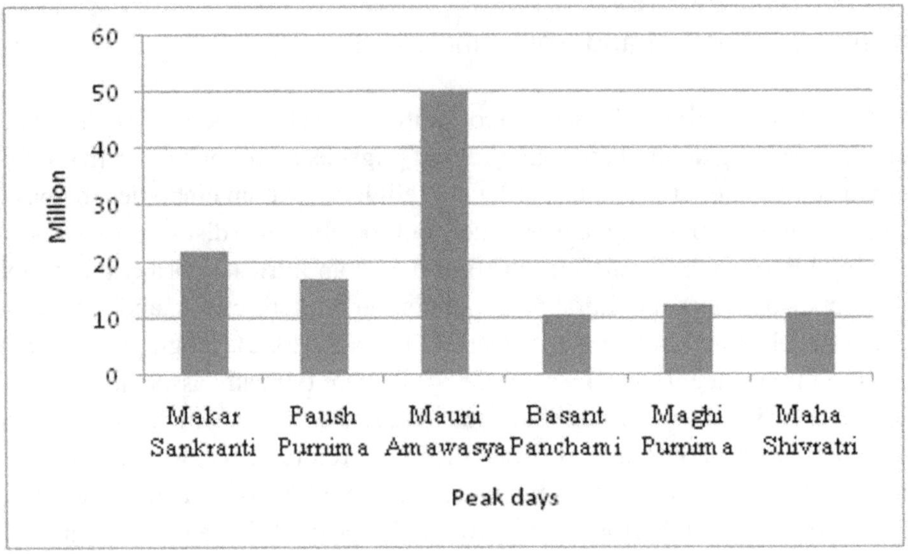

Figure 8. Procession of Peshwai
(Source: Prayagraj Mela Authority Report)

Crowd Psychology and Its Behavior During Mass Movement

S. Karthika et al. examined the matter of accessibility to large religious gatherings (Karthika et al., 2022). They hypothesized that the effectiveness of managing a large crowd in a specific scenario was greatly impacted by the conduct of different pedestrians. They verified that pedestrians preferred to select their preferred paths based on not just the distance to a specific destination but also the direction. Among several suggestions, these researchers emphasized the significance of temporary road shutdowns to avoid the influx of people into mass religious journeys. The primary element of crowd management planning is to recognize the behavior of participants. Individual behavior in a crowd is every so often prompted by the behavior of others. The people inside the crowd can also act in a different way than if they had been on their own. This is essentially decided with the aid of the form of occasion, whether or not it's religious, a teenager's festival, a sports activity occasion, a song concerts, a political gatherings, a unique precise day and time occasion primarily based on astrology, etc. Political (instability of government, inner conflicts inside the kingdom, terrorist activities, violence-affected regions, etc.) and geographical conditions (open or closed space, simple or hilly terrain, throughout the river course, season, etc.) of venue additionally have an effect on the crowd management for protection and surveillance. Based on the previous experiences, know-how, and incidences, one ought to try and decide the form of crowd predicted, i.e., age, social structure, gender, locality, traffic coming with the aid of rail, bus, non-public vehicle, airline or pedestrian, and their anticipated numbers. Promotion of packages with the aid of media, organizers, or every so often unfastened rail or bus carrier centers attracts a lot of human beings, and it ought to additionally be thought about for the estimation of human beings. For powerful crowd control, the importance of the traffic ought to be recognized, whether or not it's for political, economic, spiritual, religious, entertainment, social, etc. In the case of Kumbh Mela, the traffic mainly includes saints, kalpavasis (who remain for the duration of the complete Kumbh Mela duration) people of rural background, etc. Most people come with a single aim: to take a dip in the river and return. On peak days of bathing, a huge crowd attempts to attain the Sangam (the confluence of three rivers, i.e., Ganga, Yamuna and mystical Saraswati) to take a dip for a unique duration of time. The people come in small groups with one leader and all their belongingness. They follow the leader and move according to him because, due to the huge crowd, there is always a fear of being lost. The illegal actions of a few people can result in larger numbers following them. There is also a need to establish a lost and found system in each sector with an LED screen displayed in each sector. This should be connected with the state-of-the art communication system. Major locations should be geo-mapped and plotted on Google maps to make it easier for security personnel and visitors to find them. The crowd density during Kumbh Mela 2019 can be understood from Figure 9.

Figure 9. The crowd density during Kumbh Mela 2019
(Source: Prayagraj Mela Authority Report)

Advantages

Tourism and Local Economy

Local artisans and craftspeople often produce religious or cultural items that pilgrims may purchase as souvenirs. This supports local handicraft industries and preserves traditional craftsmanship. Pilgrimage routes can stimulate local economies by attracting tourists who spend money on accommodation, food, transportation, and souvenirs. This can lead to the development of infrastructure, job opportunities, and overall economic growth in the surrounding areas. Cultural legacy signifies one of the most crucial assets for advancement procedures, and cultural routes as cultural constituents possess the capability to rejuvenate and promote the historical region in a sustainable manner by encouraging cultural tourism (Al-Jaberi & Hasan, 2022).There are two different aspects of religious tourism in India. One is the faith of domestic tourists who have a spiritual attachment to the destination and possess religious beliefs. It may include pilgrimages, missionary travel, leisure vacations, monastery visits, faith-based camps, etc., while others are based on the faith and beliefs of the foreign tourists who have desired goals and objectives. They usually form a strong belief that all their problems will get solved, so they plan religious tourism. It is thought that the sacred ceremonies performed at Tirth will inevitably produce spiritual advantages. Tirth in Hinduism is the divine or profound pursuit of all individuals in the form of self-realization, and in that sense, it is considered to be at the pinnacle of our hierarchy of necessities. To attract and facilitate tourists during the Kumbh Mela, the State government invested around 40910 million rupees in permanent and temporary infrastructure. Around 683 projects were conceptualized, and in around 3200 hectares of the Mela area were developed. During the Kumbh 2019, 240 million devotees took part, with 1.03 million international tourists among them. In comparison, the Kumbh Mela 2013 saw 78.6 million pilgrims, including 0.35 million foreign visitors. This marked the highest attendance in the history of the Mela, surpassing the annual number of tourists Uttar Pradesh received between 2014 and 2017. According to official data from the Uttar Pradesh tourism department, the state welcomed a total of 187.1 million tourists in 2014, with 184.2 million being Indian and 2.9 million being foreign visitors. In 2015, the number rose to 209.6 million tourists, including 206.5 million Indians and 3.1 million foreigners. The records also showed that in 2016, 216.7 million tourists explored different parts of the state, with 213.5 million being Indian and 3.2 million being foreign visitors. In 2017, the state received a total of 237.5 million tourists, consisting of 233.9 million Indians and 3.78 million foreigners. However, in 2018, the number increased to 288.8 million tourists, with 285 million being Indian and 3.8 million being foreign visitors to Uttar Pradesh (Kanaujiya & Tiwari, 2023a).

Health and Wellness

Walking or traveling along pilgrimage routes encourages physical activity and outdoor engagement, contributing to better health and wellness for pilgrims. The mental and emotional benefits of the journey also play a role in overall well-being. There isn't enough focus on the limitations of involvement in large gatherings for physical health. There is proof of the beneficial impacts of engagement on psychological well-being across a range of cultural situations. Everyone agrees that it's crucial for attendees to have a strong sense of social connection when they're at an event. The research discussed above has clear policy implications, one of which is that such involvement ought to be promoted. The possibility of increasing social inclusion at some of the best-attended events in the world, such as music festivals and meetings focused on health and wellness, should be investigated by policymakers and practitioners. The mass gatherings involvement can have positive psychological and physiological effects to the extent that a shared identity is felt. The common perception of group dynamics in large meetings is not pleasant, and misconceptions like this simply prevent practical use. Our cognition changes from idiosyncratic to group-based when we identify in terms of social group membership rather than as an individual. The wide-ranging effects of this alteration in the basis for cognition include the likelihood that conducts changes when social identities change in individuals. Mass gatherings occur when there is shared attention and the opportunity for participants to see one another embodied experience. Participants can coordinate their conduct at large meetings to enable them to live out their identity-related values and beliefs. When people go to such large meetings, it's less to form a community and more to celebrate the one that already exists. Through involvement in youth groups, for instance, teenagers are faced with the difficult challenge of developing a sense of who they are and finding a place in a complicated social milieu. Other research has looked at the applicability of public involvement to the unpleasant issues brought on by the unexpected and sudden trauma of death (e.g., the suicide of a loved one). This requires the attention towards the well being of the pilgrims by providing the hygienic and pollution free environment. The water quality of the Ganga and Yamuna rivers based on the Water Quality Index (WQI) during, before, and after the Kumbh Mela 2019 has been discussed in detail (Kanaujiya & Tiwari, 2023b). The water condition was greatly impacted as a result of the different activities of the Kumbh Mela. The water condition of the Ganga and Yamuna rivers, as per the main water quality standards, was suitable solely for bathing purposes throughout the Kumbh Mela 2019.Research on how the general population reacts to terrorist attacks also highlights the importance of large-scale meetings in trauma management since participation may foster a welcoming sense of community and optimism. Following the COVID-19 pandemic, there should be a focus on restricting visitors on peak days during mass gathering events (Quadri et al., 2021).The non-following of the COVID-19 protocol all through Magh Mela-2021 had a large effect on the entire variety of instances mentioned in Prayagraj. Kumbh Mela-2021 at Haridwar had an additional effect on the surge of COVID-19 instances in Uttarakhand and India (Kanaujiya & Tiwari, 2023a).

Preservation of Heritage

Pilgrimage routes often pass through historical sites, monuments, and landmarks. The influx of pilgrims and tourists can contribute to the maintenance and preservation of these cultural heritage sites. The Kumbh Mela is more than a pilgrimage. Due to a lot of diversity in demography and geography in India, It attracts people of different natures and thinking to visit for tourism purposes. There is a vast scope of eco-tourism, spiritual tourism, historical tourism, medical tourism, religious tourism, adventure tourism, beach tourism, cultural tourism, and wildlife tourism in India. When individuals make visits to different places for religious purposes, it is called religious pilgrimage, but when it involves entertainment activities, it is called religious tourism. There are a number of religious places in India that are well known for their own unique characteristics. The Kumbh Mela offers a comprehensive view of the diverse beliefs and customs of the Hindu lifestyle. It is a commemoration of a time-honored ritual where immersing one in the sacred river is highly valued. This riverside celebration and the city that springs up around them attract millions of people, and in fact, the attendance is growing exponentially with each Kumbh. The pilgrims participate in religious discourse available there. They listen to the preaching of saints and do *kalpwas* (living a simple life during the Kumbh Mela period in camps). In earlier Kumbh mostly elderly

Figure 10. Examples of Paint My City campaign
(Source: Prayagraj Mela Authority Report)

people came to the Kumbh with the belief that they would be free from cycle of rebirth and death, but in the twenty-first century, both rural and urban elites and commoners have embraced the Kumbh Mela. The government's initiatives regarding providing facilities, amenities, and infrastructure promoted the religious tourism. For the first time in the Kumbh Mela, a Sanskriti gram and a Kala gram were developed to attract the pilgrims. Sanskriti gram was a perfect reflection of rich cultural heritage, while Kala gram was designed to showcase distinctive Indian artwork. Different cultural events were organized to exhibit the rich and diverse cultural heritage of the country. To add to the grandeur of Kumbh 2019 and make the Mela area more vibrant, over 25 temporary thematic gates were built with themes of Indian culture, tradition, and socio-religious factors. Around 1.73 million sq. ft. of street art undertaken under the Paint My City campaign as shown in Figure 10.

Economic Dimensions

Hospitality and Services

Communities along pilgrimage routes often establish accommodations, restaurants, and other services to cater to the needs of pilgrims. This creates job opportunities and stimulates local businesses. During the Kumbh Mela 2013, there was a minimum of 10 times more profit made from the initial investment (both permanent and temporary). However, during the Kumbh Mela 2019, it was anticipated to increase to a value of 1,200,000 million rupees, compared to the government's expenditure of 42,000 million rupees. In general, it was projected that there would be 60,000 million job opportunities, including 25,000 million jobs in the hospitality sector (such as tour operators, guides, airlines, hotels, local transportation, emergency services, and support systems). Additionally, around 8,500 million jobs were expected to be created in the medical and ecotourism sectors (Online document, 2019).

Transportation Infrastructure Development

The need to accommodate pilgrims can drive infrastructure development in areas that might otherwise have been overlooked. This includes the construction of roads, rest stops, and accommodations. Improved transportation infrastructure, such as roads, bridges, and public transportation, may be developed or upgraded to facilitate pilgrim travel. This can have long-term benefits for both locals and tourists. For the Kumbh Mela 2019,around 5,500 religious groups and organizations participated. There was the involvement of different departments i.e. Central, State, Indian Army, Indian Air Force, etc. for execution of the projects like broadening and beautification of roads, effective solid waste management, development of ROBs (road over bridges) and RUB(road under bridges),beautification of the city, clean toilets for all traffic junctions, electrification of all roads, drinking water at all the identified places, and development of parks and green zones in the city. For Kumbh Mela 2019,a consolidated plan was developed for the development of the city and Mela area to facilitate the pilgrims. An Integrated Command and Control Centre (ICCC) was established for crowd management through CCTV. The Integrated Traffic Management System (ITMS) was developed for traffic control and regulation. Around 500 shuttle buses and 1000 e-rickshaws were deployed on pilgrims' routes for facilitation. The aircraft movement was much higher than the routine schedule. The aircraft movement's details are given in Table 3.

Table 3. The aircraft movement at Prayagraj airport during Kumbh Mela period

Month and Year	Description	Aircraft movements (in numbers)			Passengers (in numbers)		
		Arrival	Departure	Total	Disembarked	Embarked	Total
Jan 2019	Scheduled	162	163	325	16063	15389	31452
	Non scheduled	35	32	67	206	130	336
Feb 2019	Scheduled	167	168	335	18546	17930	36476
	Non scheduled	87	86	173	488	358	846
Mar 2019	Scheduled	151	151	302	13240	13297	26537
	Non scheduled	42	43	85	28	126	254
Apr 2019	Scheduled	87	87	174	9102	7593	16695
	Non scheduled	40	40	80	119	114	233

The railway department runs 800 special trains in addition to scheduled trains for the pilgrims coming from different states of the country. The railway has commissioned 41 projects at a cost of 7000 million rupees and handled around 3.3-3.5 million pilgrims during Kumbh Mela 2019.

Cultural Exchange

Economic interactions between pilgrims and local communities foster cultural exchange, leading to the sharing of traditions, cuisine, and practices. Pilgrimage routes attract people from all walks of life who share a common purpose. This creates a sense of camaraderie and community among pilgrims as they bond over their shared experiences and stories. Pilgrimage routes often pass through regions rich in history, architecture, and cultural significance. Travelers can experience diverse traditions, customs, and landmarks that have stood the test of time. Pilgrimage routes can promote interfaith dialogue, tolerance, and understanding by bringing people of different backgrounds together on a shared journey. This can contribute to peaceful coexistence and harmony. Many pilgrimage routes are inclusive, welcoming people from various faiths and backgrounds. This fosters interfaith dialogue, tolerance, and understanding.

CONCLUSION

The Kumbh Mela is a custom that has its origins deeply embedded in the customs of the nation and Hinduism. It is also a significant occasion that draws in large numbers of people and generates income. Pilgrimage routes give pilgrims experiences of spiritual and personal growth. It enhances local tourism and the economy with preservation of heritage. It gives a boost to the growth of tertiary industries. Huge mass gatherings always present a challenge to the organizing agency. Planning for crowd control at the biggest mass gathering event is mostly hampered by the actual evaluation of attendance. In the case of a gathering like the Kumbh Mela, when a sizable proportion of pilgrims come from lower socioeconomic backgrounds and have little experience with the internet, registration for all guests is not practicable. Every participant wants to go to the main location of the event, i.e. the confluence area at Sangam in the Kumbh Mela, which is decided based on the flow of the river. As a result, venue management and crowd control are constrained by this unique location-based mass gathering event. The evaluation of crowd density in real time at a given area is made possible through crowd simulation, picture processing, RFID tags, crowd modeling, and image processing. However these techniques are quite expensive for huge crowds and have the possibility of picture duplication. When tents are built along the riverbed, the open-ended venue, makes security and surveillance control more difficult. Kumbh Mela's rising popularity creates a considerable problem for crowd control and security control. Various mass gathering events are arranged worldwide. They can exchange their expertise with one another in various fields such as event organization, novel health management initiatives, crowd control, etc. Sharing experiences and records may aid in the creation of guidelines, problem-specific solutions, and a unified strategy for public health during large gatherings. This can encourage further research and examination to discover innovative methods and practical approaches to managing public mass gatherings. This could assist the government in formulating enhanced public policies that can be efficiently implemented and enforced during large-scale events. This facilitates the shift from a reactive to a preventive model.

REFERENCES

Abi Sen, A. A., Eassa, F. A., Jambi, K., & Yamin, M.AbiSen. (2018). Preserving privacy in internet of things: A survey. *International Journal of Information Technology : an Official Journal of Bharati Vidyapeeth's Institute of Computer Applications and Management*, *10*(2), 189–200. doi:10.100741870-018-0113-4

Al-Jaberi, Z. A., & Hasan, S. A. (2022). Reviving the Cultural Route and Its Role in the Sustainability of Historical Areas-Kerbala as a Case Study. *International Journal of Sustainable Development and Planning*, *17*(6), 1737–1746. doi:10.18280/ijsdp.170607

Almutairi, M. M., Yamin, M., Halikias, G., & Abi Sen, A. A. (2021). A framework for crowd management during COVID-19 with artificial intelligence. *Sustainability (Basel)*, *14*(1), 303. doi:10.3390u14010303

Ammon, R. Jr, & Fried, G. (1999). Crowd management practices. *Journal of Convention & Exhibition Management*, *1*(2-3), 119–150. doi:10.1300/J143v01n02_05

Baranwal, A., Anand, A., Singh, R., Deka, M., Paul, A., Borgohain, S., & Roy, N. (2015). Managing the earth's biggest mass gathering event and wash conditions: Maha Kumbh mela (India). *PLoS Currents*, 7. doi:10.1371/currents.dis.e8b3053f40e774e7e3fdbe1bb50a130d PMID:25932345

Campbell, J. M., Klugar, M., Ding, S., Carmody, D. P., Hakonsen, S. J., Jadotte, Y. T, & Munn, Z. (2015). Diagnostic test accuracy: Methods for systematic review and meta-analysis. *JBI Evidence Implementation*, *13*(3), 154–162. PMID:26355602

Carter, H., Drury, J., & Amlôt, R. (2020). Social identity and intergroup relationships in the management of crowds during mass emergencies and disasters: Recommendations for emergency planners and responders. *Policing. Journal of Policy Practice*, *14*(4), 931–944.

Federal Emergency Management Agency (FEMA). (2013). *Special Events Contingency Planning for Public Safety Agencies*. Emergency Management Institute.

Gayathri, H., Aparna, P. M., & Verma, A. (2017). A review of studies on understanding crowd dynamics in the context of crowd safety in mass religious gatherings. *International Journal of Disaster Risk Reduction*, *25*, 82–91. doi:10.1016/j.ijdrr.2017.07.017

Illiyas, F. T., Mani, S. K., Pradeepkumar, A. P., & Mohan, K. (2013). Human stampedes during religious festivals: A comparative review of mass gathering emergencies in India. *International Journal of Disaster Risk Reduction*, *5*, 10–18. doi:10.1016/j.ijdrr.2013.09.003

Kanaujiya, A. K., & Tiwari, V. (2022a). Are mass gathering events hot spot for spreading of infectious diseases: The Kumbh Mela Experience. *Journal of Scientific and Industrial Research*, *81*(11), 1162–1172.

Kanaujiya, A. K., & Tiwari, V. (2022b). Crowd management and strategies for security and surveillance during the large mass gathering events: The Prayagraj Kumbh Mela 2019 Experience. *National Academy Science Letters*, *45*(3), 263–273. doi:10.100740009-022-01114-w PMID:35431383

Kanaujiya, A. K., & Tiwari, V. (2023a). The statistical analysis to find correlation between mass gathering event and COVID-19 pandemic outbreak: The Prayagraj Magh Mela 2021 experience. *Proceedings of the National Academy of Sciences. India. Section A, Physical Sciences*, *93*(1), 107–111. doi:10.100740010-022-00795-8

Kanaujiya, A. K., & Tiwari, V. (2023b). Water quality analysis of River Ganga and Yamuna using water quality index (WQI) during Kumbh Mela 2019, Prayagraj, India. *Environment, Development and Sustainability*, 1–22. doi:10.100710668-023-02907-9

Karthika, P. S., Kedar, V., & Verma, A. (2022). A walk accessibility-based approach to assess crowd management in mass religious gatherings. *Journal of Transport Geography*, *104*, 103443. doi:10.1016/j.jtrangeo.2022.103443

Koenti, I. J. (2022). Disaster Management Using a Contingency Approach in the Special Region of Yogyakarta. *IOP Conference Series. Earth and Environmental Science*, *1030*(1), 012017. doi:10.1088/1755-1315/1030/1/012017

Liro, J. (2023). The interdependencies of religious tourists' attributes and tourist satisfaction in the light of contemporary socio-cultural changes. *Current Issues in Tourism*, 1–5. doi:10.1080/13683500.2023.2214852

Mair, J., & Whitford, M. (2013). An exploration of events research: Event topics, themes and emerging trends. *International Journal of Event and Festival Management*, *4*(1), 6–30. doi:10.1108/17582951311307485

Martella, C., Li, J., Conrado, C., & Vermeeren, A. (2017). On current crowd management practices and the need for increased situation awareness, prediction, and intervention. *Safety Science*, *91*, 381–393. doi:10.1016/j.ssci.2016.09.006

Mehrotra, R., Vera, F., Eck, D., Mehta, D., & Mehta, D. (2015). Kumbh Mela: mapping the ephemeral megacity. HatjeCantz, Harvard South Asia Institute.

Pandey, A., Pandey, M., Singh, N., & Trivedi, A. (2020). KUMBH MELA: A case study for dense crowd counting and modeling. *Multimedia Tools and Applications*, *79*(25-26), 17837–17858. doi:10.100711042-020-08754-4

Persson, E., & Granberg, M. (2021). Implementation through collaborative crisis management and contingency planning: The case of dam failure in Sweden. *Journal of Risk Research, 24*(10), 1335–1348. doi:10.1080/13669877.2020.1863845

Quadri, S. A., & Padala, P. R. (2021). An aspect of Kumbh Mela massive gathering and COVID-19. *Current Tropical Medicine Reports, 8*(3), 225–230. doi:10.100740475-021-00238-1 PMID:33816058

Richards, G., Censon, D., Gračan, D., Haressy, M., Királ'ová, A., Marulc, E., Rossetti, G., Barkiđija Sotošek, M., & Sterchele, D. (2022). Event management literature: Exploring the missing body of knowledge. *Journal of Policy Research in Tourism, Leisure & Events*, 1–22. doi:10.1080/19407963.2022.2128810

Sengupta, H. (2019). Why the Kumbh Mela is an economic blessing. *Fortune India.* https://www.fortuneindia.com/polemicist/why-the-kumbh-mela-is-an-economic-blessing/102900

Sheehy, K., Vackova, P., van Manen, S., Saragih Turnip, S., Rofiah, K., & Twiner, A. (2022). Inclusive disaster risk reduction education for Indonesian children. *International Journal of Inclusive Education*, 1–17. doi:10.1080/13603116.2022.2115156

Sidiropoulos, G., Kiourt, C., & Moussiades, L. (2020). Crowd simulation for crisis management: The outcomes of the last decade. *Machine Learning with Applications, 2*, 100009. doi:10.1016/j.mlwa.2020.100009

Singh, R. P., & Rana, P. S. (2023). Geography of Hindu pilgrimage places (Tīrthas) in India. In Geography of World Pilgrimages: Social, Cultural and Territorial Perspectives, 297-322.

Soomaroo, L., & Murray, V. (2012). Disasters at mass gatherings: Lessons from history. *PLoS Currents, 4*, 4. doi:10.1371/currents.RRN1301 PMID:22453897

Tsironis, C. N. (2022). Pilgrimage and religious tourism in society, in the wake of the COVID-19 pandemic: A paradigmatic focus on 'St. Paul's Route'in the Central Macedonia Region, Greece. *Religions, 13*(10), 887. doi:10.3390/rel13100887

Verma, M., & Sarangi, P. (2019). Modeling attributes of religious tourism: A study of Kumbh Mela, India. *Journal of Convention & Event Tourism, 20*(4), 296–324. doi:10.1080/15470148.2019.1652124

World Health Organization WHO Press, Geneva, Switzerland. (2008). *Communicable Disease Alert and Response for Mass Gatherings* (June). WHO.

Yamin, M. (2019). Managing crowds with technology: Cases of Hajj and Kumbh Mela. *International Journal of Information Technology : an Official Journal of Bharati Vidyapeeth's Institute of Computer Applications and Management, 11*(2), 229–237. doi:10.100741870-018-0266-1 PMID:32289103

KEY TERMS AND DEFINITIONS

Akhada: Akhada or Akhada is an Indian word for a place of practice with facilities for boarding, lodging and training, both in the context of Indian martial artists or a sampradaya monastery for religious renunciates in Guru–shishya (mentor-disciple) tradition.

Ashura: A Muslim voluntary fast day observed on the 10th day of Muharram and especially sacred to Shiites.

COVID-19: Corona virus disease (COVID-19) is an infectious disease caused by the SARS- CoV-2 virus.

ICCC: The Integrated Command and Control Center (ICCC) acts as the "nerve center" for operations management, day-to-day exception handing and disaster management.

Kalpavasi: The pilgrims, who stay in Sangam area for whole Mela period.

Nadistuti: It literally means hymn in praise of the rivers.

RFID: Radio Frequency Identification (RFID) refers to a wireless system comprised of two components: tags and readers. The reader is a device that has one or more antennas that emit radio waves and receive signals back from the RFID tag.

Tirth: *Tirtha* is a Sanskrit word. It particularly refers to pilgrimage sites and holy places in Hinduism, Buddhism and Jainism.

Chapter 8
Pilgrimage to the "Vi" Center of Bulverket's Water Square:
Mapping the Location and Orientation of Gotland Churches

Dennis Doxtater
College of Architecture, Planning, and Landscape Architecture, University of Arizona, USA

ABSTRACT

At the cusp of Norse – Christian landscape transformation and pilgrimage, one investigates a technical ability to survey across land and ice. Two existing large bisects (Norse "vis") with vertexes at significant natural or prehistoric features, statistically compare with the likelihood of identical geometry created by random points. The Bulverket platform in Tingstäde Trask and stone church on shore create vi centered points to map three-point alignments with churches. Alignments from the Bulverket are separately tested against random phenomena statistically proving accurate, surveyed lines of churches. Thus, land surveyed azimuths to either of the vi centers or points in their systems might create the varied orientations of these churches, ranging from 14° north to 18° south of due east. At each church, pairs or triads of azimuths from other lat/long points create squares or parallelograms whose diagonals mathematically lie within one degree of church orientations. Geometric determination of church orientation may have begun with the sacred Bulverket platform square in 1130.

INTRODUCTION

The work in this chapter began as part of a larger study of early medieval stone church orientations in three areas of Scandinavia: Trondheimsfjord Norway, Storsjön Sweden, and the northern third of the island of Gotland. Theoretically, the widely diverse orientations within each region did not follow any church dictate or imposing site condition but were derived from design logic using azimuths to other landscape points, either church or natural feature in the region. This meant that these folk cultures knew of and practiced land surveying at scales well beyond individual farms. These larger scale ideas some-

DOI: 10.4018/978-1-6684-9923-8.ch008

what naturally followed good evidence of a penchant for formal geometry at scales of folk dwellings and farm layout.

A cardinally offset pattern of right-angle orientations was found in 1100's layouts of Norwegian farms studied in the author's dissertation (1981). In a wider area of Scandinavia, Lindström's documentation of grave orientations (1997, 2005), found a "*vinkelrätt*" (right angle) concept of larger landscape "system" predictably off cardinal over ten degrees. Symbolically in the Norwegian folk *tun* (cluster of farm buildings), the *stue* orientated east-west, positioned west of the *loft*, orientated opposite north-south. The western *stue* domain expressed "male" and associated with cooperative or collective relationships between individual farmers. The *loft*, symbolically opposed in position and orientation meant "female", and linked with the competitive element in Norse society, i.e. preservation of fertility and family, and of at times a warrior group (the big *hov* longhouses on larger farms may have also been oriented an offset north-south, e.g. at Hofstadir on Iceland, (Olsen 1966, 183).

The symbolism of the *loft/hov's* axis between humans (south) and spirits (north) not only exists in its south facing portal but receives greater embellishment as the south facing primary dwelling portal of the *stue* with its central fire as *axis mundi* and focal point of most important ritual. This symbolic pattern may have determined the placement of the principal portal on the south walls of many of the *fylke* stone churches around Trondheimsfjord. On Gotland, as well, many principal entrances were located on the south walls of churches, corresponding perhaps to symbolic understandings of spiritual flow up to some landscape point as North.

The two ritual domains on the farm allowed a latent family-based territory to integrate culturally, relatively peacefully with valley or fjord groups of farmers. The modified ritual idea from Bourdieu has been discussed earlier (Doxtater 1990); one kind of larger scale, integrative ritual expresses "occupation" and the other "union". The two calendrical rituals of *Jul* and *Midsommar* have opposite meanings. At winter solstice or *Jul*, the gods come out of the mountains occupying the symbolic center of the farm, the *stue*, even as expressed in much later bourgeois Sweden in Bergman's *Fanny and Alexander*: the visiting gods subordinate the family and most important architectural setting. At *Midsommar*, farm families reverse this ritual movement, journeying to some natural place and dancing around a wooden stake as cosmic center icon: the individualities of family moderate in a unification with spirits, i.e. the community becomes the gods.

While the farm *stue*, *tun* and opposed summer/winter rituals in the 1100's clearly worked from Viking concepts of landscape and dwelling, these folk were Christianizing to an extent where large farmers built small wooden stave churches nearby. But in Norway at least, it wasn't until the Reformation that the principal rituals of marriage, birth and death were moved from *stue* to church (Doxtater 1990). Thus, the Norse landscape at the time of the pilgrimages was still largely pagan, even though folk were beginning to call themselves Christian, using Biblical text and art less ritually than discursively in limited space of church interiors.

The construction of new, large stone churches during pilgrimage times in the three regions of the present initial study has been seen as continuous with Christianization in slightly earlier wooden temples. Scholars hold that these much more expensive monuments were as well evidence of the power of large farmers (Brendalsmo 2006). The driving hypothesis about azimuthal orientation logic of the stone churches, however, reveals a new kind of historic landscape analysis, one that suggests a much more collective replacement of elements of a structured Norse landscape with a more clearly collective Christian landscape of spatially integrated stone churches. "Christian" pilgrimage routes appear to have been integral to the politics and religious change of this process.

While symbolically consistent ritual at early medieval pilgrimage scales is largely unrecorded, basic elements of the Gudbrandsdalen route clearly invoke "structural" folk reverence for north-south ("vertical") axes of contact, and right angles. In the diagram of figure 1, the composition of offset. extremely accurate alignments and right angles intent on Pilgrims making contact with the largest grave mound in Scandinavia, Raknehaug to the south of the composition and with the largest gravefield, Vang at the northern end (Doxtater 2023a). The pattern does not directly link to any cathedral or church point at Trondheim (unlike the smaller, perhaps later Østerdal route mapped in Doxtater 2023b). Two things may be in play here, first the fact that St. Olav's coffin rested for decades not at the Trondheim cathedral under construction and even today cannot be located within, and second that Raknehaug exists as a terminus for an accurate north-south meridian from one of the most naturally formed possible ritual threshold—the Eidet island isthmus--well north in Trondheimsfjord very close to the latitude of Stiklestad on the mainland where the sagas say King Olav died in battle.

As mapped in figure 2, the Eidet lies accurately as a threshold on a possible ritual axis from the known pre- and post-historic *Alting* assembly site (Frostating) for the large region around Trondheimsfjord and the most visually significant mountain Heimdalshaugen (the "frame god"). The churches of Logtun and Maere align very accurately. No clarity exists in either Norwegian or Swedish website mapping about where, besides Trondheim, pilgrims would have visited if trekking to the stone Stiklestad church, (a present-day interpretation site as well). No evidence exists that devotes rowed out to the Eidet, though sites like the Alting and the Tautra monastery on Frosta peninsula have been mentioned as possibly path related. The route from the Baltic, from which St. Olav's "army" the Norse chieftains of Trondelag, has yet unpublished geometry between and orientations of three pilgrimage related stone churches with the Eidet.

The conclusion of mapping the overland route from the Oslo area suggests that while pilgrimage routes could have initiated the positioning of numerous churches, the overall landscape structure appears more Norse than Christian, even emphasizing climatic Norse sacred locations over the largest churches.

The Socio-Political Role of Large Scale, Formalized, Ritual Landscape Structure During Pilgrimage Times in Northern Gotland

King Olav made Christianizing voyages to Gotland as evidenced primarily by saga lore that says he built a church in 1029 on the peninsula called St. Olofsholm (inscription from on 1844 stone at ruin site) --brief pilgrimage discussion in Sands (2017). Another church/chapel is archaeologically recorded on the west side of Fårö (RAA number Fårö 346:1). Thus, from saga sources King Olav 's Christianization attempts on Northern Gotland occurred very close to when he continued north in the Baltic to St. Olav's harbor (Selånger), where his path to Trondheimsfjord began. The first dating of pilgrimages in Norway comes from Adam von Bremen in 1070 (Bagge 2010) describing the martyr's "tomb" in Trondheim, and the difficult overland route from Oslo (the most used route was by sea along the west coast). The Nideros cathedral, however, had just begun construction at this time, and could hardly have been the imagined goal of pilgrims; it also was never dedicated to St. Olav.

The peak of new large stone church monuments on Gotland happens around 1230, about the same period as the Mjøskastellet (castle) was laid out as the large-scale right angle between Heimdalshaugen and Gamla Uppsala, again figure 1. About a hundred years earlier, 1130, and just sixty years after the first pilgrimages were mentioned in Norway, a highly unique, geometrically precise 170 meter square wooden platform was built in the middle of Gotland's largest, but shallow lake in the north. Though archaeolo-

Figure 1. Pilgrimage related, surveyed landscape structure integrating unique prehistoric mound, gravefield, and water feature with early parish stone churches in Norway
Doxtater, 2023

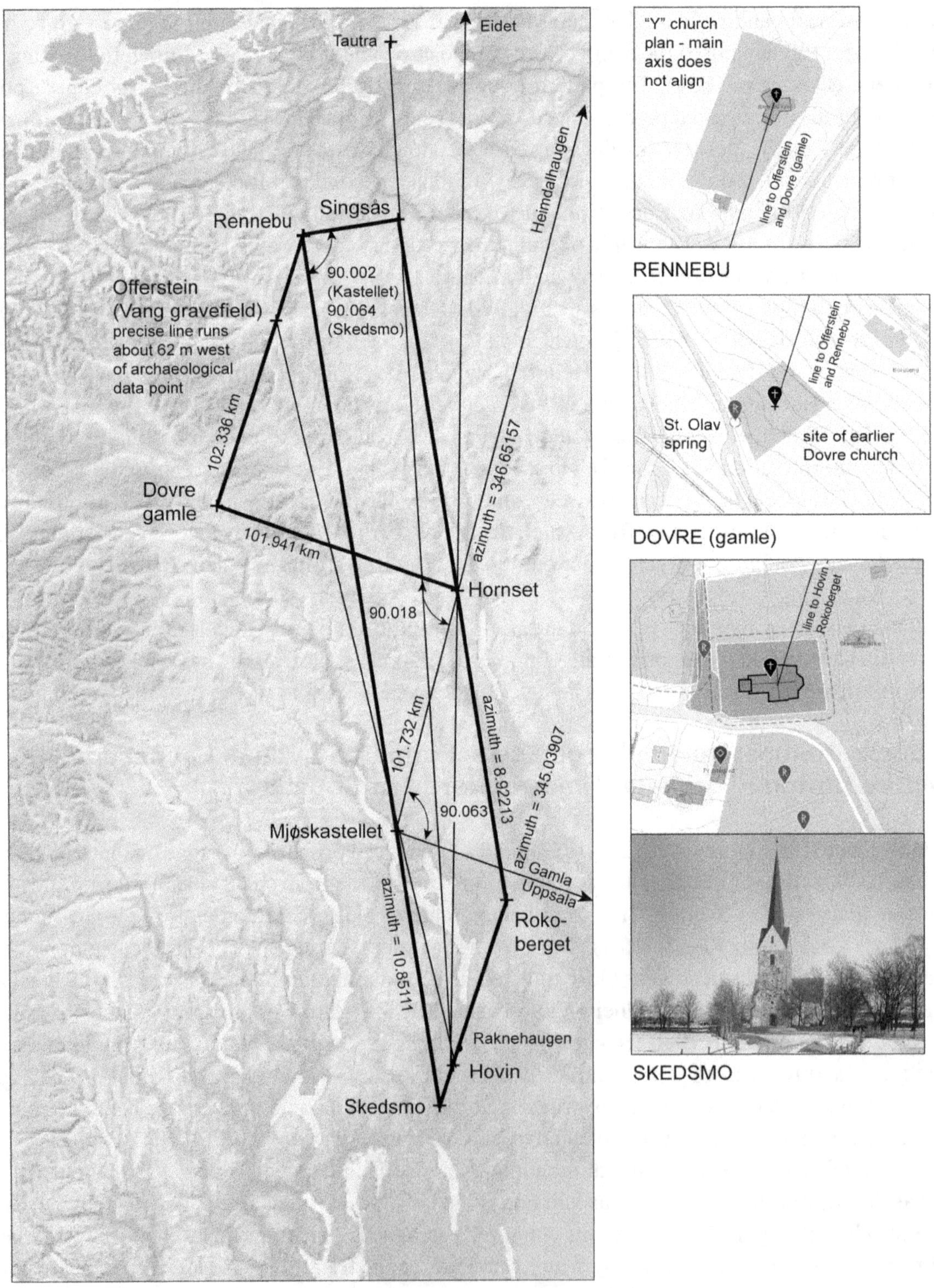

Figure 2. Four-point alignment between Logtun church (Frostating), Eidet church and isthmus point, Maere church, and summit benchmark on Heimdalhaugen.

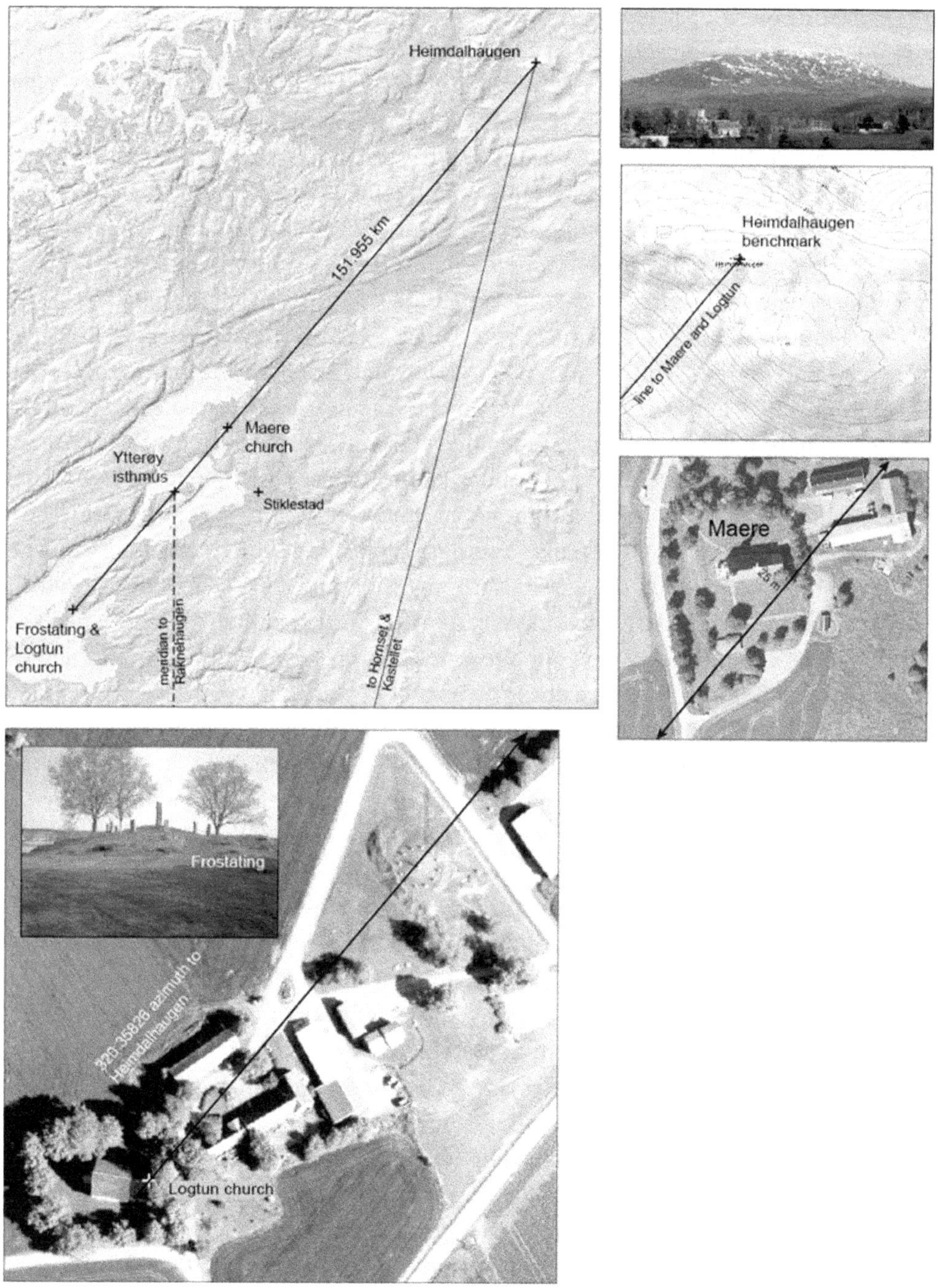

gists have only surmised a defensive purpose to this assembly place with an open water interior, its well dated coincidence with the very first of the big stone churches has not generated investigation. Does its early dating, only one lifetime after St. Olav's Christianizing on Northern Gotland, suggest a possible Baltic pilgrimage destination? Archaeologists have also not concluded its use as a new, architectural form of Ting, prehistoric Scandinavian assembly places in natural sites, though a northern Ting place, somewhat later perhaps, operates in the shadow of a huge stone church on the lake shore.

The most interesting question here, asks how a regional Baltic pilgrimage destination, and particularly geometrically integrated first stone churches meshes with conventional research about who built the new stone monuments—ignoring as it does the contemporaneous Bulverket phenomenon? What motivated either a larger farmer, some of whom may have built their own wooden chapel as in Norway, or village group of farmers want to build an architecturally impressive stone parish church? The back and forth between archaeologists Andren and Siltberg (same publication 2011) contrasts two kinds of social territoriality, one where these larger stone churches are built at or near a larger farm, and the other where they are located in relation to collectively known villages, perhaps with prehistoric continuity. In both cases, the mapping of church locations with respect to these two possibilities remains less than definitive.

On the one hand, it is as much the name of the church in relation to a nearby possibly larger farm, as much as any certainty of the farm's extent in the 12the and 13th centuries that suggests the "big man" association. Alternatively, when attempting to map long term more cooperative villages of smaller farms, churches are said to have been in the spatial interstices between farms to not restrict farming. In either event, some latitude seems to have existed about where to locate these intrusive symbolic temples—especially since churches were not located right next to or even within large prehistoric gravefields, as many are in Trondheimsjord (e.g. Alstadhaug, Vaernes, Egge, Oppdal, Orland, and many others).

The discourse about hierarchical or egalitarian power behind Gotland stone church location and building may be misleading. Symbolically, given that at this time heathen and Christian practices may well have been synchronic, an impressive architectural church "dwelling" would logically have been seen as a place where a "family" makes access to spiritual power. This would be an extended family of Christ, so to speak, with all the authority of holy father, and ultimately bishop and pope. All farmers in the area that participated in the church building process, and practicing Christian rites there, would understand this meaning, even though some farmers of the congregation may have been wealthier and more influential than others (there were no pews to designate hierarchy in churches until the Reformation, in Norway at least).

But at the same time of these new architecturally contained religious rites, people might also have been still participating more collectively in Norse rituals in the greater landscape, perhaps by or at larger gravefields, and especially at *tings*, whether more locally or at the scale of Gotland's *Alting*. In the Viking and medieval farm experience, in Norway at least, the birth, marriage and death rites of passage, all played off oppositions between the architectural focus of "center", against some natural place, whether the *tun* tree and mound (weekly and death rites) or the trip to sacred natural place on the fjord as climax to the wedding). One would expect, therefore, that a new temple should be built in subordinate relationship to a *Vi (Vé)*, or landscape place as described in the Guta Saga. This may even have been more likely to happen in the case of the larger stone churches, compared to the earlier timber structures perhaps conceptually considered part of farm building orientation meanings. There may have been significant differences in social scale between the earliest structures and those built in the 12th and13th centuries.

Assumptions of prehistoric ritual practice in Scandinavia—at any social scale--seem to be largely extensions of ideas of domestic territoriality, i.e. that the many mounds found in proximity to Iron Age and Medieval farms were the primary form of religious practice. The problem with this assumption is that the family needs less social integration than the relationship *between* farmers, and even regions of farmers. While yet unmapped, it is not unlikely that there existed some sort of formal layout of spiritual flow on Gotland's landscape, and particularly the way it would have integrated social groups larger than families, perhaps at *ting* and gravefield places. A good place to start mapping here might be much earlier in the Bronze Age; Martinsson-Wallin & Wehlin (2017) provide data points at different scales, but no investigation of possible formal, surveyed landscape patterns. In such possible systems, participants would have been aware of where the spiritual power—the fusing of social group with the gods—comes from, in other parts of Scandinavia from prominent natural features, and ultimately "North". These meanings in turn would be symbolically (homologically) associated with formal spatial practices at the scale of farm and dwellings.

Again, in the early medieval period it could be that the building of larger stone churches at times was initiated by larger farmers. But something offered by Andren in the cited discourse might be mentioned here. He speaks of *non-territorial* associations of big men or "*Godar*" on Iceland. Not discussed, however, is how the social purpose of these associations relates to architectural temples and to *Tings*. More specifically, was the reason these big men met at the *Alting* or regional *tings*, to perpetrate a dominant territoriality of their farm over neighboring farms, or was it to legitimize trade and otherwise constrain enmity among valley and fjord farm groups at much larger scales?

The issue of cultural landscape scale is interesting in another respect. To a certain extent, the introduction of Christianity refers to a much larger religious scale, made more real by the pilgrimage, to the Holy Land, Trondheimsfjord and Baltic pagan areas to the east of Gotland. If one assumes that the massive early stone churches on Gotland built at this time were conceived in part as locally scaled pilgrimage destinations themselves, thus offering greater discursive Christianization and potentially greater regional hegemony, ancient traditions of powerful natural ritual foci may have demanded some such new or revitalized foci. The memory of St. Olav, his visits, and the new pilgrimages in Norway could have suggested a re-visioned regional natural structure providing dominant spiritual to pilgrimage destinations—one perhaps seen as not unlike the power of the Eidet on the axis from Frostating to Heimdalhaugen.

LOCATING THE BULVERKET CENTER: TESTING A *VI* PATTERN AND ALIGNMENTS TO NEW CHURCHES

Migration Period (400 – 800 AD) longhouses excavated by Stenberger (1955) at Vallhager on Gotland proved to have cardinally offset *Vinkelrätt* (right angle) orientations when mapped from archaeological documents by the author (1981), and may have been symbolic of some larger, shared, formal concept of landscape, perhaps used ritually. While the location and orientation of the Bulverket follows, its formal square plan and monumental size laid out equidistant from a center point, if nothing else, speaks of right-angle symbolism. Fundamental to design formalities, *per se*, could collective ritual meaning be expressed in both Bulverket layout and accurate, straight church alignments connecting farms and villages of the land.

Rönnby and Adams (2006) considered historical and their more recent research on this 170 x 170 meter platform consisting of over 25,000 logs cut in the early 12th century and erected in the middle of Tingstäde Trask in northern Gotland, figure 3. Their interpretations suggest only a short lived need to provision and defend some particular social power. Estimated construction required 100 men about a year. Whether the organizers were Viking chieftains or just large farmers in a struggle among themselves, or with some larger territorial conflict with royal authority from mainland Sweden, still these archaeologists sensed some association with an ancient egalitarian tradition: "it is hard not to feel that there is something very "Gotlandic" about Bulverket, situated as it is in the middle of the well protected inland lake" (ibid 188).

Figure 3. Artist's rendering of Bulverket platform in Tingstäde Trask (lake) from
Rönnby and Adams (2006)

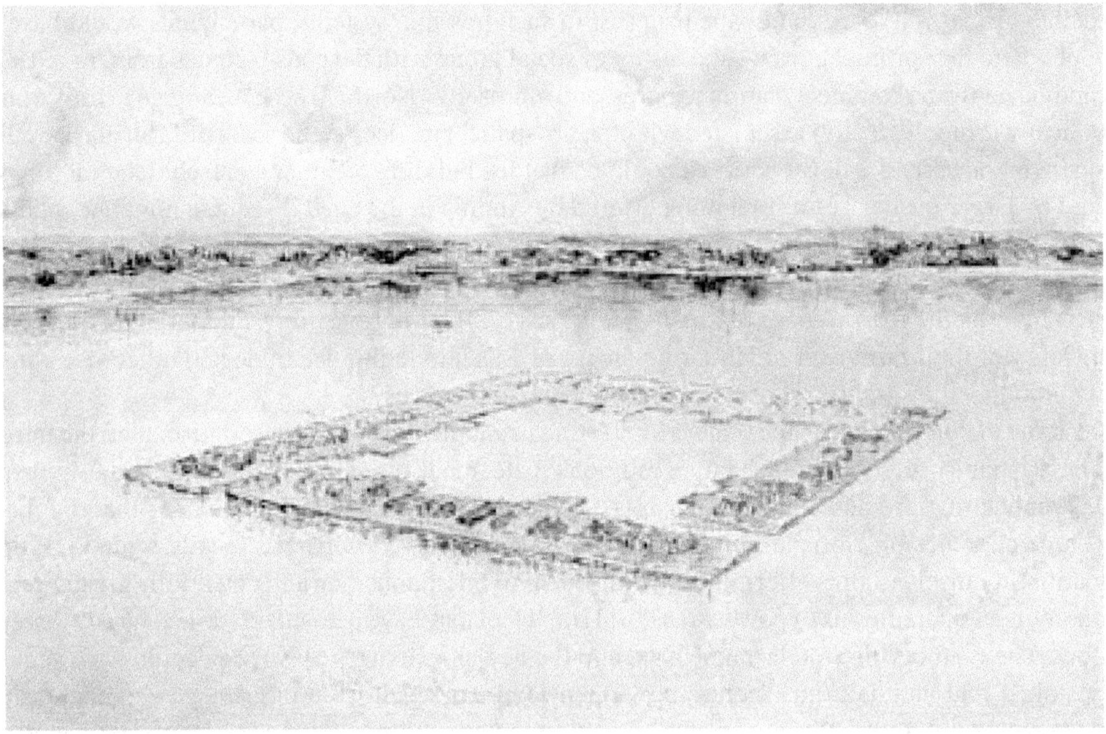

Figure 4. Zetterling's recording "towers" in winter (left) and summer (right)
Photos from Swedish Historical Museum

The detailed discussion of Zetterling's meticulous small-scale mapping of the (1935) focuses on the primary archaeological interest in documenting the remarkable timber structure—see photos in figure 3. Clearly from Zetterling's photos, the structure would offer little defense in winter when highly accessible over the ice. Alternatively, why in the lake? The only symbolic possible function made briefly in passing associates the ritual "*ting*" site and later church, Tingstäde, to the west on the shore of the lake. Good archaeology on smaller scale *ting* sites in Norway shows how temporary shelters grouped geometrically around a common open space—each building oriented in the direction of its constituent farm (Iversen 2017). While the documentation of orientation from a ritual site to constituents in the larger landscape offers good evidence of the Norse collective mind, archaeologists did not find constituent features of the platform that might be mapped at larger landscape scales.

Though focusing on the jumbled sunken timbers, figure 4, a precise formal plan was impossible for Zetterling to resurrect. He may even have been less interested in formal geometries, including processes of lake location, and the apparent non-cardinal orientation of the platform. First, nothing yet speaks to the way Norse craftsfolk would have laid out the huge square. One can imagine one scenario out on the solid ice in a typical Baltic winter. Rather than measuring 85-meter radii aligned visually to a center point, the simple but accurate technology of using tall tripods with plumb weights on thin cords for alignments would have been known within the skill set of cathedral builders of the time (the cathedral in Trondheim was under construction). Given a start point at center, pairs of tripods set about 6 meters apart can prolong a straight line close to acuity of the naked eye or 0.017° (the Romans did it many centuries earlier in Germany –Söderman 1989).

Placing the tripod pair at center, a straight line could be prolonged out to one of the eventual corners of the square. Then moving the tripod pair out to the first square corner, the opposite square corner can be aligned through the center, in this case 240.41 meters away. Getting the two legs of equal length would be measured with a unitary "rod". Projecting the perpendicular diagonal of the square could be done by measuring equal distances to a point 20-30 meters from a tripod pair at center, and prolonging that point out the requisite half diagonal distance.

However, such a process would require an orientation rationale of the two diagonals in the layout. More specifically, how was the initial center located on the frozen lake in the first place? Technically possible at the time, a much larger scale surveying process—using the same instrument pairs—possibly had created a geometric and highly symbolic rationale for the point in the lake. The precise latitude and longitude of the 170 m square center cannot be found in Rönnby and Adams, if in fact one has been calculated to date. Using Hult de Geer's mapping, however, for his biochronolgical work on dating (1935) -- "cleverly" integrated into Zetterling's work—one can tentatively determine the center point of the interior water domain.

This most unique natural (and symbolic) lake may have had symbolic association with the other most unique natural and water related Gotland feature, the narrow strait between the main island and Fårö island mapped in figure 5, Norra Gattet (the gate of the North). Not unlike the Trondheimsfjord axis, this Eidet-like point may also have been considered the symbolically most powerful threshold to North, the liminal connection between the Bulverket center and the Norse spirit world. Its position could have been surveyed as a powerful benchmark during the winter freeze over. One would not necessarily expect archaeological remains at the gate shores, given the likely prohibition of architecturalizing sacred natural features, e.g. like Horg (Olsen 1966). Like the Bulverket water center, this too might have been an invisible benchmark.

On Gotland one finds saga lore depicting early conflicts between Christians and Norse spirits during the process of locating and building first churches. The account by Luke John Murphy (2018):

One notable aspect of Guta saga's account of the earliest church building on the island is that Botair's neighbours burnt his first church, but not his second. The Gotlanders were clearly willing to destroy the second church, burning Botair and his family in in the process, but accepted Likkair's reasoning this was unacceptable þy et han standr i Vi, firir niþan klintu (because it stands at Vi/in a vé, below the crag). This has, unsurprisingly, elicited significant scholarly attention, not least due to the possibility that this Vi later became Visby, the medieval and modern capital, where the current cathedral stands at the foot of a small stoney rise. Yet precisely what it was that Botair's second church was replacing—the site's objective pre-Christian "configuration"—is not made clear in the saga. (pg. 32)

The Guta Saga was recorded several decades after the Bulverket and first monumental stone churches (Peel 1998). If the Bulverket and Norra Gattet aligned as an invisible, surveyed concept, could this be a highly symbolic "*vi*" axis among natural features on large scale Gotland?

Using today's NOAA (US National Oceanic and Atmospheric Agency) mathematically based software, one can map such possibilities, particularly at larger landscape scales (see Doxtater 2007). In the present case, calculating the azimuth of the line between the Bulverk center point and the topographically precise Norra Gattet point, its prolongation reaches up to the most northern part of Fårö, see figure 5. The northernmost topographic feature of Gotland is the Norsholmen peninsula though this name apparently only dates to the 1700's when the peninsula was still an island. On today's protected bird sanctuary, archaeologists document a remnant of earlier marginal cultural occupation as a low-walled, non-defensive circular enclosure about forty meters across, defined in 1851 as a churchyard with small chapel (*Fornsök* "Fårö 5:1"). Few architectural features remain, while a small number of human bones have been carbon dated to the 14th and 15th centuries.

Evidence of prehistoric occupation exists in separate grave fields, one of which, about 190 x 90 meters, sits at the very northernmost point of Gotland. The technically extended line from Bulverket misses the center of the ringed graveyard feature by about 49 meters, or about 20 meters from the outside of the wall (the accuracy of this line from Bulverket is about 0.06205° at 42.156 km) and extends to the tip of the island as shown in figure 5. Furthermore, a prolonged mathematically accurate line 6.927 km to the southeast of the tentative Bulverket center point, runs about 17 meters to the east of the center point of Lokrume parish church (monumental stone). Small variations in present software notwithstanding, the line comes within about one meter of the exterior east wall of the altar. Thus, one close maps a very accurate long, possibly land/ice surveyed line that includes: Lokrume, the Bulverket center, Norra Gattet, and the Norsholm ring.

Thinking hypothetically about large-scale *vis*, one can map an accurate geometry of two side rays that may have worked with the Norsholm point as sacred vertex. An eastern ray can be extended down to a large prehistoric ringed wall (*fornborg*) near the church of Halla; in terms of measurements up to Norsholm the lat/long numbers are identical between ring center and church. Such a line passes quite close to the churches of Hellvi (0.0942° or 62 meters) and Boge (0.189° or 83 meters). "Hellvi" might well be etymologically part of Gotlandic spatial concepts of "*vi*".

The area around Halla and particularly Roma, figure 6, has long been the cultural focus of Gotland, particularly with its *Alting* assembly. In her attempt to locate the archaeologically unknown location of

Figure 5. Alignment from Bulverket center point to natural threshold point, Norra Gattet, the Norsholm ring and northernmost point of Gotland

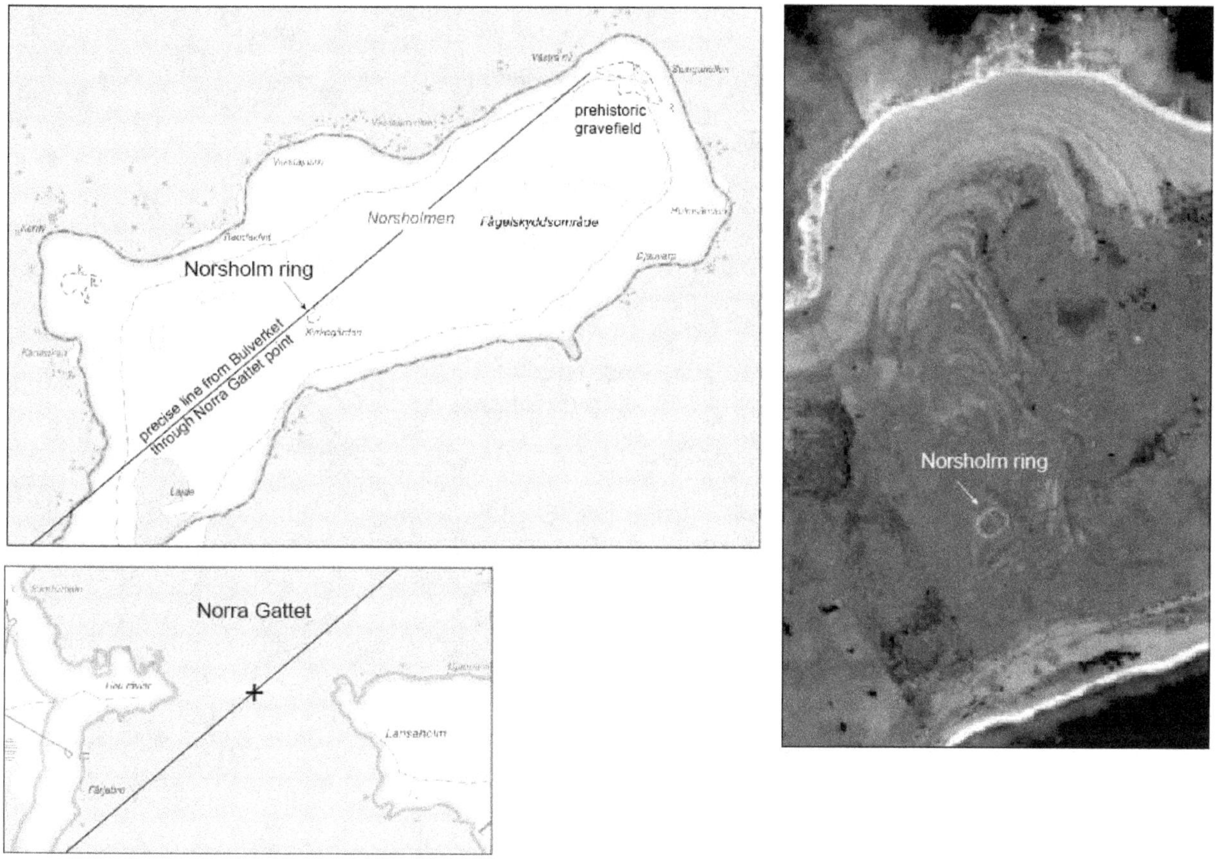

a kind of site with typically little or no architecture, Myrberg (2009) documents its existence in Viking and early Middle Ages as mentioned in the *Guta Lagh* and

Guta Saga. The name of the Cistercian monastery from 1164 may have been derived from the *all-ting* (labled "*kyrkoruin*" in the Kungsgården farm upper left in figure 6). The other highly significant site in Myrberg's investigation, one possibly influencing the location of the assembly area is "the largest burial ground on Gotland" (ibid:110) used from the Roman Iron Age through Viking periods. "Broa" meaning "the bridge" lies at the lower center of figure 6. Note the water threshold expression. The line from Norsholm to the selected point at Broa, passes three stone church sites at the following accuracies: Halla (0.11°), Hellvi (0.014°), and Boge (0.18°). And from Broa to Hellvi passes two: Halla (0.17°) and Boge (0,16°).

Myrberg's speculative conclusion locates the assembly site on a small island now nonexistent, "an island in the middle of an island" as her article's title depicts, here located about in the center of figure 6. Her detective work doesn't mention the church at Halla, which might have been the closest church to the *Alting*, just to the east of the assembly island. More importantly from a large-scale perspective, may be the location of the Iron-Age "*fornborg*" just 300 m south of Halla church. Not unlike the low walled, non-defensive ringed enclosure at Norsholm, in form at least, consider this much larger defined natural

Figure 6. Cultural center of Gotland landscape with important prehistoric and early Christian locations; alignment from Broa gravefield to Norsholm ring

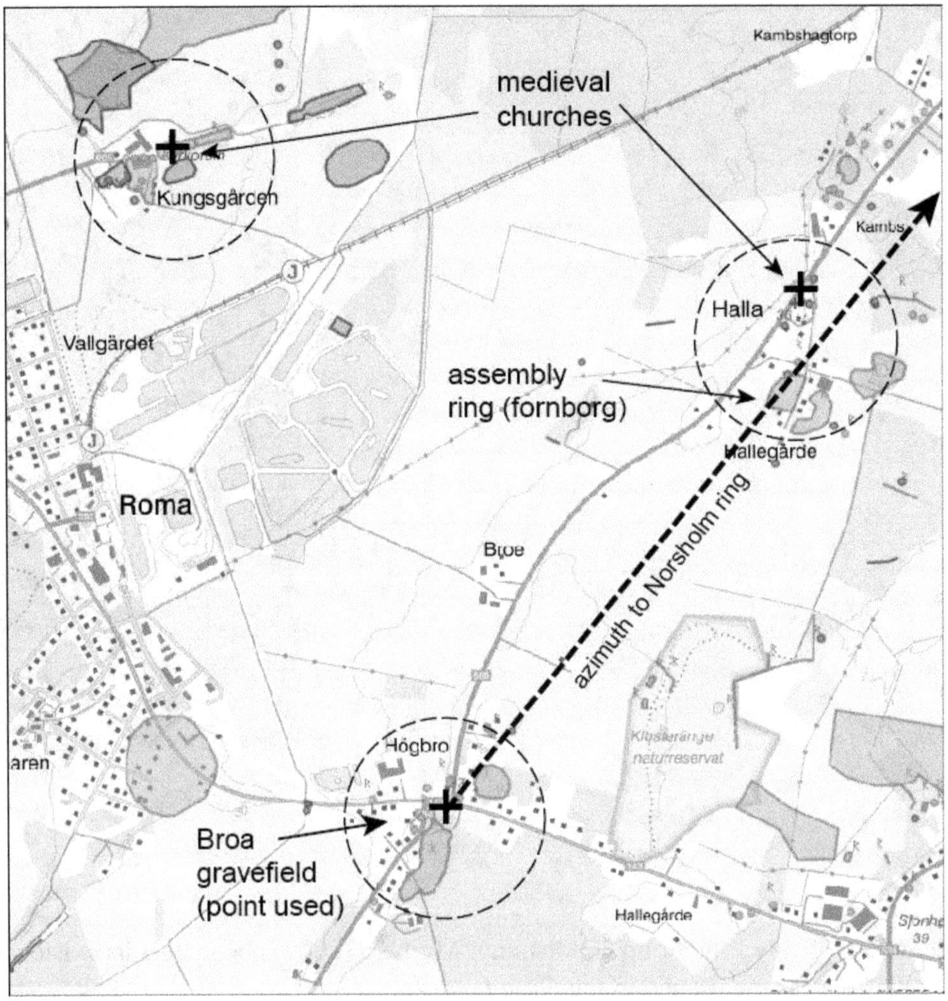

place--the outer berm being 250 m in diameter. The limited archaeological record of this site does not reveal its use, not

unlike many of these enigmatic *fornborg* places in Scandinavia; two of which in the Trondheimsfjord area seem to have clear ritual purpose in relation to larger scale landscape patterns involving early churches (at Horg and Sakshaug).

What then of a western ray from Norsholm that might pair up with a line from Halla (and the *fornborg*) perhaps including Boge and Hellvi churches? While no large, symmetrical *fornborg* exists to anchor such a complement (aside from a 500 x 700 meter prehistoric gravefield), one does find an accurate alignment between Norsholm and the two churches of Stenkyrka and Hangvar. At an accuracy of 0.142° the line from Norsholm to Stenkyrka passes about 26 meters west of the center of the Hangvar structure—missing the southeast corner some 12 meters or so. As shown in figure 7, the azimuth of the west and east rays of a Norsholm *vi* to Bulverket have a bisect accuracy of about 0.117°, one half the difference between the two angles: 11.45558° and 11.22094°. The west ray runs more accurately to the Stenkyrka structure

Figure 7. Hypothetical Norsholm and Broa Vis

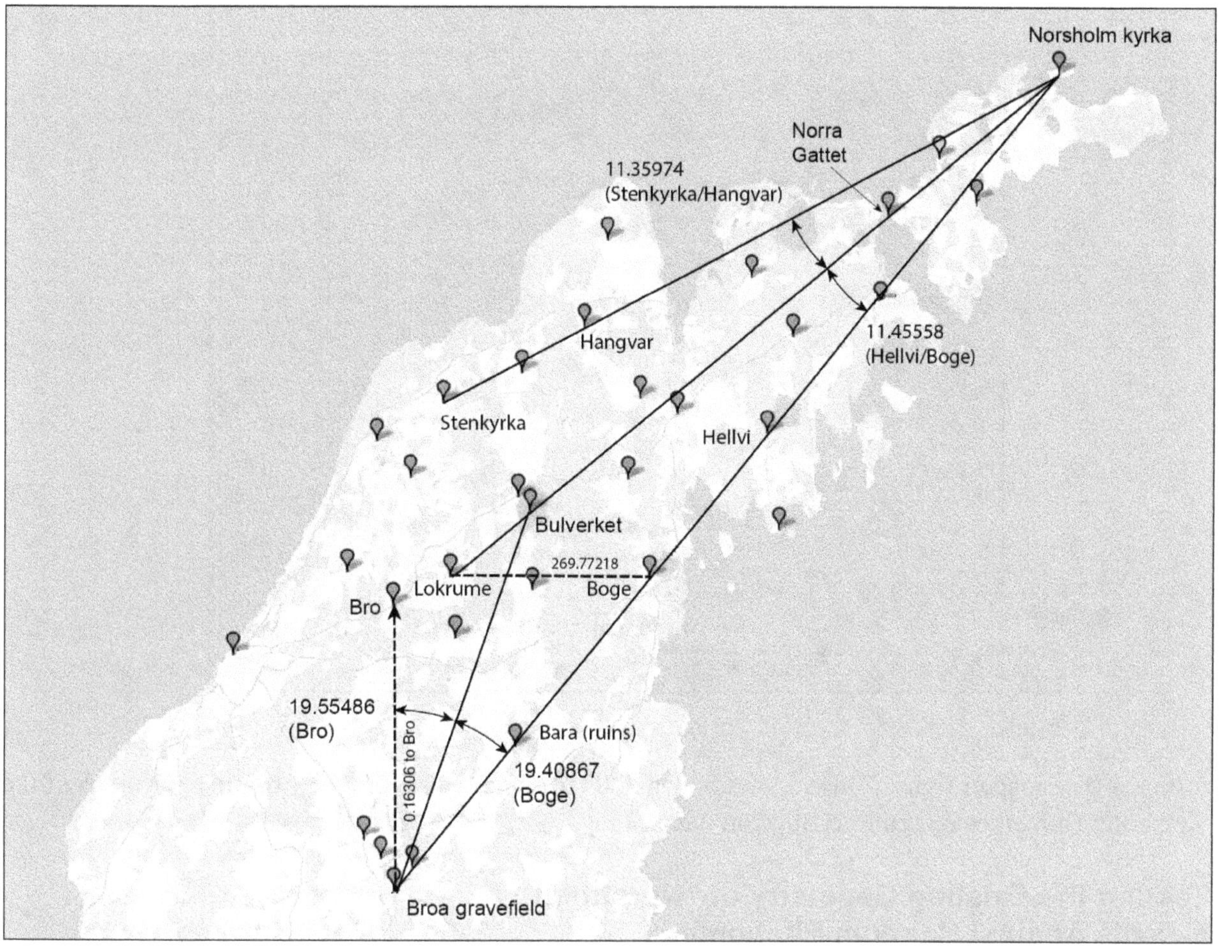

than the center of the large gravefield about 830 meters to the east, i.e. a bisect angle of 10.6780° vs. 11.45558°. The ideal bisect azimuth is about 96 meters east of the Stenkyrka center point.

Returning to the eastern ray of a Norsholm *vi*, one checks the azimuths of climax astronomical events, particularly summer and winter solstice rises and sets. As calculated in the NOAA website (https://gml.noaa.gov/grad/solcalc/sunrise.html), three azimuths map as in figure 8. Among existing points presently used, most interesting is the summer rise from either the Broa gravefield or the Halla ring—aligned as they are. The azimuth from Broa to the Norsholm ring calculates 321.17447, while the NOAA azimuth for these points and solstice rise time a thousand years ago is 320.1. From Broa the summer solstice sun sets even closer, 219.9 (from

the Visby Dom), compared to the azimuth to Broa, 219.99380. [note* The author's software uses a digital mapping convention of 360°, counter-clockwise from 0° at north around to 180° at south and on up to 360° at north again; cardinal East is 270°]

Two astronomically related cardinal directions may also be noted. A relatively good meridian (north-south) extends up from the Broa gravefield to the Bro church. The precise meridian from the estimated center of the large gravefield runs about 45 meters from the west wall of the church, some 19.347 km

Figure 8. Summer solstice rise and set points from Broa gravefield to Norsholm and Visby

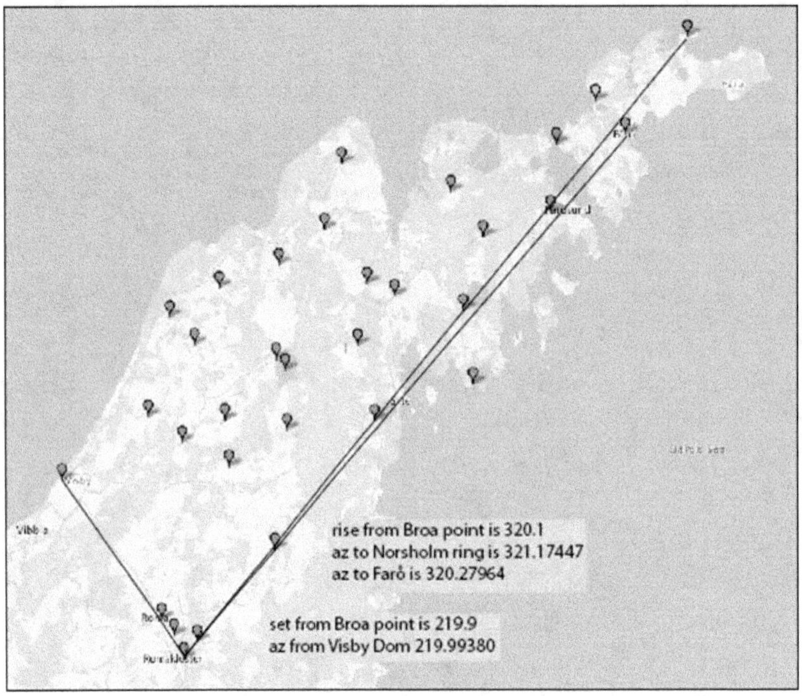

distance. The map of figure 7 also shows how a 270° true East line from the Lokrume terminus of the Norsholm/Bulverket axis runs to Boge on the east ray.

Testing the Existing Geometry of "Norsholm *Vi*" Bisects Against Random Phenomena

While one cannot include the generous alignments of archaeoastronomers—conventionally in that field within accuracy ranges up to two degrees—one can model much more precise existing patterns possibly designed and land/ice surveyed down to the limits of visual acuity. The screen shot of figure 9 shows the initial setup of points for this first test of simple patterns of three-point alignments, cardinal relationships between two points either north-south or east-west and bisects among three lines and points radiating out from a fourth point as vertex.

First, as one might imagine, given the numbers of parish stone churches in figure 7 (locations named in figure 10), some total number of coincidental or random, accurate existing patterns could be high. In the present case, however, one looks not at all largely independent patterns, but how a much smaller number creates a composite pattern suggesting design. Can one find a "module" combining some number of the three "core" patterns that can be tested against the substitution of random points in test areas around each church. A sense of the trial-and-error process of modeling a more complex module can be seen in the strings of core patterns that have been tried (left panel in the upper screen shot). In the present case, the limit of complexity can only define the Norsholm *vi* itself, without any geometry from a complementary southern *vi* from Broa and or Halla, aligned as they are with churches on the east ray to

Norsholm. Nevertheless, only involving five churches together with the Norseholm ring, Norra Gattet and Bulverket, the search string has some length:

A+A(1)+C(1)+B(4)+B(4)+B(4)+B(4)+A(2)+A(2)+A(3)+A

The accuracies of each kind of core patterns can be set differently, in this case A (alignments) 0.14° as will be explained when listing all patterns among the selected points, B (bisects) 0.06°, and C (cardinals) 0.43°. A parenthesis next to a letter states the requisite number of overlapping points with this core pattern of the sequence. The computer creates a list of all possible core patterns keeping track of which ones used in overlaps. The present module, though complex in appearance just models how a bisect from the Norsholm ring as vertex has one side ray with two aligned churches (Stenkyrka and Hangvar), the other side ray with two aligned churches (Boge and Hellvi), and a center axis with three closely aligned features with Norsholm (Norra Gattet, Bulverket, and the church of Lokrume). As mentioned Lokrume has a relatively accurate cardinal relationship to the east with the terminus of the east side ray, Boge. Accuracies of cardinal relationships will again be less precise because of their dependence on astronomical observations, rather than line of sight measurements using plumb bob instruments.

Once the search string *only* finds the stated elements and their overlaps, as shown in the upper panel of figure 9, then it can be used to find identical or very similar modules among random points--substituted for existing churches in the test of each. Using the highest deviations within each of the three core patterns of the existing, the three water related points of Norra Gattet, the Bulverket, and the Broa gravefield remain fixed, while the 29 churches (including the Norsholm ring, and two St. Olav chapels) are replaced with random points in their areas. Each set of 29 random plus 3 fixed can be searched instantaneously. In the present case, starting with 100 sets in a run, no matches are found. Then at 1,000 sets per run, matches begin to occur. In ten runs, or 10,000 sets, the existing pattern occurs 8 times, or 1 in 1,250. One such random match is shown in the lower panel of figure 9. Is the existing pattern, statistically unique as it is, just one of many unique modules in a world of random phenomena? Nevertheless, the Norsholm pattern can be taken as *possibly* designed and land/ice surveyed, especially in relation to the tentative location of an enigmatic Bulverket.

Did Surveyed Lines From the Bulverket Center Point Locate Medieval Parish Churches?

A more definitive probability can be found mapping accuracies of only church alignments to the Bulverket point. As recognized by art historians, a chart of church start dates in the *landsbygden* (farmed areas of Gotland) in Weinberg (2001: 234) begins with about six constructions some 20

years after Bulverket, or 1150, reaching a highest peak around 1200 and diminishing by 1250 with a second surge until about 1300 (reproduced as figure 10). Thus, any symbolic appropriation of a Bulverket center for aligning churches could have happened shortly after the completion of the sacred water square. These large, ultimately competitive stone churches number one hundred or more as popularly photographed across Gotland. In present work, the location of Tingstäde Trask in the northern third of Gotland suggested practical limitation of mapping, as shown in figure 11. Included separately to the south for their historical and prehistorical importance are Visby and the Cistercian cloister church at Kungsgård (1163). Additionally, three church ruins (Bara, Elinghems and Ganns) are included as well as the mentioned small chapel sites of Norsholm, St. Olav's chapel, and St. Olav's large church. The

Figure 9. Screen shot of software that tests the search module for the Norsholm vi (upper); example of 1 in 1,250 random sets that comes close to matching existing, and test areas around each church (lower)

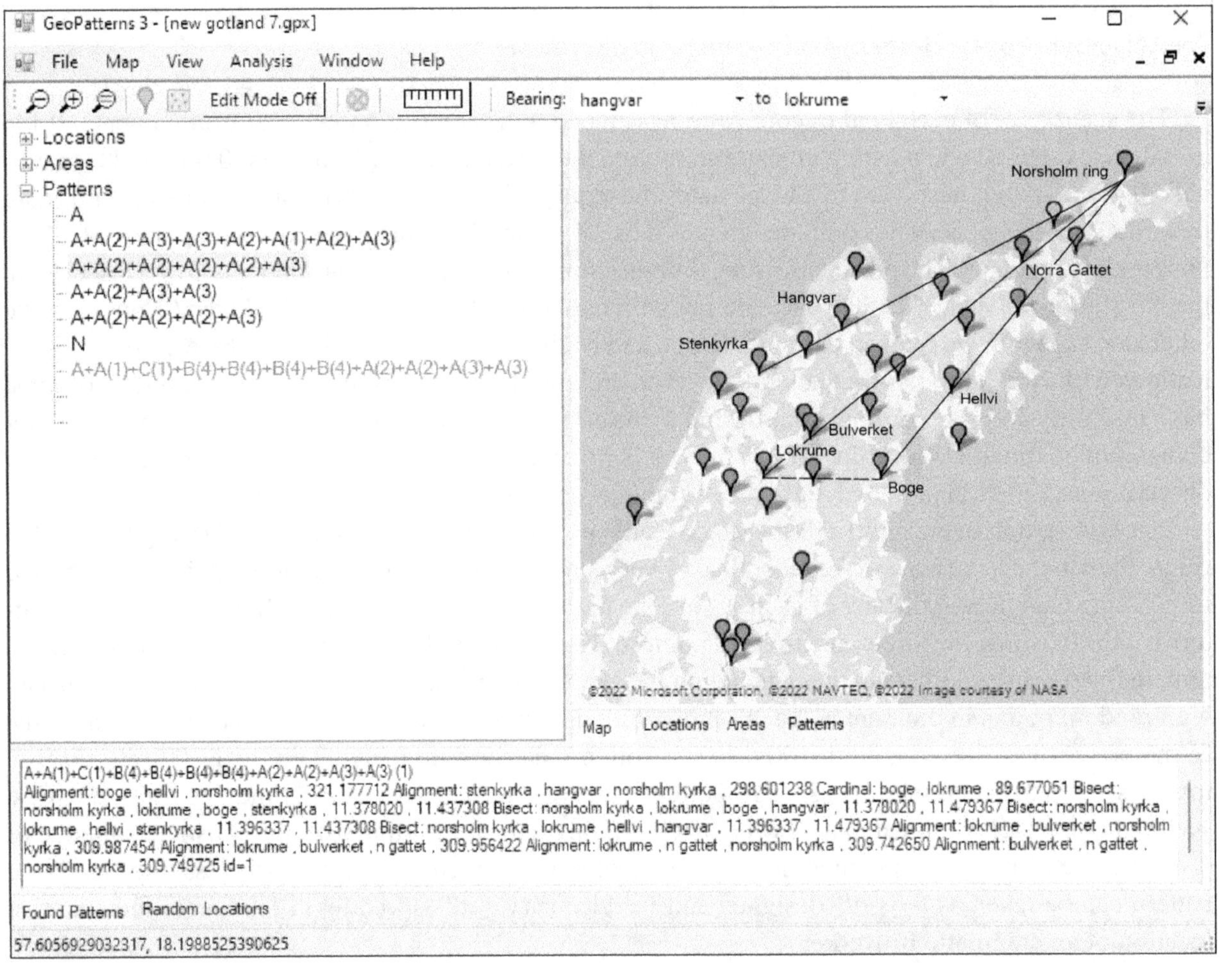

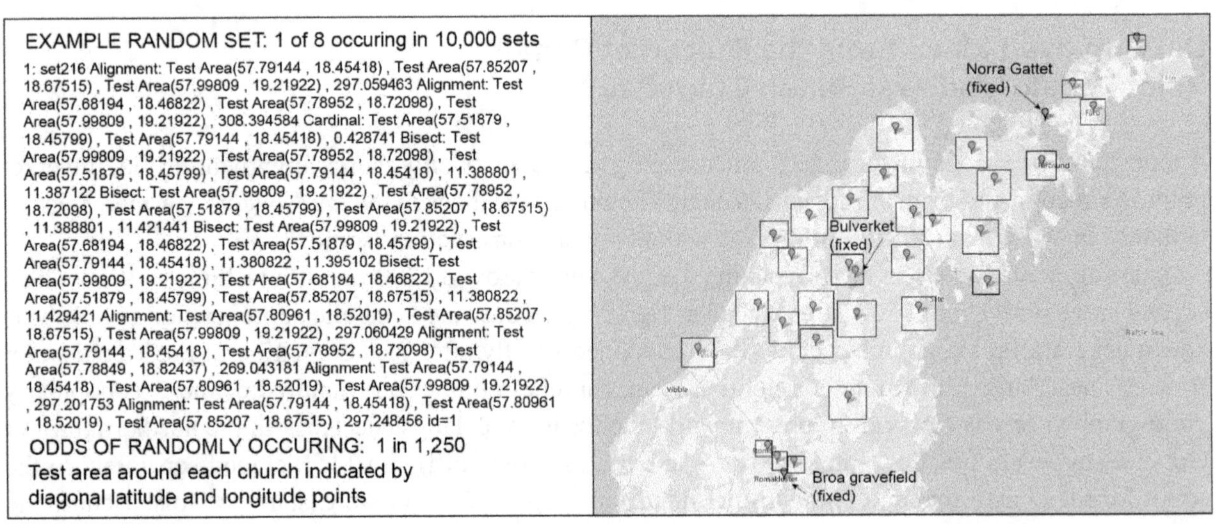

Figure 10. Church dating of parish churches on Gotland according to art historians
(Weinberg 2001)

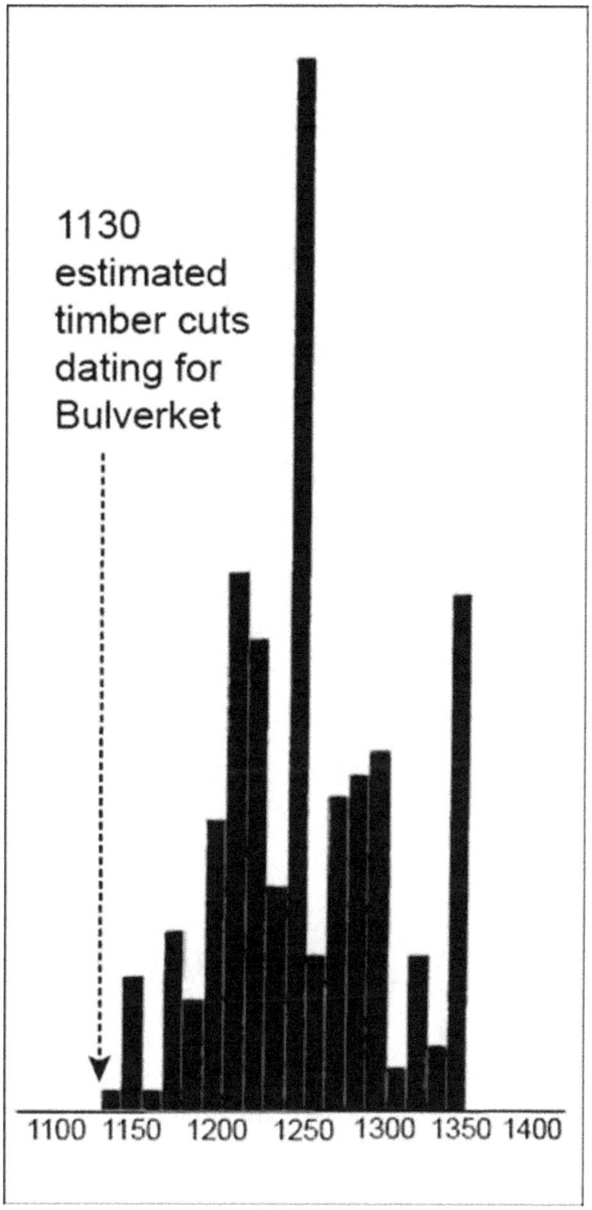

two natural points in the analysis are the Bulverket and the Norra Gattet threshold. Gotland's largest gravefield at Broa is also included for a total of 32. The map of figure 11 (aside from a small number of omitted churches to the south) resembles the early northern "third" division "Tredingen" of Gotland mentioned in the Guta Saga.

In a simpler computer task then the Norsholm - Bulverket *vi* analysis with all three kinds of core patterns, one calculates only three-point alignments among these lat/long points taken from Swedish digital maps. Beginning with the best accuracy of church alignments in the Norsholm pattern, at or under 0.06°,

Figure 11. Latitude/Longitude points used in design analysis

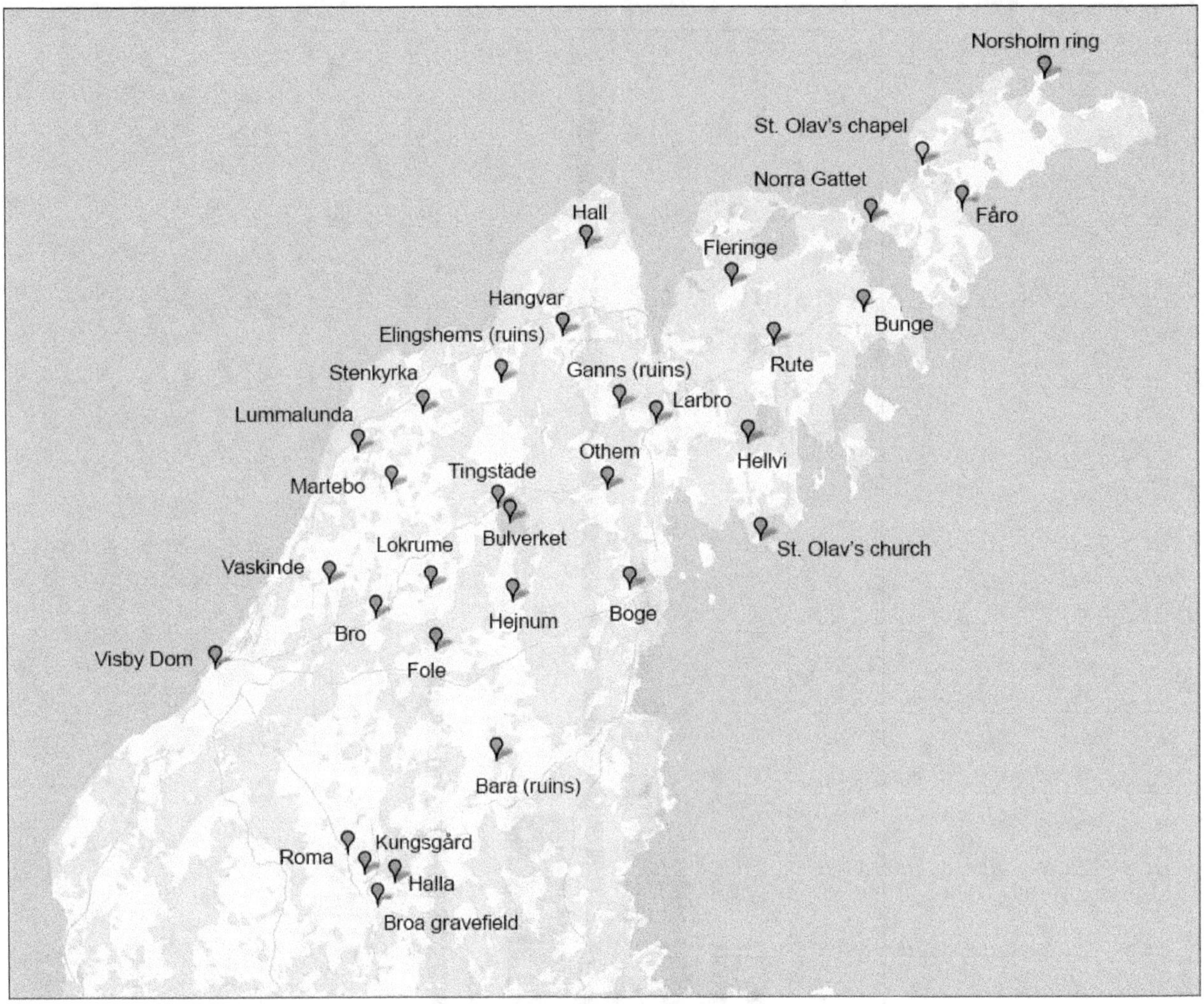

one can continue the mapping up to 0.14° looking for all relatively accurate alignments with the Bulverket. Most accurate and complex are the four three-point alignments that overlap, illustrating a possible four-point concept between Väskinde – Bulverket – Othem- Hellvi. Two of these calculate close to visual acuity at or under 0.02° deviation: Bulverket – Othem – Hellvi and Väskinde – Othem – Hellvi. The third, Väskinde – Bulverket – Hellvi is at or under 0.05° while the fourth Väskinde – Bulverket – Othem is at or under 0.06°. As already mapped, the central Norsholm axis adds an additional four three – point alignments with Bulverket that constitute a four-point alignment as well: Lokrume – Bulverket – Norra Gattet (0.04°), Lokrume – Bulverket – Norsholm (0.07°), Bulverket – Norra Gattet – Norsholm (0.09°) and Lokrume – Norra Gattet – Norsholm (0.10°). With these eight Bulverket alignments, two more exist in Bro – Bulverket – Fåro (0.04°) and Bulverket – Larbro – Rute (0.05°). All ten exist at or under 0.11°. To list angular deviations the computer averages the two calculations taken from each end with respect to the interim point. To imagine this kind of accuracy, the deviation of an interim 0.06° point exactly at the middle of a 50,000-meter line is about 26 meters.

Figure 12. List of all three-point alignments at or under 0.06°, 0.08°, and 0.14°

Alignments at or under 0.06°

bulverket , larbro , rute
bulverket , othem , hellvi
vaskinde , bulverket , othem
vaskinde , bulverket , hellvi
bro , bulverket , faro
lokrume , bulverket , n gattet

boge , hellvi , norsholm kyrka
visby domk , larbro , bunge
vaskinde , othem , hellvi
kungsgarder ruin , tingstade , hangvar
halla k , bara odekkyrka , faro

Alignments at or under 0.08°

bulverket , othem , hellvi
vaskinde , bulverket , othem
vaskinde , bulverket , hellvi
vaskinde , othem , hellvi
lokrume , bulverket , n gattet
lokrume , bulverket , norsholm kyrka
bro , bulverket , faro
bulverket , larbro , rute

boge , hellvi , norsholm kyrka
bara odekkyrka , hellvi , norsholm kyrka

visby domk , larbro , bunge
kungsgarder ruin , tingstade , hangvar
halla k , bara odekkyrka , faro

Alignments at or under 0.14°

bulverket , othem , hellvi
vaskinde , othem , hellvi
vaskinde , bulverket , othem
vaskinde , bulverket , hellvi
lokrume , bulverket , n gattet
lokrume , bulverket , norsholm kyrka
bulverket , n gattet , norsholm kyrka
lokrume , n gattet , norsholm kyrka
bro , bulverket , faro
bulverket , larbro , rute

broa gf , hellvi , norsholm kyrka
boge , hellvi , norsholm kyrka
bara odekkyrka , hellvi , norsholm kyrka
broa gf , halla k , norsholm kyrka

halla k , bara odekkyrka , faro
broa gf, bara odekkyrka , faro

vaskinde , gannes ruins , faro
tingstade , gannes ruins , st olavs ch.
kungsgarder ruin , hellvi , faro
visby domk , larbro , bunge
kungsgarder ruin , rute , n gattet
stenkyrka , hangvar , norsholm kyrka
roma , othem , larbro
kungsgarder ruin , tingstade , hangvar
broa gf, fole , elinghems odekyrka
kungsgarder, bara ruin, st.olavs ch.

Given the accuracy of these four separate alignments, one can now map in figure 12 their relationship to the lat/long point estimated from Hult de Geer's map. Keeping in mind the size of the interior water square, about 100 meters across, the four alignments run two on each side of the lat/long point used in the searches at three accuracies. In the 170 meter square the farthest deviation from the point is 14.7 meters on one side and 10.3 meters on the other. This tends to confirm that if the four alignments were surveyed in the 1100's, then the point used in the present study comes quite close to the existing center of the sacred square.

But, again, can one prove that these are not just remarkable coincidences? Yes, more so than with the test exercise of figure 9 and the Norsholm *vi*. Working only with three-point alignments and no complexity of integrated molecule patterns, this replicates early computer studies of numbers of alignments produced by random points at given accuracies in a defined area. The conclusion by archaeologists reading these results, usually created by IT others forty years ago, was that no alignments among existing features could be trusted to be designed and land surveyed by traditional cultures. The limitations of these early exercises, however, lie in the lack of methodical comparison of randomly produced patterns with those of existing possible cultural constructs. Logically, if numbers of alignments in an existing geography fall largely within a range of randomly produced patterns, then design seems improbable. The question begged in this case, however, asks about analyses where the number of patterns clearly rise to the top or even exceeds the random (see examples in Doxtater 2023, 2022, 2021, 2009). Even if the existing do not exceed the random, this does not mean designed patterns cannot also exist in the same geography, just that proving design will be more difficult. This, however, is not the present case.

For the present simplified test, one returns to the strategy of creating test areas around each of the 29 church sites shown in figure 9. Again, it may not matter that rectangular test areas vary in size as they are quickly drawn in custom software. The goal was to create areas that didn't overlap, making it possible to insert a random point in each area to substitute for the existing and where no test area contained more than one "church". A null hypothesis states that all Christian sites in the analysis were located for reasons other than surveyed large-scale, formal symbolic patterns and therefore that mapped existing patterns must be coincidental. The variation in size and topographical conditions of the test areas shouldn't inhibit the discovery of numbers of formal patterns like the existing. Nothing in test area size or topography can create in itself an unusually large number of alignments at the scale of the northern portion of a flat Gotland.

Figure 13. Distance of four alignments from estimated center point of Bulverket platform

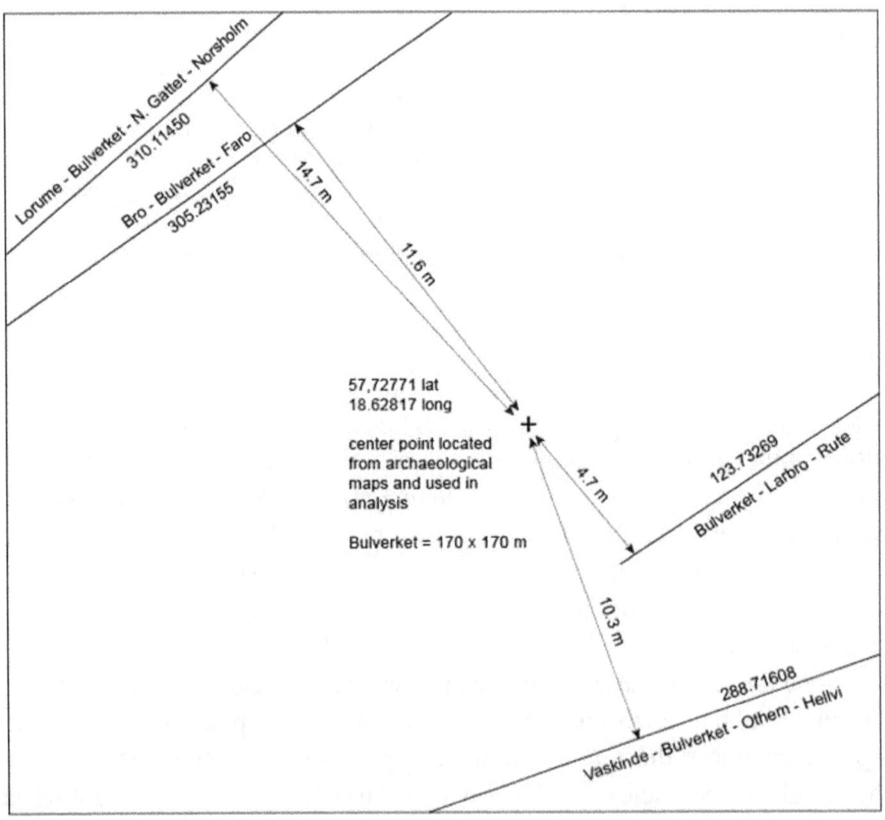

Figure 14. Graph of numbers of three-point alignments created by 100 sets of random points compared to existing (below); graph of numbers of Bulverket related alignments of 100 sets of random points compared to existing (above)

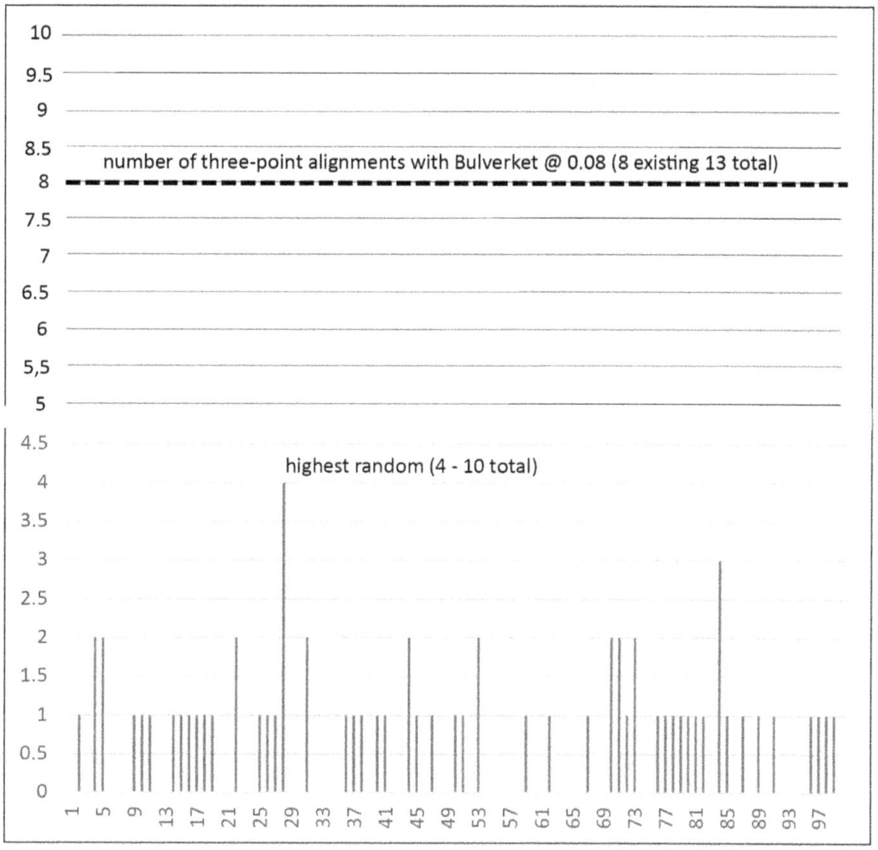

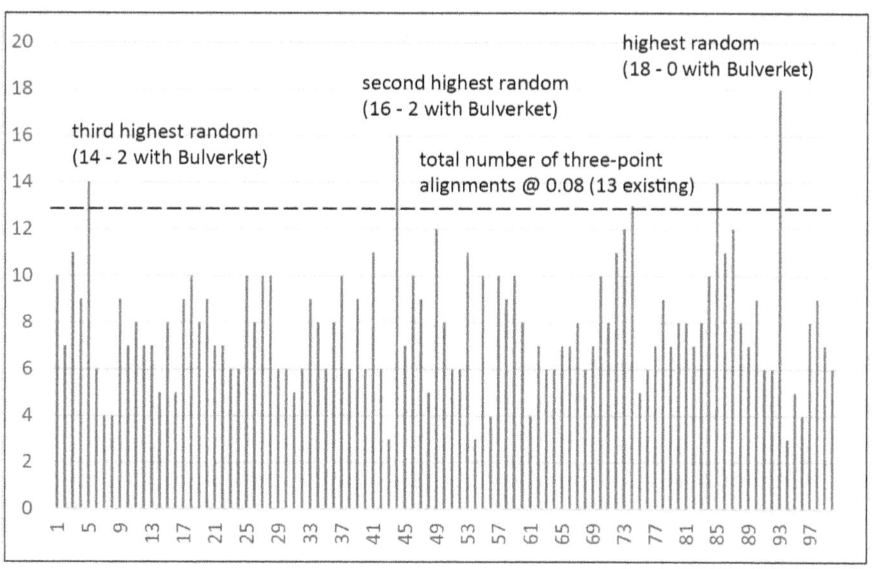

Software is set to create 100 sets of 29 random points, each substituted for an existing church. Three natural water related points remain constant without test areas: the Broa gravefield, Norra Gattet, and the Bulverket point. Accuracy is set at or less than 0.08° deviation, between the 0.06° and 0.14° of listed existing patterns. The computer calculates all three-point alignments between all possibilities of triads.

Figure 14 shows results. One first asks which of the 100 random sets creates the most three-point alignments, regardless of site points involved. The highest number is 18, while the existing generates only 13, clearly illustrating that at this accuracy impressive numbers of random alignments are created. It is true, however, that the *average* number of alignments created in the 100 sets is considerably less than the existing, i.e. 7.9. The existing 13 are higher than 96 of the 100 random sets.

Our primary interest, however, is not alignments per se, but those that use the Bulverket point in the center of the water square. Of the four highest random sets—18, 16, 14, 14-- the fixed Bulverket point occurs in a three-point alignment 0 times in the 18, and 2 times in each of the other three. The existing Bulverket three-point alignments are 8 of 13. The highest number of Bulverket alignments in the 100 sets of random points is 4, one half the existing. The average number of Bulverket alignments per set of random points is 0.66. Concluding from the graph of figure 13, the odds of 8 alignments randomly using the Bulverket point at 0.08° or under must be less than one in thousands.

IF LARGE-SCALE SURVEYING ALIGNED CHURCHES TO THE BULVERKET THEN AZIMUTHS FROM THESE SACRED POINTS MAY HAVE CREATED CHURCH ORIENTATIONS

One can now believe that most if not all churches aligned to the Bulverket as mapped in figure 15 were intentionally integrated through the process of locating and building the Bulverket and then surveying lines out to new community points of spiritual contact—this during a time of heightened pilgrimage interest. In addition to evident social cooperation in the construction of egalitarian architecture of the Bulverket—subservient as it may have been to a "Norsholm *vi*"-- subsequent positioning of churches would have required similar participation. While the terrain and smaller scales of these northern Gotland patterns presented few of the challenges of much more rugged landscape of especially Norway, still, laying out accurate lines requires numerous station-point teams and open access to areas with ancient social histories. Theoretically, designing and creating formal landscapes must have been a participatory ritual alternative to territorial conflict, though contributions from large farmers may well have been necessary.

While no records exist of Bulverket use as pilgrimage destination—or any other purpose for that matter-- large numbers of Gotlanders traveled through their landscape, establishing and cognizing sacred lines between their new churches and a larger scale sacred point. This shows considerable overlap with contemporaneous Norway and Sweden. Not highlighted in the "structuralist" mapping of the two studies shown in figures 1 and 2, the orientation of churches at integrated spatial points logically extends larger landscape symbolism—part Norse, part Christian—into the architectural meaning of first walls and portals. What then will mapping azimuths from a Bulverket "system" reveal.

Scholars have attempted to discover a rationale to medieval stone church orientations in the North by looking closely at astronomical or magnetic compass variations found in England, Denmark, Norway and Finland (Hoare & Sweet 2000, Abrahamsen 1985 and 1992, Eide 1986, and Ridderstad 2012). From this work, however, no common conclusions yet predict orientations in Scandinavia, Gotland included.

Figure 15. Bulverket system related alignments (heavy) and church orientation azimuths (light)

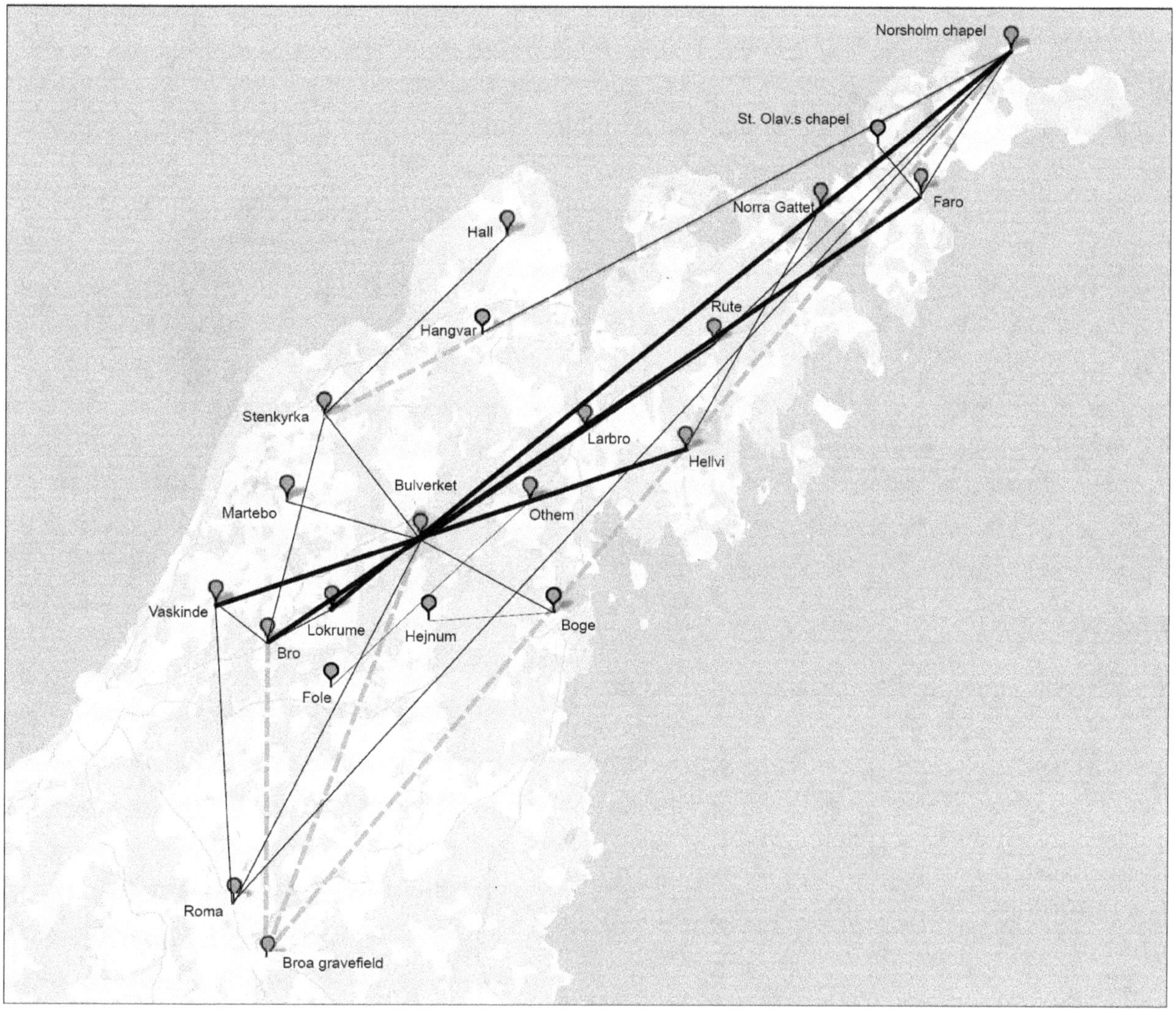

Beginning with the Bulverket platform itself, one finds no good, measured orientation for the 170 meter square. Yet Hult de Geer attempted to do so, magnetic compass readings notwithstanding. If one orients de Geer's map and its integrated Bulverket diagram, discounting his north arrow, the platform's orientation can be estimated, as shown in figure 16. Since the primary ritual role of the Bulverket phenomenon may have been the distribution of Norse landscape power to the new stone churches, its layout logically would have begun with azimuths to the two vertex features of the *vi* patterns, Norsholm and a point at Gotland's center such as Broa, both linked by summer solstice symbolism. Could these directions geometrically have created the orientation of the square? The bisect of these two azimuths from Bulverket, one north, the other south, calculates as 235.26853. As seen in figure 16, the bisect ideally would be the diagonal from the NW to SE corners, part of the initial layout of the platform. This axis, however, while expressing the bisect azimuth, may even more symbolically reveal the most important diagonal at 90°, the one that looks north, balancing the two water related azimuths to Norsholm and Broa.

Figure 16. Determining the location and orientation of the Bulverket platform from Hult de Geer's maps (above); conjectural design logic creating orientation of platform diagonals from azimuths to Norsholm and Broa gravefield

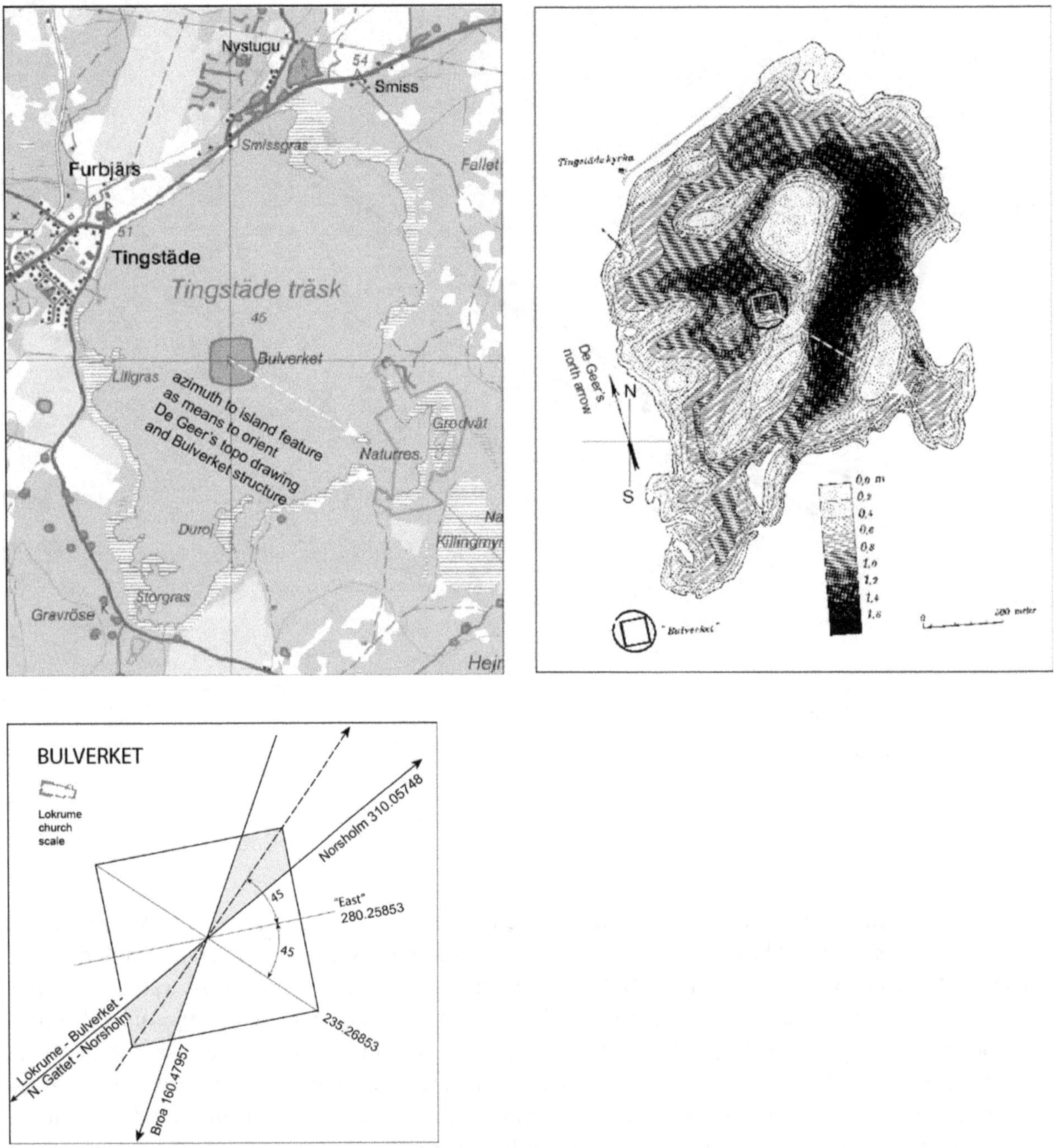

Figure 17. Square perpendicular at Lokrume determined by bisect of azimuths to Norsholm and Bro church

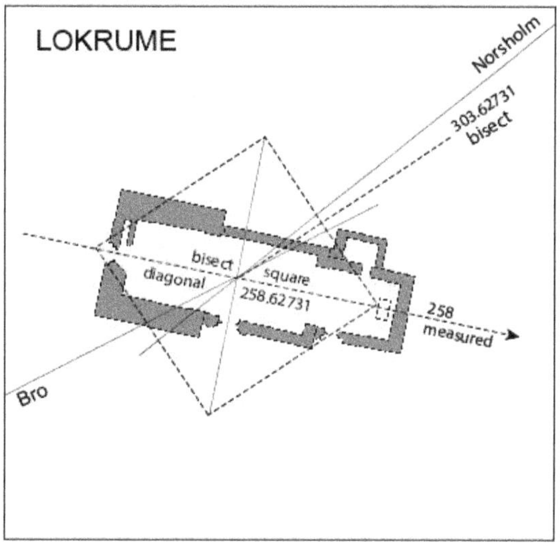

Having measured the 281° platform orientation within a couple of degrees, despite the small scale of de Geer's diagram, it is nonetheless striking that the secondary 45° bisect of the ideal "north" and "south" perpendicular calculates as 280.26853. [Is this orientation related to Gotlandic vinkelrätt concepts at Vallhagar? The presently estimated bisect diagonal of the Bulverketat about 325° is close to the 350°-330° range of Lindström's "B" cardinals, very much part of any square symbolism.]

Lokrume as the southern terminus of the Norsholm *vi* axis through Bulverket might be expected to use this axis in its initial layout, figure 17. Such geometry is possible using the Bulverket – Norsholm axis, together with an azimuth to nearby Bro. It in turn is the terminus of a meridian to Broa as part of its *vi* with Bulverket and Norsholmand, and separate alignment with the Bulverket and Fåro. Not unlike Bulverket itself, this Lokrume pair creates a bisect that defines the perpendicular "cardinals" of a square whose diagonal is close to 45° from the measured church axis of 258°. [Regarding a *vinkelrätt* concept, the axis perpendicular to the church orientation is about 348°, close to the 350° upper mark.]

The orientation and layout of Bro in figure 18 also uses an alignment through the Bulverket, reflecting its accurate alignment with Fårö. Not one but two additional lines create a parallelogram with a more complex logic of determining church axis. One of these points to neighboring Väskinde, the terminus of the four-point alignment running through the Bulverket to

Othem and Hellvi. The other azimuth runs to Stenkyrka, one of the two churches aligned as the west ray to the Norsholm vertex. This threesome of azimuths at the Bro location might have first been laid out as a northwest corner of the nave where an additional line pairs up with the Väskinde azimuth at the same angle as Bulverket – Stenkyrka to create the longitudinal nave axis. Looking at the Väskinde location, also figure 18, logically it associates with its four-point alignment through Bulverket to Othem and Hellvi, but also reciprocates to nearby Bro and its positional importance. These two azimuths create a parallelogram whose diagonal works impressively as the church axis.

At Stenkyrka, an azimuth from its location on the west ray of the Norsholm *vi* to Bulverket may have been used first, figure 19. The best second azimuth working to create another parallelogram diagonal could be that to the more isolated church of Hall. But why not a second or even third azimuth to Norsholm

Figure 18. Use of azimuths from Bulverket, Väskinde, and Stenkyrka at Bro to create equal angle of church orientation paired with Väskinde (left); Use of Bulverket and Bro azimuths at Väskinde to create parallelogram diagonal as church orientation (right)

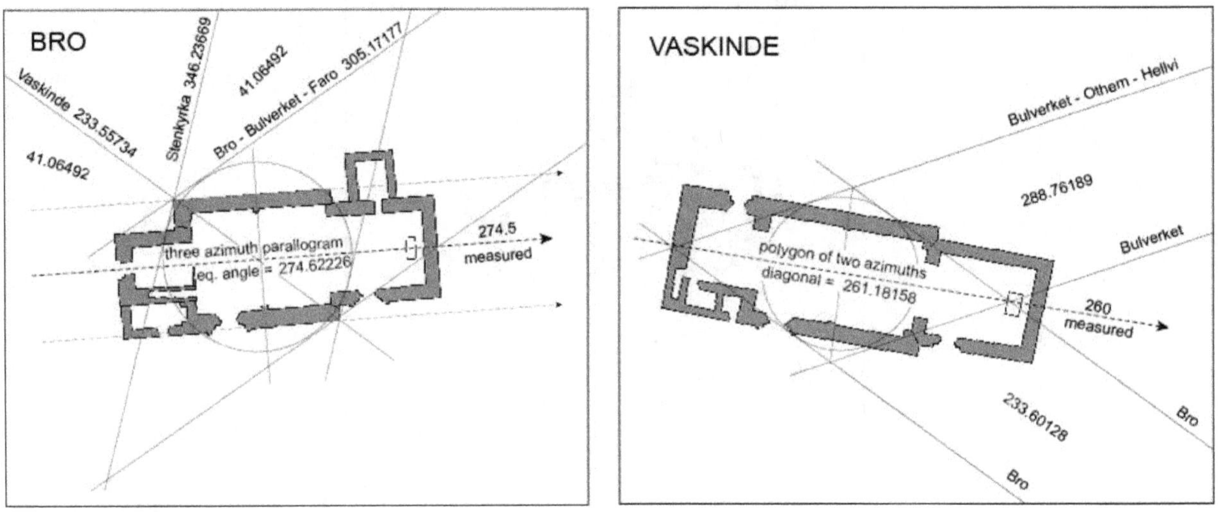

or one reciprocating to Bro? Alternatively, the church orientation calculates quite close to the direct azimuth to Lärbro sitting on an interim point of an accurate alignment with Bulverket and Rute. This, however, suggests an unusual subordination of one church over another, compared to a more socially balanced use of pairs or even triads of churches.

A formal geometry exists between Stenkyrka and Boge with respect to the Bulverket. Both lie on their respective *vi* rays to Norsholm, and both may have used azimuths from the Bulverket in their orientations. In using only the Bulverket azimuth, a 45° layout geometry of

Boge might have emulated the Bulverket square itself. As seen in figure 19, the azimuth could have first determined the interior center of the nave, the center of the altar arch and altar threshold. Speculating further, laying out a square through these three points might have generated the diagonal and church orientation.

Curiously, Boge's measured orientation equals Hangvar's, the partner to Stenkyrka on the west Norsholm *vi* ray. While Hangvar will be diagrammed as part of an alternative "system"; Boge's landscape relation to Hangvar creates a 17.516 km perpendicular between the two Bulverket determined church axes. Within or close to the one-degree margin presently used in church orientations. Again, Hangvar's perpendicular reciprocates. More precisely, Boge's Bulverket determined church perpendicular is 14.55° and the azimuth to Hangvar is 15.64225. Conversely, the perpendicular south from Hangvar's axis is 194.32° compared to the south looking azimuth between the two churches of 194.62°. If some land surveyed relationship existed between the two, Hangvar's more accurate location and orientation might have been made at a different time than Boge's earlier tie directly to Bulverket.

Lärbro, figure 20, resides on the Bulverket – Rute line, but seems not to involve the platform center point in determining its orientation. Instead, a tight parallelogram using the azimuth from its close neighbor, Hellvi (6.187 km) and cardinal East generates a diagonal of 263.76061 compared to the measured church axis of 263.5. One of the few uses of an accurate cardinal East, this line might have been first laid out from the intersection of Bulverket – Rute and a 0.05alignment from Visby Dom (cathedral) to

Figure 19. Azimuths from Bulverket and Hall to Stenkyrka that create parallelogram diagonal as church axis (left); azimuth from Bulverket to Boge creates square perpendicular as church axis (right)

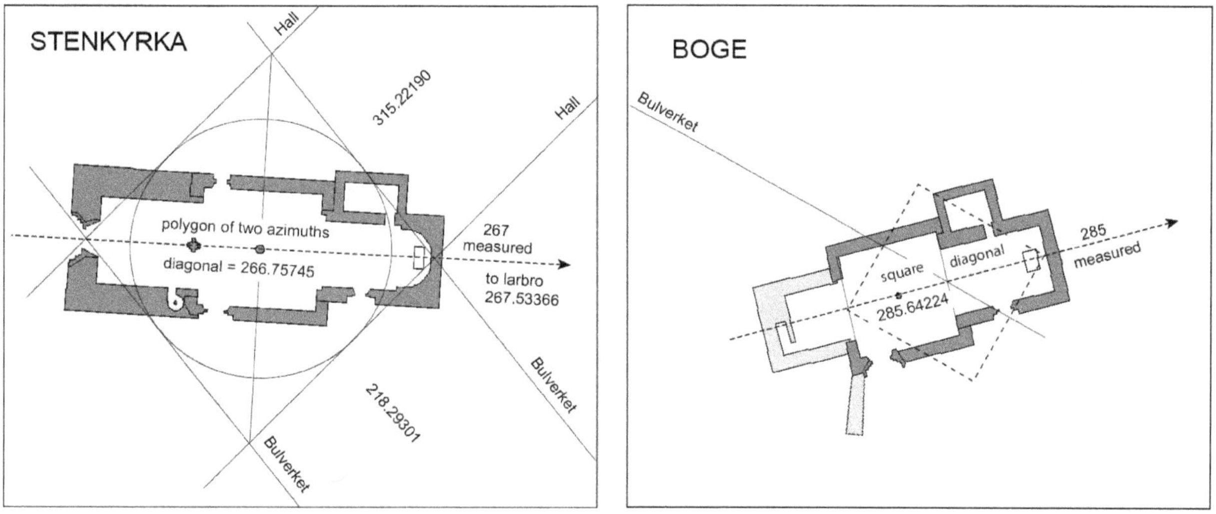

Figure 20. Azimuth to Hellvi pairs up with cardinal east to create bisect as Lärbro axis (left), azimuths to Norra Gattet and Bulverket create bisect as square perpendicular and diagonal as church axis (right)

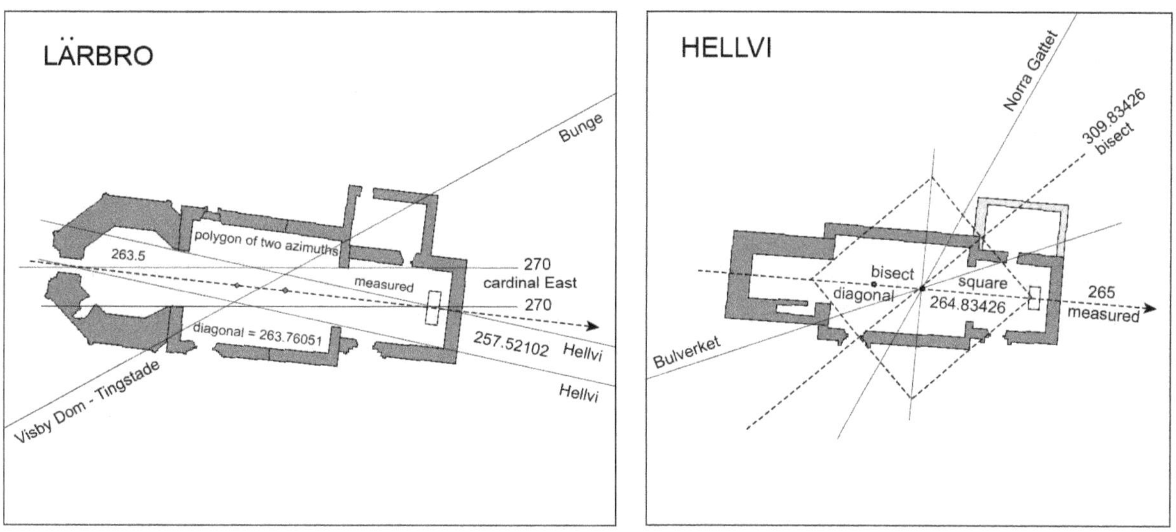

Bunge. If as indicated in plan sources, the octagonal tower was designed contemporaneously with the nave and altar, then the start point on a cardinal East could have been the octagon's west portal. Adding the Hellvi azmuth to the portal point, creates a vi whose center line defines the church axis.

Known for its early free-standing "*kastal*" or defensive tower at a strategic geographic location, as well as its octagonal bell tower, Lärbro is unique on Gotland but not dissimilar to the Nideros in Trondheim; much in the churches' sculpture evokes worship of St. Olaf (Roosval 1935:98). A parallel may exist between this *kastal* and that at Mjösa lake in Norway, figure 1, located by a large scale *vinkelrätt* pattern part of the Gudbrandsdal pilgrimage path. Perhaps a more symbolic landscape feature than defensive

Figure 21. Rute's orientation as diagonal of square perpendicular created by bisect of azimuths to Norsholm and Bulverket/Lärbro (left); Fåro's orientation as parallelogram diagonal from Norsholm and St. Olav's chapel azimuths (right)

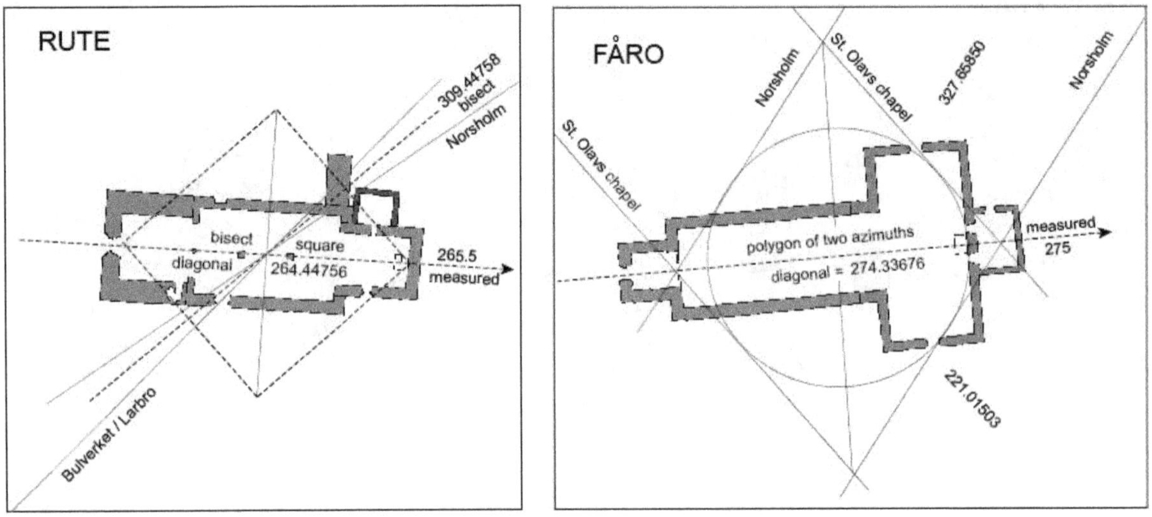

threat, the Lärbro intersection point may have expressed the alliance or integration of the Bulverket system that terminates at Rute, with one possibly focused on the Tingstäde church. As discussed in the following section, Lärbro aligns most accurately on the line from Visby Dom to Bunge—running along the Träsk shore by the church and *ting* site. The use of cardinal East in orientation logic might be associated with a greater influence of church and state, yet still paired up here with Hellvi and its prehistoric depth. The accurate line from Visby Dom to Bunge, however, does not seem otherwise to be expressed.

Hellvi's location can be seen as one of the most powerful, sitting as it does on two existing lines, the east Norsholm *vi* ray and the four-point axis with Väskinde – Bulverket – Othem. This importance seems reflected in the layout appropriation of the azimuth from Bulverket and that from Norra Gattet, perhaps an indication of some earlier formal association with this most natural Northern ritual feature. The bisect of these two azimuths at Hellvi, not unlike the pattern at Bulverket, creates an orientation 45° from the west-east diagonal of a square creating the church axis. The bisect toward the NE might have marked that corner of the nave, while running through the principal nave portal to the SE (this is a pattern in several churches in Trondheimsfjord e.g. Maere and Logtun on the Frosta – Eidet – Heimdalhaugen axis).

Rute, as the northern terminus of Bulverket – Lärbro, shares layout patterns with the powerfully positioned churches at Lokrume and Hellvi, figure 21. All three use bisects of important azimuth pairs as center lines to squares with diagonals at angles of 45°. Rute reaches out to Bulverket (and aligned Lärbro) and the Norsholm vertex point. Again, the bisect line runs from the Northeast nave corner through the nave center and south portal.

How does Fårö's location work with five existing three-point alignments? Most interesting might be the line from the meridian apex of Bro through the Bulverket to Fårö. While less direct, Fårö's use of the azimuth from Norsholm could have been associated with the *vi* to Bulverket as its eastern ray. The two three-point alignments from the Broa gravefield and Halla church up through the Bara ruins may support this symbolism with Fårö—not running all the way up to Norsholm, but closely paralleling the east *vi* axis to Halla. Two other three-point alignments run up to Fårö: Väskinde – Ganns, and Kungs-

Figure 22. St. Olav's ring and chapel, center point off 46 meters from Visby Dom line to Norsholm ring

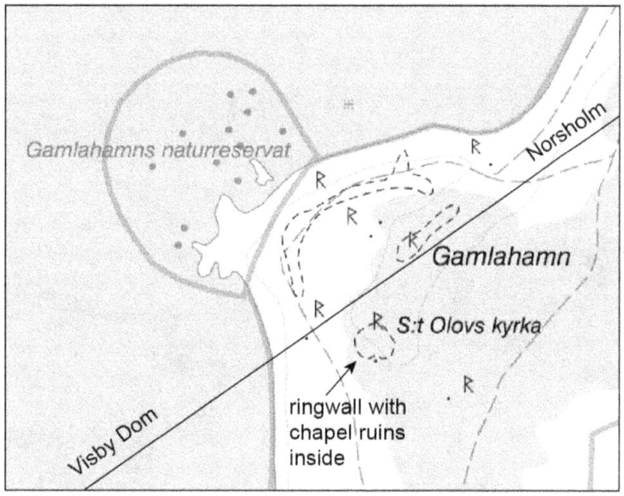

gård – Hellvi. Neither of these existing lines appear to have influenced the Fåro church layout, rather the partner to Norsholm might have been the azimuth from the small chapel dedicated to St. Olav (associated with the western vi ray?), figure 22. Three architectural points work well with this parallelogram and its diagonal as church axis, i.e. the western tower portal, the symmetrical portals of the north and south walls of the choir, and perhaps a center point in the alter space. As one of the later churches (14th century) did Fåro's layout pay homage to both a very early Norsholm – Bulverket vi, as well as later, stronger Christian elements, particularly involving St. Olav. The small ring wall enclosure and even smaller saint's chapel ruins inside, figure 22, aligns at an average accuracy equal to or less than 0.16° to the azimuth line from Visby Dom church to the Norsholm ring.

Figure 23. Martebo's orientation as bisector of azimuth to Bulverket and cardinal east (left); Hejnum's orientation as equal angle to Boge azimuth and cardinal east (right)

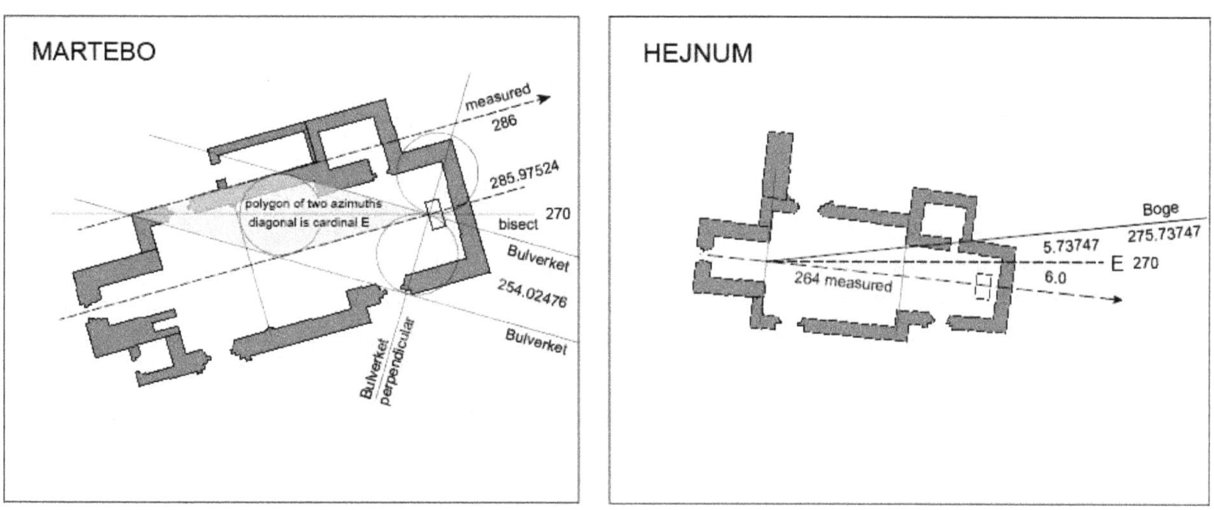

Figure 24. Othem's axis as parallelogram diagonal created by Bunge and St. Olav's church azimuths (left); angle between azimuths to Othem and Ellingshems creates equal third azimuth as church axis at Fole (right)

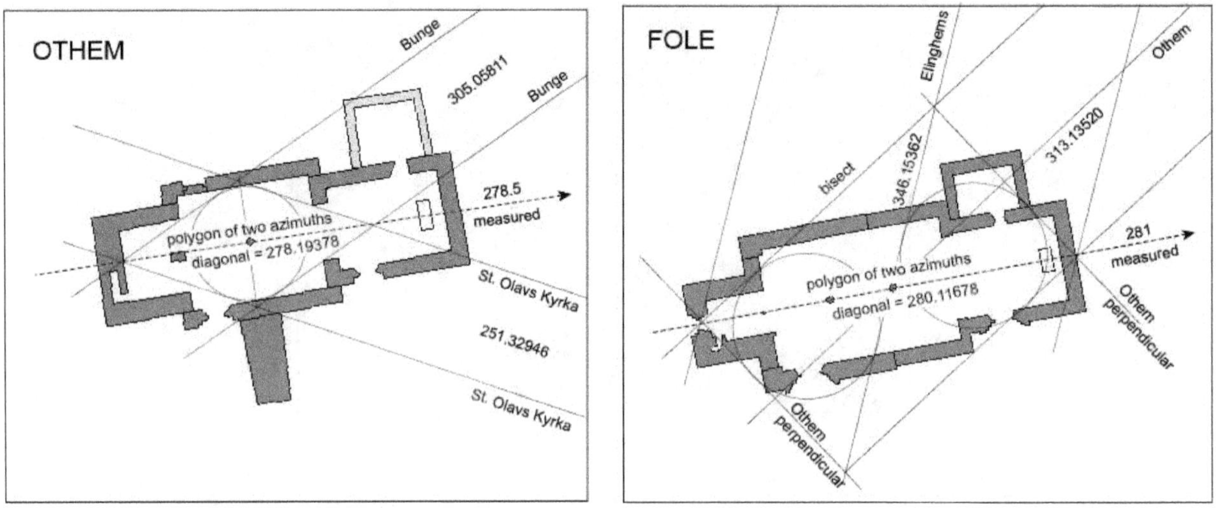

Martebo's layout may mirror Lärbro's strategy in using cardinal East as one of the two parallelogram azimuths, figure 23. Unlike Lärbro, however, Martebo's other azimuth may have come from the Bulverket point. If the first layout point was the NW nave corner, the angle between the Bulverket and cardinal East could have been emulated to the north creating the orientation of nave wall and major church axis. Hejnum as well may reflect greater Christian influence by using cardinal East, while at the same time using an azimuth to Boge with its location on the east ray of the Norsholm *vi* and singular orientational azimuth to the Bulverket.

What then of Othem, on the Väskinde – Bulverket – Hellvi line, figure 24? Like Lärbro, Othem sits on a Bulverket line, but does not appear to invoke any direct azimuthal power from the platform center when laying out orientation and plan. Curiously, a 0.135° less accurate line exists from Roma through these two Bulverket exceptions, Othem and Lärbro. Moving away from Bulverket related pattern, of course, one becomes more suspicious of random phenomena. Othem's parallelogram of Bunge and St. Olav's Kyrka shares similarities with Lärbro in the manner it may position the four jambs of the two nave arches, west and east, together with an axis perpendicular at a nave center point. These two azimuths may relate stronger to the following Tingstäde "system", particularly to Bunge. Use of the direction to St. Olav's church may have connotations as well of pilgrimage.

Fole church forms the interim point of a 0.14° line, perhaps random, that runs from the Broa grave-field up to the Ellinghems church ruin. In the present design analysis the Broa line was initially drawn in a separate layer over the correctly oriented Fole plan (the typical process). Several azimuths to other churches and North points as well as the Bulverket were tried until that to Othem became interesting. The bisect of the Ellinghems azimuth and that from Othem creates an equal ray as church orientation, 280.11678°, compared to the measured orientation of 281°. While the use of the prehistoric Broa grave-yard point seems to compete with the possible Bulverket related *vi* role of Bro, the two churches are close neighbors, 4.712 kilometers apart.

Given the high probability that thirteen early stone churches were located on land surveyed alignments with the Bulverket center point or its *vi* system, one would expect an also strong use of the Buverket point itself in the orientations of these churches. As seen in the lists of figure 25, seven may have done so. In many of these churches, their azimuths could have expressed relations to a neighbor, e.g. the possible reciprocity between Lokrume, Bro and Väskinde. The two of the nine churches on Bulverket lines that do not use the center square for orientation, Lärbro and Fåro, will be shown to also have pattern associations with an alternate *vi* system.

As for Martebo and Hejnum, neither lie on Bulverket system lines, but use azimuths to related points. Does their using cardinal East as a second azimuth suggest a greater Christian dedication, or even later construction date? While Othem lies on the Väskinde-Hellvi axis, its orientation azimuths will be shown to be part of the alternative system and could suggest a later date of construction as well. Fole, not on any line, and using an azimuth to Othem, may be part of this system overlap.

Figure 25. Summary of Bulverket related church orientations

churches on Bulverket lines including Norsholm and Broa vis	use Bulverket lines and sites for orientation
Lokrume	Norsholm, Bulverket Bro
Vaskinde	Bulverket, Othem, Hellvi, Bro
Hellvi	Bulverket
Bro	Vaskinde, Stenkyrka, Bulverket, Faro
Larbro	Hellvi
Rute	Norsholm, Bulverket
Faro	Norsholm
Boge	Bulverket
Stenkyrka	Bulverket
churches not on Bulverket lines but use for orientation	
Martebo	Bulverket, cardinal East
Hejnum	Boge, cardinal East
Fole	Othem, Ellinghems
churches on Bulverket lines but don't use for orientation	
Othem	Bunge, St. Olav's church

A TINGSTÄDE SYSTEM: A NEW *VI*, ASSOCIATED CHURCHES AND ORIENTION LOGIC

The more recent archaeology in Rönnby & Adams (2006) highlights one of the more unexpected findings about the large timber platform:

"A surprising discovery was that many of the layers of logs that comprised the caissons had subsided deep into the sediment below the construction layer. The various sediment and cultural layers are broadly horizontal but towards the edges of the caissons the construction layer and those immediately above it sweep down to the main timbers, indicating that this process started even as Bulverket was being built or soon after. It is possible that the degree of subsidence was both unexpected to the builders and progressive, perhaps accelerating as buildings were erected and that because of this the platform soon became impossible to use. The lesser degree of dip in the upper layers shows that by the time this material was deposited the rate of subsidence had slowed, perhaps at a time when less of the structure remained above the surface (182)".

Figure 26. Tingstäde church; photo by Bernt Enderborg
(from www.guteinfo.com, retrieved November 2022)

Figure 27. Tingstäde's location in relation to the Bulverket (above); orientation is angle equal to angle of Bunge and Hangvar azimuths (below)

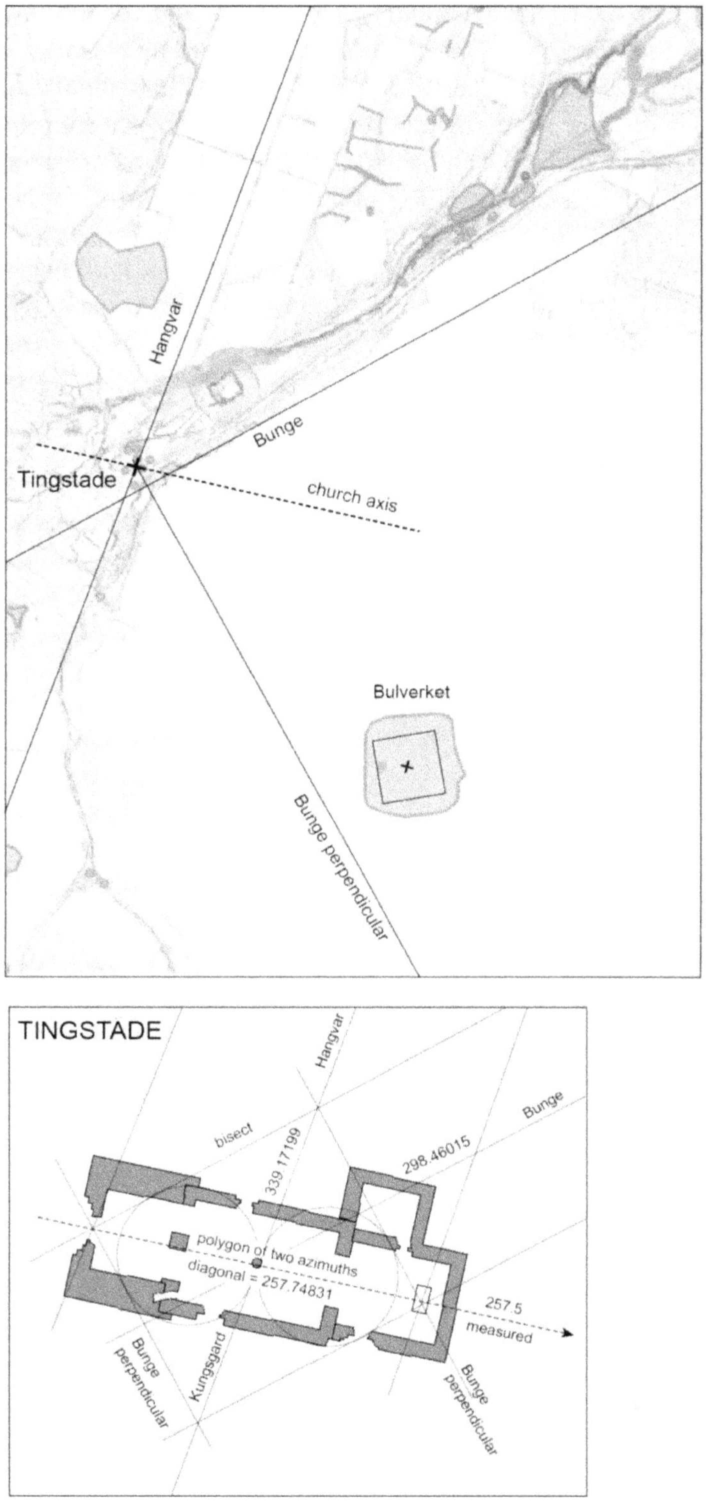

The perception of the Bulverket as above all a sacred benchmark location in the lake, may render the importance of a sinking platform somewhat differently. First, of course, the location could still have been used to land survey on the winter ice, though any *ting*-like ritual might have changed, particularly if the Norsholm *vi* was associated with summer solstice. A more interesting reason for not using the platform, however, might have been the deeper Christianization of this central ritual location by building the stone Tingstäde church on the shore, figures 26 & 27. Even though a chapel may have been built in the stone ring at the Norsholm point, the architectural symbolism of the new church and massive tower might have been an attempt to replace the power of the Bulverket point.

Pursuing this idea, though still testing large-scale surveying that may have manipulated social power, one looks more closely at two alignments that intersect at or near the Tingstäde

Church figure 28. Given the symbolic power of lines to the NE and the possibility of a Bulverket *vi* to Norra Gattet and the Norsholm ring, the accurate line from the center of the Visby Dom to Lärbro and

Figure 28. Fåro vi and Visby Dom/Bunge "system"

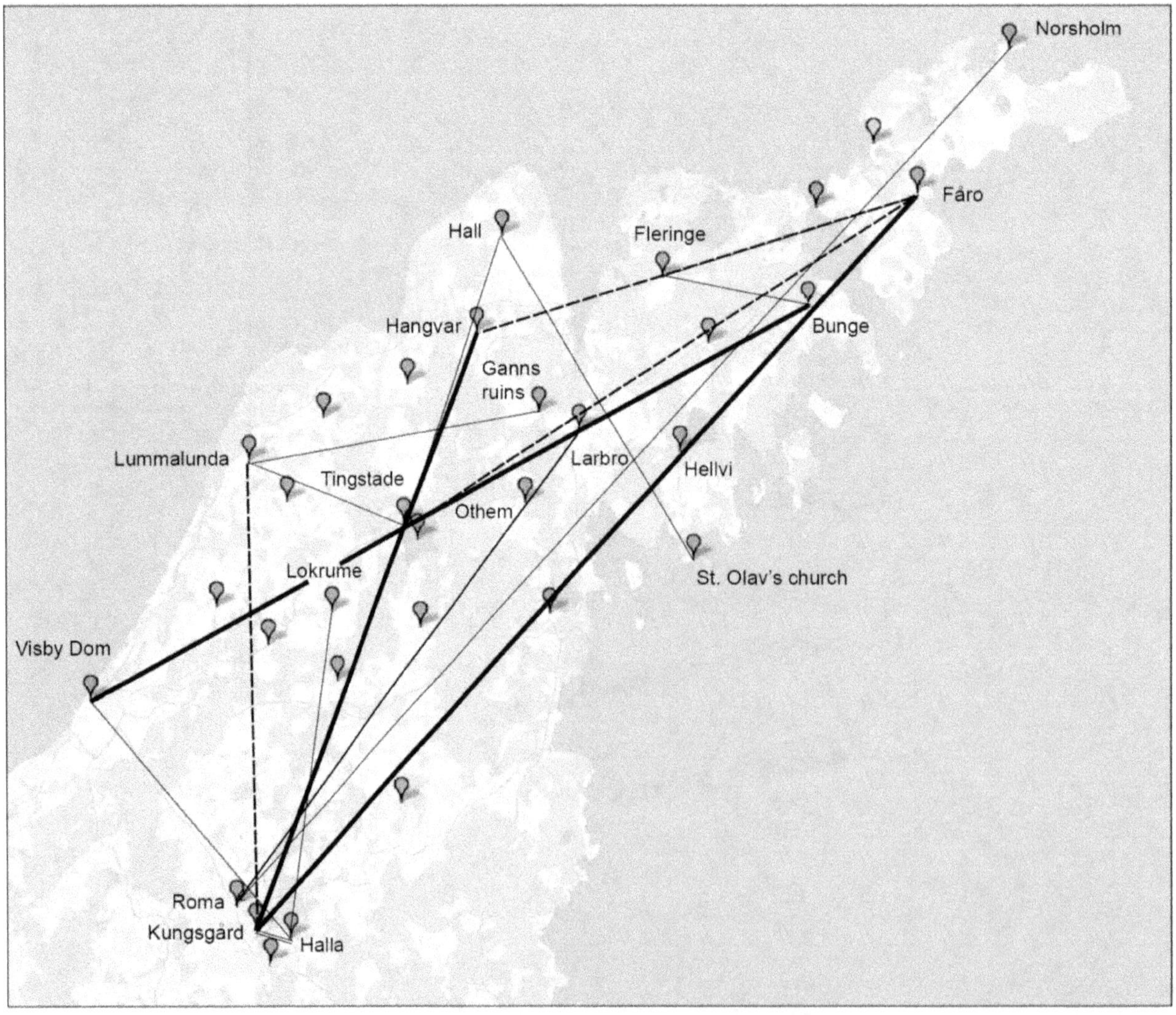

Bunge churches (under 0.08°) runs along the lake shore immediately adjacent to the Tingstäde church. The calculated distance of this less accurate alignment with the church center point is about 130 meters to the southeast. Could the long, accurate line from Visby Dom to Lärbro and Bunge have been laid out prior to locating the Tingstäde church? Perhaps the important place on the shore was a new *ting* site (location documented in Lundmark 1925), replacing the sinking Bulverket. The church could have been later built immediately in front of the non-architectural *ting* site; it continued to function in the enclosed courtyard on the north side of the church. The surveyed line from Visby Dom to Lärbro and Bunge might never have been accurate to any built feature on the lake shore, while nevertheless being close enough to be part of whatever socio-symbolic purpose this alignment served. Thus, if the church was built later, its location didn't need to be resurveyed.

One can further evaluate the symbolic relation of the church to a surveyed Visby Dom – Bunge line by looking at its principal axis, a measured 257.5. If one maps the two intersecting azimuths shown in figure 28, Bunge and Hangvar, they create a rectangle whose diagonal when laid out on thee center pillar of the nave is within a fraction of the measured number, i.e. 257.74831°. The Kungsgård – Hangvar line determines the scale of the rectangle of Bunge and its perpendicular.

Most significant perhaps, regarding a formal landscape alternative to the Bulverket as mapped in figure 27, is first that the Tingstäde church structure negates the view of the Bulverket from the *ting* site, and second that the church center point and layout do not seem to be integrated into the Bulverket point. Bunge's orientation and layout, drawn in figure 29, is consistent with that of Tingstäde giving further weight to the inclusion of the Bulverket surrogate in the longer line to Visby Dom. This azimuth generates a square perpendicular whose related diagonal is 253.54292° compared to Bunge's measured orientation of 253°.

The local history of Bunge associates with military conflict through its murals of battle and wounds from pikes and crossbows on the wooden doors of its tower. Defensible walls around the churchyard add to the image.

Figure 29. Azimuth of Visby - Tingstäde – Lärbro – Bunge is square perpendicular with diagonal as Bunge church axis (left); diagonal of parallelogram of azimuths to Fåro and Bunge from Fleringe is church axis (right)

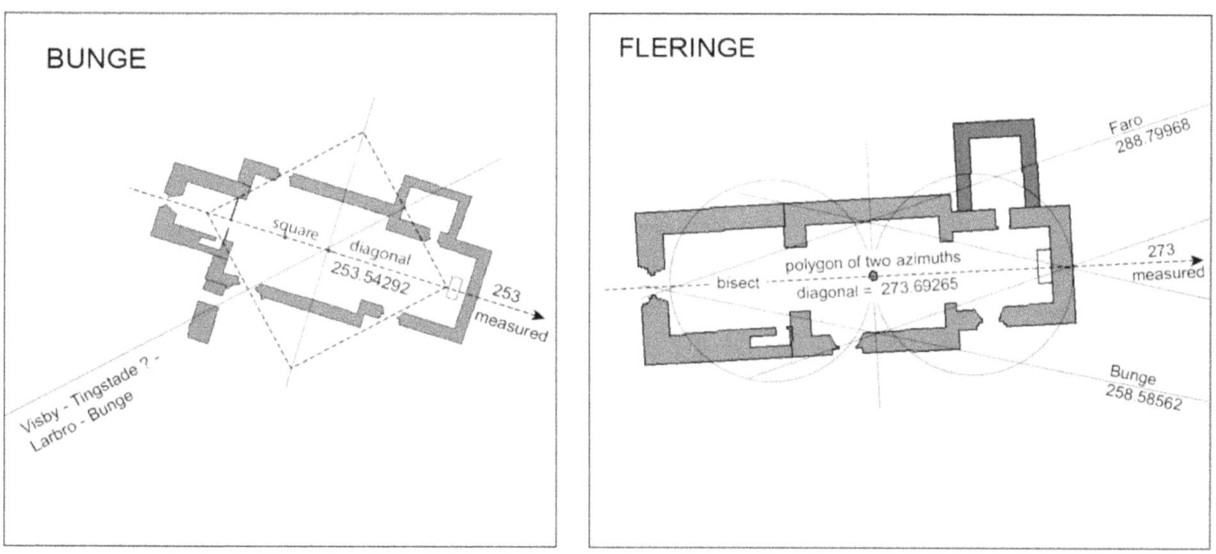

Undocumented speculation exists as to whether for a time the church was owned by a crusading Teutonic Order. No one knows who might have been fighting whom in this regard. Knights from Swedish shores in the early medieval crusaded through the heathen eastern regions of the Baltic. On the other hand, this line of Bunge – Lärbro – (Tingstäde) terminates at the fortified town of Visby, who waged a civil war with the land's farmers in 1288. Lärbro's free standing *kastal* may also contribute to the idea of power struggles here. Sand's (2017) short article on St. Olav pilgrimage on Gotland focuses on inferences about possible related activity at the large stone church built on St. Olavsholm (included in this study). She briefly comments how Lärbro (with its connectivity at the intersection of a Bulverket line and that with Bunge and Visby Dom), may have played a role in St. Olav's forceful attempts to convert. Bunge today belongs to the Church of Sweden and lies within the Diocese of Visby.

Fleringe's orientation and layout, also figure 29, does not sit on any three-point alignment at or under 0.14° and an azimuth to neighboring Bunge seems to work in its orientation logic. Also, more territorially in this area, is the nearby church at Fåro whose azimuth combines with Bunge to create a

Figure 30. Azimuths to Tingstäde and Ganns create parallelogram whose diagonal is Lummalunda axis

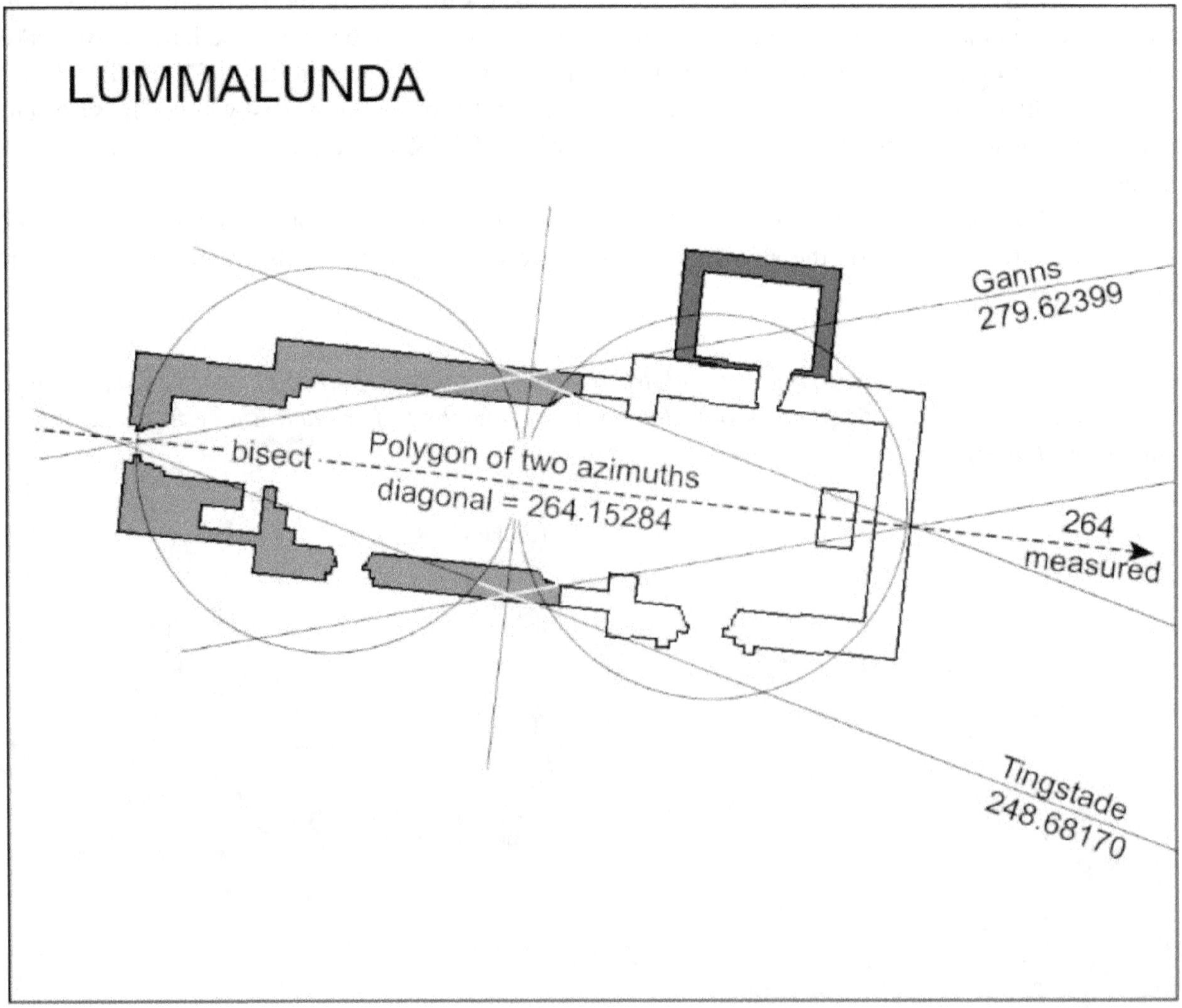

credible church axis. The long diagonal of this parallelogram calculates as 273.69265°, compared to the measured axis of 273°.

Lummalunda's location could be an alternative terminus to the prehistorically influenced west ray of a Norsholm-Bulverket *vi*. Yet it does not sit on any line of the present 0.14° list.

Other geometry, particularly involving bisects with Visby Dom, are accurate but not presently included (counterintuitively bisects with their four points are in fact far more likely to be random than three-point alignments). What can be stated about Lummalunda's layout, at least, is that an azimuth to the center of the Tingstäde church and one to the Ganns ruin creates a parallelogram similar to Fleringe, figure 30. Its long church axis diagonal calculates as 264.15284°, compared to a measured 264.

Testing a *Vi* Structure Focused on Tingstäde

If the Bunge-Visby Dom line was a surveyed artifact, and symbolically included Tingstäde, was there any "*vi*" pattern associated? No such structure emanates from Bunge, nor from Visby Dom itself. The Roma Kungsgård large chapel, however, may be more interesting. The Cistercian cloister at the "king's farm", was founded 1163-64 (*Fornsok* Roma 36:1), only two or three decades after the creation of the Bulverket point. This stylistically impressive church may have been positioned as the intersection point running through the formalizing *ting* site at Tingstäde up to Hangvar on the west ray of the Norsholm *vi*, and a line through Hellvi on an east ray (Hangvar *vi* counterpart), not to Norsholm but to the Fåro point. In terms of potential systematic *vi* structure, Fåro has *vi*-like characteristics in its vertex bisect relation to a west line to Hangvar

(but not Fleringe 364 meters off the line), an east line to Hellvi and Kungsgård, with the center line to Tingstäde, figure 31

The prospective *vi* from Fåro to Tingstäde, rays to Hangvar and Hellvi, is quite accurate: 15.063275° and 15.034083° with a precise average of 0.014°. The three-point alignment (0.087°) from Fåro through Hellvi to the Kungsgård church center is somewhat less accurate from its end. A second bisect reciprocates from Kungsgård as vertex, this using the alignment through the Tingstäde church and Hangvar as central axis. The western ray of this *vi* like structure may emulate the meridian of a more Norse and Norsholm associated line from the Broa gravefield to Bro church. The Kungsgård "meridian" is much less accurate, but may have symbolically associated with Lummalunda, perhaps related to the Bulverket west *vi* ray from Norsholm. The precise meridian from Kungsgård runs about 338 meters to the east of Lummalunda church (0.60588°). The bisect angles among the four churches of Kingsgård and Tingstäde on the central axis and Lummalunda and Hellvi on the rays are: 21.19651° and 21.14756° or an averaged accuracy of 0.024°. Given the similarities of this Tingstäde focused structure with previous test of the Norseholm pattern, how now will the Tingstäde pattern compare?

One expects less dramatic results, given the absence of both a three point alignment as west ray from Färo, and more significantly a four-point alignment as central axis. The Tingstäde molecule, shown to exist in the screen shot of figure 30, contains two alignments at or under 0.087°, one cardinal at or under 0.61°, and four bisects at or under 0.06° (two vertexes and multiple points on the two three-point alignments involved). The search string for this molecue is: A+A(1)+C(1)+B(4)+B(4)+B(4)+B(4). A run of 100 sets, where random points are substituted for the churches, does not create a match, so runs of 1000 sets are made. In this case 3 to 9 hits occur in each of 10 runs, with a total of 55 for 10,000 sets. The odds of randomly creating the existing Tingstäde/Kungsgård pattern are about 1 in 182, less than the Norsholm test, but statistically significant.

Figure 31. Kungsgard/Faro vi test map and search module (above); example of 1 in 182 random set closely reproducing existing pattern and test area at churches (below)

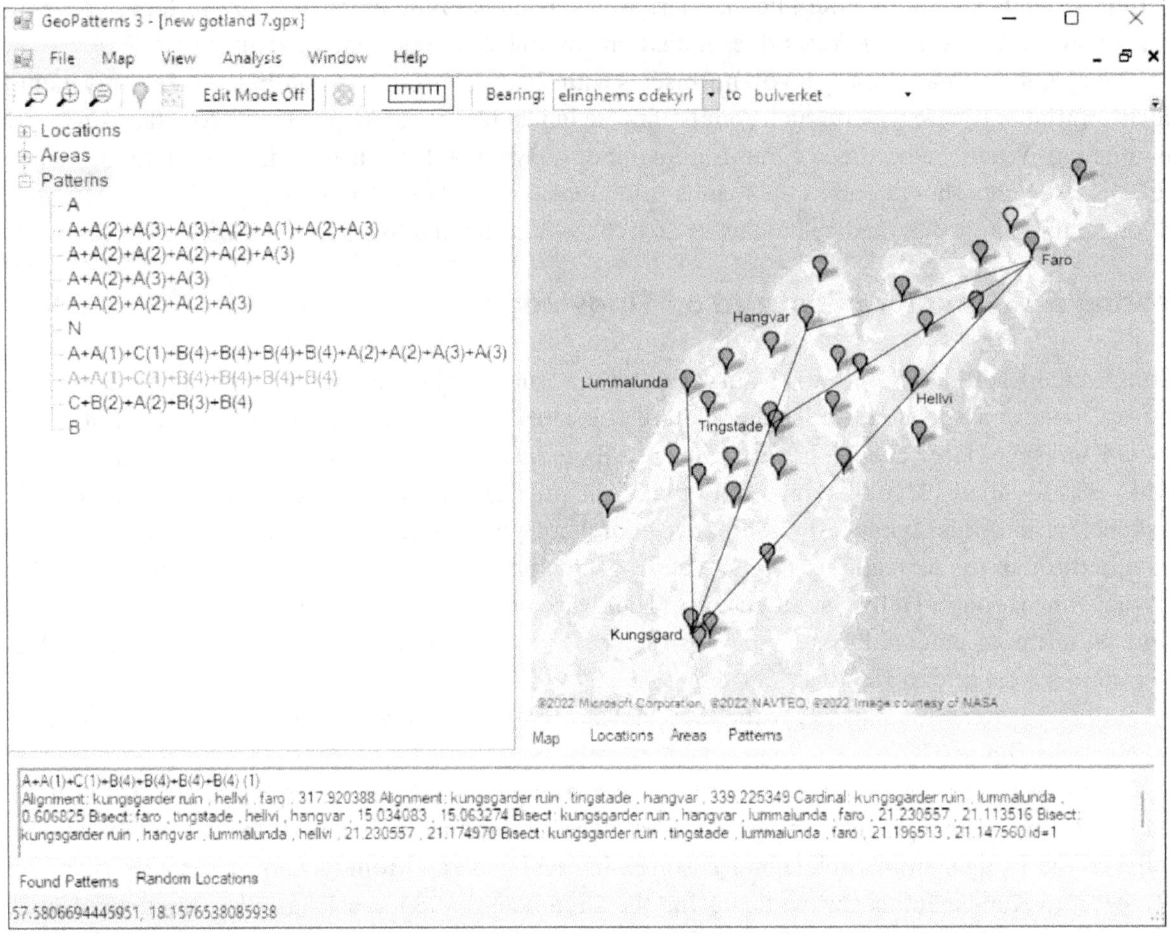

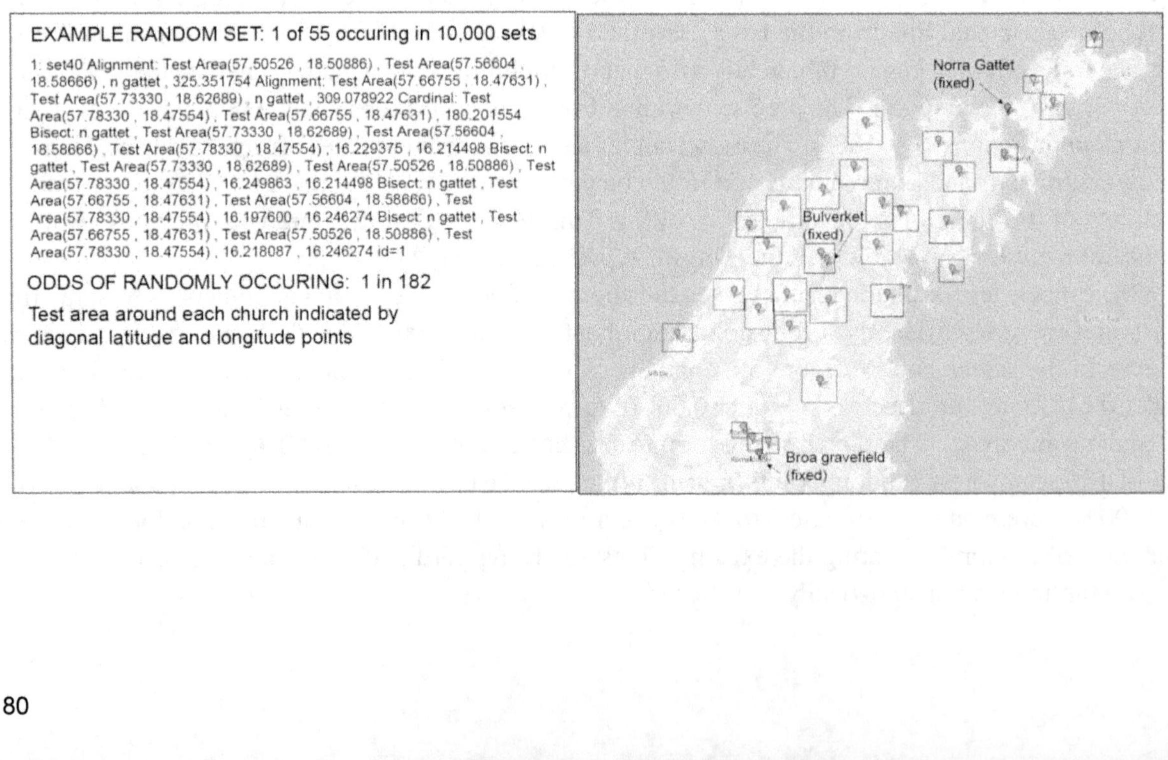

Figure 32. Azimuth angle between Tingstäde-Hangvar and Helvi/Fåro is reproduced as Halla azimuth paired with Kungsgård axis (left); Hangvar's orientation is the bisect between azimuth to Norsholm and cardinal East

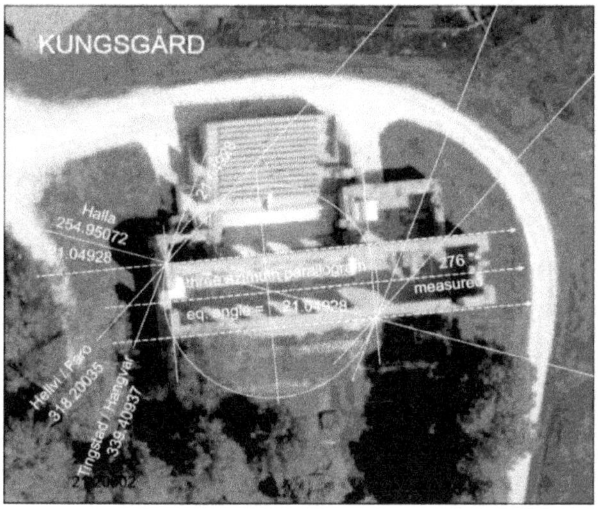

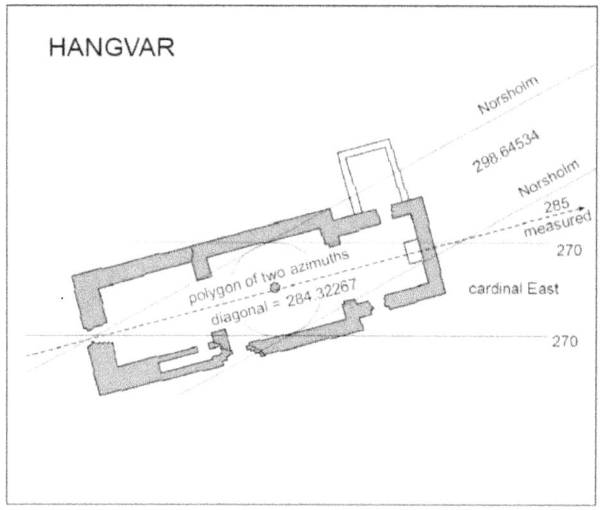

Do Other Church Orientations Integrate With a Tingstäde *Vi* System?

The alignment of Visby Dom running by the lake *ting* site through Lärbro and Bunge is not geometrically integrated with the rays of a Fåro/Kungsgård *vi* pattern. The Tingstäde orientation, along with Bunge's seems to recognize this distinction. Faro's church axis, for its part may have been linked to early post-Bulverket meanings of Norsholm and

St.Olav's chapel. What then of the vertex Kungsgård, as a north facing bisect with side rays to Lummalunda on a meridian west, Fåro/Hellvi as the east ray, and Tingstäde at the center?

Kungsgård's measured orientation as seen in figure 32 is 276°. One first tries azimuths to the two three-point alignments that terminate south at the Kungsgård chapel, i.e. to Tingstäde/Hangvar and Hellvi/Fåro. The created angle here is 21.20902°, which has no immediately understandable relation to Kungsgåard's 276°. Given the parallelogram created with three azimuths at Bro, however, a missing direction might be tried here as well. One of the most powerful locations, even in the close central Gotland vicinity is Halla and its prehistoric ring, sitting on an alignment between Broa gravefield and the Norsholm ring, (it aligns with Bara ruins and Fåro, and symblically may associate with Bara-Hellvi-Norsholm). Halla's azimuth from Kungsgård is 254.95072, and 21.04928° from Halla. Thus, beginning with the intersection of the two alignments from Tingstäde/Hangvar and Hellvi/Fåro, a third line could have been struck from that point to Halla. The Kungsgård church axis is the line that replicates the first intersection angle, but now pairing up with the azimuth to Halla and all its locational power.

What then about Hangvar's layout up at the northern terminus of the accurate alignment with Kungsgård-Tingstäde, also figure 27? It's use of the azimuth to Norsholm speaks to its "early" role in the west ray of the Bulverket focused *vi*. The second contributing azimuth may have been cardinal East. The bisect between these two is the diagonal of a parallelogram and church axis.

Now consider Visby Dom itself at the southern terminus of the Bunge – Lärbro – Tingstäd axis. Rather than link to the Bunge azimuth (proven dating of churches on this line would be important), the alliance

Figure 33. Azimuth to Halla from Visby Dom is square perpendicular with diagonal as church axis (left); azimuth to Lokrume creates square diagonal which is bisect of Kungsgård azimuth and Halla axis (right)

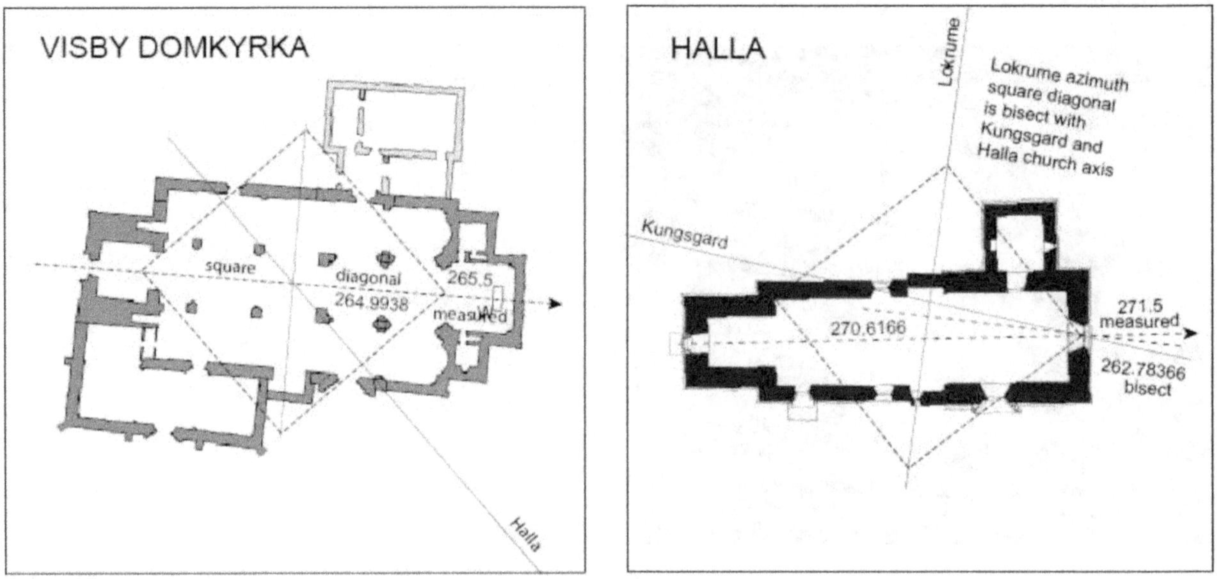

azimuth that works best is to Halla; lines to Roma and Kungsgård a couple of degrees off. If Halla, as perhaps also recognized by its reciprocial relation to Kungsgård, was perceived as the most spiritually powerful central site—its dual role in summer solstice and Norsholm east ray—then no second azimuth might have been worthy of integration.

The location of Visby Dom was undoubtedly preordained by the history of the fortified city, and could have included laying out the line to Bunge. At the time the cathedral was built, Halla's location was also prehistorically fixed associated with the *fornborg* and large-scale lines,

The first layout work might have been surveying the relatively short 18.813 km line to the Halla church as most important Norse/Christian point perhaps related to the *Alting*. Then this azimuth could have created a *vinkelrätt* square perpendicular whose diagonal is 264.9938°, compared to the measured orientation of 265.5°.

At first look, Halla's orientation seems to be a slightly off cardinal and wholly Christian East, though such axes do not exist in the present study group. Thus it may be logical that a one and one half degree variation from true East was in fact a derivation from large-scale azimuths. Recognizing Halla's importance with the *fornborg* assembly there, on the Broa - Norsholm vi ray, it could have been symbolically logical to choose the "Christian" terminus of the Norsholm-Bulverket construct at Lokrume -- 352.78366°. From this line a square could have been laid out with the Lokrume azimuth as diagonal, figure 33. The perpendicular to this diagonal is 262.78366. A second line might also have been prolonged, to reciprocate a relationship with the Kungsgård chapel. This azimuth is 254.95072°. Symbolically, the Lokrume square diagonal pairs up the azimuth to Kungsgård with the Halla orientation. If the diagonal 262.78366° is the central axis of a bisect with Kungsgård's 254.95072, then ideally the Halla axis would be an equal 7.83294°. The precise resulting axis would be close to true East, but 270.6166°. The measured orientation of 271.5° is within a degree of the ideal figure. Halla's use of these two azimuths may integrate with both Norsholm and Tingstäde "systems".

Figure 34. Azimuths from Tingstäde and St. Olav's church create parallelogram diagonal as Hall's axis (left); azimuth from Norsholm to Roma creates square perpendicular whose diagonal is church axis (right)

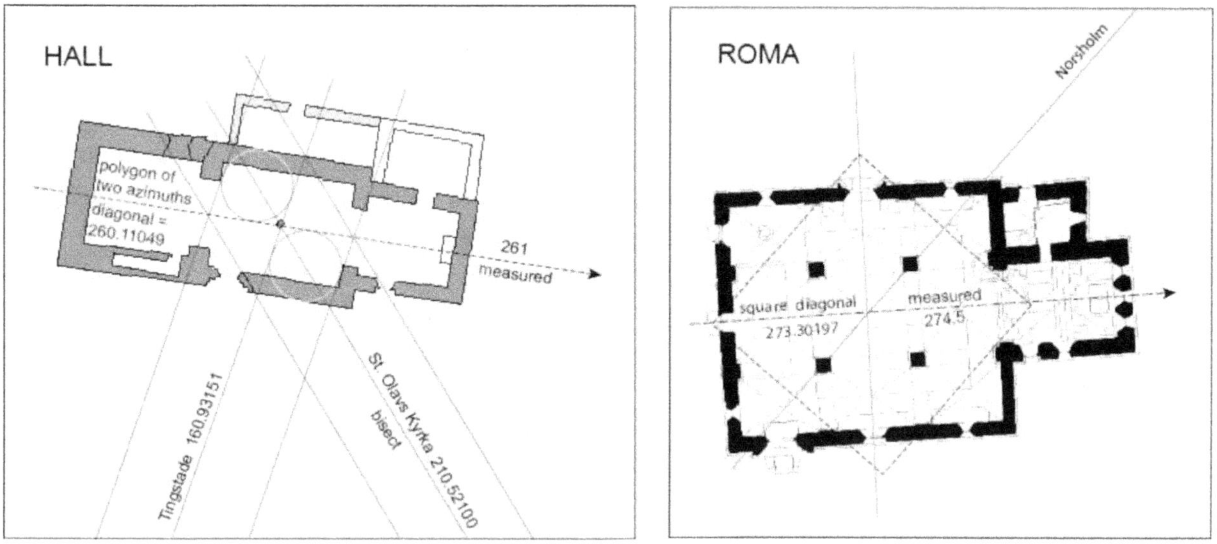

At Halla one can update introductory discussion about who built these churches, but now including the surveying of landscape lines as part of the process. It seems now possible that the alignment from Broa, through the *fornborg* at Halla, to the northernmost tip of Gotland was late Iron Age, not unlike the Trondheimsfjord axis from its *Alting* place on Frosta up to the highest north mountain, Heimdalhaugen (Doxtater 2023a). Svedjemo (2014:193) chooses the larger farm of Hallegårde near Halla church to discuss whether the church was located near or on this supposedly big man farm (*storgård*), or was part of a pre-Christian village composed of four or more farms just north of the church (the *fornborg* is not part of the discussion). Archaeologists source finds from the rich Broa gravefield to the larger Hallegård farm, and then by association, linkage of this power to the *Alting* site and Roma about two kilometers to the west. But as Svedjemo explains, the Roma bog lies between them, and was only accessed at the time by the bridge at Broa, about a five-kilometer trip. If Halla's location was land surveyed to align with a Broa center point and Norsholm, who would have organized the survey party (they could have used Boge or Hellvi as end points knowing the history of these points as part of an east ray). Logically, both large farmers and villages were involved in recruiting survey parties.

Up in the far north at Hall, a wooden church is said to have stood in the 1100's at the site of the standing stone church, most of which was constructed about a century later. This location sits on no three-point alignments found at or under 0.14°. One of the possibly Bulverket related churches, Stenkyrka on the west ray, may have used an azimuth to Hall as part of its orientational design logic. As for Hall's orientation, a parallelogram using azimuths to Tingstäde and the large St.Olav's church ruin create a diagonal of 260.11049°, compared to the measured axis of 261°. In Hall history, nothing is said about any relationship to St. Olav.

Finally, one looks at the plan of Roma in its landscape location. Not unlike Visby Dom perhaps, a single azimuth to the historically most powerful spiritual point, Norsholm creates the square perpendicular, figure 34. The SW-NE perpendicular of this square to Norsholm is 318.30197°, and its diagonal 45°, or 273.30197°, compared to the measured orientation of Roma of 274.5°. This is about 0.2° over the presently self-imposed accuracy limit of one degree variation of measured to calculated axes. One might question the cost of surveying, both economically and socially, a 69.658 line direct to Norsholm without involving alignment cooperation of church areas along the way, though none are close. As a work project, however, this length, though one of the longer on a largely featureless flat Gotland landscape, is much shorter than several hypothetical alignments in Norway, e.g. the 177.177 km line from the penisular *Frostating* to the benchmark on the mountain Heimdalhaugen.

Does the summary of formal landscape patterns listed in figure 35, and their relationships to possible azimuth bases for church orientation and layout suggest a workable theory about a "Tingstäde system"? Any kind of definitive dating of this pattern with respect to the Bulverket, however, is critical, but here must be left to more qualified others. From a design perspective, blocking the view of the Bulverket from the onshore Tingstäde site by a truly monumental stone church, as well as its total lack of azimuthal relationship to the center vi point in the lake square, together with powerful architecture at Bunge, Lärbro, Kungsgård and especially at Visby, all seem to speak about a more dominant Christian definition of a still systematic northern Gotland landscape. Yet there are connections with "earlier" Bulverket elements at Lärbro, Othem, Halla, Kungsgård, Roma and particularly apparent in the orientation of the Visby Domkyrka.

Figure 35. Summary of Tingstäde related lines and possible church orientations

churches on Tingstade lines including Faro and Kungsgard vis	use Tingstade lines and sites for orientation
Tingstade	Visby Dom, Larbro, Bunge
Bunge	Visby Dom, Tingstade, Larbro
Fleringe	Faro, Bunge
Lummalunda	Tingstade, Ganns
Kungsgard	Tingstade, Hangvar, Hellvi, Faro, Halla
churches not on Tingstade lines but use for orientation	
Halla	Kungsgard, Lokrume
Hall	Tingstade, St. Olav's church
churches on Tingstade lines but don't use for orientation	
Hangvar	Norsholm, cardinal East
Visby Dom	Halla
Roma (Othem - Larbro)	Norsholm

FINAL DISCUSSION

Initial studies of stone churches in northern Gotland were made as part of a project to determine church orientations in Trondheimsfjord, Storsjön, and northern Gotland. While mapping possibilities of relationships of church location to large-scale, formal landscape patterns, an intriguing overlap appeared with St. Olav pilgrimage routes. Leaving the Gotland component of for a bit, all these routes currently featured in tourism websites have now been close mapped at large scales. Two publications, featuring the Österdal and Gudbrandsdal routes, now begin to recognize the legitimacy of this kind cultural analysis (Doxtater 2022a, 2022b). The Gudbrandsdal route particularly, along with elements of the coastal route and the overland track replicating King Olav's saga campaign from Baltic Sweden, all point to a landscape feature in Trondheimsfjord that might have been the known spiritual portal for King Olav's Norse soul—distinct from the veneration of his bones, wherever they were. This is the most naturally formed threshold, an isthmus between two islands in the northern part of the fjord whose latitude perhaps not coincidentally aligns with Stiklestad, site of the battle and his death (though not archaeologically confirmed). This isthmus was likely already a Norse liminal place, sitting as it does on an alignment from the *Alting* site on Frosta, precisely through the prehistorically important Maere church site, up to the summit point of the mountain Heimdalshaugen.

Though no "*ve*" (Norwegian) concept can yet be associated with this central axis like with Norsholm – Bulverket, a more complex system climaxes at the natural threshold point formalizing the overland route from nascent Oslo up to Trondheimsfjord. Multiple elements in this tested pattern are large-scale, land surveyed, right angles, i.e. *vinkelrätt.* They also involve a *kastal* fortification structure on the shore of Norway's largest lake, perhaps not unlike that at Lärbro as part of its Tingstäde participation.

While there is folk tradition of pilgrimage possibilities that link the large St. Olav church on Gotland (St. Olavsholm) with Lärbro, Bunge and the Teutonic Knights, the large-scale *vi* patterns on northern Gotland at least appear to be much less driven by pilgrimage practices. Considerable structure in Norway as well seems to be indigenously self – motivated as the formalized landscape transforms to socially integrate Christianity.

Even if archaeologists and historians eventually accept some large-scale, land surveyed patterns as being cultural artifacts, it is unlikely that their ritual use will ever be known, though very likely part of an initial founding practice in an ancient symbolic landscape. These formal geometries likely involved serious cooperation in what must have been highly visible land surveying work in earlier medieval Gotland. To a certain extent it may not matter what these farmers and their families believed about any associated Norse spirituality. The most important thing, perhaps, was that the process itself may have provided the significant peaceful integration of varying realities of farm ownership—whether as big farmers or villages of smaller farmers.

What may have necessitated this landscape renovation was of course the increasing social and political power of organized Christianity. It was one thing for big farmers, or villages, to build smaller timber churches in a more territorial manipulation of social space. But rather than hoard their silver privately, it was becoming fashionable to build more monumental churches of stone in this the age of Romanesque and Gothic cathedrals. Doing so as prominent territorial entities, however, must have worked against an ancient religious ethic about a proscriptively non-architectural ritual Gotland landscape. There were no Norse temples here. Even all farm dwellings were highly constrained, essentially absent of any distinguishing style—just orientation and layout as part of some shared landscape "system". Any first sight of all the massive churches on Gotland, many within bell sounds from each other, seems amazing from any customary social, territorial perspective.

In response, one can imagine a *ting*-like convocation at Tingstäde Trask, where farmers of the northern region (Norra Tredingen?) came together to reimagine remnants of some earlier Norse landscape structure. The reason the center of the lake was chosen for the Bulverket, may have been that no one owned it—but more symbolically the center was expressly left open because water was sacred coming as it conceptually did from the Norra Gattet threshold. No founding architectural monument could be built on such a naturally sacred place, only a platform of reinvented ritual assembly, one with no stylistic territorial façade. Making decisions about the central *vi* axes would have been the first order of the day, including instruction in simple but highly accurate land surveying and the social process of organizing survey parties likely including owners of farms along proposed lines.

The possibility that the Bible was not actively present in these first assemblies on the platform logically follows, given the religious freedom given by the Church to landscape symbolism, if people practiced as they should within the Biblical iconography and texts of church interiors. The platform was not a church, only an assembly place around an invisible but cognitively known point in the middle of a lake. These land surveying processes, including the related logic of church orientation, were just typical of what farmers had been doing in the landscape for ages. While the symbolism of this large-scale geometrical work would have been discussed by the participants, perhaps for two hundred years or so, including the possible intrusive evolution of the Tingstäde "system", the record was in built form, not written documents. This integration of Norse landscape tradition with Biblical Christianity must have been a socially logical, mostly peaceful Gotland evolution.

Theoretically, text-based religion can be seen as a somewhat separate socio-cultural sphere which may thrive side by side with less discursive ritual practice in the land. This isn't so much psychological "disassociation" in the same mind, but better, perhaps associational processes in different parts of the brain that the serve different kinds of information, i.e. spatial vs. oral or textual. The cultural interface of the two is seldom articulated. For example, anthropologists may speak of chants or religious texts as ritual, when no formalized movement through a symbolically structured space is mapped. Earlier Christian churches in Scandinavia seem to have only added ritual practice to their Biblical interior during or after the Reformation. Only then, in Norway at least, does the principal, ritually structured locus of domestic dwelling, the *stue,* reorient itself to the church with its new pews and other spatial formalities. The church only then plays the primary role in the rite of passage rituals of birth, marriage, and death (Doxtater 1990). For five or six hundred years in Norway, farm societies practiced Norse related ritual in landscape settings while all the while going to church and discursively calling themselves Christian. Folk historians from the valleys and fjords recorded their ritual practices at the end of the last century, but for the most part never wrote about any sort of struggle between the two kinds of religious culture—18th century piety conflicts with the state church notwithstanding.

On Gotland, one wonders if any evidence of ritual azimuthal elements in church location, orientation, or layout can be found in the earliest extant Christian features of the interiors. One of the missing ingredients of the present paper, mentioned more than once, is a more accurate, larger scale, technically assisted, mapping of church plans and orientations. While doing so, one would also be cognizant how medieval interior features, may or may not have integrated the azimuths presently diagramed. Also possible with greater mapping precision, and continued computational power, might be random testing of how churches in their location associate with azimuths to other churches and "natural" points like

Figure 36. Comparison of two possible "systems" focused on the Bulverket and Tingstäde church

Bulverket "system": Bisect of Norsholm and Broa
Aligned with Vaskinde/Othem/Hellvi
Aligned with Larbro/Rute
Aligned with Lokrume/Norra Gattet/Norsholm
Aligned with Bro/Faro
Receives from Boge
Receives from Rute
Receives from Hellvi
Receives from Roma
Receives from Vaskinde
Receives from Stenkyrka
Receives from Martebo
Receives from Bro
Hellvi: 45 bisect of N. Gattet – Bulverket angle
Aligned with Vaskinde/Bulverket/Othem
Aligned with Bara/Norsholm chapel
Receives from Larbro
Vaskinde: Bisect of Bulverket – Bro angle
Aligned with Bulverket/Othem/Hellvi
Receives from Roma,
Receives from Bro
Bro: W/ Vaskinde - Bulverket – Stenkyrka angle
Aligned with Bulverket/Faro
Meridian from Broa gravefield
Lokrume: 45 from bisect Norsholm and Broa
Aligned with Larbro/Rute/Hellvi
Receives from Halla
Stenkyrka: Bisect of Bulverket – Hall angle
Aligned with Hangvar/Norsholm chapel
Receives from Bro
Boge: 45 from Bulverket
Aligned with Hellvi/Norsholm chapel
Rute: 45 bisect Norsholm – Bulverket angle
Aligned with Bulverket/Larbro
Martebo: Bisect of Bulverket – East angle

Tingstade "system": Bunge is bisect w Hangvar and church axis
Aligned with Ganns/St.Olavs Kyrka
Aligned with Visby Dom/Larbro/Bunge?
Receives Bunge et.al. ;
Receives Kungsgard;
Receives Lummalunda,
Receives Hall
Kungsgard: pairs with Halla equal angle to Tingstad/Hangvar – Hellvi/Faro angle
Aligned with Hellvi/Faro
Aligned with Tingstade/Hangvar
Aligned with Bara/St.Olavs Kyrka
Receives from Halla
Halla: 90 from Lokrume bisect Kungsgard – East
Aligned with Broa gravefield/Norsholm
Aligned with Broa gravefield/Bara/Faro
Receives from Visby Dom,
Receives from Kungsgard
Bunge: 45 from Larbro/Tingstade?/Visby
Aligned with Visby Dom/Larbro
Receives from Othem,
Receives from Fleringe
Hangvar: Bisect of Norsholm – East angle
Aligned with Stenkyrka/Norsholm
Receives from Kungsgard
Visby Dom: sq Halla azimuth creates diagonal
Aligned with Larbro/Bunge
Receives from Bunge/Larbro
Hall: St. Olavs Kyrka is bisect of Tingstade – church axis angle
Receives from Stenkyrka
Lummalunda: Bisect of Ganns – Tingstade angle
Receives meridian from Kungsgard
Fleringe: Bisect of Faro – Bunge angle
Roma: Square bisect to Norsholm
Aligned with Othem/Larbro

Churches on both systems
Larbro: Bisect of Hellvi – East angle
Aligned with Bilverket/Rute
Aligned with Visby Dom/Bunge
Aligned with Roma/Othem
Receives from Bunge,
Receives from Roma
Faro: Bisect of Norsholm – St. Olav's chapel
Aligned with Broa gravefield/ Halla/Bara
Aligned with Vaskinde/Ganns
Aligned with Kungsgard/Hellvi
Aligned with Bro/Bulverket
Receives from Fleringe,
Receives from Kungsgard
Othem: Bisect of Bunge – St. Olavs Kyrka angle
Aligned with Vaskinde/Bulverket/Hellvi
Aligned with Roma/Larbro
Receives from Fole,
Receives from Roma (alt)
Fole: creates Othem bisect with Ellingham
Aligned with Broa gravefield/Ellinghems

the Bulverket. For this anthropologist with an architectural background, in many cases the sources of orientation azimuths both immediately logical. Most do not seem to be random.

Given the tested patterns in northern Gotland, why, the reader has probably already asked, weren't the other two-thirds of the stone churches on the Baltic island included in the analysis? First, the present work took considerable time, despite the logic of many orientational azimuths. The volume of sketch notes on possible cultural patterns among the random is surprisingly thick. Doing the entire island at once would have made discovery of most significant patterns much more difficult. Furthermore, once the Bulverket alignments were realized at their accuracies, essentially proving the use of land surveying, it seemed appropriate to publish this piece before venturing south to the other churches and possible prehistoric sites. Serendipitously, the Bulverket focused design analysis ultimately led to a selection of churches very close to that of the northern part of the triadic division of Gotland first mentioned in Guta Saga. The medieval Gotland scholar Yrwing (1978:82) cites the first mention of the division in 1213, in which rituals are described at the scale of the entire island (alting), within each triadic area, and then at smallest scale of more local tings. Thus, the Bulverket focus may have been something symbolically unique in Norse religion on the island.

The data in figure 36 above is included as an appendix summary of the possible interrelations among sites in the present northern study.

REFERENCES

Abrahamsen, N. (1985). Romanske kirkers orienteering og den magnetiske misvisning I 1100 tallet I Danmark. *Geoskrifter, 23.*

Abrahamsen, N. (1992). Evidence for church orientation by magnetic compass in twelfth-century Denmark. *Archaeometry, 34*(2), 293–303. doi:10.1111/j.1475-4754.1992.tb00499.x

Andrén, A. (2011a). *Det Medeltida Gotland. En arkeologisk guidebok.* Historiska Media.

Andrén, A. (2011b). Kyrkor och gårder på Gotland. Svar til Tryggve Siltberg. *Fornvännen, 106*, 232–235.

Brendalsmo, J. (2006). *Kirkebygg og kirkebyggere (Ca. 1000 – 1600).* Unipub forlag.

Doxtater, D. (1981). *The Symbolism, Structure and Politics of "Center" in the Old Scandinavian Farm Culture.* [Dissertation, University of Michigan, Ann Arbor].

Doxtater, D. (1984, Summer). Spatial Opposition in Non-Discursive Expression: Architecture as a Ritual Process. *Canadian Journal of Anthropology, 4*(1), 1–17.

Doxtater, D. (1990). Socio-Political Change and Symbolic Space in Norwegian Farm Culture after the Reformation. In M. Turan (Ed.), Ethnoscapes Series: Vol. 4. *On Vernacular Architecture: Paradigms of environmental response.* Gower.

Doxtater, D. (2007). A Report on Geopatterns Software: describing and analyzing large scale geometry between Chacoan and natural sites. In Digital Discovery (pp. 200–216). Exploring New Frontiers in Human Heritage., CAA 2006.

Doxtater, D. (2009). Rethinking the Sacred Landscape: Minoan Palaces in a Georitual Framework of Natural Features on Crete. Landscape Journal, 28(1), 1 – 21.

Doxtater, D. (2017) *Minnesota River Matrix: "non-discursive" alignments of immigrant churchyards on center lines in a New Norwegian Landscape*, ca 1870-1900 (unpublished manuscript).

Doxtater, D. (2021). Probabilities of designed locations of ceremonial foci: the Chaco Meridian, temple IV at Tikal, and a large-scale sacred Adena river landscape. *Time and Mind, 14*(2), 283-326.

Doxtater, D. (2023a). Close mapping of St. Olav's Pilgrimage path through Gudbrandsdal Norway: Probabilities of a designed, land surveyed concept of a large-scale Christianized landscape. *International Journal of Religious Tourism and Pilgrimage, 11*, 1.

Doxtater, D. (2023b). Land surveying in early medieval Norway: a St. Olav pilgrimage path as a means of creating an integrated Christian society in a Viking landscape? *Landscape esearch, 48*(3), 427-452.

Eide, O. (1974). *De Toskipeded Kirker i Oslo*. [Master's thesis, University of Bergen].

Eide, O. (1986). Om Kirkers Orientering. Arkeologiske skrifter. Bergen: Historisk Museum No. 3

Enderborg, B. (2015). "Tingstäde kyrka". Guteinfo.

Hoare, P. G., & Sweet, C. S. (2000). The orientation of early medieval churches in England. *Journal of Historical Geography, 26*(2), 162–173. doi:10.1006/jhge.2000.0210

Hult De Geer, E (1935). Prehistoric Bulwark in Gotland Biochronologically Dated. *Geografiska Annaler, 17.*

Iversen, F. (2017). Tinget i Trøndelag i yngre jernalder og middelalder. *Gunneria, 81*, 71–108.

Lindström, J. (1997). The Orientation of Ancient Monuments in Sweden: A Critique of Archaeoastronomy and an Alternative Interpretation. *Current Swedish Archaeology, 5*(1), 111–125. doi:10.37718/CSA.1997.08

Lindström, J. (2005). Påsk, höstblot och jul: Sambandet mellan årliga högtider och forntida gravars orienteering. *Fornvännen, 100*, 13–28.

Lundmark, E. (1925). *Tingstäde Kyrka*. A.B. Gunnar Tisells Tekniska Förlag.

Martinsson-Wallin, H., & Wehlin, J. (2017). Stones in the South: Decoding Bronze Age ritual practices on Gotland. *Current Swedish Archaeology, 25*(1), 227–256. doi:10.37718/CSA.2017.20

Murphy, L. J. (2018). Processes of religious change in late iron age Gotland-rereading, spatialization and enculturation. In Boulton, Hawkes & Stoner (Eds) Place and Space in the Medieval World. Routledge, pg. 32 – 46.

Myrberg, N. (2009). An island in the middle of an island: on cult, laws and authority in Viking Age Gotland. In Regner, Kitzler, and Kjellström (Eds) From Ephesos to Dalcarlia. Reflections on Body, Space and Time in Medieval and Early Modern Europe. The Museum of National Antiquities, Stockholm. Studies 11, Stockholm Studies in Archaeology 48. Pg. 101 – 118.

Olsen, O. (1966). *Horg, Hov og Kirke*. H.J. Lynge & Son.

Peel, C. I. (1998). *An Edition of Guta Saga.* [Dissertation: University College London].

Ridderstad, M. (2013). Orientations of the Medieval stone churches in Finland. *Suomen museo.*

Rönnby, J., & Adams, J. (2006). Identity, threat and defiance: Interpreting the "bulwark", a 12th century lake building on Gotland Sweden. *Journal of Maritime Archaeology*, *1*(2), 170–190. doi:10.100711457-006-9008-9

Roosval, J. (1935). *Rute Setting: Sveriges Kyrkor.*

Sands, T. (2017). II: 28 Pilgrimage – Gotland. In J. Glauser (Ed.), *Handbook of Pre-Modern Nordic Memory Studies: Interdisciplinary Approaches* (pp. 601–606). Walter de Gruyter.

Siltberg, T. (2011). Kyrkolokalisering och eventualla storgårdar på Gotland. *Fornvännen*, *106*, 127–132.

Söderman, I. (1989). *Från lertavla till satellitbild.* Geographica.

Stenberger, M. (1955). *Vallhagar: a migration period settlement on Gotland/Sweden.* Munksgaard.

Svedjemo, G. (2014) *Landscape Dynamics—Spatial analyses of villages and farms on Gotland AD 200-1700.* [Dissertation Uppsala University].

Wienberg, J. (2001). Gotlands guldålder—kyrkor, konjunkturer och korståg. In Från Stad Till Land. Andrén, Ersgård, and Wienberg (Eds). Lund Studies in Medieval Archaeolog.

Yrwing, H. (1978). *Gotlands Medeltid.* Gotlandskonst.

Zetterling A. (1935) Bulverket. *Svenska fornminnesplatser.*

Chapter 9
Variety Is the Spice of Life:
A Systematic Literature Review on the Evolution of the Camino de Santiago

Bárbara Inês Marto
Universidade da Beira Interior, Portugal

Tiago Adrega
Universidade de Aveiro, Portugal

ABSTRACT

The purpose of this study is to provide a deeper understanding and uncover the main topics of discourse regarding emerging trends and follow up on the evolution of the Camino de Santiago to highlight the connections between them by looking at and comparing the papers representing this field's core. Indexed to Scopus, the authors analysed 62 papers, applying content analysis techniques to identify the main research lines. Authors found three main research perspectives: evolution in political trends and tourism strategies, the digitalisation process and its impact on the pilgrimage experience, as well as the globalisation surge in the past years. This research impacts the several stakeholders intertwined with the Camino de Santiago, be it public institutions or private operators that need to explore and understand these collective dynamics.

1. INTRODUCTION AND THEORETICAL FOUNDATIONS

A pilgrimage involves embarking on a journey to a predetermined destination with the purpose of prayer or intention setting, and ultimately returning home. Although this definition may seem uncomplicated, the concept of pilgrimage is far from straightforward. Pilgrimage is a customary practice observed in various major world religions, including Hinduism, Buddhism, Judaism, Islam, and Christianity, as well as numerous tribal communities. The act of pilgrimage entails embarking on a journey towards a sacred location, motivated by a profound sentiment, typically of a religious or devotional nature (de Sousa & da Rosa, 2020). In the Middle Ages, the Camino de Santiago (Way of St. James) was one of the most important pilgrimage routes of Christianity (Braun, 2021). It has evolved from a medieval Christian

DOI: 10.4018/978-1-6684-9923-8.ch009

pilgrimage to a globally renowned cultural and spiritual phenomenon and is closely intertwined with the historical, religious, and literary developments of Europe (Lois Gonzales, 2013). The Camino's origins can be traced back to the discovery of the tomb of St. James the Apostle in the 9th century and played a crucial role in uniting Christian kingdoms, particularly during the Reconquista. The foundational Codex Calixtinus and "Liber Sancti Jacobi" are the earliest and most important sources of information about the Camino de Santiago and related literature as been flourishing ever since, particularly after the revival in the late 20th century, thanks in part to the efforts of the Spanish government and various associations dedicated to its preservation and promotion (Castro, 2011).

Its historical context, foundational literature, and enduring popularity make it a fascinating subject for study and exploration. The Camino continues to be a symbol of spiritual and personal growth for countless pilgrims who traverse its ancient paths.

Now, more than ever, it represents itself as an undeniable part of the cultural identity in Europe, especially in Spain and Portugal. In Portugal, it traverses its territory from North to South, East to West, encompassing more than 1000 km of unforgettable landscape. Walking said routes is going on a quest to not only discover the country, but also ourselves. Over the past few decades, pilgrimage tourism has undergone a swift evolution in the globalized market (Chang et al., 2020).

At the same time, tourist activity has maintained a series of progressive changes, where, for instance, the different administrations and entities related to the Camino agreed, among other measures, to boost digitalization and to start using new technologies to continue developing and globalizing the Camino de Santiago (Lois-González & Somoza-Medina, 2022). The digitalisation of the Camino de Santiago is a process that began about a decade ago, through pioneering projects and the personal application of new technologies to all our daily experiences, such as real-time information or the carrying out of more procedures and actions in digital format (Lois-González & Somoza-Medina, 2022).

Internationalization and innovation in tourism are interwoven, and, in a globalizing world, there is increasing scope for tourism innovation to be shaped not only by the internationalization of capital, managers and entrepreneurs, but also by tourists and labour (Williams & Shaw, 2011). Furthermore, digital technologies affect the development and introduction of innovation in several ways and have been an advantage to a more globalized economy (Sepashvili, 2020). Globalisation has then played a pivotal role in the development and in leading to unprecedented changes in all aspects of society, be it economic or societal (Strielkowski et al., 2021). Historical and natural sites are considered as resources, assigning them not only a cultural interest, but also an economic value and social utility (Cazzani & Boriani, 2020). Pilgrimage routes are widely acknowledged as relevant tourist attractions, offering privileged conditions for local and regional development. Significant efforts and investments are made, often at regional and local levels, by different stakeholders to enhance their features and elements, and to augment visitor / pilgrim experiences. (Ambrósio et al., 2019).

The different meanings with which tourism activated by the Way of St. James is defined refer to the different definitions that are attributed to each tourist practice, but also to the different manners in which it is possible to interpret the experience of the Way (Moscarelli, 2021). Several studies have debated how the Saint James Way relates to economic development (Azevedo, 2021; Hortelano Mínguez & Fernández Sangrador, 2022; Moscarelli, 2021; Urrutia et al., 2018). In recent years, the growing number of tourists and pilgrims that travel the various Ways of Saint James, part of the soft tourism typology, allows them to play a key role in the process of development and construction of the territory, creating various opportunities for development of the territories where these routes pass, especially the rural towns and communities (Azevedo, 2021).

In the case of a slow travel, for example, the direct impacts could be those related to the pilgrims' accommodation services, such as hostels, bars or restaurants in the places at beginning or at the end of the stage but at the same time should be considered indirect impacts which are not produced in the places which experience the actual passage of pilgrims, or induced, feeding both direct and indirect impacts (Moscarelli, 2021).

However, despite this growing economic flow entered by the territory, as mentioned by some authors, some socioeconomic indicators also show that it has not been the expected engine to advance in the long-awaited local development of rural areas. Public institutional actions and the efforts of private entrepreneurs in order to reinforce and intensify the Jacobean benefits have not been enough to compensate for the negative demographic variables. The possible causes of local slackness center on the inherited starting disadvantages that have weighed down job opportunities aimed at young people and women and to attract new neighbors (Moscarelli, 2021).

It has been discussed how the positive pilgrims' dynamics has yet to lead to the rise of population registry on the municipalities crossed by Jacobean routes (Hortelano Mínguez & Fernández Sangrador, 2022). From the inverse point of view, if these rural areas were not crossed by the Saint James Way and did not have the resources linked to the natural and cultural heritage, the gap would be deeper and the difficulties for this region to reduce the divergences would be greater (Urrutia et al., 2018). Tourism activities enhance diversification and differentiation of local products/services, playing a crucial part in local economies (Lima & Eusébio, 2010). In the past years there has been significant investment in rehabilitation and regeneration of historical heritage, with the purpose of creating tourism accommodation in rural areas in Portugal (Barroco, Cristina; Antunes, Joaquim; Amaro, 2011). The impact on local and regional development created by rural tourism has been highly emphasized in political and cultural contexts, as well as academic, sometimes creating high expectations (Kastenholz, 2005). Additionally, (Barroco, Cristina; Antunes, Joaquim; Amaro, 2011) stress that rural tourism plays an important role in defining the tourism system where they are located and, it is at the local and regional scale that a significant part of the tourism system is organized. It is precisely on these geographical scales that, when framed within national policies defined for tourism, local actors are involved in the dynamization of resources, heritage and the creation process for strategies that will value and affirm territories. Cultural routes are, therefore, excellent strategies for local tourism dynamization, especially in rural areas. Furthermore, they open the door to inter-regional, intermunicipal, cross-border and international cooperation conventions (Sánchez & Ullate, 2017).

As per the same author, the Saint James' Ways deeply impact, on a social and economic level, the places and communities around the landmarks included in the routes, creating endless opportunities. These routes have had a surprisingly relevant socio economic impact. It is estimated that each pilgrim spends about 38€ per stage, resulting in a yield of 100 million euros, on which 11 million euros refer to the Portuguese routes (Federación Española de Asociaciones de Amigos del Camino de Santiago, 2017). The growing tourism value of the Ways of Saint James has also had repercussions on the development of the villages in several ways. The main consequence is the tourist development of these villages, where structures and new services are created, allowing a new vitality of these places (Azevedo, 2021). As initially referred, the Saint James Way comprises more than just the arrival at the cathedral (Santos, 2002; Steil & Carneiro, 2008). That said, more and more pilgrims are motivated to undertake this specific pilgrimage so as to incorporate the spiritual, social and heritage experience. These routes are a healthy, sustainable, environmentally responsible, social-friendly, and territorial cohesion-generating type of tourism, which can thus increase its socioeconomic impact in the coming years with its definitive digital transition (Sepashvili, 2020). There has thus been a resurgence in the number of pilgrims as a result of a militant effort favoured by the proliferation of Jacobean associations (Lois González, 2013). Consequently, there has been a slow but steady increase in foreign pilgrims, as seen in the statistical reports provided by the pilgrim's office in Santiago de Compostela (Oficina de Acogida al Peregrino Catedral de Santiago, 2021). For instance, according to the data sourced above, with the exception of the COVID-19 pandemic years (2020 and 2021), more than 45% of the pilgrims walking the Camino de Santiago since 2015, on average, were foreigners (non-Spanish citizens). 2019 set the record for 58% of the pilgrims walking the routes being from foreign countries, which in absolute numbers translates to 201 211 pilgrims in total. In 2022, 45% were foreigners, translating to a total of 199 073 foreign pilgrims. Indubitably, the internationalisation of the Saint James Way is worth exploring, as it is a prominent and relevant phenomenon (Gonzalo et al., 2012; Mróz et al., 2019; Schrire, 2006), and a systematic literature review on this topic is called for, with the main objectives of providing a deeper understanding and uncovering what the main topics of discourse on this specific subject are, ultimately leading to future research avenues for other scholars to draw upon (Paul & Criado, 2020). With this in mind, the following research questions were advanced:

RQ1: What are the main currents of thought regarding the evolution of the Camino de Santiago coming into 2023?

RQ2: Where should research converge in the future?

2. METHODOLOGY

This study is a systematic literature review of the published articles regarding the evolution of the Camino de Santiago. The authors searched the Scopus database and the query was as follows: (TITLE-ABS-KEY ("camino de santiago") OR TITLE-ABS-KEY ("saint james way") AND TITLE-ABS-KEY (internationalization*) OR TITLE-ABS-KEY (globalization*) OR TITLE-ABS-KEY (evolution) OR TITLE-ABS-KEY (demography) OR TITLE-ABS-KEY (statistics) OR TITLE-ABS-KEY (analysis) OR TITLE-ABS-KEY (pilgrims)). Filters were applied to language (English), category (Management or Business or Economics) and document type (article or early access or review). This database was chosen since it comes as one of the world's largest curated abstract and citation databases, with a broad global and regional coverage of scientific journals, conference proceedings, and books, all while ensuring only the highest quality data is indexed through rigorous content selection and re-evaluation by an independent Content Selection and Advisory Board (Baas et al., 2020). Study selection was a multi-stage process performed by both authors. After the aforementioned identification phase, a screening followed - the articles were selected by both authors, using an Excel pro forma that outlined quality and relevance thresholds, based on the explicit inclusion and exclusion criteria:

- The defined inclusion criteria were: (i) focus on internationalisation of the Saint James Way; (ii) articles published in peer-reviewed journals; and (iii) articles published in English;
- The defined exclusion criteria were: (i) studies investigating the Saint James Way but not related to internationalisation; (ii) reviews, editorials and conference papers.

The title and abstract were screened first, followed by full article reading for eligibility. The conflicting articles were evaluated against two quality appraisal criteria: (i) the extent to which they engaged with existing literature and (ii) the extent of fit/alignment among research questions, design and execution. Automation tools were not used, in line with the modest number of records identified through database searching. The authors independently extracted the following information from selected studies: publishing information (author, year, journal, country, number of citations), methodology used, main objectives, findings, key contributions and research gaps identified. The selected studies were fully reviewed, and the required data were extracted and summarized. The titles, abstracts and results of quality evaluations were surveyed based on the PRISMA checklist and Excel was used to organize and analyze the data. Due to the exploratory and qualitative data of the study, bias assessment, effect measures, sensitivity analyses and certainty assessment were not performed. To provide a structured approach to the review, the authors identified key themes that emerged from the data and organized the papers accordingly.

3. RESULTS ANALYSIS

3.1. Descriptive

The results of the selection process are summarized in figure 1. In the identification phase, 134 studies were found. Initial title and abstract screening resulted in 62 articles. After discussion of conflicting articles and full-text assessment for eligibility, 26 studies were finally included to assess the results.

The evolution of publications and respective citations can be appreciated in figure 2. Although the first article dates from 2006, one can appreciate that it was a recent surge in academia, with the majority of articles being published in the last 10 years, particularly in the last five (77% of the articles). Worth noting, one particular article, from Lois González (2013), accounts for 41% of the citations.

Regarding the geographical origin of the studies (as seen in table 1), the majority are from European countries (69%), with a denser expression from nations with a more present Catholic tradition, like Poland (19,2%) and the Iberian Peninsula (34,6%). The majority of the studies used a qualitative approach for analysis (69,2%). The International Journal of Religious Tourism and Pilgrimage was the journal with the most publications (with a total of 6 - 23,1%) and Mróz, the author with the most publications, contributed with three studies (11,5%) since 2019.

A summary of the exploratory results of the included articles on the evolution of the Camino de Santiago is described in detail in table 1 (annex).

3.2. Discussion

Europe, Policies, Heritage, and Transformation

The Camino de Santiago is a multifaceted phenomenon, deeply rooted in Europe (Gonzalo et al., 2012). In the past academia has mostly focused on the spheres of heritage (Chemin, 2016; Orszt & Raszeja, 2022; Schrire, 2006), economic development (Lois González, 2013; Moscarelli, 2021) or expansion (Gonçalves & Costa, 2020; Gonzalo et al., 2012; Lois González, 2013), yet, in recent times, a new trend has risen to a great degree, as a result of digitalization and globalization (de Sousa & da Rosa, 2017). Assuredly, the last few decades have been accompanied by a reinterpretation of the place of religion and its associated phenomena in society (Lois González, 2013). The re-invention and re-branding of European pilgrimage routes, more specifically the Camino de Santiago, reveals a political discourse that

Figure 1. Flow diagram of the study selection process

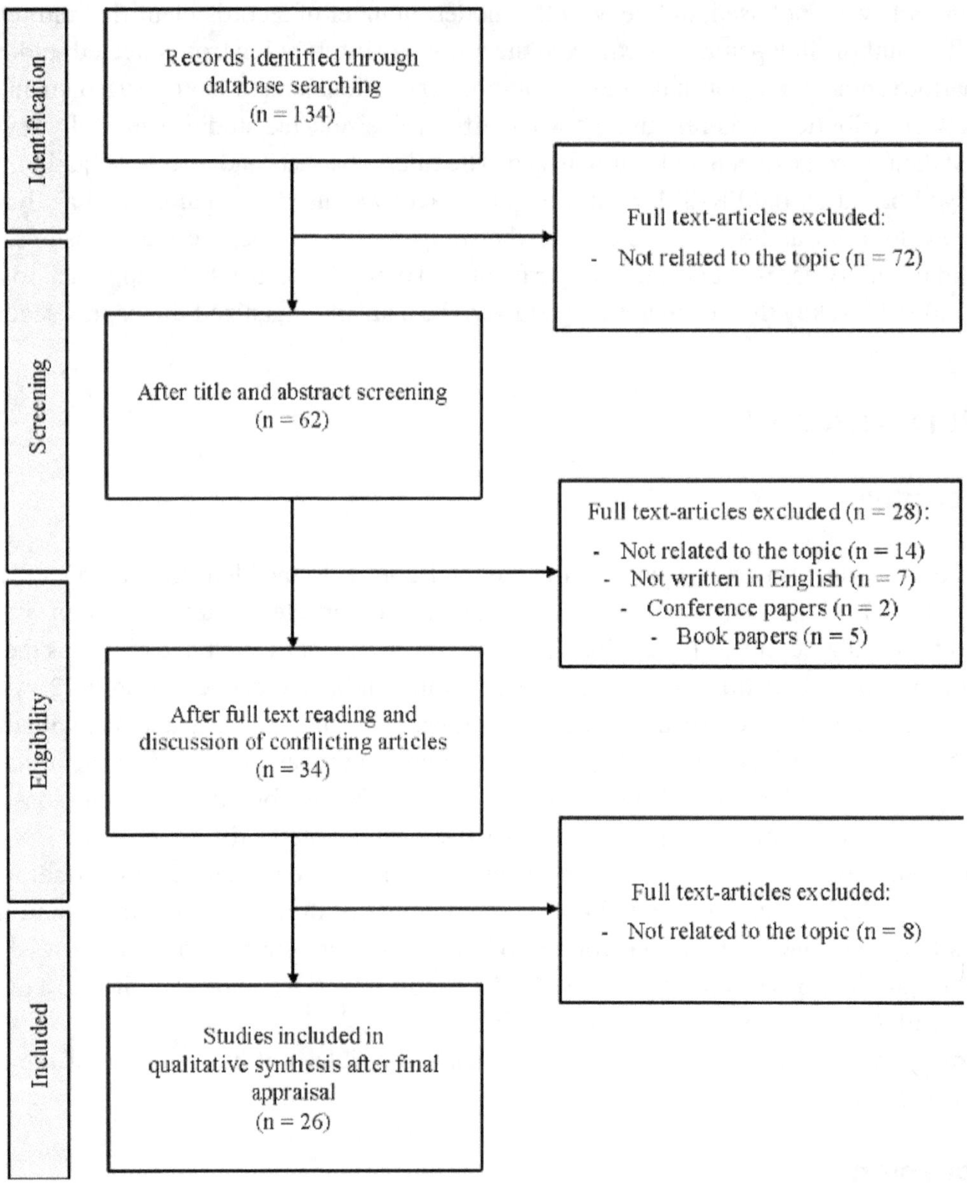

includes presumptions about a wide range of people and cultures with the aim of fostering a European cultural unity to a politico-economic project that tends to depend on the idea of integration (Chemin, 2016). This allows for a greater understanding of the renewal of the Camino de Santiago. For instance, the renaissance of the Camino could never have been considered to be a success in the absence of the massive increase in the number of people travelling it, something that started to become apparent in the 1990s (Lois González, 2013). If, on one hand, the richness of forms and materials found in Galicia and northern Portugal bring a variety of data and draw a picture connecting to the landscape and its inhabitants and interplay with the European heritage ideal on a face-to-face context (Orszt & Raszeja, 2022;

Figure 2. Evolution of the number of publications and citations over the analysis period

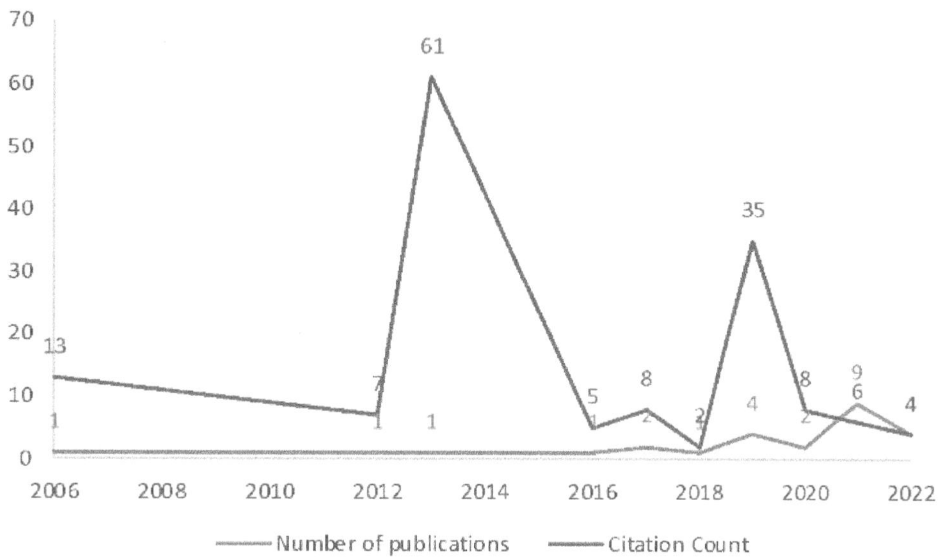

Table 1. Characterization of the included studies

Geographical setting	n	%
Poland	5	19,2%
Spain	5	19,2%
Portugal	4	15,4%
USA	3	11,5%
Brazil	2	7,7%
Other	7	26,9%
Methodology	**n**	**%**
Qualitative	18	69,2%
Mixed	4	15,4%
Quantitative	4	15,4%

Schrire, 2006). Opposing viewpoints, on the other hand, have underlined the difficult interplay between patrimony and tourism, two concepts ruled by individuals with competing interests. A route with a religious and spiritual component that passes through multiple Spanish and Portuguese autonomous regions (with transferred authorities) and a route taken by travellers with diverse backgrounds add to the issue (Gonzalo et al., 2012). The discourses among some EU representatives, as well as those of other agencies and organizations, constantly reify the European pilgrimage routes as something constant, fixed in time, overarched by something greater than the individual, and recognized by all as having cultural and historical value, much like how the EU is portrayed as being larger than the member states that make it up (Chemin, 2016).

Economic Development

Following up on what was aforementioned, the same author reiterated how tourism, being such an important slice of the economy of many European states, cannot be dissociated from the pervasive economic and political imperatives (Chemin, 2016). It has been shown that pilgrims have a positive impact on real gross value added in some regions (Domingues Martinho, 2021). Conversely, data still points to the existence of a very moderate impact of the Camino de Santiago, in the sense that the development of tourism activities linked to the Camino is not sufficient to reverse the demographic and economic decline of these rural areas (Moscarelli, 2021; Urrutia et al., 2018), hence being important to incorporate and look at this topic in a much broader way, as per the same author. The revival of the Camino can thereby be explained by a combination of factors. Firstly, the use of the shrine as a traditional referent by the most reactionary sectors of the Catholic Church and the Franco regime during its initial period and the 1970 onwards mentality, when the Camino was rediscovered as an expression of the unity of Western Europe: the reinvention of history in terms of territorial identities with a newly democratic Spain in search of its foundations, numerous towns and cities striving to make their mark in a context of competitiveness, having all helped to give the pilgrim's route new impetus (Lois González, 2013). Additionally, in the Portuguese context, emerging as a main motivation for visiting and helping cities' cultural activities agendas after the investment and promotions made to attract pilgrims/travellers (Gonçalves & Costa, 2020).

Globalisation, Digitalisation, and Expansion

Finally, numerous people have acknowledged the spiritual, mental, and physical benefits of the Camino "package" and as has been shown, the replication of the "new" Camino is having a variety of effects on both practice and notions of pilgrimage across Europe and the UK, translating into the Camino "exportation" phenomenon (Bowman & Sepp, 2019; Mróz et al., 2019). Furthermore, the digital acceleration due to COVID-19 had great impact on its *modus operandi* and all the entities involved. Even though the digitalisation of the Camino started about a decade ago, it was accelerated due to the pandemic, and the investment made by the Spanish tourism entities, for instance, should be seen as a positive attempt to transform this tourism model (Lois-González & Somoza-Medina, 2022). This research came as the turning point to strike up debate about the virtual potential of the Camino routes. Along the same lines, it has been asserted how the pandemic opened the door for virtual pilgrimages, temporarily replacing the physical presence, and clarifying how it can actually reconstruct its fundamental characteristics, without distorting its core (Mróz, 2021). Ergo, even the pilgrim customer journey seems to now include new stages in the decision process path, such as online platforms or social media (de Sousa & da Rosa, 2017). It has been shown that long-distance hiking decisions are typically made as a result of inadvertent exposure and most hikers convert after their trip is over, acting as internet advocates for other prospective hikers afterwards. (Basil, 2022). Accordingly, general online information seems to be the strongest predictor of intention to use a pilgrimage app across several nationalities (Amaro et al., 2019). Another topic that seems to be unveiled in academia is the experience of international pilgrims on the Camino, due to worldwide similarities, or semblances. For instance, both Chinese and western pilgrims seem to undergo similar external and internal journeys, even though each group experiences the pilgrimage within their respective sociocultural framework (Zhang et al., 2021). More so, in the study developed by Seryczyńska & Duda (2021), all the pilgrims interviewed, in spite of their nationality, seem to undergo a profound transformation in which virtue promotes happiness. Similarly, in this case, while studying German pilgrims, it was demonstrated that even after returning, participants demonstrate lasting effects, such as the feeling of community and friendly manners, shaping the course of their future lives (Braun, 2021). Ultimately, the Camino is now described as a meeting place of spaces of different religions and cultures in a climate of dialogue and mutual respect (Seryczyńska, 2021). Some specific factors, including the political atmosphere, seem to also play a part in the increased popularity of the Camino among foreigners. By way of illustration, the social and economic upheavals that occurred when Poland entered the European Union in 2004 were significant elements that influenced the development of Poles' pilgrimages to Santiago de Compostela over the last fifteen years. The gradual and constant improvement of the lifestyle of Poles supported by social programmes led to an increase in the tourist, religious, and religious-cognitive journeys of Poles (Mróz, 2021). Likewise, nowadays there are even virtual leadership programs, designed to mimic the real Camino experience, proven to have the same long-lasting effects aforementioned, offering the opportunity to experience and participate in the transformative powers of a pilgrimage without having to physically travel to the chosen destination (Gehrke, 2021). Also, along the lines of the digitalization process that the Camino de Santiago has undergone, some authors expand on the notion that the Camino is no longer the same: the ritual, experience and narrative has changed due to the presence of media shaping the experience, expanding the Camino beyond a spatial-territorial dimension (de Sousa & da Rosa, 2020). The effects of digital devices on spiritual connections are no longer one-dimensional but are consistently in flux (Jenkins & Sun, 2019). Some authors portray a darker picture, advancing some first thoughts on the consequences of the mediatization of pilgrimage, stating that the media productions put into circulation different meanings about the Camino embodied by the subjects through complex negotiation processes, resulting in emerging conflicts associated with different core values and belief systems (de Sousa & da Rosa, 2017). The intimate pilgrim experience has become a media product that, when distributed, conflicts with both the storytelling and the actual pilgrimage experience. The more media circulation, the more the public sphere changes this intimate experience through different narratives and expectations (de Sousa & da Rosa, 2020). Digital technologies can therefore play multiple and competing roles in the experiences individuals understand as spiritual (Jenkins & Sun, 2019). In their groundbreaking study, Nickerson & Eng (2017) were the first to attempt to try and understand the role, as well as impact, of mobile technology in a pilgrimage experience. The authors found that mobile technologies are used extensively by pilgrims, although pilgrims did not consider the technology to be essential. Technology impacts the Camino experience in both positive and negative ways, and both similarities and differences between American and European pilgrims were found in the results (Nickerson & Eng, 2017). *De rigueur*, modern digital trends have both positive and negative socio-cultural effects on the Camino de Santiago. While they have increased accessibility, streamlined logistics, and facilitated global awareness, they have also raised concerns about overcrowding and the potential erosion of traditional aspects of the pilgrimage. Locals play a crucial role in adapting to these changes, preserving their cultural heritage, and finding ways to engage with and benefit from the digital transformation of the Camino (Samartim, 2022). Balancing modernity with tradition remains an ongoing challenge for this historic pilgrimage route.

A conceptual framework was conceived for organizing all the above-mentioned themes, inspired by the Camino itself (Figure 3). Just like the Camino, there is a common ground that supports its tradition and international weight, clearly identified in the collected papers, which were heritage and European commonality. This convention and cohesion solidified the Camino as a sacred legacy that deserved respect and attention towards respectful exploration and honored communication. The road is further

Figure 3. Conceptual framework for evolution of the Camino de Santiago

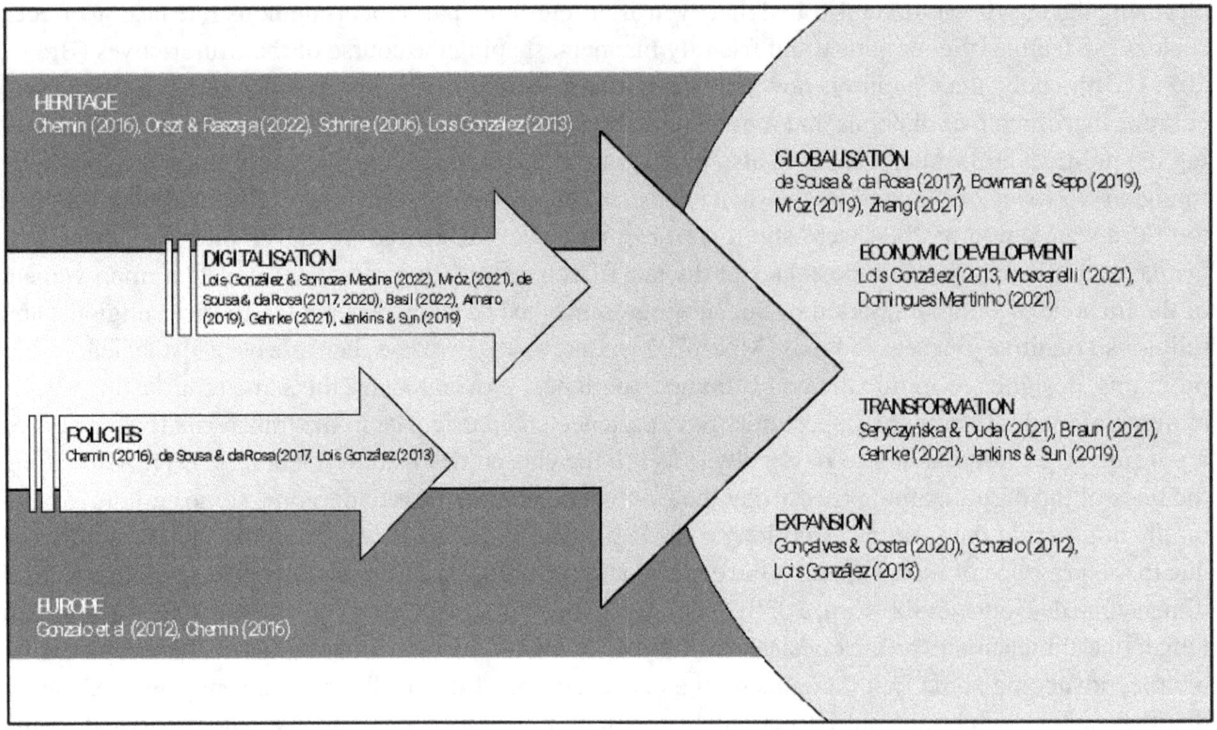

fortified with the political and legal incentives to promote the economic and social growth needed, and with the increasing digitalisation, either through social networks, either applications or other digital channels, all contributing to align with modern expectations. Finally, just like the Camino, this road leads to a globalised reach, economic development, transformative interaction and holistic expansion.

Future Research Avenues

A critical analysis of the research profile and the themes drawn from the review allowed the authors to identify gaps in the literature and opportune research questions, providing a path for future research.

Zhang et al. (2021), after analyzing how cross-cultural encounters from the Camino de Santiago transform individuals and communities and inform the sustainable and inclusive management of global culture, pointed out that a promising line of research could consider how the 'best practice' of this European heritage route could cross-fertilize the preservation, management, and tourism development of Chinese cultural itineraries. Additionally, evaluations of the effects of targeted marketing strategies among Chinese tourists could also be investigated, such as in first- and second-tier Chinese cities, or among lovers of outdoor activities in China. In a similar perspective, from the Portuguese point of view, Domingues Martinho (2021) incites to perform a global characterization of the several Portuguese contexts travelled through by the Camino, as support for an integrated and focused strategy to promote the different potentialities waiting to be appreciated in both a sustainable and planned way. The variety of St. James Way routes that cross different municipalities, with distinct and particular realities, calls for specific studies to complement the gathered data and integrate a comprehensive approach.

On the other hand, Mróz (2021), presents a different future research perspective, focusing on a historical standpoint, through the study of the biographies of medieval Compostela pilgrims and a comprehensive appraisal of the traces of the cult of St. James and pilgrimages of residents of Central and Eastern Europe over time.

Finally, from the digital angle, Amaro et al. (2019) and Nickerson & Eng (2017) consider that a future line of research could investigate the acceptance of a pilgrimage app with storytelling or could explore the information embedded in the use of mobile technology and smartphone apps for more fruitful results. And Jenkins & Sun (2019) believe in the impact of exploring the extent to which information and communication technologies transform spiritual dimensions of intimacy across life domains and religious contexts. They also underscore that reflexive engagement with digitized interaction rituals is key to addressing the tension, ambivalence and uncertainties that emerge at the intersection of tradition, modernity, and contemporary mediatization.

CONCLUSION

This study depicts the development and evolution of the Camino de Santiago in a digital, globalised world, and is aimed at analysing the main currents of thought regarding the evolution of the Camino de Santiago coming into 2023, as well as related future research avenues.

Our research identified: (1) the trends in policies that result in greater unity, such as the integrated development of the Camino in its entirety, due to the collective effort put in by the different Spanish and Portuguese regions (Chemin, 2016; de Sousa & da Rosa, 2017; Lois González, 2013). We see now how the political, economical and tourism spheres can not be disassociated from each other (Chemin, 2016); (2) the trends in digitalisation, as a result of the digital acceleration caused by the COVID-19 pandemic (Lois-González & Somoza-Medina, 2022), that allow for a different interpretation and experimentation of the Camino, such as virtual pilgrimages (Gehrke, 2021; Mróz, 2021) ot the exportation/recreation of these routes into other countries (Bowman & Sepp, 2019; Mróz et al., 2019), the mediatization, such as the role of social media and other sources of information directly impact the expectation and experience of pilgrims (de Sousa & da Rosa, 2017; Jenkins & Sun, 2019; Nickerson & Eng, 2017); (3) the trends in globalisation that sparked interest in studying different cultures and nationalities walking the camino, and analysed multiple different, but, at the same time, similar journeys (Braun, 2021; Mróz, 2021; Seryczyńska, 2021; Seryczyńska & Duda, 2021; Zhang et al., 2021). Our findings show that the Camino is indeed no longer the same (de Sousa & da Rosa, 2020; Jenkins & Sun, 2019; Seryczyńska, 2021) and has been subject to deep and powerful changes to keep the route relevant and attractive, while at the same time maintaining its core values ablaze. It is suggested that future investigation tackles the spheres aforementioned. For instance, on an economic/political sphere, it is important to investigate the true monetary potential of each pilgrim in all the different routes, how to balance the supply/demand sides of a typically religious route that is gaining traction and popularity every year, or even delve deeper into the customer (pilgrim's) journey and analyse its touchpoints. From the digitalisation phenomenon point of view, it is crucial to tackle how to improve the preceding customer journey and understand how technology can be of help to travellers. Are pilgrims using apps on the way? Are they relying on technology for research/ implementation/ experimentation of the Camino? More so, how can digitalisation and technology make the way more sustainable? In the globalisation sphere, it is noteworthy to understand the main markets involved and harness their potential. How much does a foreign pilgrim spend, as opposed to a domestic pilgrim? What are the main motivations for non-believers to walk the Camino? What is the market potential and saturation level before it becomes "too much to handle"? These are all questions that have yet to be answered and would certainly be relevant in the period we are going through.

Albeit, this study offers several relevant contributions to the theoretical body. Firstly, we add to the literature by providing an updated systematic literature review on the evolution of the Camino de Santiago in all its spheres, enhancing academia's understanding of said routes, identifying, evaluating, as well as synthesising research results. Secondly, we identify various topics of discourse, pointing out early trends and slight shifts regarding this theme that can ultimately lead to significant changes in the academia's standpoint and approach thus far regarding the Camino. From a practical perspective, our research impacts the several stakeholders intertwined with the Camino de Santiago, be it public institutions or private operators that need to explore and understand the dynamics of the aforementioned route. Hence, managerial and implications for academics are as follows:

Implications for Private Entities

It is forthcoming to assume that marketing and tourism professionals can use said framework so as to integrate this knowledge in previously developed customer journeys. This allows, for instance, to tackle the overall value of each pilgrim, resulting in fundamental structural changes in business strategies, ultimately leading to changes in yield and increased earnings.

Implications for Public Policies/Entities

As route tourism and, specifically, the Saint James Way has been an ongoing debate for both Portuguese and Spanish public entities, it is high time that a more holistic and all-around approach was done on how exactly aforementioned routes are (or are not) worthy of development/investment. This study tackles this thematic, creating feasible and realistic budget allocations and strategic agendas.

Implications for the Communities/Municipalities

Consequently, municipalities and communities in which the routes go through are direct benefactors of pilgrimage studies. This study is of importance to the various players: distributors, retailers, HORECA sector (hotels, restaurants, and cafés), pharmacies, as well as pilgrim dedicated local shops.

Implications for Tourism/Marketing Professionals

By adding experience levels to pilgrimage studies, how the Saint James Way impacts local economies and ultimately, addressing the rural problematic, it is expected that marketing and tourism professionals can develop sustainable and comprehensive business strategies. Segmenting, studying persona behavior and market analysis are a crucial part of a business strategy, thus being of great help to aforementioned professionals.

Implications for Academia

Through detailed research and analysis, this study might serve as an essential resource for students, researchers, local authorities, municipalities, and policymakers. Not only does it address the issue of fragmented experiences, it also provides a comprehensive understanding of the complex relationship between the Camino routes and various societal aspects, contributing to its transformation and revitalization.

The findings of this analysis point to limitations towards research design, databases, and the protocol chosen. First of all, the research design applied was based on keyword searches, thus reducing the scope of the study. Secondly, funnelling the research to only one database, in this case, Scopus, might very well have neglected some relevant published work regarding the evolution, digitalisation and globalisation of the Camino de Santiago presented on other databases like WOS, for instance. Due to this fact, another limitation comes from the fact that this study does not reflect the general state of the evolution of the Camino de Santiago, not the complete trends going into 2023 to their full extent, rather than the state of it according to the protocol applied by the authors. Different protocols and databases might come in handy to get a more complementary view of this theme regarding future research.

REFERENCES

Amaro, S., Duarte, P., & Antunes, A. (2019). Determinants of intentions to use a pilgrimage app: A cross-cultural comparison. *International Journal of Religious Tourism and Pilgrimage*, *7*(2), 19–30.

Ambrósio, V., Fernandes, C., Silva, G., & Cabral, A. (2019). A conceptual model for assessing the level of development of Pilgrimage Routes. *International Journal of Religious Tourism and Pilgrimage*, *7*(2), 94–104.

Azevedo, P. (2021). The Ways of Saint James in Trás-Os-Montes and Alto Douro as an Example of Soft Tourism in Rural Areas. *European Countryside*, *13*(2), 314–329. doi:10.2478/euco-2021-0020

Baas, J., Schotten, M., Plume, A., Côté, G., & Karimi, R. (2020). Scopus as a curated, high-quality bibliometric data source for academic research in quantitative science studies. *Quantitative Science Studies*, *1*(1), 377–386. doi:10.1162/qss_a_00019

Barroco, C., Antunes, J., & Amaro, S. (2011). Turismo em Espaço Rural: Tendências e Oportunidades. *Gestão de Bens Comuns e Desenvolvimento Regional Sustentável*, 666–683.

Basil, M. D. (2022). Understanding people's motivations for a long-distance hiking trip. *Leisure Studies*, *00*(00), 1–14. doi:10.1080/02614367.2022.2115108

Bowman, M., & Sepp, T. (2019). Caminoisation and Cathedrals: Replication, the heritagisation of religion, and the spiritualisation of heritage. *Religion*, *49*(1), 74–98. doi:10.1080/0048721X.2018.1515325

Braun, A. (2021). Pilgering Researchers or Researching Pilgrims: Experiences from Four Student Projects on the Camino de Santiago 2016-2019. *International Journal of Religious Tourism and Pilgrimage*, *9*(6), 109–116. https://api.elsevier.com/content/abstract/scopus_id/85127203717

Castro, B. L. (2010). El "Codex Calixtinus", primera guía del Camino de Santiago. *Cuadernos de la Cátedra de Patrimonio y Arte Navarro*, (5), 125–130.

Cazzani, A., & Boriani, M. (2020). *The Role of Historic Roads to Preserve and Valorize the Landscape*. Cycling & Walking for Regional Development.

Chang, A. Y. P., Li, M., & Vincent, T. (2020). Development and validation of an experience scale for pilgrimage tourists. *Journal of Destination Marketing and Management, 15*(November 2019), 100400. doi:10.1016/j.jdmm.2019.100400

Chemin, J. E. (2016). Re-inventing Europe: The case of the Camino de Santiago de Compostela as European heritage and the political and economic discourses of cultural unity. *International Journal of Tourism Anthropology*, *5*(1–2), 24–46. 10.1504/IJTA.2016.076851

de Sousa, M. T., & da Rosa, A. P. (2017). Faith, entertainment, and conflicts on the camino de santiago (The way of St. James): A case study on the mediatization of the pilgrimage experience on facebook groups. *ESSACHESS - Journal for Communication Studies, 10*(2), 145–169.

de Sousa, M. T., & da Rosa, A. P. (2020). The mediatization of camino de santiago: Between the pilgrimage narrative and media circulation of the narrative. *Religions*, *11*(10), 1–19. doi:10.3390/rel11100480

Domingues Martinho, V. J. P. (2021). Dimensions of the Saint James' Way Pilgrimage: Portuguese Socioeconomic Impacts. *International Journal of Religious Tourism and Pilgrimage*, *9*(6), 12–25. doi:10.21427/95em-2y12

Federación Española de Asociaciones de Amigos del Camino de Santiago. (2017, June). *Revista Peregrino, 171*, 32–50.

Gehrke, J. M. (2021). The leadership pilgrimage: How a virtual pilgrimage transforms leaders. *International Journal of Religious Tourism and Pilgrimage*, *9*(2), 55–62.

Gonçalves, F. J. B., & Costa, C. (2020). Contribution of caminos de santiago to the sustainable development of tourism, in Barcelos | Contributo dos caminhos de santiago para o desenvolvimento sustentável do turismo, em Barcelos. *Journal of Tourism and Development*, *2020*(34), 65–79.

Gonzalo, M. C. P., Angulo, A. D., & De Heredia, J. J. I. (2012). Touristic and territorial dimension of the "Ruta Norte" of the way of saint james in the basque country: Different ideas, valuations and proposals for management ofamultifaceted phenomenon [Dimensión territorial y turística de la ruta norte del camino de. *Boletín de la Asociación de Geógrafos Españoles*, *58*, 177–474. https://www.scopus.com/inward/record.uri?eid=2-s2.0-84860490826&partnerID=40&md5=f9ee02592df435437649239efa3e908b

Hortelano Mínguez, L. A., & Fernández Sangrador, L. (2022). Aportación del Camino de Santiago al desarrollo local: Características territoriales y repercusiones económicas en el tramo palentino. *Investigaciones Geográficas*, *2022*(78), 153. doi:10.14198/INGEO.19925

Jenkins, K., & Sun, K. C. Y. (2019). Digital Strategies for Building Spiritual Intimacy: Families on a "Wired" Camino. *Qualitative Sociology*, *42*(4), 567–585. doi:10.100711133-019-09432-0

Lima, J., & Eusébio, M. C. (2010). A importância da segmentação do mercado turístico, de acordo com as despesas que os visitantes realizam no destino, para o desenvolvimento económico local: o caso da Covilhã. 1, 87–99.

Lois González, R. C. (2013). The Camino de Santiago and its contemporary renewal: Pilgrims, tourists and territorial identities. *Culture and Religion*, *14*(1), 8–22. doi:10.1080/14755610.2012.756406

Lois-González, R. C., & Somoza-Medina, X. (2022). The Necessary Digital Update of the Camino de Santiago. In Lecture Notes in Networks and Systems: Vol. 482 LNNS. Springer International Publishing. doi:10.1007/978-3-031-06825-6_26

Moscarelli, R. (2021). Slow tourism, public funding and economic development. A critical review on the case of the way of St. James in galicia. *Revista Galega de Economia*, *30*(3), 1–16. doi:10.15304/rge.30.3.7522

Mróz, F. (2021). Poles travelling to Compostela in time and space. *Journal of Cultural Geography*, *38*(2), 206–234. doi:10.1080/08873631.2020.1864086

Mróz, F., Mróz, Ł., & Krogmann, A. (2019). Factors conditioning the creation and development of a network of Camino de Santiago routes in Visegrád group countries. *International Journal of Religious Tourism and Pilgrimage*, *7*(5), 56–71.

Nickerson, R. C., & Eng, J. (2017). Use of mobile technology and smartphone apps on the Camino de Santiago: A Comparison of American and European Pilgrims. *Atas Da Conferencia Da Associacao Portuguesa de Sistemas de Informacao*, *17*, 260–269. doi:10.18803/capsi.v17.260-269

Oficina de Acogida al Peregrino Catedral de Santiago. (2021). *La Peregrinación a Santiago en 2021*. Oficina de Acogida al Peregrino Catedral de Santiago.

Orszt, M., & Raszeja, E. (2022). Historical rural architecture of North Portugal and Spanish Galicia: Local vernacular forms and concept of adaptation, case study of Porreiras. *Vitruvio*, *7*(2), 46–59. doi:10.4995/vitruvioijats.2022.18845

Paul, J., & Criado, A. R. (2020). The art of writing literature review: What do we know and what do we need to know? *International Business Review*, *29*(4), 101717. doi:10.1016/j.ibusrev.2020.101717

Samartim, R., & Pazos-Justo, C. (2022). Impacts of the Ways in the Local Community of Santiago de Compostela: Results of Ongoing Research. In E. J. Torres Feijó, M. F. Rodríguez Prado, & E. Carral Vilariño (Eds.), *The Way of Saint James, tourism, and local community* (pp. 42–59). Universidad del País Vasco / Euskal Herriko Unibertsitatea.

Sánchez, P., & Ullate, M. (2017). Tourism Evolution of Cultural Pilgrimage Routes: the Case of St James Ways. In M. Ullate (Ed.), *Cultural Management and Governance for European Pilgrimage Routes* (pp. 27–40). Religious Tourism and Thermal Tourism.

Santos, X. M. (2002). Pilgrimage and Tourism at Santiago de Compostela. *Tourism Recreation Research*, *27*(2), 41–50. doi:10.1080/02508281.2002.11081219

Schrire, D. (2006). The Camino de Santiago: The interplay of European heritage and new traditions. *Ethnologia Europaea*, *36*(2), 69–86. doi:10.16995/ee.1008

SepashviliE. (2020). Supporting Digitalization: Key Goal for National Competitiveness in Digital Global Economy. *Economia Aziendale Online, 11*(2), 191–198. doi:10.13132/2038-5498/11.2.191-198

Seryczyńska, B. (2021). Manifestations of Religious Freedom in the Context of the Camino de Santiago. *International Journal of Religious Tourism and Pilgrimage*, *9*(6), 1–11.

Seryczyńska, B., & Duda, T. (2021). How Is Fortitude Among Pilgrims on the Camino de Santiago Expressed and Formed? Clues from a Study of Polish Pilgrims. *Pastoral Psychology*, *70*(5), 541–556. doi:10.100711089-021-00959-0

Steil, C. A., & Carneiro, S. S. (2008). Peregrinação, Turismo e Nova Era: Caminhos de Santiago de Compostela no Brasil. *Religião & Sociedade*, *28*(1), 105–124. doi:10.1590/S0100-85872008000100006

Strielkowski, W., Grebennikova, V., Razinkina, E., & Rudenko, E. (2021). Relationship between globalization and internationalization of higher education. *E3S Web of Conferences, 301*, 1–9. doi:10.1051/e3sconf/202130103006

Urrutia, X. A. M., Urrutia, D. C. M., Larenas, P. C., Urrutia, E. K. M., & Ocaña, J. M. (2018). The French Way of St. James as an engine in the invigoration of rural municipalities in Galicia. *Revista de Economia e Sociologia Rural*, *56*(3), 425–436. doi:10.1590/1234-56781806-94790560304

Williams, A. M., & Shaw, G. (2011). Internationalization and innovation in tourism. *Annals of Tourism Research*, *38*(1), 27–51. doi:10.1016/j.annals.2010.09.006

Zhang, K., Labajo, V., Ramos, I., & Del Valle-Brena, A. G. (2021). A guest at home: The experience of chinese pilgrims on the camino de santiago. *Sustainability (Basel)*, *13*(19), 1–15. doi:10.3390u131910658

APPENDIX

Table 2. Summary of findings of the included studies

Study	Main Objective	Findings	Key Contributions
Orszt & Raszeja (2022)	Provide a village renewal concept which aims to adapt the unused agricultural settlements into pilgrim units	Richness of forms and materials, which can be found in the historic fabric of Spanish Galicia and Northern Portugal, brings a variety of data to study about the connection of the landscape and its inhabitants through architecture.	Contributes to the body of knowledge regarding cultural landscape heritage protection, a mostly overlooked aspect in tourism.
Lois-González & Somoza-Medina (2022)	Strike up debate about the virtual potential of the Camino routes	Even though the digitalisation of the Camino started about a decade ago, it was accelerated due to the pandemic. The investment made by the Spanish tourism entities should be seen as a positive attempt to transform this tourism model.	Sheds light on the status quo of these popular routes and tackles the much necessary shake up of the existing situation.
Basil (2022)	Explore the psychological motivations to undertake long-distance hiking	The decision process for long-distance hiking mostly arises through accidental exposure and once people commit, intensive planning is required. Once the journey ends, most hikers become devotees and serve as online evangelists to other potential hikers.	Provides a deeper understanding behind the psychological motivations of undertaking a long-distance hike and its aftereffects.
Mróz et al. (2022)	Analyse the contemporary forms of replacement of pilgrimage	The COVID-19 pandemic opened the door for virtual pilgrimages, temporarily replacing the physical presence on a sacred place.	Clarifies how other types of pilgrimage, i.e. virtual experience, can, in fact, reconstruct its fundamental characteristics, without distorting the idea.
Zhang et al. (2021)	Identify the main dimensions and attributes that shape the experience of the Camino de Santiago for Chinese travelers as a tourism product, by exploring the similarities and differences between their experiences and that of Western pilgrims	Authenticity and harmony are observed to be the key elements that contribute to a satisfying and transformative experience for Chinese pilgrims, where they find a cultural-spiritual center close to their traditional values, yet distant from their everyday social practices. Both Chinese and Western pilgrims undergo similar external and internal journeys, although each group travels in its respective sociocultural framework.	Explores how chinese travelers experience the Camino and provides effective international promotional strategies to increase the Camino's visibility among chinese travelers.
Seryczyńska & Duda (2021)	Addresses the links between the Camino de Santiago and the pilgrims' virtue of fortitude using the concept of virtue developed by Aquinas in the thirteenth century based on the classical philosophy of Aristotle	For many pilgrims the Camino is an experience of profound internal transformation and development in light of the Thomistic approach to moral virtues. Virtue promotes happiness.	Shares the theological perception on virtue formation, where transformation happens under the influence of a good act.
Braun (2021)	Describe the project, its planning, its implementation, and its conclusion, as well as some experiences and impressions of the participating students on the Camino	Even after returning home, the project participants demonstrate lasting effects. The feeling of community, friendly manners and the transformative power shapes the course of their future lives.	Shares a personal report of experience based on the ethnographic research approach, facilitating the replication of student projects both on the Camino or in other pilgrimage trails.

continued on following page

Table 2. Continued

Study	Main Objective	Findings	Key Contributions
Seryczyńska (2021)	Analyses the positive manifestations of religious freedom among pilgrims on the Way of St James	The results of the study indicate that the Camino pilgrimage is linked to the experience of religious freedom by pilgrims to a greater extent than in their daily lives. Pilgrims emphasise both the aspect of freedom in religious practices, such as participation in a pilgrim's blessing rite, holy Mass or prayer of the rosary, as well as discussions on religious issues. Camino is described by the pilgrims as a meeting place of spaces of different religions and cultures in a climate of dialogue and mutual respect.	Elucidates how religious diversity is played out while on the Camino, thus opening a discussion on the evolution of religion itself, as well as pilgrim's motivations.
Domingues Martinho (2021)	Analyse the context of the Way of St. James' pilgrimage, in general, and subsequently the socioeconomic dimensions of the pilgrimage within the specific Portuguese framework.	The results show that the St. James' Way pilgrims are mostly male, travel on foot, have both religious and other motivations, are between 30 and 60 years of age, come from Spain and a great deal of them start from Sarria. Travelling via the French Way, a large number are from Madrid and Andalusia and are students, employees, self employed, retired, technicians and teachers. Finally, it was estimated that each pilgrim had, over the period 2004-2018, a positive impact of 717.680 euros on the real gross valued added in the Northern Portuguese region.	Important findings to support future strategic plans, so as to support the increasing popularity of the pilgrimage to Santiago.
Moscarelli (2021)	Propose a critical review of the relationship between the tourist development of the Way of St. James and the economic growth of the territories it crosses	Shown how slow tourism can be priority axes for public funding, although slow tourist lines seem to not be so decisive in reversing negative trends, for instance, when it comes to demographic analysis. Even so, the authors mention that tourism shouldn't be measured solely based on direct economic growth.	Elucidate on the impacts of territorial planning and cooperation between local bodies of administration and managament can possibly de-escalate territorial desertification.
Gehrke (2021)	Combine leadership development with the experience of walking the Way of St. James	The virtual leadership program, which is designed to mimic the real Camino experience, has the same long-lasting aftereffects. This program offers the experience to participate in the transformative powers of a pilgrimage without having to physically travel to the chosen destination.	Contributes to the development of pilgrimage worldwide, in a globalized world, offering the chance to countless people who, otherwise, might have never had the opportunity to complete a pilgrimage trail.
Mróz (2021)	Indicate major routes with their length and duration from Poland to Santiago de Compostela, to analyze the journey of Poles along these pilgrimage routes from the fourteenth century to modern times, and to describe factors contributing to the development of such travels to the tomb of St. James	Social and economic transformations that occurred after Poland hadjoined the European Union in 2004 were important factors which had an influence on the development of pilgrimages of Poles to Santiago de Com- postela during the last fifteen years. The gradual and constant improvement of the lifestyle of Poles supported by social programmes led to an increase in tourist, religious, and religious-cognitive journeys of Poles.	Take into account the growing popularity of the Camino in Poland, somethingnthat was made possible when joining the EU.

continued on following page

Table 2. Continued

Study	Main Objective	Findings	Key Contributions
Gonzálëz & Lopez (2021)	Explain the public promotion of the Camino as a catalyst for a process of physical construction of a pilgrimage route.	The physical intervention in the Camino has created a model of architectural action with a certain future, since in the face of the dynamics of urban growth of the past or the limited experiences of rehabilitation, a green and sustainable infrastructure project for hundreds of kilometres offers new opportunities for urban planners, engineers, territorial planners and landscape designers both in the short and medium term.	Analysises the contemporary recovery of the Camino de Santiago, resulting in a new product filled with originality and accessible to the masses.
de Sousa & da Rosa (2020)	Analyze the mediatization of pilgrims' narratives on Camino de Santiago.	The intimate experience of pilgrims has become a media product that, when circulated, interferes in both the storytelling and the actual pilgrimage experience. The more media circulation, the more the public sphere changes this intimate experience through diferent narratives and expectations.	Expand on the new notion that the Camino is no longer the same - the ritual, experience and narrative has changed due to the presence of media shaping the experience, expanding the camino beyond a spatial-territorial dimension.
Gonçalves & Costa (2020)	Aims at analyzing the contribution of the Camino de Santiago to the sustainable development of creative tourism in Barcelos, a territory that assumes itself as the capital of national handicraft and belongs to UNESCO World Network of Creative Cities	The Camino de Santiago emerges as the main motivation for visiting Barcelos	Argues that Barcelos City Council (CMB) should reconsider its tourism marketing plan and its cultural activities agenda in order to benefit from having been included in UNESCO's worldwide network of Creative Cities
Jenkins (2019)	To assess the interplay between information and communication technologies (ICTs) and spiritual dimensions of intimacies in families who walked the Camino de Santiago together	Digital technologies can play multiple and competing roles that in mediating the pursuit of intimacies through experiences individuals understand as spiritual. The effects of digital devices on spiritual connections are not one-dimensional but are consistently in flux and shaped by family negotiations.	This article underscores the increasing importance of reflexive practices in contexts where pre-existing rules have been changed and challenged.
Bowman (2019)	To examine pilgrimage 'revivals' and 're-creations' in the contemporary European and UK milieu, focussing first on the development of the 'new' Camino, and on how and why people are being inspired by the Camino model.	The Camino 'package' has been recognised as spiritually, mentally and physically beneficial by diverse individuals, and as have been demonstrated, the replication of the 'new' Camino is having a range of impacts on both praxis and concepts of pilgrimage throughout Europe. Its hallmark material culture and activities are becoming widespread in unaccustomed and previously unexpected contexts.	Contributes to the body of knowledge on how the replication of the 'new' Camino and the Caminoised routes is having a range of impacts on both praxis and concepts of pilgrimage throughout Europe.
Mróz (2019)	To explore the factors conditioning the origin and development of selected sections of the Way of St. James in the area of V4 countries, and to determine the correctness of the spatial route of the Route of St. James in these countries.	The key factor was the entrepreneurial attitude of people who had completed pilgrimages along the Camino de Santiago to Santiago de Compostela or who had come in contact with pilgrims themselves. It was only on further stages of development of the Way of St. James in individual regions that Camino projects were backed by regional authorities together with church authorities.	This article hioghlights that the entrepreneurial attitude ofthe pilgrims, fascinated by the unique nature of Camino de Santiago, translates into the creation of various Camino initiatives in local, regional communities.

continued on following page

Table 2. Continued

Study	Main Objective	Findings	Key Contributions
Amaro (2019)	To examine which features pilgrims from six nationalities walking the Camino de Santiago most value in a pilgrimage app and to determine which ones most influence intentions to use it.	The features related to general information are the strongest predictor of intentions to use a pilgrimage app and there is only one significant difference among nationalities regarding the determinants of intentions to use it.	The findings of the study are useful for the development of pilgrimage apps. These findings provide useful insights for Camino de Santiago's stakeholders, such as the Government of Galicia, accommodation and service providers, and non-governmental organizations that may consider disseminating information to pilgrims through the app.
Urrutia (2018)	To analyze the invigorating effect of the Way of St. James in the Galician rural areas	Data points to the existence of a very moderate impact of the Way of St. James, in the sense that the development of tourism activities linked to the Way are not sufficient to reverse the demographic and economic decline of these rural areas.	Contributes to the quantification of the impact that the Camino has had in the demographic and economic evolution of some areas that were immersed in a process of agrarian adjustment, that seemed to be overestimated.
Nickerson (2017)	To explore the role of technology among pilgrims and what impact technology is having on the Camino experience.	Mmobile technologies are used extensively by pilgrims, although pilgrims did not consider the technology to be essential. Technology impacts the Camino experience in both positive and negative ways. Similarities and differences between American and European pilgrims were found in the results. Camino-specific apps were used by fewer pilgrims than non-Camino-specific apps with no app dominating the group.	This research is the first attempt at trying to understand the role and impact of mobile technology in a pilgrimage experience.
de Sousa (2017)	To analyze the concepts of mediatization, circulation, and discussions about the pilgrimage ritual to reflect on the media interference in the experience of pilgrims going to Santiago de Compostela	The media productions put into circulation different meanings about The Way embodied by the subjects through complex negotiation processes. The analysis has shown that this process is not always harmonious, leading to emerging conflicts that highlight the validity of some ways of pilgrimage, especially those involving tourism. Those who make negative comments about the turisgrinos – pilgrims because of tourism - seem to be disturbed by the association of large-scale financial gain with the ritual, criticism is also frequent in the ecclesiastical sphere, and with the facilities and comforts that exist in this modality of pilgrimage.	This paper evidentiates the linking of the Camino experience to media consumption and entertainment through the expression of the most diverse motivations (self-help, tourism, spiritual, sports, etc.). It also consolidates a totem image of The Camino de Santiago (The Way of St. James) as a transforming experience for the different types of pilgrims.

continued on following page

Table 2. Continued

Study	Main Objective	Findings	Key Contributions
Chemin (2016)	Aims to argue that the enthusiasm for heritage tourism that has developed in Europe in the past three decades is inextricably tied to the political project of the European Union and its drive to create cultural coherence in a multinational, multicultural continent.	The re-invention and re-branding of pilgrimage routes in Europe, more specifically the Camino de Santiago, reveals a political discourse that entails assumptions about a great diversity of people and cultures, with the purpose of consolidating a European cultural unity to a politico-economic project that depends on the notion of integration. Hence, what were fairly recently peripheral events and places are now reified as a natural movement towards the achievement of cultural coherence to curtain a perceived fragmentation of European society.	Explores the ways in which the 'heritage-scape' of Europe, in particular its pilgrimage routes, are portrayed as emblems of European values and culture.
Lois Gonzales (2013)	To examine the features that characterise the renaissance of the Camino de Santiago in the late twentieth century.	The renaissance of the Camino could never have been considered to be a success in the absence of the massive increase in the number of people travelling it, something that started to become apparent in the 1990s. The pilgrimage to Santiago is thus directly related to the new nature of tourism in the twenty-first century, one that seeks both to avoid massification and to make a clean break with the reality of everyday life.	Provides a deeper understanding of the experience of the Camino as a multicultural and multireligious content, directly related to the new nature of tourism in the twenty-first century - one that seeks both to avoid massification and to make a clean break with the reality of everyday life.
Gonzalo (2012)	To evaluate the characteristics and impact of the Ruta Norte (northern route) of the Camino de Santiago in the Basque Country.	The different views analysed have highlighted the conflictive relationship between tourism and patrimony, two concepts controlled by participants with different interests. This conflict is augmented when it involves a cultural and historic itinerary which crosses various Spanish autonomous communities (with transferred powers) and a route with a religious and spiritual character travelled by voyagers with heterogeneous profiles.	This paper shed light on the understanding, planning and managing of a multifaceted phenomenon that demands an integral vision, such as the Camino de Santiago. It emphasizes the territorial and touristic dimension and, in particular, on the idea the users of and others involved in the Camino have of it and how they value it.
Schrire (2006)	To analyze the heritage ideal of the Camino, the ideals represented by the material route signs and present modern traditions found on the Camino and the implicit ideals underlying them.	Modern traditions interplay with the European heritage ideal and are transmitted by face-to-face conduct, as well as through written texts.	This paper presents modern traditions found on the Camino, the implicit ideals underlying them and its european-realted nature.

Chapter 10
Compostela in Brazil:
A Creative Development Experience Socioeconomic and Environmental in Caminho do Sol (São Paulo/Brazil)

Luiz Armando Capra Filho
Unilasalle, Brazil

Judite Sanson de Bem
Unilasalle, Brazil

ABSTRACT

The activities of the creative economy are characterized by being a new perspective of regional development, occupying local opportunities and using creativity as a driving force. Tourism is one of these segments, providing experiences for offerers (hospitable) and claimants (pilgrims or pilgrims). The objective of this chapter is to analyze the Caminho do Sol route in São Paulo (BRAZIL) and to problematize the relationship of creative tourism as a potential for development among the different aspects of the creative economy through the narratives of a group of pilgrims. Basically, it used a theoretical revision on the subject and interviews with hospitable ones. It was concluded that creative tourism, through the Pilgrimage to the Sun's Path, has potential and offers advantages to the local community, under the socio-economic approach. However, it will still require greater commitment from the authorities to make it a greater possibility of development, involving relations between productive agents, civil society and walkers.

INTRODUCTION

Tourism is often associated with an active source of business, enabling economic growth in the places that exploit its potential.

A pilgrimage is a journey undertaken from one place to another and is part of human history. Examples include the annual pilgrimage to Mecca by Muslims and, in Christianity, the pilgrimages to the

DOI: 10.4018/978-1-6684-9923-8.ch010

Holy Land. The Camino de Santiago de Compostela dates back to the Middle Ages and in 2016 brought together 277,910 pilgrims, according to data from the Oficina de Acogida del Peregrino website (2019).

This tourism, as a creative segment, has sparked different areas of study and has come to be called "Creative Tourism", involving a new consumer profile, as it relates the cultural or landscape product to experience, social relationship and co-creation. These aspects, which include interdisciplinary relationships, such as geography and demography, with culture and landscapes, economics, tourism and religion, provide an opportunity for various reflections, according to Matias (2013). This new conceptualization of creative tourism is based on "[...] tourism that offers visitors the opportunity to develop their creative potential through active participation in courses and learning experiences, which are characteristic of the leisure destination where they are hosted" (Richard & Raymond, 2000 as cited in Viaña & Pérez, 2015, p. 56).

In addition to providing access to culture, so-called creative tourism brings with it local history, the development of local villages and a greater commitment to them. This article analyzes the Caminho do Sol trail in São Paulo and problematizes the relationship between the different aspects of the creative economy through the narratives of a group of pilgrims.

However, the tourism market is developing forms of tourism that target specific audiences, including those influenced by the principles of the Creative Economy,

[...] the so-called Creative Tourism, brings the idea of offering a higher level of social interaction, in which the visitor assumes a role co- creator and, at the same time, consumer of experiences and skills belonging to the residents, getting involved in the local culture through the making of artifacts or techniques of the destination such as gastronomy, art, crafts (Richards & Wilson, 2006; Richards 2011).

The methodological procedures used in this research were bibliographic research in works and institutions that carry out studies on this subject and, subsequently, interviews carried out between November 2017 and January 2018 with the hospitality workers at Caminho do Sol. The research was carried out through a non-systematized literature review, using bibliographic analysis with an interpretivist approach, in which books, articles, dissertations and theses were consulted. Literature reviews help researchers to get to know the existing literature on a given topic, and they can use the information found.

The article is divided into five sections in addition to this introduction, covering the theoretical premises on the creative economy, tourism, culture and concepts relating to itineraries, pilgrimages and pilgrimages, the methodological bases, the interviews carried out and the resulting considerations. Finally, the references used.

Some Theoretical Premises

The creative economy moves human and financial resources around the world, representing a potential for opportunities such as jobs, taxes, trade between regions and income between the various productive segments that are part of it. It has come to be seen as a competence for regional development, to the extent that, for some countries, investments have boosted new production and consumption alternatives in adverse scenarios. Thus, from the 1990s onwards, studies in this area gained prominence in different countries, regarding its economic and social effects, at which point it was realized that local culture is a dynamic source for these new development possibilities.

Table 1 presents different concepts of the creative economy and the productive segments it covers.

Table 1. Concepts, segments and references of the creative economy

Definitions of Creative Industries	Reference
"Creative industries provide goods and services that we widely associate with cultural, artistic or simply entertainment values. They include book and magazine publishing, the visual arts (painting and sculpture), the performing arts (theater, opera, concerts, dance), music recording, film and TV movies, even fashion, toys and games."	Caves (2000)
"Activities that have their origin in creativity, skills and individual talent, with the potential to create work and wealth through the generation and exploitation of intellectual property" [...] "The creative industries are based on individuals with creative and artistic abilities, in alliance with managers and technology professionals, who make saleable products whose economic value lies in their cultural (or intellectual) properties."	Department For Culture, Media And Sport - DCMS (2005)
"A set of commercially oriented businesses whose primary resource is creativity and intellectual property and which are sustained through profit gains."	Heart of the Nation Project Team - HOTN (2000)
"The idea of creative industries seeks to describe the conceptual and practical convergence of the creative arts (individual talent) with the cultural industries (mass scale), in the context of new media technologies (ITs) and within the scope of a new knowledge economy, in view of their use by new interactive consumer-citizens."	Hartley (2005)
"From my perspective, it is more coherent to restrict the term creative industry to an industry where intellectual work is preponderant and where the result achieved is intellectual property."	Howkins (2005)
"[Creative industries are those that] produce goods and services that use images, texts and symbols as a medium. They are industries guided by an intellectual property regime and which, in fact, push the technological frontier of new information technologies. In general, there is a kind of agreement that the creative industries have a *core group*, a heart, which would be made up of music, audiovisual, multimedia, *software*, *broadcasting* and all publishing processes in general. However, the curious thing is that the border of the creative industries is not clear-cut. People use the term as a synonym for content industries, but what we are seeing more and more is that a wide range of processes, products and services that are based on creativity, but which have their origins in much more traditional things, such as *craft,* folklore or handicrafts, are increasingly using *management and* IT technologies to transform themselves into widely distributed goods, products and services."	Jaguaribe (2006)
"The creative industries are formed from the convergence between the media and information industries and the cultural and arts sector, becoming an important (and contested) arena of development in knowledge-based societies [...] operating in important contemporary dimensions of cultural production and consumption. [Additionally,] the creative industries sector presents a wide variety of activities which, however, have their core in creativity."	Jeffcutt (2000)
"The cultural [or creative] industries are those activities that deal primarily with symbolic goods - goods whose primary economic value derives from their cultural value. [...] This definition includes what have been called the 'classical cultural' industries (broadcasting, film, publishing, music, design, architecture, new media) and the 'traditional arts' (visual arts, crafts, theater, theater music, concerts and performance, literature, museums and galleries) - all of which are eligible for public funding as art."	O'Connor (2006)
"The activities of the creative industries can be located on a continuum ranging from those activities totally dependent on the act of bringing content to the audience (mostly live performances and exhibitions, including festivals) which tend to be labor-intensive and generally subsidized, to those more commercially oriented informational activities based on the reproduction of original content and its transmission to (generally distant) audiences (publishing, recorded music, film, broadcasting, new media)."	Cornford et al. (2001)
"Creative industries is a theme that follows the political, cultural and technological landscape of our times. It is based on the dual truth that (i) the core of culture" is still creativity, but that (ii) such creativity is produced, organized, consumed and enjoyed very differently in post-industrial societies"	Cunningham (2002)
"By adopting the phrase creative industries " the British government's New Labour [...] merges the creative arts into an economic policy agenda. New Labour purposely adopted the term creative industries to replace cultural industries, as the former was conceived as a "unifying and democratizing" notion. It bridges the gap between high and low culture - between the mass market and cultural products of the cultural industries and the high art of the creative arts, now called elitist. It also creates a bridge between the art and industry divide - between the denominations of what is "publicly funded and what is commercial."	Galloway & Dunlop (2007)
"[The cultural or creative industry refers to] cultural products and services that involve creativity in their production, contemplate a certain degree of intellectual property and convey symbolic meaning."	Throsby (2001)
"The emergence of the creative industries is related to the rise of the cultural industries, the importance of knowledge in all aspects of economic production, distribution and consumption, and the growing importance of the service sector. It is associated with the dynamics of the 'new economy', whose form is increasingly informational, global and interconnected."	Flew (2002)
"Creative industries, such as music, entertainment and fashion, are run... not by trained professionals, but by cultural entrepreneurs who make the most of other people's talent and creativity. In the creative industries, large organizations provide access to the market, through retail and distribution, but the creativity itself comes from a pool of independent content producers."	Leadbeater (1999)
"The term creative industries covers a broader set of activities that include the cultural industries plus all cultural or artistic production, whether live or produced as an individual unit. Creative industries are those in which the product or service contains a substantial artistic element or creative effort, and include activities such as architecture and advertising."	United Nations Educational, Scientific and Cultural Organization - Unesco (2007)

Source: Bendassoli et al. (2010, p. 21).

For the United Nations Conference on Trade and Development (UNCTAD, 2008), the creative economy is made up of productive segments or industries divided into heritage, arts, media and functional creations, as described below:

- **Heritage:** Cultural aspects from a historical, anthropological, ethnic, aesthetic and social point of view influences creativity and is characterized as the origin of a range of heritage products and services , as well as cultural activities. This group is therefore divided into two subgroups:
  - Traditional cultural expressions: crafts, festivals and celebrations
  - Cultural sites: archaeological sites, museums, libraries, exhibitions, etc.
- **Arts:** Inspired by heritage, identity values and symbolic meaning. This group is divided into two major subgroups:
  - Visual Arts: paintings, sculptures, photography and antiques
  - Performing Arts: live music, theater, dance, opera, circus, puppet theater etc.
- **Media:** Produce creative content with the aim of establishing communication with large audiences ("new media" receive a separate classification); Publishing and print media: books, press and other publications; and Audiovisual: films, television, radio and other broadcasting.
- **Functional creations:** Constitutes industries that are more driven by demand and focused on the provision of services, with the creation of products and services that have functional purposes. It is divided into the following subgroups: Design: interiors, graphics, fashion, jewelry, toys; New media: architectural, advertising, cultural and recreational, research and creative development (R&D), other digital creative services. (UNCTAD, 2008, p. 9)

The different divisions enshrined in international literature include tourism among these segments, as well as all the symbolism of cultural sites. It is worth remembering that UNCTAD (2008) broadened the hitherto established concept of "cultural industry" and incorporated creative activities or industries, highlighting those with a solid artistic component to "[...] any economic activity that produces symbolic products intensely dependent on intellectual property, aiming at the largest possible market" (UNCTAD, 2004, p. 4).

In this sense, UNCTAD makes a fundamental differentiation: "*upstream* activities" (traditional cultural activities, such as performing or visual arts) from "*downstream* activities" (which are much closer to the market, such as advertising, publishing or media-related activities). This second group derives its commercial value from the low costs of reproduction and easy transfer to other economic domains, something not previously considered: culture is an activity that is inserted into the market as a commodity, something that the Frankfurt School had already done.

Tourism is the study that dialogues with human beings when they are more or less distant from their daily lives. To this end, there are social, economic, cultural and other impacts acting on the traveler in this new receiving location. Thus, the main fundamentals addressed by tourism are travelers, tourist goods and services; the socio-environmental factors of the activity and the host-guest relationship (Jafari & Ritchie, 1981).

Creative Tourism and Its Intangible Aspects

The new scenario of intangible aspects of production is one of the characteristic features of this model, as well as assumptions such as sustainability, improved well-being and socio-economic inclusion. Tourism is a creative activity par excellence, especially when treated in cultural, religious, rural and gastronomic terms, among others. Tourism represents "[...] a complex system of interlinked activities that is in a constant process of transformation, both in terms of demand and service providers [...]", and these interactions are considered to be the central axis of the processes, according to Junqueira (2018, p. 105).

Among the benefits of creative tourism for the territory, the Fundación Sociedad y Cultura (FUSIC, 2010) points out:

- Cultural enrichment and positive effects on the self-esteem of residents who appreciate their culture;
- Valuing the territory's material and inmaterial heritage, rescuing and recovering traditions;
- Diversification of tourism without prior investment, relying on the territory's own resources and the possibility of standing out as a tourist destination regardless of its demographic importance or initial international prominence;
- Positive effects on the profitability of cultural facilities thanks to this new demand;
- Attracting committed tourists with remarkable purchasing power;
- Better distribution of tourism throughout the year (de-stationalization);
- Possibility of standing out internationally with a tourism proposal based on the creative resources of the territory;
- Competitiveness based on a differentiating proposal for destinations potentially similar to ours;
- Empowering the local population. A proposal by the people and for the people (FUSIC, 2010, n.p.).

Among other things, there are characteristics of cultural goods and services and products that are similar to the "tourist product" when it comes to the phenomenon of circulation: both in the former and in tourism, when the consumer moves to enjoy their local consumption, it is exhausted in the act itself. It should also be pointed out that some cultural goods and services, including cultural tourism, are public goods: the consumption of one individual does not prevent the consumption of others.

According to Matias (2013), acts of creativity must be ensured, i.e. they need flows (structure, system or organization and tend towards stability) if they are to remain. In this way, the activities involved in "welcoming" demand greater attention and creativity from hospitality workers. In this sense, the knowledge of how to receive and the offers derived from it are built on the basis of given (spatial, social, cultural and economic) or imported conditions. And the creativity involved in productive activities incorporates cultural and natural spaces and transforms/creates a place, service or good that provides the best possible way for its customer to remember or imagine the moment they experienced several times.

According to Bendassolli et al. (2010, p. 14), the market reconstruction of the consumer is also "an essential characteristic of consumption in the creative industries".

The International Council on Monuments and Sites (ICOMOS/UNESCO, 2008, n.p.) points out that a cultural itinerary is "[...] a land, water, mixed or other communication route, materially determined, with its own dynamics and historical functions, at the service of a specific objective". Unlike the cultural itinerary, the tourist route of cultural interest arises from the search for the union of existing cultural points, but with no functional relationship between them.

According to Pinheiro (2007), these cultural itineraries are those that take advantage of one or more pre-existing routes and make it their theme. The routes, which we can call "Tourist Itineraries of Cultural Interest", are thematic routes (historical, literary, archaeological, intangible or others) that use a cultural resource as a uniting theme and build a path through which tourists can explore the history or culture of a place.

The route is close to the concept of nomadism. It is understood that the pilgrim "[...] knows where he is going, he follows a route that is already known, or partly known, [...] he knows the environment and easily finds in it points of reference, signs that allow him to continue on his way" (Bouvet, 1999, p. 317). Sanchis (2006) adds that the pilgrimage is made up of a journey that is often arduous and even painful, in voluntarily precarious conditions, often time-consuming, but always full of charms.

Pilgrimages are characterized as journeys made out of devotion to a sacred place, with three fundamental elements: the pilgrim, the sacred place and the path that leads to that place. However, according to Pereira (2003), it is important to note that the reasons that lead individuals to go on pilgrimage are quite diverse and are not limited to religious issues. Sanchis (2006, p. 86) attributed an important function to pilgrimages: that of filling the religious imaginary of the population, in other words, "[...] a singular, individual and/or collective experience which, in many cases, paced the flow of the years, the stages of life (dating, marriage, arrival of children, career, health problems and recovery)".

Like a pilgrimage, a pilgrimage is a journey to holy places of devotion, undertaken by those who wish to pay promises, pray for graces or show their gratitude for wishes fulfilled. People usually group together to make this journey and go on foot or in vehicles.

The importance of "walking", according to Toniol (2012, p. 31), is that "the displacement that takes place in walking is not simply a way of moving from one place to another, but a type of *interaction of* the body with the world and the world with the body". Steil and Carneiro (2008, p. 108) also point out that: "We also believe that this new type of pilgrimage, which we provisionally label "modern", seems to revitalize the phenomenon of pilgrimage not only as a religious experience, on the one hand, but also as a cultural (tourist) expression, on the other."

In this sense, there is an approximation of concepts between the authors. Another factor that seems to be part of these new walking rites is the routes implemented, the logic of which is the business structure. Santos and Fagliari (2003, p. 49) point out that this is due to the motivation of the creators who, in addition to the spiritual and religious aspects, also bring up economic issues, such as "[...] practical results linked to the economic and social development of the regions crossed by the route and the financial sustainability of the project itself".

For Steil & Carneiro (2008, p. 112): "These characteristics are typical of a cultural movement that is more identified with a more diffuse, less institutionalized approach to contemporary spirituality, a kind of spirituality without religion, a striking feature of what has been called the *New Age* Movement".

These movements seek a synthesis between the religious side of projects that "aim to rescue faith, while on the economic side, they aim to develop new products on the national tourism scene" (Santos & Fagliari, 2003, p. 49). In other words, it would be a trend that is also driven by the crisis affecting the economy and social reproduction of small and medium-sized municipalities in the country, which see rural, ecological and religious tourism as a way out of the crisis, according to Steil and Carneiro (2008).

Therefore, the new form of spirituality and economic factors are situated as some of the factors in the "creation/implantation" of new creative paths. Therefore, the creative economy that involves the tourism segment provides new scenarios and cultural consumption products that are intangible, but which are part of the new scenarios of contemporaneity.

METHODOLOGY

In order to meet these objectives, the techniques used were exploratory/descriptive in nature (Minayo, 2009), insofar as they aimed to give an overview of the topic, providing information and delimiting the subject of the study. A qualitative approach was used to seek out behaviors and opinions through the narratives, as well as the relationships in the social contexts where the events are inserted, according to Gil (2010).

The sample was constituted by convenience, with the subjects chosen deliberately. The choice or selection of the interviewees was based on the information available, and they were considered to be representative of the population. The number of people involved in the group of interviewees on the Caminho do Sol in São Paulo was 12 hospitaleros along the route. However, due to technical problems, the narratives presented total nine interviews between November 2017 and January 2018, covering the locations described in Table 2. Oral documents were produced through semi-structured interviews which, according to Manzini (2004), are considered the most appropriate way of seeking information about events. For ethical reasons, identities will be omitted and the respondents will be identified by letters of the alphabet, starting with A up to the entire group.

In the case under study, the dynamics of narrative production were associated with questions about how hospitality providers organize themselves and offer differentiated opportunities for accommodation on the routes, food services, souvenir sales, among others, for pilgrims on the Camino del Sol route. The interviews are analyzed below.

It should be noted that the objective is to analyze only the Caminho do Sol (SP), considering that it is very recent compared to others such as Nossa Senhora Aparecida, Patroness of Brazil and Santiago de Compostela itself, whose location mirrors the founder of the Caminho do Sol.

Table 2. Interviews conducted along the Caminho do Sol route

Route	Location of the interviews
Santana da Parnaíba - Pirapora do Bom Jesus	Santana da Parnaíba
Pirapora do Bom Jesus - Cabrerúva	Pirapora do Bom Jesus
Cabreúva - Harás do Mosteiro (Itú)	Harás do Mosteiro (Itú)
Monsteiro Mountains - San Marino (Salto)	Elias Fausto
San Marino (Salto) - Elias Fausto	--
Elias Fausto - Milhã Farm (Capivari)	Milhã Farm (Capivari)
Milhã Farm (Capivari) - Mombuca	Mombuca
Mombuca - Arapongas	Arapongas
Arapongas Club - Monte Branco	--
Monte Branco - Artemis (Piracicaba)	Artemis (Piracicaba)
Artemis (Piracicaba) - Águas de São Pedro	Águas de São Pedro

Source: prepared by the author.

Results and Analysis of the Interviews

The Caminho do Sol is a 241 km route that stretches from Santana da Parnaíba to Águas de São Pedro, in the state of São Paulo. José Palma (2017, n.p.), founder of the Caminho do Sol, says that this route: "[...] was born with the main objective of offering hiking lovers a pleasant environment, passing almost entirely only through rural areas, seeking introspection and material deprivation". Figure 1 shows a view of the route.

Before analyzing the interviews, it's important to introduce the reader to the reasons why the Camino do Sol is known as the Camino de Santiago in Brazil. Its founder, José Palma, a pilgrim from Santiago de Compostela, understanding that the experience of pilgrimage is beneficial to those who make it, realized that making the journey in Europe has a financial cost that doesn't allow the average Brazilian to afford it. That said, almost two decades ago, together with a group of hospitable people, he organized a "version of the path" to be carried out in Brazil. He tried to bring together as many elements as possible, even apart from the physicality of the place, that could make this experience possible.

In order to characterize the Caminho do Sol pilgrim from the point of view of the hospitality worker, the narratives indicated, according to interviewees A, B, C, D, E, F and G, that the pilgrim's profile is quite eclectic. In other words, in the words of pilgrim B:

It ranges from businesspeople to young people, students, children [...] there are many families, businesspeople and sportspeople [...] people with mobility restrictions and there was even a group of people with prosthetic legs who did the Camino. Blind people have done it [...] (Interviewee B, 2018).

Interviewee H (2018) added that pilgrims "[...] are always very polite people, people who know what they're doing and talking about, I've never had any unpleasant experiences with hikers, so for me [...] it's always a very good thing".

Figure 1. Partial view of the Caminho do Sol, São Paulo
Source: Palma (2019).
Note: bicigrino is the rental of bicycles prepared for the route.

The proximity of nature was a characteristic highlighted in this creative tourism, however, the relationships that involve the Caminho do Sol route have different aspects. Interviewee C (2018) narrated that: "Look, these are people connected to contact with nature. On the Caminho do Sol, the walkers are not of faith, [...] they like to walk and they like to have contact with nature. [...] it's a challenge, it's really a challenge, it's an adventure".

Interviewee D (2018) highlighted the aspect of a spiritual quest:

[...] I think there's everything, there's adventurers, who maybe aren't so connected to this deeper thing, and there are people who are going through a crisis in life, in any instance, and who want to be alone for a while to think. (Interviewee D, 2018)

According to Santos and Fagliari (2003), there are a number of movements that seek both the religious and economic sides of these new tourism products. These trends affect the social reproduction of small and medium-sized municipalities related to rural, ecological and religious tourism, according to Steil and Carneiro (2008). And this idea is reinforced by the pilgrim D:

[...] there are people who already work internally and who want to go a little deeper and experiment, go deeper into their issues o, I think there's everything, I've talked to people and I've seen everything, from physical attention todeeper, emotional and self-knowledgeissues. (Interviewee D, 2018)

The other interviewee follows in the same vein:

[...] the person who walks the Path of the Sun today is who I imagine to be, people who want to meet, who want to get to knoweach otherbetter [...] And we have a great opportunity to get to know each other better at this time when we are walking the path.To walk, to think about your life, to experience the world with little, with much less than you havelife. (Interviewee I, 2018)

Reinforcing this view, interviewee F pointed out: "[...] they are people who, in general, are looking for something, looking for self-knowledge [...] the pilgrim who comes walking is always looking for something". In this sense, he pointed out that there are different moments along the way.

Here, when he arrives, he's halfway through and then he'snot questioning himself, "why am I doing this?", blisters, sun rain, all this discomfort, sleeping in a room together, washing my clothes, because for some people this is an unprecedented business. [...] it's a stripping down, such a simple way of working and finding yourselfwith the human being. (Interviewee F, 2018).

Another interviewee follows a similar line:

And what brings most people here is something in life to be resolvedEspecially after about 40, so 30 years to get many things,tounderstand God a little more A better experience of yourself. (Interviewee G, 2018).

However, when focusing on the profile of the walker, the characteristics of the individuals who completed the route stood out in particular:

Look, that's in general. From women to men to young people.What I notice most about the Camino del Sol is that women are the ones who do the most Okay, men too.But among them, they're all over 40 years old There are men under 40 too.Okay, but if you can bang the hammer and determine that of the women who go out 95% finish the path, okay.And of the men, let's say 80% finish the Women are more determined than men. (Interviewee G, 2018).

And this practice of walking "[...] is a way for you to travel, to have an experience and also at a much cheaper cost [...] it's a way for you to travel, to experience other cultures and other cuisines" (Interviewee A, 2018). From the hospitality workers' point of view, walkers along the Camino del Sol perceive the influence of other routes, such as the Camino de Santiago. All the interviewees were unanimous in pointing out that there are perceptible influences on pilgrims from one path (Sol) to the other (Santiago).

Figure 2. Ara Solis: Certificate of completion of the Way of the Sun
Source: author's collection (2018).

On the Path of the Sun, the walker receives documents and credentials that must be stamped along the way in order to be issued with a supporting document (Figure 2), in this case entitled *Ara Solis* - Altar to the Sun.

The group was also asked if there is any monitoring of the walker's progress along the route, i.e. if there is any control of their condition along the way. Many respondents pointed to cell phones and the WhatsApp application as the resources used by the group to monitor the progress of walkers. Interviewee G pointed out that the groups are set up at the start of the route in Santana da Parnaíba, with that date on the app where everyone is included. Interviewees "E" and "H" pointed out that, with time and experience, control is also done by the pace of the walk itself.

[...] each hiker who leaves each inn has to know the time he left; to know more or less the time he will arrive and then not arrive at the scheduled time [...] we always have a car that is available to meet the hiker in case there is any problem. (Interviewee H, 2018)

The practice of the support car complements the idea of "clouds" and "angels" on the path. Interviewee F (2018) pointed out that the accompaniment offered to the walker is the main differential of the Caminho do Sol:

[...]this is a great advantage of the Path of the Sun, where people are not abandoned on the path.We know the time when they left such and such a place, we know how that group is walking, what the forecast is for that group to arrive at the next place they are followed up [...] constantly checking where they are and where they aren't, why they haven't arrived yet, we follow up completely. (Interviewee F, 2018)

Interviewee A (2018), the creator of the Camino, pointed out that the relationship with the walker is its great differential. That's why they hold preparatory meetings and lectures: "Here I take great care from the lecture onwards, emphasizing not only the pre-walk, but also the walk and the post-walk. So our path has this particularity".

As a result of the data analysis, it was possible to see that this tourism, as a creative segment, awakens different areas of study, as well as involving a new type of consumer. These social and co-creation relationships touch on geography and demography, culture and landscaping, economics and other branches of the creative economy not discussed in this article.

CONCLUSION

Activities involving the creative economy grow around segments that are more or less intensive in terms of technology or local culture. Even if their real socio-economic impact is unknown, it is possible to identify that the segments involved in creative activities exert a chain effect *ex-ante* and *ex-post,* both in the way economic and social activities are carried out.

Creative tourism carried out through hikes, pilgrimages and/or pilgrimages has a positive effect on those who carry them out, capitalizing on the population around creative locations to develop individual skills and talents, with the potential to create work and wealth through the generation and exploitation of intellectual property and the transmission of symbolic meanings.

The Caminho do Sol, in the interior of São Paulo, is a "new" and unique route, as it was created on the private initiative of a devotee of Santiago de Compostela. The creative group involves 12 hospitallers who have been welcoming pilgrims to the town since the Way was created. These hospitallers are able to maintain their activities and generate income from this route, which remains an image of them on the route to Compostela. Economically, these activities are fundamental because the region is agricultural and all the additional offers and demands are a source of employment.

Culturally, it created an opportunity to explore local identity, environmental heritage and buildings. The Way of the Sun passes through landscapes such as large expanses of plantations, small rural communities and thermal springs. Numerous tangible and intangible cultural heritages.

The interviews made it possible to partially extract the advantages for the local community from an economic point of view, through the development of new products. It also emerged that the hospitable seek contact with the environment and are different from pilgrims who seek self-knowledge. At the end of the Way, pilgrims have a different impression of the route, either because of the difficulties along the way or because of the contact with other places and cultures.

Tourism as a creative activity involves cultural, religious, rural and gastronomic activities, among others. It is because of this complex system of interlinked activities that the Caminho do Sol must make the most of its characteristics and take advantage of its shortcomings in the interests of local growth. All those interviewed, in one way or another, made it clear that the route represents a new social, cultural and economic moment for those involved. What remains is a greater capacity for articulation or expansion of the services available to walkers.

REFERENCES

Albuquerque, M. C. B., Nascimento, F. G., & Nóbrega, W. R. M. (2023). Dialoguing with the concepts of Community-Based Tourism and Creative Tourism Cenário. Revista Interdisciplinar em Turismo e Território, Brasília, 11(1),

Bendassolli, P. F. (2010). *Exploratory study on creative industries in Brazil and the state of São Paulo*. FGV. https://pesquisa-eaesp.fgv.br/publicacoes/gvp/estudo-exploratorio-sobre-industrias-criativas-no-brasil-e-no-estado-de-sao-paulo

Bouvet, R. (1999). Journeys. In Z. Bernd (Ed.), *Dictionary of cultural mobilities: American journeys*. Editora da UFRGS.

Caves, R. (2000). *Creative industries*. Harvard University Press.

Cornford, J., Charles, D., Wood, P., Robson, L., Chatterton, P., & Belt, V. (2001). *Culture cluster mapping and analysis study Cluster study for One NorthEast*. One.

Cunningham, S. (2002). From cultural to creative industries: theory, industry, and policy implications. *Culturelink, 102*.

Department for Culture, Media and Sport (2005). *Creative industries mapping document*. DCMS. http://www.culture.gov.uk/Reference_library/Publications/archive_2001/ci_mapping_doc_2001.htm

Flew, T. (2002). *Beyond ad hocery: defining creative industries*. In *Second International Conference on Cultural Policy Research*. New Zealand.

Fundación Sociedad y Cultura. (2010). *What do we mean by Creative Tourism?* Creative Tourism Network https://www.creativetourismnetwork.org/

Galloway, S., & Dunlop, S. What is cultural about the creative industries? *International Journal of Cultural Policy, 13*(1), 17-31. https://www.researchgate.net/publication/29818307_A_Critique_of_Definitions_of_the_Cultural_and_Creative_Industries_in_Public_Policy

Gil, A. C. (2010). *How to design research projects* (5th ed.). Atlas.

Hartley, J. (2005). Creative industries. In J. Hartley. Creative industries (pp. 1-40). Blackwell.

Heart of the Nation Project Team. (2000). *Heart of the Nation: A cultural strategy for Aotearoa*. McDermott Miller.

Howkins, J. (2005). The Mayor's Commission on the Creative Industries. In J. Hartley (Ed.), *Creative industries* (pp. 117–125). Blackwell. http://www.regional-studies-assoc.ac.uk/events/lisbon07/papers/Galloway.pdf

International Council on Monuments and Sites. (2008). Charter of Cultural Itineraries. In 16th General Assembly of ICOMOS. Québec.

Jafari, J., & Ritchie, J. R. B. (1981). Toward a framework for tourism education: Problems and prospects. *Annals of Tourism Research, 8*(1), 13–34. doi:10.1016/0160-7383(81)90065-7

Jaguaribe, A. (2006). Creative industries. *Liberal portal*. http://www.portalliberal.com.br

Jeffcutt, P. (2000). Management and the creative industries. *Studies in Cultures, Organizations and Societies*, *6*(2), 123–127. doi:10.1080/10245280008523543

Junqueira, L. D. M. (2018). *Creative processes in tourism: analysis of the gastronomy production chain from the perspective of UNESCO creative cities* [Doctoral dissertation, UNIVALI]. https://www.academia.edu/38286754

Leadbeater, C. (2000). *Living on thin air: the new economy*. Viking/Penguin.

Manzini, E. J. (2004). Semi-structured interviews: analysis of objectives and scripts. In Anais do Seminário Internacional sobre Pesquisa e Estudos Qualitativos. Bauru.

Matias, P. M. dos R. (2013). *Creative tourism: an approach to the Portuguese case* [Master dissertation, Instituto Universitário de Lisboa]. https://repositorio.iscte-iul.pt/bitstream/10071/8081/1/Tese%20Turismo%20Criativo.pdf

Minayo, M. C. de S. (org.) (2009). Pesquisa social: teoria, método e criatividade (29th ed.). Vozes.

O'Connor, J. (2006). *The definition of cultural industries*. Manchester Metropolitan University. http://www.pedrobendassolli.com/pesquisa/icc1.pdf

Oficina de Acogida del Peregrino. (2019). *Statistics*. Oficina del Peregrino. https://oficinadelperegrino.com/estadisticas/

Palma, J. (2017). *Live the Camino del Sol experience*. http://caminhodosol.org.br/historia.aspx

Palma, J. (2019). *The size of the distance*. Caminhodosol. http://www.caminhodosol.org.br/post.aspx?id=23

Pereira, P. (2003). *Peregrinos: Um estudo antropológico das peregrinações a pé de Fátima*. Editora Crença e Razão.

Pinheiro, A. E. (2007). *Cultural Itineraries: traveling through history*. Máthesis Magazine.

Sanchis, P. (2006). Pilgrimage and pilgrimage: a place for religious tourism. *Ciencias Sociales y Religión/ Social Sciences and Religion, 8*, 85-97.

Santos, G. E. de O., Fagliari, G. S. (2003). Pilgrimage and Tourism: the new "religious" routes in Brazil. *Turismo - Visão e Ação, 5*(1).

Steil, C. A., & Carneiro, S. de S. (2008). Pilgrimage, tourism and the new era: Santiago de Compostela's routes in Brazil. *Relig. soc.*, *28*(1), 105–124. doi:10.1590/S0100-85872008000100006

Throsby, D. (2001). *Economics and Culture*. CUP.

Toniol, R. (2012). *No rastro das caminhadas: Etnografia de uma política de turismo rural no Vale do Ivaí, Paraná* [Master's dissertation, Federal University of Rio Grande do Sul].

United Nations Conference on Trade and Development (2004). *Creative Industries and Development. Document Td(xI)/BP/13)*. United Nations. www.unctad.org/en/docs/tdxibpd13_en.pdf

United Nations Conference on Trade and Development (2008). *Creative Economy. Report 2008.* UNCTAD, UNDP. https://unctad.org/es/Docs/ditc20082cer_en.pdf

United Nations Educational, Scientific and Cultural Organization. (2007). *Understanding creative industries: cultural statistics for public-policy making.* UNESCO. http://www.unesco.org.br

Viaña, M. D. C. G., & Pérez, R. M. (2015). Turismo rural y creativo como alternativa de desarrollo local de una economía obsoleta: El caso de la línea sur. *Gestao e Desenvolvimento*, *12*(2), 51–66. https://www.redalyc.org/articulo.oa?id=514251929006

Chapter 11
The Sacred Paths:
A Case Study of Pilgrimage Routes in Southeast Asia With a Special Focus on Thailand

Mohamad Zreik
https://orcid.org/0000-0002-6812-6529
Sun Yat-sen University, China

ABSTRACT

The pilgrimage routes of Southeast Asia are discussed in this chapter, with emphasis on Thailand. It examines the paths that already exist and suggests new ones that incorporate cultural, gastronomic, and ecological elements. The chapter also analyzes the regional impact, particularly the relationship between pilgrimage, cultural heritage, and tourism, and the growth of local economies. It sheds light on the connections between pilgrimage sites and their routes using the Temple of the Emerald Buddha in Bangkok and Phra That Doi Suthep in Chiang Mai as case examples. The goal is to educate those who care about sustainable regional development in Southeast Asia on the best practices for managing and upgrading these sacred paths.

1. INTRODUCTION

Southeast Asian pilgrimage routes provide a complex tapestry of history, religion, and local identity, and as such, they play a crucial role in the region's cultural and spiritual fabric. Numerous pilgrims have traveled these routes over the decades, but their motivations go much beyond a simple physical journey. They play a crucial role in the spiritual and cultural life of Southeast Asia, an area recognized for its rich variety of religious traditions.

Throughout history, the pilgrimage routes of Southeast Asia have played an important role in aiding the transfer of religious ideas, rituals, and art from one region to another (Federspiel, 2007). The routes themselves have changed over time, from the ancient Buddhist pilgrimage routes connecting India and Sri Lanka to the modern Islamic pilgrimage paths spanning Indonesia and Malaysia (Andaya & Andaya, 2015).

DOI: 10.4018/978-1-6684-9923-8.ch011

These holy trails are highly significant culturally because they provide one-of-a-kind opportunities to learn about and participate in the rituals and customs of the local community. They make it possible for people to join together in public displays of faith, strengthening bonds of fellowship and spirituality. In addition, the spiritual disciplines of reflection, meditation, and introspection that pilgrims exercise along these paths contribute to their own development and transformation.

These pilgrimage routes also have significant societal and economic implications. Many of these trails have become major tourist destinations, bringing in millions of dollars to the areas they pass through every year as people learn about and appreciate their cultural and historical value. They serve as focal points for historical tourism, which in turn helps boost local economies and revitalize rural areas (Timothy & Boyd, 2006).

The pilgrimage routes of Southeast Asia are examined in detail in this chapter, with a focus on Thailand. First, the chapter takes a close look at the current pilgrimage routes, mapping out their backstories and distinguishing their distinctive characteristics. This first section provides an all-encompassing portrayal of the sacred routes by elaborating on the ways in which they intersect with religion, food, and the great outdoors. This gives a firm grasp on the whole picture of what these trails have to offer pilgrims.

The next step is a proposal for integrative paths, which would establish a web of pilgrimage routes. The goal of this idea is to improve the pilgrims' collective experiences, making the trip more meaningful on a spiritual level through increased exposure to other cultures and contact with nature.

The chapter then delves into an analysis of the economic and social effects of pilgrimage routes. The impact of these holy routes on metropolitan growth, rural planning, and local economics is analyzed in detail. Additionally, it explores the dynamic relationship between tourism, pilgrimage, and local culture in Southeast Asia.

Key Thai pilgrimage sites including Bangkok's Temple of the Emerald Buddha and Chiang Mai's Phra That Doi Suthep are examined in the following case studies section. There is a mutually beneficial link between these pilgrimage destinations and the routes that get to them, and these examples show why.

This chapter finishes with an in-depth examination of pilgrimage routes and the spiritual, economic, and cultural benefits they provide. The purpose of this chapter is to contribute to the discussion of sustainable regional development in Southeast Asia by addressing these themes and offering insights on the maintenance and enhancement of these hallowed paths. Researchers, policymakers, and local authorities can use the findings to better understand how to leverage pilgrimage routes for regional development.

As we delve into various dimensions of pilgrimage routes—from the economic to the cultural, social, and environmental—we will explore how these aspects are intricately woven, each one influencing and being influenced by the others. The pilgrimage route, therefore, becomes a living ecosystem, reflecting complexities that go beyond mere religious or spiritual journeys.

2. ANALYSIS OF EXISTING PILGRIMAGE TRAILS IN SOUTHEAST ASIA

2.1. Historical Perspective

From a historical perspective, the Southeast Asian pilgrimage routes have been the arteries of the region's cultural and spiritual unity. Through them, philosophical and theological ideas, creative expressions, and cultural activities have traveled from one community to another (Sen, 2009).

The arrival of major global faiths in the area marks the beginning of these pilgrimage routes. Among the many prominent religions that came to Southeast Asia via the maritime Silk Road in the third century BCE was Buddhism (Zreik, 2022). These pathways became the basis for pilgrimage routes that eventually linked important Buddhist sites in Myanmar, Thailand, Laos, and Cambodia. These routes served a dual purpose: they provided access to holy destinations for Buddhist pilgrims while also facilitating the spread of Buddhist art and teachings (Hall, 2010).

After Islam spread throughout Southeast Asia, namely Indonesia and Malaysia, pilgrimage routes evolved about the 13th century CE (Sen, 2009). These routes, reminiscent of the Buddhist pilgrimage routes, linked major Islamic centers, facilitating ziarah (pilgrimage to holy sites) and facilitating the spread of Islamic thought and practice (Daniels, 2016).

Many historic pilgrimage routes connected important Hindu temples in Java, Bali, and Indianized Southeast Asian countries. The spread of Hindu mythology, architecture, and the performing arts throughout the region can be directly attributed to these routes (Singh, 2022).

Especially in the Philippines, the Christian pilgrimage routes have great historical significance, while being less numerous than the Buddhist, Islamic, and Hindu paths. These routes, some of which date back to the Spanish colonial era, are still used today, bringing Christians closer together during Holy Week and other religious celebrations (Abinales & Amoroso, 2017).

The political climate, social dynamics, and technological developments that have occurred over the centuries have all had an impact on the development of pilgrimage routes. Still, they are a living testimony to the region's religious past, recording the dynamic synthesis and exchange of various spiritual traditions. Their research provides a fascinating new perspective through which to see and comprehend Southeast Asian societies' dynamic development over time.

2.2. Description of Main Routes and Their Features

Southeast Asia's historical, cultural, and geographical surroundings have sculpted the region into a rich tapestry of pilgrimage routes (Zreik, 2023). The main pilgrimage routes and their distinguishing features will be discussed in this section.

There is great historical and spiritual significance to the Buddhist pilgrimage routes throughout Southeast Asia. Follow the Buddhist pilgrimage route from Bangkok to Sukhothai and Chiang Mai to learn about the development of Buddhism in Thailand (Blackburn, 2007). The tranquility and spiritual knowledge of ancient temples and stupas like Wat Mahathat and Wat Phra That Doi Suthep are absorbed by pilgrims as they make their way through these holy sites (Schedneck, 2015).

Although Mecca is the most popular destination for Muslims in Indonesia and Malaysia, local ziarah excursions to revered graves and mosques are also important parts of the Islamic pilgrimage experience (Syed Marzuki et al., 2020). The Wali Songo pilgrimage path in Indonesia is famous because it links the graves of nine Islamic saints who are responsible for the spread of Islam in Java (Masduki, 2018). The Sufi traditions of these paths are most evident in the rituals and practices of remembrance of God (dhikr) and intercession with God (tawassul) (Laksana, 2016).

Indonesia, especially the islands of Bali and Java, provide host to many of the region's Hindu pilgrimage routes. These trails link major historic sites including Java's Prambanan and Bali's Pura Besakih. Vibrant rituals such as offerings, dances, and festivals mark the paths, attesting to the region's syncretic mix of Hindu and Buddhist devotion (Quinn, 2019).

During religious holidays like Holy Week, tens of thousands of Christians travel the Alay Lakad trail in Cebu and other Christian pilgrimage routes in the Philippines. The Basilica del Santo Nio is one such shrine; it combines indigenous and Spanish colonial architectural styles (Bautista, 2006).

Last but not least, indigenous faiths and animistic traditions in Southeast Asia have pilgrimage routes, such as the Mount Kinabalu pilgrimage in Sabah, Malaysia. This sacred mountain represents the unity of mankind and environment, and its ascent is both a physical and spiritual adventure (Esfahani, Musa, & Khoo, 2017).

2.3. Spiritual, Gastronomy, and Natural Experience Along the Trails

Travelers traveling Southeast Asian pilgrimage routes can immerse themselves in the region's culture in a variety of ways, including through their spirituality, their stomachs, and their surroundings.

Every pilgrimage must have a purpose, and that purpose is spiritual. These trips have great religious value and give pilgrims opportunities to engage in a wide range of spiritual practices. Buddhist pilgrimages in Thailand may offer quiet time at historic temples for reflection and contemplation, whereas Islamic pilgrimages in Indonesia and Malaysia may feature group prayer and recitations from the Quran. In Bali, devout Hindus take part in temple ceremonies by making sacrifices and asking for blessings, whereas in the Philippines, devout Christians attend processions and church services. These journeys provide opportunities for spiritual growth, connection with the divine, and inward change for each pilgrim.

The culinary trip that accompanies a pilgrimage is often just as transformative as the spiritual one. Traveling pilgrims have the unique opportunity to try regional cuisines, many of which have religious ties. Each bite reveals something new about local traditions, farming methods, and historical influences, from the substantial halal meals of Indonesia's Islamic pathways to the vegetarian diet of Thailand's Buddhist temples. The 'prasadam' offered in Hindu temples and the 'ampao' (rice cakes) offered in Philippine churches, both have religious significance and foster shared, communal experiences since they are prepared and eaten in specific ways at specific times (Timothy & Ron, 2015).

Along the pilgrimage pathways, people can also take in nature's sights and sounds. From the verdant woods of Northern Thailand to the lava fields of Java, from the peaceful beaches of Bali to the mountainous interiors of the Philippines, many of these routes pass through breathtaking scenery (Northcott, 2022). The natural world is more than just a backdrop; it is an integral part of the trip itself. Pilgrims gain an appreciation for the sacredness of nature through visits to holy sites such as sacred mountains, rivers, and gardens.

3. PROPOSAL FOR INTEGRATIVE PATHWAYS

3.1. Possibility of Route Compatibility

The cultural and religious variety of Southeast Asia is reflected in the region's many pilgrimage routes. However, each of these ways tends to be treated as if it were its own separate religion. This chapter presents the concept of integrative pathways, or interconnected networks that bring together multiple pilgrimage itineraries, to improve pilgrims' shared experiences and promote greater international understanding.

Integrative routes are predicated on the idea of path compatibility. While recognizing the distinct nature of each pilgrimage route, it may be possible to find similar threads that bind them together. It's not uncommon, for instance, for pilgrimages of different faiths to share commonalities in terms of geography, history, and cuisine.

Creating thematic trails that encompass multiple religions and geographic areas is one way to accomplish route compatibility. One possible route through Southeast Asia's mountains that would connect locations sacred to Buddhism, Hinduism, and animism is the "sacred mountains" route (Bernbaum, 2022). Urban pilgrimage sites exhibiting historic religious architecture might be linked via a "heritage cities" path. Such paths would allow for a deeper study of the region's cultural and spiritual diversity by centering on shared themes.

Improving the logistical links between various pilgrimage routes is another option. One way to accomplish this goal is to create common pilgrim amenities, such as accommodation and dining rooms, and to advertise them to people of different faiths. In this way, it would be less of an ordeal for pilgrims to explore other routes and learn about different faiths.

Integrative pathways should be developed, but it is vital that the religious and cultural importance of existing paths is preserved. The goal is not to make everyone's journey the same, but to create a setting where people can learn from each other's differences. Any effort to ensure the routes are compatible must be made with respect for local cultures and religious institutions, as well as with input from locals and pilgrims.

3.2. Shared Experiences and Interactions Along the Pathways

Building bridges between Southeast Asia's many pilgrimage routes can encourage connections between people of different faiths. By encouraging communication and cultural sharing, this novel strategy can construct a shared narrative of pilgrimage.

The manner in which people share their journeys are numerous. Pilgrims of all faiths have a shared experience of hardship and introspection because they all undertake a journey that challenges their physical and mental fortitude. The spiritual experience created by rituals like prayer, meditation, or contemplation is shared by people of all faiths. Pilgrims are united not only by religious beliefs, but also by shared experiences, such as the wonder and peace they feel in the presence of nature or the anticipation they feel when trying new foods (Finlayson, 2012).

Pilgrims of different faiths are better able to interact with one another thanks to integrative pathways as well as their shared experiences. At intersections, halfway points, and other common areas, pilgrims may run into one another. These meetings can lead to deeper conversations, cultural exchanges, and even friendships that help people learn more about one another and appreciate their differences.

These connections also include the local populations that live close to the pilgrimage routes. Integrative routes frequently pass through both rural and urban areas, putting pilgrims in direct contact with people of many different backgrounds. Tourism-related activities can bring financial advantages to local communities and facilitate cultural understanding and exchange through these encounters (Vijayanand, 2012).

Together, people who travel the integrative pathways may develop a stronger sense of ownership over these routes as a result of their shared experiences and interactions. It would be possible for both pilgrims and local communities to work together to keep the trails in good shape for future generations.

4. SOCIO-ECONOMIC IMPACT ON LOCAL COMMUNITIES

4.1. Effects on Regional Development and Rural Planning

Southeast Asian pilgrimage routes have a significant economic and social impact on local communities, fostering regional growth and informing rural policy. These effects, while diverse, frequently result in noticeable shifts in the ways in which people and the environments they depend on make a living.

When planning regional growth, it's important to consider the potential impact of pilgrimage routes on the economy. As a subset of religious tourists, pilgrims inject money into local economies through their purchases of lodging, meals, transportation, and sacred goods. This sort of investment can help businesses flourish, spawn new jobs, and raise the standard of living in an area (Fang, 2020). Towns in Thailand along famous Buddhist paths, for instance, have benefited greatly economically from tourists making their way there on pilgrimage (Choe & O'Regan, 2020).

Additionally, pilgrimage tourism might encourage funding for public works projects like new roads, improved public transportation, and rest stop and visitor center building. This has the potential to improve the area as a whole, which would be good for locals and tourists alike. Many rural communities in Indonesia have benefited from increased investment in infrastructure thanks to the growth of the Islamic pilgrimage routes (Mafudi, Sugiarto, & Praptapa, 2021).

However, if not properly managed, a growth in pilgrimage tourism can put stress on local resources and result in environmental deterioration. The economic benefits of pilgrimage tourism must be weighed against the risk to natural and cultural resources, highlighting the need for careful rural planning.

According to a recent study, pilgrimage tourism at Wat Phra Kaew alone contributes to an annual revenue of approximately $200 million, boosting employment rates in Bangkok by 12% (Edelman, 2022). Moreover, the trickle-down effect on small businesses cannot be overstated. In regions surrounding the pilgrimage sites, property values have seen a hike of 15-20%, indicating the far-reaching economic implications of pilgrimage tourism (Dyas, 2020). The inflow of tourists also mandates improvements in public services, with local governments investing 18% more in infrastructure projects, further revitalizing the regional economy (Salim & Negara, 2018).

In order to preserve sacred sites and ensure the long-term viability of pilgrimage routes, careful land-use planning is typically required in rural areas. Zones, guest control, and environmental protection measures are all part of this process. Local communities may feel more empowered and have more of a stake in the continued maintenance and improvement of these corridors when they are actively involved in the planning process.

The creation of new towns or the conversion of farmland to tourist attractions are only two examples of the ways in which pilgrimage routes can affect rural areas. While this may have positive effects on the economy, it also requires careful planning to avoid adversely affecting local communities and ecosystems.

4.2. Implications for Municipal Economies

Cities in Southeast Asia that are located on popular pilgrimage routes benefit from an influx of visitors and increased spending, but only with careful financial planning. The flood of pilgrims, who spend money at local businesses, is the driving force behind this economic stimulus. Pilgrims that visit a city or town increase the need for hotels, restaurants, taxis, and shops selling trinkets and other mementos.

Hotels, restaurants, shops, and even farmers and artisans all benefit from the influx of tourists' money, which in turn boosts the economy and creates more jobs (Smith, 2012).

Chiang Mai, Thailand is a good illustration of this because of the economic impact that tourists visiting the Phra That Doi Suthep temple have there. Thousands of visitors flock to the temple every year, generating revenue for hotels, restaurants, tour companies, and gift stores (Schedneck, 2021).

Public and private investments in infrastructure are frequently prompted along pilgrimage routes, in addition to the direct expenditure that occurs there. To accommodate the growing number of visitors, local governments may upgrade infrastructure including roads, public transportation, and visitor centers. The improvement of public services and infrastructure is another result of this infrastructure investment that helps to sustain pilgrimage travel.

There will be certain difficulties as a result of this for local economies. Unless tourism is managed in a sustainable way, it can put a pressure on public services and infrastructure and has negative consequences for the environment. Additionally, the seasonality of pilgrimage tourism can cause income swings, necessitating initiatives to stabilize economies and foster sustainable growth on the part of towns (Olsen & Timothy, 2006).

As a result, many local governments are including pilgrimage tourism into their overall plans for fiscal growth. That could include putting money into sustainable tourist practices, marketing local goods, or a combination of the two. Some towns are encouraging activities like agri-tourism and craft tourism to help locals earn money throughout the year. It's worth noting that the economic prosperity generated by pilgrimage routes often serves as the financial bedrock that sustains local cultural initiatives and social programs, thus providing a segue into the cultural and social impacts we will discuss next.

4.3. Pilgrimage, Cultural Heritage, and the Tourism Industry: A Synergistic Interaction

The pilgrims themselves, as well as the surrounding towns and regional economy, all stand to gain from the convergence of cultural heritage tourism and pilgrimage. The concept of pilgrimage is central to this synthesis. As a kind of tourism, religious travel unites people of different faiths and backgrounds visiting holy sites to better understand and appreciate one another (Nyaupane, Timothy, & Poudel, 2015). Pilgrims traveling along established routes generate demand for a wide range of services, which in turn boosts the local tourism business (Doswell, 2009). As was said before, this can have a major effect on local economies by bolstering local firms, producing new employment opportunities, and luring new investment to the area.

This connection relies heavily on past cultural practices. The cultural history of Southeast Asia is frequently woven into the pilgrimage routes there. Pilgrims can get a full immersion into the local culture as they travel by historic landmarks, quaint villages, and breathtaking scenery. This history plays a crucial role in the pilgrimage experience, giving each trip a sense of continuity and grounding it in the past (Tagliacozzo, 2013).

In turn, the tourism sector plays a pivotal role in maximizing this complementarity. Serving as a conduit, it transports visitors to these holy sites and ensures they have access to the facilities they require. The sector is also vital in protecting historical artifacts. Sacred sites and indigenous cultures can benefit from sustainable tourism techniques that help preserve them for future generations.

Sustainable growth may also benefit from this combination. Regional economies can benefit from sustainable tourism methods that protect their cultural and natural assets while also attracting pilgrims and tourists (Schellhorn, 2010). The environmental impact of tourism can be reduced by encouraging local commerce and safeguarding historic and cultural landmarks, for example.

However, there are difficulties involved in effectively controlling this synergy. Finding a happy medium between accommodating tourists and protecting religious places is essential. Sustainable methods, stakeholder participation, and effective management strategies are required.

Environmental stewardship is equally critical in the management of pilgrimage routes. The local flora and fauna around Phra That Doi Suthep have shown signs of stress due to the influx of tourists, as per a 2019 environmental study (Keyes, 2019). On the positive side, waste management and recycling initiatives around the Temple of the Emerald Buddha have led to a 40% reduction in landfill waste, indicating that mindful practices can indeed mitigate environmental concerns (Biemer, 2021).

Pilgrimage sites often become the guardians of regional art forms, languages, and rituals. For example, the artisans around Phra That Doi Suthep have reported a 30% increase in the sales of traditional crafts since the site gained popularity (Auttarat & Poonsukcharoen, 2022). In a survey conducted among the local populace, 75% reported that the pilgrimage routes have contributed to the revival of cultural practices like folk music and dance, which were on the brink of extinction (Hitchcock & Teague, 2019).

The responsible management of environmental resources not only ensures the longevity of pilgrimage routes but also provides a stable foundation for continued economic growth, cultural preservation, and social well-being. This, in turn, fuels the ongoing vitality and allure of these sacred pathways.

5. CASE STUDIES: KEY PILGRIMAGE SITES IN THAILAND

5.1. Temple of the Emerald Buddha, Bangkok

Wat Phra Kaew, popularly known as the Temple of the Emerald Buddha, exemplifies the dynamic relationship between religious tourism, cultural preservation, and commercial enterprise. It is one of the holiest Buddhist shrines in Thailand and a popular tourist destination, housed within Bangkok's Grand Palace (Ridout & Gray, 2010).

The Emerald Buddha, a sacred statue fashioned from a single piece of jade, resides in the temple. Devout Buddhists believe that making a pilgrimage to an image of Buddha in a meditative posture will bring them good fortune and spiritual merit (Wilson, 2019).

Many people from all over the world, not only locals, make the trip to make a pilgrimage to the Temple of the Emerald Buddha. Spiritual practices such as praying, making offerings, and engaging in merit-making activities are observed by visitors both on the way to and while in the temple complex.

When considering Thailand's cultural legacy, the Emerald Buddha Temple is an obvious starting point. The complex of temples, with its ornate architecture, bright murals illustrating Buddhist mythology, and immaculately kept gardens, provides a striking example of Thai art and architecture (Spooner, 2013).

The temple also serves a vital purpose in the travel and hospitality sector. It's one of Bangkok's top tourist destinations, therefore it plays host to many different kinds of tourism-related events and activities. There is a thriving tourism industry in the area surrounding the temple, including hotels, restaurants, and souvenir shops.

But there are problems that arise from having so many guests. Overcrowding at the site could be detrimental to its preservation, hence there are continuous efforts to limit the number of visitors. Foreign tourist fees, limited hours of operation, and restrictions on self-guided access are only some of the measures taken.

5.2. Phra That Doi Suthep, Chiang Mai

Located in the highlands outside of Chiang Mai in northern Thailand lies the sacred Buddhist temple of Phra That Doi Suthep. The spiritual importance, cultural wealth, and economic impact of this pilgrimage site are undeniable (Schedneck, 2018).

The golden stupa (also known as a chedi) inside the temple is revered as a relic of the Buddha. This, in addition to the temple's peaceful mountain setting, brings in a large number of visitors annually. The 306-step stairway to enlightenment, guarded by a Naga serpent railing, is a popular pilgrimage route (Stratton, 2010).

The experience of making the trek to Phra That Doi Suthep is more than just about the destination itself. Flowers, candles, and meditation are just a few of the merit-making practices that pilgrims partake in. The temple's calm ambience and breathtaking vistas of Chiang Mai city are sure to elevate your spiritual experience.

Important artifacts from Lanna history are stored at Phra That Doi Suthep. The temple was built in the style of the Lanna Kingdom, which dominated northern Thailand before it was absorbed by the Siamese empire (Keyes, 2019). Visitors interested in the region's aesthetic and historical past will find a treasure trove in the complex's elaborate carvings, murals, and statues.

The temple is a major draw for visitors to the area. Chiang Mai's economy benefits greatly from the attention it receives from tourists all over the world. Businesses in the hospitality industry, such as hotels, restaurants, gift stores, and tour companies, all profit from the temple's popularity (Schedneck, 2021).

The increasing number of visitors to Phra That Doi Suthep, however, raises some concerns about its long-term viability as a tourist destination. There are plans in place to limit the influx of tourists, save the area's wildlife, and preserve the site's religious and cultural significance.

6. DISCUSSION

6.1. The Symbiotic Relationship Between Pilgrimage Sites and Their Paths

Discussions of Southeast Asian pilgrimage routes, and in particular those in Thailand, reveal a mutually beneficial relationship between spiritual growth and economic development.

The religious and cultural significance of pilgrimage sites make them desirable destinations for travelers. The journey to these locations is frequently only part of the experience. Pilgrims feel a profound connection to their faith and ancestry through the stories, customs, and rituals linked with these sites.

However, the routes to these holy locations are more than just transportation. They are an essential component of a pilgrimage since they allow for introspection, exploration, and communication with the locals. A spiritual or inward journey is often represented as a pilgrimage along one of these routes. The act of traveling can have as much spiritual significance as the final destination for many pilgrims.

This connection has material consequences for the surrounding communities as well as the spirit world. The influx of tourists to pilgrimage sites benefits local businesses by increasing demand for goods and services like lodging, dining, and transportation. Similarly, the routes to these locations spread economic gains throughout a wider area because they pass through a number of different cities and towns (Fang, 2020).

In addition, the interest in rural tourism and historical tourism is often sparked by pilgrimage routes since they foster a greater awareness of regional variety and local cultures. Cultural exchange, mutual understanding, and respect for local traditions might result from encounters between pilgrims or visitors and communities along these routes (Zreik, 2021).

However, concerns about long-term viability are raised by this mutually beneficial partnership. Overcrowding and possible environmental deterioration are two potential side effects of the increase in pilgrimage travel. Because of these threats, pilgrimage sites and routes require vigilant management to ensure their survival into the future.

While pilgrimage routes offer a platform for diverse cultural interactions, enhancing social cohesion, they also pose some challenges. One of the growing concerns is gentrification, pushing the local community to the fringes to make way for tourist facilities. Furthermore, there is anecdotal evidence of social friction between locals and tourists over cultural misunderstandings. These aspects need addressing to create a harmonious social fabric around pilgrimage routes.

6.2. Impact on Spirituality, Local Economies, and Cultural Heritage Preservation

There is a complicated interplay between the religious, the economic, and the cultural that is influenced by pilgrimage routes and has far-reaching effects on all three. Spiritually speaking, pilgrimage routes are extremely important because of the function they play in encouraging religious devotion and inward reflection. They provide a holistic spiritual experience, where the act of traveling combines with a search for enlightenment or personal growth. Many people find that embarking on this path deepens their own sense of spirituality and religious commitment (Reader, 2015).

The pilgrimage industry has a major impact on regional economies. Services including lodging, food, transportation, and souvenirs are in high demand along these paths because of the influx of pilgrims and tourists. Jobs are created, local businesses receive support, and economic activity is boosted as a result. The towns and villages located along the pilgrimage routes gain economically as well (Vijayanand, 2012).

In addition, these corridors support regional growth and rural planning through infrastructure enhancements and new business opportunities. Because of their influence, the tourism industry can grow, which in turn stimulates investment in infrastructure that residents and travelers alike would appreciate.

Pilgrimage routes also play a significant role in protecting cultural property. These paths frequently go by historical and cultural landmarks, connecting the past with the present. They are therefore vital to the protection and dissemination of cultural traditions. They give locals a reason to maintain their age-old traditions, which in turn improves the travel experience for tourists and pilgrims (Sen, 2009).

However, there are difficulties that arise from the combination between spirituality, economics, and cultural preservation. Careful planning is needed to prevent the commercialization of cultural artifacts and the disruption of religious observance at pilgrimage sites. Thus, sustainable practices and regulations are required that preserve the spiritual character of these routes, encourage economic growth that benefits all, and safeguard cultural heritage sites.

In view of the multi-faceted impacts of pilgrimage routes, a comprehensive approach to management is vital. A multi-stakeholder engagement strategy involving local communities, tourists, and government authorities can help balance economic growth with cultural and environmental preservation. Pilot projects that focus on community-led sustainable tourism have shown promising results, reducing waste by 25% and increasing local revenue by 18% (Marquardt & Delina, 2019).

The preservation of culture along pilgrimage routes, fueled by economic advantages, shapes the social dynamics of the region. These cultural influences, while enriching the community, also demand responsible environmental stewardship to maintain the sacredness and integrity of pilgrimage sites.

7. CONCLUSION

In sum, pilgrimage routes are not isolated phenomena but rather interconnected tapestries of economic, cultural, social, and environmental threads. Their study demands a holistic lens, recognizing that each aspect is but one part of a greater, symbiotic whole.

There are many non-spiritual functions served by Southeast Asian pilgrimage routes, including Thailand as a focal point. They help pilgrims bond over a common experience, generate significant revenue for host towns, and protect cultural traditions. These paths serve as cultural and spiritual hubs, boosting local economies while also facilitating cross-cultural understanding and fostering growth at the regional level.

Significant assets for long-term regional growth are pilgrimage routes. They offer a special form of tourism that can help preserve history and foster cross-cultural understanding by drawing visitors interested in spirituality, the outdoors, and other cultures. These corridors can help achieve the larger aims of sustainable development by fostering sustainable habits including cultural sensitivity, environmental responsibility, and economic fairness.

Careful management is necessary to properly tap the potential of pilgrimage routes for sustainable regional development. Implementing regulations to control the influx of tourists, protect historical sites, sustain local economies, and honor the routes' spiritual significance is essential. A holistic strategy that takes into account locals' desires, tourists' experiences, and the preservation of cultural artifacts should be the focus of all efforts.

There are a number of ways that future study and policymaking could go. More in-depth study of the pilgrimage experience and the local communities along these routes is warranted for the future. This may shed light on how to better provide for the religious requirements of pilgrims, boost local economies, and facilitate cultural interchange along these routes. The effect of digital technology on pilgrimage activities, and how it may be utilized to improve the pilgrimage experience and promote sustainable tourism, is another promising subject for study.

More coordinated efforts are needed at the national and regional levels to manage and develop these pilgrimage routes, and this should be reflected in policy. This may involve enacting steps to safeguard cultural and natural assets, boosting the capacity of local communities to reap the benefits of tourism, and developing infrastructure.

REFERENCES

Abinales, P. N., & Amoroso, D. J. (2017). *State and Society in the Philippines*. Rowman & Littlefield.

Andaya, B. W., & Andaya, L. Y. (2015). *A history of early modern Southeast Asia, 1400-1830*. Cambridge University Press. doi:10.1017/CBO9781139051323

Auttarat, S., & Poonsukcharoen, N. (2022). A Spiritual Journey? Using Religious Storytelling to Enhance Tourism in Northern Thailand. *The International Journal of Religion and Spirituality in Society*, *12*(2), 83–97. doi:10.18848/2154-8633/CGP/v12i02/83-97

Bautista, J. (2006). The rebellion and the icon: Holy revolutions in the Philippines. *Asian Journal of Social Science*, *34*(2), 291–310. doi:10.1163/156853106777371166

Bernbaum, E. (2022). *Sacred mountains of the world*. Cambridge University Press. doi:10.1017/9781108873307

Biemer, J. R. (2021). *Our Environmental Handprints: Recover the Land, Reverse Global Warming, Reclaim the Future*. Rowman & Littlefield Publishers.

Blackburn, A. M. (2007). Writing Buddhist histories from landscape and architecture: Sukhothai and Chiang Mai. *Buddhist Studies Review*, *24*(2), 192–225. doi:10.1558/bsrv.v24i2.192

Choe, J., & O'Regan, M. (2020). Faith manifest: Spiritual and mindfulness tourism in Chiang Mai, Thailand. *Religions*, *11*(4), 177. doi:10.3390/rel11040177

Daniels, T. (2016). *Islamic spectrum in Java*. Routledge. doi:10.4324/9781315590059

Doswell, R. (2009). *Tourism: How effective management makes the difference*. Routledge. doi:10.4324/9780080519463

Dyas, D. (2020). *The Dynamics of Pilgrimage: Christianity, Holy Places, and Sensory Experience*. Routledge. doi:10.4324/9781003094968

Edelman, D. J. (2022). Managing the urban environment of Bangkok, Thailand. *Current Urban Studies*, *10*(1), 73–92. doi:10.4236/cus.2022.101005

Esfahani, M., Musa, G., & Khoo, S. (2017). The influence of spirituality and physical activity level on responsible behaviour and mountaineering satisfaction on Mount Kinabalu, Borneo. *Current Issues in Tourism*, *20*(11), 1162–1185. doi:10.1080/13683500.2014.987733

Fang, W. T. (2020). *Tourism in emerging economies*. Springer Singapore. doi:10.1007/978-981-15-2463-9

Federspiel, H. M. (2007). *Sultans, shamans, and saints: Islam and Muslims in Southeast Asia*. University of Hawaii Press.

Finlayson, C. C. (2012). Spaces of faith: Incorporating emotion and spirituality in geographic studies. *Environment & Planning A*, *44*(7), 1763–1778. doi:10.1068/a44580

Hall, K. R. (2010). *A history of early Southeast Asia: Maritime trade and societal development, 100–1500*. Rowman & Littlefield Publishers.

Hitchcock, M., & Teague, K. (Eds.). (2019). *Souvenirs: The Material Cultre of Tourism*. Routledge. doi:10.4324/9781315187457

Keyes, C. F. (2019). *Thailand: Buddhist kingdom as modern nation state*. Routledge. doi:10.4324/9780429308710

Laksana, A. B. (2016). *Muslim and Catholic pilgrimage practices: Explorations through Java*. Routledge. doi:10.4324/9781315597034

Mafudi, M., Sugiarto, S., & Praptapa, A. (2021). Emerging Opportunities for Halal Tourism in Rural Areas: Insights from Indonesia. *Fokus Bisnis: Media Pengkajian Manajemen Dan Akuntansi*, *20*(1), 16–26. doi:10.32639/fokusbisnis.v10i1.726

Marquardt, J., & Delina, L. L. (2019). Reimagining energy futures: Contributions from community sustainable energy transitions in Thailand and the Philippines. *Energy Research & Social Science*, *49*, 91–102. doi:10.1016/j.erss.2018.10.028

Masduki, A. (2018). Pilgrimage as a New Way to Define and Characterize the Sainthood. *DINIKA: Academic Journal of Islamic Studies*, *3*(2), 221–238. doi:10.22515/dinika.v3i2.114

Northcott, M. S. (2022). *God and Gaia: Science, Religion and Ethics on a Living Planet*. Taylor & Francis. doi:10.4324/9781003110750

Nyaupane, G. P., Timothy, D. J., & Poudel, S. (2015). Understanding tourists in religious destinations: A social distance perspective. *Tourism Management*, *48*, 343–353. doi:10.1016/j.tourman.2014.12.009

Olsen, D. H., & Timothy, D. J. (2006). Tourism and religious journeys. In *Tourism, religion and spiritual journeys* (pp. 1–21). Routledge.

Quinn, G. (2019). *Bandit Saints of Java: How Java's eccentric saints are challenging fundamentalist Islam in modern Indonesia*. Monsoon Books.

Reader, I. (2015). *Pilgrimage: A very short introduction*. OUP Oxford. doi:10.1093/actrade/9780198718222.001.0001

Ridout, L., & Gray, P. (2010). *The Rough Guide to Bangkok*. Penguin.

Salim, W., & Negara, S. D. (2018). Infrastructure development under the Jokowi administration: Progress, challenges and policies. *Journal of Southeast Asian Economies*, *35*(3), 386–401. doi:10.1355/ae35-3e

Schedneck, B. (2015). *Thailand's international meditation centers: tourism and the global commodification of religious practices*. Routledge. doi:10.4324/9781315697284

Schedneck, B. (2018). Religious Others, Tourism, and Missionization: Buddhist 'Monk Chats' in Northern Thailand. *Modern Asian Studies*, *52*(6), 1888–1916. doi:10.1017/S0026749X16001013

Schedneck, B. (2021). *Religious tourism in northern Thailand: encounters with Buddhist monks*. University of Washington Press.

Schellhorn, M. (2010). Development for whom? Social justice and the business of ecotourism. *Journal of Sustainable Tourism*, *18*(1), 115–135. doi:10.1080/09669580903367229

Sen, T. T. (2009). *Cheng Ho and Islam in Southeast Asia*. Institute of Southeast Asian Studies. doi:10.1355/9789812308399

Singh, R. P. (2022). Heritage Value of Religious Sites of Hinduism: Asian Linkages and Reuse for Cultural Regeneration. In *Regenerating Cultural Religious Heritage: Intercultural Dialogue on Places of Religion and Rituals* (pp. 55–79). Springer Nature Singapore. doi:10.1007/978-981-19-3470-4_5

Smith, V. L. (Ed.). (2012). *Hosts and guests: The anthropology of tourism*. University of Pennsylvania Press.

Spooner, A. (2013). *Thailand Dream Trip*. Footprint Travel Guides.

Stratton, C. (2010). *What's What in a Wat: Thai Buddhist Temples: Their Purpose and Design*. Silkworm books.

Syed Marzuki, S. Z., Abdullah, H., Ab Halim, R., Buyong, S. Z., & Zreik, M. (2020). Purchasing behaviour on halal food products during movement control order (MCO): Quantitative evidence from covid-19 pandemic. [AEJ]. *ASEAN Entrepreneurship Journal*, *6*(2), 16–21.

Tagliacozzo, E. (2013). *The longest journey: Southeast Asians and the pilgrimage to Mecca*. Oxford University Press.

Timothy, D. J., & Boyd, S. W. (2006). Heritage tourism in the 21st century: Valued traditions and new perspectives. *Journal of Heritage Tourism*, *1*(1), 1–16. doi:10.1080/17438730608668462

Timothy, D. J., & Ron, A. S. (2015). Religious heritage, spiritual aliment and food for the soul. In *Heritage Cuisines* (pp. 104–118). Routledge. doi:10.4324/9781315752525-14

Vijayanand, S. (2012). Socio-economic impacts in pilgrimage tourism. *International Journal of Multidisciplinary Research*, *2*(1), 329–343.

Wilson, J. (2019). Buddhism Without Merit: Theorizing Buddhist Religio-Economic Activity in the Contemporary World. *Journal of Global Buddhism*, *20*, 87–104.

Zreik, M. (2021). Academic Exchange Programs between China and the Arab Region: A Means of Cultural Harmony or Indirect Chinese Influence? *Arab Studies Quarterly*, *43*(2), 172–188. doi:10.13169/arabstudquar.43.2.0172

Zreik, M. (2022). Historical Developments of China's Xinjiang Province or Western Region. *Indikator: Jurnal Ilmiah Manajemen dan Bisnis, 6*(2), 54 - 62. doi:10.22441/indikator.v6i2.15069

Zreik, M. (2023), "USA–Myanmar relations: democratization and beyond", Southeast Asia: A Multidisciplinary Journal, Vol. ahead-of-print No. ahead-of-print. doi:10.1108/SEAMJ-02-2023-0018

KEY TERMS AND DEFINITIONS

Cultural Exchange: The sharing and intermingling of cultural practices, beliefs, and traditions among pilgrims and local communities, contributing to a more diverse and enriched environment.

Cultural Heritage: The traditions, practices, landmarks, and artifacts that represent the shared history and identity of the community along a pilgrimage route.

Economic Impact: The influence of pilgrimage routes on the local and regional economies, including job creation, tourism revenue, and infrastructural development.

Environmental Stewardship: Responsible management and conservation of natural resources along pilgrimage routes to ensure their sustainability for future generations.

Hospitality Economy: The sector of the economy that caters to the needs of pilgrims and tourists, including lodging, food, and other services, often closely linked with the economic impact of pilgrimage routes.

Pilgrimage Route: A designated path or series of paths that religious or spiritual seekers follow to reach a sacred destination, often involving stops at various significant sites along the way.

Sacred Sites: Specific locations along a pilgrimage route that hold religious or spiritual significance, often serving as places for rituals, prayers, or meditations.

Social Dynamics: The relationships, interactions, and community structures that form and evolve around pilgrimage routes, affecting both the pilgrims and the local residents.

Spiritual Capital: The accumulation of spiritual significance and value associated with pilgrimage routes, influencing not only individual pilgrims but also the broader social and cultural context.

Sustainable Tourism: Tourism practices that minimize negative environmental and socio-cultural impacts while providing economic benefits to local communities, particularly relevant to pilgrimage routes.

Chapter 12
Pilgrims' Opinions About Pilgrimage Routes:
The Specific Case of the Portuguese Inner Way of Santiago de Compostela

Vítor João Pereira Domingues Martinho
Agricultural School and CERNAS-IPV Research Centre, Polytechnic Institute of Viseu, Portugal

João Augusto Guerra da Rocha Nunes
School of Education, Polytechnic Institute of Viseu, Portugal

Maria Lúcia de Jesus Pato
Agricultural School and CERNAS-IPV Research Centre, Polytechnic Institute of Viseu, Portugal

Liliana Andrade de Matos Castilho
School of Education, Polytechnic Institute of Viseu, Portugal

Carlos Miguel Pipa
Promover – Consultores, Lda., Portugal

Luís Maia Rodrigues
Independent Researcher, Portugal

Beatriz Topete Lopes Almeida
School of Education, Polytechnic Institute of Viseu, Portugal

ABSTRACT

This research intends to collect information from the pilgrims about the pilgrimage routes to Santiago de Compostela, focusing on the Portuguese Inner Way. For that, a questionnaire was implemented in September 2022 to collect data from the opinion of a random sample of seven pilgrims. This information was analysed through qualitative approaches following Atlas.ti procedures. The main findings obtained highlight that the Portuguese Inner Way requires some physical preparation, considering the effort needed for some parts of the itinerary. In this context, alternative paths are proposed for some parts of the route. In addition, the lack of pilgrims' logistic services and the need for more effective preservation of the itineraries are also suggested. The Catholic sanctuary of Senhora dos Milagres in Pindelo dos Milagres may be a suggestion to become an assistance point.

DOI: 10.4018/978-1-6684-9923-8.ch012

1. INTRODUCTION

Pilgrimage routes have gained importance in recent decades for many reasons (Reader, 2007). These motives include spiritual or religious reasons, cultural or historical reasons, physical or mental challenges and personal growth (where people reflect on their lives and gain perspective on their place in the world). The relevance of these itineraries also increased, because the pilgrims desire to contact with nature and the places on the routes, including for touristic reasons (particularly for urban people), as argued by many researchers (Blom et al., 2016; Lois González, 2013; Nilsson & Tesfahuney, 2016).

If there are many pilgrimage routes around the world, the most known and important ways in Europe include the Camino de Santiago (Lois-González et al., 2018). This is a network of pilgrimage routes in Spain that leads to the Cathedral of Santiago de Compostela, where the remains of the apostle Saint James are believed to be buried.

In the context mentioned above, the several pilgrims of the Camino de Santiago can walk the diverse itineraries of this route, where the religious and the tourist perspective have their relevance (Martinho & Nunes, 2020). According to Martinho and Nunes (2020), the Camino de Santiago Route crosses several European countries and regions with diverse impacts on the socio-economic dynamics. The public authorities recognize the importance of these itineraries for the development of the respective communities (Amaro et al., 2018) and usually have an interest in their promotion. However, the Camino the Santiago Route has several pilgrimage paths (Martinho & Nunes, 2020), some of them with more difficult parts, less well known and promoted, and others still needing special attention by the local authorities, specifically in terms of maintenance, signs and pilgrims assistance. This is particularly evident in the Region of Viseu, more specifically between Viseu and Castro Daire, at a distance of about 40 km.

Given the rise in Pilgrimage routes, the scarcity of literature concerning the motivations of people to take the itineraries (Amaro et al., 2018) and the perceptions of the same, this study aims to collect information from the pilgrims about the pilgrimage routes to Santiago de Compostela, focusing on the Portuguese Inner Way, namely in the region of Viseu.

In terms of methodologically, the information analysed in this study was obtained from an interview implemented in September of 2022 in a random sample of seven pilgrims. This information was analysed through qualitative approaches following Atlas.ti (ATLAS.ti, 2019) procedures.

The paper consists of four sections after the introduction. Section 2 explores the literature review, while Section 3 presents the methodology of the study. The results of the study are presented in Section 4. Finally, in the end section (5), the discussion, the main conclusions, limitations, as well as the study's contribution to knowledge and practice, are presented.

2. LITERATURE SURVEY

Santiago de Compostela is an extraordinary phenomenon in the contemporary religious/spiritual universe. The unique characteristics of the Jacobean Route, its rituals, symbols, and practices, the relevant historical and cultural aspects behind it, as well as its socioeconomic impacts, all contribute to that exceptional circumstance. The large numbers of pilgrims who annually make their way to Santiago de Compostela are living testimonies of the relevance of said phenomenon. In fact, statistics published by the Pilgrims Office (Oficina de Acogida al Peregrino, 2023) show how a large number of people of different nationalities, from different socio-cultural groups, different genders, and ages, annually travel great distances to complete the Jacobean pilgrimage. Between 2007 and 2021, in 15 years, more than 3 million people completed the journey and obtained their Compostela, a document that attests to the completion of the pilgrimage. From these data, it can be seen that the number of pilgrims who annually reach Santiago has always been increasing over for years. This increase was particularly pronounced in the Xacobeo years, such as 2010. In 2020, the pandemic naturally cut off the flow of pilgrims due to pandemic restrictions, with only 54,144 individuals completing the pilgrimage. However, in 2021, the number grew exponentially, with 178,912 pilgrims completing the journey.

To understand this reality it is necessary to acknowledge the underlying motivations for the pilgrimage. During the medieval period, pilgrims were mainly motivated by religious issues related to the idea of penance, and the miraculous power of relics (García de Cortázar, 1994). In the Modern Era, especially after the 16th century, the reinforcement of post-Tridentine piety reinforced the power of pilgrimage as a form of worship and religious practice (Fernandes, 2014; Lacarra y de Miguel, 1966; Penteado, 2000). In the contemporary period, the reasons are different, mainly due to the profound social and cultural changes resulting from what has been called the process of secularization, and the transformation of society itself. Pilgrims are turning more and more into tourists. Experience, knowledge, leisure and consumption of goods are fundamental variables for many pilgrims in the context of pilgrimage to Santiago (Collins-Kreiner, 2010; Turner & Turner, 1995). In this sense, some consider the pilgrimage to be close to what is called religious tourism (Faria et al., 2022). Whether they are tourists or pilgrims, or both, the pilgrims of Santiago are mainly motivated by spiritual issues. In a survey carried out by, Kim et. al (2016), in 2015, in which 104 pilgrims answered the survey, it was concluded that spiritual reasons were invoked by 45.2% of individuals, religious reasons by 27.9%, cultural experience by 24% and sports activities by 2.9%. Amaro et. al. (2018) published a study in 2018, which covers 1140 pilgrims, which reveals that spiritual motivations appear first in the universe of the travellers' intentions to walk the Way. Even those who are manifestly atheist, invoke reasons that can be framed in the spiritual sphere, namely being in contact with nature or something superior or finding a meaning for life (Farias et al., 2019). This spirituality fits into the New Age movement of reapproaching man to nature, that occurred in the Western world after the 1960s (Hanegraaff, 1996; Heelas, 1996; Lois-González & Santos, 2015). Sacred spaces are imbued with a special power in the imagination of man. Certain places are seen as "power spots". People believe that they descend from the energies that are preserved there and that result from existing forces in nature itself. They are mountainous spaces, typically constituted by specific natural elements, such as unusual rock formations or waterfalls. Some of these places are marked by the intersection between human action in a certain historical era that is materialized, for example, through religious structures. The fusion between the natural and cultural elements reinforces the power of these spaces in the imagination of man, as essential spaces for human well-being and happiness. Pilgrims motivated by spiritual reasons seek energy that emanates from the earth, where the energies that emanate from nature merge with the cultural traits of ancient civilizations. They do so individually, in a self-spiritual experience, imbued by nostalgia for the natural world, through a notably sensory experience (Ivakhiv, 2003). Kim et al. (2019) observe that for pilgrims who walk the Jacobean route for religious reasons, the way is what it has always been, a place of pilgrimage. For those who claim to be non-religious, the motivations to walk the Way are mainly related to nature, heritage and physical activity. However, the experience of many non-religious travellers does not allow us to consider that they fit into the secular field. The spiritual experience is of a personal and self-interpretative nature that fits into post-secular religiosity. In this perspective, secular is part of religion, and the path is predominantly "religious". On the other hand, the spiritual religiosity of the modern pilgrim does not necessarily manifest itself in clear contrast to traditional religiosity. There are common points, such as rituals and forms. Moreover, many non-religious people find spiritual significance in the attendance of the masses. Furthermore, religion in the contemporary period is characterized by its diversity. Vilaça (2017) reinforces the idea that contemporary religion is composed of diverse rituals and expressions of belonging and passage, and pilgrimage is a moment of detachment from the existence of the daily routine.

Regarding the works specifically about the pilgrims who travel along the Portuguese routes, the same tendencies are observed. Fabio et al. (2016) reveal through the diary analysis method of pilgrims, that they seek authenticity, adventure, and interculturality. Regarding the Central Portuguese Route, the most crowded way of the Santiago routes that cross Portugal, Fernandes et al. (2012) stated that the main reasons underlying the pilgrims' decision to walk the way are the following: leisure and recreation (39%); religious (35%); cultural (33%). The pilgrims value the well-being they obtain by travelling the Central Portuguese Way, which results from the enjoyment of the surrounding natural and cultural heritage (Faria et al., 2022; Duarte, 2016). Recent studies witness the relevance of spiritual reasons that are particularly valued by the pilgrims who travel the Portuguese routes, namely inner well-being, contact with nature and cultural heritage (Rodrigues, 2022). In a study focused on the Caminho Português Interior de Santiago, based on field observation and 32 interviews, Pereiro (2017) testified that this route is mainly described as a religious or spiritual experience, a metaphor for life, as a desire "to escape and recover by changing", of cultural knowledge.

3. MATERIAL AND METHODS

The information analysed in this study was obtained from a questionnaire implemented in September 2022 in a random sample of seven pilgrims. This questionnaire, following, for example, the developments of Martinho et al. (2022) has the structure presented in table 1. With this structure was intended to listen to the pilgrims about the pilgrimage routes, specifically the Portuguese Inner Way and particularly about the itinerary in the municipality of Castro Daire (district of Viseu).

Table 1. Structure of the questionnaire implemented

Questions group	Question text
I	Sociodemographic data
II	Do you usually walk the Portuguese Inner Way of Santiago de Compostela in the municipality of Castro Daire?
III	How did you find out about the existence of the Portuguese Inner Way?
IV	Do you think that the Portuguese Inner Way is well promoted and valued by public institutions? Why do you think so?
V	Do you think it is relevant that the Inner Way, as far as its route is concerned, is made from historical evidence that proves that pilgrims in the past walked the same paths?
VI	Perceptions on the route of the Portuguese Inner Way to Santiago de Compostela, namely in the municipality of Castro Daire (positive and negative aspects)
VII	Motivations for following the routes of the Portuguese Inner Way of Santiago de Compostela in the municipality of Castro Daire. Would you do it again?
VIII	How can the Portuguese Inner Way be promoted to attract more pilgrims?

Table 2. Sociodemographic data for the sample characterisation

Questionnaire identification	Age group	Gender	Highest completed educational level	Residence zone	Marital status	Current Professional activity
D1	53	Male	Bachelor in forestry production	Viseu	Married	Bank employee
D2	40	Male	The ninth year of schooling	Viseu	Single	Policeman
D3	61	Male	Twelfth year of schooling	Viseu	Married	Pre-retired
D4	36	Male	Twelfth year of schooling	Viseu	Single	Works for the Red Cross
D5	51	Male	Twelfth year of schooling	Viseu	Married	Bank employee
D6	68	Male	Master in Health Sociopsychology	Viseu	Married	Retired
D7	59	Male	PhD in Sports Sciences	Viseu	Divorced	Professor of Higher Education

Table 2 presents the information for the sample characterisation, considering the data from sociodemographic variables. All the pilgrims questioned are male and have residences around Viseu. This is a mere coincidence and is related to the difficulty we had in identifying pilgrims that know the Portuguese Inner Way, have walked it and are available to answer our questions.

This information was analysed through qualitative approaches and following Atlas.ti software (2019) procedures and the results are presented in the next section, namely through word clouds and networks. To carry out this qualitative assessment a quotation and coding system was created as presented in table 3. Each questionnaire has seven quotations and each code has a groundedness (number of quotations coded by a code) equal to 1.

4. RESULTS THROUGH QUALITATIVE ANALYSIS

This section was divided into seven subsections, one for each question group, the exception for the sociodemographic variables group. This question group was already analysed in the previous section for material and methods. The codes considered in this section are the same as already identified in the section above.

4.1. Identification of the Pilgrims That Already Travelled the Portuguese Inner Way in the Municipality of Castro Daire

Figures 1 and 2 highlight that the majority of the questioned pilgrims already travelled the itinerary of the Portuguese Inner Way in the municipality of Castro Daire. Some of them did this route more than one time, walking or by bicycle.

Table 3. Quotation and coding system

Codes	Questionnaire1	Questionnaire2	Questionnaire3	Questionnaire4	Questionnaire5	Questionnaire6	Questionnaire7	Totals
D1.II	1	0	0	0	0	0	0	1
D1.III	1	0	0	0	0	0	0	1
D1.IV	1	0	0	0	0	0	0	1
D1.V	1	0	0	0	0	0	0	1
D1.VI	1	0	0	0	0	0	0	1
D1.VII	1	0	0	0	0	0	0	1
D1. VIII	1	0	0	0	0	0	0	1
D2.II	0	1	0	0	0	0	0	1
D2.III	0	1	0	0	0	0	0	1
D2.IV	0	1	0	0	0	0	0	1
D2.V	0	1	0	0	0	0	0	1
D2.VI	0	1	0	0	0	0	0	1
D2.VII	0	1	0	0	0	0	0	1
D2. VIII	0	1	0	0	0	0	0	1
D3.II	0	0	1	0	0	0	0	1
D3.III	0	0	1	0	0	0	0	1
D3.IV	0	0	1	0	0	0	0	1
D3.V	0	0	1	0	0	0	0	1
D3.VI	0	0	1	0	0	0	0	1
D3.VII	0	0	1	0	0	0	0	1
D3. VIII	0	0	1	0	0	0	0	1
D4.II	0	0	0	1	0	0	0	1
D4.III	0	0	0	1	0	0	0	1
D4.IV	0	0	0	1	0	0	0	1
D4.V	0	0	0	1	0	0	0	1
D4.VI	0	0	0	1	0	0	0	1
D4.VII	0	0	0	1	0	0	0	1
D4. VIII	0	0	0	1	0	0	0	1
D5.II	0	0	0	0	1	0	0	1
D5.III	0	0	0	0	1	0	0	1
D5.IV	0	0	0	0	1	0	0	1
D5.V	0	0	0	0	1	0	0	1
D5.VI	0	0	0	0	1	0	0	1
D5.VII	0	0	0	0	1	0	0	1
D5. VIII	0	0	0	0	1	0	0	1
D6.II	0	0	0	0	0	1	0	1
D6.III	0	0	0	0	0	1	0	1

Table 3. Continued

Codes	Questionnaire1	Questionnaire2	Questionnaire3	Questionnaire4	Questionnaire5	Questionnaire6	Questionnaire7	Totals
D6.IV	0	0	0	0	0	1	0	1
D6.V	0	0	0	0	0	1	0	1
D6.VI	0	0	0	0	0	1	0	1
D6.VII	0	0	0	0	0	1	0	1
D6. VIII	0	0	0	0	0	1	0	1
D7.II	0	0	0	0	0	0	1	1
D7.III	0	0	0	0	0	0	1	1
D7.IV	0	0	0	0	0	0	1	1
D7.V	0	0	0	0	0	0	1	1
D7.VI	0	0	0	0	0	0	1	1
D7.VII	0	0	0	0	0	0	1	1
D7. VIII	0	0	0	0	0	0	1	1
Totals	7	7	7	7	7	7	7	49

Note: In the column codes, each code was obtained from a combination of the questionnaire identification (table 2) and question group (table 1).

Figure 1. Network between the seven questionnaires for the second questions group

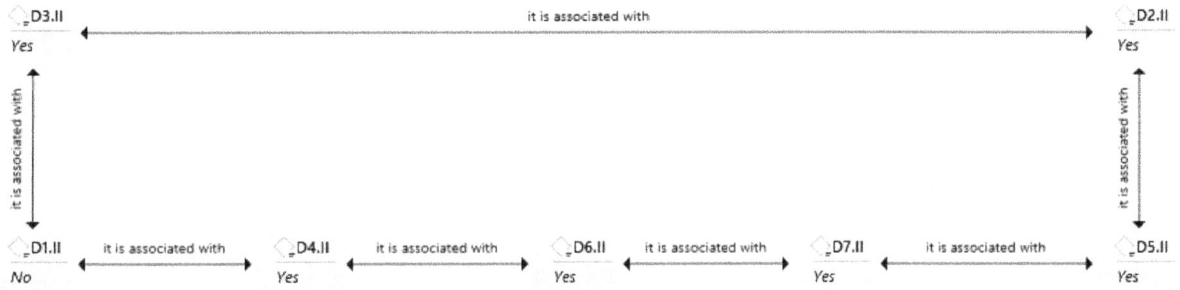

The municipality of Castro Daire is more or less in the middle of the path between Viseu and Lamego, two towns in the Centre-North of Portugal. This part of the pilgrimage route has mountains with a beautiful landscape for spiritual meditation and contact with nature, but requires some physical effort.

4.2. The Main Ways the Pilgrims Found the Existence of the Portuguese Inner Way

In general, the pilgrims found the existence of the Portuguese Inner Way talking with friends, from websites and after travelling other routes of the Santiago de Compostela Way (figures 3 and 4). In fact, some pilgrims referred that the first experience occurred after an invitation from friends and after returning alone because enjoyed it very much the experience.

Figure 2. Word cloud for the seven questionnaires and the second questions group

Figure 3. Network between the seven questionnaires for the third questions group

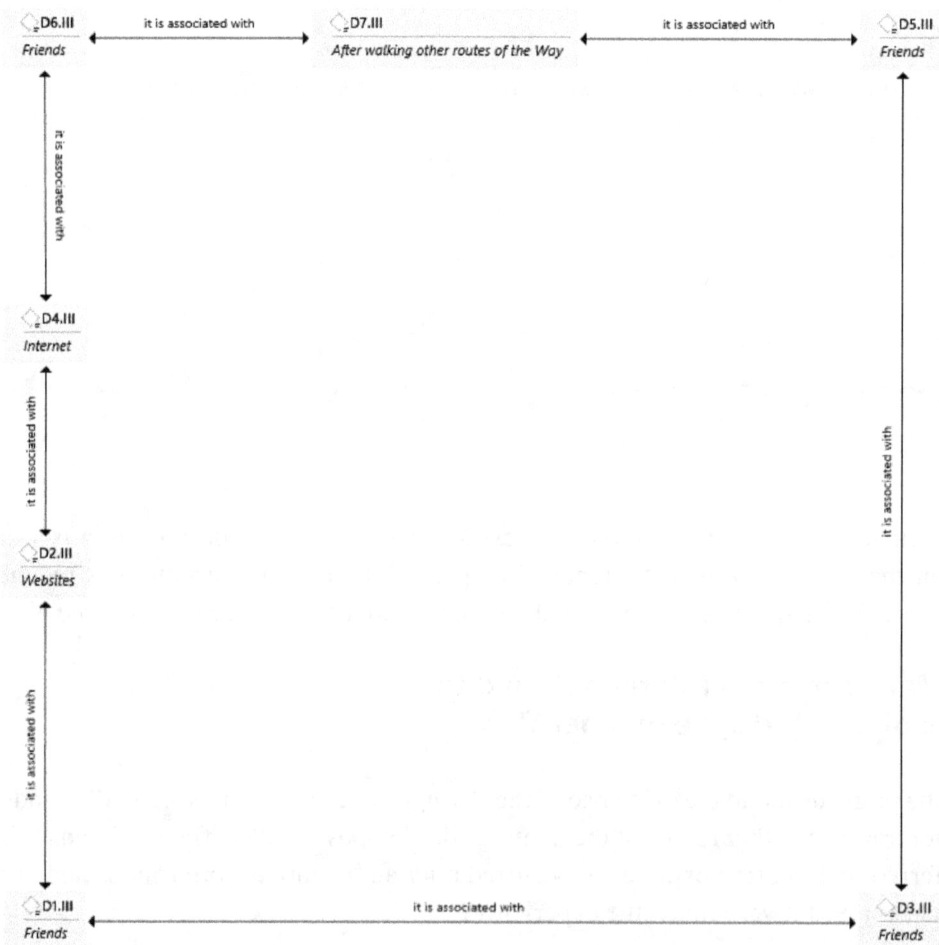

Figure 4. Word cloud for the seven questionnaires and the third questions group

Other pilgrims said that travelled the Portuguese Inner Way after travelling other Portuguese routes, highlighting these itineraries create in some circumstances healthy additive behaviours and crossing more one path is like to win more a trophy or an award.

4.3. Opinions About the Promotion of the Portuguese Inner Way by the Public Institutions

The pilgrims consider that this Way could be better promoted, organised and preserved (figures 5 and 6). The pilgrims feel that in some parts of the routes seems that the Way was forgotten by the local authorities. This is visible in the lack of maintenance of the paths that cross in some parts of dense forests and mountains and the lack, or unadjusted, identifications that support the pilgrims to avoid travelling unnecessary kilometres.

In addition, it seems that the socioeconomic importance of these itineraries is not properly recognised by the stakeholders and this discourages appropriate maintenance and effective promotion of these trails.

Figure 5. Network between the seven questionnaires for the fourth questions group

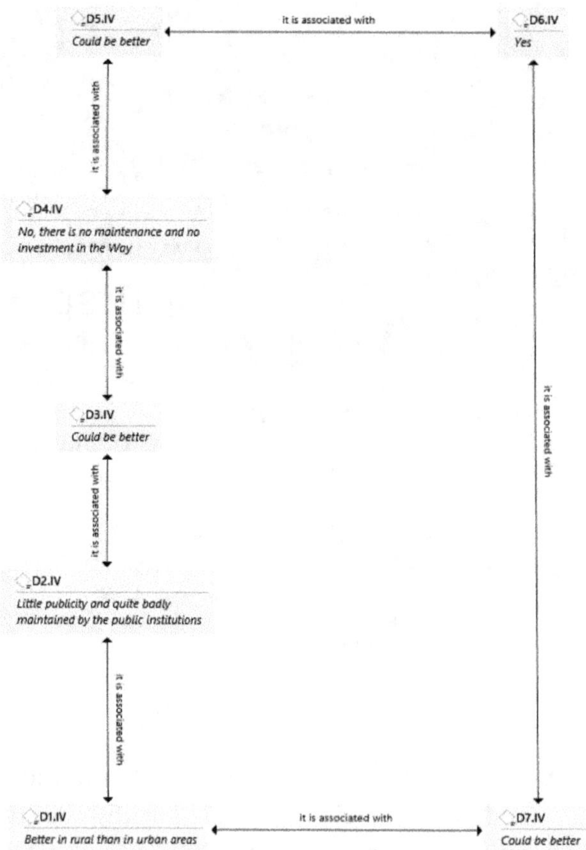

Figure 6. Word cloud for the seven questionnaires and the fourth questions group

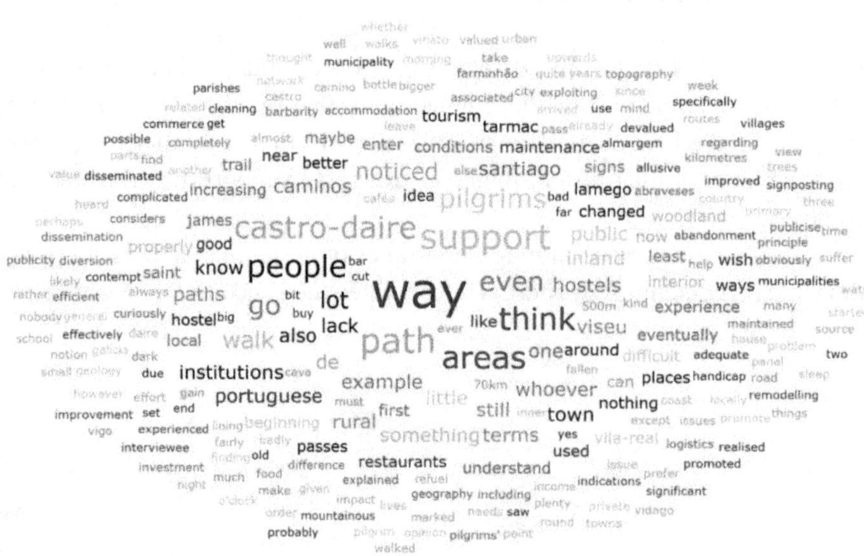

4.4. Importance of the Historical Records to Design the Pilgrimage Routes

Generally, the pilgrims consider it important that the pilgrimage itineraries are designed considering historical records related to the routes followed by the pilgrims in other decades and centuries. Consider, also, relevant that this historical information is interlinked with religious and commercial dimensions (figures 7 and 8).

Nonetheless, in some cases the historical records are considered irrelevant to the design of these paths, because the most important are the spiritual experiences, the contact with nature, talking with other pilgrims and knowing other cultures and realities.

Figure 7. Network between the seven questionnaires for the fifth questions group

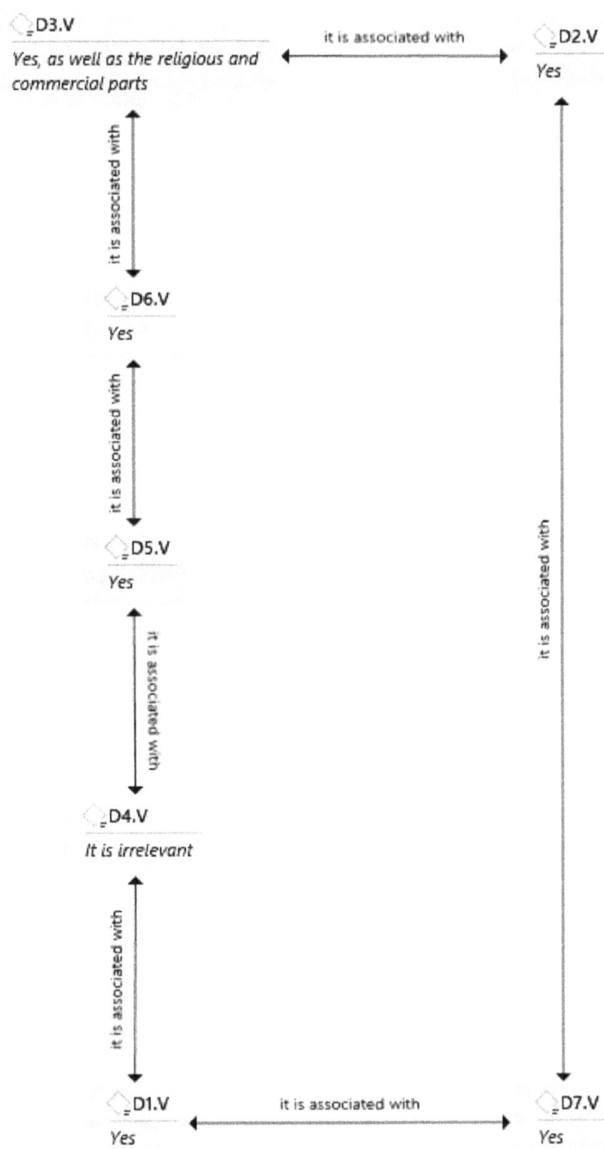

Figure 8. Word cloud for the seven questionnaires and the fifth questions group

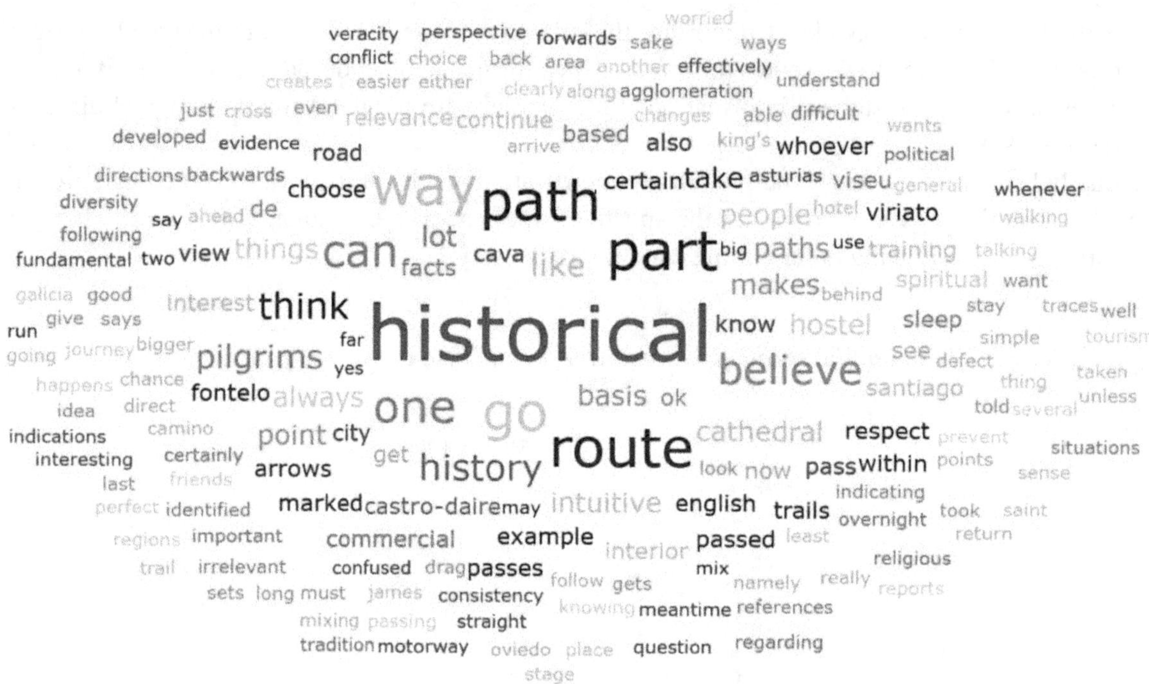

4.5. Perceptions About the Routes of the Portuguese Inner Way

The pilgrims perceive the Inner Way in Portugal as having problems with identification, requiring physical preparation and missing assistance and service points. In any case, the pilgrims after finishing the routes have the feeling that they want to come back soon (figure 9 and table 4).

Considering the harshness of the itinerary between Viseu and Lamego, namely over the municipality of Castro Daire, the pilgrims highlight the need for more assistance points in this part of the Way. The consideration of the catholic sanctuary of Senhora dos Milagres in Pindelo dos Milagres (São Pedro do Sul) as a point of assistance for the pilgrims could be a suggestion (Martinho & Nunes, 2020). Another solution to improve the pilgrimage in this route is to change or create alternative itineraries, specifically in Castro Daire, where the pilgrims could cross the village.

Figure 9. Network between the seven questionnaires for the sixth questions group

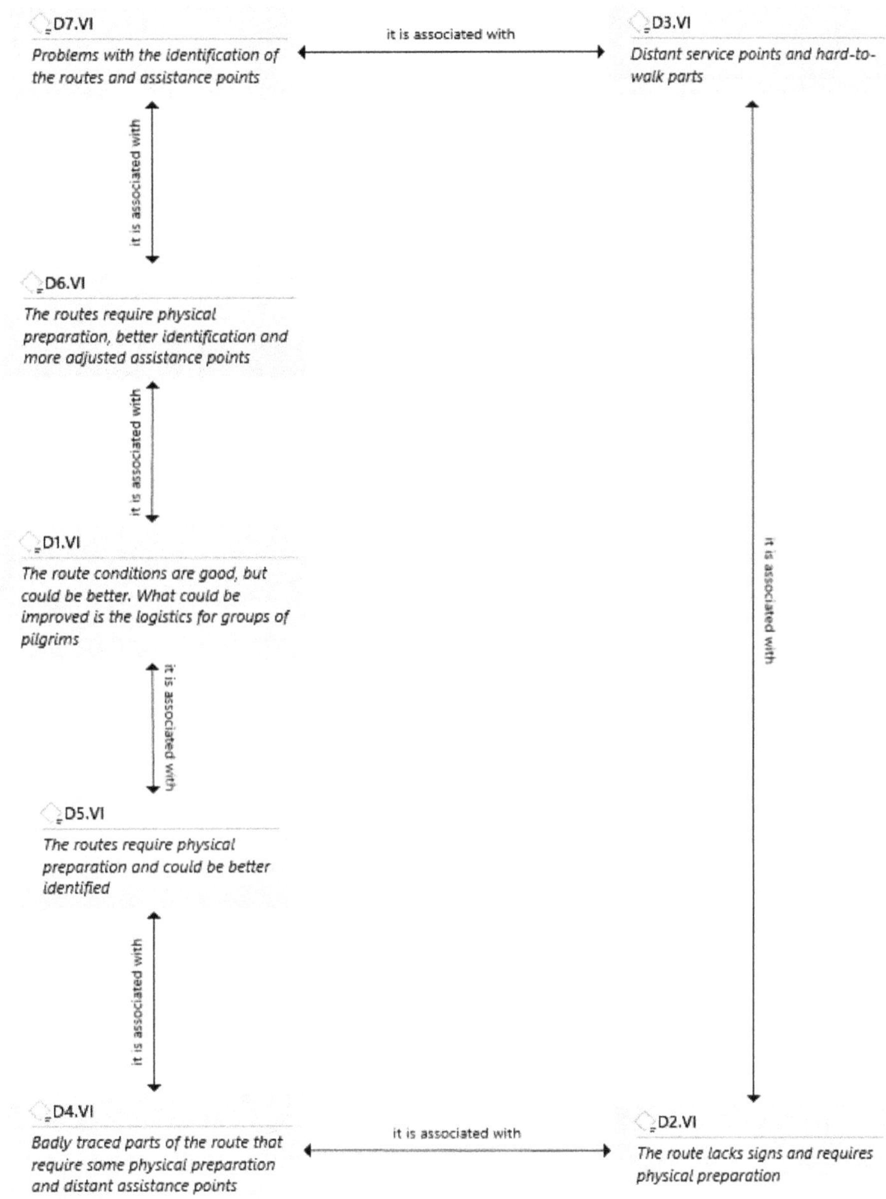

Table 4. Top 20 words with the highest occurrences for the sixth questions group

Word	D1.VI	D2.VI	D3.VI	D4.VI	D5.VI	D6.VI	D7.VI	Total
path	5	3	9	4	0	1	2	24
go	3	0	1	14	4	0	0	22
people	9	0	2	6	0	1	3	21
route	6	0	4	1	3	1	2	17
walk	1	1	0	9	3	0	3	17
like	2	1	3	2	0	1	7	16
way	2	1	4	6	2	0	1	16
physical	1	1	4	1	2	1	5	15
pilgrims	0	1	6	1	1	1	4	14
us	3	0	2	2	0	1	5	13
back	2	0	0	2	5	1	2	12
make	1	1	1	4	1	1	3	12
preparation	1	1	1	1	2	1	5	12
think	8	0	1	2	0	0	1	12
feel	1	0	0	4	0	1	5	11
points	1	0	4	5	0	1	0	11
can	0	1	4	3	0	0	2	10
going	4	0	0	1	3	0	2	10
well	3	1	3	0	1	0	2	10
areas	1	0	2	1	0	1	4	9

4.6. Motivation to Travel in the Inner Way

The main motivations to travel the Portuguese Inner Way are related to spirituality, talking with other people, contact with nature, tasting other gastronomy and religious, health and knowledge reasons (figure 10 and table 5). The sportive reasons are also presented as motivations to cross these paths.

Nonetheless, some of the questioned pilgrims refer that there are no specific reasons to travel over the pilgrimage routes. Sometimes, travel on these itineraries is more a question of well-being and good feelings.

Figure 10. Network between the seven questionnaires for the seventh questions group

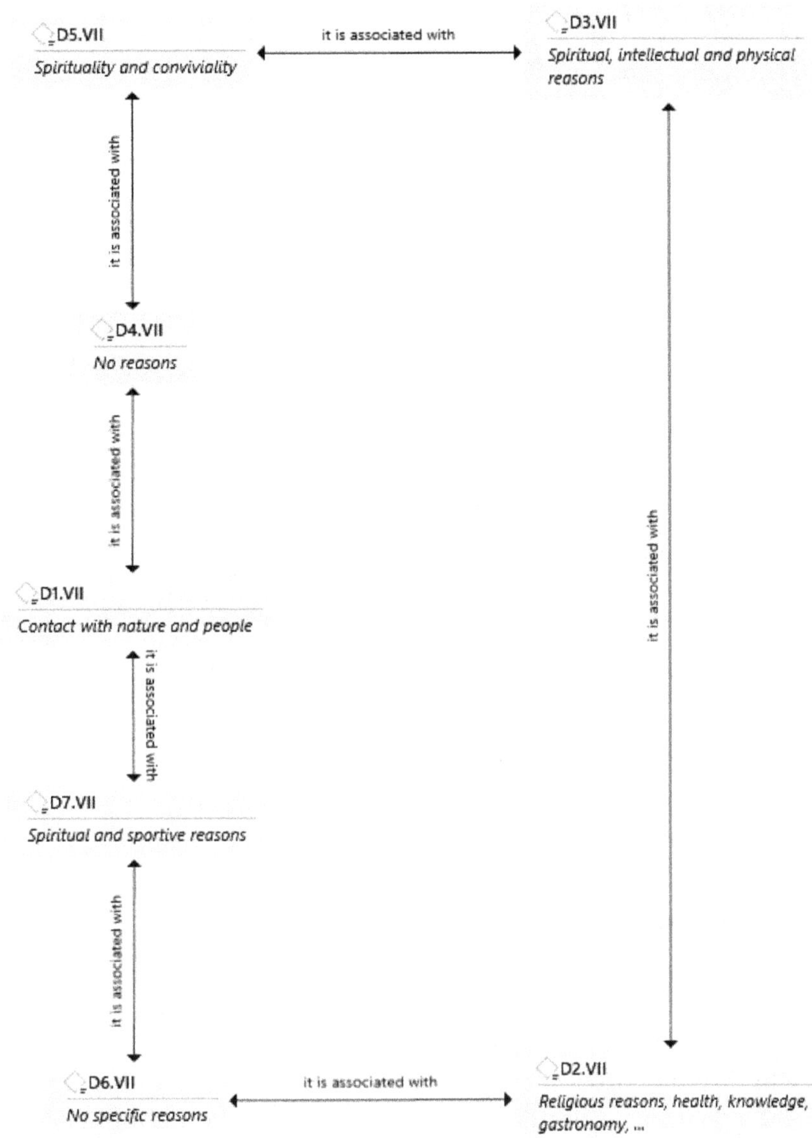

Table 5. Top 20 words with the highest occurrences for the seventh questions group

Word	D1.VII	D2.VII	D3.VII	D4.VII	D5.VII	D6.VII	D7.VII	Total
santiago	0	0	5	2	0	0	0	7
people	2	0	4	0	0	0	0	6
also	0	1	2	0	0	0	2	5
always	0	1	2	0	0	0	2	5
go	0	0	1	3	0	1	0	5
part	0	0	1	0	4	0	0	5
path	0	0	5	0	0	0	0	5
reasons	1	2	1	0	0	0	1	5
religious	1	1	0	0	2	0	1	5
spiritual	0	0	1	0	2	0	2	5
us	0	0	3	0	0	1	1	5
alone	0	0	1	1	0	0	2	4
certain	0	0	4	0	0	0	0	4
compostela	0	0	2	2	0	0	0	4
life	0	0	4	0	0	0	0	4
never	1	0	2	0	0	0	1	4
sure	0	0	3	0	1	0	0	4
will	0	0	4	0	0	0	0	4
camino	2	0	1	0	0	0	0	3
everything	0	0	2	0	1	0	0	3

4.7. Suggestion to Better Promote the Inner Way

To improve the promotion of the Inner Way in Portugal, it is suggested to better involve the commercial part, better and more adjusted publicity, recognise the importance of these routes for the rural localities, be aware of the WOM (Word of Mouth) and creating a "guide of the way" (figures 11 and 12).

Nonetheless, some pilgrims consider that the current strategy is fine and no more promotion is needed. In any case, there is some work to do to improve the conditions of the routes and the promotion strategy has here a determinant role to play to attract more pilgrims, increasing the dynamics of these paths and creating positive externalities.

Figure 11. Network between the seven questionnaires for the eighth questions group

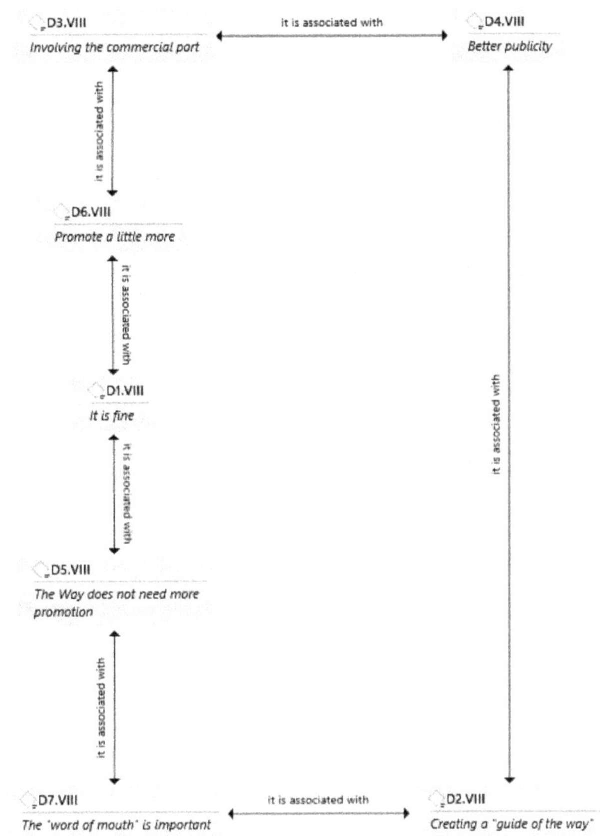

Figure 12. Word cloud for the seven questionnaires and the eighth questions group

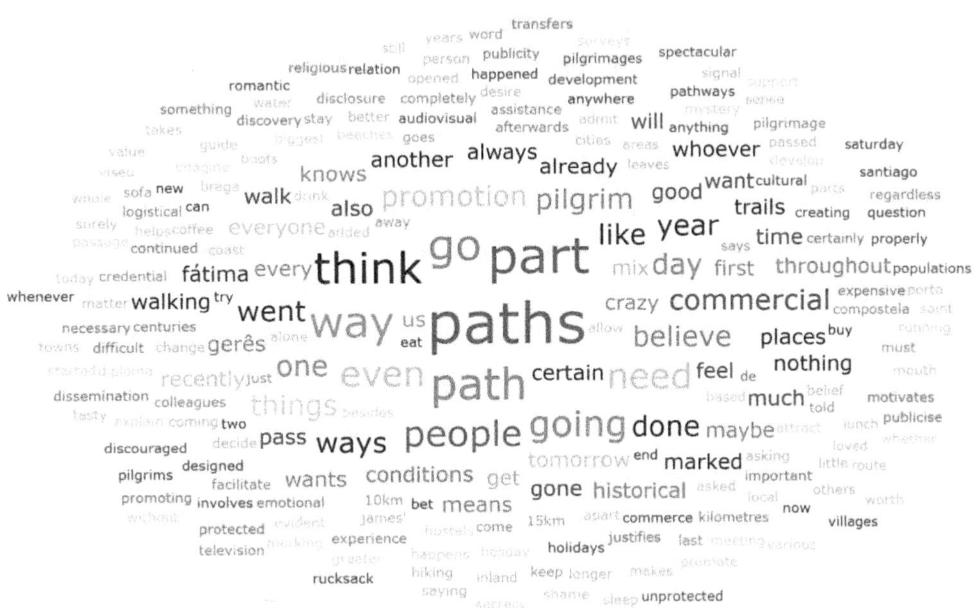

5. DISCUSSION AND CONCLUSION

This research aimed to understand the perceptions and opinions of the pilgrims about the pilgrimage itineraries to Santiago de Compostela, giving special emphasis to the Portuguese Inner Way. To achieve these objectives, an interview was carried out in September 2022 to collect information from a random sample of seven pilgrims. These data were explored with qualitative methodologies, taking into account the procedures proposed by the software Atlas.ti.

The literature review highlights the motivations of the pilgrims to Santiago de Compostela and they are related to spiritual and religious reasons, as well as to cultural, historical, physical, mental and touristic motives (Lois-González & Santos, 2015). In any case, spiritual motivations appear between the most important reasons. This route is one of the most famous pilgrimage itineraries. The literature also shows the difficulties found by the pilgrims in many paths of the route, namely in the Portuguese Inner Way.

The results obtained about the opinions and perceptions about the Portuguese Inner Way confirm the difficulties felt by the pilgrims on some paths of this route, particularly in the municipality of Castro Daire, because of the mountains require some physical preparation. Nonetheless, these paths have beautiful landscapes, appropriate for spiritual meditation. Generally, the pilgrims knew this Way talking with friends, from the internet and when travelling in other itineraries. The pilgrims agree that this route could be better organised, promoted and preserved, because in some parts maintenance and proper identifications are missing. Therefore, to improve the route a better relationship between the public (local authorities and local associations), private (economic agents) and other stakeholders, to better comprehend what role to play in the overall improvement and development of the Route based on existing good practices, would be useful (Ambrósio et al., 2019). These pilgrims gave more importance to the spiritual dimensions, contact with nature, talking with other pilgrims and contact with other cultures, than to the historical records. The lack of appropriate assistance points was another problem identified for this itinerary, as well as the need to be created alternative routes in some paths. Some of the motivations presented are related to well-being and good feelings. For the future, it is suggested to involve the commercial part, more adjusted publicity, recognise the importance of these routes for rural development, be aware of the importance of the WOM and create a "guide of the Way".

In summary, the motivations naturally impact the way pilgrims perceive the Way. Environmental, as well as heritage issues are relevant to pilgrims, who are increasingly interested in embarking on both, an exterior and interior journey. The issue of sustainability of the Santiago path is essential. The conditions and maintenance of the routes, pilgrims' support network, hostels, contact with nature and cultural heritage are fundamental aspects, all the more so as the pilgrim is increasingly becoming a tourist and seen as such. As the majority of pilgrims are those who are motivated by spiritual/religious reasons, the Way must provide conditions for those who seek these realities. Otherwise, those pilgrims will travel the Jacobean Ways no more.

ACKNOWLEDGMENT

This work is funded by National Funds through the FCT-Foundation for Science and Technology, I.P., within the scope of the project Refª UIDB/00681/2020 and the initiative "i2a-CERNAS/Verão com Ciência" in 2022. This research is also funded by the Promover - Consultores, Lda company. Furthermore, we would like to thank the CERNAS Research Centre and the Polytechnic Institute of Viseu for their support. This study was carried out under the project "Proposta de traçado para o Caminho Português Interior de Santiago no concelho de Castro Daire" (CERNAS-IPV/2022/007).

REFERENCES

Amaro, S., Antunes, A., & Henriques, C. (2018). A closer look at Santiago de Compostela's pilgrims through the lens of motivations. *Tourism Management, 64*, 271–280. doi:10.1016/j.tourman.2017.09.007

Ambrósio, V., Fernandes, C., Silva, G., & Cabral, A. (2019). A conceptual model for assessing the level of development of Pilgrimage Routes. *International Journal of Religious Tourism and Pilgrimage, 7*(2). Advance online publication. doi:10.21427/h2yb-hs41

ATLAS.ti. (2019). *Scientific Software Development GmbH [ATLAS.ti, version 8.4.26.0]* [Computer software]. https://atlasti.com

Blom, T., Nilsson, M., & Santos, X. (2016). The way to Santiago beyond Santiago. Fisterra and the pilgrimage's post-secular meaning. *European Journal of Tourism Research, 12*, 133–144. doi:10.54055/ejtr.v12i.217

Collins-Kreiner, N. (2010). Geographers and Pilgrimages: Changing Concepts in Pilgrimage Tourism Research. *Tijdschrift voor Economische en Sociale Geografie, 101*(4), 437–448. doi:10.1111/j.1467-9663.2009.00561.x

Duarte, A. C. F. (2016). *Caminhos de Santiago: O Caminho Português como fator de desenvolvimento turístico no concelho de Barcelos* [Universidade do Porto]. https://repositorio-aberto.up.pt/handle/10216/87059

Fabio, C., Gian, C., Anahita, M., Fabio, C., Gian, C., & Anahita, M. (2016). New Trends of Pilgrimage: Religion and Tourism, Authenticity and Innovation, Development and Intercultural Dialogue: Notes from the Diary of a Pilgrim of Santiago. *AIMS Geosciences, 2*(2), 152–165. doi:10.3934/geosci.2016.2.152

Faria, C. A. P., Remoaldo, P. C., & de Fátima da Silva Vieira Martins, M. (2022). Landscape and Senses in a Portuguese Municipality on the Way of St. James: Potential Impacts on the Well-Being of Pilgrims. *Journal of Religion and Health*. doi:10.100710943-022-01617-2 PMID:35925457

Farias, M., Coleman, T. J. III, Bartlett, J. E., Oviedo, L., Soares, P., Santos, T., & Bas, M. del C. (2019). Atheists on the Santiago Way: Examining Motivations to Go On Pilgrimage. *Sociology of Religion, 80*(1), 28–44. doi:10.1093ocrelry019

Fernandes, C., Pimenta, E., Gonçalves, F., & Rachao, S. (2012). A new research approach for religious tourism: The case study of the Portuguese route to Santiago. *International Journal of Tourism Policy*, *4*(2), 83–94. doi:10.1504/IJTP.2012.048996

Fernandes, P. A. (2014). *Caminhos de Santiago*. Secretariado Nacional para os Bens Culturais da Igreja / Turismo de Portugal.

García de Cortázar, J. Á. (1994). El hombre medieval como 'Homo Viator': Peregrinos y viajeros. *IV Semana de Estudios Medievales: Nájera, 2 al 6 de agosto de 1993, 1994*. https://dialnet.unirioja.es/servlet/articulo?codigo=554277

Hanegraaff, W. J. (1996). *New Age Religion and Western Culture: Esotericism in the Mirror of Secular Thought* (Vol. 72). Brill. https://brill.com/display/title/1474

Heelas, P. (1996). *The New Age Movement: The Celebration of the Self and the Sacralization of Modernity* (1st ed.). Blackwell Publishers.

Ivakhiv, A. (2003). Orchestrating Sacred Space: Beyond the 'Social Construction' of Nature. *Journal for the Study of Religion, Nature and Culture*, *8*(1). doi:10.1558/ecotheology.v8i1.1642

Kim, B., Kim, S. S., & King, B. (2016). The sacred and the profane: Identifying pilgrim traveler value orientations using means-end theory. *Tourism Management*, *56*, 142–155. doi:10.1016/j.tourman.2016.04.003

Kim, H., Yilmaz, S., & Ahn, S. (2019). Motivational Landscape and Evolving Identity of a Route-Based Religious Tourism Space: A Case of Camino de Santiago. *Sustainability (Basel)*, *11*(13), 13. Advance online publication. doi:10.3390u11133547

Lacarra y de Miguel, J. M. (1966). Las peregrinaciones a Santiago en la Edad Moderna. *Principe de Viana*, *27*(102), 33–46.

Lois González, R. C. (2013). The Camino de Santiago and its contemporary renewal: Pilgrims, tourists and territorial identities. *Culture and Religion*, *14*(1), 8–22. doi:10.1080/14755610.2012.756406

Lois-González, R. C., & Santos, X. M. (2015). Tourists and pilgrims on their way to Santiago. Motives, Caminos and final destinations. *Journal of Tourism and Cultural Change*, *13*(2), 149–164. doi:10.1080/14766825.2014.918985

Lois-González, R. C., Santos, X. M., & Romero, P. T. Z. (2018). The Camino de Santiago de Compostela: The most important historic pilgrimage way in Europe. In *Religious pilgrimage routes and trails: Sustainable development and management* (pp. 72–87). Cabi Digital Library. https://www.cabidigitallibrary.org/doi/10.1079/9781786390271.0072

Martinho, V. J. P. D., Bartkiene, E., Djekic, I., Tarcea, M., Barić, I. C., Černelič-Bizjak, M., Szűcs, V., Sarcona, A., El-Kenawy, A., Ferreira, V., Klava, D., Korzeniowska, M., Vittadini, E., Leal, M., Bolhuis, D., Papageorgiou, M., & Guiné, R. P. F. (2022). Determinants of economic motivations for food choice: Insights for the understanding of consumer behaviour. *International Journal of Food Sciences and Nutrition*, *73*(1), 127–139. doi:10.1080/09637486.2021.1939659 PMID:34148490

Martinho, V. J. P. D., & Nunes, J. (2020). Camino de Santiago: The routes in the region of Viseu. *Pasos (El Sauzal)*, *18*(3), 3. doi:10.25145/j.pasos.2020.18.025

Nilsson, M., & Tesfahuney, M. (2016). Performing the "post-secular" in Santiago de Compostela. *Annals of Tourism Research*, *57*, 18–30. doi:10.1016/j.annals.2015.11.001

Oficina de Acogida al Peregrino. (2023). *Oficina del Peregrino | Catedral de Santiago de Compostela*. https://oficinadelperegrino.com/

Penteado, P. (2000). Peregrinações e santuários. In C. M. Azevedo (Ed.), *História Religiosa de Portugal* (Vol. 2, pp. 346–359). Círculo de Leitores.

PereiroX. (2017). Turiperegrinos portugueses no caminho português interior de Santiago de Compostela. *Revista Turismo & Desenvolvimento, 1*(27/28), Article 27/28. doi:10.34624/rtd.v1i27/28.8515

Reader, I. (2007). Pilgrimage growth in the modern world: Meanings and implications. *Religion*, *37*(3), 210–229. doi:10.1016/j.religion.2007.06.009

Rodrigues, G. F. M. (2022). *Estudo da dinâmica da procura do Caminho Português da Costa em contexto de pandemia*. Instituto Politécnico de Viana do Castelo.

Turner, V. W., & Turner, E. L. B. (1995). *Image and Pilgrimage in Christian Culture: Anthropological Perspectives*. Columbia University Press.

Vilaça, H. (2017). Pilgrims And Pilgrimages Fatima, Santiago De Compostela And Taizé. *Nordic Journal of Religion and Society*, *23*(2), 137–155. doi:10.18261/ISSN1890-7008-2010-02-03

Chapter 13
Current Pilgrimage Routes:
Considering Historical Records to Rethink Them

Vítor João Pereira Domingues Martinho
Agricultural School and CERNAS-IPV Research Centre, Polytechnic Institute of Viseu, Portugal

João Augusto Guerra da Rocha Nunes
School of Education, Polytechnic Institute of Viseu, Portugal

Maria Lúcia de Jesus Pato
Agricultural School and CERNAS-IPV Research Centre, Polytechnic Institute of Viseu, Portugal

Liliana Andrade de Matos Castilho
School of Education, Polytechnic Institute of Viseu, Portugal

Carlos Miguel Pipa
Promover – Consultores, Lda., Portugal

Luís Maia Rodrigues
Independent Researcher, Portugal

Beatriz Topete Lopes Almeida
School of Education, Polytechnic Institute of Viseu, Portugal

ABSTRACT

This study intends to analyse the several dimensions of pilgrimage routes, highlighting insights that may be interesting outcomes for researchers, policymakers, pilgrims and organisations related to the spaces covered by these ways. To achieve these aims, a systematic literature review based on bibliographic data was considered, as well as the assessment of historical records. The analysis of historical records, namely those from Roman times, is important to identify the origins of the routes and, in this way, better justify their itineraries. As main insights, it is worth mentioning the importance of the Ways of Santiago de Compostela for these contexts associated with the pilgrimage routes. This highlights that some of this knowledge may be considered as a benchmark to show the dimensions of other routes related to other pilgrimages, such as those related to the shrines of Mary, Our Lady.

DOI: 10.4018/978-1-6684-9923-8.ch013

1. INTRODUCTION

Pilgrimage ways are not often itineraries for the pilgrims' comfort, because of the characteristics of these routes and the energy needed to follow them, nonetheless these roads are places to contact with the landscape that surrounds these ways and to reflect on human life (Mao & Liu, 2014; Ambrósio, 2020). Religious dimensions motivate pilgrims to travel the pilgrimage itineraries, but there are other motivations, such as those related to tourism, culture and contact with nature. From this perspective, pilgrimage ways have cultural, social, environmental and economic impacts (Martinho, 2022b). This is a kind of geotourism with relevant contributions to the different dimensions of sustainability. In these frameworks the catholic shrines of Mary, Our Lady, such as that of Nossa Senhora dos Milagres in Pindelo dos Milagres (São Pedro do Sul, Portugal), may bring relevant contributions for the pilgrimage phenomena (Martinho et al., 2017).

The historical records about the pilgrimage routes contain relevant insights about the history of these ways and the respective lived experiences which may be important supports to better understanding of their current dimensions (such as, about female pilgrimage) (Barlar, 2022), including the photographic archives (Brush, 2017). The contributions to the pilgrimage routes' understanding are relevant (Valles, 2007), for a long time (Brush, 2018), about the diverse contexts (Christie, 2006) and from different perspectives (Corio, 2021).

The historical information about the Roman era is important to (re)design the routes followed by the pilgrims in our days. In fact, it is known that the pilgrims in past centuries used the Roman roads to achieve the holy spaces of their destination (Martinho & Nunes, 2020), including in Asia Minor (Ozturk, 2021). The infrastructures from the Roman Empire continue to be used for several centuries after this era (Dallai, 2004). The itineraries of the pilgrimage roads worldwide, over the times, were interrelated with the dynamics of the territories (Ehrlich, 2006). But also influenced the choices of the populations (Ehrlich, 2008), inspired artists (Espòsito, 2009), promoted allegorical representations (Heyman, 2013) and interconnected religious communities of different countries (Powers & Attreed, 2018).

The pilgrimage to the shrine of Saint James in Santiago de Compostela motivates researchers, considering their dimensions (Urrutia-Aparicio et al., 2022). There are several ways of pilgrimage to Santiago de Compostela from the more diverse European points, including Polish (Mróz, 2021a), Portuguese and others. The interest in this sacred place increased significantly after the Xacobeo of 1993, due to its worldwide promotion (Fernández et al., 2013). The growth of the associated cultural tourism in northwestern Spain has had positive economic impacts for the crossed municipalities (Lois González & Somoza Medina, 2003).

Considering the frameworks described above, pilgrimage routes are, in fact, places of geodiversity, namely in terms of landscape, history, culture and heritage, which through adjusted strategies and plans can bring relevant added value to the populations crossed.

Considering the importance of the pilgrimage routes for the communities crossed by their itineraries, the increased interest by the pilgrims in these ways, the relevance of the historical records for the (re) design of these itineraries and the scarce research concerning the topic, the objective of this research is to bring a broader perspective about the dimensions of the pilgrimage routes and present an approach to identify the historical records of the routes that justify their itineraries. Indeed, a search in the Scopus database shows the lack of documents for the topics "pilgrimage routes" and "bibliometric". There is here a gap that may be addressed with this research. The idea is to first explore the topic "pilgrimage routes" through bibliometric analysis and then with a literature survey based on this bibliometric assessment.

In addition and more specifically, it is intended to bring more insights into the Portuguese Inner Way to Santiago de Compostela, following, for example, the study of Martinho (2022b). There is, indeed, a field to be explored in the several dimensions of the Portuguese Inner Way, namely about its history, dynamics and the interrelationships between the routes and the surrounding contexts (Martinho & Nunes, 2020).

After this introductory section, this study is organized into five more sections, for material and methods, results for bibliometric data, insights from the scientific literature, historical records on the roots of the pathways, and discussion and conclusions.

2. MATERIALS AND METHODS

Considering the objectives proposed for this research, a search on the Scopus (2022) database for the topic "pilgrimage routes" was carried out on 9 September 2022 within the "Article title, Abstract and Keywords". From this search 186 documents were obtained that were first assessed considering bibliographic data and after analysed deeper through literature review based on the insights obtained with the bibliometric approaches. In practice, from the 186 documents found for this topic was selected a sample through bibliographic coupling links, following, for example, Martinho (2022a). Taking into account the Scopus database makes it possible to obtain a greater number of documents compared to other platforms (Web of Science (2022), for example). The bibliometric approaches were carried out with the VOSviewer software (van Eck & Waltman, 2010, 2022; VOSviewer, 2022) and considering their procedures. The consideration of just one topic allowed obtaining more documents from the database and finding documents on the different dimensions of pilgrimage itineraries in a broader perspective. The consideration of the topic in the plural did not affect the research results. In fact, the results for "pilgrimage route" or "pilgrimage route*" are similar.

More specifically, for the bibliometric approaches, co-occurrence (author keywords as items) and bibliographic coupling (countries, sources and documents as items) links were considered. Full counting was considered for both kinds of links and 1 as the minimum number of occurrences of an author keyword for the co-occurrence links and 1 as the minimum number of occurrences of a country and source for the bibliographic coupling links were used as input information. For the documents as items and bibliographic coupling links, 0 as the minimum number of citations of a document was taken into account. In figures, each colour indicates a cluster and the distance among items symbolises the relatedness. Considering the great number of items in each case, the links (number of links of a keyword, for example, with other keywords) as metrics were taken into account to identify the top 25 author keywords, countries, sources and documents (Martinho, 2022c). It could be considered other criteria (Bhatta & Ohe, 2020), nonetheless that considered in this study seems more adjusted for the research here carried out. In the co-occurrence links, the relatedness is based on the number of documents where the author keywords appear together and in the bibliographic coupling links the relatedness is based on the number of references the countries and sources share (van Eck & Waltman, 2022). Based on the bibliometric assessment, a systematic literature review was performed for the top 25 documents with the highest links. The correlations between variables were analysed through the Pearson (Pearson, 1896; Pearson & Filon, 1898) and Spearman coefficients (Spearman, 1987). The consideration of co-occurrence links is useful to highlight the keywords used by the authors and, thus, show trends in the scientific literature. Bibliographic coupling links allow you to identify relevant and networked items.

Bibliometric analysis in this specific case is useful because it allows highlighting networks between items (countries and sources, for example), as well as showing relevant insights from the literature and identifying relevant documents related to the topic addressed (Martinho, 2022a).

Additionally to this first approach to highlight the insights from the scientific literature, historical records about the pilgrimage routes from the historical archives and other historical documents were assessed, namely to highlight the itineraries followed by the pilgrims in other centuries. For example, the Roman roads were followed by the pilgrims to Santiago de Compostela in past centuries and this may bring relevant outputs to rethink the current itineraries of some routes, in agreement with the findings of Martinho and Nunes (2020).

3. RESULTS FOR BIBLIOMETRIC DATA

This section has two parts, one for the co-occurrence links and another for the bibliographic coupling links. In the figures presented in this section, the dimension of the circles associated with each item represents the number of occurrences for the author keywords, the number of documents for the countries and sources and the number of citations for the documents. In tables, the metrics associated with the author keywords are those obtained by the documents where these items appear and the metrics related to countries and sources are those received by the documents published by these items. The normalised citations metrics correct the citations from the influence of the time, because the older documents receive more citations (van Eck & Waltman, 2022).

Figure 1. Network visualisation map obtained with bibliographic data from Scopus, co-occurrence links and author keywords items for the topic "pilgrimage routes"

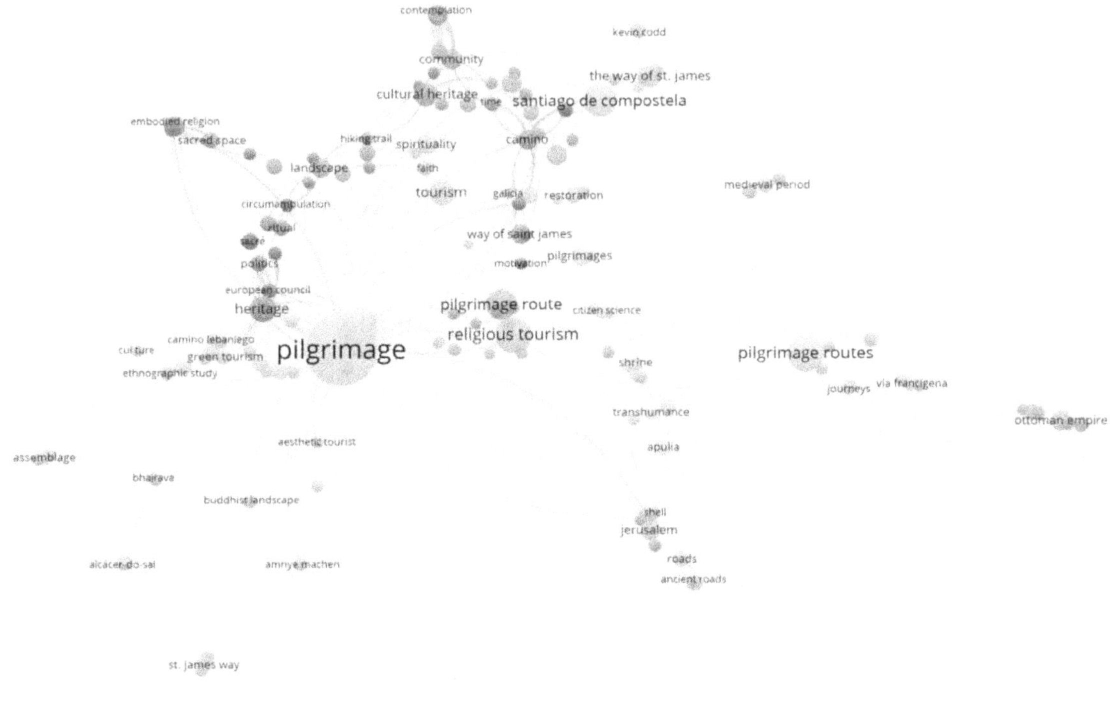

Table 1. Top 25 author keywords items with the highest links metrics, considering bibliographic data from Scopus and co-occurrence links for the topic "pilgrimage routes"

Author keywords	Links	Occurrences	Average publication Year	Average Citations	Average normalised Citations
pilgrimage	184	37	2016	12	1
pilgrimage routes	55	10	2012	11	0
Camino de Santiago	49	12	2017	18	1
Santiago de Compostela	45	8	2018	7	1
religious tourism	29	9	2017	12	1
community	27	3	2017	5	1
heritage	25	5	2012	30	1
pilgrimage route	25	7	2019	8	3
tourism	23	5	2014	9	3
Camino	21	3	2016	9	2
motives	20	2	2021	3	2
sacred space	19	2	2016	14	2
cultural heritage	17	4	2014	6	1
politics	17	2	2014	7	1
sacred	16	2	2016	6	2
Apulia	15	2	2015	0	0
devotion	15	1	2019	0	0
early Christian pilgrimage	15	1	2019	0	0
early Christianity	15	1	2019	0	0
Egeria	15	1	2019	0	0
embodied religion	15	1	2019	0	0
female pilgrims	15	1	2019	0	0
fourth century	15	1	2019	0	0
gender	15	1	2019	0	0
itineraria	15	1	2019	0	0

3.1. Co-Occurrence Links and Author Keywords Items

Figure 1 and table 1 highlight that the author keywords with the highest links metrics are, for example, the following: pilgrimage; pilgrimage routes; Camino de Santiago; Santiago de Compostela; religious tourism; community; heritage; sacred space; devotion; early Christianity; and itineraria. These findings show the importance of the Ways of Santiago de Compostela for the contexts of the pilgrimage routes. In addition, these routes are also ways for tourism and contact with nature, where the rural landscape and the heritage may contribute to the dynamics of these itineraries.

In general and considering the whole information exported from the VOSviewer, the author keywords with the highest links are also those with the great number of occurrences. The correlation among the links and the average citations and the average normalised citations is non-existent. The top 25 author keywords appear in documents published between 2012 and 2021.

3.2. Bibliographic Coupling Links and Countries and Sources Items

Spain, United Kingdom, United States, Poland, Portugal, Hong Kong, Italy, Macau, Australia and Canada are the countries with the highest number of links, showing the importance of researchers affiliated with institutions from these countries for the network (figure 2 and table 2). These results confirm again the importance of the Ways of Santiago de Compostela for the frameworks of the pilgrimage routes. Some of these countries are places of origin of pilgrims who travel the pilgrimage routes, namely to Santiago de Compostela and perhaps this explains, at least in part, the interest of authors affiliated to the respective institutions. In this case, considering the whole information from the software, the countries with the highest number of links are also those with a great number of documents, citations and normalised citations. The correlations between the number of links and the average publication year, average citations and average normalised citations do not exist.

The sources with the highest number of links are the following (figure 3 and table 3): international journal of religious tourism and pilgrimage; revista galega de economia; tourism management; journal of cultural geography; mobilities; and rivista geografica italiana. These results reveal that, in fact, the pilgrimage routes have religious dimensions, but also a touristic, wellness and health perspective. Taking into account the whole information, the correlations between the number of links and the citations, normalised citations, average citations and average normalised citations are relevant. The correlations among the links and the number of documents are not so strong.

Figure 2. Network visualisation map obtained with bibliographic data from Scopus, bibliographic coupling links and countries items for the topic "pilgrimage routes"

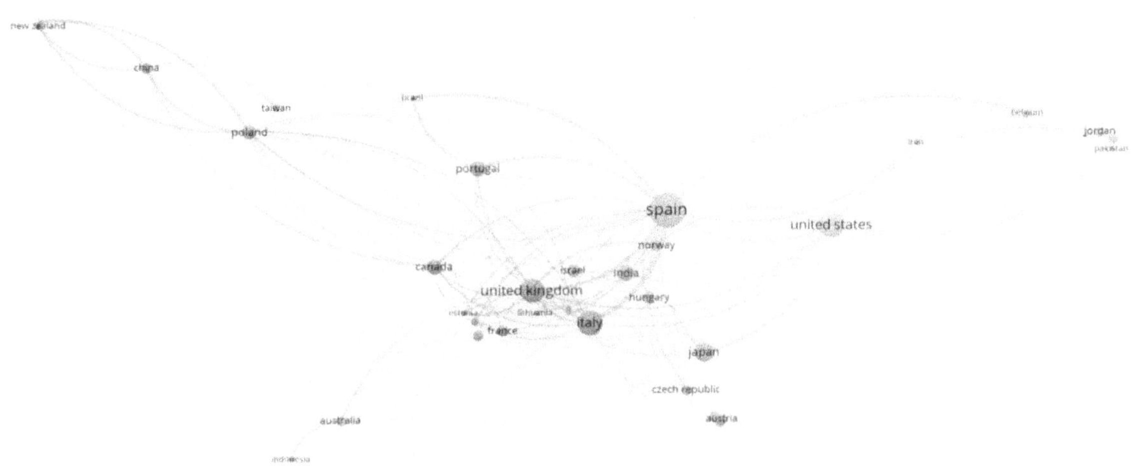

Table 2. Top 25 countries items with the highest links metrics, considering bibliographic data from Scopus and bibliographic coupling links for the topic "pilgrimage routes"

Countries	Links	Documents	Citations	Normalised Citations	Average publication Year	Average Citations	Average normalised Citations
Spain	28	36	169	39	2018	5	1
United Kingdom	24	17	250	18	2015	15	1
United States	24	20	163	17	2012	8	1
Poland	23	6	120	18	2016	20	3
Portugal	23	7	2	1	2021	0	0
Hong Kong	21	1	57	6	2016	57	6
Italy	21	19	98	24	2017	5	1
Macau	21	1	57	6	2016	57	6
Australia	20	3	49	8	2012	16	3
Canada	18	7	11	8	2016	2	1
Japan	18	11	41	9	2012	4	1
France	17	4	35	5	2015	9	1
Lithuania	17	1	2	1	2020	2	1
Estonia	16	1	12	3	2019	12	3
Hungary	16	4	19	4	2018	5	1
Sweden	16	2	16	2	2017	8	1
India	15	8	48	12	2014	6	2
Norway	15	4	9	4	2019	2	1
Czech Republic	13	3	9	2	2017	3	1
Israel	13	5	20	4	2017	4	1
Turkey	12	3	7	1	2018	2	0
China	9	4	21	8	2020	5	2
Brazil	7	1	0	0	2022	0	0
Taiwan	7	2	16	5	2016	8	3
Iran	6	1	3	2	2020	3	2

4. INSIGHTS FROM THE SCIENTIFIC LITERATURE FOR THE PILGRIMAGE ROUTES UNDERSTANDING

The documents presented in table 4 will be analysed deeper in this section through a literature review based on bibliometric approaches. For the whole information from the VOSviewer software, there are correlations among the number of links and the number of citations and normalised citations, but not for strong coefficients.

These documents reveal that the pilgrimage routes are ways with their own specific characteristics, sometimes shared by different religions. In any case, these itineraries of pilgrimage allow unique experiences for the pilgrims and hikers (Vistad et al., 2020) in terms of contact with other cultural and

Figure 3. Network visualisation map obtained with bibliographic data from Scopus, bibliographic coupling links and sources items for the topic "pilgrimage routes"

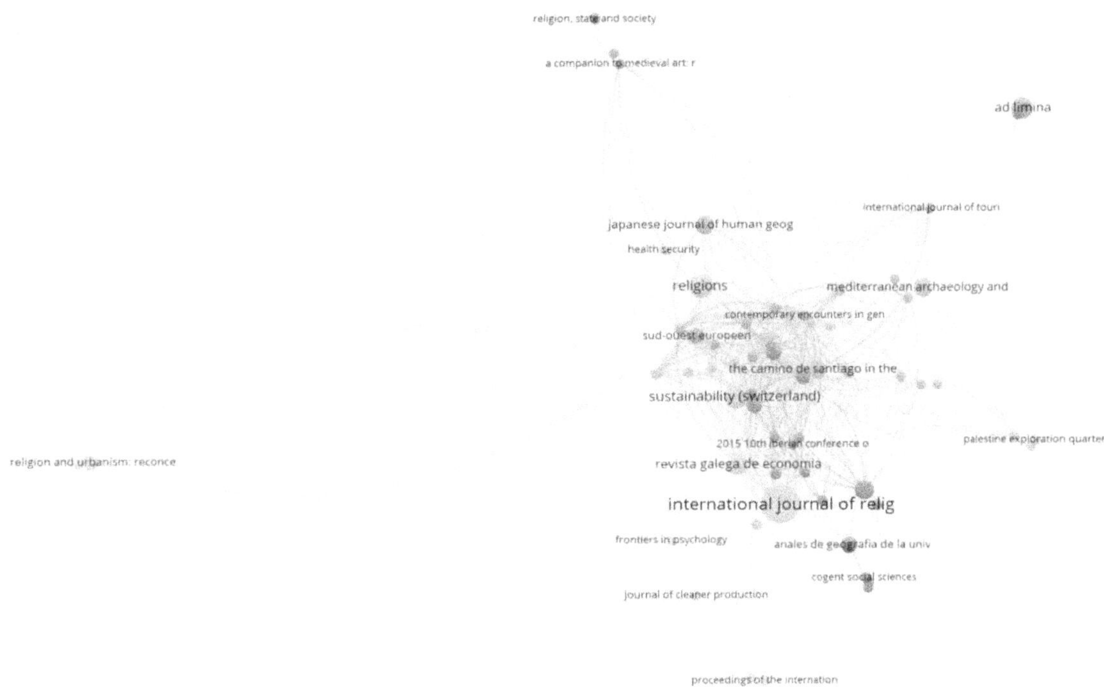

ecological realities and self-reflection (Ambrósio, 2020). The potentialities of the routes for the local development of the crossed municipalities could be better addressed with more adjusted coordination and planning (Ambrósio & Fernandes, 2022). The management of pilgrimages may play here a determinant role in better considering the various dimensions of the associated particularities (Liutikas, 2020). The pilgrimage ways have socioeconomic impacts on the crossed communities and the related activities, considering the needs of the pilgrims before, during and after the journey (González et al., 2021).

The relevance of the Camino to Santiago de Compostela led to its replication in some countries of origin of the pilgrims (Caminoisation), revitalising older pilgrimage routes and creating new ways (Bowman & Sepp, 2019). The ways of Saint James are between of the most known itineraries, nonetheless, its popularity increased in the last years, after decades of oblivion over the last century. The St. James Way is structured and organised since the Middle Ages (Cazaux, 2011). In the Middle Age, the Way of Saint James, Rome and Jerusalem were the most important itineraries of pilgrimage (González & López, 2012). But, it is worth mentioning that the first pilgrims arrived in Santiago in the 9th century (Fernández et al., 2016). The announcement of the Way as the First European Cultural Route by the Council of Europe, and as a UNESCO World Heritage Site, in 1987 and 1993, respectively, contributed to the rediscovery of the respective itineraries (Lois González et al., 2016). These itineraries to the shrine of Saint James motivated researchers from the different fields of science and multidisciplinary discussions about their characteristics and representations, such as the following: masculinities and spiritualities of capitalism (Gemzöe, 2016); narratives and experiences of pilgrims-authors (Genoni, 2011), pilgrims experiences (Kim et al., 2016); pilgrims motivations and perceptions (Oviedo et al., 2014); geography of sacred and pilgrimage spaces (López, 2014); pain on pilgrimage and experiences of transformation (Luik, 2012);

Table 3. Top 25 sources items with the highest links metrics, considering bibliographic data from Scopus and bibliographic coupling links for the topic "pilgrimage routes"

Sources	Links	Documents	Citations	Normalised Citations	Average publication Year	Average Citations	Average normalised Citations
International Journal of Religious Tourism and Pilgrimage	45	13	24	10	2020	2	1
Revista Galega de Economia	42	4	0	0	2021	0	0
Tourism Management	38	2	196	7	2007	98	3
Journal of Cultural Geography	36	1	2	1	2021	2	1
Mobilities	34	1	23	2	2016	23	2
Rivista Geografica Italiana	34	1	7	1	2014	7	1
The Camino de Santiago in the 21st Century: Interdisciplinary Perspectives and Global Views	34	3	4	1	2015	1	0
Documents D'analisi Geografica	33	1	27	4	2012	27	4
Journal of Outdoor Recreation and Tourism	29	2	20	5	2019	10	2
Religion	29	1	12	3	2019	12	3
Suomen Antropologi	29	1	5	1	2012	5	1
Tourism and Hospitality Research	29	1	17	2	2016	17	2
Contemporary Encounters in Gender and Religion: European Perspectives	28	1	1	0	2016	1	0
Journal of Religion and Health	28	2	26	15	2020	13	8
Review of Religious Research	27	1	38	4	2014	38	4
Tourism	27	1	22	3	2011	22	3
Journal of Heritage Tourism	26	3	49	6	2015	16	2
Studies in Travel Writing	26	1	12	2	2011	12	2
Religions	25	5	28	13	2019	6	3
Hungarian Geographical Bulletin	22	1	14	2	2013	14	2
Performing the Reformation: Religious Festivals in Contemporary Wittenberg	22	1	0	0	2010	0	0
Sustainability (Switzerland)	22	5	39	12	2019	8	2
The Way of the 88 Temples: Journeys on the Shikoku Pilgrimage	21	1	0	0	2013	0	0
Folia Geographica	20	1	4	2	2020	4	2
The Mirage of the Saracen: Christians and Nomads in the Sinai Peninsula in Late Antiquity	17	1	6	1	2014	6	1

from faith to tourism (Moscarelli et al., 2020); cultural heritage as touristic products (Murray & Graham, 1997); Polish travellers (Mróz, 2021a); multidisciplinary and global perspectives (Sánchez & Hesp, 2015); alternative routes, such as the *Nós* Way (Vila et al., 2021).

Table 4. Top 25 documents items with the highest links metrics, considering bibliographic data from Scopus and bibliographic coupling links for the topic "pilgrimage routes"

Documents	Title	URL	Links	Citations	Normalised Citations	Publication Year
Kim B. (2016) (Kim et al., 2016)	The sacred and the profane: identifying pilgrim traveler value orientations using means-end theory	https://doi.org/10.1016/j.tourman.2016.04.003	48	57	6	2016
Mróz F. (2021) (Mróz, 2021a)	Poles travelling to compostela in time and space	https://doi.org/10.1080/08873631.2020.1864086	47	2	1	2021
Lois González R.C. (2016) (Lois González et al., 2016)	From sacred place to monumental space: mobility along the way to st. James	https://doi.org/10.1080/17450101.2015.1080528	44	23	2	2016
Lopez L. (2014) (López, 2014)	Reflections on the sacred space: the way of st. James (spain) [riflessioni sullo spazio sacro: il cammino di san giacomo di compostella (spagna)		44	7	1	2014
Lois González R.C. (2012) (González & López, 2012)	The way of st. James: an approximation to its polysemic character from the viewpoint of cultural and tourism geography	https://doi.org/10.5565/rev/dag.6	41	27	4	2012
González R.C.L. (2021) (González et al., 2021)	Socio-economic impact of cultural itineraries: the camino de santiago and other pilgrimage routes	https://doi.org/10.15304/rge.30.3.7938	38	0	0	2021
Sánchez S. (2015) (Sánchez & Hesp, 2015)	<Introduction the camino de santiago in the 21st century: interdisciplinary perspectives and global views	https://doi.org/10.4324/9781315709147-7	37	1	0	2015
Vila N.A. (2021) (Vila et al., 2021)	Tourist spending along the way of saint james. The nós way as an alternative pilgrimage route to santiago	https://doi.org/10.15304/rge.30.3.7466	36	0	0	2021
Ambrósio V. (2020) (Ambrósio, 2020)	A shared pilgrimage road in israel and palestine: from utopia to reality		36	0	0	2020
Liutikas D. (2020) (Liutikas, 2020)	Management of pilgrimages in lithuania: resources, stakeholders and projects		36	2	1	2020
Bowman M. (2019) (Bowman & Sepp, 2019)	Caminoisation and cathedrals: replication, the heritagisation of religion, and the spiritualisation of heritage	https://doi.org/10.1080/0048721x.2018.1515325	36	12	3	2019
Castro Fernañdez B.M. (2016) (Fernández et al., 2016)	Historic city, tourism performance and development: the balance of social behaviours in the city of santiago de compostela (spain)	https://doi.org/10.1177/1467358415578473	36	17	2	2016
Luik E. (2012) (Luik, 2012)	Meaningful pain suffering and the narrative construction of pilgrimage experience on the camino de santiago		36	5	1	2012
Mróz F. (2021) (Mróz, 2021b)	The impact of covid-19 on pilgrimages and religious tourism in europe during the first six months of the pandemic	https://doi.org/10.1007/s10943-021-01201-0	35	21	14	2021

Table 4. Continued

Documents	Title	URL	Links	Citations	Normalised Citations	Publication Year
Genoni P. (2011) (Genoni, 2011)	The pilgrim's progress across time: medievalism and modernity on the road to santiago	https://doi.org/10.1080/13645145.2011.565580	34	12	2	2011
Murray M. (1997) (Murray & Graham, 1997)	Exploring the dialectics of route-based tourism: the camino de santiago	https://doi.org/10.1016/s0261-5177(97)00075-7	34	139	1	1997
Oviedo L. (2014) (Oviedo et al., 2014)	Rise of pilgrims on the camino to santiago: sign of change or religious revival?	https://doi.org/10.1007/s13644-013-0131-4	33	38	4	2014
Vistad O.I. (2020) (Vistad et al., 2020)	Long-distance hikers and their inner journeys: on motives and pilgrimage to nidaros, norway	https://doi.org/10.1016/j.jort.2020.100326	32	4	2	2020
Gemzöe L. (2016) (Gemzöe, 2016)	Working the way to santiago de compostela: masculinities and spiritualities of capitalism	https://doi.org/10.1007/978-3-319-42598-6_4	32	1	0	2016
Cianca J. (2019) (Cianca, 2019)	Written by the body: early christian pilgrims as sacred placemakers		31	0	0	2019
Miles S. (2017) (Miles, 2017)	Remembrance trails of the great war on the western front: routes of heritage and memory	https://doi.org/10.1080/1743873x.2016.1242589	31	15	2	2017
Irimiás A. (2013) (Irimiás & Michalkó, 2013)	Religious tourism in hungary - an integrative framework		31	14	2	2013
Cazaux F. (2011) (Cazaux, 2011)	To be a pilgrim: a contested identity on saint james' way		31	22	3	2011
Moscarelli R. (2020) (Moscarelli et al., 2020)	Who is interested in developing the way of saint james? The pilgrimage from faith to tourism	https://doi.org/10.3390/rel11010024	30	13	7	2020
Ambrósio V. (2022) (Ambrósio & Fernandes, 2022)	Assessing the development of the portuguese way to santiago in times of pandemic	https://doi.org/10.21427/2qgp-8b75	25	0	0	2021

The pilgrimage routes have historical roots and their knowledge is crucial to (re)design the current itineraries. Some of these roots come from Late Antiquity (Cianca, 2019). The history of the 20th century and the consequences of the World Wars impacted the pilgrimage and religious contexts (Irimiás & Michalkó, 2013). The events from the World Wars have been considered to promote emerging pilgrimage routes as Remembrance Trails and forms to transmit memories (Miles, 2017). More recently, the Covid-19 pandemic also had implications on the pilgrimage dynamics (Mróz, 2021b).

5. HISTORICAL RECORDS ABOUT THE ROOTS OF THE ROUTES – "CAMINO INTERIOR" IN THE REGION OF VISEU IN PORTUGAL AS AN EXAMPLE

The Caminho Português Interior de Santiago is a Jacobean pilgrimage route that departs from Viseu, in Portugal, to Santiago de Compostela. It is a route that crosses the interior of Portugal towards Santiago de Compostela: from Viseu it heads north, through Lamego and Chaves, then enters Galicia, passing through Ourense to Santiago. The route is about 385 km long, 205 of which in Portuguese territory and the rest in Galicia (Município de Chaves, 2022).

This route is very old, as is the case with other routes that existed in Portuguese territory. The existence of sea and land routes was documented in the 12th century. Both departed from Coimbra; the one travelling by sea passed through Montemor, the mouth of the river Vouga, heading to the mouth of the river Douro to later reach the river Minho and the region of Galicia. Regarding the land pilgrimage route is mentioned the following (Rei, 2009):

"The road from Coimbra to Santiago, by land: from Coimbra to the village of Avô (Âbuh), a journey; from Abûh to the village of Outeiro, a journey; and from there until the first lands of Portugal, a journey. And the path crosses the breadth of the land of Portugal in one day; and there is the village of Vila Nova de Gaia (Bûna Qâr), which is on the banks of the Douro River, which is the Zamora River; and you can cross it in traffic service boats. From this village to the river Minho, to the fortress of Abraqa, sixty miles, that is, two journeys. From the Abraqa fortress to the city of Tuy, two journeys. It is a small, beautiful and fertile city. From Tuy to Santiago, a journey [...]".

Some findings consider that this route would pass through the interior of Portugal, mainly through the region of Viseu through an itinerary that went from Coimbra to Avô, near Serra da Estrela, and from there to S. Miguel do Outeiro, next to Viseu, to then continue inland, through Lamego towards Braga. The correspondence they highlight between (Abûh) and Outeiro, with the localities of Avô and S. Miguel do Outeiro, respectively, leads them to consider this possibility (Debasa, 2009). There are, however, findings which reveal that this reference would correspond, roughly, to what is now called the Portuguese Central Way: from Coimbra, the route headed towards Águeda (Abûh), Oliveira de Azeméis (Outeiro), crossing the Douro River in Vila Nova de Gaia, then to Braga and from there to Tui in Galicia (Molins, 1998). In any case, despite the difficulties in specifying routes of the Way for such remote times, it is credible that the interior of the territory was traversed by pilgrims in the twelfth century. Other outcomes pointed out the existence of communication routes that linked Coimbra and Viseu, and Viseu to Salamanca. In Salamanca passed the Via de la Plata, an important medieval road that connected the south to the north of the peninsula. In turn, from Viseu, there was a road that passed through Lamego towards Chaves. At a time, in the twelfth century, when the region passed under Christian rule, the means of communication were safely crossed by travellers, among whom were, of course, pilgrims. It should be added that at this time the cult of Santiago de Compostela increased effectively, as a result of the action of the Compostela Bishop Diego de Gelmírez, endowed with the political and religious skills, to succeed in making Compostela the main centre of peninsular pilgrimage (promoting the construction of the Cathedral; obtaining from the papacy the dignity of the archdiocese for Compostela) (Singul, 1999). On the other hand, people in the late Middle Ages travelled/circulated in contexts of pilgrimage through various geographical spaces, with Compostela being their guiding light. The movement of pilgrims bound for the Apostle's tomb increased considerably after the twelfth century (de Cortázar, 1994).

Thus, during the Middle Ages, it is credible that the Camino of the Interior (Viseu-Lamego-Chaves-Ourense-Santiago) established itself as a Jacobean pilgrimage route. In 1431, the people of Viseu asked Pope Eugene IV for authorization to build a hospital for the poor, the pilgrims and the sick (Magalhães, 2011). Among the pilgrims would surely be some whose destination was Santiago, taking into account that long-distance pilgrimages, especially the Jacobean pilgrimage, were very much in vogue in the Middle Ages, motivated by prayer and penance, by the misfortunes of life but also by evasion and discovery (de Cortázar, 1994). In addition, in Viseu there are documentary references to several inns of medieval foundation, namely the inns of Soar, S. Martinho and Trindade; near the city of Viseu, there was another one known as "the bath of the Dão", which already existed in 1267 (Rosa, 2016). As is the case today, pilgrims, especially the poorest, benefited in the past from these assistance institutions. Some, on their way to Santiago, found shelter and support there.

In the early Modern Period, the Jacobean pilgrimage in the region of Viseu remained alive. In the commitment of the Misericórdia de Viseu, dated 1624, it is mentioned that the Hospital of Regueira, which was dependent on the Misericórdia, "assists and shelters pilgrims and passengers" (Santa Casa da Misericórdia de Viseu, 2010). This Hospital already existed in 1509. After the foundation of Misericórdia de Viseu in 1516, it became part of this assistance institution. It should be noted that the Misericórdia de Viseu, like other Misericórdias in the country, played an active role in poverty alleviation (Abreu, 2014).

In the 18th century, pilgrims heading to or returning to Santiago de Compostela continued to pass through Viseu. They relied on city institutions. For example, Friar António de S. Bruno passed through Viseu in 1720 in the context of a Jacobean pilgrimage; in 1735 Father Manuel de Andrade traversed the city. There were also pilgrims from abroad, such as Father Manuel Rodrigues, from Aragão, and António Lino, from Italy (Rome). They were all poor pilgrims. As can be seen, Portuguese, as well as foreign pilgrims, passed through Viseu (Martinho & Nunes, 2020). They usually travelled on their own. They used the city's institutions for the journey, alms and charity being essential for their journey. The role of the episcopal power in this context should be underlined. Pilgrims, just like the poor, received alms from the bishops or chapters because of the state of poverty they lived in. As a form of charity and care, the episcopal power was obliged, by canonical determination, to take care of the poor and sick and therefore, annually, part of the diocesan income was allocated to alms for the poor (Paiva, 2004).

In the 19th and 20th centuries, the Camino in the region of Viseu, similar to other Portuguese Ways, went into decline on account of various reasons. The renewal of religious practices was a major factor, visible, for example, in the loss of splendour of transnational pilgrimages and the affirmation of regional and national pilgrimages, such as the pilgrimages of Nossa Senhora dos Remédios (Lamego), Lapa (Sernancelhe), both in the region of Viseu, or the pilgrimage to Fátima (Leiria). The affirmation of other beliefs or atheism/agnosticism also contributed to the decline of the Camino, with fewer people considering these forms of piety relevant (Penteado, 2000).

However, at the end of the 20th century, the Jacobean pilgrimage was revitalized. As part of the renewed interest in the Way, there was a resurgence of the pilgrimage to Santiago, which eventually led to the reactivation of the Portuguese Ways that had been dormant for a long time. During their journey, pilgrims were now seeking not only spirituality. They also sought to enjoy the culture and heritage associated with the paths, as well as the spirit of evasion and discovery. Thus, the Portuguese Ways gained new life, becoming once again pilgrims' routes (Gomes & Florêncio, 2020; Pereiro, 2017).

Alongside the renaissance of the Portuguese Ways, a renewed bibliographic interest in the subject arose. Indeed, publications linked to the Portuguese routes proliferated. These are mainly studies of a tourist, heritage, ethnographic or anthropological nature. It is, however, surprising that there have not emerged more studies in the historiographical field, especially regarding the *Caminho Interior*. In other words, works of a historiographical nature are scarce. They are mainly related to the definition of routes and the study of the cultural heritage that shapes them. These are often individual references that appear in studies of a more general nature (related with the history of Galicia and history of Portugal) or studies of a religious nature, such as the work entitled *D. Pedro e a organização da Diocese of Braga* by Avelino Jesus da Costa (da Costa, 1959). Joaquim Veríssimo Serrão was one of the first authors to study the Portuguese paths to Santiago, as the background theme of a work, precisely in the book *Os Caminhos Portugueses de Santiago*, published in 1974. It refers to the routes followed by pilgrims in the Middle Ages, more specifically in the 13th century, highlighting the Lisbon-Coimbra-Porto route. He also refers to the inland path, which starts in Viseu, towards Lamego. In the city of Lamego, the way forks into two routes, one that went through Braga and another that went towards Chaves (Serrão, 1974).

Baquero Moreno was another author who first addressed the issue. His works were relevant to be able to glimpse the Portuguese paths in the Medieval Period. With the work entitled *Vias Portuguesas de Peregrinação a Santiago de Compostela*, he aimed to reconstruct the main Portuguese routes in the medieval period. He sought to observe the Ways to Santiago on the main routes of communication used in the medieval period by travellers, considering that among the migrants there would surely be pilgrims. He drew the map with the main Portuguese pilgrimage routes. With regards to the interior of the country, he referred to the road that led from Coimbra to Viseu and from there to Lamego, as an important means of communication in the region. From Lamego he would head towards Chaves and then penetrate Galicia towards Santiago. The contribution of this study was crucial to define the routes of the Portuguese Ways to Santiago (Moreno, 1986).

More recently, Martinho and Nunes discussed issues related to the Portuguese routes in their work *Caminho de Santiago: the routes in the region of Viseu*. Through a bibliographic analysis in the Web of Science, it was possible to perceive the interest that the Ways of Santiago arouse in the scientific literature, in particular the one that focuses on the interests and motivations of pilgrims. The motivations are of various kinds, mostly involving questions of evasion and discovery, life experiences, as well as religious and spiritual motivations. Pilgrims also highlight the historical and heritage value of the roads to Santiago as a motivating element for embarking on the pilgrimage and discovering the impact of the roads on local and regional development, especially on economic development. This work also sought to deepen the knowledge of the history of the Caminho Portugues Interior de Santiago, through studies of the routes and the experiences of pilgrims in the past. It was possible to understand the relevance of the *Caminho Interior* in the past, from medieval times to the 18th century. Viseu was an important location for countless pilgrims who passed through the city in the context of a Jacobean pilgrimage. These authors also discuss the route followed by pilgrims in the region of Viseu, tracing the Roman road that linked Viseu to Lamego and from there continuing to Chaves (Martinho & Nunes, 2020).

Historical references relating to the Portuguese roads to Santiago appear in travel guidebooks. The resurgence of paths and the renewed interest on the part of the public led to the proliferation of this type of literature. In 2007 the work by Francisco Rodríguez Iglesias entitled *A grande obra dos Caminhos de Santiago Iter Stellarum* was edited and published. It is a work in several volumes, illustrated with numerous photographs, that seeks to look at the routes and cultural heritage that make up the peninsular paths. There is a section about the Portuguese Ways. It shows the route, based on documentary and material references. However, the references were not always well read and interpreted. Despite considering that pilgrimage paths in the past were made through ancient Roman roads, the course on the Roman road was not taken into consideration in the definition of the route between Viseu and Castro Daire, especially between Almargem and Mões. On the other hand, some evidence, such as chapels in honour of Santiago, as they seem to suggest, cannot be considered proof of the passage of the Way, since the cult of Santiago cannot and should not be limited to the pilgrimage (Iglesias, 2007).

There are other studies of the same type, although of smaller dimension and made to illustrate the pilgrim, referring to routes, cultural heritage, and highlighting some historical aspects of the path. The Caminho Português Interior de Santiago, as well as other Portuguese Ways, are referenced by Carlos Gil, in the work *Por Caminhos de Santiago* (Gil & Rodrigues, 2000) and by Paulo Almeida Fernandes in the book *Caminhos de Santiago* (Fernandes, 2014). These are two examples of studies, which, like others, refer mainly to some historical and cultural aspects of the Portuguese routes. For instance, Carlos Gil investigates the identification of certain Portuguese routes and the Way in which they follow ancient Roman routes. Paulo Almeida Fernandes highlights the paintings by Grão Vasco, one of the most important Portuguese painters of the 16th century, born in Viseu.

In short, this means that the historical and documentary references relating to the Caminho Português Interior de Santiago are sparse and limited because historiography did, strangely, not keep up with the renewed public interest in the Jacobean pilgrimage. Historiographic studies are important to better understand this form of past piety, underlining its importance, as well as for uncovering traces with historical accuracy, traces that respect the millenary paths.

One might think that the lack of historical sources obstructs the studies about the *Camino Interior*. However, some sources enable investigating both the pilgrims and the routes they took in the past.

José Marques referred to the following regarding the Jacobean pilgrimage routes in Portugal: "In the medieval and modern period, the major road axes continued to follow the Roman communication routes. The secondary roads were mainly frequented by the local populations" (Marques, 1997). More recently, Vasco Mantas recognized the persistence of Roman roads in some regions of the country as means of communication in the Modern Period, continuing to be used by travellers in the 16th century (Mantas, 2014).

Several studies uncover the Roman roads in the interior of Portugal. The Roman road that linked the cities of Viseu and Lamego was studied by Jorge de Alarcão and Inês Vaz. Alarcão traces the main Roman communication routes in Portuguese territory, among which was the one linking Viseu to Lamego (Alarcão, 2002). The studies of João L. Inês Vaz allowed us to trace the route in concrete terms. In this regard, Inês Vaz mentions that the Roman way:

"After leaving Viseu, it would go to Abraveses, Campo, Lordosa, Bigas (where there should have been a 'mansio'), Calde, Almargem, Cabrum River, Adenodeiro, Arcas, Ponte Pedrinha, Castro Daire, Mezio, Ponte de Reconcas. There, the route would fork towards Lamego and, to the west, leading to the capital located in Cárquere and crossing the Douro in the area of Caldas de Aregos" (Vaz, 2000).

He also states that these roads were used for centuries, "only being destroyed or altered by roads opened between the 18th and 20th centuries".

Confronting the Roman roads with documentary sources contributes to a more effective discernment of pilgrimage routes. The Modern Period saw the publishing of several maps of Portugal where villages and main communication routes were specified. Itineraries also emerged, indicating the means of communication and distances between locations. As far as cartography is concerned, from old maps, between Viseu and Castro Daire, for example, it is possible to infer the localities where the route passed, namely Campo, Almargem, Rio de Mel and Mamouros. As far as itineraries are concerned, the Land Route of Portugal (*Roteiro Terrestre de Portugal*) by João Baptista de Castro, published in the mid-18th century, should be pointed out. The author states that he relied on knowledge of the territory and information from the Post Office of the various provinces of the kingdom. He also mentions that he consulted documentation on the existing means of communication, namely information from the magistrates in response to a ruling by King D. Filipe III, back in 1638. Regarding the route from Viseu to Lamego, which includes nine leagues, João Baptista de Castro indicates that the route passed through Campo, Almargem, Rio de Mel, Mamouros, Castro de Aire, Ouvida; Bigorne; Cruz e Lamego (Castro, 1753).

Written sources, compared with other types of sources, such as chancellery books, or sources referring to the management of Misericórdias, hospitals or shelters through the reference in the documentation to the poor, pilgrims and patients who frequented these same places, also make it possible to prove the existence of pilgrimage routes. There are, nevertheless, other relevant sources of assistance for the study of pilgrimage in the past that should be expounded. The registration of alms, in the chapter or mitre funds, shed light on the origins of pilgrims, paths and motivations. In the Archive of Viseu (Arquivo Distrital de Viseu), for example, there is documentation with records of alms attributed to pilgrims who passed through this city in the 18th century (Arquivo Distrital de Viseu, 2022).

Passports, both internal and external, had become mandatory in Portugal for internal travel from the mid-18th century. Therefore, they constitute important sources for getting to know pilgrims and pilgrimage routes. Passports were issued by the central administration or, in the case of internal migrants, by municipal councils. Some migrants were pilgrims and, along with their name, the route they were travelling was registered, too.

The parish memoirs of 1758 (Memórias Paroquiais de 1758), written by parish priests with references to various aspects of the respective parishes, can also be useful in studying the pilgrimage phenomenon and routes followed by pilgrims (Cardoso, 1758). In the region of Viseu, the parish priest of Rio de Mel, in 1758, said that in this village there was a "wooden bridge, at the bottom of the place of Rio de Mel, where people who went from the city of Lamego to Viseu, and from Viseu to these parts and Lamego would cross when it was raining" (Arquivo Nacional Torre do Tombo, n.d.-a). This route of communication was so important that at the end of the Modern Period, in 1822, complaints were made by the population to repair the road and improve the connections between the two cities (Oliveira, 2002).

Finally, inquisitorial sources can also serve to observe the pilgrim reality/pilgrimage routes. Some pilgrims were targeted by the Inquisition for heresy reasons. The records of the proceedings make it possible to understand the motivations behind the pilgrimages, as well as the routes travelled and the experiences lived by pilgrims of the past. For example, Guilherme Boroa travelled pilgrimage routes in the region of Viseu and Lamego in the 16th century and through the inquisitorial process – he was condemned for Protestantism – it is possible to know where he went and with whom he contacted in the context of the pilgrimage to Santiago (Arquivo Nacional Torre do Tombo, n.d.-b).

6. DISCUSSION AND CONCLUSION

This research, it was intended to analyse the several dimensions of the pilgrimage routes and to bring more insights into the Portuguese Inner Way to Santiago de Compostela. Relatively to the Way to Santiago, the objective is to highlight information related to the routes and their relationships with historical records, showing that in some cases it could be interesting to rethink the itineraries, considering the historical data about the Roman roads. To achieve these objectives, 186 documents were considered from the Scopus database on a search performed on 9 September 2022 for the topic "pilgrimage routes". This information was first assessed with bibliometric data and after through a systematic literature review for the top 25 documents (those with the highest number of links with other documents). In addition, to rethink the itineraries of the Portuguese Inner Way to Santiago de Compostela, historical information from historical archives was taken into account.

This bibliometric assessment shows the several dimensions of the pilgrimage itineraries, namely those associated with religion, tourism, ecology, environment, culture and heritage. In fact, the pilgrims intend not only to achieve the final destination of their journeys, but also to enjoy the dynamics and the surrounding frameworks of the routes, from a perspective of wellness and healthy experiences. Currently the pilgrimage has religious, tourist and cultural dimensions, with environmental and economic impacts on the municipalities crossed. This richness of pilgrimage routes from a geodiversity perspective creates an enormous socio-economic potential to be explored by the respective populations. Bibliometric data also reveal the importance of the Camino de Santiago de Compostela for discussions on pilgrimage routes.

The review of the literature based on bibliometric assessments highlights that the pilgrimage routes are famous worldwide for the most different destinations and in some cases shared by pilgrims who believe in distinct religions. The socioeconomic impact of these itineraries is relevant for the crossed places and associated activities, considering the consumption of the pilgrims from the beginning until the end of the pilgrimage. Nonetheless, there are yet potentialities to be explored in these routes that require more adjusted management and coordination. Specifically, the Camino to Santiago de Compostela is sometimes replicated in some countries (Caminoisation). The first pilgrims arrived at Santiago de Compostela in the 9th century. The Saint James Way is structured since the Middle Ages and after decades of forgetfulness in the 20th century, increased its relevance in the more recent years, namely after 1993 with its declaration as a UNESCO World Heritage Site and the international promotion of the Xacobeo'93. The literature shows also that there are also emerging pilgrimage routes, in some cases as alternatives to the current itineraries and in other cases as itineraries to remember and transmit the memory of past landmark events (such as those related to the World Wars).

The Caminho Português Interior de Santiago is a Jacobean pilgrimage route that departs from Viseu, in Portugal, to Santiago de Compostela. Since Middle Ages, the region of Viseu was visited by pilgrims and the city was equipped with institutions dedicated to assisting the underprivileged, including some pilgrims. Hospital da Regueira, which already existed in 1509, and which became part of the Misericórdia of the city founded in 1516, provided support to pilgrims passing through Viseu. It was not the only institution in the city that supported pilgrims on their way to Compostela. For example, in the 18th century, religious institutions also gave alms to poor pilgrims who transited through this region in the contexts of the Jacobean pilgrimage. The route went across ancient Roman roads. It is possible to locate the Roman roads in Viseu, thanks to the studies of Jorge Alarcão and Inês Vaz. It is also possible to trace the main pilgrimage routes by comparing Roman roads to the cartography of the modern period or other documentary sources. Long-distance pilgrimage waned in the 19th century and much of the 20th century. But at the end of the latter, the ways of Santiago came back to life. The renewed interest in the pilgrimage led to the existence of bibliographic production, mostly of a tourist and economic nature, considering the impact that the Way to Santiago can have on local and regional development. However, with regards to the Caminho Português Interior de Santiago, publications, especially those of a historiographic nature, are scarce, which shows that this route has not received the due interest. These studies are relevant to find out about the existence of pilgrims, reinforcing the importance of routes and correcting possible mistakes in tracing the Way through historical-patrimonial evidence.

This paper gives a wider perspective about the dimensions of the pilgrimage routes worldwide. Considering the limited number of studies about the pilgrimage routes and bibliometric analysis, this research has its novelty and may highlights relevant insights about the pilgrimage itineraries around the world, identify trends and open new perspectives for future studies. The specific interest in this research about the Camino de Santiago aimed to identify its historic roots of these routes that, in some cases, come from the Roman era, in an itinerary that receive annually pilgrims from the different parts of the world (Martinho, 2022b). In addition, there are here insights about the roots of the Camino de Santiago that may support the crossed municipalities to better (re)design the itineraries based on the history of the routes and these approaches may be spread for other pilgrimage ways worldwide. As main limitation of this research, of referring the focus on the Santiago de Compostela Way. For future research, it is suggested to spread the approaches here addressed to other pilgrimage routes worldwide.

ACKNOWLEDGMENT

This work is funded by National Funds through the FCT-Foundation for Science and Technology, I.P., within the scope of the project Refª UIDB/00681/2020 and the initiative "i2a-CERNAS/Verão com Ciência" in 2022. This research is also funded by the Promover - Consultores, Lda company. Furthermore, we would like to thank the CERNAS Research Centre and the Polytechnic Institute of Viseu for their support. This study was carried out under the project "Proposta de traçado para o Caminho Português Interior de Santiago no concelho de Castro Daire" (CERNAS-IPV/2022/007).

REFERENCES

Abreu, L. (2014). *O poder e os pobres. As dinâmicas políticas e sociais da pobreza e da assistência em Portugal (séculos XVI-XVIII)*. Gradiva. https://www.academia.edu/8139032/ABREU_L_O_poder_e_os_pobres_As_din%C3%A2micas_pol%C3%ADticas_e_sociais_da_pobreza_e_da_assist%C3%AAncia_em_Portugal_s%C3%A9culos_XVI_XVIII_

Alarcão, J. (2002). *O domínio Romano em Portugal*. Publicações Europa-América.

Ambrósio, V. (2020). A shared pilgrimage road in Israel and palestine: From utopia to reality. [Scopus.]. *International Journal of Religious Tourism and Pilgrimage*, *8*(6), 48–58.

Ambrósio, V., & Fernandes, C. (2022). Assessing the Development of the Portuguese Way to Santiago in Times of Pandemic. *International Journal of Religious Tourism and Pilgrimage*, *9*(6). doi:10.21427/2qgp-8b75

Arquivo Distrital de Viseu. (2022). *Archive of Viseu.* Arquivo distrital de Viseu. https://digitarq.advis.arquivos.pt/

Arquivo Nacional Torre do Tombo. (n.d.-a). Memorias paroquiais. *Pindelo dos Milagres, 29*(175).

Arquivo Nacional Torre do Tombo. (n.d.-b). *Tribunal do Santo Ofício. Inquisição de Lisboa, proc. 660.* Inquisição de Lisboa.

Barlar, S. H. (2022). Romeras, Rameras, and Royals: Female Pilgrims on the Camino de Santiago in Medieval and Early Modern Spain. In Women and Pilgrimage (pp. 15–24). CABI International; Scopus. doi:10.1079/9781789249392.0002

Bhatta, K., & Ohe, Y. (2020). A Review of Quantitative Studies in Agritourism: The Implications for Developing Countries. *Tourism and Hospitality*, *1*(1), 1. Advance online publication. doi:10.3390/tourhosp1010003

Bowman, M., & Sepp, T. (2019). Caminoisation and Cathedrals: Replication, the heritagisation of religion, and the spiritualisation of heritage. *Religion*, *49*(1), 74–98. doi:10.1080/0048721X.2018.1515325

Brush, K. (2017). Medieval art through the camera lens: The photography of arthur kingsley porter and lucy wallace porter. *Visual Resources, 33*(3–4), 252–294. *Scopus*. Advance online publication. doi:10.1080/01973762.2017.1349623

Brush, K. (2018). Blazing 'the Way' Arthur Kingsley Porter's First Trip to Northern Spain (1920). [Scopus.]. *Ad Limina*, *9*(9), 225–245.

Cardoso, L. (1758). *Memórias Paroquiais do padre Luís Cardoso ou Dicionário Geográfico.* Arquivo Nacional Torre do Tombo.

Castro, J. B. (1753). *Roteiro Terrestre de Portugal. Mappa de Portugal Antigo e Moderno. Lisboa: Na off. Patricarcal de Francisco Luiz Ameno.*

Cazaux, F. (2011). To be a pilgrim: A contested identity on Saint James' Way. [Scopus.]. *Tourism (Zagreb)*, *59*(3), 353–367.

Christie, J. J. (2006). Inca copacabana: A reconstruction from the perspective of the carved rocks. [Scopus.]. *Anthropos*, *101*(1), 179–201.

Cianca, J. (2019). Written by the Body: Early Christian Pilgrims as Sacred Placemakers. *International Journal of Religious Tourism and Pilgrimage*, *7*(1). Advance online publication. doi:10.21427/kam9-y363

Corio, A. (2021). From cabestany to tuscany: Times and vectors of the artistic path of an 'itinerant' maestry. [Scopus.]. *Iconographica*, *2021*, 38–48.

da Costa, A. de J. (1959). *O bispo D. Pedro e a organização da diocese de Braga.* Faculdade de Letras da Universidade de Coimbra.

Dallai, L. (2004). From villa to monastery: Topography along the Gulf of Baratti and archaeological documentation on Poggio San Leonardo. *Archeologia Medievale, 31*, 433-440+559-560. Scopus.

de Cortázar, J. Á. G. (1994). *El hombre medieval como 'Homo Viator': Peregrinos y viajeros*. 11–30. https://dialnet.unirioja.es/servlet/articulo?codigo=554277

Debasa, A. M. C. (2009). La peregrinacion jacobea en la literatura árabe Medieval. *De Madrid al Camino. Boletín Informativo de La Asociación de Amigos de Los Caminos de Santiago de Madrid*, 8–11.

Ehrlich, M. (2006). The route of the first crusade and the Frankish roads to Jerusalem during the 12th century. [Scopus.]. *Revue Biblique*, *2*, 263–283.

Ehrlich, M. (2008). The organization of space and hierarchy of cities in the royal latin of Jerusalem. [Scopus.]. *Cahiers de Civilisation Medievale*, *51*(3), 213–222.

Espòsito, A. (2009). The language of the Chanson de Sainte Foy: Why the Hispanic manner matters. *Romance Quarterly, 56*(1), 21–32. *Scopus*. doi:10.3200/RQTR.56.1.21-32

Fernandes, P. A. (2014). *Caminhos de Santiago*. Secretariado Nacional para os Bens Culturais da Igreja / Turismo de Portugal.

Fernández, B. M. C., González, R. C. L., & Lopez, L. (2016). Historic city, tourism performance and development: The balance of social behaviours in the city of Santiago de Compostela (Spain). *Tourism and Hospitality Research*, *16*(3), 282–293. doi:10.1177/1467358415578473

Fernández, P. M., González, D. R., & Novello, S. (2013). Value added, authenticity and loyalty during the 2010 Xacobeo event: A tourists perception perspective. [Scopus.]. *Cuadernos de Turismo*, *31*, 225–244.

Gemzöe, L. (2016). Working the Way to Santiago de Compostela: Masculinities and Spiritualities of Capitalism. In L. Gemzöe, M.-L. Keinänen, & A. Maddrell (Eds.), *Contemporary Encounters in Gender and Religion: European Perspectives* (pp. 77–101). Springer International Publishing. doi:10.1007/978-3-319-42598-6_4

Genoni, P. (2011). The pilgrim's progress across time: Medievalism and modernity on the road to Santiago. *Studies in Travel Writing*, *15*(2), 157–175. doi:10.1080/13645145.2011.565580

Gil, C., & Rodrigues, J. (2000). *Por caminhos de Santiago: Itinerários portugueses para compostela (3ª* (P. D. Quixote, Ed.).

Gomes, L. E., & Florêncio, F. (2020). Os Caminhos Portugueses a Santiago de Compostela—Fragmentos Holísticos da Patrimonialização. *Antropologia Portuguesa*, *37*(37), 37. doi:10.14195/2182-7982_37_2

González, R. C. L., Eade, J., & Carballo-Penela, A. (2021). Impacto socioeconómico dos itinerarios culturais: O Camiño de Santiago e outras rutas de peregrinación. *Revista Galega de Economía*, *30*(3), 3. doi:10.15304/rge.30.3.7938

González, R. C. L., & López, L. (2012). El Camino de Santiago: Una aproximación a su carácter polisémico desde la geografía cultural y el turismo. *Documents d'Analisi Geografica*, *58*(3), 3. doi:10.5565/rev/dag.6

Heyman, A. (2013). Sirens chanting in Auvergne- Velay: A story of exegetical pilgrimage on the via podiensis. [Scopus.]. *Ad Limina*, *4*(4), 69–115.

Iglesias, F. R. (2007). *A grande obra dos Caminhos de Santiago: Iter Stellarum*. Hércules de Ediciones.

Irimiás, A., & Michalkó, G. (2013). Religious tourism in Hungary—An integrative framework. [Scopus.]. *Hungarian Geographical Bulletin*, *62*(2), 175–196.

Kim, B., Kim, S. S., & King, B. (2016). The sacred and the profane: Identifying pilgrim traveler value orientations using means-end theory. *Tourism Management*, *56*, 142–155. doi:10.1016/j.tourman.2016.04.003

Liutikas, D. (2020). Management of Pilgrimages in Lithuania: Resources, Stakeholders and Projects. *International Journal of Religious Tourism and Pilgrimage*, *8*(2). doi:10.21427/j8w8-cw12

Lois González, R. C., Castro Fernández, B. M., & Lopez, L. (2016). From Sacred Place to Monumental Space: Mobility Along the Way to St. James. *Mobilities*, *11*(5), 770–788. doi:10.1080/17450101.2015.1080528

Lois González, R. C., & Somoza Medina, J. (2003). Cultural tourism and urban management in northwestern Spain: The pilgrimage to Santiago de Compostela. *Tourism Geographies*, *5*(4), 446–460. *Scopus*. doi:10.1080/1461668032000129164

López, L. (2014). Riflessioni sullo spazio sacro: Il cammino di San Giacomo di Compostella (Spagna). *Rivista Geografica Italiana*, *121*(3), 289–309.

Luik, E. (2012). Meaningful pain suffering and the narrative construction of pilgrimage experience on the Camino de Santiago. [Scopus.]. *Suomen Antropologi*, *37*(2), 24–43.

Magalhães, V. L. (2011). O Hospital Novo da Misericórdia de Viseu. Assistência, poder e imagem. *Viseu: Santa Casa da Misericórdia de Viseu.*

Mantas, V. G. (2014). Vías romanas e viagens transfronteiriças no século XVI. In M. C. Villalón (Ed.), *Viajes, viajeros y obra pública. Extremadura entre España y Portugal* (pp. 85–108). Universidad de Extremadura, Servicio de Publicaciones., https://dialnet.unirioja.es/servlet/articulo?codigo=5158678

Mao, Y., & Liu, X. (2014). The systemic protection and utilization of ancient temples and pilgrimage roads in western suburbs of Beijing. *World Congr. Int. Fed. Landsc. Archit., IFLA*. Scopus. https://www.scopus.com/inward/record.uri?eid=2-s2.0-84954126191&partnerID=40&md5=a8bc8d0b4f6027013062910ba05e9b1f

Marques, J. (1997). Viajar em Portugal nos séculos XV e XVI. *História: revista da Faculdade de Letras da Universidade do Porto, 14*, 91–121.

Martinho, V. J. P. D. (2022a). Bibliographic Coupling Links: Alternative Approaches to Carrying Out Systematic Reviews about Renewable and Sustainable Energy. *Environments (Basel, Switzerland)*, *9*(2), 2. doi:10.3390/environments9020028

Martinho, V. J. P. D. (2022b). Dimensions of the Saint James' Way Pilgrimage: Portuguese Socioeconomic Impacts. *International Journal of Religious Tourism and Pilgrimage*, *9*(6). doi:10.21427/95em-2y12

Martinho, V. J. P. D. (2022c). Impacts of the COVID-19 Pandemic and the Russia–Ukraine Conflict on Land Use across the World. *Land (Basel)*, *11*(10), 10. doi:10.3390/land11101614

Martinho, V. J. P. D., & Nunes, J. (2020). Camino de Santiago: The routes in the region of Viseu. *Pasos (El Sauzal)*, *18*(3), 3. doi:10.25145/j.pasos.2020.18.025

MartinhoV. J. P. D.SerraA. B.DuqueE. (2017). Santuários católicos: O caso da Senhora dos Milagres em Pindelo dos Milagres. *Theologica, 52*(1–2). doi:10.34632/theologica.2017.44

Miles, S. (2017). Remembrance Trails of the Great War on the Western Front: Routes of heritage and memory. *Journal of Heritage Tourism, 12*(5), 441–451. doi:10.1080/1743873X.2016.1242589

Molins, M.-J. V. (1998). En torno a Riba Coa y Al-Andalus. *O Tratado de Alcanices e a Importância Histórica Das Terras de Riba-Côa. Atas Do Congresso Histórico Luso-Espanhol*, 131–152.

Moreno, H. B. (1986). Vias portuguesas de peregrinação a Santiago de Compostela na Idade Média. *História: revista da Faculdade de Letras da Universidade do Porto, 3*, 77–88.

Moscarelli, R., Lopez, L., & Lois González, R. C. (2020). Who Is Interested in Developing the Way of Saint James? The Pilgrimage from Faith to Tourism. *Religions, 11*(1), 1. doi:10.3390/rel11010024

Mróz, F. (2021a). Poles travelling to Compostela in time and space. *Journal of Cultural Geography, 38*(2), 206–234. *Scopus*. doi:10.1080/08873631.2020.1864086

Mróz, F. (2021b). The Impact of COVID-19 on Pilgrimages and Religious Tourism in Europe During the First Six Months of the Pandemic. *Journal of Religion and Health, 60*(2), 625–645. doi:10.100710943-021-01201-0 PMID:33611686

Município de Chaves. (2022). *Caminho Português Interior de Santiago*. Chaves. https://www.chaves.pt/pages/223

Murray, M., & Graham, B. (1997). Exploring the dialectics of route-based tourism: The Camino de Santiago. *Tourism Management, 18*(8), 513–524. doi:10.1016/S0261-5177(97)00075-7

Oliveira, J. N. (2002). *A Beira Alta de 1700 a 1840 gentes e subsistências*. Palimage Editores.

Oviedo, L., de Courcier, S., & Farias, M. (2014). Rise of Pilgrims on the Camino to Santiago: Sign of Change or Religious Revival? *Review of Religious Research, 56*(3), 433–442. doi:10.100713644-013-0131-4

Ozturk, H. S. (2021). New Inscriptions from Nikaia XIV - Nikaia to Leukai/Lefke: Settlements, Milestones, Roman Road and Maurice Bridge. *Libri(Turkey), 7*, 1–15. *Scopus*. doi:10.5281/zenodo.4475599

Paiva, J. P. (2004). O episcopado e a 'assistência' em Portugal na Época Moderna (séculos XVI-XVII). In L. Abreu (Ed.), *Igreja, caridade e assistência na Península Ibérica (sécs* (Vol. XVI-XVIII, pp. 167–196). Edições Colibri e CIDEHUS-UE. https://books.openedition.org/cidehus/197 doi:10.4000/books.cidehus.197

Pearson, K. (1896). Mathematical Contributions to the Theory of Evolution. III. Regression, Heredity, and Panmixia. *Philosophical Transactions of the Royal Society of London. Series A, Containing Papers of a Mathematical or Physical Character, 187*, 253–318. doi:10.1098/rsta.1896.0007

Pearson, K., & Filon, L. N. G. (1898). Mathematical Contributions to the Theory of Evolution. IV. On the Probable Errors of Frequency Constants and on the Influence of Random Selection on Variation and Correlation. *Philosophical Transactions of the Royal Society of London. Series A, Containing Papers of a Mathematical or Physical Character, 191*, 229–311. doi:10.1098/rsta.1898.0007

Penteado, P. (2000). Peregrinações e Santuários. In C. M. Azevedo (Ed.), *História Religiosa de Portugal* (Vol. 2, pp. 346–359). Círculo de Leitores.

PereiroX. (2017). Turiperegrinos portugueses no caminho português interior de Santiago de Compostela. *Revista Turismo & Desenvolvimento, 1*(27/28), Article 27/28. doi:10.34624/rtd.v1i27/28.8515

Powers, J. F., & Attreed, L. C. (2018). Justice, conflict, and dispute resolution in Romanesque art: The ecclesiastical message in Spain. *GESTA-International Center of Medieval Art, 57*(1), 5–22. *Scopus*. doi:10.1086/695771

Rei, A. (2009). Coimbra e a sua região, segundo as fontes geográficas árabes. In *Olhares Sobre a História. Estudos oferecidos a Iria Gonçalves* (pp. 493–499). Caleidoscópio. https://www.academia.edu/11928778/Coimbra_e_a_sua_regi%C3%A3o_segundo_as_fontes_geogr%C3%A1ficas_%C3%A1rabes

Rosa, M. de L. P. (2016). A vivência do cristianismo pelos fiéis leigos: A experiência do sagrado cristão. In J. P. Paiva (Ed.), História da Diocese de Viseu (pp. 517–568). Diocese de Viseu I Imprensa da Universidade de Coimbra.

Sánchez, S. S., & Hesp, A. (2015). Introduction The Camino de Santiago in the 21st Century: Interdisciplinary Perspectives and Global Views. In *The Camino de Santiago in the 21st Century*. Routledge. doi:10.4324/9781315709147

Santa Casa da Misericórdia de Viseu. (2010). *Compromisso da Misericórdia de Viseu (reedição do compromisso de 1624). Viseu: Santa Casa da Misericórdia de Viseu.* Viseu: Santa Casa da Misericórdia de Viseu.

Scopus. (2022). *Scopus database*. https://www.scopus.com

Serrão, J. V. (1974). *Os caminhos portugueses de Santiago*. Fundação Calouste Gulbenkian.

Singul, F. (1999). Historia cultural do Camiño de Santiago. *Galáxia (São Paulo).*

Spearman, C. (1987). The Proof and Measurement of Association between Two Things. *The American Journal of Psychology*, *100*(3/4), 441–471. doi:10.2307/1422689 PMID:3322052

Urrutia-Aparicio, M., Belmonte, J. A., & González-García, A. C. (2022). Land-and Skyscapes of the Camino de Santiago: An Astronomy and World Heritage Sustainable Approach. *Sustainability (Switzerland), 14*(5). *Scopus*. doi:10.3390u14053047

Valles, J. G. (2007). Pilgrimage roads in Spain and Japan. In Pilgr. And Spirit. Quests in Jpn. (pp. 10–14). Routledge; Scopus. doi:10.4324/9780203318508

van Eck, N. J., & Waltman, L. (2010). Software survey: VOSviewer, a computer program for bibliometric mapping. *Scientometrics*, *84*(2), 523–538. doi:10.100711192-009-0146-3 PMID:20585380

van Eck, N. J., & Waltman, L. (2022). *Manual for VOSviewer version 1.6.18*. Centre for Science and Technology Studies (CWTS), Leiden University. https://www.vosviewer.com/documentation/Manual_VOSviewer_1.6.18.pdf

Vaz, J. L. I. (2000). A Romanização. In Por terras de Viriato: Arqueologia na região de Viseu (pp. 163–164). Governo Civil; Museu Nacional de Arte Antiga.

Vila, N. A., Brea, J. A. F., & Muñiz, D. R.-T. (2021). Consumo turístico durante o Camiño de Santiago. O Camiño Nós como ruta alternativa de peregrinación a Santiago. *Revista Galega de Economía*, *30*(3), 3. doi:10.15304/rge.30.3.7466

Vistad, O. I., Øian, H., Williams, D. R., & Stokowski, P. (2020). Long-distance hikers and their inner journeys: On motives and pilgrimage to Nidaros, Norway. *Journal of Outdoor Recreation and Tourism*, *31*, 100326. doi:10.1016/j.jort.2020.100326

VOSviewer. (2022). *VOSviewer—Visualizing scientific landscapes—Version 1.6.18*. VOSviewer. https://www.vosviewer.com//

Web of Science. (2022). *WoS database*. Web of Science. https://www.webofscience.com

Chapter 14
Nine Pagoda, Nine Chinese Vegetarian House, and Nine Church Pilgrimage:
Current Practice in Indochina in the Post-COVID-19 Pandemic Crisis Situation

Saitin Sim
Shantou University, China

Viroj Wiwanitkit
Chndigarh University, India

Amnuay Kleebayoon
Independent Researcher, Cambodia

ABSTRACT

The chapter "Nine Pagoda, Nine Chinese Vegetarian House, and Nine Church Pilgrimage: Current Practice in Indochina in Post-COVID Pandemic Crisis Situation" will examine how the COVID-19 pandemic affected religious customs in Indochina. With a focus on three distinct examples—the Nine Pagoda pilgrimage, the Chinese Vegetarian House, and the Nine Church Pilgrimage in Indochina—the chapter will analyze how religious organizations and rituals have adjusted to the epidemic. The chapter will look at the difficulties these institutions have experienced since the pandemic, including as limitations on gatherings and travel, and how they have dealt with these difficulties. Furthermore, the chapter will investigate how these religious rituals have brought comfort and support to communities during a time of crisis, as well as how they may evolve in the aftermath of the pandemic. Overall, the chapter will shed light on the function of religion in Indochina during a period of crisis, as well as how it has evolved to meet the changing demands of its practitioners.

DOI: 10.4018/978-1-6684-9923-8.ch014

INTRODUCTION

Religion is a tough topic to define since it is complex and multidimensional. Religion, at its heart, is a system of ideas, practices, and rituals centered on the worship of a higher force or heavenly being. Religion frequently gives a framework for comprehending the meaning and purpose of life, as well as a sense of belonging and community. Religious practices can take many various shapes, based on a religion's distinctive beliefs and traditions. Prayer, meditation, worship services, fasting, pilgrimage, and charitable activity are examples of these disciplines. Many religions offer specific laws and guidelines for ethical and moral behavior. Religion can influence individual and community identity, as well as social, cultural, and political institutions. Religion may also be a source of contention and friction, especially when different religious groups have opposing beliefs or values.

Many religious traditions incorporate pilgrimage or other sorts of travel to sacred locations or holy places, which can be strongly tied to travel. In Islam, a notable example is Hajj. The Hajj is a pilgrimage to Saudi Arabia's holy city of Mecca that is compulsory of all able-bodied Muslims who can afford to make the journey. The Hajj is performed during the month of Dhu al-Hijjah and consists of a number of rites, including circumambulating the Kaaba, a cube-shaped edifice in the middle of Mecca's Great Mosque. Another example is the Hindu Kumbh Mela. The Kumbh Mela is a great pilgrimage that takes place in four distinct locales in India every 12 years. Millions of Hindus flock to the hallowed rivers to bathe and participate in religious rites and ceremonies. Another example is the Camino de Santiago in Christianity, which is a pilgrimage route traveled by Christians for over a thousand years. The road travels to St. James' tomb in the Spanish city of Santiago de Compostela and is regarded as a spiritual journey of self-discovery and introspection. The Wailing Wall in Judaism is another example. The Wailing Wall in Jerusalem is a holy monument that Jewish pilgrims from all over the world visit. The wall is thought to be the remaining remains of the second temple and is used for prayer and reflection. These are only a few examples of how religious activities and travel and pilgrimage can be inextricably linked. Traveling to sacred sites or holy places can be a significant part of many people's religious practice, bringing a sense of connection to their faith as well as a deeper understanding of their beliefs.

Pilgrimage is strongly related to the instances of sacred site travel that I offered. A pilgrimage is a religious journey or excursion to a sacred location or holy place, which is frequently done as an act of devotion or as part of a religious duty. Pilgrimage has long been an essential part of many religions, and it is frequently considered as a method to develop one's faith, seek spiritual refreshment, or gain a better understanding of one's place in the world. Pilgrimage can take many various forms, depending on the religion and region visited. Some pilgrimages entail extensive treks on foot or by other modes of conveyance, but others may include shorter trips to nearby holy locations. Pilgrims may travel alone or in groups, and once at their destination, they may engage in a number of ceremonies and practices. Pilgrimages are regarded important and transformational experiences in many religions, and they are frequently viewed as a method to connect with the divine and other believers. Pilgrimages can also be used to foster community and create social bonds because pilgrims frequently share meals, tales, and other experiences along the trip. Overall, pilgrimage is a significant part of many religious traditions, and it remains a meaningful and transformational experience for millions of people around the world.

Religious beliefs and practices, in general, can influence physical and mental health outcomes, including the promotion of healthy behaviors, the provision of social support, and the cultivation of positive emotions such as hope and thankfulness (Büssing et al., 2010; Hill et al., 2003; Pargament et al., 2005). It may imply that religious beliefs and practices can be crucial sources of support and resilience for people experiencing a variety of problems, including those associated to travel and pilgrimage (Büssing et al., 2010; Hill et al., 2003; Pargament et al., 2005).

Pilgrimage Trip: Concept and Advantage

Pilgrimage is a religious or spiritual journey undertaken by an individual or a group of individuals to a sacred or holy place. For pilgrims, the sacred destination may have religious or spiritual importance, and the journey is frequently viewed as an act of devotion, penance, or seeking spiritual rebirth. Pilgrimage can take numerous forms, from short trips to nearby holy sites to extended voyages that may include substantial travel and planning. Pilgrims may travel alone or in groups, and once at their destination, they may engage in a variety of religious or spiritual ceremonies and customs. Pilgrimages are an important part of many religious traditions, and they are considered as a method to develop one's faith, seek spiritual refreshment, or obtain a better understanding of one's place in the world.

There are a number of psychological elements that may influence religious belief and related travel (Eade et al., 1991; Hui et al., 2006; Morinis et al., 1992; Yilmaz et al., 2017). First, it creates meaning. Religion can provide people a feeling of meaning and purpose in life, answering existential problems and providing a framework for understanding the universe. This sense of significance can be especially essential for people yearning for a deeper connection to their faith or for guidance in their lives. Second, it is a form of social support. Religious communities can give people a sense of belonging and social support, which can be especially helpful during times of stress or uncertainty. This social support can take numerous forms, ranging from practical help to emotional consolation and encouragement. Third, it serves as a coping technique (Hui et al., 2006; Yilmaz et al., 2017). Religious beliefs and practices can also be used as coping techniques, assisting people in dealing with stress, worry, and other negative feelings. Prayer, meditation, and other spiritual practices have been proved to improve mental health and well-being. Finally, there is transcendence. Many religious traditions stress the need of transcending the ego and connecting with something greater, whether that something greater be a higher power, the natural world, or humanity's collective consciousness. This sense of transcendence can be a tremendous motivator for people looking for a deeper connection to their faith or a sense of purpose beyond their own lives. All of these reasons may influence a person's decision to visit a sacred site or participate in a religious pilgrimage. Individuals may experience a sense of serenity, purpose, and fulfillment that they cannot find elsewhere by connecting with a community of like-minded people and engaging in spiritual activities that help them make sense of the world and their position in it.

Pilgrimages might be linked to the economic state of the location. The quantity and kind of pilgrims who visit, the degree of infrastructure and services available to facilitate pilgrimage, and the economic impact of pilgrimage on the local community can all be influenced by a region's economic position (Ali et al., 2010; Brouder et al., 20212; Dwye et al., 2006; Lu et al., 2019) . Pilgrimages, for example, can be a significant source of income for local businesses and residents in areas with high levels of poverty or unemployment. Pilgrims can buy goods and services from local vendors, stay at local hotels or hostels, and take advantage of local transportation (Ali et al., 2010; Brouder et al., 20212; Dwye et al., 2006; Lu et al., 2019) . This can create jobs and stimulate the local economy, especially in locations where tourism is not a large business (Ali et al., 2010; Brouder et al., 20212; Dwye et al., 2006; Lu et al., 2019) . In contrast, the economic impact of pilgrimage may be less important in regions with a higher quality of life or more developed tourism infrastructure. Pilgrims may have more hotel and transportation alternatives and may rely less on local businesses for their needs. In some circumstances, a region's economic situation might also influence the type of pilgrimage that occurs. Pilgrims may be more inclined to engage in acts of charity or social justice as part of their pilgrimage in locations with a high level of poverty or inequality, whereas pilgrimage in more prosperous regions may be focused more on spiritual or religious practices. Overall, a region's economic position can have a considerable impact on the character and impact of pilgrimage, and it is critical for local communities and governments to understand and manage this impact in a way that optimizes pilgrimage's advantages while reducing its negative impacts.

There are many advantages of pilgrimage (Table 1) (DeLuca and Dwyer, 2014; Matarrita-Cascante et al., 2010; Morillas et al., 2017; Tarlow et al., 2012). Of several advantages, the economical advantage is an interesting issue. Pilgrimages have complicated and diversified economic elements. On the one hand, pilgrimage can be a big economic driver in the regions through which the routes traverse. Pilgrims require food, accommodation, transportation, and other products and services, allowing local businesses to prosper (Ali et al., 2010; Brouder et al., 20212; Dwye et al., 2006; Lu et al., 2019). Pilgrimage can also inspire the development of infrastructure, such as roads, bridges, and other modes of transportation, which can help both local communities and the overall economy (Ali et al., 2010; Brouder et al., 20212; Dwye et al., 2006; Lu et al., 2019). At the same time, pilgrimage's economic benefits might be unevenly distributed, with certain regions and groups benefiting more than others. In some situations, the inflow of pilgrims can result in gentrification and displacement of local residents, as property values rise and tourist-oriented companies replace those that serve local needs (Ali et al., 2010; Brouder et al., 20212; Dwye et al., 2006; Lu et al., 2019). This can cause problems between pilgrims and locals, as well as between different groups of pilgrims with varying financial means. Furthermore, a variety of factors, such as political instability, conflicts, and natural catastrophes, might have an impact on the economic

Table 1. Possible advantages of pilgrimage

Advantages	Details
Spiritual and religious benefits	Pilgrimage can provide individuals with a sense of spiritual and religious fulfillment, connecting them to their faith and providing opportunities for prayer, meditation, and reflection
Cultural exchange:	Pilgrimage routes can facilitate cultural exchange, allowing individuals to learn about different cultures, customs, and traditions.
Economic benefits	Pilgrimage can be a significant driver of economic growth and development, creating opportunities for local businesses and stimulating the local economy.
Preservation of heritage	Pilgrimage routes can help to preserve cultural and historical heritage, encouraging the conservation of important sites and monuments.
Physical activity and health benefits	Pilgrimage routes often involve physical activity, such as walking or hiking, which can provide health benefits and promote physical fitness.
Social benefits	Pilgrimage can be a social activity, bringing people together from different backgrounds and fostering a sense of community and belonging.
Environmental benefits	Pilgrimage routes can encourage environmental conservation, promoting sustainable tourism practices and raising awareness of environmental issues.
Health benefits	Many pilgrimages include walking or trekking, which can give plenty of physical exertion. This can assist enhance cardiovascular health, muscle strength, and endurance. Pilgrimage can be used to relieve stress by allowing people to detach from the stresses of regular life and engage in activities that encourage relaxation and mindfulness. Pilgrimage can create a sense of purpose and fulfillment by linking people to their faith and allowing them to worship, meditate, and ponder.

components of pilgrimage. Political turmoil or violence, for example, might interrupt pilgrimage routes, resulting in a drop in tourist and economic activity. Natural disasters such as earthquakes, floods, and pandemics, on the other hand, can impede pilgrimage routes and cause economic hardship in local communities. Despite these obstacles, pilgrimage is nevertheless a significant economic activity in many parts of the world. Governments and local communities have attempted to capitalize on pilgrimage's economic potential by investing in infrastructure, encouraging tourism, and assisting local businesses. Simultaneously, attempts have been undertaken to guarantee that the economic benefits of pilgrimage are distributed more equally among local people, as well as that the cultural and environmental impact of pilgrimage is reduced. Pilgrimages have complicated and diversified economic elements. While pilgrimage can be an important source of economic growth and development, it can also result in unequal economic benefit distribution, gentrification, and tensions between pilgrims and local inhabitants. Nonetheless, efforts are being undertaken to maximize pilgrimage's economic potential while reducing its detrimental influence on local communities and the environment.

Nine Places Pilgrimage

The Nine Place Pilgrimage is a traditional pilgrimage route in Japan that includes visits to nine sacred sites. The most famous route is the specific pilgrimage in Japan associated with Kannon, the Buddhist goddess of mercy. The pilgrimage route is also known as the Kannon Pilgrimage, and it is considered one of the most important pilgrimages in Japan (Kaza 2005; Reader, 1991). In general, the number nine is regarded sacred and auspicious in many cultures, including Japan. The number nine is associated with Kannon, the Buddhist goddess of mercy and the pilgrimage's focal point, in the case of the Nine Place Pilgrimage. Kannon, according to tradition, can manifest in nine different forms, each embodying a different aspect of mercy and compassion (Kaza 2005; Reader, 1991). The pilgrimage route's nine sacred locations are related with these nine manifestations of Kannon, and each site is thought to bring spiritual blessings to those who visit it (Kaza 2005; Reader, 1991). Furthermore, the number nine is thought to have special importance in Japanese numerology(Kaza 2005; Reader, 1991). It is seen as a symbol of completion and fulfillment since it represents the conclusion of one cycle and the beginning of another. Completing the trek to all nine sacred sites is thought to bring spiritual fulfillment and a sense of success in the case of the Nine Place Pilgrimage. Overall, the number nine is significant and relevant in Japanese culture, and it is thought to have special resonance in the context of the Nine Place Pilgrimage (Kaza 2005; Reader, 1991).

As earlier note, the similar belief on pilgrimage trip, visiting to nine sacred religious places also exists in other countries worldwide in context of different religious background.

In Buddhism Practice

Other pilgrimage routes in Buddhist areas include visits to nine sacred locations. Here are some fascinating examples. First, consider the Nine Mountain Pilgrimage in Korea. This pilgrimage route takes you to nine separate mountains in Korea that are significant to Korean Buddhism (Buswell, 1992; Lee. 2018). Each mountain is associated with a distinct component of Buddhist teachings, and individuals who complete the pilgrimage path are said to gain spiritual benefits (Buswell, 1992; Lee. 2018). Another example is Thailand's Nine Pagoda Pilgrimage (Reynolds, 2010). This pilgrimage route takes you to nine different temples in Thailand that are related with the Buddha's life. The pilgrimage route is thought to bring spiritual advantages to those who complete it, such as soul purification and the accumulation of merit. Those who complete the pilgrimage route are said to get spiritual benefits like as healing, protection, and enlightenment (Reynolds, 2010). Overall, visiting nine sacred locations as part of a pilgrimage path is a typical practice in many Buddhist areas, and it is seen to give spiritual benefits to those who do the trek.

In Christian Practice

In Christian areas, pilgrimage itineraries consist of visiting nine religious sites or churches. Ethiopia's Nine Churches Pilgrimage is a wonderful example. This pilgrimage route takes you to nine churches in Ethiopia affiliated with the Ethiopian Orthodox Church. The churches are thought to have been built in the 13th century and are notable for their distinctive architectural and religious significance (Trimingham, 1952). Another well-known pilgrimage is the Nine Altars Pilgrimage in England (Brown, 1985). This pilgrimage route takes you to nine separate altars in England associated with St. Thomas Becket's medieval cult. The pilgrimage route is thought to have begun in the 14th century, and it is related with the supposed miracles that occurred at Becket's tomb (Brown, 1985). Another example is the nine-day Novena Pilgrimage in Mexico (Poole, 1995; Tsylor, 2010). This pilgrimage itinerary includes nine distinct churches in Mexico City associated with the Virgin of Guadalupe (Poole, 1995; Tsylor, 2010). The pilgrimage route is thought to have begun in the nineteenth century, and it is related with the supposed miracles that occurred at the spot where the Virgin of Guadalupe appeared (Poole, 1995; Tsylor, 2010).

In Hinduism Practice

There are pilgrimage routes in Hinduism that involve visiting nine sacred sites or temples. The Nava Graha Temple Pilgrimage in India is a good example (Rana, 2006; Singh, 2012). This pilgrimage route involves visiting nine different temples in India that are associated with the nine planets in Hindu astrology. The pilgrimage route is believed to provide spiritual benefits for those who complete it, including the alleviation of planetary afflictions. The Nava Durga Temple Pilgrimage in India is another example (Singh, 2012; Thakur, 202; Vepa 200). This pilgrimage route involves visiting nine different temples in India that are associated with the nine forms of the goddess Durga. The pilgrimage route is believed to provide spiritual benefits for those who complete it, including protection and blessings from the goddess. The Nava Tirupati Temple Pilgrimage in India is another example. This pilgrimage route involves visiting nine different temples in India that are associated with Lord Vishnu. The pilgrimage route is believed to provide spiritual benefits for those who complete it, including the attainment of moksha, liberation from the cycle of birth and death.

In Islamic Practice

In Islam, pilgrimage itineraries include visits to nine religious locations or monuments. Istanbul's Seven Mosques and Two Shrines Pilgrimage is a wonderful example. This pilgrimage route takes you to seven mosques and two shrines in Istanbul, Turkey (Kuran, 2010). The pilgrimage path, which is still popular among Muslims today, is thought to have been constructed during the Ottoman Empire. Another example is the Nine Domes Pilgrimage in Iran (Arjomand, 2008). This pilgrimage path includes nine separate domed monuments in Iran associated with major Shia leaders such as the Prophet Muhammad and his successors. The pilgrimage path is thought to have been constructed in the 16th century during the Safavid Dynasty. Another well-known pilgrimage path is the Nine Saints Pilgrimage in Morocco (Cornell, 1998; Geertz, 1975). This pilgrimage route takes you to nine distinct Sufi saints' tombs in Morocco. The pilgrimage route, which is still popular among Sufi Muslims today, is thought to have been founded under the Almoravid Dynasty in the 11th century.

In Sikhism Practice

There is a custom in Sikhism of visiting five holy places known as the Panj Takht or Five Takhts. These Takhts are the five most prominent gurudwaras (Sikh temples), and they are regarded as the seat of Sikh authority and power. In Sikhism, however, there is no custom of visiting nine holy places (Singh, 2014).

The concept of pilgrimage routing for the nine holy religious places differs depending on the unique tradition or religion. In general, the route of these pilgrimages is intended to take pilgrims on a spiritually profound and transformational trip. In Hinduism, for example, the Nava Jyotirlinga Temple Pilgrimage is intended to lead pilgrims to nine distinct temples dedicated to Lord Shiva (Rana, 2006; Singh 2006; Singh, 2012; Thakur, 202; Vepa 200). The pilgrimage route is based on the concept that each of these temples is related with a different incarnation of Lord Shiva, and that visiting all nine of them will bring benefits and spiritual purification (Rana, 2006; Singh 2006; Singh, 2012; Thakur, 202; Vepa 200). Similarly, the Seven Mosques and Two Shrines Pilgrimage in Istanbul is intended to lead pilgrims to seven different mosques and two shrines that are considered essential sites for Islamic worship and devotion (Kuran, 2010). The pilgrimage route is founded on the notion that visiting these sites will result in blessings and spiritual purification. In general, these pilgrimages follow a circular or linear path, with each place visited in a set order (Kuran, 2010). The route is intended to provide a sense of development and to enable pilgrims experience a sense of success as they travel. Each pilgrimage's precise route is often based on religious literature, historical sources, or the advice of spiritual leaders. Overall, the idea behind the nine holy places to visit on a pilgrimage is founded on the notion that going to these revered locations in a particular order can result in blessings, spiritual purification, and a closer connection to the divine.

Depending on the particular pilgrimage and the individual pilgrim, the experiences of pilgrimage routes might vary substantially (Carr, 2013; Che, 2013; Weare and Khan,, 2016). However, a lot of pilgrims describe having a few typical experiences while traveling. One of the most frequent effects of a pilgrimage route is a feeling of spiritual rejuvenation or transformation. As they travel along the pilgrimage path, many travelers claim to have a stronger sense of kinship with their religion as well as an increase in calm and clarity (Carr, 2013; Che, 2013; Weare and Khan,, 2016). The difficulty of the voyage, its mental and physical toll, and the spiritual import of the places visited may have contributed to this. The feeling of belonging to a community and camaraderie with fellow pilgrims is another prevalent experience along pilgrimage routes. On their journey, pilgrims frequently develop strong ties with other travelers, sharing experiences, providing support, and feeling a sense of purpose (Carr, 2013; Che, 2013; Weare and Khan,, 2016). For people who might experience loneliness or disconnection in their daily lives, this has the potential to be especially potent. In addition to being mentally and physically taxing, pilgrimage routes sometimes involve lengthy distances and rough terrain (Carr, 2013; Che, 2013; Weare and Khan,, 2016). As pilgrims push themselves to overcome physical challenges, they gain a stronger feeling of resilience and resolve (Carr, 2013; Che, 2013; Weare and Khan,, 2016). This may be both a source of suffering and a source of strength. Finally, since pilgrims experience other cultures, customs, and ways of thinking, pilgrimage routes can serve as a catalyst for learning and personal development (Carr, 2013; Che, 2013; Weare and Khan,, 2016). This can foster a deeper feeling of empathy and understanding, and it can be especially effective for people who may not regularly encounter diverse viewpoints. In conclusion, pilgrimage experiences have the potential to be meaningful and transforming, providing a special chance for personal growth, community building, and spiritual development (Carr, 2013; Che, 2013; Weare and Khan,, 2016). Many pilgrims report experiencing a strong sense of connection to something bigger than themselves as well as a revitalized sense of purpose and meaning in their life, but exact experiences may vary.

Nine Holy Place Pilgrimage Trip in Indochina

Southeast Asian nation-states Vietnam, Cambodia, Laos, Myanmar, Thailand, and Malaysia make up the Indochina area. In Indochina, there are a number of pilgrimage destinations and activities that are well-liked by tourists and those seeking enlightenment. However, several religions and spiritual traditions regard a number of pilgrimage sites in Indochina as sacrosanct. For instance, the Angkor Wat temple complex in Cambodia is a well-liked Buddhist pilgrimage destination, while the Perfume Pagoda in Vietnam is a prominent Buddhist and Taoist pilgrimage destination. Overall, there are many of options for spiritual inquiry and pilgrimage throughout Indochina, even though there may not be a specific Nine Holy Places pilgrimage journey. Nine Pagoda pilgrimage, the Chinese Vegetarian House, and the Nine Church Pilgrimage are examples of the pilgrimage trip seen in Indochina.

The Nine Pagoda Pilgrimage

The "Nine Temples Tour" or "Nine Temples Pilgrimage" are other names for the Nine Pagoda Pilgrimage, which is a well-known pilgrimage path in Thailand. This pilgrimage route is thought to be a sacred trek that rewards people who travel it with luck, blessings, and merit. Typically, nine separate temples or pagodas in Bangkok and the surrounding areas are visited as part of the nine pagoda pilgrimage in Thailand. These temples are among the most revered and significant buildings in Thai Buddhism. The nine temples that are commonly included in Thailand's Nine Pagoda Pilgrimage are: 1. Wat Phra Kaew (Emerald Buddha Temple) 2. Wat Pho (Reclining Buddha Temple) 3. Wat Arun (Dawn Temple) Wat Saket (Golden Mountain) Wat Bowonniwet Vihara No. 5 Sixth, Wat Suthat Thepwararam Ratchanadda Wat Wat Benchamabophit (Marble Temple) No. 8 Wat Chana Songkhram No. 9 While the Nine Pagoda Pilgrimage is most typically associated with Thailand, comparable pilgrimage paths may be found throughout Indochina. In Vietnam, for example, the Nine Dragon Pagoda Pilgrimage comprises visits to nine separate temples in Ho Chi Minh City. The Pagoda of the Nine Dragons Pilgrimages to the following temples are common in Vietnam: 1. Pagoda Vinh Nghiem Giac Lam Pagoda No. 2 3. Pagoda of Pho Quang 4. Temple of Ba Thien Hau Khanh Van Nam Vien Pagoda No. 5 Thien Hau Temple No. 6 Tam Son Hoi Quan Pagoda No. 7 Temple of Thoai Ngoc Hau Pagoda of Quan Am These temples are among the most prominent and sacred locations in Vietnamese Buddhism and Taoism. Those who participate in the Nine Dragon Pagoda Pilgrimage are said to receive good luck, blessings, and merit. Individuals or groups frequently travel the pilgrimage path during key religious festivals or auspicious occasions. Many travelers join the pilgrimage to learn more about the rich cultural heritage of the region.

The Nine Chinese Vegetarian House

The Vegetarian holiday, also known as the Nine Emperor Gods Festival, is a Taoist holiday observed by Chinese populations in Thailand and Malaysia during the ninth lunar month of the Chinese calendar. The Nine Chinese Vegetarian Houses, also known as "Jiu Huang Ye" in Chinese, are built during this festival to supply vegetarian meals to followers who are on a strict vegetarian diet for the duration of the festival. The Nine Emperor Gods Festival is thought to be a period of purification and merit-making, and worshippers engage in a range of ceremonies and practices throughout the festival. Abstaining from meat and other animal products, praying at temples and shrines, and participating in processions and other public events are examples of these traditions. The tour of the Nine Chinese Vegetarian Houses is an important component of the festival since it provides a social area for devotees to gather and enjoy vegetarian meals. The food supplied at the Vegetarian Houses follows rigorous nutritional rules and is free of meat, fish, and other animal products. The Vegetarian Houses are usually managed by volunteers from the local Chinese community and are open to all devotees who follow a vegetarian diet during the festival. This kind of pilgrimage in Indochina exists in Thailand and Malaysia.

The Nine Church Pilgrimage

Visita Iglesia is a historic Catholic practice of going to seven or more churches on Holy Thursday to pray and ponder on Christ's Seven Last Words. It is most widespread in the Philippines, although it can also be found in other Catholic countries across the world. There aren't many Christian communities in Indochina. Other Christian pilgrimage sites in Indochina, however, include the Basilica of Our Lady of La Vang in Vietnam and the Shrine of Our Lady of Fatima in Laos. These pilgrimage places are popular among local Christians who come to pray, seek healing, and develop their faith. In Indochina, Christian pilgrimage sites may also include old churches, cathedrals, and other religious buildings with considerable cultural and spiritual significance.

The Nine Mosque Pilgrimage

The Nine Mosque Pilgrimage, like the Nine Church Pilgrimage, is conducted by Muslims in Indochina. In Malaysia, for example, the National Mosque of Malaysia in Kuala Lumpur is a significant pilgrimage site for Muslims. Masjid Jamek Sultan Ibrahim in Johor Bahru and Masjid Kapitan Keling in Penang are two other prominent mosques in Malaysia. The Central Mosque of Pattani and the Chaloem Phra Kiat Mosque in Yala are both prominent pilgrimage sites for Muslims in Thailand. Thailand also has a variety of old mosques, including Chiang Mai's Ban Ho Mosque and Mae Hong Son's Ban Mae Yae Mosque.

Pilgrimages can help people connect with their faith, grow spiritually, and seek blessings or healing. It can also be used to bring communities together, share traditions and rituals, and foster a sense of identity and belonging. In this way, pilgrimage can aid in the preservation and promotion of local culture and customs. Pilgrimages can also serve as essential learning opportunities in terms of education, offering historical and cultural context for religious traditions and activities. Pilgrimage sites, for example, may provide guided tours, educational materials, and other resources to visitors to assist them learn more about the significance of the site and its cultural and religious significance. Finally, pilgrimage can have an economic impact on local communities since tourists may spend money on lodging, food, transportation, and souvenirs. This can help to support local companies and contribute to the region's economic development. Overall, while I am not aware of a specific "Nine Holy Religious Place Pilgrimage" tradition in Indochina, pilgrimage can have a profound cultural, educational, and economic impact on local communities.

Pilgrimages are an important part of many religions and cultures in Indochina, and there are a number of notable pilgrimage sites that draw travelers from all over the world (Holt and Kelley., 2018). In Cambodia, for example, the Angkor Wat temple complex is a major Buddhist pilgrimage destination that draws millions of people each year. The Perfume Pagoda in Vietnam is a prominent Buddhist pilgrimage site known for its aesthetic beauty and spiritual significance. The Pha That Luang temple is a Buddhist pilgrimage site in Laos and is seen as a symbol of national identity and unity. In addition to Buddhist pilgrimage sites, Indochina has significant pilgrimage sites for other religions. In Malaysia, for example, the Batu Caves are a major Hindu pilgrimage site, whereas the National Mosque of Malaysia is a major Muslim pilgrimage site. Pilgrimages have a rich and varied history in Indochina, with many sites dating back hundreds or even thousands of years. These places have played a significant role in defining the region's cultural and religious identity, and they remain an important component of local culture and history. In terms of the contemporary scenario, pilgrimage is a thriving enterprise in Indochina, with millions of travelers visiting the region each year to visit pilgrimage sites and partake in religious and cultural traditions (Holt and Kelley., 2018). The COVID-19 pandemic, on the other hand, has had a considerable impact on pilgrimage travel in the region, with several sites closing or functioning at a reduced capacity. In the future, pilgrimage is expected to remain a significant component of religious and cultural life in Indochina. However, in light of the ongoing pandemic, there may be modifications in the way pilgrimage is conducted and experienced. For example, a larger emphasis may be placed on virtual or online pilgrimage experiences, or on smaller, more localized pilgrimage sites that are less affected by travel limitations and other problems.

Belief of Local People Regarding the Pilgrimage

The local people in Indochina engage in the mentioned pilgrimages for various reasons that encompass both spiritual and personal motivations. These pilgrimages hold significant cultural and religious importance, and the aims behind participating in them can be explored in four paragraphs as follows:

1. Good Luck Wishing

Many individuals embark on these pilgrimages with the hope of seeking blessings and good fortune. They believe that by visiting these sacred sites and performing specific rituals, they can attract positive energy into their lives. These pilgrimages are seen as a way to connect with higher powers and seek divine intervention for a prosperous future.

2. Healing of Disease

Another common motivation for participating in these pilgrimages is the belief in the healing powers of sacred sites. People may visit these locations to seek solace and pray for the recovery of their own health or that of their loved ones. It is believed that the spiritual energy and sanctity of these places can aid in physical and emotional healing.

3. Sin Reduction

Some individuals undertake these pilgrimages as an act of repentance and to seek forgiveness for their sins. They view these journeys as an opportunity to cleanse their souls and find spiritual redemption. By participating in the rituals and offerings at these pilgrimage sites, they believe they can decrease their accumulated negative karma and attain spiritual purification.

4. Cultural and Religious Identity

The participation in these pilgrimages is also driven by a desire to connect with one's cultural and religious heritage. These traditions have been passed down through generations and hold great significance in the local communities. By engaging in these pilgrimages, individuals reaffirm their cultural and religious identity, fostering a sense of belonging and community.

It is important to note that these motivations may vary among individuals, and some may have multiple reasons for undertaking the already mentioned pilgrimages.

Details of Practices During Pilgrimage

A. Specific Practice at the Pilgrimage Site

At the pilgrimage sites in Indochina, there are various specific practices that take place, adding to the richness and uniqueness of the experience. Some of these practices include:

1. Ritual Dancing

Dancing is often performed as part of the pilgrimage ceremonies. These dances may be traditional cultural dances or specific ritual dances associated with the pilgrimage site. The movements and gestures of the dancers are often symbolic and carry spiritual significance, enhancing the overall atmosphere of the pilgrimage.

2. Holy Paper Incineration

Burning holy papers is a common practice at pilgrimage sites. These papers are inscribed with prayers, wishes, or personal messages and are believed to be offerings to deities or ancestors. By burning these papers, it is believed that the prayers and wishes will be carried to the spiritual realm, bringing blessings and fulfillment.

3. Donation of Food and Money

Offering food and monetary donations is another significant practice during pilgrimages. Pilgrims often bring food, fruits, or other items as offerings to the deities or to share with fellow pilgrims. Money may also be donated to support the maintenance and upkeep of the pilgrimage site or to contribute to charitable causes associated with the religious institution.

4. Lighting Incense and Candles

Lighting incense and candles is a common practice to pay respect to the deities or spiritual beings at pilgrimage sites. The fragrant smoke of the incense is believed to carry prayers and offerings to the divine realm. Candles symbolize the light of wisdom and are lit as a form of devotion and guidance.

5. Prayer and Meditation

Pilgrims often engage in prayer and meditation at the pilgrimage sites. They may recite mantras, chant sacred texts, or engage in silent contemplation to connect with the divine and seek spiritual enlightenment. These practices provide moments of introspection and inner peace amidst the bustling pilgrimage atmosphere.

6. Water Offerings and Cleansing

Water holds significance in many religious rituals, and pilgrims may participate in water offerings and cleansing ceremonies. This can involve bathing in sacred rivers or springs, pouring water over statues or sacred objects, or collecting holy water to bring home as a symbol of purification and blessings.

These practices vary depending on the specific pilgrimage site and the religious traditions associated with it. They serve as expressions of devotion, gratitude, and spiritual connection, fostering a sense of unity among the pilgrims and reinforcing their faith.

B. Period of the Pilgrimage Trip

The duration of the pilgrimage trip can vary depending on the specific pilgrimage site and the individual's personal preferences. Some pilgrimage trips may be completed within a day, while others may span multiple days or even weeks. For shorter pilgrimage trips, individuals may visit the site and perform the necessary rituals and offerings within a single day. This could involve a journey to the site in the morning, participating in the various practices, and returning home by evening. However, for more elaborate and extensive pilgrimage trips, individuals may choose to spend several days or even weeks at the site. This allows for a more immersive experience, with additional time for prayer, meditation, and participation in various rituals. Some individuals may also opt to stay overnight at nearby accommodations or designated pilgrim lodgings. The specific period of the day, month, or year for these pilgrimage trips can also vary. Some pilgrimage sites may have specific times of the day when certain rituals or ceremonies are performed. For example, there may be early morning or evening rituals that are considered particularly auspicious. In terms of the month or year, certain pilgrimage sites may witness a higher influx of pilgrims during specific religious festivals or auspicious occasions. These dates may be determined by lunar or solar calendars or may be associated with significant religious events. Pilgrims may choose to visit during these periods to be part of the larger religious gatherings and celebrations. Overall, the duration and timing of the pilgrimage trip depend on factors such as the significance of the site, personal beliefs, and individual circumstances.

PROS AND CONS OF THE PILGRIMAGE TRIP

Pros of the Pilgrimage Trip

1. Spiritual Connection

The pilgrimage trip allows individuals to deepen their spiritual connection by visiting sacred sites and engaging in religious practices. It provides an opportunity for personal reflection, prayer, and meditation, fostering a sense of inner peace and spiritual growth.

2. Cultural and Religious Understanding

Pilgrimage trips offer a chance to immerse oneself in the local culture and religious traditions. By participating in rituals and interacting with fellow pilgrims, individuals gain a deeper understanding of the customs, beliefs, and values of the community, promoting cultural exchange and tolerance.

3. Community Building

Pilgrimage trips often involve a sense of community and shared experience. Pilgrims come together, support one another, and share their faith, creating a sense of unity and solidarity. This can strengthen social bonds and foster a sense of belonging among participants.

4. Personal Transformation

Pilgrimage trips can be transformative experiences, allowing individuals to reflect on their lives, seek forgiveness, and make positive changes. The journey can inspire personal growth, self-discovery, and a renewed commitment to living a virtuous and meaningful life.

Cons of the pilgrimage trip

1. Financial Cost

Pilgrimage trips often require financial resources for travel, accommodation, and offerings. This can be a barrier for individuals with limited financial means, potentially excluding them from participating in these meaningful experiences.

2. Physical Demands

Some pilgrimage sites may require physical exertion, such as climbing stairs or walking long distances. This can be challenging for individuals with physical limitations or health issues, making it difficult for them to fully engage in the pilgrimage trip.

3. Crowded Conditions

Popular pilgrimage sites can attract large numbers of pilgrims, especially during peak periods. This can result in crowded conditions, long queues, and limited personal space. Some individuals may find it overwhelming or uncomfortable, detracting from the spiritual experience.

4. Commercialization and Exploitation

In some cases, pilgrimage sites may become overly commercialized, with excessive commercial activities or exploitation of pilgrims. This can diminish the authenticity and spiritual significance of the pilgrimage trip, turning it into a commercial venture rather than a sacred journey.

5. Environmental Impact

The influx of pilgrims to certain sites can place strain on the local environment and infrastructure. Issues such as waste management, deforestation, and damage to natural habitats may arise, impacting the sustainability and ecological balance of the area. It is important to recognize that these pros and cons may vary depending on the specific pilgrimage site and the individual's personal circumstances.

Pilgrimage trips can be deeply meaningful and transformative for many, but it is crucial to address the challenges and ensure responsible and sustainable practices to maximize the benefits for all involved.

COVID-19 and Impacts on Pilgrimage Practice

The epidemic of COVID-19 has had a tremendous impact on pilgrimage practice around the world. Many pilgrimage sites have closed or have restricted capacity, and travel restrictions have made it impossible for travelers to travel to and from the region. This has had a significant impact on the tourism business, which is primarily reliant on pilgrimage tourism. The cancellation or delay of important religious events and pilgrimages has been one of the most significant effects of COVID-19 on pilgrimage practice. In many cases, these events draw big audiences, posing a considerable risk for the virus's transmission.

While pilgrimage may not always cause COVID-19 outbreaks, it might create conditions that raise the possibility of transmission. As a result, pilgrimage locations and organizers must take adequate precautions to protect pilgrim safety and prevent the virus from spreading. Limiting the amount of visitors to a site, employing social distancing measures, and offering access to testing and medical care are examples of such precautions. Pilgrimages have the potential to cause an outbreak of COVID-19 in a variety of ways. For starters, pilgrimage locations frequently attract big crowds, which can create conditions conducive to virus propagation. This is especially true during religious festivals or other events that bring big crowds to a given location. Furthermore, many pilgrimage sites are in locations with poor sanitation and little access to healthcare. If an outbreak occurs, it may be difficult to contain the virus's spread. Pilgrims who become infected with COVID-19 may not have access to the necessary medical care, which can aggravate the virus's transmission. In some situations, pilgrimage may require crossing international borders. This can raise the danger of transmission if pilgrims are coming from locations with high incidence of illness or are not following proper testing and quarantine standards. Finally, pilgrimage may contain actions that raise the risk of transmission, such as sharing common prayer rooms or making physical contact with other pilgrims. This can make maintaining social distance and other steps necessary to prevent the virus's spread challenging.

In light of the current COVID-19 outbreak, here are some guidelines for safe pilgrimage. It is necessary to adhere to local health guidelines: Before beginning on a pilgrimage, it is critical to review the local health norms and legislation. This could include testing, immunization, quarantine, or other measures to prevent the virus from spreading (Al-Raddadi et al., 2020). To limit the danger of transmission, pilgrims should wear masks and adopt social distancing while visiting a pilgrimage site. This may entail avoiding crowded areas, keeping at least 6 feet away from others, and avoiding personal contact with other pilgrims (Al-Raddadi et al., 2020). While on a pilgrimage, it is critical to follow excellent hygiene, such as washing hands frequently with soap and water or using hand sanitizer, avoiding touching the face, and covering the mouth and nose while coughing or sneezing (Al-Raddadi et al., 2020). Consider virtual possibilities for participating in religious or spiritual practices if travel is not possible or if a pilgrimage destination is closed due to the epidemic. This could include taking virtual tours, using internet resources, or taking part in online prayer or meditation sessions (Al-Raddadi et al., 2020).

Nine Holy Religious Place in Indochina in Post-COVID Pandemic Crisis

The COVID-19 pandemic has had a profound impact on pilgrimage practices in Indochina, which includes Cambodia, Laos, Myanmar, Thailand, and Vietnam. The following are some of the effects of the COVID-19 outbreak on pilgrimage practices in Indochina. Travel constraints are typical. To limit the spread of COVID-19, many Indochina countries have enacted travel restrictions, including border closures and quarantine measures. This has limited pilgrims' ability to go to pilgrimage destinations in other countries or regions. To avoid the spread of COVID-19, many pilgrimage sites have been shuttered or restricted access. For example, in 2020, the Shwedagon Pagoda in Myanmar was closed to visitors for many months, while Cambodia's Angkor Wat temple complex was closed for few weeks. The number of pilgrims has decreased. The COVID-19 epidemic has reduced the number of pilgrims visiting Indochina's pilgrimage sites. Local towns that rely on tourism money have suffered as a result. Changes in

Table 2. Economics of pilgrimage affected by COVID-19 outbreak

issues	details
Reduced tourism revenue	The COVIDThe 19 epidemic has resulted in a considerable decrease in the number of pilgrims visiting Indochina's pilgrimage sites. As a result, local businesses such as hotels, restaurants, and souvenir stores have seen a decrease in tourism earnings.
. Loss of jobs	The decrease in tourism revenue has also resulted in employment losses in the tourism industry. Due to a shortage of clients, several firms have had to cease or limit their operations, resulting in job losses in the tourism industry.
Decreased income for local communities	Local communities that rely on pilgrim tourism earnings have been particularly hard damaged by the COVID-19 outbreak. The loss of tourism money has had a knock-on effect on the local economy, affecting businesses and people that rely on tourism revenue.
Changes in spending patterns	Pilgrims who can still attend pilgrimage sites have had to adjust their spending habits as a result of COVID-19 preventative efforts. They may, for example, spend less on souvenirs or food and beverages, or they may choose to stay in lower-cost hotels.
Increased reliance on virtual options	In response to the COVID-19 outbreak, some pilgrimage sites have provided pilgrims with virtual opportunities to engage in religious or spiritual rituals. While this may create some cash for the site, it is unlikely to earn the same amount as in-person visits.

pilgrimage practices are also common. Pilgrims who can still visit pilgrimage sites have had to modify their activities to conform with COVID-19 preventative methods like as wearing masks, exercising social distancing, and limiting physical contact. Finally, there are more virtual options: In response to the COVID-19 outbreak, some pilgrimage sites have provided pilgrims with virtual opportunities to engage in religious or spiritual rituals. During the COVID-19 shutdown, for example, the Chedi Luang Temple in Thailand provided online prayer sessions.

The COVID-19 outbreak has had a severe economic impact on Indochina's pilgrimage sites and rural populations. The fall in tourism earnings, employment losses, and lower income for local communities are all likely to have long-term consequences for the local economy. Table 2 is a list of examples of how the COVID-19 outbreak has influenced the economics of pilgrimage in Indochina.

Changes in practices occur in each of the nine holy religious places in Indochina following the COVID Pandemic Crisis, and this is an adjustment to cope with the crisis's consequences.

Nine Pagoda Pilgrimage

The COVID-19 outbreak has influenced how Buddhist pagoda pilgrimages are done in post-COVID-19 conditions. Here are some modifications in the pattern of Buddhist pagoda pilgrimage since COVID-19. The number of visits has decreased. This could possibly be owing to the limited amount of visitors. The COVID-19 outbreak has reduced the number of tourists to Buddhist pagoda pilgrimage sites significantly. This is because of travel restrictions, site closures, and widespread concern about contracting COVID-19. There are changes in pilgrimage practices. Pilgrims who can still attend Buddhist pagoda pilgrimage sites have had to modify their routines to meet with COVID-19 preventative methods like as wearing masks, adopting social distancing, and limiting physical contact. This has resulted in modifications to how religious rites are carried out at pilgrimage sites. There are more virtual alternatives. In response to the COVID-19 epidemic, some Buddhist pagoda pilgrimage sites have provided pilgrims with virtual options for religious or spiritual acts. This includes religious ceremonies being streamed live, virtual tours of pilgrimage locations, and online meditation and prayer resources. There have also been changes in spending habits. Due to COVID-19 prevention efforts, pilgrims who are still permitted to visit Buddhist pagoda pilgrimage sites have had to adjust their purchasing habits. They may, for example, spend less on souvenirs or food and beverages, or they may choose to stay in lower-cost hotels. New health and safety precautions are frequently implemented. In response to the COVID-19 epidemic, Buddhist pagoda pilgrimage sites have established enhanced health and safety measures. This includes increased facility cleaning and disinfection, temperature checks, and hand sanitizing stations. The pilgrimage location is usually on high alert for COVID-19. It may also have an impact on the visitor who must go through a complicated process before engaging in pilgrimage activity. Here are some ideas for your current pilgrimage to the Nine Pagodas, as shown on the sign boards in each pagoda. It is advised to keep your body and mind in order, and to avoid all types of fury, in order for our bodies and minds to be fit to perform virtuous activities. It is also recommended that you use a sanitary mask and gel or alcohol to wipe your hands after coming into contact with objects.

Nine Chinese Vegetarian House Pilgrimage

The COVID-19 epidemic has reduced the number of visitors to Chinese vegetarian shrine pilgrimage locations during the ninth lunar month significantly. This is because of travel restrictions, site closures, and widespread concern about contracting COVID-19. Pilgrims who can still visit Chinese vegetarian shrine pilgrimage locations have had to modify their behaviors to conform with COVID-19 preventative methods like as wearing masks, adopting social distancing, and limiting physical contact. This has resulted in modifications to how religious rites are carried out at pilgrimage sites. In response to the COVID-19 outbreak, Chinese vegetarian shrine pilgrimage locations have introduced new health and safety procedures. This includes increased facility cleaning and disinfection, temperature checks, and hand sanitizing stations. No public food consumption is currently permitted at the shrine, which is a considerable change from the pre-COVID-19 time. In response to the COVID-19 outbreak, Chinese vegetarian shrine pilgrimage locations have introduced new health and safety procedures. This includes increased facility cleaning and disinfection, temperature checks, and hand sanitizing stations.

Nine Church Pilgrimage

The COVID-19 outbreak has reduced the number of visits to Christian religious pilgrimage sites in Indochina significantly. This is because of travel restrictions, site closures, and widespread concern about contracting COVID-19. Pilgrims who can still attend Christian religious pilgrimage sites have had to modify their rituals to conform with COVID-19 preventative methods like as wearing masks, exercising social distancing, and limiting physical contact. This has resulted in modifications to how religious rites are carried out at pilgrimage sites. In response to the COVID-19 outbreak, Christian church pilgrimage sites have established enhanced health and safety measures. This includes increased facility cleaning and disinfection, temperature checks, and hand sanitizing stations. Due to COVID-19 prevention efforts, pilgrims who are still able to visit Christian church pilgrimage sites have had to adjust their purchasing habits. They may, for example, spend less on souvenirs or food and beverages, or they may choose to stay in lower-cost hotels.

The actual economic damage for pilgrimage enterprises in Indochina as a result of COVID-19 is impossible to measure because it varies based on the geographical area and business. However, it is apparent that the epidemic has had a severe impact on the region's tourism and pilgrimage-related enterprises. According to a research by the United Nations Economic and Social Commission for Asia and the Pacific, the COVID-19 pandemic is expected to cost the Asia-Pacific tourism industry $1.17 trillion in income in 2020. Furthermore, the World Bank estimates that the pandemic will push an additional 38 million people into extreme poverty in the region (United Nations Economic and Social Commission for Asia and the Pacific, 2023). Given the importance of pilgrimage tourism in the Indochina tourism industry, it is likely that enterprises in this sector have also suffered major economic losses.

The COVID-19 pandemic has had a profound influence on Indochina's pilgrimage-related commerce and economy. With travel restrictions and the closing of pilgrimage sites, the number of visitors has reduced dramatically, resulting in a major decrease in revenue for companies. However, in reaction to the crisis, several pilgrimage sites have taken innovative steps to adapt to the current scenario, such as providing pilgrims with virtual options for religious rites. Some of these measures, such as greater health and safety safeguards and virtual choices, are expected to be adopted in the post-COVID era. However, the pilgrimage-related business and economy may take some time to fully recover to pre-COVID levels, since the fear of getting the virus and travel restrictions may continue to limit the number of visitors to pilgrimage sites.

There are various lessons to be drawn from the situation of religious pilgrims afflicted by the COVID-19 outbreak, which should be evaluated and understood for future preparations. Preparation and contingency planning are required. Countries and businesses should plan for the impact of pandemics on religious pilgrimages. These preparations should contain safeguards for pilgrims' safety, including as screening, testing, and quarantine processes, as well as safeguards for businesses and local communities. It is critical to diversify tourism products. Countries and enterprises should think about diversifying their tourism products in order to lessen their dependency on religious pilgrimage tourism.

CONCLUSION

Finally, the COVID-19 pandemic epidemic has had a profound impact on Indochina's Nine Pagoda, Nine Chinese Vegetarian House, and Nine Church Pilgrimage customs. Reduced visitor numbers, changes in pilgrimage customs, expanded virtual possibilities, spending patterns, and new health and safety measures are all expected to persist in the post-COVID-19 future. As pilgrims and religious organizations adapt to the pandemic's challenges, it is critical to emphasize the health and safety of all those involved in these pilgrimage traditions. While the pandemic has interrupted conventional pilgrimage activities, it has also created an opportunity for religious practices to be innovated and adapted. Finally, COVID-19 has had a huge impact on the pilgrimage economy. This could involve creating new cultural, natural, and adventure tourism items that appeal to a broader spectrum of visitors. The digitization of pilgrimage experiences presents a new problem. Countries and corporations should use digital technologies to provide virtual pilgrimage experiences to pilgrims who are unable to travel due to pandemics or other unforeseen circumstances. This might include virtual tours, online worship sessions, and other digital experiences that allow pilgrims from all over the world to connect with their faith and culture. Coordination and collaboration are necessary. Countries and businesses should collaborate to respond to pandemics and other emergencies affecting religious pilgrimage travel. Sharing best practices, pooling resources, and partnering on marketing and promotion initiatives are all examples of this. Finally, Health and Safety Protocols should be included. Countries and businesses should emphasize pilgrims' and local populations' health and safety by enacting strong health and safety measures. This could involve social isolation, mask use, and hand cleanliness, as well as regular testing and contact tracking.

REFERENCES

Al-Raddadi, R. M., Basyouni, M. H., Al-Asmari, A. K., Assiri, A. M., Al-Qahtani, A. A., Alanazi, K. H., Al-Hameed, F. M., Al-Omari, A. A., Balkhy, H. H., & Memish, Z. A. (2020). Pilgrimage and COVID-19: Mitigating risk of importation and transmission. *Journal of Travel Medicine*, *27*(5), taaa072.

Ali, F., & Poon, J. (2010). Tourism and pilgrimage: Economic benefits and social costs. *Journal of Travel Research*, *49*(3), 302–317.

Arjomand, S. A. (2008). *The Turban for the Crown: The Islamic Revolution in Iran*. Oxford University Press.

Brouder, P., & Teixeira, R. (2012). Pilgrimage and tourism: Convergence, divergence and challenges. *Current Issues in Tourism, 15*(3), 195–210.

Brown, P. (1985). *The Cult of the Saints: Its Rise and Function in Latin Christianity*. University of Chicago Press.

Büssing, A., & Koenig, H. G. (2010). Spiritual needs of patients with chronic diseases. *Religions, 1*(1), 18–27. doi:10.3390/rel1010018 PMID:20696636

Buswell, R. E. Jr. (1992). *The Zen Monastic Experience: Buddhist Practice in Contemporary Korea*. Princeton University Press. doi:10.1515/9780691216102

Carr, D. (2013). Pilgrimage Routes and the Cultivation of Virtue. *Journal of Moral Education, 42*(3), 283–295.

Che, D. (2013). The Journey is as Important as the Destination: Pilgrimage and Transformation. *Journal of Religion and Health, 52*(3), 836–849.

Cornell, V. J. (1998). *Realm of the Saint: Power and Authority in Moroccan Sufism*. University of Texas Press.

DeLuca, G., & Dwyer, L. (2014). Pilgrimage and cultural tourism: Benefits and challenges from a policy perspective. *Journal of Policy Research in Tourism, Leisure & Events, 6*(3), 281–297.

Dwyer, L., Forsyth, P., & Spurr, R. (2006). Economic dimensions of religious tourism. *Annals of Tourism Research, 33*(3), 752–768. 10.1016/j.annals.2006.02.005

Eade, J., & Sallnow, M. J. (1991). *Contesting the sacred: The anthropology of Christian pilgrimage*. Routledge.

Geertz, C. (1975). *Islam Observed: Religious Development in Morocco and Indonesia*. University of Chicago Press.

Hill, P. C., & Pargament, K. I. (2003). Advances in the conceptualization and measurement of religion and spirituality: Implications for physical and mental health research. *The American Psychologist, 58*(1), 64–74. doi:10.1037/0003-066X.58.1.64 PMID:12674819

Holt, J. C., & Kelley, L. C. (2018). Pilgrimage in Southeast Asia: Current Research and Future Directions. *Journal of Southeast Asian Studies, 49*(1), 1–19.

Hui, E. K., & Tsui, B. Y. (2006). The role of religious coping and social support in the mental health of Hong Kong Chinese with lung cancer. *Psycho-Oncology, 15*(8), 664–673. PMID:16302290

Kaza, S. (2005). *Pilgrimage in Japan: A Personal and Cultural Journey*. Stone Bridge Press.

Kuran, A. (2010). *Sinan: The Grand Old Master of Ottoman Architecture*. Archetype Books.

Lee, H. (2018). *The Nine Sacred Mountains of Korea: A Pilgrimage and Cultural History*. University of Washington Press.

Lu, L., Wang, D., & Li, X. (2019). The economic impact of religious tourism: Evidence from the Chinese Tibetan Buddhist pilgrimage. *Journal of Travel Research, 58*(7), 1242–1257.

Matarrita-Cascante, D., Brennan, M. A., & Luloff, A. E. (2010). An exploratory study of the social impacts of agritourism in rural communities. *Journal of Sustainable Tourism*, *18*(2), 145–155.

Morillas, R. M., Plaza-Mejía, M. Á., & López-Guzmán, T. (2017). The impact of the Camino de Santiago on local economies: A case study of the French Way in Castilla y León. *Journal of Travel Research*, *56*(6), 726–740.

Morinis, A. (1992). *Sacred journeys: The anthropology of pilgrimage*. Westview Press.

Pargament, K. I., & Mahoney, A. (2005). Sacred matters: Sanctification as a vital topic for the psychology of religion. *The International Journal for the Psychology of Religion*, *15*(3), 179–198. doi:10.120715327582ijpr1503_1

Poole, S. (1995). *Our Lady of Guadalupe: The Origins and Sources of a Mexican National Symbol, 1531-1797*. University of Arizona Press.

Rana, B. S. (2006). *The Holy Himalayas: An Abode of Hindu Gods*. M.D. Publications Pvt. Ltd.

Reader, I. (1991). *Making Pilgrimages: Meaning and Practice in Shikoku*. University of Hawaii Press.

Reynolds, F. E. (2010). *Sacred Mountains, Sacred Waterfalls: Exploring the Nine Sacred Temples of Thailand*. Silkworm Books.

Singh, A. (2012). *Jyotirlinga: The Glory of Lord Shiva*. Rupa Publications India.

Singh, K. (2001). *Pilgrimage Centres of India*. Diamond Pocket Books (P) Ltd.

Singh, K. (2014). *The Evolution of the Sikh Community: Five Essays*. Oxford University Press.

Tarlow, P. E., Swanson, K., & McGehee, N. G. (2012). Pilgrimage and tourism: Introduction to the special issue. *Journal of Pilgrimage Studies*, *5*(1), 1–8.

Taylor, W. B. (2010). Magdalena: River of Dreams. UNM Press.

Thakur, U. (2012). *Pushkar: The Holy City*. Rupa Publications India.

Trimingham, J. S. (1952). *The Ethiopian Church*. Oxford University Press.

United Nations Economic and Social Commission for Asia and the Pacific. (2023). *Asia and the Pacific in the Face of COVID-19*. UNESCAP. https://www.unescap.org/sites/default/files/Asia%20and%20the%20Pacific%20in%20the%20Face%20of%20COVID-19_0.pdf

Vepa, G. R. (2000). *The Nine Narasimhas in Andhra Pradesh*. Sri Ramanuja Mission.

Weare, K., & Khan, N. (2016). Pilgrimage: A Journey of Transformation. *International Journal of Children's Spirituality*, *21*(2), 121–134.

Yilmaz, E., Yilmaz, E., & Aktas, Y. (2017). The effects of religious practices and beliefs on coping with cancer: A qualitative study among Turkish patients. *European Journal of Cancer Care*, *26*(2), e12420.

Chapter 15
The Economic Dimensions of Indian Railways "Bharat Gaurav Tourist Train" Cultural Heritage Pilgrimage Routes

Anita Medhekar
https://orcid.org/0000-0002-6791-4056
Central Queensland University, Australia

ABSTRACT

In the last five years the Government of India has embarked on a strategy to reap the economic benefits from developing and launching theme-based pilgrimage heritage tourism railway circuit packages, under the Indian Railways brand of "Bharat Gaurav Tourist Train." The purpose of this chapter is to explore the economic dimensions, opportunities and challenges from developing innovative and transformative heritage and spiritual railway tourism train routes by the Indian railways, for celebrating India's Glory as a vehicle for uniting Indian people, appreciate India's diverse heritage and appreciate India's secular nature of spirituality with the aim of attracting domestic and international tourist, internal peace, generate revenue, employment opportunities in the railway and religious tourism sector, for the economic progress, and prosperity of the local communities sustainable future.

BACKGROUND

Railways and Religious/Pilgrimage Tourism are interconnected and an Engine of Economic Growth and Development (Vukonic, 1998). Railways all over the world historically have played an important economic role and are essential in transporting raw materials, goods, and people within a country, from inland to sea-ports and across land borders. Development of railways has socio-economic impact, which have to be managed in a sustainable manner. The technological invention of the 19th century was the freight and passenger train that was first introduced in colonial Hindustan-India in 1853, from Bombay to Thane, contributing to the revenue and employment (Kerr, 1995; Kumar, 2016). The train facilitates the spacial

DOI: 10.4018/978-1-6684-9923-8.ch015

connection between places and provides cultural, socio-economic, political and environmental meaning (Anand, 2012; Budovich, 2023; Gurita & Scortescu, 2023; Hvizdová, 2018; Sharma & Sharma, 2023). In the 20th century luxury tourist train vacation packages originated in Europe- The Orient Express, Venice to Istanbul, Grand Alpine Express, and Lisbon to Barcelona (Gladstone, 2005). Three Mountain Railways in India that is the Darjeeling Himalayan Railway, the Nilgiri Mountain Railway, and the Kalka-Shimla Railways are listed as the world heritage railway sites by United Nations Educational, Scientific and Cultural Organization (Coulls, 1999).

Indian Railway is the world's largest monopoly state-owned enterprise (Roy & Kulshrestha, 2021). Railway is the life-line of the Indian economy's supply chain and is very important in connecting the length and breadth of the Indian subcontinent, from the states of Kashmir in the North to Kanyakumari in the South; from Arunachal Pradesh in the extreme East to Ahmedabad in the West; for transporting people and bulk material goods, but also are specially designed offering specialised theme based packaged tours for different religious and pilgrimage routes across the Indian states. India has centuries old religious heritage and is dotted with tangible cultural heritage religious/pilgrimage routes, monuments, and places of worship across the length and breadth of the country (Kumar & Singh, 2015).

According to Turner and Turner 1978 "a tourist is half a pilgrim, if a pilgrim is half a tourist" (p.20). This paper defines 'Railway Tourism' as an organised rail tourism pilgrimage packages along a specified religious route, using the railway transport from one destination to another giving the passengers on-train and off-train experience, with a combination of sightseeing at local historical pilgrimage sites, national parks, forts, shopping, and spiritual places combining it with rail, bus, and hotel stay for local sightseeing. India is a secular country representing different cultures, food, music, and people from diverse racial and spiritual orientations. In the last five years the Indian railways have embarked on an integrated strategy to reap the benefits from these cultural heritage and spiritual tourism related pilgrimage circuits/routes (Haq & Medhekar, 2013). Indian railways branding and innovative product development strategy in developing and launching special tourist train routes and journeys lasting form a week to three weeks packages under the Indian Railways brand of "Bharat Gaurav Tourist Trains" (BGTT) packages, literally translated as "Indian Glory Train" or Journey Celebrating India's Glory (https://www.irctctourism.com/bharatgaurav).

As India celebrates its 75th independence day, on the 15th of August 2023, the aim of the government was to develop new tourist rail-routes and launch the BGTT heritage pilgrimage circuits from the year 2022 onwards. Indian Railways BGTT are theme-based heritage pilgrim packages, which have different dimensions of tourist circuits covering cultural heritage, pilgrimage, spirituality, diverse geographical landscape, food, UNESCO heritage sites, holy rivers, and centuries old pilgrimage/religious routes for each state, appealing to the tastes and religious/spiritual orientation of different consumers. On one hand railway tourism circuits are used as a vehicle for peace and uniting the people of India given its religious diversity, and on the other hand as an economic development strategy to develop infrastructure facilities for the domestic tourists, increase inter-state connectivity, promote religious tourism, and create jobs in the railway, hospitality, and the spiritual tourism sector (Haq & Medhekar, 2013), for 66% of youth population in India, below the age of 35 (ILO, 2023). India is blessed with centuries old built heritage, spiritual places of worship, monuments surrounded by gardens, palaces and forts linked to the major religious and spiritual beliefs (Medhekar & Haq, 2009). Domestic tourism has matured in India post-pandemic since the launching of affordable special religious/pilgrimage tourism related train circuits/routes and packages mainly catering to Buddhist, Sikh, and Hindu religions, besides secular cultural heritage routes. The Indian government has spent $30 billion in 2021-22, an increase of 15% in the railway budget from the previous fiscal year for launching tourist trains. The government's tourism policy and the economic dimensions of BGTT pilgrimage packages with detailed itinerary for religious train tourism circuits/routes in India will be explored and analysed with the purpose to identify challenges for promoting pilgrimage tourism through specially built BGTT along the cultural heritage pilgrimage routes, fostering connectivity, social transformation, economics progress and prosperity in India.

The purpose of this chapter is: (i) To examine the Indian government's tourism policy to develop the organised religious pilgrimage train route packages. (ii) To explore the economic dimensions of "BGTT" pilgrimage routes with detailed packaged itinerary developed by the Indian railways for spiritual/religious tourism in India. (iii) To propose developing heritage pilgrimage tourist train circuits/routes for uniting Indian people, appreciate India's diversity and respect Indian secular nature of spirituality with the aim for internal domestic stability, economic progress, and prosperity via pilgrimage tourism routes. (iv) Identify and recommend a PPPs framework for "BGTT" circuit packages as vehicle for promoting pilgrimage tourism in the country. This paper aims to identity the Indian railways strategy as an innovative transformative heritage Pilgrimage journey celebrating India's Glory and creating economic development and employment opportunities in the railway hospitality and pilgrimage sector for the youth and the local communities for their sustainable future.

This chapter is structured as follows. The first section introduces the growing importance and significance of railway tourism route development. Section-2 provides the literature review on the economic dimension of railway special tourists trains for economic progress, specifically in case of India. Section-3 discusses the case study example in relation to theme based 'Bharat Gaurav Train' pilgrimage packages developed for promoting domestic and international tourism. Section-4 discusses the challenges and opportunities of reaping the economic benefits from developing these themes based pilgrimage routes. This is followed by discussions and recommendations for managerial and policy implications, conclusion and future research directions to advance the knowledge regarding the economic benefits of developing theme based pilgrimage train routes for revenue generation, economic development, employment opportunities and progress.

LITERATURE REVIEW

Economic Dimension of Railway Tourism

Railways all over the world have played a significant role in connecting places and people, bringing about socio-cultural and economic transformation. Development of railways for transporting freight, people and theme based tourist trains provides direct and indirect integrated economic development benefits to the regions having a significant multiplier effect on small and medium businesses, employment, output, and income (Astanakulov et al., 2022; Blanquart & Koning, 2017; Chakraborty, 2011; Choudhary, 2018; Hsiao-Hsien et al., 2021; Hvizdová, 2018; Kumar & Komaraiah, 2014; Wang et al., 2023). The 4 point vision-2020 of the Indian railways is to be (i) geographically and socially inclusive, (ii) strengthen national integration, (iii) generate large-scale employment opportunities and (iv) environmental sustainability to reduce carbon foot-print, besides introduce high-speed rail that is grounded, with low-grip transport system to reduce travel time, latest technology, augment capacity for freight and passenger services, telecommunication, adopt digitisation, world class safety and service quality, security, investment, introduce tourist trains and public-private partnerships (Ravi, 2019).

Railways have a significant economic dimension in providing socio-economic benefit to the regions it passes through and it is intertwined with pilgrimage tourism, (i) contributing to the Gross Domestic Product (GDP) in terms of revenue generation and profits from the sale of tickets, catering and diversified tourism pilgrimage packages. (ii) Pilgrimage tourism routes, creates employment opportunities in the railway products, catering, and related service sector supporting the pilgrimage routes. (iii) Railways connect mining and agriculture regions with markets and are a catalyst to drive industrial development, along the railway routes. (iv) Provides opportunities for small and medium business enterprises to develop gift/souvenir shops and fast food outlets on platform and within the vicinity of the railway stations such as hotel, restaurants, pharmacies, and shopping malls. (v) Railway routes broaden regional tourism development opportunities (rural, cultural, heritage, religious), (vi) increased revenue/income for the government, and (vii) appreciate land value and property near the railway station (Ali & Mir, 2018; Anand, 2012; Astanakulov et al., 2022; Blanquart & Koning, 2017; Budovich, 2023; Hsiao-Hsien et al., 2021; Ravi, 2019; Vukonic, 1998).

Blanquart and Koning (2017) conclude that besides the short-term economic effects of high speed railway trains on local production and tourism. The long-term cultural and socio-economic benefit from railways leads to an increase in mass tourism, growth of new infrastructure development, and relocation of businesses from the cities to the regions. However, their research findings conclude that there is greater variability as the economic impacts are conditional upon other factors such as city size, facilities, industry structures, and distance from the urban areas. Whereas study by Ravi (2019) for Asian Development Bank Institute on socio-economic development due to introduction of high-speed trains in India, concluded that it achieved economies of scale, employment creation, revenue generation, and profit for the railways suburban, medium-distance, enhanced communication technologies and for the passenger high-speed trains are faster, safer, comfortable, and affordable for millions of Indians. Cheng-Fei and Kuan-Yang (2017), explored through experts' opinion to determine the factors for attractiveness of on-board and off-board heritage railway tourism experience in Taiwan and that integrating rail-road tourism experiences provides diversified products and enhances the attractiveness of niche heritage railway tourism. The determinants identified for attractiveness of on-board/off-board heritage railway tourism experiences are- (i) tourism attractions along the railway route, (ii) accessibility to the railway station, (iii) facilities provided on-the railway station and in the train, and (iv) complementary on-board railway services like free-Wi-Fi, information, safety and security.

Bokov et al. (2022), very rightly mention that worldwide Railway *"Industry is showing clear signs of a renaissance, as evident by significant increase in service offerings"* Bokov et al. (2022, p.2179), in terms of organised tourism packages and new routes by railways to cater to demand of diverse groups of customers from different countries. Historically, railways are an important part of transport infrastructure for connecting remote villages, and for carrying bulk cargo of goods and resources from the mining towns to the industry or the seaports for export, supports development of iron and steel heavy industry, and also for intercity transportation of people daily for short-distance local travel and also long-distance tourism journeys, having a significant socio-economic impact to promote heritage, religious and pilgrimage tourism, which drives economic progress and prosperity of the country and has a positive spillover effects on the local regions it passes through (Blanquart & Koning, 2017; Bo Zhou & Ningqiao, 2017; Bokov et al., *2022;* Budovich, 2023; Gurita & Scortescu, 2023; Hvizdová, 2018; Piera et al., 2022; Sang & Lin, 2021; Sharma & Sharma, 2023; Vukonic, 1998).

Colin and Bird (2014) in their book provide a global perspective on niche Railway Heritage Tourism related issues and trends. The contributing chapter authors have highlighted the diversification of tourism by developing railway heritage tourism routes from the 1950's onwards in UK, Canada, Australia, and America. Alpu (2015) studies customer satisfaction derived from high-speed inter-city train services from Ankara to Istanbul in Turkey looking at service attributes of physical condition of the railway station, train, food services, information, and railway personnel behaviour. To measure Indian Railway Service Quality for ticketing, railway platform and on-board services Vanniarajan and Stephen (2008) identified and developed an instrument measuring three factors reliability, assurance, and empathy. Survey findings from a sample size 500, on Indian railways by Agarwal (2008) identified that customers were satisfied if the railway employer behaved politely with the customer at the point of service delivery.

Nandan (2010) study identified five determinants of passenger satisfaction on service quality at railway platforms in India, in order of importance refreshments, behavior towards passengers, efficient information system, basic facilities, and security. Singla (2015), has studied the perception of Indian tourists, about Indian railways service quality on customer satisfaction and found that the tourists are not satisfied with the railway facilities and services, as Indian railways caters to the needs of domestic Indian tourists from diverse income, religious backgrounds, and geographical areas. Kanimozh and Sherlin (2016) have examined the income generating role of the Indian railways in domestic tourism. However, Indian railway infrastructure needs to be maintained and developed for the safety of the passengers and positive travel experience. Kumar and Komaraiah (2015) have identified poor quality and quantity of Indian railway infrastructure, service quality and word-of-mouth from family and friends plays a significant role to attract foreign tourists. Therefore, in order to promote Indian railway tourism packages to foreign tourist, railway infrastructure needs to be maintained for safety and service quality.

Ali and Mir (2018) note that Indian railways have applied a pragmatic approach to reinvent and develop business in order to meet the socio-economic and environmental objectives of Sustainable Development, that meet the needs of the present generation, without compromising the needs of the future generations, and is more energy efficient than the road and air transport. They have further identified that in order to develop sustainable rail transport system, the ten fundamental requirements are required: (i) customer driven, (ii) affordable to all- social inclusion, (iii) create employment/employer of choice, (iv) Providing an start-end journey, (v) being carbon smart, (vi) energy efficient, (vii) reducing our environmental foot-print, (viii) supporting the other sectors of economy, (ix) optimum use of railway resources, and (x) being transparent and accountable in terms of revenue earned, profit, loss, efficiency, safety and security.

Sang and Lin (2021) have measured the customer satisfaction of Yunnan-Vietnam railway heritage tourism site based on five indicators from previous research: natural landscape, cultural character, transportation and facilities, safety, services, and the regions sustainable development. Their findings concluded that high value of satisfaction rating related to personal safety, staff services, railway technology, hospitality of locals, and regional sustainable development was experienced by the customers. Whilst lower rating was scored for enjoyment of exploring, environmental quality, accessibility by public transports, the comfort of train experience and related facilities (hotel, accommodation, restaurants, shopping). This indicates that the future of rail pilgrimage tourism depends on integrated urban planning around the railway station such as construction of all facilities required by the railway tourist hotels, transport, conservation and protection of railway relics and the natural environment having a positive socio-economic impact.

When it comes to the environment in order to reduce pollution impact on climate change, tourism by railways can achieves economies of scale by transporting 50,000 people in an hour compared to 2500 by a freeway-lane and is environmentally friendly as greenhouse gas emission is five time less than road transport (NSW Transport, 2023). For example, to transport 1000 people, one train with eight carriages are required, it is seven times safer than road per/kilometer per/passenger, reduces traffic congestion costs, noise pollution, and relief from rising fuel costs. Therefore, railway transport is more sustainable, cost and energy efficient, as the negative externality in terms of air, noise pollution, infrastructure damage, and accidents, is lower than using road transport.

Bešinović (2020), provides a systematic literature review of the impacts of disruptions and resilience on railways, and provides a research agenda for building resilience in the railway transport industry post-pandemic, which is essential for an efficient functioning of the society and the economy. Peira et al. (2022) have recently published a systematic literature review of railway tourism, linked with historic railway sites which are now abandoned and cultural sites in the town located nearby. Recent empirical study findings by Astanakulov et al. (2022), on socio-economic and environmental impact of religious/pilgrimage tourism in Turkey, highlight that government initiated integrated and diversified planned approach to developing pilgrimage tourism in Turkey not only optimized revenue for the government with strategic foreign direct investment but also led to sustainable development, employment, and economic prosperity of town resorts with pilgrim sites into tourism hubs. This approach is also supported by recent studies that development of religious tourism has positive economic benefits (Budovich, 2023; Hsiao-Hsien et al., 2021; Sharma & Sharma, 2023) and adopted by the Indian government by integrated tourism development with special themed based tourist trains for cultural heritage and religious/pilgrimage tourism, and using it as an engine of economic development, growth and revitalizing the regions.

Indian Railways and Tourism Policy

Subsidiary of the Indian Railways, called as Indian Railway Catering and Tourism Corporation (IRCTC) was established in 1999. Railways tourism development policies aim to promote domestic and also inbound-international tourism having a multiplier effect on other railway related supporting sectors of the economy, such as heritage religious/pilgrimage tourism packages, online reservation system and catering on-train, with base kitchen on key railway stations to cater to freshly cooked food for long-distance tourist trains (Kumar, 2016). As the Indian economy progresses and with growing middle class there is a tremendous increase in demand for affordable domestic tourism and special tourist train travel packages by diverse groups of consumers, such as school excursions, senior citizen, pilgrimage packages, diaspora descendants visiting India to connect with their roots, heritage, pilgrimage, overseas and domestic back-packers.

Indian railways also play a very important role for promoting Indian heritage and religious tourism to domestic and international travellers, through their '*Incredible India*' advertising campaigns (Kanimozhi & Sherlin, 2016; Kumar & Komaraiah, 2014). The Indian tourism policy has used famous Bollywood stars like Amir khan and Amitabh Bachan for advertising and promoting inbound tourism by its famous slogan in Sanskrit "*Athiti Devo Bhavah*", translated literally as "*Guest is God*". Indian railways promotes tourism by offering different promotional tourist packages, such as luxury trains like palace on Wheels and the Maharaja Express, and special theme-based tourist trains (heritage or spiritual), and charter train options. Dogra and Sharma (2020), assess the India's first luxury train 'Maharaja Express' by interviewing *n=83* railway employees and travel agents concerns about service and surveying *n=157* foreign tourist from 20 countries on their perspectives about the luxury train satisfaction and service quality.

Tourists from all over the world can now book online Indian Railways tourism packages, which also provide options for taxi, hotel, and air bookings on the online railway reservation platform (Jain & Gupta, 2012). Subramanian (2022) explored the adoption, and diffusion of technologies since the colonial times from railway development, rail engineering to telegraphic communication and present-day internet. To take advantage of the emerging internet related online business model and be competitive with other transport like airways and road the Indian Railways since 2008 adopted the internet-based communication technologies in every aspect of the railways, for online ticket reservation booking portal and secure e-payment facilities in order to manage the increasing volume of tourism demand and passenger traffic (Choudhary, 2018; Subramanian, 2022).

Themed Rail Pilgrimage Routes

Collins-Kreiner (2016), applies the product-life-cycle model and describes how pilgrimage tourism has gone through transformation to a holistic secular tourism, with religious tourism at the core. Whereas Polus et al. (2022), stress that three core elements connect tourism and pilgrimage in the 21st century- by (i) meaning, (ii) ritual, and (iii) transformation that the pilgrims go through after the spiritual journey with a purpose to perform ritual to gain an authentic experience, inner spiritual growth, and enlightenment. Special pilgrimage tourist train route packages, where passengers live on-board the train for a week or two and it provides them with unique heritage pilgrimage experience on/off-board the train journey. These trains are designed with all comforts and provide customer-oriented services as they get in a four to five-star hotel and much more with onboard dinning and off-board sightseeing tours by bus to cultural, heritage, and spiritual tourism sites with a combination of hotel accommodation. Organized tourism packages/itineraries by rail covering cultural and historical sites was developed in Russia being a vast country and by 1983, Russia had 1,600 railway tours. For example, Circum-Baikal railway and Luxury Imperial Russian Train which covered territories of present day five countries, aimed at wealthy Russians and foreign tourists (Bokov et al.,2022). Further Russian Heritage Railway company, which was founded in 2014, includes itineraries which cover abandoned heritage railway lines, stations, and local attractions. This results into preserving and conserving heritage sites and reaping the economic benefits from special interest niche railway tourism.

The importance and value of heritage railway tourism sites in Asia according to Sang and Lin (2021) depends on five factors: (i) railways colonial historical background, (ii) railway engineering technology used (horseshoe curve-U-turn line, loop/spiral line, loop, switchback/zig-zag line, and specially designed engines for mountain rail track, (iii) quality of landscape that the train passes. High landscape has higher value in terms of tourist attraction and socio-economic development. (iv) Railway architecture which includes local culture, history, railway station itself and geography. (v) Overall Railway heritage as a means of transporting people and goods, development of mining towns, agriculture, villages, and seaports connecting via, the railway lines played an important in transforming rural agricultural societies to modern industrial tourism towns. To develop theme-based spiritual pilgrimage railway circuits for different religions were proposed for India by Medhekar and Haq (2012) to target different customers as per their religious/spiritual orientation. Development and promotion of theme based spiritual and cultural heritage tourism railway circuit trains have a positive spill-over socio-cultural and economic impact on the other sectors of the economy such as, tour guides with multi-lingual skills and knowledge of local culture and history, hospitality, accommodation, local transport, and souvenir shops. Gurita and Scortescu, (2023) findings for religious tourism and sustainable development in Romania, also conclude that developing and improving infrastructure facilities can create favourable business environment for tourism development opportunities for the locals in hospitality, hotel, restaurant, shops, and improve quality of life and sustainable development.

Figure 1. Buddhist circuit

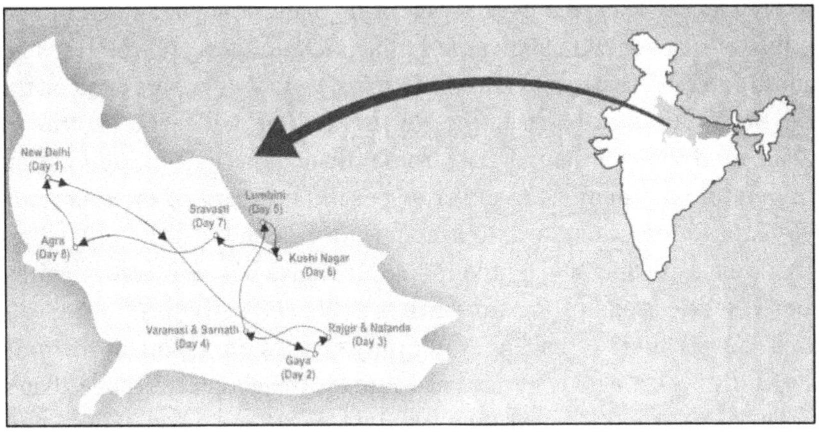

The first religious pilgrimage route developed by the Indian Railways, have different touristic and complementary dimensions such as the Buddhist Circuit Tourist Train (Figure-1) "Maha-parinirvan Express" was the first to be launched in 2007 solely by the Indian Railway Catering and Tourism Corporation (IRCTC) and Buddhist heritage sites including Buddha's birthplace, Lumbini in Nepal, taking the route from Delhi, Gaya, Nalanda, Sarnath, Kushinagar, Lumbini, Varanasi, Banaras, Agra, and Delhi.

This route not only takes the foot-steps of buddha but also brings the Buddhist pilgrims and researchers from Burma, Japan, Korea, Thailand, and other secular spiritual tourist in contact with other pilgrims, vegetarian food gastronomy and diverse nature and geography of the country that train passes through between the two states of Uttar Pradesh, Bihar, and bordering country Nepal (Medhekar & Haq, 2012; 2022).

CASE STUDY: INDIAN RAILWAY, TOURISM DEVELOPMENT, PROMOTION AND ECONOMY—BGTT- HERITAGE PILGRIMAGE TOURISM RAIL ROUTES

The Indian Government Railway Ministry has its own budget, which is separate to the central government budget. Railways have always played a significant role providing great value to the Indian economy contributing to the Gross Domestic Product (GDP), connecting places, tourism, providing society safe-travel options, and being environmentally sustainable due to lower carbon emissions and congestion costs. Indian railways have provided employment opportunities in the railways related industries, products, and services During the pandemic, the railways saw a decline in the domestic travel. Railway industry has been innovative in product development during the pandemic period and various pilgrimage tourism-based niche railway routes have been developed to promote domestic and international tourism. Significant investment has been made in the Indian railways in the last two years, developing new niche heritage pilgrimage tourism routes, tourism, and transport infrastructure.

A separate Bharat Gaurav train policy was approved on 23-November-2021, the Indian railways with the initiative of the central government have embarked on developing and identifying theme-based tourist circuits, in order to tap the extensive and rich tourism potential of India, with the brand name of 'Bharat Gaurav" (translated: The Pride of India) to promote domestic pilgrimage/secular heritage tourism under the banner of "Dekho Apna Desh" (translated: See Your Own Country), providing a holistic experience to the travellers. In 2022, the BGTT were fully operational and inaugurated and step-by-step tourism circuit trains were launched to showcase India's rich cultural and religious heritage places and monuments to domestic and international visitors. The first train was inaugurated on the 14th of July 2022 from Coimbatore in the South to Srinagar in the North. Most of the Bharat Gaurav train journeys start and terminate in Delhi, and some of them depart from railway junctions located within other states. The BGTT routes have multiple destinations to cover as per the itinerary of the tour and passengers board and deboard at particular destinations for sightseeing via bus and also hotel stay as required. Bharat Gaurav Tourist Train routes are operated by the Indian Railways in collaboration with the private operator providing on-board services and off-board tourism visits and activities.

The theme-based railway tourism packages not only creates employment for millions of people in India in the railway industry, but also generates revenue for the economy, given that the Indian railway budget is independent of the central government budget. Further, Indian railways also crates job opportunities in other sectors which support the railway industry such as tourism operators, travel agents, hospitality, hotels, local bus and taxi services, restaurant business, souvenirs shops and other shopping arcades and outlets located in and outside the railway station premises. The Indian railway offer wide range of themed-based religious/pilgrimage packages, ranging from one week to 21 days, and are operated on a revenue generating market demand-based business model and commercial viability of the circuit. These tarins are operated in partnership with Indian Railways Catering and Tourism Corporation Ltd. (IRCTC) and private service providers who run the packaged circuit itinerary and provide all on/off board services to the train-passengers.

The service providers have the flexibility to plan the pilgrimage themed itineraries for the BGTT circuit. The pilgrims experience all meals on board, dining and lounge carriages, rail restaurants, off-train tourism experience by bus to local heritage and pilgrimage sites, tour guides, hotel stay, travel insurance and transfers are covered in the packaged deal. The main aim is to promote affordable domestic tourism in particular (see your own country) and also to attract international tourists and Indian diaspora to explore their cultural roots and heritage, though BGTT heritage pilgrimage routes. The passengers also experience the diverse landscape of India from the windows, remote villages, and possible sighting of wildlife, besides those who travel to remember the past and have a nostalgic experience.

These Bharat Gaurav Theme Train inauguration was promoted on YouTube based on day-to-day itinerary and one could experience the journey virtually to get a taste of the various packaged heritage pilgrimage tours. Promotion and advertising niche BGTT pilgrims packages provides revenue, supports local business, and promotes cultural heritage and spiritual tourism of different religions in particular regions and states. Form the exterior the trains are highly decorative and colourful, with local Indian art painted on the trains, such as temples, dancing figures, and heritage temples and monuments. They have a mix of Sleeper AC/non/AC- third, second and first-class carriages. They contain 600-700 seats, pantry and kitchen on board serving regional cuisines in the rail restaurant, common area, library, boardgames, shoe-shine, room-service staff, electronic safe in each cabin, washroom, shower facilities, and CCTV cameras for security. Government has offered subsidy to the passengers travelling the pilgrimage route. The following examples of BGTT pilgrimage circuits promotion Figures (2, 3, 4 & 5) provides the Indian railway pilgrimage routes introduced in 2022, linked with Lord Rama, Shridi Saints footsteps, 9-Sikh temples, Goddess-Vishnodevi, Northern and Southern Indian heritage temples and pilgrimage circuits (IRCTC, 2023).

Figure 2. BGTT- Ramayana and Shridi Pilgrimage routes
Source: IRCTC Goodle Image

Figure 3. BGTT Guru Sikh Krupa and Shridi Saibaba train pilgrimage routes
Source: IRCTC - Goodle Image

Figure 4. BGTT: North India pilgrimage and south India pilgrimage
Source: IRCTC - Goodle Image

Figure 5. BGTT-Jyotirlinga Pilgrimage and Vaishno Devi Pilgrimage
Source: IRCTC - Goodle Map Image

Table -1 provide the names of the theme based Indian Railway circuits year of inauguration.

ECONOMIC DIMENSION OF HERITAGE PILGRIMAGE TRAIN CIRCUITS

Pilgrimage routes and railways in the contemporary world is intertwined. Economic benefits from pilgrimage tourism by railways, in terms of GDP and other indicators of employment generation are numerous, infrastructure development, services, freight, and passenger transport having a positives socio-economic and environmental positive spillover effect on all sectors of the economy related to the pilgrimage tourism. Railways are also socially beneficial, efficient, and inclusive, in being affordable in a populous country and connecting regional remote villages and towns. Railways help to unit and integrate the geographically, culturally, and a spiritually diverse country like India, suitable for long-distance travel at least cost, supports the development of industry and agriculture in the regions, but also promotes tourism activities by launching innovative special BGTT theme-based heritage pilgrimage packages. Indian Railways have reduced environmental impact such as fewer accidents, low congestion, carbon emission, and pollution costs, having positive health benefit and being socially responsible.

Opportunities

1. *Railway station Routes Revival and Restoration*: Abandoned railway heritage sites of India, railway tracks, and railway stations could be restored and partly converted to museums or railway restaurants of past years serving tradition foods. Similarly, railway stations in India across borders with neighbouring countries of Pakistan, Nepal, and Bangladesh could be restored and made operational to promote travel, tourism, and peace between countries as niche railway heritage pilgrimage tracks, covering Buddhist, Hindu, Islamic, and Sikh pilgrimage sites across borders, providing memorable nostalgic experience to train enthusiast and pilgrimage/religious tourists such as Kartarpur Sikh temple cross-border in Pakistan.
2. *Religious monuments and Railway infrastructure development and maintenance:* For the safety of the religious pilgrims and railway crew, it is essential to maintain, repair, and upgrade existing

Table 1. Theme based Indian railway train and Bharat Gaurav train circuits

	Rail Circuits	Start Year	Indian Railway Trains (Heritage Pilgrimage routes)
A	Palace on Wheels (Luxury train) Cultural Heritage	1982 8 days	Is a luxury train showcasing Rajasthan states royal heritage .The train was refurbished and relaunched in 2009 in partnership with Rajasthan Tourism Development Cooperation.
B	Maharaja Express (Luxury train) Cultural Heritage	2010 7 days	Luxury train equal to the Orient Express- covers the golden triangle route Mumbai, Udaipur, Jodhpur, Jaipur, Bikaner, Ranthambore, Agra, Delhi covering Rajasthan state and UNESCO world heritage sites. It is a joint venture by IRCTC and Cox & Kings travel agency.
C	The Golden Chariot (luxury) Cultural Heritage	2008 7 days	Pride of Karnataka state -Vijayanagar Kingdom taking the route from Bangalore to Goa, covering the heritage sites in the states of Kerala, Tamil Nadu, and Pondicherry.
D	Deccan Odyssey (Luxury) Heritage Pilgrimage	2004 8 days	This train is run by Maharashtra Tourism Development Coopetition, covering heritage and spiritual sites in Maharashtra's Konkan coast in Goa
E	Buddhist Rail Circuit Heritage Pilgrimage	2007 8 days	Buddhist pilgrimage sites, covering three Indian states and Lumbini in Nepal, the birthplace of Buddha www.irctcbuddhisttrain.com/ https://www.youtube.com/watch?v=IfMs5ni-STI
F	Bharat Darshan Heritage Pilgrimage	2016 14 days	Most affordable train starts form various states capital city covering the golden triangle and cultural spiritual pilgrimage heritage sites.
Bharat Gaurav Tourist Trains: Theme based train circuits started in 2022 Public-Private Partnerships			
1	BGTT: Karnataka - Heritage Pilgrimage	2022 8 days	Religious pilgrimage and heritage tourism temples in Karnataka state
2	BGTT: BabaSaheb Ambedkar Yatra Heritage Pilgrimage	2022 8 days	Visits religious places and Buddhist temple sites connected with Dr Ambedkar-writer of Indian constitution and fighting for the rights of socially backward class in India. (New Delhi, Mhow, Nagpur, Buddhist Sites of Gaya, Rajgir, Nalanda, and Sanchi)
3	BGTT: Royal Rajasthan Tour Heritage Pilgrimage	2022 12 days	Starting from Kolkata, and covering destination of Mount Abu, Ajmer, Bikaner, Chittorgarh, Jaipur, Jaisalmer, Jodhpur & Udaipur. Thes package covers cultural and religious pilgrimage sites.
4	BGTT: South Indian Hindu Temples Heritage Pilgrimage	2022 11 days	Visit South Indian key ancient temple sites – Kanyakumari, Madurai, Mallikarjun, Rameswaram and Tirupathi are heritage and religious pilgrimage route of famous ancient Hindu temples in South India.
5	BGTT: Ramayana express Heritage Pilgrimage	2022 18 days	Also known as Dekho Apna Desh (see your country) Ramayana Circuit, starting point Delhi covering many states and also connecting spiritual places linked with Lord-Ram, Ayodhya birthplace of God-Ram and Janakpur https://www.youtube.com/watch?v=5cAmEGPb8CY
6	BGTT: Guru Sikh Krupa Yatra Holiest Sikh 9 sites Heritage Pilgrimage	2022 10 days	This Sikh pilgrimage takes you to the 9 holiest Sikh shrines in India: Sri-Kesgarh Sahib (Lucknow); Sri-Kiratpur Sahib, Sri-Fatehgarh Sahib, Sri-Akal Takht (Amritsar);- Sri-Damdama Sahib (Bhatinda); Sri-Hazur Sahib (Nanded); Sri-Gurunanak Sahib (Bidar); Sri-Harmandirji Sahib (Patna), Sei-Hemkunt Sahid (Uttarakhand)
7	BGTT: Shridi Saibaba Pilgrimage	2022 5 days	Train runs along the western coast from Coimbatore to Shirdi covering the pilgrimage route of Shridi Saibaba - Tirupur, Salem, Dharmavaram, Mantrayalam, and Shridi
8	BGTT: Bharat Nepal Ashtha yatra- Heritage Pilgrimage	2023 10 days	This train starts from Punjab-Jallandhar train station and covers cultural and spiritual heritage sites of Ayodhya, Kathmandu, Varanasi, and Prayag Raj in Allahabad.
9	BGTT: Puri Ganga Sagar Bhavya Kashi Yatra-Heritage Pilgrimage	2023 10 days	Train starts from Indore and cover 6 most important spiritual destinations for the Hindus- Puri, Konark, Bhubaneswar, Kolkata, Deodar, Varanasi, and Ayodhya.

continued on following page

Table 1. Continued

	Rail Circuits	Start Year	Indian Railway Trains (Heritage Pilgrimage routes)
10	BGTT: Rameswaram Tirupati Dakshin Darshan Yatra	2023 10 days	Train starts from Indore and covers five spiritual destinations - Rameswaram, Tirupati, Madurai, Kanyakumari, and Thiruvananthapuram- with centuries old temples in South India.
11	BGTT: Punya Teerth Yatra - Heritage Pilgrimage	2023 12 days	Train starts from Kochuveli and Puri, Konark, Kolkata, Kashi, Gaya, Haridwar, Gaya, Sarnath, Varanasi, Ujjain, Ayodhya, and Allahabad.
12	BGTT: North- East Discovery Heritage Pilgrimage	2023 15 days	Train covers eastern states, starting from Guwahati, Sivasagar, Jorhat and Kaziranga in Assam; Unakoti, Agartala and Udaipur in Tripura; Dimapur and Kohima in Nagaland; Shillong and Cherapunji in Meghalaya, and Arunachal Pradesh.
13	BGTT: Garvi Gujarat Heritage Pilgrimage	2023 8 days	Train will depart from Delhi Safdarjung railway station. It will cover cultural heritage and spiritual sites of Gujarat state-Champaner, Somnath, Dwarka, Nanageshwar, Beyt Dwarka, Ahmedabad- heritage city, Modhera and Patan.
14	BGTT: Ayodhya Janakpur Heritage Pilgrimage	2023 7 days	Train will depart from Delhi Safdarjung railway station covering all heritage pilgrimage sites at Ayodhya, Janakpur (Nepal) Nandigram, Sitamarhi, Varanasi, and Prayagraj.
15	BGTT: Punya Kshetra Yatra Heritage Pilgrimage	2023 9 days	This train is for the two Telegu speaking states of Andhra Pradesh and Telangana. Train will depart from Secunderabad and cover most ancient key heritage and spiritual places in Eastern & Northern part - Puri, Konark, Gaya, Varanasi, Ayodhya and Prayagraj.
16	BGTT: Sainagar Shirdi Heritage Pilgrimage	2023 8 days	Southern Railway Bharat Gaurav train will depart from Madurai to spiritual places of Sainagar Shirdi and Pandharpur, Maharashtra state.
17	BGTT: Rampath Yatra Heritage Pilgrimage	2023 8 days	Starting from Pune and covering religious pilgrimage sites in Ayodhya, Chitrakoot, Jabalpur, Prayag, and Varanasi.
18	BGTT: SAAT (7) Jyotirlinga Darshan Yatra - Heritage Pilgrimage	2023 10 days	Train will start from Rajkot in Gujarat, and cover spiritual sites of Bhimshankar, Girshneshwar, Mahakaleshwar, Mallikarjun, Omkareshwar, Parli and Trambakeshwar
19	BGTT: Vaishno Devi Uttar Bharat Darshan Heritage Pilgrimage	2023 11 days	Starting from Kolkata and covering north Indian heritage spiritual pilgrimage sites of various Hindu and, Buddhist, and Sikh Gods from Agra, Ayodhya, Golden temple, Haridwar, Katra, Mathura, Rishikesh and Wagha border Sikh Temples.
20	BGTT: Jyotirlinga Dwarka-Shridi Yatra Heritage Pilgrimage	2023 11 days	Starting from Indore and covering heritage spiritual Aurangabad, Dwarka, Kevadiya, Nasik, Prabhati, Pune, Shridi and Somnath

Source: Indian Railways Catering and Tourism Corporation https://www.irctctourism.com/ https://www.irctctourism.com/bharatgaurav

religious places, infrastructure and develop new railway stations and pilgrimage routes for better connectivity for the religious tourists as railways are more environmentally friendly.

3. *Employment:* Railway stations and pilgrimage routes and places provides employment opportunities for millions of Indian youths off and on the pilgrimage routes for proving different types of services to the pilgrims. These jobs are highly specialised and can range from IRCTC pilgrims information desk, multi-lingual tour guides, souvenir shops, railway engineering, electrician, internet technology, catering, concierge services, platform services like ticketing, luggage handling, travel shops, disability wheel-chair support for pilgrims, health and hygiene, railway first-aid clinic with doctor and nurse, tourism information, to high top-level management and administration roles like finance, management, advertising and promotion.

4. *Revenue Generation:* Train services whether freight, people, or pilgrims tourist train packages generate income. Luxury, Pilgrims themed packages can be promoted to high income domestic as well as overseas pilgrims.
5. *Authorized Travel and Tourism Agents:* Indian railways has authorised travel and tourism agents/ operators who can sell BGTT luxury train tickets and heritage pilgrim/religious tourism packages. The authorised travel agents get a commission from 18-25% of each total ticket price, providing good returns to the travel agents and the luxury pilgrims theme train package service providers.
6. *Integrated restaurants, and other retail services:* BGTT pilgrim train package development provides opportunities for other integrated supporting services closer to the railway station for the pilgrims. For example, taxi and bus services, hotel, accommodation, restaurants, pharmacy, clinic, besides shopping for essential travel goods and souvenirs in the surrounding areas of the railway station.
7. *Railway museum and pilgrims souvenir shop:* Railway museums can be established at one end of the railway station with static display of the old equipment used, old trains and engines, names of station masters from early 1857 onwards when the different routes were introduced, railway memorabilia, pottery and cutlery used etc. steam engine ride and whistle to smell the coal on the premises of the railway station to capture the past experiences and nostalgia. For example, in Australia when passengers travel by the luxury train Ghan, from Darwin to Adelaide, there is a railway souvenir shop on and off train for the passengers.
8. *Developing rural and heritage pilgrimage routes:* Indian railways in partnership with rural farmers (growing grapes wine, sugarcane, dairy, fruits) and UNESCO and Indian Archaeological Society listed secular heritage religious pilgrimage sites, can be develop, and promote these niche secular spirituality pilgrimage routes.
9. *On-board Dining car contribution to diverse religious food:* The theme-based pilgrimage trains have the opportunity to hire specialises chefs in cuisines related to diverse religious events/festivals from different states in India, creating employment opportunities, and proving a unique religious gastronomic experience for the pilgrims.

Challenges

Demand for fast and low-cost freight and tourist transportation is growing in India. With rising middle class and large number of youth population, there is an increase in demand for domestic tourism. Therefore, innovative BGTT heritage pilgrimage packages related to other minority religions and sustained investment in railway infrastructure will help India to face the challenges of maintaining and developing efficient state-of-the-art, safe, and healthy railway services and infrastructure facilities to cater to the millions of domestic as well as foreign pilgrims /religious tourists.

The following challenges are faced by the Indian railways along the pilgrimage routes.

1. Regular maintenance of railway tracks and machines to prevent accidents.
2. Health and safety of the employees and pilgrims to prevent health emergency.
3. Land ownership and beautification around the railway property and pilgrim site.
4. Railways must take note of passengers complaints, reply promptly, and take actions to fix the issues, to provide better, reliable, and safe railway services and onboard-off-board pilgrimage experience. In order to retain customers, a customer relationship officers should be employed.

5. Fencing, maintaining gardens and planting trees along the track of the railway property. This not only provides better view to the passengers, but also can keep the railway tracks safe from vandalism. Development and maintenance of railway stations and railways surrounding property and land.
6. Effective railway human resources management practices and providing skills and training related to pilgrimage routes and religious tourism.
7. Regular maintenance and repair for safety of the pilgrims and staff, railway engines, locomotives, carriages, and infrastructure that support the building and operations of the railways must be serviced, maintained, and upgraded.
8. Financial planning for the railway budget, new rail tourism product development and branding project for innovative pilgrimage routes.
9. Different prices can be charged for different pilgrimage routes based on days on train, age, students, pensioners, disabled, armed forces personnels, group booking, peak/off-peak season and time, railway carriage category, distance, and value adding quality and authenticity of product life-cycle and innovative service.
10. It is important to integrate the services of railways with other service providers like taxi, bus, airways, and hotel booking with the railways bookings with IRCTC registered authorised agents, for pilgrims convenience.
11. Development of hotels, restaurants, shops selling essential travel goods pharmacies, medical facilities, railway clinic and accommodation services around the railway station for the convenience of the religious tourists.

The themed based religious pilgrimage train packages to be operational and profitable throughout the year with full booking capacity, must be advertised and promoted to low- and middle-income budget travellers, and also high income domestic as well as foreign tourists of northern and southern hemisphere, catering to every one's taste, income, and religious orientations.

DISCUSSION AND RECOMMENDATIONS

In a country like India with largest population in the world, short and long-distance trains are the cheapest way to travel safely and are also environmentally friendly, compared to road. Concerns regarding marketing cultural heritage and spiritual tourism are about the commercial profit motive purpose of the vendors but also commodification of cultural heritage and spirituality. Finney, Orwig, and Spake (2009) suggest that marketing should be "without causing offense for seeming overly commercial" (p.149). Pilgrimage and religious tourism promote religious motivation, though people also travel to religious destinations and places for various motives, to appreciate and respect various spiritual sites, for awareness about other culture, faith, heritage, spiritual education, knowledge, personal goals, meditation, secular outlook and for peace in the world (Haq & Medhekar, 2013). Pilgrims are taking a train trip to experience every aspect of on/off-board railway pilgrimage. Pilgrims satisfaction is likely to influence their positive word-of-mouth recommendation to family and friends to take the religious pilgrimage by Bharat Gaurav Tourist Trains Train routes.

This chapter recommends that besides providing BGTT religious tourism routes for mainstream Hindu, Sikhs, and Buddhist pilgrims, it is also important to showcase and cover other rich religious diversity related to religious heritage buildings and places for Sufi-Shrines, Mosques, Zoroastrianism Fire Temples, and Synagogues, in India for minority religions for example- Bahai, Bohra, Christianity, Islam, Judaism, Jainism, Sufism, and Zoroastrianism. There are centuries old places of worship belonging to minority religions of Judaism and Zoroastrianism who were persecuted in Iran and Iraq and given asylum in India. This will capture minority religious tourists and those who are secular to take the BGTT pilgrimage routes and attract domestic and foreign tourists from all over the world throughout the year for spiritual journey in India carting to their cultural heritage and spiritual orientation, taste, and preferences. Further, the following recommendations can be made to meet the future growth in demand for developing innovative long distance rail tourism routes for different tourism segments such as farm, cultural, heritage, and religious pilgrimage:

1. *Adopting internet communication technology*: Railways have also adopted technological change in terms of digitilisation and online booking facilities since Covid-19, to keep up with the airways competition and customer convenience. Online booking platform needs to be made user friendly, well integrated with other services bookings required by the tourists and internet free Wi-Fi facilities onboard the train.
2. *Maintaining and upgrading railway infrastructure:* To meet the future demand, rail infrastructure needs to be upgrade and maintained for safety of the employees and pilgrims to avoid any disastrous accidents.
3. *Developing new railway stations and routes: R*ailways could consider developing new railway stations to connect remote villages famous for its places of worship and pilgrim sites that it passes through, as this will have a positive multiplier effect and encourage small businesses to be established around the railway station and create employment opportunities for the locals in the railways and railway-station platform services and thus reduce rural to urban migration in search of jobs.
4. *Food safety:* Hygienic catering service from the train kitchen for fresh warm food, safe bottled drinking water and cold fridge facility is essential so that passengers do not fall sick on-board the train due to food poisoning.
5. *On-board train nursing staff and medical clinic:* Since the pandemic experience, in the long-distance passenger trains and Bharat Gaurav Tourist pilgrim theme-based Trains, it is also important to have a carriage for medical clinic with a doctor and two first-aid trained paramedic railway nurses (male and female for cultural sensitivity) and on-board travel essential goods, toiletry items and pharmacy shop with prescriptive and non-prescriptive medicines, first-aid for passengers requiring aspirin, fever tablet, or cough syrup and attending to any health emergencies on the train.
6. *Integrating transport services:* To meet the future demand, rail and road infrastructure needs to be integrated and well connected for transporting tourists and linking them to other local transport services like local trains, metro, bus, taxi, and airport services for convenience of the passengers.
7. *Skilled labour for railway jobs:* With an increase in demand for BGTT services, there will also be an increase in demand for skilled railway engineers, other levels of management skills, required such as front office, catering, railway security, multi-lingual tour guide, railway tourism pilgrims on-board/off-board information, and technology personnels to maintain digital online booking platform.

Figure 6. Public-private partnerships for Bharat Gaurav tourist train pilgrimage routes

Public-Private Partnerships For BGTT Pilgrimage Routes

1. Government
2. Indian Railways IRCTC
3. Tourism Department
4. IRCTC- BGTT Online Booking Platform for Pilgrim Packages
5. BGTT- Pilgrimage Tour Packages
6. Integrated Transport Services
7. Hotel and Hospitality
8. Private Providers on &off Board Train Services for BGTT Packages
9. Religious Organisations
10. Railway Safety & Security
11. Shopping and Souvenir
12. Health: First-Aid, Wheelchair Access, and Availability

8. *Enhanced customer experience:* Government, railway industry and its supporting private sector service providers for BGTT pilgrim routes, must work together to enhance customer/pilgrims experience from booking, rail travel, catering, to arrival at the destination and transport connectivity beyond rail journey.
9. *On-board souvenir shop:* The BGTT theme-based heritage pilgrims tourist trains have the opportunity to sell state specific handicraft, spiritual/religious souvenirs, similar to duty free shopping in the plane. The shop can be located in the lounge areas of the train, which is next to the dining car, as well as on the railway stations waiting room for BGTT- pilgrims/passengers.
10. *Railway track and onboard security:* Railway police and security on board BGTT for the passengers and the crew is important for security, sustainability and to prevent any accidents and deaths due to terrorism or poor maintenance of the railway tracks.
11. *Public-private partnerships*: All stakeholders- Government's railway and tourism department, private service providers, and minority religious representative should work together to improve pilgrimage railway services offering, and open new innovative pilgrimage routes for other minority religious places such as BGTT- Islamic, Jewish, Jains, and Zoroastrian heritage and pilgrim across India and adopt disruptive innovative technologies to improve rail efficiency. Figure 6 proposes a stakeholders public-private-partnership model for developing Bharat Gaurav Tourist Train- Heritage Pilgrimage Routes.

CONCLUSION

The social-economic benefits and opportunities are infinite and priceless, connecting people and places and promotes sustainable tourism development. Presently, the current model of Indian "Bharat Gaurav' Tourist Train packaged holidays are very suitable for high-end global and local tourists, which not only provides an economic benefit to the country, people, and places it passes through, but also a diverse geography and a rich cultural heritage experience. The challenges for the future of BGTT- heritage pilgrimage railway tourism route development is that government needs to diversify the pilgrimage tourism experience and provide as well as promote other minority pilgrimage routes and make it more affordable to all low/middle-income groups budget travellers in particular and to make it all inclusive.

Future research can explore with qualitative in-depth interviews tourist experience and satisfaction with the Bharat Gaurav Tourist Train pilgrimage journeys. In-depth interviews can also be conducted with the BGTT senior railway staff, registered travel agents, stakeholders, and on-board staff responsible for service delivery in the Bharat Gaurav Tourist Train. BGTT's service quality can also be measure through a quantitative survey applying service quality construct to measure pilgrims satisfaction, loyalty, quality of the product/service, reliability and responsibility of the staff and overall passenger experience on BGTT, between domestic and foreign tourists.

Furthermore, in terms of understanding the expectations and perceptions of BGTT pilgrimage packages the market demand from domestic and foreign tourists and the supply-side stakeholders can identify factors for developing, new products and pilgrimage routes to improve and market the Indian BGTT to potential train tourists. The socio-economic multiplier effect of BGTT pilgrimage circuit development on small and medium businesses, employment, output, and income can be studied for different pilgrim routes and compared to identify the success factors. This Indian model of BGTT cultural heritage and religious themes-based tourist trains can be developed in other developing countries of West Asia, Africa, Southeast Asia, and within the Indian subcontinent in partnership with neighbouring countries, like the BGTT-Buddhist Circuit is in partnership between India and Nepal, or Islamic, Hindu, and Sikh circuit with Pakistan. Themes based tourist train heritage pilgrimage routes development thus offers not only social, economic, and environmental benefits to the wider community but also promotes national integration, appreciation, understanding and and respect for all religions. Indian Railway Tourism BGTT need to continuously innovate and improve the product and service quality for pilgrims/religious tourist satisfaction and sustainability of the pilgrimage train routes.

REFERENCES

Agarwal, R. (2008). Public transportation and customer satisfaction: The case of Indian railways. *Global Business Review*, *9*(2), 257–272. doi:10.1177/097215090800900206

Ali, S., & Mir, A. A. (2018). The pragmatic approach of Indian railways in outlasting the sustainable development. *Journal of Management Research and Analysis*, *5*(1), 57–60.

Alpu, O. (2015). A methodology for evaluating satisfaction with high-speed train services: A case study in Turkey. *Transport Policy*, *44*, 151–157. doi:10.1016/j.tranpol.2015.08.004

Ananad, V. (2012). Socio-Economic Impacts in Pilgrimage Tourism. *International Journal of Multidisciplinary Research*, *2*(1), 329–343.

Astanakulov, O., Goyipnazarov, S., & Nasurova, K. (2022). The study of pilgrimage in aspects of the economy of tourism organization. *Economic Annals-XXI*, *200*(11-12), 42–54. doi:10.21003/ea.V200-07

Bešinović, N. (2020). Resilience in railway transport systems: A literature review and research agenda. *Transport Reviews*, *40*(4), 457–478. doi:10.1080/01441647.2020.1728419

Blanquart, C., & Koning, M. (2017). The local economic impacts brought by high-speed railways: Theories and facts. *European Transport Research Review*, *9*(12).

Budovich, L. S. (2023). The impact of religious tourism on the economy and tourism industry. *Hervormde Teologiese Studies*, *79*(1), a8607. doi:10.4102/hts.v79i1.8607

Bukov, M., Matveeva, N., Veretennikova, I., & Troittskaya, N. (2022). Formation of tourist trains on international and domestic routes. *Transportation Research Procedia*, *63*, 2179–2185. doi:10.1016/j.trpro.2022.06.245

Chakraborty, S. (2011). Developing an integrated tourism circuit in Gar Mandaran-Kamarpukur-Joyrambati in the state of West Bengal, India. *South Asian Journal of Tourism and Heritage*, *4*(1), 144–155.

Cheng-Fei, L., & Kuan-Yang, C. (2017). Exploring factors determining the attractiveness of railway tourism. *Journal of Travel & Tourism Marketing*, *34*(4), 461–474. doi:10.1080/10548408.2016.1182460

Choudhary, A. B. (2018). An Impact of Recent Technological Reforms in Indian Railways on its revenue and its Influence on the Passenger Satisfaction in Terms of Services. *International Journal of Innovative Technology and Exploring Engineering*, *8*(2S), 90–95.

Collins-Kreiner, N. (2016). The lifecycle of concepts: The case of 'Pilgrimage Tourism'. *Tourism Geographies*, *18*(3), 322–334. doi:10.1080/14616688.2016.1155077

Coulls, A. (1999). Railways as world heritage sites. *The World Heritage Convention*. Paris: ICOMOS.

Dogra, J., & Sharma, K. V. R. (2020). Assessment of Luxury Trains in India: A Case Study of Maharajas' Express. *Journal of Tourismology*, *6*(2), 185–200. doi:10.26650/jot.2020.6.2.0002

Gladstone, D. L. (2005). *From Pilgrimage to Package Tour*. Routledge.

Gurita, G., & Scortescu, F. (2023). Religious Tourism & Sustainable Development of the Economy in the Context of Globalization in the Northeast Area of Romania. *Sustainability (Basel), 15*(6), 12128. doi:10.3390u151612128

Haq, F., & Medhekar, A. (2013). Branding Spiritual Tourism as an Innovation for Peace between India and Pakistan. *International Journal of Social Entrepreneurship and Innovation*, *2*(5), 404–414. doi:10.1504/IJSEI.2013.059312

Hsiao-Hsien, H., Ying, L., Jao-Chuan, L., & Zhou-Fu, L. (2021). Research on the Development of Religious Tourism and the Sustainable Development of Rural Environment and Health. *International Journal of Environmental Research and Public Health, 18*(5), 2731. doi:10.3390/ijerph18052731 PMID:33800416

Hvizdová, E. (2018). Religious Tourism and its Socio-Economic Impact. *European Journal of Science and Theology*, *14*(2), 89–98.

International Labour Organisation (ILO). (2023). *Decent Work for Youth in India.* ILO. https://www.ilo.org/newdelhi/info/WCMS_175936/lang--en/index.htm

Jain, P., & Gupta, R. (2012). Trend Analysis of Online Tourism in Indian Railway. *HSB Research Review, 6*(2), 37-41.

Kanimozhi, S., & Sherlin, P.D. (2016). Role of Indian Railways in Tourism Industry. *Tourism and Travel Management*, 5(7), 69.

Kerr, I. J. (1995). *Building the Railways of the Raj.* Oxford University Press.

Kumar, A., & Singh, P. (2015). Cultural Heritage Tourism of Ayodhya-Faizabad. *The Geographer*, *62*(2), 66–74.

Kumar, R. G. (2016). *Indian Railway Catering &Tourism Corporation Ltd: A Force to Reckon with.* ResearchGate. https://www.researchgate.net/publication/339472624_Indian_Railway_Catering_and_Tourism_Corporation_Ltd_-A_Force_to_Reckon_with_Submitted_by_Force_to_Reckon_with

Kumar, V., & Komaraiah, J. B. (2014). Role of Indian Railways in Promotion of Tourism in India: A Case Study of Foreign Tourists. *Journal of the Humanities and Social Sciences*, *19*(1), 22–32. doi:10.9790/0837-19192232

Medhekar, A., & Haq, F. (2009). Growth of spiritual tourism in India: A public private partnership approach. *International Journal of Business Intelligence & Management*, *1*, 1–12.

Medhekar, A., & Haq, F. (2012). Development of Spiritual Tourism Circuits: The Case of India. *Journal of Global Business Review*, *2*(2), 212–218.

Medhekar, A., & Haq, F. (2022). Promoting Trade and economic relations via Buddhist Spiritual Tourism Circuit between India and Southeast Asia. In A. Medhekar & H. Kaur (Eds.), *Evaluating Trade and Economic Relations Between India and Southeast Asia* (pp. 167–185). IGI Global Publishing. doi:10.4018/978-1-7998-5774-7.ch009

Nandan, G. S. (2010). Determinant of customer satisfaction on service quality: A study of railway platforms in India. *Journal of Public Transportation*, *13*(1), 97–113. doi:10.5038/2375-0901.13.1.6

Peira, G., Guidice, A. L., & Miraglia, S. (2022). Railway and Tourism: A Systematic Literature Review. *Tourism and Hospitality*, *3*(1), 69–79. doi:10.3390/tourhosp3010005

Polus, R., Carr, N., & Walters, T. (2022). Conceptualizing the changing faces of pilgrimage through contemporary tourism. *International Journal of Sociology of Leisure*, *5*(3), 321–335. doi:10.100741978-022-00109-7

(2014). Railway Heritage and Tourism: Themes, Issues and Trends. InColin, M. V., & Bird, G. R. (Eds.), *Railway Heritage and Tourism: Global Perspective*. Channel View Publications.

Ravi, N. (2019). Speed and Socioeconomic Development: Influence of Indian Railways. *ADBI working paper series Number-952*. ABD. https://www.adb.org/sites/default/files/publication/503516/adbi-wp952.pdf

Roy, S., & Kulshrestha, M. (2021). Performance Assessment Study of Indian Railways- Case of Low Efficiencies in Large Government Monopoly. *Transportation Research Record: Journal of the Transportation Research Board*, *2675*(11), 1272–1284. doi:10.1177/03611981211025516

Sang, K., & Lin, G. (2021). A system for measuring the satisfaction of railway heritage tourism: The case of Yunnan–Vietnam Railway. *Environmental Research: Infrastructure and Sustainability*, *1*(015001), 015001. doi:10.1088/2634-4505/abf1cf

Sharma, R., & Sharma, P. (2023). Spiritual Tourism and its Impact on the Economy. *Academy of Marketing Studies Journal*, *7*(5), 1–15.

Singla, A. (2015). The Effect Of Perceived Service Quality On Customer Satisfaction In Indian Railways. *International Journal Of Research In Business Management, 3*.

Subramanian, R. (2022). Evolution and Diffusion of ICTs in the Indian Railways: A Historical Analysis. *Journal of International Technology and Information Management*, *31*(2), 4. doi:10.58729/1941-6679.1498

Transport NSW. (2023). *Why is rail travel a better choice for the environment?* Transport NSW. https://www.transport.nsw.gov.au/projects/environment-and-safety/sydney-trains-environment-and-sustainability/why-rail-travel-a

Turner, V., & Turner, E. (1978). Introduction: Pilgrimage as a limonoid phenomenon. In V. Turner & E. Turner (Eds.), *Image and Pilgrimage in Christian Culture* (pp. 1–39). Columbia University Press.

Vanniarajan, T., & Stephen, A. (2008). Railqual and passenger satisfaction: An empirical study in Southern railways. *Asia Pacific Business Review*, *4*(1), 64–75. doi:10.1177/097324700800400107

Vukonic, B. (1998). Religious Tourism: Economic values or an Empty Box? *Zagreb International Review of Economics & Business*, *1*(1), 83–94.

Weng, S. L., Suntikul, W., & Chen, Z. (2023). Tourism development and induced social change. *Annals of Tourism Research*, *4*(1), 100088. doi:10.1016/j.annale.2023.100088

Zhou, Bo., & Ningqiao, L. (2017). The impact of high-speed trains on regional tourism economies: Empirical evidence from China. *Tourism Economics*, *24*(2). 10.1177/1354816617749

ADDITIONAL READING

Chakraborty, V., & Dutta, S. (2022). Indian railway infrastructure systems: global comparison, challenges, and opportunities. *Proceedings of the Institute of Civil Engineering*. ICE Virtual Library. 10.1680/jsmic.22.00014

Geary, D. (2008). Destination enlightenment: Branding Buddhism and spiritual tourism in Bodhgaya, Bihar. *Anthropology Today*, *24*(3), 11–14. doi:10.1111/j.1467-8322.2008.00584.x

Prasad, R. (2012). Time-Sense': Railways and Temporality in Colonial India. *Modern Asian Studies*, *47*(4), 1252–1282. doi:10.1017/S0026749X11000527

Rizal, P., & Asokan, R. (2013). Role Of Transportation In Tourism Industry In Sikkim State, India. *International Journal of Innovative Research and Development*, 2.

KEY TERMS AND DEFINITIONS:

Heritage Tourism: The economics significance of heritage tourism is growing. It is defined as an activity where people visit to see or study, centuries old historical archaeological sites, monuments, cities, places of workshops, forts, railway stations, battlegrounds, and museums preserving heritage objects and artifacts.

National Unity: Railways can promote national unity in diversity in a country like India, with diverse languages, geography, and cultural practices. Railways special tourists trains can By connect the country and make it possible for people to experience diverse culture and heritage in different states in India.

Railway Tourism: Railway tourism describes the travel experience by train, which is slowing seeing the countryside pass by, experience onboard food, and at different destinations experience diverse geographical landscape, cultural heritage linked sites, monuments, places of worship, or going down memory lane in the past.

Social Transformation: Railway Tourism can drive and bring about a positive social change and transformation in the economies of the cities the train connects and passes through. For example, it induces regional development and development of infrastructure facilities, roads, hotels, restaurants, market for local artifacts, preserving/conserving local heritage sites, and numerous job opportunities for multilingual informed tour guides, security, bus drivers etc.

Spiritual Tourism: Visiting places of worship of different religions is defined as spiritual/religious/ or faith-based tourism. For example, pilgrims go for annual pilgrimage to Mecca in Saudi Arabia, Kumbh mela in India, Vatican in Rome, Lady of Fatima in Portugal.

Compilation of References

(2014). Railway Heritage and Tourism: Themes, Issues and Trends. InColin, M. V., & Bird, G. R. (Eds.), *Railway Heritage and Tourism: Global Perspective*. Channel View Publications.

Abad-Galzacorta, M., Guereno-Omil, B., Makua, A., Iriberri, J. L., & Santoma, R. (2016). Pilgrimage as tourism experience: The case of the Ignatian Way. *International Journal of Religious Tourism and Pilgrimage*, *4*(4), 48–66.

Abi Sen, A. A., Eassa, F. A., Jambi, K., & Yamin, M.AbiSen. (2018). Preserving privacy in internet of things: A survey. *International Journal of Information Technology : an Official Journal of Bharati Vidyapeeth's Institute of Computer Applications and Management*, *10*(2), 189–200. doi:10.100741870-018-0113-4

Abinales, P. N., & Amoroso, D. J. (2017). *State and Society in the Philippines*. Rowman & Littlefield.

Abrahamsen, N. (1985). Romanske kirkers orienteering og den magnetiske misvisning I 1100 tallet I Danmark. *Geoskrifter, 23*.

Abrahamsen, N. (1992). Evidence for church orientation by magnetic compass in twelfth-century Denmark. *Archaeometry*, *34*(2), 293–303. doi:10.1111/j.1475-4754.1992.tb00499.x

Abreu, L. (2014). *O poder e os pobres. As dinâmicas políticas e sociais da pobreza e da assistência em Portugal (séculos XVI-XVIII)*. Gradiva. https://www.academia.edu/8139032/ABREU_L_O_poder_e_os_pobres_As_din%C3%A2micas_pol%C3%ADticas_e_sociais_da_pobreza_e_da_assist%C3%AAncia_em_Portugal_s%C3%A9culos_XVI_XVIII_

Agarwal, R. (2008). Public transportation and customer satisfaction: The case of Indian railways. *Global Business Review*, *9*(2), 257–272. doi:10.1177/097215090800900206

Ahmad, N. M., Sohail, R., & Ahmad, M. M. (2022). Impact of Religious Tourism on the Development of Smokeless Industry in Pakistan. *Global Social Sciences Review*, *VII*(II), 77–89. doi:10.31703/gssr.2022(VII-II).08

Ahmed, M., Ahmed, S., & Abbas, R. (2022). Tourism in Pakistan, Challenges and Opportunities. *Journal of Social Sciences Review*, *2*(3), 130–137. doi:10.54183/jssr.v2i3.102

Akdeniz, E., & Erön, A. (2020). Evaluations of the temple ruins in Thyateira. *Anatolian Studies*, *23*, 159–192.

Alarcão, J. (2002). *O domínio Romano em Portugal*. Publicações Europa-América.

Albuquerque, M. C. B., Nascimento, F. G., & Nóbrega, W. R. M. (2023). Dialoguing with the concepts of Community-Based Tourism and Creative Tourism Cenário. Revista Interdisciplinar em Turismo e Território, Brasília, 11(1),

Ali, F., & Poon, J. (2010). Tourism and pilgrimage: Economic benefits and social costs. *Journal of Travel Research*, *49*(3), 302–317.

Ali, S., & Mir, A. A. (2018). The pragmatic approach of Indian railways in outlasting the sustainable development. *Journal of Management Research and Analysis*, *5*(1), 57–60.

Al-Jaberi, Z. A., & Hasan, S. A. (2022). Reviving the Cultural Route and Its Role in the Sustainability of Historical Areas-Kerbala as a Case Study. *International Journal of Sustainable Development and Planning*, *17*(6), 1737–1746. doi:10.18280/ijsdp.170607

Almuhrzi, H. (2020). Islamic tourism: Management of travel destinations. *Journal of Heritage Tourism*, *15*(4), 480–482. doi:10.1080/1743873X.2019.1658351

Almutairi, M. M., Yamin, M., Halikias, G., & Abi Sen, A. A. (2021). A framework for crowd management during COVID-19 with artificial intelligence. *Sustainability (Basel)*, *14*(1), 303. doi:10.3390u14010303

Alpu, O. (2015). A methodology for evaluating satisfaction with high-speed train services: A case study in Turkey. *Transport Policy*, *44*, 151–157. doi:10.1016/j.tranpol.2015.08.004

Al-Raddadi, R. M., Basyouni, M. H., Al-Asmari, A. K., Assiri, A. M., Al-Qahtani, A. A., Alanazi, K. H., Al-Hameed, F. M., Al-Omari, A. A., Balkhy, H. H., & Memish, Z. A. (2020). Pilgrimage and COVID-19: Mitigating risk of importation and transmission. *Journal of Travel Medicine*, *27*(5), taaa072.

Álvarez, F.-E., Hurtado, R., & Rivas, O. (1999). La economía de Dios: La construcción de un santuario cristiano según los *carmina natalicia* de Paulino de Nola. *Arys*, *2*, 275–300.

Amaro, S., Antunes, A., & Henriques, C. (2018). A closer look at Santiago de Compostela's pilgrims through the lens of motivations. *Tourism Management*, *64*, 271–280. doi:10.1016/j.tourman.2017.09.007

Amaro, S., Duarte, P., & Antunes, A. (2019). Determinants of intentions to use a pilgrimage app: A cross-cultural comparison. *International Journal of Religious Tourism and Pilgrimage*, *7*(2), 19–30.

Ambrósio, V. (2020). A shared pilgrimage road in Israel and palestine: From utopia to reality. [Scopus.]. *International Journal of Religious Tourism and Pilgrimage*, *8*(6), 48–58.

Ambrósio, V., & Fernandes, C. (2022). Assessing the Development of the Portuguese Way to Santiago in Times of Pandemic. *International Journal of Religious Tourism and Pilgrimage*, *9*(6). doi:10.21427/2qgp-8b75

Ambrósio, V., Fernandes, C., Silva, G., & Cabral, A. (2019). A conceptual model for assessing the level of development of Pilgrimage Routes. *International Journal of Religious Tourism and Pilgrimage*, *7*(2), 94–104.

Amigos de Tongobriga. (n.d). *Associação de amigos de tongobriga: Caminhos romanos e de peregrinação*. Amigos de Tongbriga. https://amigosdetongobriga.pt/caminhos-romanos-e-de-peregrinacao/

Ammon, R. Jr, & Fried, G. (1999). Crowd management practices. *Journal of Convention & Exhibition Management*, *1*(2-3), 119–150. doi:10.1300/J143v01n02_05

Ananad, V. (2012). Socio-Economic Impacts in Pilgrimage Tourism. *International Journal of Multidisciplinary Research*, *2*(1), 329–343.

Andaya, B. W., & Andaya, L. Y. (2015). *A history of early modern Southeast Asia, 1400-1830*. Cambridge University Press. doi:10.1017/CBO9781139051323

Andrén, A. (2011a). *Det Medeltida Gotland. En arkeologisk guidebok*. Historiska Media.

Andrén, A. (2011b). Kyrkor och gårder på Gotland. Svar til Tryggve Siltberg. *Fornvännen*, *106*, 232–235.

An, J., Wan Zainon, W. M. N., & Zainon, W. (2023). An interactive visualization of location-based reviews using word cloud and OpenStreetMap for tourism applications. *Spatial Information Research, 31*(2), 235–243. doi:10.100741324-022-00492-z

Argüelles, P. (2021). Peligros, inseguridades y problemas del viajero visigodo. *Espacio, Tiempo y Forma. Serie III, Historia Medieval,* (34), 15–36. doi:10.5944/etfiii.34.2021.28413

Arjomand, S. A. (2008). *The Turban for the Crown: The Islamic Revolution in Iran.* Oxford University Press.

Arquivo Distrital de Viseu. (2022). *Archive of Viseu.* Arquivo distrital de Viseu. https://digitarq.advis.arquivos.pt/

Arquivo Nacional Torre do Tombo. (n.d.-a). Memorias paroquiais. *Pindelo dos Milagres, 29*(175).

Arquivo Nacional Torre do Tombo. (n.d.-b). *Tribunal do Santo Ofício. Inquisição de Lisboa, proc. 660.* Inquisição de Lisboa.

Arsanjani, J. J., Mooney, P., Helbich, M., & Zipf, A. (2015). An Exploration of Future Patterns of the Contributions to OpenStreetMap and Development of a Contribution Index. *Transactions in GIS, 19*(6), 896–914. doi:10.1111/tgis.12139

Arshad, M. I., Iqbal, M. A., & Shahbaz, M. (2018). Pakistan tourism industry and challenges: A review. *Asia Pacific Journal of Tourism Research, 23*(2), 121–132. doi:10.1080/10941665.2017.1410192

Astanakulov, O., Goyipnazarov, S., & Nasurova, K. (2022). The study of pilgrimage in aspects of the economy of tourism organization. *Economic Annals-XXI, 200*(11-12), 42–54. doi:10.21003/ea.V200-07

ATLAS.ti. (2019). *Scientific Software Development GmbH [ATLAS.ti, version 8.4.26.0]* [Computer software]. https://atlasti.com

Auttarat, S., & Poonsukcharoen, N. (2022). A Spiritual Journey? Using Religious Storytelling to Enhance Tourism in Northern Thailand. *The International Journal of Religion and Spirituality in Society, 12*(2), 83–97. doi:10.18848/2154-8633/CGP/v12i02/83-97

Avcı, E. (2011). *Evaluation of the faith tourism potential of Izmir in terms of travel agencies.* (Thesis No. 312364) [Master's thesis, Adnan Menderes University]. YÖK National Thesis Center.

Avcı, E. (2020). Selçuk/Ephesus, the city where beliefs meet. Eda Avcı, Tolga Akcan & Devrim Ertürk (Eds.), An interdisciplinary view of a UNESCO city in Selçuk (pp. 21-36). Çizgi Bookstore.

Aydın, M. (2022). *History of religions with its main lines, history, belief and worship.* Ensar Publications.

Azevedo, P. (2021). The Ways of Saint James in Trás-Os-Montes and Alto Douro as an Example of Soft Tourism in Rural Areas. *European Countryside, 13*(2), 314–329. doi:10.2478/euco-2021-0020

Baas, J., Schotten, M., Plume, A., Côté, G., & Karimi, R. (2020). Scopus as a curated, high-quality bibliometric data source for academic research in quantitative science studies. *Quantitative Science Studies, 1*(1), 377–386. doi:10.1162/qss_a_00019

Babut E.-Ch. (1908). Paulin de Nole, Sulpice Sévère, Saint Martin. *Recherches de chronologie. Annales du Midi: revue archéologique, historique et philologique de la France méridionale, 20* (77), 18-44. doi:10.3406/anami.1908.6830

Babut E.-Ch. (1910). Paulin de Nole et Priscillien. *Revue d'histoire et de littérature religieuses, 1*, 97-130, 252-275.

Balcı, F. (2011). *An investigation on the relationship between psychological and subjective well-being and religious beliefs* [Master's thesis, Uludag University]. YÖK National Thesis Center.

Balducci, F. (2021). Is OpenStreetMap a good source of information for cultural statistics? The case of Italian museums. *Environment and Planning. B, Urban Analytics and City Science*, *48*(3), 503–520. doi:10.1177/2399808319876949

Baranaydın, F., & Baranaydın, D. (2019). Apocalyptic churches. *Academy Journal of Social Sciences*, *6*(17), 213–228.

Baranwal, A., Anand, A., Singh, R., Deka, M., Paul, A., Borgohain, S., & Roy, N. (2015). Managing the earth's biggest mass gathering event and wash conditions: Maha Kumbh mela (India). *PLoS Currents*, 7. doi:10.1371/currents.dis.e8b3053f40e774e7e3fdbe1bb50a130d PMID:25932345

Bari, M. W., & Khan, Q. (2020). Pakistan as a destination of religious tourism. In Global Development of Religious Tourism. IGI Global. doi:10.4018/978-1-7998-5792-1.ch001

Barlar, S. H. (2022). Romeras, Rameras, and Royals: Female Pilgrims on the Camino de Santiago in Medieval and Early Modern Spain. In Women and Pilgrimage (pp. 15–24). CABI International; Scopus. doi:10.1079/9781789249392.0002

Barman, N. (2022). Economic activities and commercial spaces in Philadelphia, a unique provincial city of Byzantium (XI-XIV centuries). *Journal of Medieval Studies*, *5*(2), 488–497.

Barroco, C., Antunes, J., & Amaro, S. (2011). Turismo em Espaço Rural: Tendências e Oportunidades. *Gestão de Bens Comuns e Desenvolvimento Regional Sustentável*, 666–683.

Basil, M. D. (2022). Understanding people's motivations for a long-distance hiking trip. *Leisure Studies*, *00*(00), 1–14. doi:10.1080/02614367.2022.2115108

Batisstón, D. (2006). *Mens nova me fateor:* Paulino de Nola, poeta cristiano. *Circe*, *10*(1), 59–73.

Bauman, Z. (1996). From pilgrim to tourist or a short history of identity. *Questions of cultural identity*, *1*, 18-36.

Bautista, J. (2006). The rebellion and the icon: Holy revolutions in the Philippines. *Asian Journal of Social Science*, *34*(2), 291–310. doi:10.1163/156853106777371166

Belhassen, Y., Caton, K., & Stewart, W. P. (2008). The search for authenticity in the pilgrim experience. *Annals of Tourism Research*, *35*(3), 668–689. doi:10.1016/j.annals.2008.03.007

Bendassolli, P. F. (2010). *Exploratory study on creative industries in Brazil and the state of São Paulo*. FGV. https://pesquisa-eaesp.fgv.br/publicacoes/gvp/estudo-exploratorio-sobre-industrias-criativas-no-brasil-e-no-estado-de-sao-paulo

Berardi, C. C. (2019). *Sul cammino di San Nicola e di San Michele*. Progedit.

Bernbaum, E. (2022). *Sacred mountains of the world*. Cambridge University Press. doi:10.1017/9781108873307

Berti, E. (2012). *Itinerari Culturali del Consiglio d'Europa tra ricerca di identità e progetto di paesaggio*. Firenze University Press. doi:10.36253/978-88-6655-142-3

Bešinović, N. (2020). Resilience in railway transport systems: A literature review and research agenda. *Transport Reviews*, *40*(4), 457–478. doi:10.1080/01441647.2020.1728419

Bhatta, K., & Ohe, Y. (2020). A Review of Quantitative Studies in Agritourism: The Implications for Developing Countries. *Tourism and Hospitality*, *1*(1), 1. Advance online publication. doi:10.3390/tourhosp1010003

Bianco, R. (2016). La Apulia nel camino de Santiago. Culto e iconografia di San Giacomo di Compostella in Apulia. *Ad Limina*, *7*, 83–112.

Biemer, J. R. (2021). *Our Environmental Handprints: Recover the Land, Reverse Global Warming, Reclaim the Future*. Rowman & Littlefield Publishers.

Bitton-Ashkelony, B. (2005). *Encountering the Sacred: The Debate on Christian Pilgrimage in Late Antiquity.* California Scholarship online. https://doi.org/ doi:10.1525/california/9780520241916.003.0002

Blackburn, A. M. (2007). Writing Buddhist histories from landscape and architecture: Sukhothai and Chiang Mai. *Buddhist Studies Review, 24*(2), 192–225. doi:10.1558/bsrv.v24i2.192

Blanquart, C., & Koning, M. (2017). The local economic impacts brought by high-speed railways: Theories and facts. *European Transport Research Review, 9*(12).

Blom, T., Nilsson, M., & Santos, X. (2016). The way to Santiago beyond Santiago. Fisterra and the pilgrimage's post-secular meaning. *European Journal of Tourism Research, 12*, 133–144. doi:10.54055/ejtr.v12i.217

Bona, K., Seongseop, K., & Brian, K. (2020). Religious tourism studies: Evolution, progress, and future prospects. *Tourism Recreation Research, 45*(2), 185–203. doi:10.1080/02508281.2019.1664084

Booth, A. D. (1982). Sur la data de naissance de Saint Paulin de Nole. *Echos du monde claassique: Classica views, XI* (1-1), 56-64.

Botella-Carrubi, D., Curras Mostoles, R., & Escrivá-Beltrán, M. (2019). Penyagolosa trails: From ancestral roads to sustainable ultra-trail race, between spirituality, nature, and sports. A case of study. *Sustainability (Basel), 11*(23), 6605. doi:10.3390u11236605

Bouvet, R. (1999). Journeys. In Z. Bernd (Ed.), *Dictionary of cultural mobilities: American journeys*. Editora da UFRGS.

Bowman, M., Johannsen, D., & Ohrvik, A. (2020). Reframing Pilgrimage in Northern Europe: Introduction to the Special Issue. *Numen, 67*(5-6), 439–452. doi:10.1163/15685276-12341597

Bowman, M., & Sepp, T. (2019). Caminoisation and Cathedrals: Replication, the heritagisation of religion, and the spiritualisation of heritage. *Religion, 49*(1), 74–98. doi:10.1080/0048721X.2018.1515325

Božić, S., & Tomić, N. (2016). Developing the cultural route evaluation model (CREM) and its application on the Trail of Roman Emperors. Serbia. *Tourism Management Perspectives, 17*, 26–35. doi:10.1016/j.tmp.2015.11.002

Brakke, D. (2001). Jewish flesh and Christian spirit in Athanasius of Alexandria. *Journal of Early Christian Studies, 9*(4), 453–481. doi:10.1353/earl.2001.0055

Branco, J. A. C. (2010). *Itinerário inédito do séc. XVIII dum caminho de santiago, com passagem por Ponte de Lima: Pontedelimacultural.pt.* https://pontedelimacultural.pt/Blog.asp?t=paginas&pid=2247&mpid=2246

Brandenburg, A., & Carroll, M. (1995). Your Place or Mine? The Effect of Place Creation on Environmental Values and Landscape Meanings. *Society & Natural Resources, 8*(5), 381–398. doi:10.1080/08941929509380931

Braun, A. (2021). Pilgering Researchers or Researching Pilgrims: Experiences from Four Student Projects on the Camino de Santiago 2016-2019. *International Journal of Religious Tourism and Pilgrimage, 9*(6), 109–116. https://api.elsevier.com/content/abstract/scopus_id/85127203717

Brendalsmo, J. (2006). *Kirkebygg og kirkebyggere (Ca. 1000 – 1600).* Unipub forlag.

Brouder, P., & Teixeira, R. (2012). Pilgrimage and tourism: Convergence, divergence and challenges. *Current Issues in Tourism, 15*(3), 195–210.

Brown, L. (2016). Tourism and pilgrimage: Paying homage to literary heroes. *International Journal of Tourism Research, 18*(2), 167–175. doi:10.1002/jtr.2043

Brown, P. (1985). *The Cult of the Saints: Its Rise and Function in Latin Christianity.* University of Chicago Press.

Brown, P. (2018). *El culto a los santos*. Ed. Sígueme.

Brumec, S., Lavrič, M., & Naterer, A. (2023). Examining Motivations to Walk the Camino de Santiago: A Typology of Pilgrims. *Pastoral Psychology*, *72*(4), 479–500. doi:10.100711089-023-01071-1

Brush, K. (2017). Medieval art through the camera lens: The photography of arthur kingsley porter and lucy wallace porter. *Visual Resources, 33*(3–4), 252–294. *Scopus*. Advance online publication. doi:10.1080/01973762.2017.1349623

Brush, K. (2018). Blazing 'the Way' Arthur Kingsley Porter's First Trip to Northern Spain (1920). [Scopus.]. *Ad Limina*, *9*(9), 225–245.

Budak, D. (2012). *Evaluation of the lives of saints and saints who lived in Anatolia in terms of the history of religions.* (Thesis No. 350764) [Master's thesis, Necmettin Erbakan University]. YÖK National Thesis Center.

Budhathoki, N. R., & Haythornthwaite, C. (2013). Motivation for Open Collaboration: Crowd and Community Models and the Case of OpenStreetMap. In American Behavioral Scientist, 57(5). doi:10.1177/0002764212469364

Budovich, L. S. (2023). The impact of religious tourism on the economy and tourism industry. *Hervormde Teologiese Studies*, *79*(1), a8607. doi:10.4102/hts.v79i1.8607

Bukov, M., Matveeva, N., Veretennikova, I., & Troittskaya, N. (2022). Formation of tourist trains on international and domestic routes. *Transportation Research Procedia*, *63*, 2179–2185. doi:10.1016/j.trpro.2022.06.245

Büssing, A., & Koenig, H. G. (2010). Spiritual needs of patients with chronic diseases. *Religions*, *1*(1), 18–27. doi:10.3390/rel1010018 PMID:20696636

Bustamante, A., Sebastia, L., & Onaindia, E. (2021). On the representativeness of openstreetmap for the evaluation of country tourism competitiveness. *ISPRS International Journal of Geo-Information*, *10*(5), 301. doi:10.3390/ijgi10050301

Buswell, R. E. Jr. (1992). *The Zen Monastic Experience: Buddhist Practice in Contemporary Korea*. Princeton University Press. doi:10.1515/9780691216102

Butler, A. (1750). *Live of the Saints.* (revised by P. Burns). Burns & Oates Search Press Limited (reed.1995).

Çakmak, T. F. (2014). *The place and importance of faith tourism in touristic destination marketing: The example of Göbekli Tepe.* [Master's thesis, Istanbul University]. YÖK National Thesis Center.

Caldo, C. (1990). Regione e cultura: la presenza religiosa in Piemonte. In C. Lanza Dematteis (Ed.), *Interpretare una regione. Geografa del Piemonte che cambia* (pp. 51–69). Ed. Libreria Cortina.

Campbell, J. M., Klugar, M., Ding, S., Carmody, D. P., Hakonsen, S. J., Jadotte, Y. T, & Munn, Z. (2015). Diagnostic test accuracy: Methods for systematic review and meta-analysis. *JBI Evidence Implementation*, *13*(3), 154–162. PMID:26355602

Cardia, G. (2018). Routes and itineraries as a means of contribution for sustainable tourism development. In V. Katsoni & K. Valander (Eds.), *Innovative approaches to tourism and leisure* (pp. 17–33). Springer Nature Switzerland., doi:10.1007/978-3-319-67603-6_2

Cardini, F., & Musarra, A. (2019). *Il grande racconto delle crociate*. Il Mulino.

Cardoso, L. (1758). *Memórias Paroquiais do padre Luís Cardoso ou Dicionário Geográfico.* Arquivo Nacional Torre do Tombo.

Carr, D. (2013). Pilgrimage Routes and the Cultivation of Virtue. *Journal of Moral Education*, *42*(3), 283–295.

Carter, H., Drury, J., & Amlôt, R. (2020). Social identity and intergroup relationships in the management of crowds during mass emergencies and disasters: Recommendations for emergency planners and responders. *Policing. Journal of Policy Practice*, *14*(4), 931–944.

Castro, J. B. (1753). *Roteiro Terrestre de Portugal. Mappa de Portugal Antigo e Moderno. Lisboa: Na off. Patricarcal de Francisco Luiz Ameno.*

Castro, B. L. (2010). El "Codex Calixtinus", primera guía del Camino de Santiago. *Cuadernos de la Cátedra de Patrimonio y Arte Navarro*, (5), 125–130.

Caucci von Saucken, P. (Ed.). (1999). Il mondo dei pellegrinaggi. Roma, Santiago, Gerusalemme. Jaca Book.

Caves, R. (2000). *Creative industries*. Harvard University Press.

Cazaux, F. (2011). To be a pilgrim: A contested identity on Saint James' Way. [Scopus.]. *Tourism (Zagreb)*, *59*(3), 353–367.

Cazzani, A., & Boriani, M. (2020). *The Role of Historic Roads to Preserve and Valorize the Landscape*. Cycling & Walking for Regional Development.

Chakraborty, S. (2011). Developing an integrated tourism circuit in Gar Mandaran-Kamarpukur-Joyrambati in the state of West Bengal, India. *South Asian Journal of Tourism and Heritage*, *4*(1), 144–155.

Chang, A. Y. P., Li, M., & Vincent, T. (2020). Development and validation of an experience scale for pilgrimage tourists. *Journal of Destination Marketing and Management, 15*(November 2019), 100400. doi:10.1016/j.jdmm.2019.100400

Che, D. (2013). The Journey is as Important as the Destination: Pilgrimage and Transformation. *Journal of Religion and Health*, *52*(3), 836–849.

Cheer, J. M., & Lew, A. A. (2017). Understanding tourism resilience: Adapting to social, political, and economic change. In J. M. Cheer, & A. A. Lew (Eds.). Tourism, resilience and sustainability: Adapting to social, political and economic change, (pp. 3-17). Routledge.

Chélini, J., & Branthomme, H. (2004). *Le vie di Dio. Storia dei pellegrinaggi cristiani dalle origini al Medioevo*. Jaca Book.

Chemin, J. E. (2016). Re-inventing Europe: The case of the Camino de Santiago de Compostela as European heritage and the political and economic discourses of cultural unity. *International Journal of Tourism Anthropology*, *5*(1–2), 24–46. 10.1504/IJTA.2016.076851

Cheng-Fei, L., & Kuan-Yang, C. (2017). Exploring factors determining the attractiveness of railway tourism. *Journal of Travel & Tourism Marketing*, *34*(4), 461–474. doi:10.1080/10548408.2016.1182460

Choe, J., & O'Regan, M. (2020). Faith manifest: Spiritual and mindfulness tourism in Chiang Mai, Thailand. *Religions*, *11*(4), 177. doi:10.3390/rel11040177

Choudhary, A. B. (2018). An Impact of Recent Technological Reforms in Indian Railways on its revenue and its Influence on the Passenger Satisfaction in Terms of Services. *International Journal of Innovative Technology and Exploring Engineering*, *8*(2S), 90–95.

Christian, W. A., Jr. (1972). *Person and God in a Spanish Valley*. Seminar Press.

Christie, J. J. (2006). Inca copacabana: A reconstruction from the perspective of the carved rocks. [Scopus.]. *Anthropos*, *101*(1), 179–201.

Cianca, J. (2019). Written by the Body: Early Christian Pilgrims as Sacred Placemakers. *International Journal of Religious Tourism and Pilgrimage*, *7*(1). Advance online publication. doi:10.21427/kam9-y363

Civil, Z. (2003). *Hajj in terms of the sociology of religion.* [Master's thesis, Marmara University]. YÖK National Thesis Center. Culture and Tourism Ministry. Laodicea Church. https://kvmgm.ktb.gov.tr/TR-157979/denizli-ili-laodikeia-kilisesi-koruma-ve-onarim-calismalarina-avrupa-birligi-kulturel-miraseuropa-nostra-awards-mansiyon-odulu-verildi.html Retrieved October 9, 2023.

Cohen, E. (1992). Pilgrimage and Tourism: Convergence and Divergence. In E. A. Morinis & V. W. Turner (Eds.), *Sacred Journeys: the anthropology of pilgrimage* (pp. 47–61). Greenwood Press.

Coleman, S., & Eade, J. (2004). *Reframing Pilgrimage. Cultures in Motion.* Routledge. doi:10.4324/9780203643693

Collins-Kreiner, N. (2010). Geographers and Pilgrimages: Changing Concepts in Pilgrimage Tourism Research. *Tijdschrift voor Economische en Sociale Geografie, 101*(4), 437–448. doi:10.1111/j.1467-9663.2009.00561.x

Collins-Kreiner, N. (2010). Researching pilgrimage: Continuity and transformations. *Annals of Tourism Research, 37*(2), 440–456. doi:10.1016/j.annals.2009.10.016

Collins-Kreiner, N. (2010). The Geography of Pilgrimage and Tourism: Transformations and Implications for Applied Geography. *Applied Geography (Sevenoaks, England), 20*(1), 153–164. doi:10.1016/j.apgeog.2009.02.001

Collins-Kreiner, N. (2016a). Dark tourism as/is pilgrimage. *Current Issues in Tourism, 19*(12), 1185–1189. doi:10.1080/13683500.2015.1078299

Collins-Kreiner, N. (2016b). The lifecycle of concepts: The case of 'pilgrimage tourism'. *Tourism Geographies, 18*(3), 322–334. doi:10.1080/14616688.2016.1155077

Collins-Kreiner, N. (2018). Pilgrimage-tourism: Common themes in different religions. *International Journal of Religious Tourism and Pilgrimage, 6*(1), 8–17. doi:10.21427/D73428

Collins-Kreiner, N., & Gatrell, J. D. (2006). Tourism, heritage and pilgrimage: The case of haifa's baha'i gardens. *Journal of Heritage Tourism, 1*(1), 32–50. doi:10.1080/17438730608668464

Corio, A. (2021). From cabestany to tuscany: Times and vectors of the artistic path of an 'itinerant' maestry. [Scopus.]. *Iconographica, 2021*, 38–48.

Cornell, V. J. (1998). *Realm of the Saint: Power and Authority in Moroccan Sufism.* University of Texas Press.

Cornford, J., Charles, D., Wood, P., Robson, L., Chatterton, P., & Belt, V. (2001). *Culture cluster mapping and analysis study Cluster study for One NorthEast.* One.

Coulls, A. (1999). Railways as world heritage sites. *The World Heritage Convention.* Paris: ICOMOS.

Courcelle, P. (1947). Paulin de Nole et saint Jérome. *REL, XXV*, 250–280.

Cozzo, P. (2021). *In cammino.* Carocci.

Culture and Tourism Ministry. (2023). *Pergamon Church.* MUZE. https://muze.gov.tr/muze-detay?SectionId=BAZ01&DistId=MRK

Culture and Tourism Ministry. (2023). *Philadelphia Church.* MANISA. https://manisa.ktb.gov.tr/TR-152050/incilde-adi-gecen-7-kiliseden-ucu.html

Culture and Tourism Ministry. (2023). *Sardis Church.* MANISA. https://manisa.ktb.gov.tr/TR-73017/artemis-mabedi.html

Culture and Tourism Ministry. (2023). *Thyateira Church.* https://www.kulturportali.gov.tr/turkiye/manisa/gezilecekyer/thyateira-akhisar-tepe-mezarligi Retrieved October 9, 2023.

Cunningham, S. (2002). From cultural to creative industries: theory, industry, and policy implications. *Culturelink, 102*.

da Costa, A. de J. (1959). *O bispo D. Pedro e a organização da diocese de Braga*. Faculdade de Letras da Universidade de Coimbra.

Dallai, L. (2004). From villa to monastery: Topography along the Gulf of Baratti and archaeological documentation on Poggio San Leonardo. *Archeologia Medievale, 31*, 433-440+559-560. Scopus.

Damari, C., & Mansfeld, Y. (2016). Reflections on pilgrims' identity, role and interplay with the pilgrimage environment. *Current Issues in Tourism, 19*(3), 199–222. doi:10.1080/13683500.2014.957660

Daniels, T. (2016). *Islamic spectrum in Java*. Routledge. doi:10.4324/9781315590059

de Cortázar, J. Á. G. (1994). *El hombre medieval como 'Homo Viator': Peregrinos y viajeros*. 11–30. https://dialnet.unirioja.es/servlet/articulo?codigo=554277

de Sousa, M. T., & da Rosa, A. P. (2017). Faith, entertainment, and conflicts on the camino de santiago (The way of St. James): A case study on the mediatization of the pilgrimage experience on facebook groups. *ESSACHESS - Journal for Communication Studies, 10*(2), 145–169.

de Sousa, M. T., & da Rosa, A. P. (2020). The mediatization of camino de santiago: Between the pilgrimage narrative and media circulation of the narrative. *Religions, 11*(10), 1–19. doi:10.3390/rel11100480

Debasa, A. M. C. (2009). La peregrinacion jacobea en la literatura árabe Medieval. *De Madrid al Camino. Boletín Informativo de La Asociación de Amigos de Los Caminos de Santiago de Madrid*, 8–11.

Deffontaines, P. (1948). *Géographie et religions*. Gallimard.

DeLuca, G., & Dwyer, L. (2014). Pilgrimage and cultural tourism: Benefits and challenges from a policy perspective. *Journal of Policy Research in Tourism, Leisure & Events, 6*(3), 281–297.

Demircan, Ş. (2014). *The importance of faith tourism in local development: The case of Midyat*. [Master's Thesis, Sıtkı Koçman University]. YÖK National Thesis Center.

Demircioğlu, A. (2020). Introducing the cities of Ghazali in the context of religious tourism. In Global Development of Religious Tourism. IGI Global. doi:10.4018/978-1-7998-5792-1.ch003

Department for Culture, Media and Sport (2005). *Creative industries mapping document*. DCMS. http://www.culture.gov.uk/Reference_library/Publications/archive_2001/ci_mapping_doc_2001.htm

Derin, H. (2004). *Worship in divine religions (the example of pilgrimage in Islam and its comparison with other religions)*. [Master's thesis, Uludağ University]. YÖK National Thesis Center.

Desmulliez, J. (2006). Paulin de Nole: Du gouverneur de Campanie à l'évêque de Nole, ruptures e continuités. *Cahiers du Centre Gustav Glotz, 17*(1), 267–275. doi:10.3406/ccgg.2006.915

Di Giovine Michael, A., & Elsner, J. (2016). Pilgrimage tourism. In H. Jafari Jafar and Xiao (Ed.), Encyclopedia of Tourism (pp. 722–724). Springer International Publishing. doi:10.1007/978-3-319-01384-8_146

Di Giovine, M. A., & Choe, J. (2019). Geographies of religion and spirituality: Pilgrimage beyond the 'officially' sacred. *Tourism Geographies, 21*(3), 361–383. doi:10.1080/14616688.2019.1625072

Digance, J. (2003). Pilgrimage at contested sites. *Annals of Tourism Research, 30*(1), 143–159. doi:10.1016/S0160-7383(02)00028-2

Dogra, J., & Sharma, K. V. R. (2020). Assessment of Luxury Trains in India: A Case Study of Maharajas' Express. *Journal of Tourismology*, *6*(2), 185–200. doi:10.26650/jot.2020.6.2.0002

Domingues Martinho, V. J. P. (2021). Dimensions of the Saint James' Way Pilgrimage: Portuguese Socioeconomic Impacts. *International Journal of Religious Tourism and Pilgrimage*, *9*(6), 12–25. doi:10.21427/95em-2y12

Dorrell, D. (2019). Using openstreetmap as a source of religious mapping data in an oer human geography textbook. In Open Educational Resources (OER) Pedagogy and Practices. doi:10.4018/978-1-7998-1200-5.ch006

Doswell, R. (2009). *Tourism: How effective management makes the difference*. Routledge. doi:10.4324/9780080519463

Downe-Wamboldt, R. N. (1992). Content analysis: Method, applications, and issues. *Health Care for Women International*, *13*(3), 313–321. doi:10.1080/07399339209516006 PMID:1399871

Doxtater, D. (1981). *The Symbolism, Structure and Politics of "Center" in the Old Scandinavian Farm Culture.* [Dissertation, University of Michigan, Ann Arbor].

Doxtater, D. (2007). A Report on Geopatterns Software: describing and analyzing large scale geometry between Chacoan and natural sites. In Digital Discovery (pp. 200–216). Exploring New Frontiers in Human Heritage., CAA 2006.

Doxtater, D. (2009). Rethinking the Sacred Landscape: Minoan Palaces in a Georitual Framework of Natural Features on Crete. Landscape Journal, 28(1), 1 – 21.

Doxtater, D. (2017) *Minnesota River Matrix: "non-discursive" alignments of immigrant churchyards on center lines in a New Norwegian Landscape*, ca 1870-1900 (unpublished manuscript).

Doxtater, D. (2021). Probabilities of designed locations of ceremonial foci: the Chaco Meridian, temple IV at Tikal, and a large-scale sacred Adena river landscape. *Time and Mind, 14*(2), 283-326.

Doxtater, D. (2023b). Land surveying in early medieval Norway: a St. Olav pilgrimage path as a means of creating an integrated Christian society in a Viking landscape? *Landscape esearch, 48*(3), 427-452.

Doxtater, D. (1984, Summer). Spatial Opposition in Non-Discursive Expression: Architecture as a Ritual Process. *Canadian Journal of Anthropology*, *4*(1), 1–17.

Doxtater, D. (1990). Socio-Political Change and Symbolic Space in Norwegian Farm Culture after the Reformation. In M. Turan (Ed.), Ethnoscapes Series: Vol. 4. *On Vernacular Architecture: Paradigms of environmental response*. Gower.

Doxtater, D. (2023a). Close mapping of St. Olav's Pilgrimage path through Gudbrandsdal Norway: Probabilities of a designed, land surveyed concept of a large-scale Christianized landscape. *International Journal of Religious Tourism and Pilgrimage*, *11*, 1.

Duarte, A. C. F. (2016). *Caminhos de Santiago: O Caminho Português como fator de desenvolvimento turístico no concelho de Barcelos* [Universidade do Porto]. https://repositorio-aberto.up.pt/handle/10216/87059

Duccio, D. (2005). *La filosofia del camminare*. Cortina Editore.

Dwyer, L., Forsyth, P., & Spurr, R. (2006). Economic dimensions of religious tourism. *Annals of Tourism Research*, *33*(3), 752–768. 10.1016/j.annals.2006.02.005

Dyas, D. (2020). *The Dynamics of Pilgrimage: Christianity, Holy Places, and Sensory Experience*. Routledge. doi:10.4324/9781003094968

Eade, J., & Sallnow, M. J. (1991). *Contesting the sacred: The anthropology of Christian pilgrimage*. Routledge.

Ebanista, C. (2007). Paolino di Nola e l'introduzione della campana in Occidente. *Dal fuoco all'aria. Tecniche, significati e prassi nell'uso delle campane dal Medioevo all'età Moderna*, a cura di Fabio Redi e Giovanna Petrella, 325-353.

Edelman, D. J. (2022). Managing the urban environment of Bangkok, Thailand. *Current Urban Studies*, *10*(1), 73–92. doi:10.4236/cus.2022.101005

Ehrlich, M. (2006). The route of the first crusade and the Frankish roads to Jerusalem during the 12th century. [Scopus.]. *Revue Biblique*, *2*, 263–283.

Ehrlich, M. (2008). The organization of space and hierarchy of cities in the royal latin of Jerusalem. [Scopus.]. *Cahiers de Civilisation Medievale*, *51*(3), 213–222.

Eide, O. (1974). *De Toskipeded Kirker i Oslo*. [Master's thesis, University of Bergen].

Eide, O. (1986). Om Kirkers Orientering. Arkeologiske skrifter. Bergen: Historisk Museum No. 3

Enderborg, B. (2015). "Tingstäde kyrka". Guteinfo.

Erbaş, A. (2002). Hajj in non-Islamic religions. *Sakarya University Faculty of Theology Journal*, *5*, 97–121.

Erdoğan, A. (2020). The ancient city of Smyrna (Bayrakli) in the Classical Period. Olcay Pullukçuoğlu Yapucu, Aylin Ü. Erdem & Aytekin Erdoğan (Eds.), A city in pursuit of the past: İzmir (pp. 17-29). Ege University Press.

Erdoğan, O. (2013). *Philadelphia / Alaşehir in the Middle Ages*. [Master's thesis, Akdeniz University]. YÖK National Thesis Center.

Esfahani, M., Musa, G., & Khoo, S. (2017). The influence of spirituality and physical activity level on responsible behaviour and mountaineering satisfaction on Mount Kinabalu, Borneo. *Current Issues in Tourism*, *20*(11), 1162–1185. doi:10.1080/13683500.2014.987733

Espòsito, A. (2009). The language of the Chanson de Sainte Foy: Why the Hispanic manner matters. *Romance Quarterly*, *56*(1), 21–32. *Scopus*. doi:10.3200/RQTR.56.1.21-32

Fabio, C., Gian, C., Anahita, M., Fabio, C., Gian, C., & Anahita, M. (2016). New Trends of Pilgrimage: Religion and Tourism, Authenticity and Innovation, Development and Intercultural Dialogue: Notes from the Diary of a Pilgrim of Santiago. *AIMS Geosciences*, *2*(2), 152–165. doi:10.3934/geosci.2016.2.152

Fabre, P. (1948). *Essai sur la chronologie de l'oeuvre de Saint Paulin de Nole*. Publications de la faculté des lettres de l'université de Strasbourg.

Fang, W. T. (2020). *Tourism in emerging economies*. Springer Singapore. doi:10.1007/978-981-15-2463-9

Faria, C. A. P., Remoaldo, P. C., & de Fátima da Silva Vieira Martins, M. (2022). Landscape and Senses in a Portuguese Municipality on the Way of St. James: Potential Impacts on the Well-Being of Pilgrims. *Journal of Religion and Health*. doi:10.100710943-022-01617-2 PMID:35925457

Farias, M., Coleman, T. J. III, Bartlett, J. E., Oviedo, L., Soares, P., Santos, T., & Bas, M. D. C. (2019). Atheists on the Santiago Way: Examining motivations to go on pilgrimage. *Sociology of Religion*, *80*(1), 28–44. doi:10.1093ocrelry019

Federación Española de Asociaciones de Amigos del Camino de Santiago. (2017, June). *Revista Peregrino, 171*, 32–50.

Federación española de asociaciones de amigos del camino de Santiago. (n.d.). *Hospitaleros voluntários*. Federación española de asociaciones de amigos del camino de Santiago. https://www.caminosantiago.org/cpperegrino/hospitaleros/hospitaleros.asp

Federal Emergency Management Agency (FEMA). (2013). *Special Events Contingency Planning for Public Safety Agencies*. Emergency Management Institute.

Federspiel, H. M. (2007). *Sultans, shamans, and saints: Islam and Muslims in Southeast Asia*. University of Hawaii Press.

Feldman, J. (2017). Key figure of mobility: The pilgrim. *Social Anthropology. Social Anthropology, 25*(1), 69–82. doi:10.1111/1469-8676.12378

Ferah, H. (2012). *Number symbolism in religions and folk beliefs*. [Master's thesis, Süleyman Demirel University]. YÖK National Thesis Center.

Fernandes, P. A. (2014). *Caminhos de Santiago*. Secretariado Nacional para os Bens Culturais da Igreja / Turismo de Portugal.

Fernandes, C., Pimenta, E., Gonçalves, F., & Rachao, S. (2012). A new research approach for religious tourism: The case study of the Portuguese route to Santiago. *International Journal of Tourism Policy, 4*(2), 83–94. doi:10.1504/IJTP.2012.048996

Fernández, B. M. C., González, R. C. L., & Lopez, L. (2016). Historic city, tourism performance and development: The balance of social behaviours in the city of Santiago de Compostela (Spain). *Tourism and Hospitality Research, 16*(3), 282–293. doi:10.1177/1467358415578473

Fernández, P. M., González, D. R., & Novello, S. (2013). Value added, authenticity and loyalty during the 2010 Xacobeo event: A tourists perception perspective. [Scopus.]. *Cuadernos de Turismo, 31*, 225–244.

Finlayson, C. C. (2012). Spaces of faith: Incorporating emotion and spirituality in geographic studies. *Environment & Planning A, 44*(7), 1763–1778. doi:10.1068/a44580

Flew, T. (2002). *Beyond ad hocery: defining creative industries*. In *Second International Conference on Cultural Policy Research*. New Zealand.

Flori, J. (2003). *La Guerra santa. La formazione dell'idea di crociata nell'Occidente cristiano*. Il Mulino.

Forlani, F., Picciotti, A., & Splendiani, S. (2023). Improving tourism resilience through Cultural Routes. An exploratory analysis of the Italian case "Via Francigena". *Turistica, 32*(1), 45–70.

Frend, W. H. C. (1969). Paulinus of Nola and the Last Century of the Western Empire. *Journal of Roman Studies, 59*(1/2), 1–11. doi:10.2307/299842

Fundación Sociedad y Cultura. (2010). *What do we mean by Creative Tourism?* Creative Tourism Network https://www.creativetourismnetwork.org/

Galliano, G. (2002). Per l'analisi del rapporto geografia-religione. La letteratura geografica. *Geotema, 18*, 3–31.

Galloway, S., & Dunlop, S. What is cultural about the creative industries? *International Journal of Cultural Policy, 13*(1), 17-31. https://www.researchgate.net/publication/29818307_A_Critique_of_Definitions_of_the_Cultural_and_Creative_Industries_in_Public_Policy

García de Cortázar, J. Á. (1994). El hombre medieval como 'Homo Viator': Peregrinos y viajeros. *IV Semana de Estudios Medievales: Nájera, 2 al 6 de agosto de 1993, 1994*. https://dialnet.unirioja.es/servlet/articulo?codigo=554277

García Ferrando, M. (2006). *Postmodernidad y deporte: Entre la individualización y la masificación: encuesta sobre hábitos deportivos de los españoles, 2005*. Centro de Investigaciones Sociológicas.

Garrod, B. (2008). Exploring place perception, a photo-based analysis. *Annals of Tourism Research, 35*(2), 381–401. doi:10.1016/j.annals.2007.09.004

Gayathri, H., Aparna, P. M., & Verma, A. (2017). A review of studies on understanding crowd dynamics in the context of crowd safety in mass religious gatherings. *International Journal of Disaster Risk Reduction, 25*, 82–91. doi:10.1016/j.ijdrr.2017.07.017

Geary, P. (1978). *Furta Sacra. Thefts of relics in the Middle Ages*. Princeton University. doi:10.1515/9781400820207

Geertz, C. (1975). *Islam Observed: Religious Development in Morocco and Indonesia*. University of Chicago Press.

Gehrke, J. M. (2021). The leadership pilgrimage: How a virtual pilgrimage transforms leaders. *International Journal of Religious Tourism and Pilgrimage, 9*(2), 55–62.

Gemzöe, L. (2016). Working the Way to Santiago de Compostela: Masculinities and Spiritualities of Capitalism. In L. Gemzöe, M.-L. Keinänen, & A. Maddrell (Eds.), *Contemporary Encounters in Gender and Religion: European Perspectives* (pp. 77–101). Springer International Publishing. doi:10.1007/978-3-319-42598-6_4

Genoni, P. (2011). The pilgrim's progress across time: Medievalism and modernity on the road to Santiago. *Studies in Travel Writing, 15*(2), 157–175. doi:10.1080/13645145.2011.565580

Gibelli, M. C. (2007). Piano strategico e pianificazione strategica: Un'integrazione necessaria. *Archivio di Studi Urbani e Regionali, 89*, 211–222.

Gil, A. C. (2010). *How to design research projects* (5th ed.). Atlas.

Gil, C., & Rodrigues, J. (2000). *Por caminhos de Santiago: Itinerários portugueses para compostela (3ª* (P. D. Quixote, Ed.).

Gladstone, D. L. (2005). *From Pilgrimage to Package Tour*. Routledge.

Gökdeniz, A. (1996). Religious travels in international tourism movements and Türkiye. *Anatolia, 7*(1), 101–103.

Goldsmith, R. C. (1940). *Paulinus´ Churches at Nola. Texts, translations, and commentary*. N.V. Noord-Hollandsche Uitgevers Maatschappij.

Gomes, L. E., & Florêncio, F. (2020). Os Caminhos Portugueses a Santiago de Compostela—Fragmentos Holísticos da Patrimonialização. *Antropologia Portuguesa, 37*(37), 37. doi:10.14195/2182-7982_37_2

Gonçalves, F. J. B., & Costa, C. (2020). Contribution of caminos de santiago to the sustainable development of tourism, in Barcelos | Contributo dos caminhos de santiago para o desenvolvimento sustentável do turismo, em Barcelos. *Journal of Tourism and Development, 2020*(34), 65–79.

González, R. C. L., Eade, J., & Carballo-Penela, A. (2021). Impacto socioeconómico dos itinerarios culturais: O Camiño de Santiago e outras rutas de peregrinación. *Revista Galega de Economía, 30*(3), 3. doi:10.15304/rge.30.3.7938

González, R. C. L., & López, L. (2012). El Camino de Santiago: Una aproximación a su carácter polisémico desde la geografía cultural y el turismo. *Documents d'Analisi Geografica, 58*(3), 3. doi:10.5565/rev/dag.6

Gonzalo, M. C. P., Angulo, A. D., & De Heredia, J. J. I. (2012). Touristic and territorial dimension of the "Ruta Norte" of the way of saint james in the basque country: Different ideas, valuations and proposals for management ofamultifaceted phenomenon [Dimensión territorial y turística de la ruta norte del camino de. *Boletín de la Asociación de Geógrafos Españoles, 58*, 177–474. https://www.scopus.com/inward/record.uri?eid=2-s2.0-84860490826&partnerID=40&md5=f9ee02592df435437649239efa3e908b

Griffe, E. (1966). *La Gaule chrétienne à l'époque romaine. T.II: Des origines chrétiennes a la fin du IVe siècle.* Nouvelle éd. Rev. Et Augm.

Grimaldi, F. (1993). *La Historia della chiesa di Santa Maria de Loreto.* Carilo.

Gündüz, Y. (2016). *Faith tourism in terms of cultural heritage: The case of Turkey* [Master's thesis, Istanbul University]. YÖK National Thesis Center.

Guriţă, D., & Scortescu, F. I. (2023). Religious Tourism and Sustainable Development of the Economy in the Context of Globalization in the Northeast Area of Romania. *Sustainability (Basel), 15*(16), 12128. doi:10.3390u151612128

Güzel, F. Ö. (2010). A new dynamic within the scope of touristic product diversification: Faith tourism. *Süleyman Demirel University Visionary Journal, 2*(2), 87–100.

Hall, K. R. (2010). *A history of early Southeast Asia: Maritime trade and societal development, 100–1500.* Rowman & Littlefield Publishers.

Hanegraaff, W. J. (1996). *New Age Religion and Western Culture: Esotericism in the Mirror of Secular Thought* (Vol. 72). Brill. https://brill.com/display/title/1474

Haq, F., & Medhekar, A. (2013). Branding Spiritual Tourism as an Innovation for Peace between India and Pakistan. *International Journal of Social Entrepreneurship and Innovation, 2*(5), 404–414. doi:10.1504/IJSEI.2013.059312

Harrison, V. (2006). The pragmatics of defining religion in a multi-cultural world. *International Journal for Philosophy of Religion, 59*(3), 133–152. doi:10.100711153-006-6961-z

Hartley, J. (2005). Creative industries. In J. Hartley. Creative industries (pp. 1-40). Blackwell.

Harwood, T. G., & Garry, T. (2003). An overview of content analysis. *The Marketing Review, 3*(4), 479–498. doi:10.1362/146934703771910080

Heart of the Nation Project Team. (2000). *Heart of the Nation: A cultural strategy for Aotearoa.* McDermott Miller.

Heelas, P. (1996). *The New Age Movement: The Celebration of the Self and the Sacralization of Modernity* (1st ed.). Blackwell Publishers.

Heidari, A., Yazdani, H. R., Saghafi, F., & Jalilvand, M. R. (2018). The perspective of religious and spiritual tourism research: A systematic mapping study. *Journal of Islamic Marketing, 9*(4), 747–798. doi:10.1108/JIMA-02-2017-0015

Herrero Pérez, N. (2011). La posmodernización de la tradición. Nuevos retos para la gestión del patrimonio. *Revista de Antropología Social, 20*(0), 293–307. doi:10.5209/rev_RASO.2011.v20.36270

Heyman, A. (2013). Sirens chanting in Auvergne- Velay: A story of exegetical pilgrimage on the via podiensis. [Scopus.]. *Ad Limina, 4*(4), 69–115.

Hill, P. C., & Pargament, K. I. (2003). Advances in the conceptualization and measurement of religion and spirituality: Implications for physical and mental health research. *The American Psychologist, 58*(1), 64–74. doi:10.1037/0003-066X.58.1.64 PMID:12674819

Hitchcock, M., & Teague, K. (Eds.). (2019). *Souvenirs: The Material Cultre of Tourism.* Routledge. doi:10.4324/9781315187457

Hoare, P. G., & Sweet, C. S. (2000). The orientation of early medieval churches in England. *Journal of Historical Geography, 26*(2), 162–173. doi:10.1006/jhge.2000.0210

Holt, J. C., & Kelley, L. C. (2018). Pilgrimage in Southeast Asia: Current Research and Future Directions. *Journal of Southeast Asian Studies*, *49*(1), 1–19.

Hortelano Mínguez, L. A., & Fernández Sangrador, L. (2022). Aportación del Camino de Santiago al desarrollo local: Características territoriales y repercusiones económicas en el tramo palentino. *Investigaciones Geográficas*, *2022*(78), 153. doi:10.14198/INGEO.19925

Howkins, J. (2005). The Mayor's Commission on the Creative Industries. In J. Hartley (Ed.), *Creative industries* (pp. 117–125). Blackwell. http://www.regional-studies-assoc.ac.uk/events/lisbon07/papers/Galloway.pdf

Hsiao-Hsien, H., Ying, L., Jao-Chuan, L., & Zhou-Fu, L. (2021). Research on the Development of Religious Tourism and the Sustainable Development of Rural Environment and Health. *International Journal of Environmental Research and Public Health*, *18*(5), 2731. doi:10.3390/ijerph18052731 PMID:33800416

Hui, E. K., & Tsui, B. Y. (2006). The role of religious coping and social support in the mental health of Hong Kong Chinese with lung cancer. *Psycho-Oncology*, *15*(8), 664–673. PMID:16302290

Hult De Geer, E (1935). Prehistoric Bulwark in Gotland Biochronologically Dated. *Geografiska Annaler*, *17*.

Hung, K., Yang, X., Wassler, P., Wang, D., Lin, P., & Liu, Z. (2017). Contesting the commercialization and sanctity of religious tourism in the Shaolin Monastery, China. *International Journal of Tourism Research*, *19*(2), 145–159. doi:10.1002/jtr.2093

Hvizdová, E. (2018). Religious Tourism and its Socio-Economic Impact. *European Journal of Science and Theology*, *14*(2), 89–98.

Hyde, K. F., & Harman, S. (2011). Motives for a secular pilgrimage to the Gallipoli battlefields. *Tourism Management*, *32*(6), 1343–1351. doi:10.1016/j.tourman.2011.01.008

Iglesias, F. R. (2007). *A grande obra dos Caminhos de Santiago: Iter Stellarum*. Hércules de Ediciones.

Iips. (2022a). *Potential of religious tourism in Pakistan*. https://iips.com.pk/potential-of-religious-tourism-in-pakistan/#:~:text=Challenges%20of%20Religious%20Tourism%20in%20Pakistan&text=inadequate%20infrastructure%20is%20one%20of,since%20there%20are%20limited%20resources

Iips. (2022b). *Religious tourism and its potential in Pakistan*. Iqbal Institute of Policy Studies – IIPS. https://iips.com.pk/religious-tourism-and-its-potential-in-pakistan/

Illiyas, F. T., Mani, S. K., Pradeepkumar, A. P., & Mohan, K. (2013). Human stampedes during religious festivals: A comparative review of mass gathering emergencies in India. *International Journal of Disaster Risk Reduction*, *5*, 10–18. doi:10.1016/j.ijdrr.2013.09.003

Imarisio, C. S. (2011). Il paesaggio e i segni della religione. Problemi di metodo e casi di studio. *Ambiente Società Territorio*, *56*, 17–21.

International Council on Monuments and Sites. (2008). Charter of Cultural Itineraries. In 16th General Assembly of ICOMOS. Québec.

International Labour Organisation (ILO). (2023). *Decent Work for Youth in India*. ILO. https://www.ilo.org/newdelhi/info/WCMS_175936/lang--en/index.htm

Irfan, E., & Ali, Y. (2020). Religious tourism in Pakistan: Scope, obstacles & strategies. *Journal of Convention & Event Tourism*, *22*(2), 134–154. doi:10.1080/15470148.2020.1852990

Irimiás, A., & Michalkó, G. (2013). Religious tourism in Hungary—An integrative framework. [Scopus.]. *Hungarian Geographical Bulletin*, *62*(2), 175–196.

Işık, B. (2022). *A study to determine the faith tourism potential of seven churches in the Aegean region within the scope of touristic product diversification.* [Master's thesis, Katip Celebi University]. YÖK National Thesis Center.

Ivakhiv, A. (2003). Orchestrating Sacred Space: Beyond the 'Social Construction' of Nature. *Journal for the Study of Religion, Nature and Culture*, *8*(1). doi:10.1558/ecotheology.v8i1.1642

Iversen, F. (2017). Tinget i Trøndelag i yngre jernalder og middelalder. *Gunneria*, *81*, 71–108.

Ivona, A. (2023). Network of saints, network of roads. Apulia crossroads of pilgrimages. In L. Lopez (Ed.), *Geography of world pilgrimages. Social, cultural and territorial perspectives* (pp. 53–75). Springer Nature Switzerland. doi:10.1007/978-3-031-32209-9_4

Ivona, A., & Privitera, D. (2022). L'attrattività dei piccoli borghi. La resilienza come strumento per una nuova centralità. *IL CAPITALE CULTURALE. Studies on the Value of Cultural Heritage*, *25*, 157–178. doi:10.13138/2039-2362/2836

Jackowski, A. (2000). Religious tourism-problems with terminology. *Peregrinus Cracoviensis*, *10*, 63–74.

Jafari, J., & Ritchie, J. R. B. (1981). Toward a framework for tourism education: Problems and prospects. *Annals of Tourism Research*, *8*(1), 13–34. doi:10.1016/0160-7383(81)90065-7

Jaguaribe, A. (2006). Creative industries. *Liberal portal*. http://www.portalliberal.com.br

Jain, P., & Gupta, R. (2012). Trend Analysis of Online Tourism in Indian Railway. *HSB Research Review*, *6*(2), 37-41.

Jeffcutt, P. (2000). Management and the creative industries. *Studies in Cultures, Organizations and Societies*, *6*(2), 123–127. doi:10.1080/10245280008523543

Jenkins, K., & Sun, K. C. Y. (2019). Digital Strategies for Building Spiritual Intimacy: Families on a "Wired" Camino. *Qualitative Sociology*, *42*(4), 567–585. doi:10.100711133-019-09432-0

Jenkins, W., & Chapple, C. (2011). Religion and Environment. *Annual Review of Environment and Resources*, *36*(1), 441–463. doi:10.1146/annurev-environ-042610-103728

Jensen, J. S. (2014). *What is religion?* Routledge Taylor and Francis Group.

Jimura, T. (2016). World heritage site management: A case study of sacred sites and pilgrimage routes in the Kii mountain range, Japan. *Journal of Heritage Tourism*, *11*(4), 382–394. doi:10.1080/1743873X.2016.1146287

Jokar Arsanjani, J., & Bakillah, M. (2015). Understanding the potential relationship between the socio-economic variables and contributions to OpenStreetMap. *International Journal of Digital Earth*, *8*(11), 861–876. doi:10.1080/17538947.2014.951081

Jones, A. H., Martindale, J. R., & Morris, J. (1971). The prosopography of the Later Roman Empire, Vol. I. (260-395 a. C.). Cambridge University Press.

Junqueira, L. D. M. (2018). *Creative processes in tourism: analysis of the gastronomy production chain from the perspective of UNESCO creative cities* [Doctoral dissertation, UNIVALI]. https://www.academia.edu/38286754/Processos_Criativos_no_Turismo_An%C3%A1lise_da_cadeia_produtiva_da_gastronomia_sob_a_perspectiva_das_cidades_criativas_Unesco?auto=downloadHYPERLINK "https://www.academia.edu/38286754/Processos_Criativos_no_Turismo_An%C3%A1lise_da_cadeia_produtiva_da_gastronomia_sob_a_perspectiva_das_cidades_criativas_Unesco?auto=download&campaign=weekly_digest"&HYPERLINK "https://www.academia.edu/38286754/Processos_Criativos_no_Turismo_An%C3%A1lise_da_cadeia_produtiva_da_gastronomia_sob_a_perspectiva_das_cidades_criativas_Unesco?auto=download&campaign=weekly_digest"campaign=weekly_digest

Kaçar, F., & Türker, N. (2020). A research on travel motivations and religious place perceptions of faith tourism visitors in the context of Hagia Sophia. *Journal of Tourism and Management*, *1*(1), 40–63.

Kanaujiya, A. K., & Tiwari, V. (2022a). Are mass gathering events hot spot for spreading of infectious diseases: The Kumbh Mela Experience. *Journal of Scientific and Industrial Research*, *81*(11), 1162–1172.

Kanaujiya, A. K., & Tiwari, V. (2022b). Crowd management and strategies for security and surveillance during the large mass gathering events: The Prayagraj Kumbh Mela 2019 Experience. *National Academy Science Letters*, *45*(3), 263–273. doi:10.100740009-022-01114-w PMID:35431383

Kanaujiya, A. K., & Tiwari, V. (2023a). The statistical analysis to find correlation between mass gathering event and COVID-19 pandemic outbreak: The Prayagraj Magh Mela 2021 experience. *Proceedings of the National Academy of Sciences. India. Section A, Physical Sciences*, *93*(1), 107–111. doi:10.100740010-022-00795-8

Kanaujiya, A. K., & Tiwari, V. (2023b). Water quality analysis of River Ganga and Yamuna using water quality index (WQI) during Kumbh Mela 2019, Prayagraj, India. *Environment, Development and Sustainability*, 1–22. doi:10.100710668-023-02907-9

Kanimozhi, S., & Sherlin, P.D. (2016). Role of Indian Railways in Tourism Industry. *Tourism and Travel Management*, 5(7), 69.

Kanthi, N. S., & Purwanto, T. H. (2016). Application of OpenStreetMap (OSM) to Support the Mapping Village in Indonesia. *IOP Conference Series: Earth and Environmental Science*. IOP Science. 10.1088/1755-1315/47/1/012003

Kartal, E. (2019). *Religious belief and meaning*. [Master's thesis, Yıldırım Beyazıt University]. YÖK National Thesis Center.

Karthika, P. S., Kedar, V., & Verma, A. (2022). A walk accessibility-based approach to assess crowd management in mass religious gatherings. *Journal of Transport Geography*, *104*, 103443. doi:10.1016/j.jtrangeo.2022.103443

Kartopu, A. (2009). *Different views on the definition of religion in the history of religions* [Master's thesis, Çukurova University]. YÖK National Thesis Center.

Kassa, T. T. (2020). *Emperor Constantine I and his place in the history of Christianity*. [Master's thesis, Uludag University]. YÖK National Thesis Center.

Kato, K., & Progano, R. N. (2017). Spiritual (walking) tourism as a foundation for sustainable destination development: Kumano-kodo pilgrimage, Wakayama, Japan. *Tourism Management Perspectives*, *24*, 243–251. doi:10.1016/j.tmp.2017.07.017

Kaza, S. (2005). *Pilgrimage in Japan: A Personal and Cultural Journey*. Stone Bridge Press.

Kerr, I. J. (1995). *Building the Railways of the Raj*. Oxford University Press.

Keser, Y. (2019). *The seven churches mentioned in St. John's book of Revelation and their archaeological condition from past to present.* [Master's thesis, Necmettin Erbakan University]. YÖK National Thesis Center.

Keyes, C. F. (2019). *Thailand: Buddhist kingdom as modern nation state.* Routledge. doi:10.4324/9780429308710

Kim, B., Kim, S. S., & King, B. (2016). The sacred and the profane: Identifying pilgrim traveler value orientations using means-end theory. *Tourism Management, 56*, 142–155. doi:10.1016/j.tourman.2016.04.003

Kim, H., Yilmaz, S., & Ahn, S. (2019). Motivational Landscape and Evolving Identity of a Route-Based Religious Tourism Space: A Case of Camino de Santiago. *Sustainability (Basel), 11*(13), 13. Advance online publication. doi:10.3390u11133547

Koenti, I. J. (2022). Disaster Management Using a Contingency Approach in the Special Region of Yogyakarta. *IOP Conference Series. Earth and Environmental Science, 1030*(1), 012017. doi:10.1088/1755-1315/1030/1/012017

Kong, L. (1990). Geography and Religion. Trends and Prospects. *Progress in Human Geography, 3*(3), 355–371. doi:10.1177/030913259001400302

Köse, S. (2019). *The social importance of pilgrimage.* (Thesis No. 602373) [Master's thesis, Ondokuz Mayıs University]. YÖK National Thesis Center.

Küçük, M. A. (2015). *Religious places in Turkey in terms of faith tourism (Example of Judaism and Christianity).* Berikan Publishing House.

Kumar, R. G. (2016). *Indian Railway Catering &Tourism Corporation Ltd: A Force to Reckon with.* Research Gate. https://www.researchgate.net/publication/339472624_Indian_Railway_Catering_and_Tourism_Corporation_Ltd_-A_Force_to_Reckon_with_Submitted_by_Force_to_Reckon_with

Kumar, A., & Singh, P. (2015). Cultural Heritage Tourism of Ayodhya-Faizabad. *The Geographer, 62*(2), 66–74.

Kumar, V., & Komaraiah, J. B. (2014). Role of Indian Railways in Promotion of Tourism in India: A Case Study of Foreign Tourists. *Journal of the Humanities and Social Sciences, 19*(1), 22–32. doi:10.9790/0837-19192232

Kunt, S. (2014). *The seven churches within the framework of St. John's book of Revelation and the place of these churches in the history of Christianity.* [Master's thesis, Ankara University]. YÖK National Thesis Center.

Kunt, S., & Güngör, A. İ. (2017). Seven churches within the framework of St. John's book of Revelation and the place of these churches in religious tourism in Türkiye. *Journal of Gazi University Faculty of Tourism, 1*, 71–92.

Kuran, A. (2010). *Sinan: The Grand Old Master of Ottoman Architecture.* Archetype Books.

Kurmanaliyeva, A., Rysbekova, S., Duissenbayeva, A., & Izmailov, I. (2014). Religious tourism as a sociocultural phenomenon of the present "The unique sense today is a universal value tomorrow. This is the way religions are created and values are made.". *Procedia: Social and Behavioral Sciences, 143*, 958–963. doi:10.1016/j.sbspro.2014.07.534

Lacarra y de Miguel, J. M. (1966). Las peregrinaciones a Santiago en la Edad Moderna. *Principe de Viana, 27*(102), 33–46.

Lagrange, F. (1881). Histoire de Saint Paulin de Nole. Librairie Pussiel frères.

Laksana, A. B. (2016). *Muslim and Catholic pilgrimage practices: Explorations through Java.* Routledge. doi:10.4324/9781315597034

Laterza, L. E. (2013). Culto mariano e percorsi di pellegrinaggio: La Madonna di Loreto in Apulia. *Ad Limina, 4*, 249–274.

Leadbeater, C. (2000). *Living on thin air: the new economy.* Viking/Penguin.

Lee, H. (2018). *The Nine Sacred Mountains of Korea: A Pilgrimage and Cultural History*. University of Washington Press.

Lefebvre, H. (1974). *La Production de l'espace*. Anthropos.

Lefeuvre, A. (1980). Religious tourism and pilgrimage: On the move. *Vatican City: Pontifical Commission on Migration and Tourism, 10*(30), 80–81.

Levine, G. J. (1986). The Geography of Religion. *Transactions of the Institute of British Geographers, 11*(4), 428–440. doi:10.2307/621934

Lienhard, J. T. (1977). *Paulinus of Nola and Early Western Monasticism. With a Study of the Chronology of His Works and an Annotated Bibliography, 1879-1976*. Peter Hanstein Verlag.

Lima, J., & Eusébio, M. C. (2010). A importância da segmentação do mercado turístico, de acordo com as despesas que os visitantes realizam no destino, para o desenvolvimento económico local: o caso da Covilhã. 1, 87–99.

Lindström, J. (1997). The Orientation of Ancient Monuments in Sweden: A Critique of Archaeoastronomy and an Alternative Interpretation. *Current Swedish Archaeology, 5*(1), 111–125. doi:10.37718/CSA.1997.08

Lindström, J. (2005). Påsk, höstblot och jul: Sambandet mellan årliga högtider och forntida gravars orienteering. *Fornvännen, 100*, 13–28.

Liro, J. (2023). The interdependencies of religious tourists' attributes and tourist satisfaction in the light of contemporary socio-cultural changes. *Current Issues in Tourism*, 1–5. doi:10.1080/13683500.2023.2214852

Liutikas, D. (2020). Management of Pilgrimages in Lithuania: Resources, Stakeholders and Projects. *International Journal of Religious Tourism and Pilgrimage, 8*(2). doi:10.21427/j8w8-cw12

Lois González, R. C. (2013). The Camino de Santiago and its contemporary renewal: Pilgrims, tourists and territorial identities. *Culture and Religion, 14*(1), 8–22. doi:10.1080/14755610.2012.756406

Lois González, R. C., Castro Fernández, B. M., & Lopez, L. (2016). From Sacred Place to Monumental Space: Mobility Along the Way to St. James. *Mobilities, 11*(5), 770–788. doi:10.1080/17450101.2015.1080528

Lois González, R. C., & Somoza Medina, J. (2003). Cultural tourism and urban management in northwestern Spain: The pilgrimage to Santiago de Compostela. *Tourism Geographies, 5*(4), 446–460. *Scopus*. doi:10.1080/1461668032000129164

Lois-González, R. C., & Somoza-Medina, X. (2022). The Necessary Digital Update of the Camino de Santiago. In Lecture Notes in Networks and Systems: Vol. 482 LNNS. Springer International Publishing. doi:10.1007/978-3-031-06825-6_26

Lois-González, R. C., Santos, X. M., & Romero, P. T. Z. (2018). The Camino de Santiago de Compostela: The most important historic pilgrimage way in Europe. In *Religious pilgrimage routes and trails: Sustainable development and management* (pp. 72–87). Cabi Digital Library. https://www.cabidigitallibrary.org/doi/10.1079/9781786390271.0072

Lois-González, R. C., & Santos, X. M. (2015). Tourists and pilgrims on their way to Santiago. Motives, Caminos and final destinations. *Journal of Tourism and Cultural Change, 13*(2), 149–164. doi:10.1080/14766825.2014.918985

Longo, L. (2008). Cammini d'Europa e "Via Francigena della Capitanata". In V. Vecchione, P. Pazienza, M. Russo, R. Infante, L. Longo, M. Del Giudice, & R. Guglielmi (Eds.), *LA VIA FRANCIGENA DELLA CAPITANATA* (pp. 38–49). Dipartimento di Scienze Economiche, Matematiche e Statistiche.

López, L. (2014). Riflessioni sullo spazio sacro: Il cammino di San Giacomo di Compostella (Spagna). *Rivista Geografica Italiana, 121*(3), 289–309.

Luik, E. (2012). Meaningful pain suffering and the narrative construction of pilgrimage experience on the Camino de Santiago. [Scopus.]. *Suomen Antropologi*, *37*(2), 24–43.

Lu, L., Wang, D., & Li, X. (2019). The economic impact of religious tourism: Evidence from the Chinese Tibetan Buddhist pilgrimage. *Journal of Travel Research*, *58*(7), 1242–1257.

Lundmark, E. (1925). *Tingstäde Kyrka*. A.B. Gunnar Tisells Tekniska Förlag.

Luz, N. (2020). Pilgrimage and religious tourism in Islam. *Annals of Tourism Research*, *82*, 102915. doi:10.1016/j.annals.2020.102915

MacCannell, D. (1976). *The tourist: A new theory of the leisure class*. Schocken.

Madrigal, M. (2017). *First Century Anatolian Churches*. Academia. https://www.academia.edu/42885860/B%C4%B0R%C4%B0NC%C4%B0_Y%C3%9CZYIL_ANADOLU_K%C4%B0L%C4%B0SELER%C4%B0. Retrieved August 4, 2023.

Madrigal, M. (2014). *First Century Anatolian Churches*. The Bible and Archeology.

Mafudi, M., Sugiarto, S., & Praptapa, A. (2021). Emerging Opportunities for Halal Tourism in Rural Areas: Insights from Indonesia. *Fokus Bisnis : Media Pengkajian Manajemen Dan Akuntansi*, *20*(1), 16–26. doi:10.32639/fokusbisnis.v10i1.726

Magalhães, V. L. (2011). O Hospital Novo da Misericórdia de Viseu. Assistência, poder e imagem. *Viseu: Santa Casa da Misericórdia de Viseu.*

Mair, J., & Whitford, M. (2013). An exploration of events research: Event topics, themes and emerging trends. *International Journal of Event and Festival Management*, *4*(1), 6–30. doi:10.1108/17582951311307485

Malis, J., Masilka, D., & Janeckova, K. (2023). The solo pilgrim phenomenon on the Journey to Santiago de Compostela in Spain. *Journal of Heritage Tourism*, *18*(5), 575–593. doi:10.1080/1743873X.2023.2201451

Mantas, V. G. (2014). Vías romanas e viagens transfronteiriças no século XVI. In M. C. Villalón (Ed.), *Viajes, viajeros y obra pública. Extremadura entre España y Portugal* (pp. 85–108). Universidad de Extremadura, Servicio de Publicaciones., https://dialnet.unirioja.es/servlet/articulo?codigo=5158678

Manzini, E. J. (2004). Semi-structured interviews: analysis of objectives and scripts. In Anais do Seminário Internacional sobre Pesquisa e Estudos Qualitativos. Bauru.

Mao, Y., & Liu, X. (2014). The systemic protection and utilization of ancient temples and pilgrimage roads in western suburbs of Beijing. *World Congr. Int. Fed. Landsc. Archit., IFLA*. Scopus. https://www.scopus.com/inward/record.uri?eid=2-s2.0-84954126191&partnerID=40&md5=a8bc8d0b4f6027013062910ba05e9b1f

Margry, P. J. (Ed.). (2008). *Shrines and pilgrimage in the modern world. New itineraries into the sacred*. Amsterdam University. doi:10.5117/9789089640116

Marquardt, J., & Delina, L. L. (2019). Reimagining energy futures: Contributions from community sustainable energy transitions in Thailand and the Philippines. *Energy Research & Social Science*, *49*, 91–102. doi:10.1016/j.erss.2018.10.028

Marques, J. (1997). Viajar em Portugal nos séculos XV e XVI. *História: revista da Faculdade de Letras da Universidade do Porto, 14*, 91–121.

Martella, C., Li, J., Conrado, C., & Vermeeren, A. (2017). On current crowd management practices and the need for increased situation awareness, prediction, and intervention. *Safety Science*, *91*, 381–393. doi:10.1016/j.ssci.2016.09.006

Martínez Muñoz, E., Escribano, J., & Pérez Cosín, J. V. (2019). El desarrollo local como satisfactor de salvaguarda del patrimonio rural en un contexto de inflación patrimonial: El caso de los peregrinos Les Useres (Castellón). *Revista PH: Instituto Andaluz del Patrimonio Histórico, 27*(98), 380–381. doi:10.33349/2019.98.4499

Martínez, J. (1973). Paulino de Nola e Hispania. [BIEH]. *Boletín del Instituto de Estudios Helénicos, V*(2), 27–33.

Martinho, V. J. P. D. (2022a). Bibliographic Coupling Links: Alternative Approaches to Carrying Out Systematic Reviews about Renewable and Sustainable Energy. *Environments (Basel, Switzerland), 9*(2), 2. doi:10.3390/environments9020028

Martinho, V. J. P. D. (2022c). Impacts of the COVID-19 Pandemic and the Russia–Ukraine Conflict on Land Use across the World. *Land (Basel), 11*(10), 10. doi:10.3390/land11101614

Martinho, V. J. P. D., Bartkiene, E., Djekic, I., Tarcea, M., Barić, I. C., Černelič-Bizjak, M., Szűcs, V., Sarcona, A., El-Kenawy, A., Ferreira, V., Klava, D., Korzeniowska, M., Vittadini, E., Leal, M., Bolhuis, D., Papageorgiou, M., & Guiné, R. P. F. (2022). Determinants of economic motivations for food choice: Insights for the understanding of consumer behaviour. *International Journal of Food Sciences and Nutrition, 73*(1), 127–139. doi:10.1080/09637486.2021.1939659 PMID:34148490

Martinho, V. J. P. D., & Nunes, J. (2020). Camino de Santiago: The routes in the region of Viseu. *Pasos (El Sauzal), 18*(3), 3. doi:10.25145/j.pasos.2020.18.025

MartinhoV. J. P. D.SerraA. B.DuqueE. (2017). Santuários católicos: O caso da Senhora dos Milagres em Pindelo dos Milagres. *Theologica, 52*(1–2). doi:10.34632/theologica.2017.44

Martinsson-Wallin, H., & Wehlin, J. (2017). Stones in the South: Decoding Bronze Age ritual practices on Gotland. *Current Swedish Archaeology, 25*(1), 227–256. doi:10.37718/CSA.2017.20

Masduki, A. (2018). Pilgrimage as a New Way to Define and Characterize the Sainthood. *DINIKA: Academic Journal of Islamic Studies, 3*(2), 221–238. doi:10.22515/dinika.v3i2.114

Matarrita-Cascante, D., Brennan, M. A., & Luloff, A. E. (2010). An exploratory study of the social impacts of agritourism in rural communities. *Journal of Sustainable Tourism, 18*(2), 145–155.

Matias, P. M. dos R. (2013). *Creative tourism: an approach to the Portuguese case* [Master dissertation, Instituto Universitário de Lisboa]. https://repositorio.iscte-iul.pt/bitstream/10071/8081/1/Tese%20Turismo%20Criativo.pdf

Matthews, J. M. (1975). Western Aristocracies and Imperial Court (364-425). Clarendon Press; Oxford University Press.

Medhekar, A., & Haq, F. (2009). Growth of spiritual tourism in India: A public private partnership approach. *International Journal of Business Intelligence & Management, 1*, 1–12.

Medhekar, A., & Haq, F. (2012). Development of Spiritual Tourism Circuits: The Case of India. *Journal of Global Business Review, 2*(2), 212–218.

Medhekar, A., & Haq, F. (2022). Promoting Trade and economic relations via Buddhist Spiritual Tourism Circuit between India and Southeast Asia. In A. Medhekar & H. Kaur (Eds.), *Evaluating Trade and Economic Relations Between India and Southeast Asia* (pp. 167–185). IGI Global Publishing. doi:10.4018/978-1-7998-5774-7.ch009

Mehrotra, R., Vera, F., Eck, D., Mehta, D., & Mehta, D. (2015). Kumbh Mela: mapping the ephemeral megacity. HatjeCantz, Harvard South Asia Institute.

Miles, S. (2017). Remembrance Trails of the Great War on the Western Front: Routes of heritage and memory. *Journal of Heritage Tourism, 12*(5), 441–451. doi:10.1080/1743873X.2016.1242589

Minayo, M. C. de S. (org.) (2009). Pesquisa social: teoria, método e criatividade (29th ed.). Vozes.

Minghini, M., & Frassinelli, F. (2019). OpenStreetMap history for intrinsic quality assessment: Is OSM up-to-date? *Open Geospatial Data. Software and Standards*, *4*(1), 9. doi:10.118640965-019-0067-x

Mobasheri, A., Zipf, A., & Francis, L. (2018). OpenStreetMap data quality enrichment through awareness raising and collective action tools—Experiences from a European project. *Geo-Spatial Information Science*, *21*(3), 234–246. doi: 10.1080/10095020.2018.1493817

Molins, M.-J. V. (1998). En torno a Riba Coa y Al-Andalus. *O Tratado de Alcanices e a Importância Histórica Das Terras de Riba-Côa. Atas Do Congresso Histórico Luso-Espanhol*, 131–152.

Mooney, P., Corcoran, P., & Winstanley, A. C. (2010). Towards quality metrics for OpenStreetMap. *Proceedings of the 18th SIGSPATIAL International Conference on Advances in Geographic Information Systems GIS 10*, (pp. 514–517). ACM. 10.1145/1869790.1869875

Moreno, H. B. (1986). Vias portuguesas de peregrinação a Santiago de Compostela na Idade Média. *História: revista da Faculdade de Letras da Universidade do Porto, 3*, 77–88.

Morillas, R. M., Plaza-Mejía, M. Á., & López-Guzmán, T. (2017). The impact of the Camino de Santiago on local economies: A case study of the French Way in Castilla y León. *Journal of Travel Research*, *56*(6), 726–740.

Morinis, A. (1992). *Sacred journeys: The anthropology of pilgrimage*. Westview Press.

Moscarelli, R. (2021). Slow tourism, public funding and economic development. A critical review on the case of the way of St. James in galicia. *Revista Galega de Economia*, *30*(3), 1–16. doi:10.15304/rge.30.3.7522

Moscarelli, R., Lopez, L., & Lois González, R. C. (2020). Who Is Interested in Developing the Way of Saint James? The Pilgrimage from Faith to Tourism. *Religions*, *11*(1), 1. doi:10.3390/rel11010024

Mratschek, S. H. (2002). Der Briefwechsel des Paulinus von Nola: Kommunikation und soziale Kontakte zwischen christlichen Intellektuellen, Hypomnemata 134. Vandenhoeck & Ruprecht.

Mratschek, S. H. (2001). Multis enim notissima est sanctitas loci: Paulinus and the gradual rise of Nola as a center of Christian hospitality. *Journal of Early Christian Studies*, *9*(4), 511–533. doi:10.1353/earl.2001.0059

Mróz, F. (2021). Poles travelling to Compostela in time and space. *Journal of Cultural Geography*, *38*(2), 206–234. do i:10.1080/08873631.2020.1864086

Mróz, F. (2021b). The Impact of COVID-19 on Pilgrimages and Religious Tourism in Europe During the First Six Months of the Pandemic. *Journal of Religion and Health*, *60*(2), 625–645. doi:10.100710943-021-01201-0 PMID:33611686

Mróz, F., Mróz, Ł., & Krogmann, A. (2019). Factors conditioning the creation and development of a network of Camino de Santiago routes in Visegrád group countries. *International Journal of Religious Tourism and Pilgrimage*, *7*(5), 56–71.

Município de Chaves. (2022). *Caminho Português Interior de Santiago*. Chaves. https://www.chaves.pt/pages/223

Murphy, L. J. (2018). Processes of religious change in late iron age Gotland-rereading, spatialization and enculturation. In Boulton, Hawkes & Stoner (Eds) Place and Space in the Medieval World. Routledge, pg. 32 – 46.

Murray, M., & Graham, B. (1997). Exploring the dialectics of route-based tourism: The Camino de Santiago. *Tourism Management*, *18*(8), 513–524. doi:10.1016/S0261-5177(97)00075-7

Musti, D. (1988). *Strabone e la Magna Grecia: città e popoli dell'Italia antica*. Ed. Programma.

Myrberg, N. (2009). An island in the middle of an island: on cult, laws and authority in Viking Age Gotland. In Regner, Kitzler, and Kjellström (Eds) From Ephesos to Dalcarlia. Reflections on Body, Space and Time in Medieval and Early Modern Europe. The Museum of National Antiquities, Stockholm. Studies 11, Stockholm Studies in Archaeology 48. Pg. 101 – 118.

Nandan, G. S. (2010). Determinant of customer satisfaction on service quality: A study of railway platforms in India. *Journal of Public Transportation, 13*(1), 97–113. doi:10.5038/2375-0901.13.1.6

Nickerson, R. C., & Eng, J. (2017). Use of mobile technology and smartphone apps on the Camino de Santiago: A Comparison of American and European Pilgrims. *Atas Da Conferencia Da Associacao Portuguesa de Sistemas de Informacao, 17*, 260–269. doi:10.18803/capsi.v17.260-269

Nilsson, M., & Tesfahuney, M. (2016). Performing the "post-secular" in Santiago de Compostela. *Annals of Tourism Research, 57*, 18–30. doi:10.1016/j.annals.2015.11.001

Nolan, M. L., & Nolan, S. (2018). *Christian pilgrimage in modern Western Europe*. UNC Press Books.

Norman, A., & Cusack, C. M. (Eds.). (2015). *Religion, pilgrimage and tourism*. Routledge.

Northcott, M. S. (2022). *God and Gaia: Science, Religion and Ethics on a Living Planet*. Taylor & Francis. doi:10.4324/9781003110750

Nyaupane, G. P., Timothy, D. J., & Poudel, S. (2015). Understanding tourists in religious destinations: A social distance perspective. *Tourism Management, 48*, 343–353. doi:10.1016/j.tourman.2014.12.009

O'Connor, J. (2006). *The definition of cultural industries*. Manchester Metropolitan University. http://www.pedrobendassolli.com/pesquisa/icc1.pdf

O'Mara, S. (2021). Biopsychosocial Functions of Human Walking and Adherence to Behaviourally Demanding Belief Systems: A Narrative Review. *Frontiers in Psychology, 12*, 654122. doi:10.3389/fpsyg.2021.654122 PMID:34421710

Oficina de Acogida al Peregrino Catedral de Santiago. (2021). *La Peregrinación a Santiago en 2021*. Oficina de Acogida al Peregrino Catedral de Santiago.

Oficina de Acogida al Peregrino. (2023). *Oficina del Peregrino | Catedral de Santiago de Compostela*. https://oficinadelperegrino.com/

Oficina de Acogida del Peregrino. (2019). *Statistics*. Oficina del Peregrino. https://oficinadelperegrino.com/estadisticas/

Olcay, A., & Albuz, N. (2016). Faith tourism and its contribution to the promotion of Turkey. Mehmet Özdemir (Ed.), Media and Türkiye in international promotion (pp. 199-229). Dora Publishing House.

Oliveira, J. N. (2002). *A Beira Alta de 1700 a 1840 gentes e subsistências*. Palimage Editores.

Olsen, D. H., & Timothy, D. J. (2006). Tourism and religious journeys. In *Tourism, religion and spiritual journeys* (pp. 1–21). Routledge.

Olsen, D. H., Trono, A., & Fidgeon, P. R. (2018). Pilgrimage trails and routes: the journey from the past to the present. In D. H. Olsen & A. Trono (Eds.), *Religious pilgrimage routes and trails: Sustainable development and management* (pp. 1–13). CABI. doi:10.1079/9781786390271.0001

Olsen, O. (1966). *Horg, Hov og Kirke*. H.J. Lynge & Son.

Orszt, M., & Raszeja, E. (2022). Historical rural architecture of North Portugal and Spanish Galicia: Local vernacular forms and concept of adaptation, case study of Porreiras. *Vitruvio, 7*(2), 46–59. doi:10.4995/vitruvioijats.2022.18845

Oviedo, L., de Courcier, S., & Farias, M. (2014). Rise of Pilgrims on the Camino to Santiago: Sign of Change or Religious Revival? *Review of Religious Research*, *56*(3), 433–442. doi:10.100713644-013-0131-4

Ozturk, H. S. (2021). New Inscriptions from Nikaia XIV - Nikaia to Leukai/Lefke: Settlements, Milestones, Roman Road and Maurice Bridge. *Libri(Turkey), 7*, 1–15. *Scopus*. doi:10.5281/zenodo.4475599

Paiva, J. P. (2004). O episcopado e a 'assistência' em Portugal na Época Moderna (séculos XVI-XVII). In L. Abreu (Ed.), *Igreja, caridade e assistência na Península Ibérica (sécs* (Vol. XVI-XVIII, pp. 167–196). Edições Colibri e CIDEHUS-UE. https://books.openedition.org/cidehus/197 doi:10.4000/books.cidehus.197

Palma, J. (2017). *Live the Camino del Sol experience.* http://caminhodosol.org.br/historia.aspx

Palma, J. (2019). *The size of the distance.* Caminhodosol. http://www.caminhodosol.org.br/post.aspx?id=23

Pandey, A., Pandey, M., Singh, N., & Trivedi, A. (2020). KUMBH MELA: A case study for dense crowd counting and modeling. *Multimedia Tools and Applications*, *79*(25-26), 17837–17858. doi:10.100711042-020-08754-4

Parejo, J. A. (2006). De la región a la ciudad. Un nuevo enfoque de la historia industrial española contemporánea. *Revista de Historia Industrial*, *30*, 53–102.

Pargament, K. I., & Mahoney, A. (2005). Sacred matters: Sanctification as a vital topic for the psychology of religion. *The International Journal for the Psychology of Religion*, *15*(3), 179–198. doi:10.120715327582ijpr1503_1

Paul, J., & Criado, A. R. (2020). The art of writing literature review: What do we know and what do we need to know? *International Business Review*, *29*(4), 101717. doi:10.1016/j.ibusrev.2020.101717

Paul, O. (2014). *Sanctity and Pilgrimage in Medieval Southern Italy, 1000-1200.* Cambridge University Press.

Pazos, A. M. (2014). Introduction. In A. M. Pazos (Ed.), *Redefining pilgrimage: New perspectives on historical and contemporary pilgrimages* (pp. 1–6). Ashgate Publishing, Ltd.

Pazos, A. M. (Ed.). (2020). *Nineteenth-Century European Pilgrimages: A New Golden Age* (1st ed.). Routledge. doi:10.4324/9780429198892

PBS. (2018). *6th Population & Housing Census 2017.* PBS. https://www.pbs.gov.pk/sites/default/files//population_census/National.pdf

Pearson, K. (1896). Mathematical Contributions to the Theory of Evolution. III. Regression, Heredity, and Panmixia. *Philosophical Transactions of the Royal Society of London. Series A, Containing Papers of a Mathematical or Physical Character*, *187*, 253–318. doi:10.1098/rsta.1896.0007

Pearson, K., & Filon, L. N. G. (1898). Mathematical Contributions to the Theory of Evolution. IV. On the Probable Errors of Frequency Constants and on the Influence of Random Selection on Variation and Correlation. *Philosophical Transactions of the Royal Society of London. Series A, Containing Papers of a Mathematical or Physical Character*, *191*, 229–311. doi:10.1098/rsta.1898.0007

Pedreschi, L. (1966). Aspetti geografici di alcuni centri religiosi italiani. *Bollettino della Società Geografica Italiana*, *IX*(7), 333–443.

Peel, C. I. (1998). *An Edition of Guta Saga.* [Dissertation: University College London].

Peira, G., Guidice, A. L., & Miraglia, S. (2022). Railway and Tourism: A Systematic Literature Review. *Tourism and Hospitality*, *3*(1), 69–79. doi:10.3390/tourhosp3010005

Penteado, P. (2000). Peregrinações e santuários. In C. M. Azevedo (Ed.), *História Religiosa de Portugal* (Vol. 2, pp. 346–359). Círculo de Leitores.

Penteado, P. (2000). Peregrinações e Santuários. In C. M. Azevedo (Ed.), *História Religiosa de Portugal* (Vol. 2, pp. 346–359). Círculo de Leitores.

Pereira, P. (2003). *Peregrinos: Um estudo antropológico das peregrinações a pé de Fátima*. Editora Crença e Razão.

PereiroX. (2017). Turiperegrinos portugueses no caminho português interior de Santiago de Compostela. *Revista Turismo & Desenvolvimento, 1*(27/28), Article 27/28. doi:10.34624/rtd.v1i27/28.8515

Persson, E., & Granberg, M. (2021). Implementation through collaborative crisis management and contingency planning: The case of dam failure in Sweden. *Journal of Risk Research, 24*(10), 1335–1348. doi:10.1080/13669877.2020.1863845

Pinheiro, A. E. (2007). *Cultural Itineraries: traveling through history*. Máthesis Magazine.

Pinto, J. M. (2019). Um homem do caminho. (1st ed). Lavra: Letras e coisas.

Piscitelli T. (1989). *Paolino di Nola. Epistole ad Agostino*. Stranae Nolane, 2.

Podda C., Secchi P., & Lampreu S. (2020). Turismo religioso e sviluppo delle aree rurali. Considerazioni sul caso della Sardegna. *Bollettino della Società Geografica Italiana, 14, 3*(2), 39-54. DOI: . doi:10.36253/bsgi-1227

Polus, R., Carr, N., & Walters, T. (2022). Conceptualizing the changing faces of pilgrimage through contemporary tourism. *International Journal of Sociology of Leisure, 5*(3), 321–335. doi:10.100741978-022-00109-7

Poole, S. (1995). *Our Lady of Guadalupe: The Origins and Sources of a Mexican National Symbol, 1531-1797*. University of Arizona Press.

Post, F. (2022). Religious tourism in Pakistan. *The Frontier Post*. https://thefrontierpost.com/religious-tourism-in-pakistan-2/

Powers, J. F., & Attreed, L. C. (2018). Justice, conflict, and dispute resolution in Romanesque art: The ecclesiastical message in Spain. *GESTA-International Center of Medieval Art, 57*(1), 5–22. *Scopus*. doi:10.1086/695771

Quadri, S. A., & Padala, P. R. (2021). An aspect of Kumbh Mela massive gathering and COVID-19. *Current Tropical Medicine Reports, 8*(3), 225–230. doi:10.100740475-021-00238-1 PMID:33816058

Quinn, G. (2019). *Bandit Saints of Java: How Java's eccentric saints are challenging fundamentalist Islam in modern Indonesia*. Monsoon Books.

Ramos, C. M. Q., & Mafé-García, A. (2018). Analysis of the contribution of ICT to cultural and religious tourism: In communicating religious heritage to visitors and tourists. In Handbook of Research on Socio-Economic Impacts of Religious Tourism and Pilgrimage. doi:10.4018/978-1-5225-5730-2.ch010

Ramsay, W. M. (1904). *The letters to the seven churches of Asia*. Hodder and Stoughton.

Rana, B. S. (2006). *The Holy Himalayas: An Abode of Hindu Gods*. M.D. Publications Pvt. Ltd.

Ravi, N. (2019). Speed and Socioeconomic Development: Influence of Indian Railways. *ADBI working paper series Number-952*. ABD. https://www.adb.org/sites/default/files/publication/503516/adbi-wp952.pdf

Reader, I. (1991). *Making Pilgrimages: Meaning and Practice in Shikoku*. University of Hawaii Press.

Reader, I. (2007). Pilgrimage growth in the modern world: Meanings and implications. *Religion, 37*(3), 210–229. doi:10.1016/j.religion.2007.06.009

Reader, I. (2015). *Pilgrimage: A very short introduction*. OUP Oxford. doi:10.1093/actrade/9780198718222.001.0001

Rei, A. (2009). Coimbra e a sua região, segundo as fontes geográficas árabes. In *Olhares Sobre a História. Estudos oferecidos a Iria Gonçalves* (pp. 493–499). Caleidoscópio. https://www.academia.edu/11928778/Coimbra_e_a_sua_regi%C3%A3o_segundo_as_fontes_geogr%C3%A1ficas_%C3%A1rabes

Revelation. To the Church in Ephesus. https://www.biblegateway.com/passage/?search=Revelation%202&version=NIV Retrieved July 15, 2023.

Revelation. To the Church in Laodicea. https://www.biblegateway.com/passage/?search=Revelation%203&version=NIV Retrieved August 9, 2023.

Revelation. To the Church in Pergamum. https://www.biblegateway.com/passage/?search=Revelation%202&version=NIV Retrieved August 7, 2023.

Revelation. To the Church in Philadelphia https://www.biblegateway.com/passage/?search=Revelation%203&version=NIV Retrieved August 8, 2023.

Revelation. To the Church in Sardis. https://www.biblegateway.com/passage/?search=Revelation%203&version=NIV Retrieved August 8, 2023.

Revelation. To the Church in Smyrna. https://www.biblegateway.com/passage/?search=Revelation%202&version=NIV Retrieved July 15, 2023.

Revelation. To the Church in Thyatira. https://www.biblegateway.com/passage/?search=Revelation%202&version=NIV Retrieved August 7, 2023.

Reynolds, F. E. (2010). *Sacred Mountains, Sacred Waterfalls: Exploring the Nine Sacred Temples of Thailand*. Silkworm Books.

Richards, G., Censon, D., Gračan, D., Haressy, M., Kiráľová, A., Marulc, E., Rossetti, G., Barkiđija Sotošek, M., & Sterchele, D. (2022). Event management literature: Exploring the missing body of knowledge. *Journal of Policy Research in Tourism, Leisure & Events*, 1–22. doi:10.1080/19407963.2022.2128810

Ridderstad, M. (2013). Orientations of the Medieval stone churches in Finland. *Suomen museo*.

Ridout, L., & Gray, P. (2010). *The Rough Guide to Bangkok*. Penguin.

Rinschede, G. (1992). Forms of religious tourism. *Annals of Tourism Research*, *19*(1), 51–67. doi:10.1016/0160-7383(92)90106-Y

Rocca, G. (2003). Luoghi, itinerari e assetti spaziali nella vita di una comunità religiosa. Il caso dell'Ordine Somasco. *Geotema*, *21*, 76–97.

Rodrigues, G. F. M. (2022). *Estudo da dinâmica da procura do Caminho Português da Costa em contexto de pandemia*. Instituto Politécnico de Viana do Castelo.

Rönnby, J., & Adams, J. (2006). Identity, threat and defiance: Interpreting the "bulwark", a 12th century lake building on Gotland Sweden. *Journal of Maritime Archaeology*, *1*(2), 170–190. doi:10.100711457-006-9008-9

Roosval, J. (1935). *Rute Setting: Sveriges Kyrkor*.

Rosa, M. de L. P. (2016). A vivência do cristianismo pelos fiéis leigos: A experiência do sagrado cristão. In J. P. Paiva (Ed.), História da Diocese de Viseu (pp. 517–568). Diocese de Viseu | Imprensa da Universidade de Coimbra.

Rot, E., Mikinac, K., & Bogdan, S. (2014). General characteristics of religious tourism in Croatia. *UTMS Journal of Economics (Skopje)*, *5*(1), 79–87.

Roy, S., & Kulshrestha, M. (2021). Performance Assessment Study of Indian Railways- Case of Low Efficiencies in Large Government Monopoly. *Transportation Research Record: Journal of the Transportation Research Board*, *2675*(11), 1272–1284. doi:10.1177/03611981211025516

Ruíz, A. (2011). Viajes y prácticas culturales en las provincias romanas de Hispania y la Galia. Iglesias, J. M., Ruíz, A. (eds.), Viajes y cambios de residencia en el mundo romano. Universidad de Cantabria, 203-204.

Salim, W., & Negara, S. D. (2018). Infrastructure development under the Jokowi administration: Progress, challenges and policies. *Journal of Southeast Asian Economies*, *35*(3), 386–401. doi:10.1355/ae35-3e

Samartim, R., & Pazos-Justo, C. (2022). Impacts of the Ways in the Local Community of Santiago de Compostela: Results of Ongoing Research. In E. J. Torres Feijó, M. F. Rodríguez Prado, & E. Carral Vilariño (Eds.), *The Way of Saint James, tourism, and local community* (pp. 42–59). Universidad del País Vasco / Euskal Herriko Unibertsitatea.

Sánchez, P., & Ullate, M. (2017). Tourism Evolution of Cultural Pilgrimage Routes: the Case of St James Ways. In M. Ullate (Ed.), *Cultural Management and Governance for European Pilgrimage Routes* (pp. 27–40). Religious Tourism and Thermal Tourism.

Sánchez, S. S., & Hesp, A. (2015). Introduction The Camino de Santiago in the 21st Century: Interdisciplinary Perspectives and Global Views. In *The Camino de Santiago in the 21st Century*. Routledge. doi:10.4324/9781315709147

Sanchis, P. (2006). Pilgrimage and pilgrimage: a place for religious tourism. *Ciencias Sociales y Religión/Social Sciences and Religion, 8*, 85-97.

Sands, T. (2017). II: 28 Pilgrimage – Gotland. In J. Glauser (Ed.), *Handbook of Pre-Modern Nordic Memory Studies: Interdisciplinary Approaches* (pp. 601–606). Walter de Gruyter.

Sang, K., & Lin, G. (2021). A system for measuring the satisfaction of railway heritage tourism: The case of Yunnan–Vietnam Railway. *Environmental Research: Infrastructure and Sustainability*, *1*(015001), 015001. doi:10.1088/2634-4505/abf1cf

Santa Casa da Misericórdia de Viseu. (2010). *Compromisso da Misericórdia de Viseu (reedição do compromisso de 1624). Viseu: Santa Casa da Misericórdia de Viseu.* Viseu: Santa Casa da Misericórdia de Viseu.

Santos, G. E. de O., Fagliari, G. S. (2003). Pilgrimage and Tourism: the new "religious" routes in Brazil. *Turismo - Visão e Ação, 5*(1).

Santos, X. M. (2002). Pilgrimage and Tourism at Santiago de Compostela. *Tourism Recreation Research*, *27*(2), 41–50. doi:10.1080/02508281.2002.11081219

Santus, D. (1990). La geografia della religione. Una rassegna. *Rivista Geografica Italiana*, *XCVII*(2), 251–259.

Sarılar Özdemir, M. (2021). Thyateira and its coins in the Hellenistic Period. Engin Akdeniz, Barış Gür & Nihal Akıllı (Eds.), 11 years for Thyateira (articles on the results of the 2011-2021 excavations) (pp. 185-205). Dokuz Eylul University Press.

Schedneck, B. (2015). *Thailand's international meditation centers: tourism and the global commodification of religious practices*. Routledge. doi:10.4324/9781315697284

Schedneck, B. (2018). Religious Others, Tourism, and Missionization: Buddhist 'Monk Chats' in Northern Thailand. *Modern Asian Studies*, *52*(6), 1888–1916. doi:10.1017/S0026749X16001013

Schedneck, B. (2021). *Religious tourism in northern Thailand: encounters with Buddhist monks*. University of Washington Press.

Schellhorn, M. (2010). Development for whom? Social justice and the business of ecotourism. *Journal of Sustainable Tourism*, *18*(1), 115–135. doi:10.1080/09669580903367229

Schrire, D. (2006). The Camino de Santiago: The interplay of European heritage and new traditions. *Ethnologia Europaea*, *36*(2), 69–86. doi:10.16995/ee.1008

Scriven, R. (2014). Geographies of pilgrimage: Meaningful movements and embodied mobilities. *Geography Compass*, *8*(4), 249–261. doi:10.1111/gec3.12124

Scriven, R. (2020). Pilgrim and path: The emergence of self and world on a walking pilgrimage in Ireland. *Cultural Geographies*, *27*(2), 261–276. doi:10.1177/1474474019876622

See, L., Fritz, S., Perger, C., Schill, C., McCallum, I., Schepaschenko, D., Duerauer, M., Sturn, T., Karner, M., Kraxner, F., & Obersteiner, M. (2015). Harnessing the power of volunteers, the internet and Google Earth to collect and validate global spatial information using Geo-Wiki. *Technological Forecasting and Social Change*, *98*, 324–335. doi:10.1016/j.techfore.2015.03.002

Sengupta, H. (2019). Why the Kumbh Mela is an economic blessing. *Fortune India*. https://www.fortuneindia.com/polemicist/why-the-kumbh-mela-is-an-economic-blessing/102900

Sen, T. T. (2009). *Cheng Ho and Islam in Southeast Asia*. Institute of Southeast Asian Studies. doi:10.1355/9789812308399

SepashviliE. (2020). Supporting Digitalization: Key Goal for National Competitiveness in Digital Global Economy. *Economia Aziendale Online, 11*(2), 191–198. doi:10.13132/2038-5498/11.2.191-198

Serrão, J. V. (1974). *Os caminhos portugueses de Santiago*. Fundação Calouste Gulbenkian.

Seryczyńska, B. (2021). Manifestations of Religious Freedom in the Context of the Camino de Santiago. *International Journal of Religious Tourism and Pilgrimage*, *9*(6), 1–11.

Seryczyńska, B., & Duda, T. (2021). How Is Fortitude Among Pilgrims on the Camino de Santiago Expressed and Formed? Clues from a Study of Polish Pilgrims. *Pastoral Psychology*, *70*(5), 541–556. doi:10.100711089-021-00959-0

Severn, P. (2019). A history of Christian pilgrimage. *International Journal for the Study of the Christian Church*, *19*(4), 323–339. doi:10.1080/1474225X.2019.1692274

Sharma, R., & Sharma, P. (2023). Spiritual Tourism and its Impact on the Economy. *Academy of Marketing Studies Journal*, *7*(5), 1–15.

Sharpley, R. (2009). Tourism, Religion and sirituality. In T. Jamal & M. Robinson (Eds.), *The Sage Handbook of Tourism*. Sage. doi:10.4135/9780857021076.n14

Shaukat, R. (2023, May). The economy of religious tourism. *The News*. https://www.thenews.com.pk/tns/detail/1074402-the-economy-of-religious-tourism#:~:text=As%20per%20the%20Pakistan%20Tourism,tourists%20visit%20Pakistan%20every%20year

Sheehy, K., Vackova, P., van Manen, S., Saragih Turnip, S., Rofiah, K., & Twiner, A. (2022). Inclusive disaster risk reduction education for Indonesian children. *International Journal of Inclusive Education*, 1–17. doi:10.1080/13603116.2022.2115156

Sheldon, P., & Daniele, R. (Eds.), *Social Entrepreneurship and Tourism. Tourism on the Verge*. Springer., doi:10.1007/978-3-319-46518-0

Sheller, M. (2014). The new mobilities paradigm for a live sociology. *Current Sociology*, *62*(6), 789–811. doi:10.1177/0011392114533211

Shinde, K. A. (2010). Entrepreneurship and indigenous enterpreneurs in religious tourism in India. *International Journal of Tourism Research*, *12*, 523–535. doi:10.1002/jtr.771

Sidiropoulos, G., Kiourt, C., & Moussiades, L. (2020). Crowd simulation for crisis management: The outcomes of the last decade. *Machine Learning with Applications*, *2*, 100009. doi:10.1016/j.mlwa.2020.100009

Siltberg, T. (2011). Kyrkolokalisering och eventualla storgårdar på Gotland. *Fornvännen*, *106*, 127–132.

Şimşek, C. (2013). Studies in the ancient city of Laodikeia. *Colloquium Anatolicum*, *12*, 15–36.

Singh, K. (2001). *Pilgrimage Centres of India*. Diamond Pocket Books (P) Ltd.

Singh, R. P., & Rana, P. S. (2023). Geography of Hindu pilgrimage places (Tīrthas) in India. In Geography of World Pilgrimages: Social, Cultural and Territorial Perspectives, 297-322.

Singh, A. (2012). *Jyotirlinga: The Glory of Lord Shiva*. Rupa Publications India.

Singh, K. (2014). *The Evolution of the Sikh Community: Five Essays*. Oxford University Press.

Singh, R. P. (2022). Heritage Value of Religious Sites of Hinduism: Asian Linkages and Reuse for Cultural Regeneration. In *Regenerating Cultural Religious Heritage: Intercultural Dialogue on Places of Religion and Rituals* (pp. 55–79). Springer Nature Singapore. doi:10.1007/978-981-19-3470-4_5

Singla, A. (2015). The Effect Of Perceived Service Quality On Customer Satisfaction In Indian Railways. *International Journal Of Research In Business Management, 3*.

Singul, F. (1999). Historia cultural do Camiño de Santiago. *Galáxia (São Paulo)*.

Sivan, H. (1996). The Death of Paulinus' brother. *Rheinisches Museum für Philologie. Neue Folge*, *139*(2), 170–179.

Slavin, S. (2003). Walking as Spiritual Practice: The Pilgrimage to Santiago de Compostela. *Body & Society*, *9*(3), 1–18. doi:10.1177/1357034X030093001

Smith, V. L. (Ed.). (2012). *Hosts and guests: The anthropology of tourism*. University of Pennsylvania Press.

Söderman, I. (1989). *Från lertavla till satellitbild*. Geographica.

Sołjan, I., & Liro, J. (2022). The changing roman catholic pilgrimage centres in Europe in the context of contemporary socio-cultural changes. *Social & Cultural Geography*, *23*(3), 376–399. doi:10.1080/14649365.2020.1739322

Soomaroo, L., & Murray, V. (2012). Disasters at mass gatherings: Lessons from history. *PLoS Currents*, *4*, 4. doi:10.1371/currents.RRN1301 PMID:22453897

Sorabella, J. (2011). Pilgrimage in Medieval Europe. In *Heilbrunn Timeline of Art History*. New York: The Metropolitan Museum of Art, 2000–. http://www.metmuseum.org/toah/hd/pilg/hd_pilg.htm

Spearman, C. (1987). The Proof and Measurement of Association between Two Things. *The American Journal of Psychology*, *100*(3/4), 441–471. doi:10.2307/1422689 PMID:3322052

Splendiani, S., Forlani, F., Picciotti, A., & Presenza, A. (2023). Social Innovation Project and Tourism Lifestyle Entrepreneurship to Revitalize the Marginal Areas. The Case of the via Francigena Cultural Route. *Tourism Planning & Development*, *20*(5), 938–954. doi:10.1080/21568316.2022.2161616

Spooner, A. (2013). *Thailand Dream Trip*. Footprint Travel Guides.

Steil, C. A., & Carneiro, S. S. (2008). Peregrinação, Turismo e Nova Era: Caminhos de Santiago de Compostela no Brasil. *Religião & Sociedade*, *28*(1), 105–124. doi:10.1590/S0100-85872008000100006

Stenberger, M. (1955). *Vallhagar: a migration period settlement on Gotland/Sweden*. Munksgaard.

Stopani, R. (1992). *La Via Francigena del sud. L'Appia Traiana nel medioevo*. Le Lettere.

Stratton, C. (2010). *What's What in a Wat: Thai Buddhist Temples: Their Purpose and Design*. Silkworm books.

Strielkowski, W., Grebennikova, V., Razinkina, E., & Rudenko, E. (2021). Relationship between globalization and internationalization of higher education. *E3S Web of Conferences, 301*, 1–9. doi:10.1051/e3sconf/202130103006

Stroheker, K. F. (1963). Spanische Senatoren der spätrömischen und westgotischen Zeit. *Madrider Mitteilungen*, *4*, 107–132.

Subramanian, R. (2022). Evolution and Diffusion of ICTs in the Indian Railways: A Historical Analysis. *Journal of International Technology and Information Management*, *31*(2), 4. doi:10.58729/1941-6679.1498

Sumption, J. (1993). *Monaci santuari pellegrini. La religione nel Medioevo*. Ed. Riuniti.

Svedjemo, G. (2014) *Landscape Dynamics—Spatial analyses of villages and farms on Gotland AD 200-1700*. [Dissertation Uppsala University].

Syed Marzuki, S. Z., Abdullah, H., Ab Halim, R., Buyong, S. Z., & Zreik, M. (2020). Purchasing behaviour on halal food products during movement control order (MCO): Quantitative evidence from covid-19 pandemic. [AEJ]. *ASEAN Entrepreneurship Journal*, *6*(2), 16–21.

Szerb, A. B., Bakucz, M., & Martínez-Cortijo, F. J. (2016). The impact of the santiago pilgrimage way on rural Spain. The case of the French Way (Northern Spain). *Journal of Tourism Challenges and Trends*, *9*(1), 47.

Tagliacozzo, E. (2013). *The longest journey: Southeast Asians and the pilgrimage to Mecca*. Oxford University Press.

Tala, M. L., & Padurean, A. M. (2008). Dimensions of religious tourism. *Amfiteatru Economic*, *10*, 242–253.

Tarlow, P. E., Swanson, K., & McGehee, N. G. (2012). Pilgrimage and tourism: Introduction to the special issue. *Journal of Pilgrimage Studies*, *5*(1), 1–8.

Tasneem, S., Khawar, M., & Hayat, R. (2022). Cultural Tourism in Pakistan: Prospects and Challenges. *Pakistan Vision, 23*(2).

Taylor, W. B. (2010). Magdalena: River of Dreams. UNM Press.

Terre di Mezzo Editore. (2022). *La Via Francigena nel Sud*. https://www.terre.it, Trono, A. (2012). *Via Francigena. Cammini di Fede e Turismo Culturale*. Congedo Editore.

Thakur, U. (2012). *Pushkar: The Holy City*. Rupa Publications India.

Throsby, D. (2001). *Economics and Culture*. CUP.

Timothy, D. J., & Boyd, S. W. (2006). Heritage tourism in the 21st century: Valued traditions and new perspectives. *Journal of Heritage Tourism*, *1*(1), 1–16. doi:10.1080/17438730608668462

Timothy, D. J., & Olsen, D. (Eds.). (2006). *Tourism, religions and spiritual journeys*. Routledge. doi:10.4324/9780203001073

Timothy, D. J., & Ron, A. S. (2015). Religious heritage, spiritual aliment and food for the soul. In *Heritage Cuisines* (pp. 104–118). Routledge. doi:10.4324/9781315752525-14

Toniol, R. (2012). *No rastro das caminhadas: Etnografia de uma política de turismo rural no Vale do Ivaí, Paraná* [Master's dissertation, Federal University of Rio Grande do Sul].

Transport NSW. (2023). *Why is rail travel a better choice for the environment?* Transport NSW. https://www.transport.nsw.gov.au/projects/environment-and-safety/sydney-trains-environment-and-sustainability/why-rail-travel-a

Trimingham, J. S. (1952). *The Ethiopian Church*. Oxford University Press.

Trout, D. E. (1991). The dates of the ordination of Paulinus of Bordeaux and of his departure for Nola. *Revue d'Études Augustiniennes et Patristiques*, *37*(2), 237–260. doi:10.1484/J.REA.5.104642

Tsironis, C. N. (2022). Pilgrimage and Religious Tourism in Society, in the Wake of the COVID-19 Pandemic: A Paradigmatic Focus on 'St. Paul's Route' in the Central Macedonia Region, Greece. *Religions*, *13*(10), 887. doi:10.3390/rel13100887

Tuan, Y. (1977). *Space and Place: The Perspective of Experience*. University of Minneapolis Press.

Turkish Language Society. (2023). *Definition of religion*. Sozluk. https://sozluk.gov.tr/

Türkoğlu, S. (1999). *The story of Ephesus*. Archeology and Art Publications.

Turner, V. (1974). Pilgrimages as social process. Turner, V. (ed.). Dramas, Fields and Metaphors. Cornell University Press, 166-230.

Turner, V. W., & Turner, E. L. B. (1995). *Image and Pilgrimage in Christian Culture: Anthropological Perspectives*. Columbia University Press.

Turner, V., & Turner, E. (1978). Introduction: Pilgrimage as a limonoid phenomenon. In V. Turner & E. Turner (Eds.), *Image and Pilgrimage in Christian Culture* (pp. 1–39). Columbia University Press.

Tutku Tours. (2023). *Tour program sample*. Turku Tours. https://www.tutkutours.com/images/left/Seven-Churces-2021.pdf

United Nations Conference on Trade and Development (2004). *Creative Industries and Development. Document Td(xI)/BP/13)*. United Nations. www.unctad.org/en/docs/tdxibpd13_en.pdf

United Nations Conference on Trade and Development (2008). *Creative Economy. Report 2008*. UNCTAD, UNDP. https://unctad.org/es/Docs/ditc20082cer_en.pdf

United Nations Economic and Social Commission for Asia and the Pacific. (2023). *Asia and the Pacific in the Face of COVID-19*. UNESCAP. https://www.unescap.org/sites/default/files/Asia%20and%20the%20Pacific%20in%20the%20Face%20of%20COVID-19_0.pdf

United Nations Educational, Scientific and Cultural Organization. (2007). *Understanding creative industries: cultural statistics for public-policy making*. UNESCO. http://www.unesco.org.br

United Nations. (2014). *ONU News: Agência da ONU realiza primeiro congresso global sobre turismo religioso*. UN. https://news.un.org/pt/story/2014/09/1485471 (Accessed on August 3, 2023)

Urrutia-Aparicio, M., Belmonte, J. A., & González-García, A. C. (2022). Land-and Skyscapes of the Camino de Santiago: An Astronomy and World Heritage Sustainable Approach. *Sustainability (Switzerland), 14*(5). *Scopus*. doi:10.3390u14053047

Urrutia, X. A. M., Urrutia, D. C. M., Larenas, P. C., Urrutia, E. K. M., & Ocaña, J. M. (2018). The French Way of St. James as an engine in the invigoration of rural municipalities in Galicia. *Revista de Economia e Sociologia Rural*, *56*(3), 425–436. doi:10.1590/1234-56781806-94790560304

Usta, K. M. (2005). *Evaluation of Iznik in terms of faith tourism potential.* [Master's thesis, Balikesir University]. YÖK National Thesis Center.

Vallega, A. (2006). *La geografia del tempo. Saggio di geografia culturale.* Utet.

Valles, J. G. (2007). Pilgrimage roads in Spain and Japan. In Pilgr. And Spirit. Quests in Jpn. (pp. 10–14). Routledge; Scopus. doi:10.4324/9780203318508

Van Dam, R. (1985). *Leadership and community in Late Antique Gaul.* California Press University. doi:10.1525/9780520341968

van Eck, N. J., & Waltman, L. (2022). *Manual for VOSviewer version 1. 6.18.* Centre for Science and Technology Studies (CWTS), Leiden University. https://www.vosviewer.com/documentation/Manual_VOSviewer_1.6.18.pdf

van Eck, N. J., & Waltman, L. (2010). Software survey: VOSviewer, a computer program for bibliometric mapping. *Scientometrics, 84*(2), 523–538. doi:10.100711192-009-0146-3 PMID:20585380

Vanniarajan, T., & Stephen, A. (2008). Railqual and passenger satisfaction: An empirical study in Southern railways. *Asia Pacific Business Review, 4*(1), 64–75. doi:10.1177/097324700800400107

Vargas-Munoz, J. E., Srivastava, S., Tuia, D., & Falcao, A. X. (2021). OpenStreetMap: Challenges and Opportunities in Machine Learning and Remote Sensing. *IEEE Geoscience and Remote Sensing Magazine, 9*(1), 184–199. doi:10.1109/MGRS.2020.2994107

Vaz, J. L. I. (2000). A Romanização. In Por terras de Viriato: Arqueologia na região de Viseu (pp. 163–164). Governo Civil; Museu Nacional de Arte Antiga.

Vaziri, F., Nanni, M., Matwin, S., & Pedreschi, D. (2020). *Discovering Tourist Attractions of Cities Using Flickr and OpenStreetMap Data.* doi:10.1007/978-981-15-2024-2_21

Vepa, G. R. (2000). *The Nine Narasimhas in Andhra Pradesh.* Sri Ramanuja Mission.

Verma, M., & Sarangi, P. (2019). Modeling attributes of religious tourism: A study of Kumbh Mela, India. *Journal of Convention & Event Tourism, 20*(4), 296–324. doi:10.1080/15470148.2019.1652124

Via Francigena Road to Rome. (2023). *The Free App of Via Francigena.* Vie Francigene. https://www.viefrancigene.org/ en/guides-app

Viaña, M. D. C. G., & Pérez, R. M. (2015). Turismo rural y creativo como alternativa de desarrollo local de una economía obsoleta: El caso de la línea sur. *Gestao e Desenvolvimento, 12*(2), 51–66. https://www.redalyc.org/articulo.oa?id=514251929006

Vidal-González, P. (2018). Patrimonio Inmaterial y rutas senderistas como búsqueda de las raíces culturales. El caso de la provincia de Castellón. In B. Santamarina, A. Coca, & O. Beltrán (Eds.), *Antropología Ambiental. Conocimientos y prácticas locales a las puertas del Antropoceno* (pp. 217–230). Icaria.

Vidal-González, P., & Cantillo, D. (2019). *Un tesoro del patrimonio cultural: la rogativa de Culla a Sant Joan de Penyagolosa.* Diputación de Castellón y Ayuntamiento de Culla.

Vidal-González, P., & Sánchez, V. (2019). Hiking paths and Intangible Heritage: A quest for cultural roots. Cases in the province of Castellón, Spain. *Sport in Society, 22*(12), 2065–2076. doi:10.1080/17430437.2018.1551368

Vijayanand, S. (2012). Socio-economic impacts in pilgrimage tourism. *International Journal of Multidisciplinary Research, 2*(1), 329–343.

Vilaça, H. (2017). Pilgrims And Pilgrimages Fatima, Santiago De Compostela And Taizé. *Nordic Journal of Religion and Society*, *23*(2), 137–155. doi:10.18261/ISSN1890-7008-2010-02-03

Vila, N. A., Brea, J. A. F., & Muñiz, D. R.-T. (2021). Consumo turístico durante o Camiño de Santiago. O Camiño Nós como ruta alternativa de peregrinación a Santiago. *Revista Galega de Economía*, *30*(3), 3. doi:10.15304/rge.30.3.7466

Vistad, O. I., Øian, H., Williams, D. R., & Stokowski, P. (2020). Long-distance hikers and their inner journeys: On motives and pilgrimage to Nidaros, Norway. *Journal of Outdoor Recreation and Tourism*, *31*, 100326. doi:10.1016/j.jort.2020.100326

VOSviewer. (2022). *VOSviewer—Visualizing scientific landscapes—Version 1.6.18*. VOSviewer. https://www.vosviewer.com//

Vukonic, B. (1998). Religious Tourism: Economic values or an Empty Box? *Zagreb International Review of Economics & Business*, *1*(1), 83–94.

Weare, K., & Khan, N. (2016). Pilgrimage: A Journey of Transformation. *International Journal of Children's Spirituality*, *21*(2), 121–134.

Web of Science. (2022). *WoS database*. Web of Science. https://www.webofscience.com

Webb, D. (2017). *Medieval European Pilgrimage c. 700-c. 1500*. Bloomsbury Publishing..

Weber, P., & Haklay, M. (2008). OpenStreetMap: User-generated street maps. *IEEE Pervasive Computing*, *7*(4).

Weng, S. L., Suntikul, W., & Chen, Z. (2023). Tourism development and induced social change. *Annals of Tourism Research*, *4*(1), 100088. doi:10.1016/j.annale.2023.100088

Wienberg, J. (2001). Gotlands guldålder—kyrkor, konjunkturer och korståg. In Från Stad Till Land. Andrén, Ersgård, and Wienberg (Eds). Lund Studies in Medieval Archaeolog.

Williams, A. M., & Shaw, G. (2011). Internationalization and innovation in tourism. *Annals of Tourism Research*, *38*(1), 27–51. doi:10.1016/j.annals.2010.09.006

Williams, W. (1998). *Pilgrimage and Narrative in the French Renaissance: 'The Undiscovered Country*. Oxford University Press. doi:10.1093/acprof:oso/9780198159407.001.0001

Wilson, J. (2019). Buddhism Without Merit: Theorizing Buddhist Religio-Economic Activity in the Contemporary World. *Journal of Global Buddhism*, *20*, 87–104.

Woodward, S. C. (2004). Faith and tourism: Planning tourism in relation to places of worship. *Tourism and Hospitality Planning & Development*, *1*(2), 173–186. doi:10.1080/1479053042000251089

World Economic Forum. (2022). *Travel & Tourism Development Index 2021*. WEF.

World Health Organization WHO Press, Geneva, Switzerland. (2008). *Communicable Disease Alert and Response for Mass Gatherings* (June). WHO.

Yamin, M. (2019). Managing crowds with technology: Cases of Hajj and Kumbh Mela. *International Journal of Information Technology : an Official Journal of Bharati Vidyapeeth's Institute of Computer Applications and Management*, *11*(2), 229–237. doi:10.100741870-018-0266-1 PMID:32289103

Yegül, F. K. (2020). Sardes: History, architecture and urbanism. *Anatolian Studies*, *23*, 135–158.

Yılmaz, I. (2004). *Pergamon history and coins during the Roman Empire*. [Master's thesis, Istanbul University]. YÖK National Thesis Center.

Yılmaz, A. A. (2010). *History of religions*. Alter Publishing.

Yilmaz, E., Yilmaz, E., & Aktas, Y. (2017). The effects of religious practices and beliefs on coping with cancer: A qualitative study among Turkish patients. *European Journal of Cancer Care*, *26*(2), e12420.

Yordanov, V., Quang Truong, X., Thanh Thuy Pham, T., Dong Khuc, T., & Antonia Brovelli, M. (2022). Open and collaborative tools for disaster management and risk reduction. *Vietnam Journal of Hydrometeorology*, *3*(12), 33–38. doi:10.36335/VNJHM.2022(12).33-38

Yrwing, H. (1978). *Gotlands Medeltid*. Gotlandskonst.

Zetterling A. (1935) Bulverket. *Svenska fornminnesplatser.*

Zhang, K., Labajo, V., Ramos, I., & Del Valle-Brena, A. G. (2021). A guest at home: The experience of chinese pilgrims on the camino de santiago. *Sustainability (Basel)*, *13*(19), 1–15. doi:10.3390u131910658

Zhou, Bo., & Ningqiao, L. (2017). The impact of high-speed trains on regional tourism economies: Empirical evidence from China. *Tourism Economics*, *24*(2). 10.1177/1354816617749

Zreik, M. (2022). Historical Developments of China's Xinjiang Province or Western Region. *Indikator: Jurnal Ilmiah Manajemen dan Bisnis, 6*(2), 54 - 62. doi:10.22441/indikator.v6i2.15069

Zreik, M. (2023), "USA–Myanmar relations: democratization and beyond", Southeast Asia: A Multidisciplinary Journal, Vol. ahead-of-print No. ahead-of-print. doi:10.1108/SEAMJ-02-2023-0018

Zreik, M. (2021). Academic Exchange Programs between China and the Arab Region: A Means of Cultural Harmony or Indirect Chinese Influence? *Arab Studies Quarterly*, *43*(2), 172–188. doi:10.13169/arabstudquar.43.2.0172

About the Contributors

Munir Ahmad is a Ph.D. in Computer Science. over 24 years of extensive experience in spatial data development, management, processing, visualization, and quality control. He is dedicated expertise in open data, crowdsourced data, volunteered geographic information and spatial data infrastructure. A seasoned professional with extensive knowledge in the field, having served as a trainer for the latest spatial technologies. With a passion for research and over 30 publications in the same field. In 2022, he got PhD degree in Computer Science from Preston University Rawalpindi, Pakistan. He is dedicated to advancing the industry and spreading knowledge through my expertise and experience. #SpatialData #GIS #GeoTech

Beatriz Topete Lopes de Almeida, 21, has a degree in Basic Education from the Escola Superior de Educação de Viseu. At the same institution, she is currently studying for a Master's degree in Pre-School and Primary Education and is a member of the Assembly of Representatives, while also taking part in the "Carbo2Soil" research grant.

Patricia Ana Arguelles Alvarez has a PhD on Ancient History and Archaeology by UNED University of Spain. Currently Patricia is a Postdoctoral distinguised researcher in Santiago de Compostela University. She has been awarded with several postdoc fellowships in Almería University and Salamanca University. She has made international stays in Houston, Sicily, Belgium or Bosnia and Hercegovina. Patricia has been teacher at Oviedo University. Her research is focushed on the study of historical roads with special interest in Roman roads and the relation with the landscape and the travelers. She has participated in more than 50 national and international congresses.

Judite Bem is an economist, post-doctoral student in Geography UFRGS, Professor at PPG in Social Memory and Cultural Assets and at the PPG in Environmental Impact Assessment, from LaSalle University, UNILASALLE, Canoas, RS.

Luiz Capra Filho has a Master's in Social Memory and Cultural Assets – LaSalle University, Canoas, RS. University Center Professor of Serra Gaúcha – FSG. Caxias do Sul, RS. Superintendent Director of Theatro São Pedro, Porto Alegre, RS.

Josep Capsí is a lecturer in Physical Activity and Sport Sciences at the Catholic University of Valencia and Director of the Public Sport Management Master in the same institution. His research areas of interest are the social determinants of sport participation and the dynamics of sport practices. Currently, he is focused on outdoor activities research within the Hiking Research Group.

Antonietta Ivona has a PhD in Economic Geography and Territorial Organization. He is currently Associate Professor of Economic Geography and Political Geography. She is Erasmus coordinator for the Department of Economics and Finance of the University of Bari. Her research topics include territorial development and geopolitical choices. He is a member of several national and international research groups.

Ashok Kumar Kanaujiya has completed his M.Tech. in Electronics Engineering from Indian Institute of Technology (IIT) BHU, Varanasi, India. He has worked as Engineer in Bharat Heavy Electricals Limited for around one and half years. He is presently working as senior administrator in State Civil Services Uttar Pradesh (India). He has rich experience of planning and execution of Kumbh Mela-2019. He is also pursing the course of Ph.D. as working professionals from Indian Institute of Information Technology Allahabad, Prayagraj, India. He has published various International papers on crowd management, sanitation management, and environmental impacts of mass gathering events

Bárbara Marto is a PhD student in Marketing and Advertising at Universidade da Beira Interior, Portugal. Holding a master in Digital Marketing, she has solid experience on a practitioner level and has worked for numerous organisations in tourism, tech, and FMCG. Research interests encompass a multidisciplinary approach to studying tourism, economics, and consumer psychology. With a passion for understanding and unraveling the intricacies of consumer behavior in the digital age, she aims to contribute to the field through innovative research that embodies both the theoretical and practical spheres in the field of Marketing.

Anita Medhekar is a senior lecturer in economics and holds a PhD from Deakin University, Australia. She has completed her double Masters in pure Economics as well as in Education. She has taught at undergraduate and post graduate levels in India, Indonesia, and Australia and has nearly 30 years of teaching experience. Currently, she is teaching at Central Queensland University, Australia. Her research interests are in applied Health Economics, International Trade, Tourism Economics, Development Economics, Asia-Pacific Economies, Public Finance, South-Asia, Australian Economy, Bilateral Trade and Development for Peace, Supply Chains, Public Policy, and Public-Private Partnerships. She has presented papers at numerous international conferences and received best research paper wards. She has numerous refereed publications in journals, conference proceedings, edited books, and book chapters to her credit.

Diego Piay has a PhD on Archeology by Santiago de Compostela University. Currently he is Associate teacher in Oviedo University. He has conducted more than 100 archaeological projects, and he has made researcher stays in Italy. His research is focushed on the study of the Primitive Christianism during Ancient times. In particular, he is interested in the figure of Priscillian. About Priscillian he has published 4 monographs and he has published also more than 30 articles about Roman archaeology.

Carlos Miguel Pipa is a consultant, managing partner of a consultancy company and pilgrim of the ways of Santiago de Compostela.

Luís Maia Rodrigues was born on 21 February 1955, Degree in History from the University of Coimbra - 1985 Post-graduated in Business Management at the ISAG, Porto Bank officer since 1982 Vice-presidente of local charity (Misericórdia de Santar) since 1990s until 2008 1st Director of the a Care Unit of Misericórdia de Santar in Nelas Founder and President of the Portuguese Red Cross Centre in Santar for over 10 years Pilgrim from 1973 untill now Volunteer on several social associations Retired since 2015

Vineet Tiwari, PhD is Assistant Professor in the Department of Management Studies, Indian Institute of Information Technology, Allahabad, (Prayagraj) India. He has been a Post-doctoral researcher at IIM Ahmedabad, India. He has more than 12 years of industry-academia experience. His research interests span over areas like, Energy and Water Modelling and Policy Analysis, Sustainability, Green HRM, Green Supply Chain Management, Circular Economy, ESG, Sharing Economy, Crowdshipping, Crowd Management. He is teaching courses in the area of Operations and Supply Chain Management. He has worked on many international and national research and consulting projects. He has several research papers published in reputed international journals like Environment, Development and Sustainability (Springer), International Journal of Greenhouse Gas Control (Elsevier), International Journal of Emerging Markets (Emerald), Proceedings of the National Academy of Sciences, India, Section, A: Physical Sciences (Springer), National Academy of Science Letters (Springer), Information Technology for Development (Taylor & Francis), Environmental Research Letters (IOP Publishing), Journal of Business Economics and Management, Carbon Management (Taylor & Francis), Climate Policy (Taylor & Francis) etc. and presented his research work at various international conferences in India and abroad. He is also a reviewer of reputed Journals.

Leyla Tokgöz was born in 1989 in Mersin, Leyla Tokgöz completed her undergraduate education in Nevşehir University Travel Management and Tourist Guiding Education Department and received her master and doctorate degrees from Atatürk University. Leyla Tokgöz, who has national and international publications on tourism-related issues, currently has been working at Atatürk University Faculty of Tourism.

Pablo Vidal-González is professor of Social and Cultural Anthropoloy at the Catholic Universiy of Valencia, and director of his Anthropology Research Institute. He researchs the relation between people and nature, landscapes and rural areas. He is Visiting Fellow at the MacMillan Center in Yale University, USA, and Associated Researcher in URMIS, University of Paris Diderot, France.

Mohamad Zreik, a Postdoctoral Fellow at Sun Yat-sen University, is a recognized scholar in International Relations, specializing in China's Arab-region foreign policy. His recent work in soft power diplomacy compares China's methods in the Middle East and East Asia. His extensive knowledge spans Middle Eastern Studies, China-Arab relations, East Asian and Asian Affairs, Eurasian geopolitics, and Political Economy, providing him a unique viewpoint in his field. Dr. Zreik is a proud recipient of a PhD from Central China Normal University (Wuhan). He's written numerous acclaimed papers, many focusing on China's Belt and Road Initiative and its Arab-region impact. His groundbreaking research has established him as a leading expert in his field. Presently, he furthers his research on China's soft power diplomacy tactics at Sun Yat-sen University. His significant contributions make him a crucial figure in understanding contemporary international relations.

Index

G

H

I

J

K

L

M

N

O

P

Q

R

S

T

V

W

Ensure Quality Research is Introduced to the Academic Community

Become an Reviewer for IGI Global Authored Book Projects

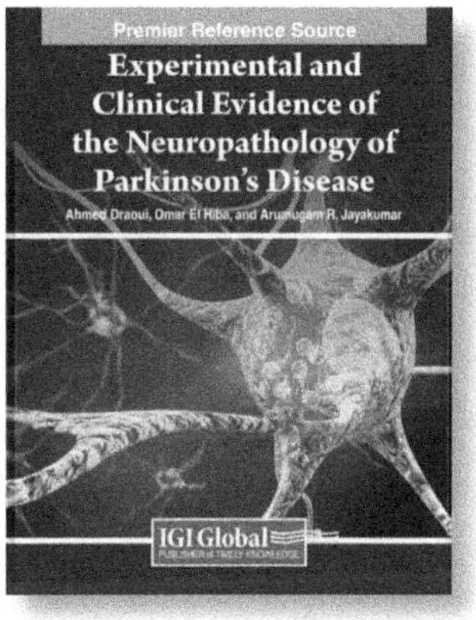

The overall success of an authored book project is dependent on quality and timely manuscript evaluations.

Applications and Inquiries may be sent to:
development@igi-global.com

Applicants must have a doctorate (or equivalent degree) as well as publishing, research, and reviewing experience. Authored Book Evaluators are appointed for one-year terms and are expected to complete at least three evaluations per term. Upon successful completion of this term, evaluators can be considered for an additional term.

If you have a colleague that may be interested in this opportunity, we encourage you to share this information with them.

www.ingramcontent.com/pod-product-compliance
Lightning Source LLC
LaVergne TN
LVHW060410300926
849162LV00006B/1391